Oxford Readings in

The Greek Novel

Oxford Readings in

The Greek Novel

Edited by

SIMON SWAIN

OXFORD
UNIVERSITY PRESS

*This book has been printed digitally and produced in a standard specification
in order to ensure its continuing availability*

OXFORD
UNIVERSITY PRESS

Great Clarendon Street, Oxford OX2 6DP
Oxford University Press is a department of the University of Oxford.
It furthers the University's objective of excellence in research, scholarship,
and education by publishing worldwide in

Oxford New York

Auckland Cape Town Dar es Salaam Hong Kong Karachi
Kuala Lumpur Madrid Melbourne Mexico City Nairobi
New Delhi Shanghai Taipei Toronto
With offices in
Argentina Austria Brazil Chile Czech Republic France Greece
Guatemala Hungary Italy Japan South Korea Poland Portugal
Singapore Switzerland Thailand Turkey Ukraine Vietnam

Oxford is a registered trade mark of Oxford University Press
in the UK and in certain other countries

Published in the United States
by Oxford University Press Inc., New York

ISBN 978-0-19-872188-8

PREFACE

The aim of this volume is to provide a selection of the most useful recent work on the ancient Greek novel for those teaching, taking courses on, or researching the subject. A knowledge of Greek is not necessary, since the most important passages cited in Greek have been translated, where this was not done already, using translations drawn from B. P. Reardon's *Collected Ancient Greek Novels*. The readings themselves have for the most part been taken from journals. Studies that are available in English-language books or that have been published very recently have been avoided in accordance with the Publisher's policy for this series, with two exceptions. The selection of pieces is not easy. Some will miss a favourite article or author. It is certainly regrettable that nothing of a suitable standard could be found within the set parameters on Xenophon of Ephesus. His absence from the Specific Studies in Part III is only partly countered by notice taken of him in the selections chosen for the General Studies, Part II, where common issues and problems are explored. A similar difficulty presented itself with Achilles Tatius: here it was felt that an exception to the general policy must be made. Those coming anew to this subject should remember that there is now a great deal of work of the highest quality to be found in books and collections that could not be drawn on for this volume. Some of this work is mentioned in the introductory Chapter I, though its main function is to discuss what the ancient Greek novel is and in particular to explain the course of its study in modern times to the present, including brief comments on the pieces chosen for the volume.

It is a pleasure to acknowledge the generous help and advice of a number of colleagues and friends, most especially Ewen Bowie, Stephen Harrison (editor of the sister-volume, *Oxford Readings in the Roman Novel*), John Morgan, and Bryan Reardon. Hilary O'Shea, Jenny Wagstaffe, and Georga Godwin at OUP have been supportive and helpful as usual. One of the assets of this series is the inclusion for an Anglophone readership of material written in other languages. Translating in a technical field is a difficult task and I am therefore especially grateful to P. G. Ruggieri, Regine May, and Thomas Schmidt for their help, hard work, and promptness. Finally I should like to thank California University Press for permission to use translations from its *Collected Ancient Greek Novels*.

S. S.

Shotteswell
May 1998

FIRST PUBLICATION SOURCES

The original titles and places of publication of the pieces collected in this volume are as follows:

E. L. Bowie, 'The Greek Novel', in P. E. Easterling and B. M. W. Knox (eds.), *The Cambridge History of Classical Literature*, i. *Greek Literature* (Cambridge, 1985), 683–99. (*Note*: the relevant pages of the Appendix of Authors and Works have not been reprinted in this volume.)

M. Fusillo, 'Les Conflits des émotions: un topos du roman grec érotique', *MH* 47 (1990), 201–21.

S. Saïd, 'La Société rurale dans le roman grec ou la campagne vue de la ville', in E. Frézouls (ed.), *Sociétés urbaines, sociétés rurales dans l'Asie Mineure et la Syrie hellénistiques et romaines*. Actes du colloque organisé à Strasbourg (Strasbourg, 1987), 149–71.

B. Egger, 'Zu den Frauenrollen im griechischen Roman. Die Frau als Heldin und Leserin', *GCN* 1 (1988), 33–66.

T. Hägg, '*Callirhoe* and *Parthenope*: The Beginnings of the Historical Novel', *Cl. Ant.* 6 (1987), 184–204.

B. P. Reardon, 'Theme, Structure and Narrative in Chariton', *YCS* 27 (1982), 1–27.

B. Effe, 'Longos. Zur Funktionsgeschichte der Bukolik in der römischen Kaiserzeit', *Hermes* 110 (1982), 65–84.

L. Cresci, 'Il romanzo di Longo Sofista e la tradizione bucolica', *A&R* 26 (1981), 1–25.

B. P. Reardon, 'Achilles Tatius and Ego-Narrative', in J. R. Morgan and R. Stoneman (eds.), *Greek Fiction: The Greek Novel in Context* (London, 1994), 80–96.

J. R. Morgan, 'The Story of Knemon in Heliodoros' *Aithiopika*', *JHS* 109 (1989), 99–113.

J. J. Winkler, 'The Mendacity of Kalasiris and the Narrative Strategy of Heliodoros' *Aithiopika*', *YCS* 27 (1982), 93–158.

M. Fusillo, 'Le Miroir de la lune. L'"Histoire vraie" de Lucien, de la satire à l'utopie', *Poétique*, 19/73 (1988), 109–35.

CONTENTS

NOTE ON THE TRANSLITERATION
OF GREEK NAMES

In a volume of reprinted work readers may expect to find both Hellenized and Latinized forms of names: e.g. Kalasiris *vs* Calasiris.

In the case of articles translated into English an attempt has been made to harmonize the spellings of the most familiar names with the forms used in the Introduction (so Lycaenion, *not* Lykainion, Cleinias, *not* Kleinias). Inevitably some inconsistencies remain.

PART I
Introductory

I

A Century and More of the Greek Novel

SIMON SWAIN

GREEK FICTION AND GREEK NOVEL IN THE HIGH ROMAN EMPIRE

The ancient Greek novel is the name we give to a series of long prose fiction texts which were written in the first few centuries AD (the period of the High Roman Empire) or not long before or after. The term 'romance' may also be used, especially for the five major surviving works (the 'ideal novels'), since these are largely concerned with romantic love.[1] In its modern meaning the word 'novel' refers to English language prose fiction of the eighteenth century and later.[2] Since it has now more or less ousted 'romance' even as a description of fiction with a sentimental or romantic storyline (cf. even 'romantic novel'), it is better for the most part to speak of the ancient novel, even though 'novel' is not a wholly appropriate name for a type of literature which was anything but realist. 'Romance' is, however, perfectly acceptable in contexts stressing erotic content or themes, and it will be used that way here.[3]

In Greek literature the novel was a late development with a very long ancestry. The question of its chronology is extremely important for deciding why it arose and what its appeal might have been

---

[1] The equivalent of 'romance' in French, German, and Italian (*roman, Roman, romanzo*) is the term for all of the ancient novels, 'romantic' or not (Spanish uses *novela*).

[2] This sense of 'novel' replaced 'history' as the term used to distinguish the new 'realistic' writing from the unrealist fiction of earlier verse or prose romance.

[3] Another term that may be mentioned now is the 'novella' (from the Italian; cf. French *nouvelle*, German *Novelle*), which has been taken up in the 20th c. in the sense of an (inset) short story dealing with a single situation or character (cf. the first literary reference of 'novel' in English to describe tales such as those of Boccaccio and the *Heptaméron*). The novella has been put forward by some classicists as the source of the ancient Greek novel—see below, pp. 20f.

to its first readers, and it is one to which I shall return throughout this introduction. Ancient Greek fiction itself is of course as old as the earliest ancient Greek literature, the Homeric epics. Ultimately the ancient romance can be traced to the same starting point. 'What is the *Odyssey*', remarked Ovid, 'but the story of a single woman wanted by many men for love?' This tongue-in-cheek assessment (*Tristia* 2. 1. 375-6) is not so wrong from the perspective of the *Odyssey*'s status as the first ancestor of the novel, since its travel, adventure, and especially the fortunes of its chaste married couple, are elements which recur in all the Greek novels. Modern scholars' ideas of the literary paternity of the novel is an area I shall be much concerned with here. For the moment it is important to stress that the novel's characteristic form—its length and its prose medium—and its characteristic mode—fiction—make it unique within Greek narrative literature. Historiography is comparable, and the connection with the sustained prose narrative of the historian has often been remarked on. Yet if the Greek novel uses many of the conventions of the historians, it is for all this quite different in its fictional aim. In the novel, then, Greek literature produced an entirely new form of writing. The importance of this for later literatures can scarcely be overemphasized. Even if 'no writings are more different than ancient *Romance* and modern *Novel*', as Clara Reeve puts it in *The Progress of Romance* (1785), the clear influence of the ancient novels, especially those of Heliodorus and Longus, on various of the great sentimental prose works of the later sixteenth and early seventeenth centuries, such as d'Urfé's vast *L'Astrée* and Sidney's no less lengthy *Arcadia*, should encourage us also to recognize their influence on the first modern novels of the seventeenth and eighteenth centuries (Sidney's Pamela, for example, is reborn in Richardson's heroine; Saint-Pierre's *Paul et Virginie* builds on d'Urfé's idyll as well as that of Longus).[4]

The point of Clara Reeve's contrast between ancient and modern was that the modern novel, unlike its ancient Greek ancestor, was

---

[4] S. L. Wolff (1912) is still useful on Sidney and his age (and also for its clear summaries of Achilles Tatius, Heliodorus, and Longus). For the *Nachleben* of Heliodorus see Weinreich (1950: esp. 368-76), for Longus see Barber (1989). In general consult Hägg (1983: 192-227) and the relevant essays in Baslez–Hoffmann–Trédé (1992), Tatum (1994), and Schmeling (1996). For influences in later Greek literature see Beaton (1988 and 1996). Note that Xenophon and Chariton were not printed until 1726 and 1750, which probably explains why they are not as important here.

'a picture of real life and manners, and of the times in which it is written'.[5] The objection is certainly true on the surface. For one of the most important generic aspects of the Greek novel—and a significant difference between it and the Roman novels of Petronius and Apuleius—is its setting in a vague or specified past. The novels either feature historical figures who tie them to a particular time (but in a very general manner) or may be said to be set 'in the past' because, with one significant exception (the *Lucius or Ass*), they completely ignore (at conscious level) the single most obvious sign of contemporary life, the Roman Empire. Yet even those novels with characters taken from history are somehow set at no determinable distance from the present. And although the Greek novel is not a straightforward reflection of 'real life and manners', its values and assumptions probably do reflect those of its writers and original readers, and this is true also of some matters of geography and social custom. The Greek novel did not create a historical age clearly distinct from that of its audience (contrast the world of epic), and the 'difference' between its readers and its past setting is no more than a difference between the real world and the world of the imagination.

The Greek novels fall into three groups according to how they survive. First, there are the five major surviving stories. These are *Chaereas and Callirhoe* by Chariton of Aphrodisias, the *Ephesian Story/Ephesian Tales* (*Ephesiaka*) by Xenophon of Ephesus, *Leucippe and Clitophon* by Achilles Tatius of Alexandria, *Daphnis and Chloe* by Longus, and the *Ethiopian Story/Ethiopian Tales* (*Aithiopika*) by Heliodorus of Emesa. These five works are known as the 'ideal novels' because their main characters are a young hero and heroine whose adventures and trials are set in the context of, or lead up to, their happy marriage. Stress is laid on faithfulness and chastity (though these are by no means maintained in all cases or always by design). Second are two lengthy summaries of novels by Iamblichus (probably also from Emesa) and Antonius Diogenes (origin unknown[6]), the *Babylonian Story/Babylonian Tales* (*Babyloniaka*) and *The Incredible Things beyond Thule*. These summaries are found in Photius' ninth-century *Library*.[7] Third are a number of short or

[5] C. Reeve (1785: 7, 110 ff.)
[6] Bowersock (1994: 38–9) suggests Aphrodisias.
[7] Codexes 94 (73b–78a) and 166 (109a–112a). They are translated in Reardon (1989: 785–93 and 777–82).

very short fragments of novels found on papyri recovered from
Egypt.[8] The three longer texts in this group are important. The so-
called *Ninus* romance is one of the earliest known Greek novels
and therefore crucial for the question of the novel's origins and
development. *Metiochus and Parthenope* is firmly tied to a particular
historical scene and is important for thinking about the role of
historical figures.[9] The *Phoenician Story/Phoenician Tales* (*Phoinikika*)
of Lollianus consists of fragments detailing a first experience of
sex at a party and a frightening religious ritual. The latter scene is
important not only for discussions of the religious dimension of the
novels but also because many have felt that it has an analogue in
Apuleius' *Metamorphoses*. Apart from these, the very short texts
which have been identified as novels are pieces which appear to be
fragments of narrative fiction with an element of romance or
adventure.

The fragments and summaries raise questions about the definition of novelistic fiction.[10] It is right to ask whether the attention
we pay to the surviving 'ideal novels' prevents us from appreciating the full diversity of ancient novelistic literature. The answer to
this question depends not only on how one defines novel and the
relation of novel to fiction, but also on what one likes and how one
reads the status of one's likes. Clearly, there are good grounds for
defining prose *fiction* as widely as possible. In which case the Greek
literature of the High Roman Empire offers considerable riches and
intriguing eccentricities, and sometimes these are called 'novels'.
One immediate distinction to be drawn is that between texts with
a stable literary form and those without one. Works such as
Alexander Romance, *History of Apollonius King of Tyre* (if it is correctly held that this Latin romance of the fifth or sixth century was
based on a Greek original), and the Aesop story (*Life of Aesop*) show
complex variant recensions in their manuscript traditions.[11] In

---

[8] See Kussl (1991), and esp. Stephens and Winkler (1995; with English translations), and Morgan (1998). Many of these are translated in Reardon (1989). New
papyrological and other (cf. Alpers 1996) fragments are noted in the *PSN* bibliographies (see n. 119).

[9] It is also of great interest as an example of reuse in later literatures: Hägg
(1984, 1985, and 1986), Utas (1984–6).

[10] For different aspects see Barwick (1928), Holzberg (1996), Kuch *et al.* (1989),
C.-W. Müller (1976), Morgan (1993), Reardon (1991), Ruiz-Montero (1996),
Selden (1994).

[11] *Alexander Romance*: Merkelbach (1977); *History of Apollonius King of Tyre*:
Kortekaas (1984), but see Schmeling (1996); Aesop: Holzberg (1992). There is also

other words, they are stories formed of shifting combinations of oral, folk-tale elements, and may be ruled out of contention, if we wish to keep the term 'novel' from becoming uselessly vague.

Within the category of high literature the task of isolating the novel from other fictional writing is not at all simple, but the attempt must be made. A good example of a text we would certainly classify as fiction and not as novel is the bizarre 'anthology' of Ptolemy Chennos (an Egyptian word meaning 'Quail'), the so-called *Strange* (or *Unusual*) *History*, which was composed in the late first or early second century AD.[12] This has recently been discussed by Glen Bowersock in his study of the rise of fiction in the High Roman Empire. He rightly designates it 'a totally irresponsible rewriting of the famous stories of the past'.[13] From the summary of the work in Photius' *Library* (codex 190, 146a-153b) we can see that Ptolemy deformed mythological and historical tales by fast and furious rewriting in a mock serious style, adding the details others had left out, such as the name of Herodotus' boyfriend. Again, this entertainment is fiction, but hardly a novel. Here, moreover, there is no continuous narrative, no characterization, no plot.

The many fictional writings of Lucian in the mid-second century come into consideration. Lucian's comic dialogues rework a shared mythological repertoire. Many of his essays such as *Alexander* or *Peregrinus* again mingle accepted fact with Lucianic invention. These pieces are no more 'novels' than the *Strange History*. But some of Lucian's fictions do look more like the real thing. *Toxaris*, *Lovers of Lies*, and *True Histories* are works of sustained prose. Yet it is their resemblance to the novels that allows us to see that they are best not classified as novels themselves. *Toxaris* consists of ten original tales on the theme of male friendship. *Lovers of Lies* has a comparable 'moral' aim, that of debunking superstition and the supernatural, which it achieves by telling a series of stories about magicians, exorcisms, ghosts, etc. (among them the first appearance of the 'sorcerer's apprentice'). The episodic nature of both these works makes them important for the development of the short story ('novella'), but not for the novel.[14] *True Histories* is of a

papyrological evidence of minor variation/innovation for Chariton (Reardon 1996: 315 n. 9) and Achilles Tatius (Russo 1955; Laplace 1983*a*; Plepelits 1996: 391-2).

[12] Καινὴ (or Παράδοξος) ἱστορία.   [13] Bowersock (1994: 24-7).

[14] The same may be said for the so-called epistolary novels: a number of these are known and have analogues with other novelistic fiction: *inter alios* Konstan and Mitsis (1990), Holzberg and Merkle (1994), P. A. Rosenmeyer (1994).

different order, for here we have one long narrative unified by a distinctive and appealing theme. Cast in two books in a historiographical form, *True Histories* is again an attack on credulity. The comic element is uppermost, and Lucian develops his story by using the comic technique of drawing out the details of the ludicrous places and creatures his narrator meets with on his fantastic journey. As a work of sustained narrative *True Histories* could well be described as a novel.[15] Yet there is no characterization, no developed focus on named persons, and it is perhaps better not so called, however convenient the label may be.[16]

The same may be said of another fictional prose work which is often (and reasonably) canvassed as a novel, Philostratus' *In Honour of Apollonius of Tyana* (*Life of Apollonius*). Aspects of the form and structure of the *Apollonius* do correspond to certain distinguishing features of various of the ancient novels, especially the themes of travel in the mysterious East, the quest for wisdom, the 'historiographical' division into eight books.[17] But the piece has in fact a deeply serious intention concerned with the changes and challenges faced by Greek culture and religion in the third century AD.[18] This, together with the absence of characterization, plot, and the type of adventures found in the novel make it less deserving of the title than the works of Lucian just discussed.

If it is allowed that both characterization and plot are essential to a definition of prose fiction as a novel, the scope of the Greek novel is not reduced at a stroke to the 'ideal novels'. Iamblichus' *Babylonian Story* has many of these features, but looks significantly different from Chariton, Longus, and the others in the way it handles them (e.g. the un-ideal tone of the many sub-stories, the homicidal jealousy of the heroine, the bizarre role-reversals and overdone love of paradox, the high degree of magic). This is truer still of Antonius Diogenes' *The Incredible Things beyond Thule*, where the hero and heroine are nothing like the young romantic protagonists of the ideal stories (and indeed have little to do with one another in the course of the work). Lollianus' *Phoenician Story* (in the 145 or so incomplete lines known to us) also looks anything other than ideal. Different too is the so-called *Iolaus* fragment (if

---

[15] Thus it is included in the translations of Reardon (1989).
[16] See below, p. 32.
[17] Cf. Reardon (1971: 189), Bowie (1978: 1663-7), G. Anderson (1986: 230-2), Billault (1991*b*).   [18] Swain (1999), cf. Elsner (1997).

we may generalize from even smaller remains). This mixture of prose and verse with a dose of obscenity has reminded editors of Petronius' *Satyrica*.[19]

Yet if a line is to be drawn round the term 'novel', Iamblichus would probably be inside it, Antonius Diogenes probably without. Consider the following. On the basis of Antonius' *Incredible Things* the editors of the standard edition of the fragmentary and summary novels rightly conclude that '[t]he teen-romance framework was not an essential feature of long prose *fiction*'. But it is more difficult to accept the implications of their remark that, '[i]f teen romance is regarded as the core of the *novel*-writing project, then Antonius' work is by definition a marginal work, not a central masterpiece.'[20] This is an objection to a long history of scholarship on the novel, which has indeed taken romance as a key defining element. There is also a strong desire to make Antonius' work into that 'central masterpiece'. *Incredible Things*, as we see from Photius, had an extremely complex structure. We are presented with a text that is highly self-conscious. According to Photius, Antonius

says that he himself is a poet of Old Comedy and that, even if he is inventing incredible lies, for most of his fictions he has the testimonies of the older writers from whom he has compiled them with much effort. He lists at the start of each book the men who have described such things before so that his incredible stories will not seem to lack testimony.[21]

If Antonius is saying that parts of *Incredible Things* were taken over from earlier writers, there is no need to look further than the ethnographical and scientific information which formed a large part of the story, though the phrase 'such things' may mean that 'the testimonies of the older writers' was no more than a series of parallel fictions. Stephens and Winkler ask whether the fictional story was a vehicle for the 'factual' information, or whether the paradoxographical and geographical accounts were meant to enhance the fiction. The latter must be right, for the claim to be a 'poet of Old Comedy' makes it difficult to believe that Antonius aimed to provide a 'serious . . . encyclopedia' of paradoxography.[22] Antonius alerts us to the fact that he is an honest fabricator, just

---

[19] On *Iolaus* (P.Oxy. 3010) consult Stephens and Winkler (1995: 358–74).
[20] Stephens and Winkler (1995: 109–10; my italics).
[21] Photius, *Library* cod. 166, 111a34–40. On this work see Borgogno (1975*b* and 1979), Di Gregorio (1968), Morgan (1985), Fusillo (1990*b*).
[22] Stephens and Winkler (1995: 103).

as Lucian in *True Histories* praises 'the poet Aristophanes, a wise man and a truthful one, whose compositions are disbelieved for no reason' (I. 29). The naming of sources and/or targets should again remind us of Lucian.[23] For like *True Histories* the *Incredible Things* is really a *satire* on the whole class of paradoxography. It certainly takes in romantic fiction during its course.[24] But geographers and paradoxographers are the principal victims. Its sheer length and complexity do indeed mark it out as a masterpiece; but a masterpiece of satire is by definition a marginal work, not a central one.

As a deformation of earlier texts Antonius Diogenes may better be classified with the works of Ptolemy the Quail and Lucian rather than with the novel. These three represent a sort of literature which is as old as Greek fiction.[25] They should also be placed against the cultural trends of their age, for they are not the only texts where the engagement with earlier literature is a source of play. As has been noted, Iamblichus' *Babylonian Story* pushes features characteristic of the five ideal novels (separations, supposed deaths, misrecognitions and look-alikes, inset tales) so far that it is more than reasonable to discern a considerable amount of intentional humour. Nevertheless, it does deploy them—which is not the case with Antonius Diogenes. Thus it is tempting to see *Babylonian Story* as a satirical rewriting of the 'ideal novel' and indeed parasitic upon its success, for the setting of *Babylonian Story* in the legendary antiquity of Mesopotamia and its firm dating to c.AD 170 suggests that it was designed to capitalize on interest in the land of Marcus Aurelius' and Lucius Verus' Parthian War. The humour of imitation is also present among the ideal novels themselves. It has been surely detected in Longus,[26] and no one could deny its presence in Achilles Tatius' *Leucippe and Clitophon*, where elements such as the near-sexual encounter of hero and heroine at the beginning of the novel and the large dose of macabre eroticism

---

[23] Stephens and Winkler (1995: 107); Swain (1992; 75-6). Cf. also *True Histories* I. 4: 'I am telling the truth, when I declare that I am a liar', etc.

[24] Judging the scale of the love-interest from Photius' information is hazardous: cf. Sandy (1994: 138); but Photius does single out the love element at the end of his summary (cod. 166, 111b37-42), where the characters of *Incredible Things* are the 'model for Sinonis and Rhodanes [Iamblichus], Leucippe and Clitophon [Achilles Tatius], Charicleia and Theagenes [Heliodorus], their adventures and wanderings and loves and capture and perils' (after Stephens and Winkler).

[25] See Aristotle, *Poetics* 2, 1448a10 ff. on early pastiche and parody of Homer. Cf. *The Battle of the Frogs and Mice* (*Batrachomyomachia*).

[26] Bretzigheimer (1988).

have led a recent commentator to talk of the author's 'dangerous straining of the boundaries of the genre'.[27] But the degree of the peril lies in the function of the strain. Boundaries are extraordinarily important in the Greek world of the early centuries AD when the Greek élite (the primary readership of the novels; see p. 27) protected its identity and heritage by enclosing itself in a thoroughgoing classicism. One aspect of this culture may help to explain the particular type of humour we are discussing. The rules which constructed Greek identity were never easy to formulate. In all *belles-lettres*, for example, it was imperative to imitate classical texts. This imitation (or 'mimesis') was constantly made problematical by the existence of rival prescriptions of the correct models and sources, which exposed the whole project to the predations of the satirist.[28] The purpose of mimesis was to pay homage to predecessors *and* to establish differences from them: but identification of these tasks was for author and reader alike a game rather than an unthinking mechanism.[29]

Imitation is also most important between the novelists. The fact that the five surviving novels (and the *Babylonian Story*) are built out of very similar elements (no matter what skilful deployments of these each novelist came up with) is the obvious proof of extensive imitation within the genre (and one which makes it difficult to decide who is imitating whom). Humour is involved here too. The presence of it in the rewritings of the novelistic formula does not signal a straining of the boundaries. It is a sign that the rules of the genre were necessarily flexible, subtle, debatable, that in laughing through them each new author knew best, a case of a challenge for recognition rather than an attempt to overturn the system the rules were designed to uphold.[30] With Iamblichus rewriting has probably changed from playfulness to satire; even so, this does not go beyond the bounds. Indeed, only in the case of one text, the *Lucius or Ass* (the older 'cousin' of Apuleius' *Metamorphoses*), should we probably see a deliberate refusal to play with

[27] Goldhill (1995: 93), an important study. See also Durham (1938). In general on the novelists' humour, G. Anderson (1982).

[28] Cf. esp. Lucian's *Lexiphanes* and *Teacher of Rhetoric*.

[29] One of the commonest examples of imitation, the rewriting of Homeric epic (esp. the *Iliad*), may be mentioned here because it produced at least one novelistic work, Dictys Cretensis' *Diary of the Trojan War* (the surviving Latin version depends on a late 1st- or 2nd-c. Greek original). See Merkle (1994, 1996).

[30] So, Goldhill (1995) is itself a challenge within the hegemonical system of the scholarly academy, an attempt to deseat Foucault, not the system.

due consideration for the rules. For here, the setting in the present, the acknowledgement of Roman military control of Greece, the total absence of romantic (but not sexual) love, the dominance of magic and superstition, and the unwillingness of an obviously educated author to classicize his language are difficult to explain in any other way.[31]

The centrality of the ideal novels in the narrative prose fiction of the High Roman Empire is clear enough. It may be added that most of the very short fragments of novels do not fail to accord with the romantic scheme. Even where the contents of the fragments are discrepant, for example in the case of Lollianus' *Phoenician Story*, to assume that the text as a whole did not purvey the values of the ideal stories may be unwarranted, the intrusion of an undestandable desire to replace the Greek novel with something more exotic, frightening, and modern.[32]

PAST READINGS OF THE GREEK NOVEL

The most important figure in the history of modern scholarship on the novel is Erwin Rohde. *Der griechische Roman und seine Vorläufer* (*The Greek Romance and its Precursors*) was first published 1876, when Rohde was only 30 years of age.[33] The quality of the writing, the breadth of the erudition, and the coherence of the ideas turned it into an immediate classic. Yet to approach *Der griechische Roman* nowadays is to approach a work which 'has long been lying in ruins, exploded by papyrus discoveries[, though] the devastation [forms] a most instructive tour, nay a necessary pilgrimage.'[34] There is indeed a tone of reverence in many of the comments made about Rohde and his book. Perhaps because he died young (at the

---

[31] *Lucius or Ass* is translated in Reardon (1989). On it see e.g. Bompaire (1988), Effe (1976), Holzberg (1984), Kussl (1990), Perry (1967: 211–35).

[32] *Iolaus*, had we more, might well join the *Ass*, as perhaps would *Tinouphis* (but note Stephens and Winkler (1995: 402): '[t]he low-status types . . . would seem to set this piece firmly in the area of criminal fiction. But . . . [t]he whole may be no more than a witty and salacious anecdote within a longer and distinctly different type of work'), and *Daulis* (if this is a novel: cf. West (1971: 96): 'generally neglected on the assumption that it is a rather freakish specimen of some other genre', quoted with approval by Stephens and Winkler (1995: 375)).

[33] All citations are taken from the pages of the fourth edition (1960).

[34] Giangrande (1962: 132).

start of 1898), perhaps because of the loyalty of his followers and pupils, perhaps because there had been nothing like it before, the work took on a saintly aura which survived the overturning of its views about the novels' dates. Indeed the main thesis, that the romance grew out of a combination of the love stories of the Hellenistic poets and literature of paradoxography and fantasy travel with a philosophical bent, was in no wise affected by the discoveries of the papyrologists.

It is crucial to understand Rohde's theories well, since the development of scholarship on the novel, even in recent times, owes a great deal to what he said. The prefaces to the three later editions of his book (in which the main text stood unchanged) make interesting reading. That of Fritz Schöll, Rohde's colleague at Heidelberg, is a pious homage, which states that, had Rohde lived, he would not have had to make any substantive changes. Schöll makes little of the major discovery of the *Ninus* romance (published by Ulrich Wilcken in 1893),[35] whose existence Rohde had noted in his personal copy.[36] The edition of Wilhelm Schmid in 1914 has a scarcely less reverential preface. His appendix of scholarship on new trends in the novel since the second edition again leaves Rohde's 'theory' and 'interpretation' virtually intact. Rohde was wrong in two things only. Antonius Diogenes' *Incredible Things* was not a proto-novel (as he had suggested), but as 'we now know' an aretalogy.[37] Secondly, the recent papyrus discoveries showed that the 'new sophistic' (i.e. the classicizing literary culture of the Greek élites in the High Roman Empire) was not responsible for merging the two formative strands of the novel, as Rohde had believed. Schmid, the great expert in this area, believed wrongly, and for reasons I shall return to, that the 'second sophistic' (as this movement is always now known) did not begin till the second century AD (a view broadly shared by Rohde). The discovery of *Ninus* and then in 1900 of a papyrus of *Chaereas and Callirhoe* dating to no later than AD 150 (suggesting that it had been composed 'about the end of the 1st century BC at the latest') convinced him that

[35] See below, pp. 17 f.
[36] E. Rohde (1960: XXII, 577), *Ninus*. Rohde also denied that fragments of *Metiochus and Parthenope*, which were published in 1895, were from a romance: ibid. 568 n. 2 (on p. 570).
[37] An allusion, cf. E. Rohde (1960: 618), to Reitzenstein (1906)—still a brilliant work—on the rise of texts ('aretalogies') which celebrated the wondrous deeds of the new Hellenistic gods. Cf. below, n. 61.

Rohde had made an error in the field in which he was himself the master.

The third new preface, that of the fourth edition of 1960, was written by Karl Kerényi, the historian of religion. Kerényi strikes a more critical tone, beginning with the savage remarks of Hermann Riefstahl on Rohde's failure to understand the 'real sense' of the genre and his consequent exclusion of works like Apuleius' *Metamorphoses* and *Lucius or Ass*. He then quotes Otto Weinreich on the 'untenable chronology' of Rohde's idea that the novel coincided with the period of the second sophistic and was a product of the practice exercises which formed the basic curriculum of the sophists (the teachers of rhetoric).[38] Kerényi goes on to trace Rohde's relations with Nietzsche and the influence on both men of the humanist Swiss historian Jacob Burckhardt. Finally he outlines Rohde's argument that the Greeks had lost their ability to express their imagination in myth as a consequence of Socrates' new teaching. This loss was followed by a vacuum, in which the only form of literature to arise (in the Hellenistic period) was the short love story. The renaissance of Greek rhetoric in the second century AD allowed the gift of imagination to be prized anew and this gave birth to the novel.[39] Rohde's vacuum was, however, a trick of the evidence 'which papyrus discoveries began to fill soon after the appearance of the book'. Furthermore Rohde suffered from an 'understandable' ignorance of a form of literature which pointed to the existence of popular story-telling long before the second sophistic, for, when he wrote, no one had a clear idea about the flood of 'oriental' cults that entered the Greek world in the Hellenistic age with their own myths and stories in which the element of creative love played an important part.

In these last comments Kerényi makes reference to his own theory of the novel's beginning, published in his 1927 book, *Die griechisch-orientalische Romanliteratur in religionsgeschichtlicher Beleuchtung* (*The Romance Literature of Greece and the Orient from a Historico-religious Perspective*). The wider background of this book (to which I shall return) was the then dominant (and still influential) belief that the conquests of Alexander brought about a crisis in Greek society. In the greatly expanded Greek world of the Hellenistic kingdoms the old social structures broke down and with them went the appeal of the traditional Olympian gods. Contact

---

[38] Kerényi in E. Rohde (1960: VII–VIII).   [39] So E. Rohde (1960: 310–87).

with the orient led to the worship of new deities, whose rites gave meaning to the individual in a social, cultic setting, and placed a special accent on the salvation of the soul. The stories of the new gods were the spur to the Greek novel.

Many pathways of scholarship derive from Rohde's literary-historical interpretation and Kerényi's alternative—and equally original—historico-religious response. The standard modern accounts of Ben Perry and Bryan Reardon stand in a direct line to Rohde. Historico-religious analysis has remained strong in German scholarship owing to the towering figure of Reinhold Merkelbach, and now sees an impressive advocate in Bowersock's *Fiction as History* (1994). Even the purely literary-structural study of the novels, which is the most important development of recent scholarship, has some dependence on these books. For the main object of the new literary work is to uncover the narrative sophistication of the individual stories, and here the old questions of chronology, of the audience and its cultural expectations, of the literary techniques deployed by other second sophistic authors, remain important, even if discussed under other headings. The religiosity of the novels comes into focus here too, for example in Winkler's and Jones's work on Lollianus and his relations with Apuleius' Isis-novel, the *Metamorphoses*.

The intellectual formation of Rohde's book has been traced by Hubert Cancik.[40] Like Nietzsche Rohde was a great admirer and friend of Richard Wagner. Cancik suggests a parallel between Wagner's influence on Nietzsche's *Der Geburt der Tragödie aus dem Geiste der Musik* (*The Birth of Tragedy from the Spirit of Music*), published in 1872, and Rohde's *Roman*. Nietzsche found in Wagner's *Musikdramen* the hope of a rebirth of the tragic free spirit that had been forced out of the world by Socratic rationalism. For Rohde the ancient romance was the product of a world in decline (partly as a result of Socratic thinking), but was also an expression of a new individualism, even if this had not flowered properly before the psychological realism of the European novel.[41] As Cancik notes, Rohde quotes from Wagner's *Siegfried* (without attribution),[42] and

---

[40] Cancik (1985: 451-6). See also Schmid (1899-1900: 88-96), Gründer (1969) for reactions to Nietzsche's book by Rohde, Wilamowitz, and Wagner.

[41] E. Rohde (1960: 404-5, cf. 6, 179, 296, 404-5, 476, 549, 583).

[42] Ibid. 544. 'Die erhabenen Schauer . . . der »seligen Öde auf sonniger Höh'«' = *Siegfried*, Act 3 Scene 3 (Siegfried approaches the rocks where Brünnhilde sleeps amidst fire).

his correspondence reveals a great love of Wagner's music. One can go further by observing the influence on Rohde of the German Romantics and their congeners. References in the footnotes of *Roman* to Dorothea von Schlegel, Novalis (the pseudonym of Friedrich Hardenberg), Schopenhauer, as well as to Rousseau combine with his enthusiasm for Wagner and close relationship with Nietzsche to suggest a disenchantment with modern urban living, the primacy of artistic creation,[43] an idealization of a pre-modern, quasi-medieval pure Nature, and a belief in romantic Love as the goal. Novalis, the chief poetic inspiration of the Romantics, had pursued the idea of *Sehnsucht*, the 'longing' that is an intrinsic part of the quest for true Love, and this notion recurs in *Roman* in, amongst other places, the most personal and significant passage in the book, the attack on Longus' *Daphnis and Chloe*.[44] Here Rohde attacks Longus for failing to share the values of the modern 'Nature-lover' (*Naturschwärmer*). Longus' 'feeling for Nature' was crystallized in the garden, that most human intrusion upon the natural, and his language, style, and storyline smacked of sophistry. The passion of his two lovers showed 'no deep psychological unfolding', but only 'loathsome, canting affectation'.[45] It is not surprising that Rohde should locate the 'deeper and fuller ring of the most powerful feelings of the heart' in the Germanic medieval tale of 'Brunhild the Valkyrie's love for Siegfried', nor that he should (probably) be thinking of Wagner's version of the story as he does so.[46]

Rohde ascribes Longus' excessive charm and mannerism to sophistic rhetoric. The importance of the second sophistic in his scheme has been noted. Its nature, and scholars' views of it in relation to the novel, requires some explanation. Rohde thought of second-sophistic rhetoric as a combination of 'atticism' (imitation of classical Attic Greek) with an 'asianist' or baroque style. His belief that the second sophistic was not established until the second century AD caused him to take the *Babylonian Story* as the first true novel and to put all other novels after it (leaving Antonius

---

[43] Cf. E. Rohde (1960: 12–13) on the transcendent imaginative Poet who reigned before rationalism.

[44] Ibid. 541–54, cf. 260.   [45] Ibid. 549.

[46] Ibid. 44, cf. 119. In the medieval German *Nibelungenlied* Siegfried's love is for Kriemhild, not Brunhild. Wagner made his Brünnhilde the major romantic interest on the basis of nordic versions (Rohde uses the familiar German names while calling the saga 'nordic').

Diogenes' first-century *Incredible Things* as an experiment in which the erotic element was as yet not fully developed). When it was discovered that a fully-fledged novel, the *Ninus* romance, had certainly been written before the end of the first century AD, if not much earlier (Wilcken suggested that the script of the papyrus might even belong to 'later Ptolemaic times'[47]), the novel's dependence on the second sophistic was apparently ended at a stroke and Rohde's scheme with it.

Atticism is one of the most extraordinary and best-documented examples of linguistic purism. It is important to be aware that it did *not* suddenly arise in the mid-second century AD. Rather it is clear from Philostratus' *Lives of the Sophists*, from the first handbooks of Attic style (Dionysius of Halicarnassus and Caecilius of Caleacte at the end of the first century BC) and atticist rhetoric (Theon of Smyrna in the first century AD), and from atticist authors like Dio Chrysostom (later first/early second century AD) that atticizing taste grew progressively stronger during the first century AD and was dominant by its end. Even then atticism was not monolithic. The precise identification of the right classical models was difficult, as has been remarked already, and competence in Attic language and literature was anyway more often a matter of belief and presentation than of reality, since the possession of classicizing culture was as much a social affair as a literary one. The proliferation of rival handbooks of Attic style and manuals of Attic lexicography is both a sign of the difficulty of the task and an indication of its value in giving the Greek élite a firm identity as Greeks whose cultural-political roots lay in the free Greek world before the coming of Rome.[48]

In the view of many nineteenth-century scholars atticism had been obliged to dislodge 'asianism', the degenerate, exuberant form of Greek prose which had become the norm in Hellenistic times. The cause of this essentially erroneous view was the habit of approaching the Greek world of the second sophistic, including its literature, from a Roman perspective. For the naming of an 'Asian' or 'Asiatic' style occurs principally in *Latin* letters of the Late Republican period. It is never found in Greek rhetorical treatises addressed to a Greek audience.[49] 'Asianism' was still remembered

---

[47] Wilcken (1893: 164); for his actual preferred dating see below, p. 18.
[48] Cf. Bowie (1970), Swain (1996).
[49] It occurs in Dionysius of Halicarnassus' prefatory work *On Ancient Orators* in

in Latin by Quintilian and Tacitus at the turn of the second century AD and this was enough to persuade scholars like Rohde and
Schmid (who followed him closely here) that it formed a major part
of the second-century revival of Greek rhetoric. It is this which
explains Rohde's chronology of the novel's birth.

In his report of the *Ninus* romance Wilcken is careful to pay
tribute to Rohde's 'classic' work, while being fully aware of the
implications of his dating of the new text. Although he suggests
initially that the work may well be Ptolemaic, the atticism and
rhetoric of the language made him decide finally on a date 'not too
far back in the first century BC'. Moreover, as he pointed out, *Ninus*
does not appear to be experimental and thus presupposed the
existence of earlier novels.[50] The main *Ninus* papyrus was reused to
record accounts which are dated to 100 or 101 AD. Owing to the
good quality of the hand and layout of the text of the novel
Wilcken was loath to believe that it could have been discarded
quickly—'at least 50-70 years must have elapsed' before the reuse
of 'such a valuable book'.

It has been recognized for some time now that the hand of the
main *Ninus* fragments actually belongs to the 'latter part of the first
century' AD (as does the fragment of a different copy).[51] The novel
was indeed discarded within a generation. We do not know when
Ninus was first written; but there is no need to date it very long
before our papyri. However, Wilcken's dating encouraged a rebellion against Rohde's totalizing masterpiece and may be said to have
shaped all major scholarship till fairly recent times. A first-century
BC beginning for the novel, something Rohde had in fact been
careful not to rule out absolutely,[52] opened up the possibility that
Petronius' *Satyrica*, in which a male homosexual couple have a
series of ribald adventures in various 'Greek' towns of southern
Italy, was a parody of a serious Greek novel similar to *Ninus*
or *Chaereas and Callirhoe*. This view was advocated especially by
the Latinist Richard Heinze shortly after Rohde's death (though

what is effectively a quotation from Cicero included to please Dionysius' Roman
friends; see Gabba (1991: 31-4). Greek denunciations of the prose of the Hellenistic
period avoid the label in the political-moral sense it acquired at Rome.

[50] Wilcken (1893: 191-3).

[51] The Berlin roll (frgs. A, B, D): Roberts (1955: no. 11a). The Oxyrhynchus
fragment (frg. C) has a similar date. Cf. Stephens and Winkler (1995: 31, 63).

[52] E. Rohde (1960: 263; cf. 387).

rumblings of dissent had been heard in his lifetime).[53] According to Heinze not only was Rohde's chronology wrong, but his idea of fusion was completely unnecessary (he noted with some justification that only *Incredible Things* showed Rohde's element of 'travel fantasy'), for the Greek *Liebesroman* had long existed in 'approximately the form . . . presupposed by Petronius'.

It is interesting that Heinze's triumphalism rests only on the destruction of Rohde's literary explanations for the novel, whereas for Rohde it had been as important to postulate social reasons for the novel's prose form and erotic focus. There is a strong connection in Rohde's mind between the rise of prose fiction and the decline (as he saw it) of the Greek world from the classical through the Hellenistic to the Roman period (the period of 'das sinkende Altertum', 'antiquity in decline'). He too noted the position of the 'individual' in the great Hellenistic cities, whose self-indulgent passion was satisfied first by erotic poetry ('the poetry of private life') and later by romantic novels celebrating the only goddess still to carry any meaning, Love.[54] Rohde talked about a total change in the construction of the sentiment (*Empfindungsweise*) as being relevant in both periods. This nexus of ideas has had a wide appeal in recent times. The rise of the isolated individual, his longing for personal stories about people just like himself, and the idea of the novel as epic in prose for the plain man are at the heart of Perry's *The Ancient Romances* (1967), and is prominent in influential modern work such as David Konstan's *Sexual Symmetry* (1994). And Rohde's conception of a fundamental change in society's *Empfindungsweise* is again relevant to Konstan and other scholars who are interested in what we now call from Michel Foucault 'the history of sexuality'.

Rohde's cultural approaches to the novel were not, however, pursued for the time being. Rather, three important literary approaches were offered. A convincing improvement on his ideas was made by Eduard Schwartz's *Fünf Vorträge über den griechischen Roman* (1896). Towards the end of these *Five Lectures* on fiction in Greek narrative literature Schwartz suggested that the ancient romance was a by-product of the 'decay' (*Zersetzung*) of Hellenistic

---

[53] Heinze (1899), cf. already Bürger (1892a), whose ideas are rejected by Rohde (1901a: 25–39). Schmid *ap*. E. Rohde (1960: 605) too dismisses the idea as 'pure supposition'. For Gärtner (1984: VIII) it 'has proved itself brilliantly true'.

[54] E. Rohde (1960: 127–8).

historiography, especially as practised at Alexandria, which moved
under the influence of an orientalized rhetoric from real history to
a self-consciously artistic 'quasi-poetry'. Schwartz was prepared to
follow Rohde (to whom he pays court) in the belief that the novel
had not properly emerged before the second century AD, though he
found in the *Ninus* romance a confirmation of his thoughts on the
development of fictional historiography. He accepted the importance of Alexandrian erotic poetry as a source of the love element
in the novel; this also suffered decay in that its material was
prosified. But he greatly played down the importance of fantasy
travel. Rohde sneered that his idea of the novel was as loose as that
of his own predecessor, A. Chassang, who had confused the novel
with all imaginative prose fiction.[55] It is, however, strange that
Rohde ignored historiography as a source for the prose structure of
the novel, since some of the novels (*Ninus, Chaereas and Callirhoe,
Metiochus and Parthenope, Ethiopian Story*) allude to 'historical'
events (the element of pseudo-history being high in all of these),
while the influence of historiographical writing and form is undeniable (Xenophon's dependence on Herodotus, Longus' imitations of Thucydides).

Otmar Schissel von Fleschenberg's *Entwicklungsgeschichte des
griechischen Romanes im Altertum* was published in 1913.[56] Some of
his odder ideas, especially his 'attempt to mechanize [the novel's]
literary development' in ten arbitrary stages (which include
Petronius and Apuleius), are probably best forgotten.[57] One of his
merits was to bring into consideration the short story or novella,
arguing that late Hellenistic collections of such tales had shown the
novelists how to use a 'frame story' (*Rahmenerzählung*) within which
they placed their heroes' central adventures. Schissel pointed to
Aristides' *Milesiaka* as a known, if lost, example. The title of this
work clearly has influenced some of our existing stories (*Ephesiaka,
Phoinikika, Aithiopika*); but most scholars would not allow a real
connection between a series of tales (cf. Lucian's *Toxaris, Lovers of
Lies*) and a novel conceived of as a unit, even if it is accepted that
Aristides couched his stories within a framework such as that used
by Boccaccio. A partial exception is Fritz Wehrli, who argued in an

---

[55] E. Rohde (1901*b*). Cf. Chassang (1862). Helm (1956) takes a similarly broad
view.
[56] *History of the Development of Greek Novelistic Fiction in Antiquity.*
[57] Cf. Schmid *ap.* E. Rohde (1960: 606–8, 612–13).

important article published in 1965 that the presence of novellas, defined as digressions or episodes of the main story, in both the Greek novels and in Petronius and Apuleius showed that they had entered prose fiction at a fairly early stage. In arguing thus Wehrli, of course, took the Hellenistic origin of the novel for granted. That the Greek novels do not share the tone of their Latin counterparts (except for *Lucius or Ass*) was to be explained by a process of 'standardization' (*Vereinheitlichung*), in which non-ideal elements were progressively marginalized, an idea which owes much to Schissel's own model of 'standardization', in which Schissel suggested appealingly that the novel eventually (in the form of Heliodorus' *Ethiopian Story*) became too moral, too interested in chastity and true love, and therefore too boring to survive.

The next major contribution was Bruno Lavagnini's fluent essay 'Le origini del romanzo greco', published in 1922. In arguing for the influence of Hellenistic historiography Lavagnini took his cue from Schwartz, but he concerned himself purely with local legends. Throwing a glance at Rohde's social-cultural concerns, Lavagnini suggested that such legends focused on stories of love because the Hellenistic age was the age of the individual who was satisfied only by the literature proper to the self—the love story. These local tales underwent a 'double elaboration'. Partly they were transformed into Alexandrian court poetry, which had no very wide appeal. Partly they were (re-)written as full-length narratives of love for the 'less cultured classes' (an educational, not a social distinction). None of these had much artistic merit (except for Longus' *Daphnis and Chloe*). In this manner Lavagnini was pleased to have dissolved the gap between the Hellenistic period and the second sophistic, which had troubled Rohde himself. Naturally, too, his thesis squared with the discovery of the *Ninus* romance and with Heinze's demonstration of the romance-origins of Petronius' *Satyrica*.[58] Lavagnini observes finally that part of the novel's inheritance from historiography (which includes the 'short narrative', a species distinct from the novella) is the setting in the past. The high regard in which contemporaries held these theories may be seen most easily in Giuseppe Giangrande's 1962 survey of the novel's develop-

---

[58] Lavagnini (1922a: 13–14); E. Rohde (1960: 176–7). The gap is in any case not a void: we can at least point to the generation of the *Alexander Romance*, and to the existence of stories in oral circulation (cf. Trenkner (1958)) and other quasi-novelistic material.

ment. He argued that the 'double elaboration' of love stories was unnecessary: a 'vertical' elaboration from Hellenistic love poetry, which was turned into prose via the (well-attested) medium of the 'school paraphrasis', explained the novel on its own.

It was at this point that the 'Hellenistic theory' of the novel (as it may be called) was turned in a radical new direction by Karl Kerényi. Kerényi's ideas about the religious meaning of the novels, which he published in 1927 (see above, p. 14), were based on the then dominant trends in the history of religion. From the end of the nineteenth century onwards a series of rationalist scholars (Bidez, Cumont, Dodds, Festugière, Murray, Nestle, Reitzenstein) sought to explain the origin of new religious interests in the Hellenistic age, such as Isis, Asclepius, Mithras, in the dissolution of traditional civic and familial structures and a crisis of faith in the old gods. The new gods appealed to isolated individuals because they could offer genuine social interaction in this world and the possibility of salvation in the next. This process culminated in Christianity. A marked feature of this body of work is its tendency to make revealing connections between 'antiquity in decline' and the twentieth century. Another feature is the idea of a debasement of Hellenism under 'oriental' influences. The extent of Semitic and Egyptian influence on Greek culture is debated today as fiercely as ever, and it would be odious to point an 'orientalist' finger at the rather simple model of corruption and decline advanced by some earlier interpreters. Rohde himself in his generation had also thought of a Graeco-oriental society, though he avoided drawing comparisons between what Dodds for example called the Age of Anxiety (the second and third centuries AD) and his own time.[59] As to Kerényi, it may be said that he was a victim of his own learning. His huge knowledge of ancient, especially Egyptian, religion, tricked him into a relentless reductionism whereby the novels' stories must be traced back to the one story of Isis and Osiris.[60] Since Apuleius' *Metamorphoses* was the most Isiac novel in ancient literature, its Greek base-text, the *Lucius or Ass*, must also have been strongly Isiac and was therefore the first Greek novel.[61] After-

[59] He was also aware of the possibility that many novellas had an eastern origin: see the lecture of 1875 published at the end of E. Rohde (1960).

[60] See e.g. Nock (1928) for an assessment of Kerényi's particular strengths and general weakness.

[61] Behind this suggestion is Reitzenstein's theory of the 'aretalogy' (see e.g. Merkelbach (1994); cf. above, n. 37) and his belief in a 2nd-c. BC date for the *Ass*

wards the connection between the novels and the Isis-story became progressively less sharp (Kerényi suggested that this offered a way of dating the novels), and the novelists did not necessarily know they were reworking a holy story.[62]

When Kerényi wrote, it had been known for nearly a century that native Egyptian literature had some part to play in the history of Greek prose. The *Nektanebos* fragment, a fictional narrative about the last Pharaoh, dates to the second century BC and is evidently a translation of a lost Demotic text. The importance of such translations has been stressed by a number of leading scholars, arguing for the transfer of an Egyptian form into Greek literature.[63] Kerényi's idea was quite different. For him an essential structural feature of Egyptian culture was incorporated and built into Greek society and expressed in a characteristically Graeco-oriental form. His religious interpretation has been elaborated in recent times by Reinhold Merkelbach, who sees the different novels as representing texts of the various different 'mystery religions of antiquity in decline'.[64] The first novels were, again, retellings of the Isis-story and Xenophon is the oldest surviving 'initiatory novel' (*Mysterienroman*).[65] The sustained intimacy of *Daphnis and Chloe* is one of the clearest cases of all.[66] Merkelbach has never denied that the novels may be read as entertainment. Indeed, their role as literature is important to their success as religious books. But only those who have been initiated in, for example, the cult of Dionysus can really understand Longus' *Daphnis and Chloe*, since almost every incident in such a text is designed to recall some aspect of the cult's ritual.

It must be said that few scholars choose to follow Kerényi and Merkelbach (Albert Henrichs is a prominent exception), though ironically many who do not have been ready to see the novel as a product of social decline.[67] This is true of perhaps the most

(which had, he argued, been part of Aristides' *Milesian Tales*). The extant version of the *Ass* must be late 1st- or 2nd-c. AD.

[62] See esp. Kerényi (1927: ch. 10).
[63] Wilcken (1905), esp. Barns (1956) followed by Reardon (1971: 328–33); cf. Stephens and Winkler (1995: introduction). The only example to survive in both languages is the *Tefnut* fragment: West (1969); Tait (1994: 212–13).
[64] Merkelbach (1962).
[65] Xenophon's redactor later changed the focus from Isis to Helios: ibid. 91, 110ff., cf. Merkelbach (1995).   [66] Merkelbach (1988). Cf. below, p. 30.
[67] Henrichs (1972), cf. Petri (1963) on Chariton. For a balanced assessment of Merkelbach see Beck (1996). On decline and the novel there is no finer essay than that of Altheim (1951).

influential English-language scholar of the novel, Ben Perry. Perry's contributions to scholarship on the Greek novel begin with a still important article on Chariton.[68] But he is best known for his 1951 Sather Lectures, *The Ancient Romances: A Literary-Historical Account of their Origins*, which were published in 1967. In this work, which also has important chapters on the comic 'romances' of Petronius, Apuleius, and Lucian (who he believed was the author of the original version of the *Ass*), Perry set himself against 'organic' models of the novel's development. He stressed three factors: the historical-cultural background, the formative influence of Xenophon's historical saga about Cyrus the Great, the *Cyropaedia*, and the crucial role of the author who first decided to write a novel 'on a Tuesday afternoon in July' prompted by Xenophon's work.[69] Perry, who did not question the early dating of *Ninus*, put the beginnings of the novel in the 'late second century BC.' It was invented to please 'Everyman', an isolated individual who might be 'on the farm or in the army' or in a large Hellenistic city. His 'open society', a 'cosmopolitan world' full of 'foreigners and expatriates', became in the Roman heyday of the novel 'essentially backward-looking, negative, and moribund in worldly affairs and prospects'. Unsurprisingly Perry suggested that '[t]he age of Greek romance was similar to that of the modern novel'.[70] The Everyman it was written for got his 'latter-day epic' in prose, 'the natural medium for a reading public'.[71]

Although Perry describes the ideas of Kerényi and Merkelbach as 'nonsense',[72] the interpretative trends that influenced them have influenced him too, and the assumed problems of Hellenistic man coincide with and reinforce the assumed Hellenistic origin of the novel. It looks today as if this picture is terribly wrong. First, there is no compelling reason to accept so early a date for the novel or for any novel. Most scholars would now agree that the earliest fully surviving novelist (Chariton) must be placed at the end of the first or the beginning of the second century AD.[73] *Ninus* and *Metiochus*

---

[68] Perry (1930).

[69] Perry (1967: 175). On the role of the *Cyropaedia* Perry acknowledges Weil (1902).

[70] Perry (1967: 6–7, 29).   [71] Ibid. 29, 72, 79.   [72] Ibid. 336 n. 17.

[73] e.g. Baslez (1992); C. P. Jones (1992). Linguistic analysis has played an important part in this trend: Ruiz-Montero (1980, 1991); Hernández Lara (1994). One other piece of evidence may be noted here: the *Callirhoe* referred to disparagingly by Persius at the end of his first *Satire* (134). If this is a reference to Chariton, Chariton

and Parthenope are not long before and it seems difficult to deny that the age of the novel is the High Roman Empire.[74] That papyrological evidence has had a part in forming this consensus makes it all the more paradoxical that a century after Rohde's death one of his principal contentions has been quietly resurrected: the novel *is* second sophistic. Secondly, the benighted and grim world of the Greeks under Rome is entirely imaginary. The evidence of archaeology, of epigraphy and numismatics, of the many literary texts of the period, if read without bias, make it plain that the second sophistic was a time of extraordinary confidence in the Greek world. We might recall that Rohde, though putting the second sophistic too late (for reasons I have sketched above), was none the less aware that Greeks of this time were not convinced of their own decline. It is easy to forget that he had stressed historical and cultural changes in the making of the novel. (He had also, by the by, assumed an 'inventor'.[75]) He realized that the second sophistic stood not only for a revival of good literature. Just as important was a 'national-hellenisches Element', a sense of Greekness reborn, and the encouragement of this by philhellene Romans such as Hadrian.[76] The love romance, as its 'most characteristic flower', was the product of a very different cultural environment from that envisaged by those who came after him.

   The Greek novels are of course about individuals wandering around the world, suffering tribulations, undergoing many bad experiences. The confidence of the Greek world in the period of their production obviously did not preclude personal anxieties (which there is no need to psychopathologize). More to the point, it did not preclude the use of these as entertainment. This storyline caught on as a literary form. But it had to remain recognizable. The adventures of the two young lovers were extreme but not impossible versions of any life. They reflect a big world picture and what can go wrong in that world for people. Young people are

had written by 'the earliest years of Nero's reign' (Reardon 1996: 317). However, Persius would seem to be refering to poetry or possibly a dramatic work: there is no guarantee that even the same story is involved, let alone Chariton's version of it.

   [74] It is unclear if the novel continued to be written into the late Empire: the matter turns on the question of whether Heliodorus is 3rd- or 4th-c. See esp. Bowersock (1994: 149–60), triumphalist on the 4th c.; and Lightfoot (1988: esp. 115–19), sensible on the 3rd c.

   [75] E. Rohde (1960: 264), 'Erfinder', 'der erste Begründer'.

   [76] Ibid. 313 ff., 319 ff.

the focus because of their enthusiasm, naïvety, conviction—but
also because (as Bourdieu somewhere remarks) the young 'have
nothing' and are 'unconditional supporter[s]' of the system they
choose to be part of. The stories of the novels are the imaginary
necessary reverse side of society's success, a harmless way of asking 'what if?' But they are not a sign of introspection or collapse,
as the happy endings make plain.

RECENT READINGS

The biggest difference between the work of the last thirty years and
what precedes it is the discovery that the novels are clever, high-
quality *literary* texts. Virtually all previous generations of scholars
have been embarrassed by their own condemnation of the novels
as works of low artistic merit (a judgement from which only
Longus was routinely excepted). There are two main reasons for
the change. One is an improvement in historians' understanding of
the cultural conditions of the Greek world under Rome. We now
have a better idea about the novelists' own expectations of their
readership and about the demand of these readers for good books.
A second is the greatly increased attention being paid to post-
classical Greek literature by Hellenists. Modern literary theory and
the highly developed critical apparatus for reading modern prose
fiction have proved particularly fruitful here, though it is sometimes true that modern criticism is invoked simply to make spontaneous responses look as if they are 'tricked out as the most
explosive stuff around'.[77] Disguising older approaches under modern ones is a game for some cultural historians too. A number of
those who want to tie the novel down in its own time have
deployed Foucauldian analysis to explain its foregrounding of
virginity, chastity, and marriage, and in many cases the effort has
paid off handsomely, bringing research on the novel into contact
with the latest thinking on gender studies and the new interpretations of early Christianity.[78]

It is not my intention (nor is it within my ability) to go through

---

[77] Eagleton (1981: 138). Bakhtin is one 20th-c. critic whose work (1981) has
encompassed the ancient romances—and has been of major influence.

[78] Cf. and ctr. Richlin (1992a: xiii–xxxiii) on the problem of Foucault's andro-
centrism.

the burgeoning modern literature on the novel. I shall say something about the pieces put into this volume and place these and some of the many good items which could not be, including books and collections, in the context of recent trends.

With regard to readership the last few years have seen real progress. First and foremost here are essays by Ewen Bowie and Susan Stephens.[79] On the basis of the novels' range of literary allusion, their utilization of rhetorical techniques learned in the academies of higher education,[80] the social and political assumptions made in the texts, and the facts of book production, circulation, and literacy, as well as a few references to novel-reading in antiquity, it is very likely that the novels' readers were found among those with access to wealth and education. We know nothing of the size of this readership (the numbers of novel papyri are so low as to be irrelevant). And we can only speculate on the distribution of the readers within this class: were they men, children, women? Furthermore, there is of course no law which makes only sophisticated readers read sophisticated texts.[81] On the subject of female readership and particularly the question of how female readers might respond to the presentation of the novels' heroines, both in a literary and in a social role, there is an outstanding essay by Brigitte Egger, which it is a pleasure to include in this volume (Ch. 5).[82] From solid historical evidence she shows that the position of women in the novels does not reflect the greater freedom of women in Greek society after the classical period and she questions the easy assumption that the heroine—often the most important *dramatis persona*—must have appealed to a female reader.

The modern work on readership squares with our general knowledge of the cultural and social life of the Greek élites.[83] If we combine this work with current thinking on the dating of the novel, it becomes increasingly untenable to divide the novels into

---

[79] Bowie (1994, 1996; cf. 1985a: 688 = below, p. 45); Stephens (1994). See also Wesseling (1988).

[80] Cf. esp. Bartsch (1989), and of older work Rommel (1923).

[81] Cf. Stramaglia (1996) on the identification of Chariton on a papyri school list of trisyllables: *if* he is right, the apparently elementary level is interesting (but tells us nothing about who included Chariton and for what reason).

[82] Egger (1988, cf. 1994a, with a much more restricted interest). See also Wiersma (1990) and Johne (1996).

[83] For the novels' contributions to this body of knowledge see e.g. recently Liviabella Furiani and Scarcella (1989).

a 'presophistic' Chariton and Xenophon and a 'sophistic' Achilles
Tatius, Heliodorus, and Longus, as does Perry (reserving for the
former a 'juvenile' readership and for the latter a lonely one).[84] The
better understanding of the true audience and dating of the novels
should encourage us to return to the old questions of why the
novel was invented and from where it came. Graham Anderson
has done more than most to disclose the qualities that made second
sophistic fiction (including the novel) appealing to its readers,[85]
though in the case of the novel he sidesteps the actual question of
invention by tracing its themes to 'the [near-eastern] fertility and
divine kingship myths of several millennia before'.[86] The two recent
attempts to suggest reasons for the rise of the novel in its own
times irrespective of its thematic ancestry—by myself and Glen
Bowersock—propose quite different answers. My own work tries to
isolate the elements in the (ideal) novel which appealed to the
Greek élite of the time. Two of the selections in this volume respond
to this interest (Saïd 1987; Hägg 1987: see below). Briefly, I argue
that the ideal Greek novel encoded the civic values of the élite. The
accent on marriage and faithfulness appealed to a group which
was beholden to the mystique of ancestry. To these readers
marriage, the perpetuation of their own kind, was of paramount
importance and interest. The change in sexual ethics in the High
Roman Empire, whereby married love was given an intellectual
credibility denied to homosexual relations,[87] is tangential to this,
for the sexuality of the novels is rather a part of the general
engagement with the free Greek past that characterizes the time of
their production.[88]

Bowersock's interest is in the rise of prose fiction under Rome.
Here the novel takes its place beside texts like Ptolemy's *Strange
History* (see above). He contends that the phenomenon is 'some

[84] Perry (1967: 98). The division, and not dissimilar thoughts on readers, is
maintained by among others Hägg (1983; 1994), on which see Bowie (1996:
95–100).

[85] See bibliography *s.v.* G. Anderson (a small selection of his work); on the novel
note esp. (1982, 1984).

[86] G. Anderson (1984: 13, cf. 217). It is as well to mention here the first modern proponent of an eastern origin for the novel, Pierre-Daniel Huet, who advanced
his thesis about Greek fiction (1671) as part of a general theory that the world's
myths represented a diffusion of the Moses story. Cf. Sandy (1996: 745–50).

[87] See esp. Foucault (1986).

[88] Cf. Beaton (1996: 12–13, 22–3, 54) on the function of the past in the
12th-c. Byzantine novels.

kind of reflection of the remarkable stories that were coming out of
Palestine precisely in the middle of the first century AD,'[89] in other
words, the accounts of Jesus. In his survey of recent literature on
the novel John Morgan suggests that Bowersock's social-cultural-
religious reading is part of an 'apparent faltering of the [literary]
critical trends [of the novel scholarship] of the early eighties'.[90] If
there is a new interest in the novel's 'didacticism' (Morgan), it has
been made possible by the new ideas about the chronology and
society of the novel. Thus Wilcken and his dating of the *Ninus*
romance are wisely ignored by Bowersock. As to society, it is true
that Kerényi's arguments have a part in the ancestry of Bowersock's thesis that fiction is a response to a particular mystery story
(Christianity) without constituting a series of mystery texts.[91] But
the book's more direct origin lies in the current interest among
historians of religion in the productive interrelations between
pagans and Christians.[92]

The historical setting of the novels should also be part of this
'didacticism'. On this important subject there is an admirable piece
by Tomas Hägg, which has been included in this volume (Ch. 6)[93]
Though he is uninterested in the reasons for the appeal of the past
in the High Roman Empire, Hägg does us the service of reviewing
the ancient novels against the criteria for labelling a modern novel
'historical', a comparison well worth exploring.[94] The urban viewpoint of the novels is surely another part of their 'didacticism'.
Scholars have sometimes been tempted to exploit the novels for
information about rural life. Suzanne Saïd has written a superb
piece on the real presentation of the rural scene, and it has been
translated for this collection (Ch. 4).[95] She explodes some of the
dumber fantasies and makes it quite plain that in the novels rural
décor forms a conscious 'other' to the urban scene, and amounts
to a re-emphasis of civic values in an age that was indeed one of
the most successful periods of urban development in the ancient
world.

[89] Bowersock (1994: 119).
[90] Morgan (1996*a*: 73).
[91] Cf. esp. Kerényi (1927: ch. 2), 'Tod und Auferstehung', with Bowersock
(1994: ch. 5), 'Resurrection'.
[92] On contact between pagan and Christian literature see e.g. Pervo (1987) and,
better, Perkins (1995: chs. 2, 4, 5, 8).   [93] Hägg (1987).
[94] Cf. Morgan (1996*b*) on the possibility of seeing the novels as a species of
Bildungsroman.   [95] Saïd (1987).

As Saïd notes, Longus has been the prime site for rival interpretations of the novelistic countryside. The interpretation of his story as literature has often turned on this question. After Erwin Rohde's condemnation *Daphnis and Chloe* was not properly rehabilitated until the famous 1937 essay of Georg Rohde (no relation), 'Longus and Bucolic'.[96] Unlike his namesake, G. Rohde thought that Longus *was* a Nature-lover. His view of *Daphnis and Chloe* as a mystical, semi-religious text has had two major influences. First is the important article of Henry Chalk.[97] Chalk argued that *Daphnis and Chloe* is an elaborate celebration of Dionysus as a creator god of Nature, and that the literary development of the heroes marks the stages of initiation into his cult. Still more determined to prove the religious truth of the story is Merkelbach, first in a chapter in his famous (or notorious) *Novel and Mystery Religion* (*Roman und Mysterium*), of 1962, secondly in a 1988 book of much value and insight devoted to Longus alone, *The Shepherds of Dionysus* (*Die Hirten des Dionysos*). Bernd Effe's 1982 piece on Longus (Effe 1982a) is an important and original survey of these attitudes and has been included in this volume (Ch. 8). He himself suggests that Longus' fling with Nature is momentary escapism designed to appeal to the readership's urban love of the country. Ultimately Erwin Rohde was right.

Two important responses to Effe should be noted. First, Gerlinde Bretzigheimer has suggested not unreasonably that the key to understanding Longus is a sophisticated, immoralist urban humour, which makes fun of everything rural.[98] Karl-Heinz Stanzel deflects the question of attitude by arguing that *Daphnis and Chloe* is virtually a *Bildungsroman*, a novel about the development of personality through experience.[99] Some will feel that any *Bildungsroman* is necessarily a critical analysis of the society which gives these experiences. And a magisterial essay by Jack Winkler, published first in a well-known volume in 1990, takes this approach further by arguing that what he calls a 'resisting reader' will discover in Longus a deliberate ambiguity about his contemporaries' attitudes to sex and marriage.[100]

Three other examples of the rich scholarship on Longus, one of which is translated below, must be mentioned. First is Richard

[96] 'Longus und die Bukolik'.
[97] Chalk (1960). Chalk and G. Rohde would have been included in this volume, had they not been reprinted several times over (Rohde, however, has not been translated into English).   [98] Bretzigheimer (1988).
[99] Stanzel (1991); cf. again Morgan (1996b).   [100] Winkler (1990).

Hunter's 1983 exploration of Longus' debt to earlier literature. A better treatment of Longus' responses to his sources is offered by Lia Cresci's 1981 article, the translation of which in this volume (Ch. 9) should complement for English-language users both Hunter and the several good articles by Michael Mittelstadt on this subject.[101] Finally, a piece which would like Winkler's have been included here, were it not available twice over in books basic to any library, is Froma Zeitlin's 1990 essay on the development of Daphnis and Chloe against the text's interplay of Art and Nature. This is essential reading for anyone thinking about the structure of this text.[102]

The standard of work on Heliodorus is as high as that on Longus. The old questions of date and author are still argued over. If Heliodorus is a product of the fourth rather than the third century, as many hold, he is surely one of the last Greek novelists of antiquity, and will have been writing for a pagan élite that was under threat from an offensive state-sponsored Christianity.[103] In the interpretation of the *Ethiopian Story* as literature one name stands out: John Morgan. In a series of articles he has done more than anyone else to elucidate the structure of the narrative and the assumptions and predilections of the author.[104] In the end only one of these articles could be included, his 1989 reading of the Cnemon tale as an immoral story of how not to love with a clear didactic message for the interpretation of the whole novel (Ch. 11).[105] Any serious student of Heliodorus must read also at least Morgan (1982). Both this paper and Winkler's 1982 study of Heliodorus' 'narrative strategy' were aired at the first international conference on the ancient novel, held in 1976 in Bangor (Wales) to mark the centenary of *Der griechische Roman*.[106] Winkler's article is long and, some may feel, self-indulgent; it is also a brilliant example of a clever reading of a text by one of the best representatives of this school of criticism and for this reason it has been included in this collection (Ch. 12). To read the piece today is to discover the

---

[101] Esp. Mittelstadt (1970).

[102] On Longus see also *inter alios* Berti (1967), Billault (1996a), Bowie (1985b), Edwards (1997), Longo (1978), Mason (1979 and 1995), McCulloh (1970), MacQueen (1990), Morgan (1997 and forthcoming), Reeve (1969), Scarcella (1968a, 1968b, 1970, and 1972b), Valley (1926), Vieillefond (1987), Young (1968 and 1971).

[103] Cf. n. 74 above.

[104] See bibliography *s.v.* Morgan.

[105] Morgan (1989a).

[106] Abstracts and menus in Reardon (1977).

forerunner of *Auctor & Actor*, the dazzling 1985 study of Apuleius' *Metamorphoses*. If the approach works better on Apuleius, that is because Apuleius' comic masterpiece is a cleverer, less straightforward text. Heliodorus' narrative sophistication is undeniable; but his moral code is surely less questionable than Apuleius'.[107]

Massimo Fusillo is another leading exponent of the narratological approach to the ancient novels. His 1989 book, *Il romanzo greco. Polifonia ed eros*,[108] is the most successful single reading of the major novelists (*Daphnis and Chloe* is excluded because of its somewhat different literary ancestry). Two of his pieces have been translated for this volume: the highly original 1990 study of emotional turmoil in the romances (Ch. 3);[109] and his study of Lucian's *True Histories* (Ch. 13).[110] The latter has been included for two reasons. First, anyone interested in the novel must pay attention also to other types of prose fiction in the same period. *True Histories* is the best of the rest (see above, pp. 7–8) and has had an important influence on later literature. Secondly, and more importantly, the work is comic. Fusillo's study of it is the best treatment known to me of how humour works in a text of this time.[111] The success of the analysis depends in part on its use of Gérard Genette's *Palimpsestes*, in which Genette deals with the question of 'hypertextuality', the 'global' reuse of a base text ('hypotext') by a later author (for example, Joyce's *Ulysses* and Homer's *Odyssey*). The application of his theories to second sophistic literature awaits exploitation. One of his realizations is the extent to which humour is present in such imitation (see above, p. 11), and this is certainly the case with Lucian. The translation of Fusillo's piece should open up a more sophisticated way of reading a phenomenon at the heart of the novels themselves.

It is not for reasons of space that no specific study of Xenophon is represented in this volume: there is a lack of quality material that is not already published in books or collections.[112] The same is

[107] On Heliodorus see also *inter alios* Altheim (1942), S. Bartsch (1989), Billault (1981b), Bowie (1995), Breitzigheimer (1998), Dowden (1996), Feuillâtre (1966), Futre Pinheiro (1987 and 1998), Hefti (1950), Karl-Deutscher (1996 and 1997), Kövendi (1966), Lightfoot (1988), Mazal (1958), Paulsen (1992), Rommel (1923), Sandy (1982a and 1982b), Scarcella (1972b), Szepessy (1957, 1975, and 1976), Walden (1894).

[108] Translated into French as *La Naissance du roman grec* (1991).

[109] Fusillo (1990a).   [110] Fusillo (1988a).

[111] See also Branham's excellent 1989 study of Lucian.

[112] On Xenophon see *inter alios* K. Bürger (1892b), Griffiths (1978), Hägg (1966,

true of work on Achilles Tatius. In his case, however, an exception has been made to the rules by including Bryan Reardon's sensible and compact 1994 study.[113]

Chariton too suffers from something of a lack of available studies in journals apart from Bryan Reardon's elegant *Yale Classical Studies* article from 1982, a self-selecting piece for any collection (Ch. 7). Here without the assistance of narratology Reardon simply tells us how the novel functions as literature.[114] He shows the same sobriety and sense that is apparent in his classic 1969 study, 'The Greek Novel', which may be said to mark the start of the novel's revival in English-language literary scholarship. Taking up many of Perry's ideas, it went beyond him in treating the texts at last as literature. It is still one of the best introductory pieces available. But for the purpose of introducing the Greek novels in this collection we have taken the opportunity of reprinting Ewen Bowie's thorough and masterly 1985 chapter of the same title (Ch. 2).[115]

To understand the ancient Greek novel is to try to understand all its components and roles at once. It is probably beyond the ability of any one author to encompass both the literary and the social-cultural dimensions. Collections of papers from scholars in the several disciplines concerned have at least the potential to offer more successful treatments of the whole picture or large sections of it, and I shall mention here five recent examples of note. One is *Le Monde du roman grec* (1992), which contains high-quality essays of literary and historical interpretation.[116] For Anglophones there is

1971a, and 1971b), Kytzler (1996), Laplace (1994a), Merkelbach (1995), O'Sullivan (1995; a major study), Papanikolaou (1973a), Ruiz-Montero (1994b), Scarcella (1977 and 1979), Schmeling (1980), Zimmerman (1949-50).

[113] Reardon (1994a). See *inter alios* G. Anderson (1997), S. Bartsch (1989), Cresci (1976 and 1978), Garnaud (1991), Goldhill (1995: 66-102), Hägg (1971a), Laplace (1983a, 1983b, 1991, and 1994b), Liviabella Furiani (1988), Mignogna (1995), Morales (1995), Napolitano (1983-4), O'Sullivan (1980), Plepelits (1980 and 1996), Rojas Álvarez (1989), Rommel (1923), Scarcella (1992), Segal (1984), Vilborg (1962), Wilhelm (1902), Willis (1990).

[114] Reardon (1982a). See also Reardon (1996) and *inter alios* Alvares (1997) Bartsch (1934), Baslez (1992), Billault (1981a and 1989), D. Edwards (1994), Egger (1994b), Gerschmann (1975), Goold (1995), Hägg (1971a, 1972, and 1987), Helms (1966), Hunter (1994), C. P. Jones (1992), Laplace (1980 and 1997), Molinié (1989), Müller (1976), Papanikolaou (1973b), Perry (1930), Petri (1963), Plepelits (1976), Ruiz-Montero (1980, 1991, and 1994a), Schmeling (1974).

[115] Bowie (1985a). Among books in the introductory category are Hägg (1983), Holzberg (1994), and Schmeling (1996).

[116] Baslez-Hoffmann-Trédé (1992).

the equally welcome publication of some of the contributions to the
second international conference on the ancient novel (ICAN II,
held at Dartmouth, NH, in 1989), *The Search for the Ancient Novel*
(1994).[117] Although it is narrower in its total coverage, *Greek
Fiction: The Greek Novel in Context* (1994) is of great importance for
placing the Greek novel against other fictional writings in the
Greek language.[118] Fourth is the large handbook edited by Gareth
Schmeling, *The Novel in the Ancient World* (1996). This is a mine of
information, and can be read with profit by those who know the
field and those who do not. Fifth, the steady activity at Groningen,
published as *Groningen Colloquia on the Novel* (*GCN*), certainly
merits mention, for the Groningen programme has played a
significant part in the last decade in maintaining and bringing on
interest in the subject. It is worth noting that all of these groups of
works contain extensive bibliographies. In addition there are many
dedicated bibliographical aids for consultation.[119]

Many individuals have contributed to the success of novel scholarship over the past thirty years. If I single out Bryan Reardon from
among them here, that is not to diminish the achievement of any
other, but to state on record that Reardon has done more by himself to stimulate novel scholarship and raise its standard. His
account in his major book, *Courants littéraires grecs* (1971), his
vision in organizing the first international conference (ICAN I), and
his long project of translation (*Collected Ancient Greek Novels*, 1989)
have been among the most important forces for good in the subject. As a result of his and others' labours, novel courses are taught
in many universities and colleges. It may be asked finally where
this work may be going. On the literary side, there is still plenty to
do from a narratological perspective, both in the classic fields
of narrative time, mode, and voice, and also with regard to the

---

[117] Tatum (1994).

[118] Morgan and Stoneman (1994).

[119] See the bibliographical review articles by Sandy (1974), Bowie and Harrison
(1993), and Morgan (1996a), the appendix to Bowie (1985a), recent pieces in
ANRW by G. Anderson (1997), Morgan (1997 [this was submitted by the author
as bibliography for 1950-92] and 1998), Ruiz-Montero (1994a and 1994b), and
esp. the bi-annual surveys by Bryan Reardon in the *Petronian Society Newsletter*,
12-13 (1982), 3-5; 15 (1984), 4-5; 16 (1986), 11-13; 19 (1989), 3-6; 21
(1991), 8-15; 24 (1994), 7-14; 26 (1996), 6-10; 28 (1998), 10-16). *PSN* offers
electronic bibliographical searches as well as other items of interest to Greek and
Latin novel students via its website (http://www.chss.monclair.edu/classics/petron/
PSNNOVEL.HTML).

organic, functionalist elements of the story. As historical research is refined, reader-response interpretation, that endless exploration of the shifting 'horizons of expectation' (which so many scholars are already engaged with), will come more and more into play. In his recent summary of modern critical approaches Massimo Fusillo points additionally to the potential of psychoanalytical readings as a means of unlocking the logic of these texts.[120] Readers of his two pieces in this collection will see that this is an approach he is at home with. The immensely sophisticated and extraordinary *Sacred Tales* of Aelius Aristides (*c.* AD 170) confirm its applicability to the novels and their age.[121] Perhaps the most productive of the modern approaches may be that mentioned last by Fusillo, that range of disparate interests he labels 'post-structuralist'. The Greek novel will never attain a dominant position within Classics. To ensure its future, it must always appeal to students of other literatures and be seen to offer scope for discovering the contemporary ideological formations that are ever sought in these. For the novels are part of a total cultural system, neither literary, nor cultural, nor historical. These *Readings* are a small contribution to the enjoyment of them in all of these areas.

[120] Fusillo (1996*a*). For guidance in this area see Ellmann (1994).
[121] The *Sacred Tales* are translated with notes in Behr (1981: 278–353).

PART II
General Studies

2

The Greek Novel

E. L. BOWIE

THE GENRE

The most influential product of Graeco-Roman literary activity is
also the most enigmatic; ancient literary theory finds no place for
prose narrative about lovers who are separated, exposed to perils
and finally reunited. Apart from two dismissive allusions in Philostratus to a work and an individual, neither certainly novelistic,
only a derogatory sideswipe in Julian betrays other writers' awareness of the genre.[1] The earliest attempt to pass a constructive
literary verdict is that of Photius about AD 855. Yet most of these
works were written by men of considerable erudition, arguably for
appreciation by educated readers. The extent to which some were
read (and the range of the form's varieties) has been demonstrated,
at least for Egypt and Antioch, by papyri and mosaics discovered
over the last eighty years.[2]

Papyrus texts have also aided chronology, although there is still
uncertainty about the novel's origins and development and its
place in the culture of the Hellenistic world. Rohde saw the genre
as a product of the Second Sophistic in which declamatory themes
and techniques operated upon a hybrid of Alexandrian love-elegy
and travel tales. He began the novel's development with Antonius
Diogenes in the first century AD and ended it with Chariton in the
fifth. The discovery in 1893 of the *Ninus* romance, probably composed in the first century BC and certainly written in a hand of the

* *Editor's note*: The relevant pages of the appendix of Authors and Works have not
been reprinted in this chapter.

[1] Philostr. *V. S.* I. 22. 524 to the *Araspes and Pantheia*, possibly a novel (cf.
below, p. 43) and id. *Epist.* 66 to Chariton, disparaging his λόγοι: this may be the
novelist; Julian, *Epist.* 89B (Bidez) 301b: ὅσα δέ ἐστιν ἐν ἱστορίας εἴδει παρὰ τοῖς
ἔμπροσθεν ἀπηγγελμένα πλάσματα παραιτητέον, ἐρωτικὰς ὑποθέσεις καὶ πάντα ἁπλῶς τὰ
τοιαῦτα 'We must eschew the fictions reported under the form of history by earlier
writers, love stories and all that sort of stuff.'

[2] Cf. also n. 14 below.

early first century AD, undermined the general theory. Moreover
Rohde's view of the novelists' order was overthrown by the publication in 1900 of a papyrus of Chariton dating from the second
century AD. Much remains disputed, but the table below presents a
provisional chronology (titles of works extant in continuous texts
are in capitals, related genres in square brackets).

It would be injudicious to use the tabulation below as the basis
for any general theory. We remain uncertain when the first and
last of our novels was written. *Ninus* might be as early as 100 BC[3]
and it has been argued that the *Aethiopica* belongs to the late fourth
century. These dates would give a span of five centuries and ground
for seeing the genre as culturally symptomatic of later Hellenism.[4]
But neither *Ninus* nor Chariton need antedate the first century AD,
and if Heliodorus were third-century the efflorescence would match
that of Philostratus' Second Sophistic. For this a purely literary
explanation is possible. The novels' rise would reflect merely the
avid reading and prolific writing of the age, their demise the decline
of a peaceful and cosmopolitan Greek world.

[*Alexander*-romance prototype ? second century BC]

[*Nectanebus*' dream   second century BC]

[JOSEPH AND ASENATH   first century BC/AD?]

Ninus   first century BC? (papyri first century AD)

Chariton, CHAEREAS AND CALLIRHOE   mid-first century BC/AD?
(papyri mid-second/early third century AD)

Metiochus and Parthenope   first century AD? (papyri second century
AD)

Iolaus   first century AD? (may influence Petronius: papyrus early
second century AD)

[*Tefnut*   first/second century AD? (demotic text second, Greek text
third, century AD)]

Sesonchosis   first/second/third century AD? (papyri third century
AD)

[?Celer, *Araspes and Pantheia*   *c.* AD 150]

Xenophon of Ephesus, ANTHIA AND HABROCOMES   mid-second
century AD? (no papyri)

Diogenes, *The Incredible beyond Thule*   early/mid-second century

---

[3] *Ninus*, Perry (1967: 153); *Joseph and Asenath*, West (1974: 79–81); Chariton,
Papanikolaou (1973*b*).

[4] As Reardon (1969: 293–4).

AD? (parodied by Lucian in 160s: papyri late second/early third century)

Lucian(?), *Metamorphoses*   AD 150-180 (no papyri)

Iamblichus, *Babyloniaca*   AD 165-180 (Photius cod. 95.10 = p. 32 ed. Habrich; no papyri)

Lollianus, *Phoenicica*   mid-second century (papyrus second half of second century AD)

Longus, DAPHNIS AND CHLOE   late second/early third century AD (no papyri).

Achilles, LEUCIPPE AND CLITOPHON   late second century AD (papyri second century and later)

Heliodorus, AETHIOPICA   early/mid-third century OR late fourth century AD (no papyri)

[Philostratus, APOLLONIUS   c. AD 230 (no papyri)]

It is uncertain what features should be seen as characterizing the genre. The five novels which survived to'influence Byzantine and European readers can reasonably be seen as a coherent group,[5] each a variant on the 'ideal' romance. The plot is one element of unity. Boy and girl of aristocratic background fall in love, are separated before or shortly after marriage and subjected to melodramatic adventures which threaten their life and chastity and carry them around much of the eastern Mediterranean. Eventually love and fortune prove stronger than storms, pirates and tyrants and the couple is reunited in marital bliss. Longus offers a variation that is recognizably germane: the horizon is the Aegean off Lesbos, but the Methymnaean sportsmen can start a war, and Daphnis and Chloe turn out to be lost aristocrats in pastoral guise. Unity can also be claimed for the genre on grounds of scale, style and treatment. Longus again diverges with four books: but Chariton and Achilles have eight, the original text of Xenophon ten,[6] as does Heliodorus. All five write careful, literary Greek, eschewing hiatus[7] and affecting particular prose rhythms, especially, it seems, in speeches. Speeches, reflections and letters are much exploited to delineate the characters' emotions, set in the foreground of the reader's attention against a backcloth of travel and adventure. These emotions and the beauties of art and nature are given a

[5] Chariton, Xenophon, Longus, Achilles and Heliodorus: as well as the last two Photius knew Iamblichus, Antonius Diogenes and 'Lucius of Patrae'.

[6] Bürger (1892b).

[7] M. D. Reeve (1971).

generous allocation of rhetoric by Achilles, Longus and Heliodorus
(too generous, indeed, for modern taste). But even Chariton, despite
his less pretentious style, loses few opportunities for emotional and
rhetorically moulded outbursts, and his neglect of Atticist predilections in syntax and vocabulary is a witness to the environment in
which he was educated rather than to a humbler intent.

Fragments show four other works to have been similar. In the
Ninus the young king of Assyria is found pleading for the hand
of Semiramis and later parted from her by shipwreck. Love and
adventure in a Near-Eastern setting also mark the *Sesonchosis* story
and Iamblichus' *Babyloniaca*. All four have stylistic pretensions and,
like Chariton, envisage a specific historical context: thus *Metiochus
and Parthenope* is linked with Polycrates' Samos. The reader can
fancy that he is enjoying a sentimental sidelight on conventional
political history. This may support the view that local history is one
ancestor of the novel, although it may only be the guise under
which novelists chose to masquerade, as suggested by the form of
title probably current in antiquity—*Ephesiaca*, *Lesbiaca*, *Ethiopica*.

But at least one example shows that a historical context could
provide a setting at a more popular level. The story of the Egyptian
Asenath's love for the biblical Joseph, a love which leads to her
conversion and marriage, is written in a monotonous and simple
Greek close to the *koine*. Its novelistic motifs show that the author
was acquainted with the genre. We do not know at what level, and
it is tempting to imagine that the author knew popular examples,
which preceded the development of the literary form. Indeed, some
have seen Graeco-Egyptian literature as an important factor in the
creation of the Greek novel.[8] But the tale of Tefnut, translated from
demotic Egyptian to Greek at some time before the third century
AD, lacks *erotica*, and the dream of Nectanebus is too short to
justify its classification with the novel. We need not, therefore,
believe that the literary novel descended from Greek translations of
Egyptian tales *via* Greek popular stories.

It might be, indeed, that less pretentious versions of the novel
were written only contemporaneously with or even after the earliest literary attempts. They certainly went on being written in the
novel's heyday. The *Phoenicica*, ascribed by the papyrus fragments
to Lollianus, seems to fall within the boundaries of the genre. There
is eroticism (but not sentimentality) and dramatic if improbable

    [8] Barns (1956); Reardon (1969: nn. 39 and 43).

incident reminiscent of Xenophon (see below, pp. 48 ff.). But there is also surprising material: the seduction of the narrator Androtimus by a girl who is not the heroine (and does not seem to have the importance to the plot of Achilles' Melite or Longus' Lycaenion, cf. below, pp. 51 and 58), and a mystery ritual in which the sacrifice of a boy so that his heart can be eaten is followed by group copulation in Androtimus' presence. The style, never elevated and sometimes crude, confirms the impression that a substantial gap separates this work from the 'ideal' romance. It is hard to believe that it is by the sophist from Ephesus, P. Hordeonius Lollianus, but it may have been circulated maliciously under his name, like the *Araspes and Pantheia* published under Dionysius of Miletus' name by his enemy Celer.[9]

Three further works exemplify a type of prose fiction clearly related to the love romance but in many respects different. Antonius Diogenes' *The Incredible beyond Thule* is known only in epitome. Love seems to have played but a small part, albeit pivotal: the narrator Deinias fell in love with Dercyllis in Thule. But the many adventures are as striking as the complex framework within which they are told (cf. Heliodorus, below, p. 54). The first location seems to have been Thule. Deinias narrates his own journey there and then gives Dercyllis' account (complete with sub-plots) of how she and her brother fled to Thule pursued by the wizard Paapis. Deinias' narrative continues with Paapis' arrival and death. The siblings after a false death regain their native Tyre: Deinias too returns via the moon, assisted by a magic wish (cf. Lucian's *True Histories* and *Wishes*). Only then do we learn that all this is being told by a Deinias living happily in Tyre with Dercyllis. The final twist is still to come; Dercyllis provides tablets for the recording of the narrative, and these, buried by the principals' graves, were discovered during Alexander's siege of Tyre and form the basis of Diogenes' book.

The 'chinese box' effect is not the only remarkable feature. Size, twenty-four books, marks it off from all the love romances save that of Iamblichus. Magic and Pythagoreanism anticipate Philostratus' work on Apollonius.[10] Furthermore Antonius claimed to be a practitioner of Old Comedy.[11] As the only claim to a literary pedigree in the novelists this merits attention, even if it only alludes

[9] Philostr. *V. S.* 1. 22. 524.   [10] Bowie (1978: 1663 ff.).
[11] Photius, *Bibl., Cod.* 166, 111a34.

to the rich vein of fantasy—humour is hard to read into the epitome! Antonius Diogenes' work does not play the vital role in the development of the genre assigned to it by Rohde, but it is a valuable index of how varied prose fiction could be.

Yet another sort of fiction is found in the *Metamorphoses* preserved in epitome by Photius and ascribed by him to Lucius of Patrae. It is very probably by Lucian, and the original of both the *Ass* in the Lucianic corpus (a work unlikely to be by Lucian) and Apuleius' *Metamorphoses*.[12] Erotic incident will have been treated without sentiment and simply as one of many sorts of adventure: magic, fantasy and travel provide a bridge to *The Incredible* of Antonius, but the obscenity (if we trust Photius) is a differentiating ingredient.

Comedy may also have been one objective of the *Iolaus* novel, known from a recent papyrus scrap in which prose and verse are mingled. Iolaus is apparently represented learning the mysteries of the eunuch priests of Cybele in order that he may pass himself off as one and thereby seduce his boy-friend. Form and tone have suggested that the work was of the sort known to us only by the Latin *Satyrica* of Petronius.

The three works just reviewed show that prose narrative fiction could take many forms. Others are also related, though they would not merit our modern term 'novel': Dio's *Euboean*, Lucian's *True Histories*, Philostratus' *Apollonius* and *Heroic Tale*. Much was left to the writer's choice. Even those who selected what seems identifiable as a particular type, the ideal love romance, could exploit, develop or parody standard motifs.

The search for origins which dominated much earlier scholarship has now few practitioners. It is clear that the writers of novels were, like contemporaries in other literary fields, highly conscious of classical works. In its many facets the novel exhibits formal resemblances to the *Odyssey*, Herodotus, Thucydides and above all Xenophon's *Cyropaedia* as well as community of content with love-poetry and New Comedy. Whatever this might tell us about origins (and that is still disputed) is less important than its bearing on the writers' intentions. All these classical forms were still popular with readers, but only historiography was being written with any distinction. The others must have offered few openings, and to a man who wished to exercise his talents in writing rather than declaim-

---

[12] Cf. *Cambridge History of Classical Literature*, i. (1985), 679; ii. (1985), 778–85.

ing, the prose narrative form, once available, offered a challenge and a guarantee of a readership. Other motives may have operated. The novel has been seen as the Hellenistic myth, expressive of man's solitude and search for union with another being, human or divine. Such a view overplays the solitude of the central characters in novels, and we do not need to explain why the adventure plot, familiar since the *Odyssey*, continued to attract the readers of our period. Love is likewise a primary ingredient of literature which calls for no special explanation. But the combination of love and religion tells us much about the spiritual life a novelist might expect his reader to find meaningful. Religion was an increasingly prominent constituent of private and public life. That suffices to explain its role in the novel, and few scholars accept Merkelbach's ingenious hypothesis that all the love romances save Chariton are mystery texts, communicating an allegory of the progress of the initiate through ordeals, death and resurrection to recognition by and union with the deity.[13] The correspondences Merkelbach noted are adequately explained by the common model of both novels and mystery ritual. That model is life, and it is about life as a Graeco-Roman reader saw it (or wished to see it) that the novelist writes.

We must assume that the writers had a better idea of their readership than we can form. Little in their erudite approach supports modern fancies that the works were intended for women or children. Like paradoxography, epistolography and the works of Lucian, the novels were more probably written as lighter reading for the intelligentsia. The preference for an Eastern setting is no guide to readership distribution, and the varied origins of the authors—Achaea, western Asia Minor, Syria and perhaps Alexandria—show the same scatter as other branches of literature. Papyri can tell us that some, but not all, were read in Egyptian towns (as well as attesting illustrated texts), and mosaics that *Ninus* and *Metiochus* were of interest to owners of villas in fourth-century Antioch.[14] Fortunately the novels were popular enough in late antiquity for the survival of several to be assured.

---

[13] Merkelbach (1962): for criticism cf. Reardon (1971: 393f.).

[14] Illustrated texts and mosaics, Weitzmann (1959: 99f.); Maehler (1976: 2) where the appearance of a Leucippe and of an unnamed daughter of Polycrates in mime is observed.

THE SURVIVING TEXTS

Chariton's *Chaereas and Callirhoe*, probably the earliest of the extant group, already shows a deft mastery of the genre, to which its apparent directness and simplicity should not blind us. Chariton professes to recount a love story (πάθος ἐρωτικὸν ἐν Συρακούσαις γενόμενον διηγήσομαι) and although he tells it straight he never drops his conscious narrative role. Most striking is his preface to the eighth and last book, where, after recapitulating the lovers' adventures, he promises a happy end:

And I also think this last chapter will give most pleasure to its readers: for it purges the grim happenings of the earlier episodes. No longer piracy and slavery and litigation and battle and endurance and warfare and capture, but now legal passions and lawful marriages. So I shall tell how Aphrodite brought the truth to light and revealed to each other the lovers each unaware of the other's identity. (8. 1. 4)

There are many other places, however, where the author is found to intervene in the thinly disguised *persona* of Tyche, manipulating the plot in the required direction (e.g. 4. 5. 3). Yet despite reminders that a story of remarkable changes of fortune is being told the reader is rarely faced with sheer improbability (unless perhaps the fortuitous capture of the pirate Theron by Syracusans which discloses to Chaereas his wife's fate, 3. 3f.). Chariton gives his narrative just enough motivation. When the couple, married through the power of Eros, have to be separated, jealousy moves Chaereas to kick Callirhoe: taken for dead, she comes to life again in her tomb. Thence Theron hales her to Ionia and sells her to a leading Ephesian, Dionysius. She marries him when she discovers she is pregnant with a child of Chaereas, who has meanwhile pursued her to Ionia and become a slave of the satrap Mithridates. He encourages Chaereas to send Callirhoe a letter whose interception gives rise to the next journey theme; Mithridates and Dionysius are summoned before the Great King in Babylon to decide the truth of their mutual accusations. Mithridates conceals Chaereas, his trump card, until the day of the trial, so that the lovers can suddenly be confronted with each other in the court room but prevented from embracing. The legal battle now shifts to possession of Callirhoe and is protracted by the king's own passion for the lovely heroine. Decision is forestalled by an Egyptian revolt. The king leaves

Babylon with Dionysius in his army and Callirhoe in his train. In despair Chaereas joins the rebels and leads them to the capture of Tyre and naval victory, while Dionysius' exploits in the victorious land campaign win him the title to Callirhoe. But she is with the women and baggage in Aradus, captured by Chaereas: briefly the author prolongs the suspense in postponing recognition, then they are reunited to sail finally to Syracuse.

The narrative has linear simplicity, untrammelled by flashbacks or subplots. Other men's passions indeed complement that of Chaereas, but they are united by having the same object, Callirhoe, whose overwhelming beauty acts as a leitmotif insistently recalling the power of Eros and Aphrodite. Beside her Chaereas is a feeble figure. We know he is handsome, but his initial and fatal jealousy is no more attractive than his recurrent despair in adversity; it is this despair and not any more positive quality which precipitates his unexpected energy and valour in the wars as he seeks that death from which a friend (created for this very purpose) has often saved him. Dionysius, on the other hand, is sympathetically drawn as an aristocrat whose impeccable behaviour derives largely from Hellenic *paideia* (1. 12. 6; 2. 5. 11; 3. 2. 6; 5. 9. 8). His thoughtful and stable character appeals strongly to the reader and seems to offer a much closer bond with Callirhoe than Chaereas' adolescent passion. For Callirhoe too is educated (1. 12. 9) and her strength of purpose is unintelligible to the barbarian eunuch trying to lure her to the king's bed: οὐκ ᾔδει δὲ φρόνημα Ἑλληνικὸν εὐγενὲς καὶ μάλιστα τὸ Καλλιρόης τῆς σώφρονος καὶ φιλάνδρου 'but he did not understand the noble spirit of a Greek, and particularly of Callirhoe, who was chaste and loyal to her husband' (6. 4. 10). Being *barbaros* does not damn the king, for he too is inhibited by *noblesse*, although his attempt to check his own infatuation by absorption in sport (6. 3. 8f.) predictably fails. Eros follows him into the field, and the eunuch's view is confirmed: φάρμακον γὰρ ἕτερον Ἔρωτος οὐδέν ἐστιν πλὴν αὐτὸς ὁ ἐρώμενος . . . ὁ τρώσας αὐτὸς ἰάσεται 'there is no other remedy for love save the beloved himself . . . the wounder shall himself heal' (6. 3. 7).[15] The king and Dionysius are both sensitive and worthy princes, but a reader who put his money on them would lose, for their outclassing by the improbable Chaereas vindicates the author's creed that love conquers all.

---

[15] An allusion to the oracle given to Telephus.

Chariton expects his readers not only to venerate Love but to admire his characters as larger than life. Callirhoe is often compared to, twice taken for, a goddess; Chaereas resembles Achilles, Nireus, Hippolytus or Alcibiades (! 1. 1. 3); and the heroic atmosphere is fostered by apt quotations from Homer.[16] Slaves (2. 1. 5), barbarians (cf. 6. 4. 10 quoted above) and the mob are deemed inferior (8. 6. 7)—although Plangon, the bailiff's wife charged with Callirhoe's care, is allowed a simple nobility—and echoes of classical orators and historians (especially Xenophon) show that the educated classes of the Greek East are envisaged as readers. They had the *paideia* of Dionysius and might dream of having his rank, and they would enjoy a tale in which Chaereas combined traits of culture heroes like Odysseus, Alexander and the Xenophon of the *Anabasis* with some features of the less known general Chabrias in Egypt in the fourth century BC.[17] They would appreciate the many reflections and speeches of the characters, rhetorical (cf. 6. 1. 4 ἐρρητόρευον) but not excessive, and such textbook touches, blending allusion and contrast, as the comment on Chaereas' return with Persian booty: ὥστε ἐνεπλήσθη πᾶσα ἡ πόλις, οὐχ ὡς πρότερον ἐκ τοῦ πολέμου τοῦ Σικελικοῦ πενίας Ἀττικῆς, ἀλλά, τὸ καινότατον, ἐν εἰρήνηι λαφύρων Μηδικῶν 'And so the whole city overflowed, not, as before after the Sicilian war, with Athenian poverty, but, most strangely, in peace with Persian spoils' (8. 6. 12). This game played between educated author and reader makes it clear that Chariton is no popular or folk writer, and the contrast between such features and the admission to his careful prose of post-classical vocabulary and syntax condemned by Atticists forces us to attribute him to a time and place where the Atticist movement had not yet triumphed.

Xenophon's Ephesian tale of *Anthia and Habrocomes* evokes little enthusiasm among modern critics. That the surviving text in five books is an epitome of an original ten[18] may be partly to blame for maladroitness of construction and motivation as well as for the flat simplicity of a style which lacks Chariton's charm. Comparison with Chariton is inevitable, for they share many themes and details, Xenophon usually being deemed the borrower.[19] Our text has little room for close observation of human emotions (albeit

[16] Cf. Papanikolaou (1973b: ch. 1).
[17] Salmon (1961).
[18] As shown by Bürger (1892b).
[19] Cf. Gärtner (1967: 2080f.). Merkelbach (1962) and Petri (1963) put Chariton after Xenophon.

speechifying is not infrequent) and throughout the action, more complex than in Chariton, divine motivation and intervention combine with melodramatic and scarcely credible incident to produce a mediocre work closer to a thriller than a novel.

Eros is seen as an active force from the start. Habrocomes, handsome, well-connected but scornful of love, is made by Eros to fall for a lovely fourteen-year-old at a procession in Ephesus. Both waste away as they try to resist their mutual passion, and the oracle at Claros obscurely enjoins a solution interpreted as marriage but predicts dreadful overseas adventures before the couple can enjoy a better fortune. Xenophon launches his pair on their travels, but they are caught, predictably, by pirates, and on the estate in Phoenicia of the pirate king Apsyrtus their beauty invites approaches to each which result in their separation. Thereafter Xenophon attempts to handle each star's fortunes alternately. Anthia's fidelity survives a marriage to a noble goatherd (his name Lampon might suggest knowledge of Longus' Lampis), a wedding to the magistrate Perilaus (eleventh-hour false death by potion which occasions a Charitonian theft of the revived heroine from her tomb), and many threats to her chastity culminating in enlistment in a brothel in Tarentum. Habrocomes' perils are chiefly to his life, and he is saved by the miraculous intervention of the Nile when he prays to Helios, as does Anthia to Isis. The pair's tribulations are recurrently linked by the person of the robber Hippothous (an aristocrat turned desperado through disaster in love); a device more ingenious than successful, for the author must ship three, not two, on separate but parallel courses from Cilicia to Egypt, thence to Italy and Rhodes for final reunion. This sometimes overtaxes his techniques of motivation; and when Hippothous captures Anthia for the second time (necessarily, to prevent her disappearance to India in the train of the tourist monarch Psammis) we are told blandly that neither recognized the other (4. 3. 6). The original text may have been more convincing, but in many details (e.g. Anthia shut in a ditch with two fierce dogs 4. 6. 3f.) the reader must have doubted if Xenophon's world were his own.

Yet realism of a sort is one of the author's objectives. His circumstantial detail about places and distances in Anatolia and his concern to give mainly realistic names to a high proportion of his characters are witnesses to that. It will not have disturbed the cultivated reader that most of these names were commoner in

Athens and mainland Greece than in the Anatolian and Near-Eastern setting of the novel. This classicism is but one indication among many that the author's intentions, at least, were literary. The role of divinities is also a mark of pretensions both literary, in the line of descent from Homer and Herodotus, and realistic: prayers to gods and miraculous responses were part of the life of second-century Greeks. It is for such reasons, and not because Xenophon is himself the prophet of a religious message whether open or cryptic, that his gods are so prominent in the narrative.

It would be unjust to neglect some grounds for commendation. His prolonged separation of the lovers and the involvement of Hippothous entail more complexity than Chariton or Achilles undertake, and it pays dividends in the denouement. Tension mounts as the three converge but fail to unite in Egypt, then Sicily and Magna Graecia: from the moment Hippothous recognizes Anthia in the slave-market at Tarentum (5. 9. 5) the reader's excitement is constantly fuelled until the climactic scene in Rhodes when Habrocomes is told that Anthia is found and runs like a maniac through the streets (5. 13. 2). Hippothous himself is a far more interesting creation than Chariton's Polycharmus and Achilles' Cleinias or Menelaus: to fashion the hero's trusty companion out of a robber whose capture of the heroine is twice vital to the plot shows ingenuity, and the mixture of good and bad in his character some awareness of the danger of polarizing heroes and villains. Although no papyri have been identified the need for an epitome and its survival to the Byzantine period are testimony enough that the work found readers.

Iamblichus' *Babyloniaca* is known chiefly from Photius' epitome. A few manuscript fragments show that in details of handling and style he had fewer pretensions than Achilles, and elements of the plot put him closest to Chariton. The beautiful couple Sinonis and Rhodanes, already wed, flee the lust of the Babylonian monarch Garmus in a series of melodramatic incidents. They are separated by the jealousy of Sinonis when Rhodanes rewards a helpful country lass with a kiss, and only reunited when Garmus sends Rhodanes at the head of his army against the Syrian monarch to whom Sinonis has allowed herself to be married out of pique. Rhodanes not only wins the war and Sinonis but even becomes king of Babylon. But if the jealousy, oriental setting and military denouement recall Chariton, the succession of false deaths (demanded by the frequency with which the pursuers are on the point of seizing the fugitives) and variety of digressive material on the ways of the Orient put the author nearer to Achilles and Heliodorus. The introductory frame (comparable to Antonius Diogenes) also serves to authenticate the narrator as an authority on the arcane lore of the East (cf. Habrich 1960: 2, 32).

The eight books of Achilles Tatius' *Leucippe and Clitophon* were probably written in the last quarter of the second century AD. Clitophon, a rich young Tyrian, falls in love with his cousin Leucippe, evacuated to Phoenicia from war-threatened Byzantium. Surprised by her mother on the point of making love they elope only to be shipwrecked in Egypt and be captured by brigands. Clitophon escapes, witnesses an apparent sacrifice of his beloved and is about to kill himself when it is revealed (to him and to the reader) that she has survived by a conjuring trick. Although reunited with Clitophon she demurs at lovemaking, and the dangerous attentions of the general Charmides are only frustrated by her sudden and death-like collapse. When she is cured they visit Alexandria and Pharos: here Leucippe is kidnapped by pirates and the pursuing hero again thinks he sees her die. Returning to Egypt he is cajoled into marriage, but not bed, with widow Melite: they go to her native Ephesus where Leucippe turns out to be living, but as Melite's slave. The 'widow's' husband is also alive, and unsuccessfully pursues Leucippe while Clitophon finally, but once only, succumbs to Melite. A trial and ordeal establish Leucippe's virginity and the couple can at last return to a wedding in Byzantium.

Achilles' treatment is rarely direct and vigorous. The florid, Asianic style, intent on conceits and short sentences, combines with rich elaboration of plot and incident to produce a baroque *tour de force* which sometimes cloys. Structurally it falls into pairs of books each presenting a different stage of the lovers' fortunes,[20] while progress is retarded by sub-plots, descriptions of the works of man or nature, and philosophic speeches and reflections. The first pair lingers over the growth of the couple's love. Only at 2. 7 does Clitophon, feigning to have been stung on the lip, deceive the shy but not unresponsive Leucippe into their first kiss by asking her to use the cure she had earlier used on her maid:

She came close to me and put her mouth close to mine, so as to work the

[20] Reardon (1971: 361).

charm, and murmured something while she touched the tip of my lips;
and I gently kissed her, avoiding all the noise of an ordinary salute, until,
in the successive opening and shutting of her lips as she murmured it, she
converted the charm into a series of kisses . . . (tr. Gaselee)

Although by the end of this book they are embarked for Egypt
Clitophon is not in bed with Leucippe but debating the merits of
boys and women with friends old and new, Clinias and Menelaus.
The second pair of books exploits separation and danger, and
adumbrates in the general Charmides the rival motif that will
dominate Books 5 and 6. Their location allows digressions on the
geography and beasts of the Nile, evocative of Herodotus. Within
Books 5 and 6 the couples Clitophon–Melite and Thersander–
Leucippe are contrasted: Book 5 culminates in the former's union,
6 in Leucippe's impassioned assertion of her virginity. The implausi-
bility of this claim prepares the way for the trial of Clitophon and
ordeal of Leucippe that are expanded to fill most of Books 7 and 8.

Within this framework sub-plots act as pendants to the love of
the smitten couple and extend the range of erotic incident. The
topic of eros is likewise pursued in many speeches and reflections
exploring its psychology, physiology and analogues in nature.
Although suffused with ill-concealed rhetoric these set in perspective the characters' actions and emotions: this cannot be said for
the many digressions (e.g. on the discovery of purple 2. 11. 5, the
phoenix 3. 25, or the elephant 4. 4) where relevance and propriety
are often ignored.

There are several counts, however, on which Achilles shows
advances on his predecessors. The setting is no longer historical.
The contemporary world of the East Mediterranean reader is envisaged and evoked with a fair measure of consistency and realism.
Only the Byzantines' Thracian war invites the reader to imagine a
particular date, less probably historical[21] than invented. In 1. 3
Clitophon takes over the narrative role from the first-person author
to whom he tells his own story as they admire a painting at Sidon
(and the ego-narrator is then forgotten, even at the end of Book 8).
This stifles questions about the truth or morality of the tale, but
carries with it the limitation that all events are seen from Clitophon's point of view—only his side of the story is continuously
told. The same bias is evident in the analyses of passion and most
glaringly in the acquiescence of both writer and Clitophon in the

[21] As argued by Altheim (1942/1948: 121–4).

latter's seduction by Melite (a male orientation which should give pause to theories of a chiefly female readership).

The seduction of the hero is one of many reversals or over-exploitations of conventions which shows Achilles apparently playing with rather than by the rules of the game. One explanation is that he is concerned to make his characters more realistic than the distant and idealized figures of Chariton or Xenophon. But set alongside the excesses of rhetoric it has been seen as an argument that he must be parodying the genre with humorous intentions. Nevertheless, there is a fine line between wit and humour. Readers of some erudition (not all of whom need have been endowed with comparable taste or intelligence) might well have taken a pleasure in Achilles' deployment of conventions that savoured the art rather than scorned the artificiality. The audience's tastes are as enigmatic as its composition (see above, p. 45). But those who endured the rhetorical gymnastics of Aristides surely appreciated similar *techne* as displayed by Achilles, and his digressions would also entertain a generation ready to seek *paideia* in that genre of *varia historia* to which, according to the Suda, he also contributed.

Read he was, and perhaps at several levels. The names of Leucippe and Clitophon given to the parents of St Galaktion of Emesa, combined with the Suda tradition that Achilles became a bishop, show he left his mark below the upper crust of culture.[22] But it was upper-class readers such as Photius whose admiration for the sophistic style and manner of Achilles overrode disapproval of his licentious subject matter and guaranteed for him and for Heliodorus extensive readership and copying in the ninth and tenth centuries (*Bibliotheca*, *Cod.* 87).

Heliodorus' *Aethiopica* is organized in ten books, but in bulk it is more than twice the length of its nearest rival, *Leucippe and Clitophon*. The length results not from mere accumulation of incident, as in Iamblichus, but from a leisurely elaboration which is especially manifested in the construction of dramatic set-pieces. Time and trouble are applied to development of plot and delineation of character alike. The work is held by many to be the best of the extant novels. Motivation is well handled, the principal characters nicely drawn, even if they may not achieve the realism of Achilles, and the sub-plots and digressions in which the sophistic author takes pleasure are carefully integrated in the story.

[22] Cf. Dörrie (1938).

But it is in the story itself, and the manner in which Heliodorus unfolds its complexities, that his superiority most clearly lies. He begins with a dramatic scene of mystery and excitement: an Egyptian strand strewn with bodies. Only Theagenes and Charicleia are alive. Apprehended by robbers they follow a perilous course up-country, the heroine attracting the attentions of Thyamis, their leader. Their companion, Cnemon, has been separated from them so that he can meet the central character Calasiris and hear his story. An Egyptian priest, Calasiris had gone to Delphi and thence brought Charicleia from her adoptive father to return to her native Ethiopia, where she had been born the white daughter of black royalty and entrusted by a priest to a visiting Delphian, Charicles. Naturally the trip to Ethiopia includes Charicleia's inamorato, Theagenes, and their shipwreck is the prelude to the dramatic opening scene. Cnemon and Calasiris duly find Charicleia, and then, at Memphis, Theagenes: here Calasiris dies and Thyamis, who turns out to be his son, is installed as priest, while the lovers are captured by the Persian satrap's wife Arsace. Her lust for Theagenes precipitates their flight and eventually an Egyptian–Ethiopian war in which they are captured by the Ethiopians and taken to be human sacrifices at Meroe. There their virginity and Charicleia's identity are established in the course of the awesome ceremony that should result in their death; they are married and consecrated priest and priestess of the Sun.

Heliodorus' Odyssean plunge *in medias res* not only gives pace and tension to the story but allows the structure to be presented to the reader from different angles. At first the Delta journey seems a pointless movement south in the hands of a Thyamis whose hieratic origins are circumstantial frills no more meaningful than the aristocratic past of Xenophon's Hippothous. Calasiris' entrance (the stage metaphor is apt to the author's approach) gives an added dimension to the characters. Although Theagenes is leaving his country for a distant and exotic land, and gives a strong impression of linear progress to the story, Charicleia, we discover, has a destiny to fulfil, and her journey is the homeward and circular movement familiar from other novels. Ambiguity also pertains to the reasons for Calasiris' visit to Delphi: he alleges at different junctures a general motive of pilgrimage (2. 26) and specific instructions from the Ethiopian queen (4. 12f.). But Heliodorus' sleight of hand conceals the flaw (if it is such) and evokes admiration rather than suspicion for such Odyssean tales whose share of truth and falsehood is elusive.

The impression that the couple is in the hands of divinity, escorted from Apollo's Delphi to the idealized Ethiopia (where he is worshipped as Helios) by a series of priests of an ascending order of sanctity, is a mixed literary blessing. It gives added point to the lovers' chastity and the adventures which imperil it, and for a reader of the third or fourth century, with strong religious convictions and a proclivity to accept divine explanations of the world's ways, it will have charged the whole story with a deeper and more coherent significance than the more casual reference to gods or fortune in the earlier writers. But the perfection required from hero and heroine impedes realistic characterization, and the reader's conviction that they will survive their perils leaves little room for nerve-racking suspense. Their union is threatened seriously on only two occasions—the opening episode of robbers and the passion of Arsace. When together they face death in Meroe we have little doubt that they will escape, and are best advised to admire Heliodorus' dramatic rendering of the occasion instead of nurturing pity or fear.

Many of these literary weaknesses are balanced by the religious intensity of the work, but we are not entitled to assume that this was the writer's chief concern. A religious stamp is indeed given by the role of Delphi, the priests and the traditionally pious Ethiopians, as well as the author's claim to be 'a Phoenician from Emesa, of the line of Helios, Theodosius' son Heliodorus'. But the personal link here established between the writer and Helios has also a literary purpose, as has Calasiris' flashback narrative. It is not for religious ends that Calasiris is brought on in the way he is, and the fact that so central a character is a priest tells us no more about Heliodorus' own commitment to religion than Philostratus' elaboration of the analogous ascetic Apollonius tells us about that sophist's Neopythagoreanism.

It might help to solve this problem of Heliodorus' priorities if his date were certain, for a location in the 220s or 230s would strengthen the case for linking him with the imperial house that sprang from Emesa and the religious propaganda that has been credited to it. To the present writer the preoccupations and presentation of Heliodorus seem too close to those of Achilles and Philostratus to make anything later than the 230s probable. A

similarity between his siege of Syene and the historical siege of
Nisibis in AD 351 has been alleged to prove a date later in the
fourth century.[23] But the similarity is vulnerable to alternative
explanations. A reader of Heliodorus should bear in mind that he
may be dealing with a contemporary of Philostratus. Although in
that age the currents of religious thought ran strongly, those of
sophistic literature were equally powerful. It is as a product of the
literary skills of the sophistic age operating in their most developed
form upon the range of models open to writers of prose fiction that
the *Aethiopica* is best seen.

The other candidate for primacy amongst extant novelists chose
an utterly different approach. Instead of augmenting scale and
complexity Longus in his *Daphnis and Chloe* presents a miniature
romance, simple in its theme, construction and narration. The
action does not range over half the Mediterranean but is confined
to the east coast of Lesbos. The lovers meet no kings or queens but
move in a world of shepherds and goatherds, a world to which
they return even when they are discovered to be foundling children
of city aristocrats. The narrative moves simply forward, professing
to expound a painting seen by the writer in a grove of the nymphs
in Lesbos, and focusing on the gradual growth of sexual awareness
and experimentation in the naïve couple until obstacles are overcome and they are united to live happily ever after.

Simplicity is not the only gain that is achieved by the choice of
a pastoral theme. Longus can revel in pictorial descriptions
(ecphraseis) of nature (indeed the whole work is a sort of ecphrasis)
and use the progress of the seasons both as a framework and as a
source of forward movement: spring (1. 9f.), summer (1. 23f.) and
autumn (2. 1f.) are at once a backcloth and a stimulus to the
development of *eros* as Daphnis, carried by the advance of the
seasons from fifteen to sixteen years, vies in naïvete with a Chloe
two years his junior. No journey is needed to create a story. But
Longus makes it clear that his work is to be compared to the
adventure-story genre. In addition to the natural agent of winter
(3. 3) conventional hazards are exploited to separate the couple.
Tyrian (!) pirates carry off Daphnis, their ship is wrecked and he is
saved by the pan-pipes of his potential rival Dorcon who is himself
fatally beaten up (1. 28f.). A war between Mytilene and Methymna

---

[23] For the arguments and their proponents cf. Reardon (1971: 334 n. 57); and
for a refutation, Szepessy (1975).

occasions Chloe's kidnapping, wondrously terminated by Pan (2. 20 f.). Finally, when the older woman Lycaenion's lesson in the act of love (3. 18) has supplemented that of old man Philetas in its theory (2. 3 f.) and ensured that Chloe's virginity will soon go the way of Daphnis', dangerous rivals are introduced to effect tension and impediment before the adolescents' recognition and marriage.

Concentration on a small and unified stage also gives Longus advantages over the other novelists. His descriptions of the rural scene at different points in the year build up a comprehensive picture in the reader's vision: we feel we are spectators of a pastoral world that is worked out and developed in all its vivid details, and only on reflection do we appreciate how selective these are, how they are sometimes less than plausible or consistent, and how many of them derive from the literary tradition of pastoral fiction, notably Theocritus, rather than from the real world they successfully suggest.

Pruning of *dramatis personae* is also an advantage: the minor figures can be picked out with small but effective touches of realism (e.g. the reluctance of the foster-parent to forgo the economic gain of purloining the infant's upper-class tokens, 1. 3. 1). On the other hand Longus makes no great effort to develop the children's characters: they are types of artless rustic teenagers, and never become individuals. Longus examines *physis*, nature, not *ethos*, character. Indeed he sometimes carries his representation of natural artlessness too far. Chloe's uncomprehending soliloquy after seeing Daphnis bathing may strike us as implausible in a country lass: νῦν ἐγὼ νοσῶ μέν, τί δὲ ὁ νόσος ἀγνοῶ· ἀλγῶ, καὶ ἕλκος οὐκ ἔστι μοι· λυποῦμαι, καὶ οὐδὲν τῶν προβάτων ἀπόλωλέ μοι. κάομαι, καὶ ἐν σκιᾶι τοσαύτηι κάθημαι . . . 'Now I am sick, but of what sickness I know not; I feel pain, and I have no wound; I am distressed, and none of my flock is lost; I burn, and am resting in all this shade . . .' (1. 14. 1). Our credulity is even more severely tested when Daphnis and Chloe get as far as lying down together, as prescribed in Philetas' treatment for *eros*, but go no further εἰδότες δὲ τῶν ἐντεῦθεν οὐδὲν . . . 'knowing nothing of what follows' (2. 11. 3). Yet this guileless innocence is required not only to spin out the action over Longus' four books but so that the gradual operation of *physis* can be celebrated.

For one clear objective of the writer is to hymn nature as a guide and god. It is from their goats and sheep that the foster-parents learn tenderness and pity for the foundlings (1. 3. 1 and 6. 1), and from a dream sent by the Nymphs that they are to be consigned to Eros (1. 7. 1). Eros, like the Nymphs, is a manifestation of nature, as is made clear in the next stage of learning, Philetas' tale. It is indeed puzzling that nature and its rural servants are inadequate to instruct the young people in the culminating act of love, and that a city girl, Lycaenion, has to lend a hand: but even here Longus insists that *physis* is the chief agent: τὸ δὲ ἐντεῦθεν οὐδὲν περιειργάζετο ξένον· αὐτὴ γὰρ ἡ φύσις λοιπὸν ἐπαίδευσε τὸ πρακτέον 'But from then on she lavished no unfamiliar craft: for nature herself taught what was then to be done' (3. 18. 4).

One feature, be it noted, is very far from natural, and that is Longus' style. Eschewing subordination and long periods in favour of participial and paratactic constructions he favours simple sentences of two, three or sometimes four members, often carefully balanced in length and similar in rhythm, with an especial prefence for tricolon, often crescendo. Within the limited compass and scale of the work the finite number of variants possible on these few patterns can be seen as binding the whole together: but even so they approach a mesmeric monotony, and they would not have sustained a longer story. Only one example can be given (see also above); Longus describes the spring which is to be the setting of awakening love:

ἦρος ἦν ἀρχὴ καὶ πάντα ἤκμαζεν ἄνθη, τὰ ἐν δρυμοῖς, τὰ ἐν λειμῶσι καὶ ὅσα ὄρεια· βόμβος ἦν ἤδη μελιττῶν, ἦχος ὀρνίθων μουσικῶν, σκιρτήματα ποιμνίων ἀρτιγεννήτων· ἄρνες ἐσκίρτων ἐν τοῖς ὄρεσιν, ἐβόμβουν ἐν τοῖς λειμῶσιν αἱ μέλιτται, τὰς λόχμας κατῆιδον ὄρνιθες· τοσαύτης δὴ πάντα κατεχούσης εὐωρίας οἱ' ἁπαλοὶ καὶ νεοὶ μιμηταὶ τῶν ἀκουομένων ἐγίνοντο καὶ βλεπομένων . . .

Spring was beginning, and all the flowers were in full bloom, in thickets, in meadows and those on the hills. By now there was the humming of bees, the calling of song birds, the gambols of the flocks' newborn young. Lambs gambolled in the hills, in the meadows the bees hummed, birds drowned the copses in song. Everything basked in these seasonable blessings, and Daphnis and Chloe, being young and tender, began to imitate what they heard and saw. (1. 9. 1-2)

Choice of words is also simple, poetry is drawn upon sparingly, and the range of vocabulary presents the reader with a mixture of current and classicizing usages such as he might expect in a writer of pretensions without pedantry.

The overall intent of the work must be judged in the light of this mannered simplicity as well as of the content. The preface makes a series of claims, balancing pleasure and instruction:

ἀνάθημα μὲν Ἔρωτι καὶ Νύμφαις καὶ Πανί, κτῆμα δὲ τερπνὸν πᾶσιν ἀνθρώποις, ὃ καὶ νοσοῦντα ἰάσεται, καὶ λυπούμενον παραμυθήσεται, τὸν ἐρασθέντα ἀναμνήσει, τὸν οὐκ ἐρασθέντα προπαιδεύσει.

A dedication to Eros and the Nymphs and Pan, and a pleasing possession for all men, which will heal the sick, comfort the distressed, will remind anyone who has loved and instruct anyone who has not. (pref. 3)

This is the traditional blend of objectives in Greek literature, (even in the Thucydides here echoed) and it is no slight to Longus to credit him with primarily literary aims. There is indeed a stronger case for seeing religious statements here than in the other novels. The novel can be seen as allegory of love, initiating the reader in the gradual unfolding of its mystery and in the essential identity of Eros with the other divine forces of nature represented by the Nymphs, Pan, Dionysus and Demeter.[24] But we can accept the author's veneration for nature without interpreting Daphnis and Chloe's progress allegorically—it need only be a microcosmic example. He wished no doubt to express a certain sort of worship for natural forces, but that wish should probably be seen as the formal rather than the proximate cause of the work's creation. For that we should look to literary intentions, and compare *Daphnis and Chloe* with Dio's *Euboean*, Alcilphron's and Aelian's rustic letters or Philostratus' *Heroic Tale* rather than with Aristides' *Sacred Discourses*.

[24] Chalk (1960), endorsed by Reardon (1969: 300-2).

3

The Conflict of Emotions: A *Topos* in the Greek Erotic Novel

MASSIMO FUSILLO

Misera Elvira, che contrasto d'affetti in sen ti nasce
(Da Ponte/Mozart, *Don Giovanni*, 3)

1. 'Why should I not, had I the heart to do it, Like to th'Egyptian thief, at point of death, Kill what I love'. In these verses of Shakespeare's *Twelfth Night* (5. 1. 115-17), the protagonist of the play, Duke Orsino, alludes to one of the characters in Heliodorus' *Aethiopica*, Thyamis, thus revealing to us how well known the Greek novel was to the Elizabethan audience. The English translation of Heliodorus had only been published in 1587; moreover, the allusion is a very cryptic one and presupposes a thorough knowledge of the Greek model. In the Renaissance and especially in the Baroque period, we know that the ancient novel was read and studied even by a non-specialized public. In particular Heliodorus was considered, both in terms of theory and invention, as a privileged model of prose epic, worthy of comparison with Homer and Virgil.[1] Today, however, even when talking to an audience of classicists, one cannot take the knowledge of these texts for granted. Their slow decline was due mainly to the increasing importance which the genre of the novel acquired from 1700 onwards and to the depreciatory judgement passed on them by romantic and idealistic critics. However, over the past twenty years, the interpretation of the ancient novel has undergone a

* This paper was given in May 1989 at a session of the Groupe Romand des Études Grecques et Latines. My special thanks go to its president Denis Knœpfler and to André Hurst.
    [1] For a panoramic view of the reception of the Greek novel, cf. Weinreich (1950/1962: 56-71) and Hägg (1983: 192-213); there is a complex study of its relation to Shakespeare in Gesner (1970). As for Heliodorus, see further Oeftering (1901) and esp. the final chapter of Sandy (1982a). Cf. also Molinié (1982).

radical change once the positivist perspective, so slow to disappear from classical philology, was finally abandoned. Thus, from studying the prehistory of the novel and its hypothetical progenitor, critics have moved toward the study of its intrinsic characteristics, often in accordance with recent theories developed in the new discipline of narratology. Today, of course, no one thinks of exalting these novels as the Baroque period did. On the contrary, they are often seen as the ancient equivalent of serialized fiction. Such a reading of the novel is partly justified by its repetitive *topoi*, its predictable narrative, its fixed characterization, and the comforting sentimentalism of its happy endings. But one should not overstate these points. Heliodorus, for instance, shows an inventiveness and profundity that should not be underestimated.[2]

Moreover, our general knowledge of the ancient novel has been significantly improved by papyrological evidence. This has indeed wrought a complete change in the relative chronology.

Nowadays, the position held by classical philologists and notably by that anthropologist of genius, Bakhtin, opposing the serious and idealistic Greek novel to the comic and realistic Roman novel, is no longer tenable.[3] One can only outline some basic trends by taking into account mixed meta-literary operations which presuppose a well established literary genre, such as the analogy between erotic and utopian novel used by Antonius Diogenes, or the assimilation to the bucolic genre in Longus' *Daphnis and Chloe*.

2. In this paper I shall restrict myself to the Greek erotic novel, which makes up a homogeneous corpus in its forms and themes. The four fully extant novels we have all follow the same narrative pattern. A couple of noble and particularly handsome adolescents fall in love with each other on their first encounter; fate separates them, they go through all sorts of misfortunes, and eventually reunite for the happy ending.

---

[2] The most thorough and complete narratological reading is Hägg (1971*a*); the functionalist approach of Ruiz-Montero (1988), although full of interesting themes, seems too schematic to me. On the tone used in this sort of consumer literature, see Scobie (1969); García Gual (1970/1988); Heiserman (1977); G. Anderson (1982); Holzberg (1986/1944: esp. 7-8).

[3] Cf. Rohde (1876/1900: 583-91), opposing realistic novel and idealistic romance; the polarity is esp. expressed by Perry (1967: chs. 2 and 3); Bakhtin (1978: ch. 3); against this dichotomy cf. F. Wehrli (1965) overstressing the opposite view. On the contribution of papyri, cf. Henrichs (1972); Szepessy (1978: 29-36); Parsons (1971).

The main novelty of this corpus is that it highlights eros. This is the principal theme to which the entire narrative is subordinated. It is an everyday, intimate, 'bourgeois' eros, and always ends with marriage, following the model of Menandrian comedy, which is imitated and amplified, rather than Alexandrian elegy, which always preserves a learned distance by the use of myth. It is far from the Sapphic eros (from which it nevertheless takes many of its themes), since this aims for an impossible satisfaction, whereas the protagonists of the Greek novel always stay bound by mutual, exclusive, monomaniac passion.

Parallelism is indeed the main narrative figure used in the novel. The couple comprises two young people of the same age, the same enviable social status, and divine beauty, going through identical adventures, always wishing to die in times of separation, and both victims of powerful rivals.[4] In a recent essay I have tried to show that this persistent parallelism is a narrative concretization of the desire for symmetry. This concept was first used by the Chilean psychoanalyst Ignacio Matte Blanco. The logic of the unconscious is neither aware of the Aristotelian principle of non-contradiction nor of the distinction between individual and class, but aims at a homogeneous and indivisible whole. This explains why at all times the language of love ends in a fusion of the persons involved (to give only one sublime example, one thinks of Wagner's *Tristan und Isolde*).[5] By setting out the two elements of the couple as two sides of one coin, the Greek novel appears to project into the narrative the collective dreams of its audience. The interesting point is not, however, this relation between a primary psychological phenomenon and a literary text (the level at which 'wild' psychoanalysis of literature usually stops), but, on the contrary, the variations which each author applies to this scheme. In the history of the Greek novel, two phases can be distinguished. The first has a simpler and more popular appearance. The work of Xenophon of Ephesus is certainly the most consolatory of all and one that uses parallelism with great rigidity, showing the two protagonists in a countless number of identical episodes. Against this, Chariton, though he is earliest of the novelists, can already be seen to be importing

---

[4] For parallelism as a narrative figure, cf. Todorov (1967: 70-3); on the Greek novel, cf. the archetypal interpretation of Marcovaldi (1969: 57-8, 69-74), and the functionalist analysis of Ruiz-Montero (1988: 83, 154, 202); Molinié (1982: pt. 1) puts more stress on the narrative discourse.

[5] Cf. Matte Blanco (1975); Fusillo (1989: esp. 186-96).

notable ambiguities by describing rivals whose attitudes are more indistinct and towards whom the author shows sympathy, sometimes in a repressed way, but sometimes explicitly. The novels of the second phase, more elaborate and complex, offer variations of a more structural type. Achilles Tatius' decision to use his male protagonist as narrator alters the parallelism by presenting the partner as a figure in flight. This fits well with his greater moral elasticity and his more marked proximity to the comic sphere, which turns his work into an ironic pastiche of the Greek novel, not unlike Petronius. Heliodorus, on the other hand, fills the couple's story with symbols and Neoplatonic values by a tragic elevation which contrasts sharply with the comic degradation in Achilles Tatius. Moreover, he lays particular emphasis on his heroine and on the fact that she finds her way back to the land of her ancestors, Ethiopia.[6]

3. Thus, in the Greek novel, one detects a centripetal force which finalizes the dominant theme of the couple's eros. However strong it may be, there is none the less an opposite, centrifugal force, which leads to a more open structure and so to polyphony. I should like to examine now an aspect which stands aside from the erotic themes, a *topos* characteristic of our corpus but one which is almost entirely neglected by modern critics: the conflict of emotions.[7] It derives from the importance attached in this type of literature to the emotive sphere. Thus criticism based on idealistic psychologism was contrary to history: one cannot expect to find in ancient texts the kind of analytical introspection which the European novel was only to attain in the 19th century and then in the Freudian period.

On the other hand, it is a mistake to believe that the characters of the Greek novels can be reduced to mere puppets manipulated by capricious fate. This judgement would indeed be partly true, but only for Xenophon's *Ephesiaca*. The other novels all show cases of pragmatic initiative and internal conflicts. One thinks of Chariton's heroine Callirhoe, torn between the desire to be faithful to the memory of Chaereas and the wish to raise their son in freedom by marrying Dionysios (2. 9–11). In the four extant erotic novels the

---

[6] The distinction between the two phases is found in Hägg (1983: 34–5); *contra* Janni (1987: xxvii n. 38). On the development and evolution of the literary genre, cf. Kuch (1989*b*).

[7] To my knowledge, the only reference to this *topos* is in Heisermann (1977: 120, 125), 'mixed contrary emotions'.

narrator often describes the state of emotions of a single character or of a group of people as the result of a conflict between a series of feelings, usually listed in a cumulative manner. The frequence with which this *topos* occurs and its novelty (to my knowledge there are no direct models or parallels in other ancient novels) clearly demonstrate that even without a theoretical codification the novelists were aware that they were dealing with a literary genre which had rules, conventions, and themes of its own, in other words that they were using a code. This is further proof that the narrative of the Greek novels is not restricted to the mechanisms of external episodes, but shows an internal dynamic based on a view of the human psyche as a field of tensions and contradictory forces, whereas the schematic way in which it is expressed comes intuitively very close to modern concepts. We may start with a particularly significant example, showing a clear meta-literary awareness. We are at the climax of Chariton's narrative, the trial at the court of the Persian Great King, Artaxerxes, where Callirhoe's husband, Dionysios, and Chaereas' master, the satrap Mithridates, confront one another. All the people involved in the trial, even Callirhoe, believe that Chaereas is dead. But Mithridates sends him a letter intended for Callirhoe in order to get her back. Dionysios intercepts the letter, believes it to be a trick to seduce Callirhoe, and accordingly accuses the satrap of adultery. By a clever manoeuvre, Mithridates makes Chaereas reappear at the very moment when he is to answer publicly for the charges brought against him. This *coup de théâtre*, the sudden resurrection of a dead man which completely overturns the issue of the trial, is a comic way of rewriting the model of judicial eloquence (in that respect the trial in Achilles Tatius is identical), and intersects with another very frequent *topos* in the Greek novel, apparent death, which points to a world based on theatrical paradox, on anti-tragic resolution, on fiction.[8]

The conflict of emotions thus appears to be underlined by a *praeteritio*: τίς ἂν φράσαι κατ' ἀξίαν ἐκεῖνο τὸ σχῆμα τοῦ δικαστηρίου; ποῖος ποιητὴς ἐπὶ σκηνῆς παράδοξον μῦθον οὕτως εἰσήγαγεν; ἔδοξας ἂν ἐν θεάτρῳ παρεῖναι μυρίων παθῶν πλήρει· πάντα ἦν ὁμοῦ, δάκρυα, χαρά, θάμβος, ἔλεος, ἀπιστία, εὐχαί, 'Who could fitly describe that

[8] Cf. Chariton 1. 4-5; Xenophon of Ephesus 3. 5-7; Achilles Tatius 3. 17-22, 5. 6-7, 7. 1-5; Heliodorus 2. 3-4. F. Wehrli (1965: 140-1) supposes the *topos* to derive from the novel, whereas Weinreich (1950/1962: 24) stresses the relation to Euripides' *Helen*. For the use of the *topos* by Shakespeare, cf. Gesner (1970: 95-8).

scene in court? What dramatist ever staged such an astonishing story? It was like being at a play packed with passionate scenes, with emotions tumbling over each other—weeping and rejoicing, astonishment and pity, disbelief and prayers' (5. 8. 2). One should pay special attention to the form in which the *topos* occurs: asyndetic accumulation of abstract nouns (or, as we shall see in some cases, of verbs). In his essay on Greek prose, J. D. Denniston has emphasized how in Greek the tendency to abstract expression often coexists with a tendency for asyndeton. However, among the examples which he cites for their stylistic significance and which were most certainly the formal models for the novelists, one misses the element of multiple contrast (Denniston only has the binary antithesis): the series is always homogeneous, as in a passage of Plato's *Laws*, which is particularly close because it deals with harmful emotions: θυμός, ἔρως, ὕβρις, ἀμαθία, φιλοκέρδεια, δειλία, καὶ ἔτι τοιάδε, πλοῦτος, κάλλος, ἰσχύς, 'anger, lust, insolence, ignorance, covetousness, cowardice, and also these—wealth, beauty, strength') (1. 649d).[9] This is a cumulation of negative concepts, whereas in the novel the new element introduced in the *topos* is the conflict between the emotions which Aristotle had clearly distinguished in the *Rhetoric*. This novelty is underlined through Chariton's explicit emulation. Moreover, the narrator's intervention reveals the poetic aim of the *topos*. It is to stupefy with a paradoxical simultaneity, immediately analysed as follows: Χαιρέαν ἐμακάριζον, Μιθριδάτῃ συνέχαιρον, συνελυποῦντο Διονυσίῳ, περὶ Καλλιρρόης ἠπόρουν, 'How happy all were for Chaereas! How glad for Mithridates! For Dionysios, how sorrowful! As for Callirhoe, they did not know what to think' (with a measured chiasma and remaining asyndetic; 5. 8. 3). The prospect defines Callirhoe's aphasic anguish: after the verbal conflict between the two rivals, in the style of theatrical stichomythia, the stress is put on the binary conflict between her love for Chaereas and her respect for Dionysios. The poetics of stupefaction is a constant feature of the Greek novel and could not fail to appeal to baroque writers. As in this case, there is often an identification with the techniques of the theatre, for we have a collective situation, with three protagonists and a chorus. I have found no parallel for this variant other than a modern form of theatre which comes close to the Greek novel, the melodrama. I

---

[9] Denniston (1965: ch. 6).

am thinking of typical group scenes (especially in Rossini) where all the characters are paralysed with stupefaction.[10]

In Heliodorus the theatricality is even more explicit and yet presents a stylistic *variatio*. Only in his *Aethiopica* can we read a story that is relatively independent from that of the couple. The story of Calasiris, the Egyptian prophet initiated in the mysteries, and of the fratricidal struggle between his sons Thyamis and Petosiris, follows the path of Euripides' *Phoenissae*. However, the end of the tragedy is turned into comedy through the timely arrival of the prophet together with Charicleia. Heliodorus uses many stage metaphors and underlines the theatrical matrix. Calasiris' arrival 'by a miracle of stagecraft' is defined as 'a second drama brought on stage to compete with the one already in progress' (7. 6. 5).[11] The slow process of recognition brings his two sons to this state of emotion: πολλὰ ἅμα καὶ ἐξ ἐναντίων ἔπασχον. ἥδοντο ἐπὶ τῷ φύντι σωζομένῳ παρ᾽ ἐλπίδας· ἐφ᾽ ᾗ κατελαμβάνοντο πράξει καὶ ἠνιῶντο καὶ ᾐσχύνοντο· τῆς ἀδηλίας τῶν ἀποβησομένων εἰς ἀγωνίαν καθίσταντο, 'they experienced many contrary emotions at one and the same time: joy at the unexpected restoration of their father, sorrow and shame at the business in which he had surprised them, and finally anguish over the uncertainties of what might ensue' (7. 7. 3).

The structure of this period is still asyndetic, but without a cumulative effect, with a chiasma between the two first sentences and a *variatio* of the two central verbs with homoioteleuton. The theatricality of the situation is amplified by the astonishment and aphasia which befall the public watching the scene from the walls of Memphis: not understanding what happens and not moving, they remain petrified, as statues.

The conflict of emotions can also be seen within an isolated character, as in Achilles Tatius. This is a private and intimate variant which comes extremely close to forms of expression adopted by the modern novel (a striking example is the penultimate chapter of Thomas Mann's *Tonio Kröger*). The love of the protagonists, a vital element in the erotic novel, takes an atypical form with Leucippe and Clitophon. Their feelings arise not in the solemn context of a religious ceremony, but, in the case of Clitophon, with the young

[10] Cf. Rossini, *Il Barbiere di Siviglia*, final act, 1; *La Cenerentola*, final act, 1 and 2. 7; *La Donna del Lago*, final act, 1.
[11] Cf. Feuillâtre (1966: 120); Fusillo (1989: 41-2); on Heliodorus' frequent use of scenic metaphors, cf. Walden (1894).

girl's very first appearance. Besides, this inspiration is neither reciprocal nor violent. It is told only from the point of view of the male protagonist, that is, by the ego-narrator identical with the ego-character, who is not yet aware of Leucippe's emotive response. This is how he records his psychological movements at that time: πάντα δέ με εἶχεν ὁμοῦ, ἔπαινος, ἔκπληξις, τρόμος, αἰδώς, ἀναίδεια, ἐπήνουν τὸ μέγεθος, ἐκπεπλήγμην τὸ κάλλος, ἔτρεμον τὴν καρδίαν, ἔβλεπον ἀναιδῶς, ἡδούμην ἁλῶναι, 'I now became a prey to a host of emotions: admiration, amazement, trembling, shame, shamelessness. I admired her generous stature, marvelled at her beauty, trembled in my heart, stared shamelessly, ashamed I might be caught' (1. 4. 5). This form of asyndetic accumulation is the most decisive. In particular one notes a liking for antithesis, as frequently in Greek prose from Gorgias onwards (especially the pairing αἰδώς-ἀναίδεια), and the reminiscence of Sapphic shivering. A feature in common with other novels is the devastating passion ('as soon as I had seen her, I was overwhelmed', 1. 4. 4) in contrast to the restraint of decency. But in Achilles Tatius this first glance is followed by a free and urbane conquest which extends over the two first books and is narrated from the same limited viewpoint as we find it here in the conflict of emotions. The narrative figures and the thematic figures, when compared with other novelists, offer a vision of eros less glorified and less crystallized, much closer to the daily round in comedy.[12]

So we end up with a framework of variants which may be used for this *topos*. On a thematic axis the conflict of emotions may imply a group of characters and assume a more theatrical dimension, or a single character, with a more psychological one. At a stylistic level it takes the form either of an asyndetic accumulation of abstract nouns or more elaborate forms based on verbs. In *Chaereas and Callirhoe* the people of Syracuse play quite an important role because of the pseudo-historic reconstruction in the novel: at their democratic assembly, they want to sail off as soon as they learn that Callirhoe is not dead but has been sold in Miletus. On the day when the delegation, chosen and led by Chaereas, is about to leave on a ship still bearing the ensign of the victory over

---

[12] Cf. Calderini (1912: 61-8); Durham (1938; still useful though outmoded by papyri); Reardon (1971: 363-5); García Gual (1970/1988: 245, 258-9); Cresci (1978); Napolitano (1983-4); Heiserman (1977: 117-30; too extreme); also Fusillo (1989: 98-109, 158-70).

Athens, the entire population, even women and children, run to the harbour: καὶ ἦσαν ὁμοῦ εὐχαί, δάκρυα, στεναγμοί, παραμυθία, φόβος, θάρσος, ἀπόγνωσις, ἐλπίς, 'prayers were joined with tears, groans of despair, words of consolation, fear, confidence, despair, hope' (3. 5. 3). Antitheses and asyndeton depict the people as participating in the love story, giving it an epic and public resonance. Chariton often points out that the people of Syracuse were even more receptive to the couple's adventures than to the famous victory over the Athenians.[13]

Xenophon of Ephesus, on the contrary, offers a rather summary example. Antheia has poisoned herself in order to escape her marriage with the rich Perilaos. The collective reaction to this death, occurring on the wedding day (following the tragic tomb/bridal chamber *topos*), is summarized in this way: θόρυβός τε πολὺς τῶν κατὰ τὴν οἰκίαν ἦν καὶ πάθη συμμιγῆ, οἰμωγή, φόβος, ἔκπληξις. οἱ μὲν ᾤκτειρον τὴν δοκοῦσαν τεθνηκέναι, οἱ δὲ συνήχθοντο Περιλάῳ, πάντες δὲ ἐθρήνουν τὸ γεγονός, 'There was a great deal of commotion in the household: they felt a welter of emotions—grief, fear, and terror. Some pitied the girl who had apparently died; others shared Perilaus's grief; while all mourned the tragedy' (3. 7. 1). This is a relatively short sequence with few contradictions, but its purpose is nevertheless to bring out the motive of apparent death and the desperate reaction of Perilaos, which ennobles him in an unusual manner.

The typology of internal conflict offers a richer and more interesting picture. In the novels of the first period, the narrative pattern is always that of an external, primary, all-knowing narrator, following the model of the Homeric (Iliadic) narrative, in contrast with more complex forms investigated by the novelists of the second period. Chariton's narrator, however, presents a more varied profile. Although he preserves a basic omniscience, he often comes close to the viewpoint of his characters in short passages where he introduces subjective elements.[14] For instance, whereas Xenophon narrates Antheia's apparent death in a panoramic, synthetic, and absolutely objective picture, the corresponding episode in Chariton appears far more elaborate. The narrative scheme

[13] On the primacy of eros over the historical atmosphere, cf. C.-W. Müller (1981: 391-2).

[14] On this distinctive psychological aspect of Chariton's narrative, cf. Hägg (1971a: 114-19); Ruiz-Montero (1988: 318-19); Stark (1984: 260); Fusillo (1989: 120-2).

retains a zero degree focalization: we readers know from the start that this is a false death and that the brigands have decided to rob the tomb. However, the narrative concentrates on Callirhoe's emotional reactions to her traumatic awakening and describes the various feelings of anguish of a 'dead' girl buried alive, resulting in a desperate monologue.[15] Her state of emotions when she hears the brigands open the tomb is described as follows: Καλλιρρόην κατελάμβανεν ὁμοῦ πάντα, φόβος, χαρά, λύπη, θαυμασμός, ἐλπίς, ἀπιστία, 'Callirhoe was gripped by a variety of emotions—fear, joy, grief, surprise, hope, disbelief' (1. 9. 3). The *topos* gains emphasis from the monologue in which the character gives several interpretations of the event, from the supernatural to the natural (which is also the reality). Although this passage has a more subjective tone, paradox and antithesis remain the dominant elements and have to be taken into account in the 'baroque' *topos* of apparent death.

The Persian episode makes up the central part of the novel. After Chaereas' resurrection the judicial issue is left unsettled as another character falls in love with Callirhoe: King Artaxerxes. The characterization of this new rival prompts an unusual form. For his eros arises not at first sight, but gradually, and leaves him torn between his public function as a judge and his destructive desire which would lead him to commit an act of adultery contrary to his own established laws. The king then tries to sublimate his feelings by indulging in his favourite pleasure, hunting, but this fails miserably and makes him succumb to the god's power. So he entrusts his eunuch with Callirhoe's seduction, but when Callirhoe rejects his advances, the eunuch is left staggered, μυρίων παθῶν μεστός, ὀργιζόμενος μὲν Καλλιρρόη, λυπούμενος δὲ ἐφ' ἑαυτῷ, φοβούμενος δὲ βασιλέα, 'seething with all kinds of emotion: he was angry with Callirhoe, sorry for himself, and frightened of the King' (6. 6. 1). This mixture of emotions has the purpose of deprecating oriental customs and passion in line with the pseudo-historiographic polemic against despotism which is present throughout the novel.[16] The King has to give up Callirhoe because of a war. Chaereas wins his wife back through one of his military feats on the side of the

---

[15] For a full treatment of this episode, cf. Reardon (1982a: 16–19).

[16] Achilles Tatius has the same episode (6. 12. 13), but without reference to history. Anti-oriental polemic is found e.g. in Chariton 6. 5. 10; 6. 7. 3, 9–10, 12. Hägg (1987) sees Chariton's narration as a historical novel comparable to those of Walter Scott.

Egyptian rebels. The conflict of emotions occurs once more when Artaxerxes reads the letter in which Chaereas announces the restoration of the queen: μυρίων παθῶν ἐπληροῦτο· καὶ γὰρ ὠργίζετο διὰ τὴν ἅλωσιν τῶν φιλτάτων καὶ μετενόει διὰ τὸ παρασχεῖν αὐτομολίας ἀνάγκην, καὶ χάριν δὲ αὐτῷ πάλιν ἠπίστατο ὅτι Καλλιρρόην μηκέτι δύναιτο θεάσασθαι. Μάλιστα δὲ πάντων φθόνος ἥπτετο αὐτοῦ, καὶ ἔλεγε· Μακάριος Χαιρέας, εὐτυχέστερος ἐμοῦ, 'the King was filled with countless emotions as he read it: he was angry at the capture of his dear ones, he regretted making Chaereas go over to his enemies, and then again he was grateful to him that he could not see Callirhoe anymore. But above all he was envious. "Happy Chaereas!" he said. "He is luckier than I" ' (8. 5. 8).

In the essay I referred to earlier, I have tried to read the topical scheme of the triangular relation between lovers and rivals as a dialectic between a repressive element, pertaining to the project of celebrating the couple's eros and therefore of giving a negative characterization to the third party, and a repressed element, introducing ambiguities and leading to a harmonious characterization of the rivals. Repressive and repressed are not meant in a sense of evaluation or transgression. On the contrary they are two important components structuring the polysemy of the literary discourse.[17]

In the Greek novel rivals can therefore be differentiated on a scale according to the degree of identification shown in the text, i.e. from zero (when a rival has the classic function of an opponent) all the way to obvious sympathy. This can be done at the light of the categories of Francesco Orlando's Freudian rhetoric. Artaxerxes falls into a high category (Orlando defines it as 'the return of a repressed element which is conscious but not accepted,' and refers to Racine's *Phèdre* as an example[18]) precisely because of this subjective split which places eros in opposition to the cultural rules.

Another rival to whom Chariton has granted an even greater space is Dionysios, a Menandrian and educated character.[19] He too gets caught in a conflict between his desire, which breaks out at the first sight of Callirhoe, and the moral code, i.e. his faithfulness to the memory of his recently deceased wife. It is a conflict between

[17] Fusillo (1989: 219–28); for the idea of a triangular desire in modern novels, cf. Girard (1961: 2).

[18] Orlando (1973); see also Orlando (1980).

[19] For the relation of this character with the comedies of Menander, cf. Borgogna (1971: 260–1).

reason and passion, as the narrator puts it schematically (2. 4. 4). But unlike Artaxerxes, Dionysios is not nurturing a desire for adultery. He marries the protagonist and always stresses the legal character of his position. In terms of the ideology of marriage in the Greek novel, this is a further positive charge.

Chariton keeps describing Dionysios' internal experience and his relation to Callirhoe in an elaborate manner (more elaborate than the same type of relation between the protagonists): when Callirhoe tells him that she had dreamed of her former husband, one notes a topical simultaneity of emotions: τούτων τῶν λόγων ἀκούσας ὁ Διονύσιος ποικίλας ἐλάμβανε γνώμας· ἥπτετο μὲν γὰρ αὐτοῦ ζηλοτυπία διότι καὶ νεκρὸν ἐφίλει Χαιρέαν, ἥπτετο δὲ καὶ φόβος μὴ ἑαυτὴν ἀποκτείνῃ· ἐθάρρει δὲ ὅμως ὅτι ὁ πρῶτος ἀνὴρ ἐδόκει τεθνηκέναι τῇ γυναικί· μὴ γὰρ ἀπολείψειν αὐτὴν Διονύσιον, οὐκ ὄντος ἔτι Χαιρέου, 'When he heard this, Dionysios was assailed by conflicting sentiments. He was seized with jealousy, that Callirhoe loved Chaereas even dead; with fear, that she would kill herself. Yet still, he was heartened by the thought that his wife thought her first husband dead, for he supposed that she would not leave Dionysios if Chaereas was no longer alive' (3. 7. 6). This passage, like the one on Artaxerxes, takes a less conventional form, since it is less interested in the paradox of accumulation.

Perry praises Chariton as the least rhetorical and the most psychological of the Greek novelists, especially in his minor characters. This idealized view, which *a priori* underestimates rhetoric, is no longer acceptable today. In fact, Chariton uses the same *topoi* as the other novelists. What distinguishes him is that he uses these features for vaguer characterizations.[20]

On the other hand, the rivals in Xenophon's *Ephesiaca* show a monolithic, univocally negative image. In the figure of Manto, the daughter of the protagonists' master, a certain margin of *empatheia* can be detected, still completely unconscious (and not obvious as with Dionysios). A reasonable narrative space is allotted to the pathological passion and the foolish obsession of her eros for Abrocomas. After reading the letter in which the protagonist rejects all her advances, Manto falls into a state of mind described by the narrator as follows: ἡ Μαντὼ ἐν ὀργῇ ἀκατασχέτῳ γίνεται καὶ ἀναμίξασα πάντα, φθόνον [καὶ], ζηλοτυπίαν, λύπην, φόβον, 'Manto

---

[20] Perry (1930: 115-23); cf. also Rakcińska (1971: 600-2); García Gual (1970/1988: 203, 218-20); Hägg (1972: 545-56).

could not control her anger. All her feelings were confused: she felt envy, jealousy, grief, and fear' (2. 5. 5). Subsequently, Xenophon uses this *topos* only for his protagonists when they reunite, that is, at the beginning and at the end of the story, following the strictly circular structure of the novel. In Book 1 Xenophon describes their first wedding night in a way which is rather unusual for such a synthetic writer, underlining their dense expectations with emotions: τοῖς δὲ ἑκατέροις πάθος συνέβη ταὐτόν, καὶ οὔτε προσειπεῖν ἔτι ἀλλήλους ἠδύναντο οὔτε ἀντιβλέψαι τοῖς ὀφθαλμοῖς, ἔκειντο δὲ ὑφ' ἡδονῆς παρειμένοι, αἰδούμενοι, φοβούμενοι, πνευστιῶντες, καιόμενοι· ἐπάλλετο δὲ αὐτοῖς τὰ σώματα καὶ ἐκραδαίνοντο αὐτοῖς αἱ ψυχαί, 'Both of them felt the same emotions and were unable to say anything to each other or to look at each other's eyes but lay at ease in sheer delight, shy, afraid, panting—and on fire. Their bodies trembled and their hearts quivered' (1. 9. 1).[21] But, as expected, the joys of marriage cannot last very long: frightened by a strange oracle, the parents decide to send their newly married children away. The anxiety caused by this departure, calmed only by the comfort of being together, is described in the following sentence: πολλὰ ἀνανοοῦντες, τοὺς πατέρας οἰκτείροντες, τῆς πατρίδος ἐπιθυμοῦντες, τὸν χρησμὸν δεδοικότες, τὴν ἀποδημίαν ὑποπτεύοντες, 'turning a host of things over their minds: pitying their parents, longing for their homeland, fearing the oracle, and feeling uneasy about the voyage' (1. 11. 1). The whole framework of the novel consists in a series of threatening episodes, which the protagonists endure separated always and overcome by a mechanical fate. Finally they meet again in Rhodes, the place of their first adventure while they were still united. The theatrical identification ends in a climax based on a mixture of contradictory feelings: κατεῖχε δὲ αὐτοὺς πολλὰ ἅμα πάθη, ἡδονή, λύπη, φόβος, ἡ τῶν πρότερον μνήμη, τὸ τῶν μελλόντων δέος, 'A host of different emotions took hold of them at once—joy, grief, fear, memory of past events, and anxiety of the future' (5. 13. 3).

As can be seen, Xenophon of Ephesus uses the *topos* in its purest form. The asyndetic accumulation, with a minor *variatio* only in the final example (moreover the asyndetic use of abstracts is found throughout the novel, in the sort of recapitulations which frequently sum up the previous episodes for the reader's benefit), puts

[21] On the structural function of this first *Liebesnacht*, cf. Schissel (1909: 30–41), in an essay stressing the dichotomic technique used in this novel.

the stress on the emotional sphere of the couple, seen as an indivisible whole.[22]

The work of Achilles Tatius is far more elaborate. Of the two basic trends in the Greek novel as described above, *Leucippe and Clitophon* is clearly dominated by the centrifugal force, by polyphony. The narrator, Clitophon, and behind him the author himself, are attracted by every kind of phenomenon and transcribe this polymorphism by using free, non-hierarchical forms of expression, often turning to the rhetoric of contrast and of competition without winners, which is identical to that of the emotional conflicts we have previously seen, suspended always in immobility. Thus Leucippe's beauty is described as a chromatic rivalry with the flowers (1. 19), the exceptional nature of a necklace as a struggle amongst gems (2. 11. 2-3), the floods of the Nile as a competition between the rivers and the earth (4. 12. 3), the charms of Alexandria as a conflict of beauty and greatness (5. 1. 6). The metaphor of the suspended, continuous, insoluble conflict, is indeed the strong point of this heterogeneous novelist, who aims to reproduce the full dynamics of reality. The *topos* we are dealing with therefore gets a particularly elaborate treatment in Achilles Tatius.

At the end of Book 2 the meeting of the two protagonists at night is disrupted by the arrival of Leucippe's mother. This avoids premarital relations and keeps up the conventions of the novelistic genre, now playfully rewritten. The (female) protagonist's state of mind when left alone in her room is objectivized by the narrator: παντοδαπή τις ἦν· ἤχθετο, ᾐσχύνετο, ὠργίζετο, 'she was caught in emotional chaos. She was vexed, ashamed, angered' (2. 29. 1). But this time the triple asyndeton is not considered enough: Clitophon adds a long excursus on these three emotions, seen as waves emanating from speech and wounding the person on various parts of the body. This is a pseudo-scientific theory, which vaguely derives from Democritus and falls within Achilles Tatius' tendency to encyclopedism; his novel is full of digressions on customs, on physical and geographical phenomena, on exotic animals and on all kinds of paradoxographic material.[23] This theoretical interest for the psychological sphere accords with the many moments when the conflict is restricted to the contrast of two emotions, a slight

---

[22] This trend towards recapitulative repetition, obviously aimed at a popular audience, is stressed by Hägg (1971a: 267-77).

[23] Cf. chiefly Rommel (1923).

variation of our *topos* (the only one, for instance, found in *Daphnis and Chloe*) which goes back to lyric poetry (Sappho and Anacreon). Shortly before the nocturnal tryst, the narrator had given an account of his mental instability caused by the tension between his fear of danger and his hope of success (2. 23. 4). Earlier still, love had created a conflict between eros and the will of his father who had planned for his son to marry his daughter by a previous marriage. In this case, the conflict had ended favourably for the narrator (1. 11 and 2. 5), but later on, when this half-sister is abducted, he is nevertheless torn between relief and sorrow (2. 18. 6). This binary mode is also applicable to the description of works of art, a minor literary genre allotted much space by Achilles Tatius, who gives it the task of putting the stresses on the macro-rhythm of the narrative. In the painting of Europa's abduction, with which the novel opens, the girls waver between joy and fear (1. 1. 7); at the beginning of Book 3, the picture of Prometheus about to be freed shows the Titan caught between hope and terror (3. 8. 7); and in the work depicting Procne and Philomela, which is the opening of Book 5, the women are laughing and frightened at the same time (5. 3. 7).[24]

An authentic accumulation of emotions can be obtained by a *coup de théâtre*, as in Chariton where it is caused by a paradoxical resurrection, but prepared by a fairly skilful effect of suspense. The novelty in Achilles Tatius' narrative technique is indeed the choice of a restricted viewpoint. Clitophon, the narrator, usually takes the position of the author of the story, just as Homer's Odysseus, but very often, unlike Odysseus and in the same way as Petronius' Encolpius, he limits the perspective to himself as an actor in the story; he is then able to introduce elements of surprise and to 'theatricalize' the phenomenon as it occurs. One important example: when Leucippe is beheaded (the scene is imitated by Shakespeare in his *Cymbeline*), Clitophon narrates the episode by giving the reader only his own perceptions as a character in the action, without any knowledge of the exchange of persons which saved his partner's life.[25] Later, when Leucippe reappears by mere

[24] On ekphrasis in Achilles Tatius, cf. Friedländer (1912: intro. 47–51); Garson (1978: 83–6); and above all, on its structural function, Sedelmeier-Stoeckl (1958: 77–90).
[25] Cf. Effe (1975: 149–51); Hägg (1971: 103–5, 131–4); Stark (1984: 262–3); Fusillo (1989: 164–70); on Odysseus as ego-narrator, cf. Suerbaum (1968); on Petronius' ego-narrator, cf. Veyne (1964).

coincidence as the slave of Melite, the widow Clitophon has married believing his beloved to be dead, the effect of surprise is repeated with the same technique. Clitophon is astonished at the sight of the slave, somehow reminding him of Leucippe, though in a state of degeneration (for the reader this is already a clearly directed sign), but he is brought to the peak of stupefaction when he is later given a letter signed by Leucippe, a peak marked by the accumulation of antithetical emotions: τούτοις ἐντυχὼν πάντα ἐγινόμην ὁμοῦ· ἀνεφλεγόμην, ὠχρίων, ἐθαύμαζον, ἠπίστουν, ἔχαιρον, ἠχθόμην, 'On reading this, my feelings exploded in all directions— I turned red; I went pale; I wondered at it; I doubted every word; I was rapt with joy and racked with distress' (5. 19. 1). An asyndetic series of six members, with an antithesis of colours in the expression of the face. It is picked up shortly afterwards as a binary conflict between pleasure and pain, the pleasure of having found the beloved and the pain of not being able to communicate with her (5. 21. 1).

In another of his generalizing *sententiae* Clitophon as narrator argues against the view which denies a direct relation between the expression of the face and the emotion of the soul. On the contrary, the one seems to him to be the mirror of the other (6. 6. 2). This theoretical statement almost seems to justify all the occasions when the protagonist describes the mental state of the other characters; Achilles Tatius indeed tends to safeguard the credibility of the ego-narrative. The physiognomy of Thersandros, Melite's first husband, believed to be dead, is contradictory. Madly in love with Leucippe, he shows all the negative characteristics of the rivals in the Greek novel: he is violent, sensual, arrogant, ready for anything, even the most illegal intrigues, in order to reach his goal. However, being a rich and noble Ionian, as Dionysios in Chariton, his character has a more elaborate depth. For example he is able to refrain from courting Leucippe because he is moved by her monologue, which he has heard in secret.[26] His amorous obsession also receives a special treatment. After Leucippe's heroic refusal, Thersandros is caught in a binary conflict between anger and love. Achilles Tatius uses this opportunity to insert a long theoretical digression on these two emotions, arising respectively in the liver and in the heart and fighting a continuous and vain struggle in each story of unrequited

---

[26] On the characterization of Thersander, cf. Sedelmeier-Stoeckl (1958: 134-5); Fusillo (1989: 222-3).

love (6. 19). After this phase of immobility, his state of mind
becomes fuller: ταῦτα ἀκούσας ὁ Θέρσανδρος παντοδαπὸς ἦν· ἤχθετο,
ὠργίζετο, ἐβουλεύετο. ὠργίζετο μὲν ὡς ὑβρισμένος· ἤχθετο δὲ ὡς ἀπο-
τυχών· ἐβουλεύετο δὲ ὡς ἐρῶν, 'On hearing this, Thersandros reacted
in several ways at once: he grieved, he raged, he plotted. He raged
as a man insulted; he grieved as man rejected; he plotted as a man
in love' (7. 1. 1). This triple asyndeton is the starting point of the
novel's last episode: Thersandros' plans, conceived from love, result
in the spectacular trial which closes the narrative.

It is not Thersandros, however, but Melite, who actually overturns the *topos* of the triangular relation in Achilles Tatius. The
description of Melite is an exceptionally positive one: she is beautiful, educated, ironic, elegant, human. Like another famous widow
of Ephesus, the matron of Petronius, this figure is the novel's incar-
nation of sensual freedom as opposed to the chastity represented by
Leucippe. This chastity imitates the mythical antithesis of Aphrodite and Artemis, referred to several times in the text (4. 1 and 8.
12), as usual without ending in a synthesis. This sympathy for the
third party, no longer repressed but openly acknowledged, and
moreover the episode of Melite as the whole, clearly demonstrate
Achilles Tatius' ironic ambivalence towards his chosen literary
genre.[27] The marriage of Melite and Clitophon is not consummated,
although this would fit with the norms of the erotic novel, since
their respective partners are believed to be dead (but the heroes of
the Greek novel never withstand the news of their partner's death
and always try to commit suicide); paradoxically, they have sexual
intercourse only once, secretly, and this is regarded as a flagrant
case of adultery since Leucippe and Thersandros are both brought
back to life. In this part of the novel, this image has a fundamental
semantic importance: after finding Leucippe's letter, which proves
that she is still alive, Melite decides to renounce this impossible
relation and goes to the prison where Clitophon is held to help him
escape with Leucippe, only asking in exchange, and in a very
elaborate manner, for a sole moment with him. Clitophon agrees,
regarding it as medicine for a mentally sick person rather than a
betrayal, but he will remain absolutely silent about this weak
moment. At the end, Melite successfully passes the test of the oath
on the Styx, by adding to the formula attesting that she did not

[27] For a re-examination of this still very controversial question, see my fuller
treatment in Fusillo (1989: 98–109); for the opposite view, cf. Hägg (1983: 53–4).

have intercourse with Clitophon the words 'in the absence of Thersandros'. This clever way of getting round the sacred rule shows the comic debasement Achilles has brought to the theme of marital fidelity, which is the ideological axis of the Greek novel.[28] The whole narrative unit devoted to the betrayal with Melite and to her half-victory in prison is introduced by a scene of conflict transcribing her mental state immediately after she has read the letter: ἐμεμέριστο πολλοῖς ἅμα τὴν ψυχήν, αἰδοῖ καὶ ὀργῇ καὶ ἔρωτι καὶ ζηλοτυπίᾳ. ᾐσχύνετο τὸν ἄνδρα, ὠργίζετο τοῖς γράμμασιν, ὁ ἔρως ἐμάραινε τὴν ὀργήν, ἐξῆπτε τὸν ἔρωτα ἡ ζηλοτυπία, καὶ τέλος ἐκράτησεν ὁ ἔρως, 'she felt her soul torn apart by conflicting emotions: shame, anger, love, and jealousy—she was ashamed to face her husband; the letter made her angry, but her anger withered away before her love, which was in turn inflamed by her jealousy. In the end her love prevailed' (5. 24. 3).

This example is less conventional in form, for it is based on polysyndeton and *variatio*, and atypical in content, because it does not end in parity but shows the victory of the erotic emotion. This victory is precisely the main novelty of the figure of Melite: unlike Thersandros, whose anger prevails over eros in the end, placing him in the classic position of an antagonist, Melite is the only rival in the Greek novel actually to help the protagonists (apart from the identical case of Lamon in Longus' *Daphnis and Chloe*). Love makes her renounce the plot which her anger or her jealousy would have dictated to her. This *topos* of the lover's renouncement is later brought out in quite disparate categories of Western culture, especially in the form of a more mature character helping a young couple. In the novel one notes a resemblance to the splendid picture of Sanseverina in Stendhal's *La Chartreuse de Parme*; as for theatre, one may think of Wagner's *Meistersinger von Nürnberg*, and (why not?) of the cinematographic masterpiece *Casablanca*. In our case, this is how Achilles Tatius' deviation from the code of the novel is resolved (he nevertheless stays within this code since the exaltation of the couple is compromised but not turned completely upside down): by asserting a vision of the world as playful, unprejudiced, mundane.

Heliodorus, on the other hand, rewrites the erotic novel in a totally different way to Achilles Tatius. The latter's is free and heterogeneous in every respect (form, themes, ideology, moralism),

[28] On the figure of Melite, cf. Cresci (1978); Segal (1984: 83–91).

his is closed, coherent, philosophically motivated. In the *Aithiopica*, the *topoi* of the novel, and therefore the conflicts of emotions, always appear in a measured and organic manner.

This novel's grand architecture is what makes it unique from a thematic as well as narrative point of view. Schematically it may be said that the other novels use a linear time for a circular story, whereas Heliodorus uses a circular time for a linear story. In the other novels the story (i.e. the level of the signified) is circular as far as it tells the adventures of two young people who fall in love with each other in their homeland, then get separated and go through a series of repetitive episodes, in spaces and times of little intrinsic value (they are simply tests for the heroes), and finally come together again in their homeland: from Syracuse back to Syracuse in Chariton, from Ephesus back to Ephesus in Xenophon, and from Tyre to Tyre in Achilles Tatius (there, however, Leucippe comes from Sidon). On the other hand, the narrative of this story (i.e. the level of the signifier) is linear since it follows the chronology of the story from the beginning to the end (only Achilles Tatius introduces some variations through the use of the first person). In the *Aithiopica*, on the contrary, the story is linear and describes the route that leads Charicleia from Delphi, where she was raised by Charicles the priest of Apollo, to her homeland Meroe, where she finds her real parents, the rulers of Ethiopia. It is a long cognitive process in which the spaces are not of repetitive character, but integrated with their distinctive features into a confrontation of culture and into a hierarchy of knowledge which reaches its peak with the utopian representation of Ethiopia inspired by the mysticism of the Gymnosophists. On the other hand, the narration is totally anti-linear: following the model of the *Odyssey*, but with an original use of mystery and suspense, it starts *in mediis rebus* with the pirates attacking the couple on the banks of the Nile, then goes back to the beginning and tells the previous episodes in the middle of the novel, where the opening scene is narrated from a different perspective, and moves on toward the final triumph (the couple's separation being very limited).[29] This reinterpretation of the novel is largely entrusted to a Neoplatonic figure, the Egyptian prophet Calasiris, who narrates the entire first part of the novel and reflects in the action the image of the author

---

[29] On the linearity of Heliodorus' story and its contrast with the erotic genre, cf. Szepessy (1957).

with the effect of a *mise en abyme*.[30] The *topos* of the conflict of emotions is introduced at a decisive moment in this story when Calasiris tells the young Athenian Cnemon that Charicles has asked him to cure Charicleia of her mysterious disease and to make her overcome her stubborn refusal of eros. This is how the prophet gets hold of the band embroidered with Ethiopian letters that she had with her when she was exposed as an infant and from which he learns of her abnormal birth, how this white princess was born of black parents, and how she was exposed by her mother to avoid all suspicion of adultery (in fact the white colour comes from a painting of Andromeda which the woman was looking at as she made love, a theme imitated by Tasso for his Clorinda).[31]

Here is how the narrator explains his reaction after reading the stunning news: ἡδονῆς δὲ ἅμα καὶ λύπης ἐνεπλήσθην. καὶ πάθος τι καινότερον ὑπέστην, ὁμοῦ δακρύων καὶ χαίρων, διαχεομένης μὲν τῆς ψυχῆς πρὸς τὴν τῶν ἀγνοουμένων εὕρεσιν καὶ τῶν χρησθέντων ἤδη τὴν ἐπίλυσιν, ἀδημονούσης δὲ πρὸς τὴν τῶν ἐσομένων ἔκβασιν, καὶ τὸν ἀνθρώπινον βίον οἰκτιζούσης ὡς ἄστατόν τι καὶ ἀβέβαιον καὶ ἄλλοτε πρὸς ἄλλα τρεπόμενον, τότε δὲ ὑπερβαλλόντως ἐν ταῖς Χαρικλείας τύχαις γνωριζόμενον ... ἐπὶ πολύ τε ἀμφίβολος εἱστήκειν, τῶν μὲν παρελθόντων οἰκτείρειν ἔχων, τῶν δὲ ἐσομένων εὐδαιμονίζειν οὐ θαρσῶν, 'I was filled with a mixture of pleasure and sadness and had the peculiar experience of being moved simultaneously to joy and tears. My heart was thankful that the mystery had been explained, that the riddle of the oracle had been solved, but it was sorely troubled about the course the future might take and filled with pity for the life of man, whose instability and insecurity, whose constant changes of direction were made all too manifest in the story of Charicleia . . . For a long time I stood there, torn between pity for past sorrows and despair for future happiness' (4. 9. 1). The passage clearly shows how the secondary narrator, more even than the primary one, uses a narrative technique based on suspense and on a restricted standpoint. Indeed, Calasiris only tells of his own perceptions and emotions, recorded quite unconventionally (there is no theatrical accumulation) and subjectively (in a scattered way later ordered by rationality) without superimposing on this his

---

[30] An ample theorization of Gide's concept of the *mise en abyme* can be found in Dällenbach (1978). On Calasiris as the oblique reflection of the author and on how to read the novel, cf. Haight (1943: 84–93); Winkler (1982) (= this volume, ch. 12).   [31] Cf. Billault (1981*b*).

knowledge as ego-narrator. On the contrary, and precisely here, Calasiris withholds the information he had as a character by using a narrative device defined by Genette as *paralipse*.[32] Shortly afterward we learn from the conversation with Charicleia that he had been commissioned by the queen of Ethiopia, Persinna, to search for the exposed girl and that he had asked for the band only to confirm that she was really Charicleia. Thus his reaction when reading the text is more than just an indistinct emotion, it is in fact an identification. This dissimulation has baffled modern critics: for Hefti Persinna's commission to Calasiris is a double role which is not very well interwoven with the oracle of Apollo, while Sandy sees in this development the cunning of an ambivalent, learned magician figure; only Winkler, in his study with the beautiful Jamesian title 'What Kalasiris Knew', has given this continuous postponement of information, which is the main feature of the novel, its true sense. Calasiris' narrative strategy reflects the complex meaning of the novel, i.e. that the divine truth is uncovered by degrees, by progressive clues.[33] So, for the 'narratee' Cnemon as well as for us readers, the reading of the band transmits a true emotional reaction, for Calasiris wavers between his pity for the past, his joy over the present revelation, and his fear of the future, but only in part: the queen's commission is hidden from us and deferred until the dramatic moment when it is revealed to the person affected, the protagonist.

The episode of the band is part of the long process through which Calasiris makes Charicleia become aware of her eros for Theagenes by using the Neoplatonic principle of gradual maieutics upon which Heliodorus' narrative and ideology are based. Through a psychoanalytic therapy *ante litteram*, Calasiris resolves all the moral and religious inhibitions which kept Charicleia from even admitting to the idea of love and which induced her, unlike Achilles Tatius' rather nonconformist heroine, to imitate the behaviour of Euripidean heroines, especially Phaedra. In fact, a verbal confession of eros is never spoken by Charicleia, not even at the end, but by Calasiris himself, who explains to the girl her state of mental love and provokes in her an aphasic turmoil described as follows:
ἱδρῶτι πολλῷ διερρεῖτο τούτων εἰρημένων, ὦ Κνήμων, καὶ δήλη

---

[32] Genette (1972: 93–4, 211–12).
[33] Hefti (1950: 72–8; doublets); Sandy (1982: 141–67), following E. Rohde (1876/1900: 477–8); Winkler (1982: pt. 3 = below, pp. 329–50).

παντοίως ἦν χαίρουσα μὲν ἐφ' οἷς ἤκουσεν, ἀγωνιῶσα δὲ ἐφ' οἷς ἤλπιζεν, ἐρυθριῶσα δὲ ἐφ' οἷς ἑάλωκεν, 'At these words, Cnemon, rivers of perspiration began to run down her face, and there could be no doubt that she was prey to all kinds of emotion: joy for what she heard, anguish for what she hoped, shame for what had been detected in her' (4. 11. 1). The *topos*, used here in Heliodorus' favourite form of symmetrical expression, synthesizes the long phase of the story which deals with the conflict between the girl's increasing desire and her restraining sense of virginal decency. It is the last moment of stupefaction before the total acceptance of eros, based on the ideal of marriage and chastity.

Apart from these two examples, which fit very well into this key-episode, the *topos* of the conflict of emotions occurs again in the spectacular ending to the novel. The recognition of Charicleia by the two Ethiopian monarchs comes about gradually, as a piece of theatre. When Queen Persinna sees the band she had embroidered, she has no more doubts and is prostrated by her emotions, just like Charicleia earlier: τρόμῳ τε καὶ παλμῷ συνείχετο, καὶ ἱδρῶτι διερρεῖτο, χαίρουσα μὲν ἐφ' οἷς εὕρισκεν, ἀμηχανοῦσα δὲ πρὸς τὸ τῶν παρ' ἐλπίδας ἄπιστον, δεδοικυῖα δὲ τὴν ἐξ Ὑδάσπου τῶν φανερουμένων ὑποψίαν τε καὶ ἀπιστίαν, ἢ καὶ ὀργήν, ἂν οὕτω τύχῃ, καὶ τιμωρίαν, 'She was seized with a fit of palpitations, perspiration streamed from every pore, as joy at the return of what had been lost combined with perplexity at this incredible and unlooked-for turn of events, and with fear that Hydaspes might be suspicious and incredulous of these relevations, possibly even angry and vengeful' (10. 13. 1). The plot moves on in stages until the final recognition by Hydaspes, who is caught in a binary conflict between his fatherly affection and his kingly resolve. Later, after a series of delays and difficulties of various types, Theagenes is eventually saved too and his relationship with Charicleia is uncovered. The novel then reaches its end. It is worthwhile reading the following description of collective feelings because it confers a public dimension on the outcome of this private intrigue rather than setting up a *mise en abyme* of the intended effect on the people:

ὁ δῆμος δ' ἑτέρωθεν σὺν εὐφήμοις ταῖς βοαῖς ἐξεχόρευε, πᾶσα ἡλικία καὶ τύχη συμφώνως τὰ γινόμενα θυμηδοῦντες, τὰ μὲν πλεῖστα τῶν λεγομένων οὐ συνιέντες, τὰ ὄντα δὲ ἐκ τῶν προγεγονότων ἐπὶ τῇ Χαρικλείᾳ συμβάλλοντες, ἢ τάχα καὶ ἐξ ὁρμῆς θείας, ἢ σύμπαντα ταῦτα ἐσκηνογράφησεν, εἰς ἐπίνοιαν τῶν ἀληθῶν ἐλθόντες. ὑφ' ἧς καὶ τὰ

ἐναντιώτατα πρὸς συμφωνίαν ἡρμόζετο, χαρᾶς καὶ λύπης συμπεπλεγ-
μένων, γέλωτι δακρύων συγκεραννυμένων, τῶν στυγνοτάτων εἰς ἑορτὴν
μεταβαλλομένων, γελώντων ἅμα τῶν κλαιόντων καὶ χαιρόντων τῶν
θρηνούντων, εὑρισκόντων οὓς μὴ ἐζήτουν καὶ ἀπολλύντων οὓς εὑρηκέ-
ναι ἐδόκουν, καὶ τέλος τῶν προσδοκηθέντων φόνων εἰς εὐαγεῖς θυσίας
μεταβαλλομένων. 'The populace cheered and danced for joy where
they stood, and there was no discordant voice as young and old,
rich and poor, united in jubilation, for though they had understood
very little of what was said, they were able to surmise the facts of
the matter from what had already transpired concerning
Charicleia; or else perhaps they had been brought to a realization
of the truth by the same divine force that had staged this whole
drama and that now produced a perfect harmony of diametric
opposites: joy and sorrow combined; tears mingled with laughter;
the most hideous horror transformed to celebration; those who
wept also laughed; those who grieved also rejoiced; they found
those whom they had not sought and lost those whom they
thought to have found; and finally the offering of human blood,
which all had expected to see, was transformed into a sacrifice free
of all stain' (10. 38. 4).

The meta-literary impact of this passage makes it a true poetic
declaration. Stripped of its typically Heliodorian religious accents, it
may give us an idea of the significance of the entire Greek novel
and help formulate a conclusion of its development. The conflict of
emotions is one of the features through which the Greek novel imitates and rivals the theatre of the classical period by expanding and
amplifying it in such a way as to order and create ambivalent
responses. Laughter and tears mix together because they are the
result of the contradictory lines of the plot, which is meant to puzzle the reader with its complex ramifications. The psychological
conflict reflects the dynamism of life, which the novel, being the
open form *par excellence*, as defined by the young Lukács,[34] means
to channel in its globality, lighting on several different levels of
expression, from comic to tragic. However, polyphony does not
mean unsolved contradictions; on the contrary, it aims at over-
coming them. This final passage of Heliodorus thus highlights the
fact that the poetics of the novel are anti-tragic and consolatory.
All dissonances are resolved harmoniously in the triumph of eros.

[34] Lukács (1968), partly following the Hegelian theory of the novel as a bourgeois epic; Bakhtin's theories are not very far from this view.

4

Rural Society in the Greek Novel, or The Country Seen from the Town

SUZANNE SAÏD

The Greek novel, just as much as Petronius' *Satyricon*[1] or Apuleius' *Golden Ass*,[2] merits special attention from those interested in the economic and social history of the Roman Empire, according to E. Bowie.[3] The five extant Greek love and adventure novels (*Chaereas and Callirhoe*, *The Ephesian Tale*, *Leucippe and Clitophon*, *Daphnis and Chloe*, and *The Ethiopian Story*) offer a picture of the countryside and its inhabitants that is remarkably coherent for works so distant from one another in time and space. The novels extend over at least two centuries, possibly even five. All depends on the date chosen for the first of them, *Chaereas and Callirhoe*—first century BC for some,[4] first century AD or even mid-second century AD for others[5]—and for the last, *The Ethiopian Story*—dated by some to the third century because of the important place accorded to the cult of the Sun,[6] whereas others tend to bring it down to the mid-fourth century on the basis of apparent similarities between the siege of Syene in the story and the siege of Nisibis (AD 450) in Julian.[7] According to tradition, the authors of these novels came from various cities in Asia Minor (Chariton from Aphrodisias in Caria, Xenophon from Ephesus, Longus from Lesbos, Heliodorus from Emesa in Syria) or in Egypt (Achilles Tatius from Alexandria).

To add to the genre's diversity, we may recall that the plots of these works are located at various fictitious times which are not

---

[1] Cf. Veyne (1961).   [2] Cf. Millar (1981).   [3] Cf. Bowie (1977: 91).
[4] Papanikolaou (1973*b*); Hägg (1983:6).
[5] So Perry (1967), Reardon (1971), and Molinié (1979/1989).
[6] This opinion prevailed until van der Valk (1941), and is still defended by Hägg (1983:59) and G. Anderson (1984: 91).
[7] On this comparison and possible conclusions from it, see van der Valk (1941), Colonna (1950), and Schwartz (1967).

always easy to determine. Accuracy is possible to a certain extent in the case of *Chaereas and Callirhoe*, since the heroine's father, Hermocrates of Syracuse, is a historical figure who made a name for himself in the Peloponnesian War at the time of the Sicilian Expedition, and because the end of the novel refers to a well dated historic event, the revolt of Egypt (371–345 BC). As for the other novels, the dating is even vaguer. In *Daphnis and Chloe* the war between Methymna and Mytilene seems to point to a time when the Greek cities were still independent. With regard to the *Ethiopian Story* it can be said only that it belongs to a time when Egypt was still under Persian rule; while in Achilles Tatius, although Alexandria is the capital of Egypt, the country is governed by a 'satrap'[8] (but we know from Philostratus that this title could also be borne by a Roman magistrate[9]). *The Ephesian Tale* mentions an 'eirenarch'[10] in Cilicia and a 'governor' (ἄρχων)[11] in Egypt and seems to refer to the Roman period, even though Rome itself is never mentioned.[12]

It should also be noted that, except for *Daphnis and Chloe* where the action is restricted to Lesbos, the geographical space of the novels is a broad one: it encompasses Byzantium and Thrace to the north, South Italy and Sicily to the west, Asia Minor as far as Babylon to the east, Egypt and even Ethiopia (in Heliodorus) to the south.

The homogeneous representation of rural society in the novels, then, certainly constitutes a phenomenon of special interest to historians. But the question is how to interpret it. It seems hazardous to me to accept (or criticize) it, as some have,[13] as first-degree evidence. Thus the lack of a reference to cultivated fields in *The Ephesian Tale* has actually led to the conclusion that the second century was a time of general decline in agricultural production, with an increasing proportion of fallow land.[14] Proof of rural depopulation has been drawn from a passage where the brigands are described as walking with their prisoners 'on a *long* desert road' (3.

---

[8] Achilles Tatius 4. 11. 1, 13. 4.

[9] *Lives of the Sophists* 1. 22. 3 (524).

[10] Xenophon of Ephesus 2. 13. 3. On these magistrates, first mentioned in a Carian inscription of 116 or 117, see Dalmeyda (1926: 33 n. 1).

[11] Xenophon of Ephesus 3. 12. 6; 4. 2. 1, 9; 4. 1. 2.; 5. 3. 1, 5. 2.

[12] On the absence of Rome from imperial Greek literature, see Bowie (1974).

[13] Scarcella (1970, 1972a, 1977).

[14] Scarcella (1977: 250).

12. 1).[15] In fact the Greek novels do not give us, nor do they aim
to give us, an undistorted view of reality. On the contrary they try
to construct a 'plausible' image of it,[16] that is, one in accord with
the author's prejudices as a townsman[17] and with the expectations
of the reader, who also appears to be from a well-to-do urban background and to have enough education and free time to indulge in
the reading of texts written in Greek for his own pleasure.[18] This
constructed image is necessarily selective and distorted in certain
aspects, but it also reveals the attitude of the Hellenized élite of the
Roman Empire towards rural life and therefore deserves the attention of historians of mentalities.

In this article I should like to highlight this attitude through a
series of examples (exhaustivity would go beyond the limits of an
article). My analysis will be based on the four novels in which the
heroes, all members of the Greek or Hellenized élite (the Ethiopian
princess in *The Ethiopian Story* bears the Greek name of her adoptive father and has spent all of her childhood in Greece), do nothing but traverse the countryside, and also on those passages in
Longus where the people depicted live ordinarily in towns. From
this analysis I shall extract two contradictory images: the negative
image of a countryside full of brigands and barbarians who only
arouse fear and contempt; but also a positive one describing it as
a sweet refuge offering within the protective walls of a garden the
delights of nature artistically and carefully reshaped. These two
representations presuppose an identical exclusion, namely of cultivated fields, of agricultural work and of the people engaged in it—
not surprisingly since the novels are narrated from the perspective
of the heroes, that is of landowners living in town on the income
of their estates and showing no interest in people who ranked
lower than them in education (Hellenized cities versus 'barbarian'
countrymen) and social status (the rural population of Greek
novels being mainly constituted by slaves, even more than in 'real'
life). I shall then test this urban view against the picture of rural
life as found in the only extant 'pastoral' novel, Longus' *Daphnis
and Chloe*.

---

[15] Ibid. 259.

[16] The expression is taken from Bowie (1977: 94).

[17] Cf. MacMullen (1974a: 28); 'Ancient writers represented an urban culture,
even those few like Plutarch who chose to live most of their lives in a rural setting'.

[18] Hägg (1983: 90 ff.).

THE HORRORS OF THE COUNTRYSIDE

In the Greek novel as much as in reality towns were safe and civilized places opposed to a countryside which formed a zone of insecurity and savagery. Letters by contemporary writers, from Seneca[19] down to Symmachus,[20] attest the urban population's reluctance to venture outside the city walls because of its fear of brigands.[21] The only guarantee of security was, as in the case of Dio in the *Euboicos*, to have been shipwrecked and to wear nothing but a shabby coat.[22]

In the novels of Xenophon of Ephesus,[23] Achilles Tatius,[24] and Heliodorus,[25] this image of a dangerous countryside full of bandits could certainly be illustrated from descriptions of 'herdsmen' (ποίμενες)[26] and 'cattlemen' (βουκόλοι)[27] living in the area of the Nile mouth.[28] This 'treacherous crew' (ἄπιστον τὸ βουκόλων γένος)[29] is indeed represented in a wholly negative light. Herdsmen look repulsive;[30] they all speak a barbarian language;[31] they are 'gullible'[32] and stupid;[33] their customs are primitive: they fight with clods of earth[34] and eat fish which has been dried in the sun;[35] their deeds are dictated by passion[36] and individual interest;[37] their habits are cruel: they practise human sacrifice and anthropophagy.[38] But nowhere are the herds of these strange 'herdsmen' ever mentioned, and the pastoral character of these people seems only to lie in their name. As Heliodorus puts it, 'they are called men and herdsmen' (καλοῦνται μὲν ἄνθρωποι καὶ βουκόλοι), 'though in fact they are brigands' (λῃσταὶ δέ, 2. 24. 1).[39] This description, probably a more or less distant and distorted echo of an historical

---

[19] Seneca, *Letters* 123.   [20] Symmachus, *Letters* 2. 22.
[21] On the presence of bandits in the Roman Empire, see MacMullen (1967: 255-68) and B. Shaw (1984: 8-12).
[22] *Euboicos* 7. 8-10, 11.   [23] Cf. 3. 12. 1-2.
[24] Cf. 3. 9. 2-15. 6 and 4. 11. 1-18. 1.   [25] Cf. 1. 1-33.
[26] Xenophon of Ephesus 3. 12. 2.   [27] In Achilles Tatius and Heliodorus.
[28] Xenophon of Ephesus 3. 12. 1; Achilles Tatius 4. 11-12 and Heliodorus 1. 5. 1-6. 2.
[29] Heliodorus 2. 17. 4.
[30] See the description in Achilles Tatius 3. 9. 2 and Heliodorus' remark on the 'Herdsmens' long, shaggy hair' (2. 20. 5).
[31] Achilles Tatius 3. 10. 2-3.   [32] Heliodorus 2. 18. 1 ὑπόκουφος.
[33] Heliodorus 1. 7. 2.   [34] Achilles Tatius 3. 13. 2-3.
[35] Heliodorus 1. 5. 4.   [36] Ibid. 2. 12. 5.
[37] Ibid. 1. 32. 4.   [38] Achilles Tatius 3. 15. 1-5.
[39] See also 6. 13. 2.

event attested in Cassius Dio and the *Historia Augusta*,[40] reveals an
ideological structure which changes all enemies of the Roman
order into savage and inhuman beings[41] and assimilates them to
'most dangerous beasts',[42] thus legitimating campaigns against
them. But is not the choice of this *nom de guerre* revealing in itself?
To explain how the name of this peaceful profession came to be
associated with an ethnic group famous principally for brigandage,
it has been suggested that there was a conscious identification of
the Egyptian 'rebels' with the 'herdsmen' who in times past had
been mandated by the Pharaohs to guard the site of Pharos and to
prevent strangers from entering Egypt,[43] according to Strabo.[44]
Attention has also been drawn to the importance of cattle-rearing
in the everyday economy of the marshy Nile delta.[45] Could not this
name be taken as revealing the attitude of an élite who made of
every herdsman a potential brigand[46] and readily confused fishermen and pirates, as can be shown in certain passages of Achilles
Tatius?[47]

One is certainly on safer ground in *The Ephesian Tale*, a novel
where the country is assimilated to a forest (ὕλη), symbol of danger
and death.[48] The heroine is indeed taken 'into the thickest part of
the wood' (2. 11. 3) where she is to be killed. The forest is also the
place where the shipwrecked fall into the hands of the brigand
Hippothous,[49] and where the latter prepares for human sacrifice.[50]
This novel also depicts 'villages' (κῶμαι) in Asia Minor[51] and in

[40] Cf. Cassius Dio 72. 4. 1-2 and *SHA, Vita Marc.* 21. 2 and *Vita Avid. Cassii* 6.
7. On the historical problem of the revolt of the 'Herdsmen' in the era of Marcus
Aurelius, in 171, see Schwartz (1967: 540-2) and Winkler (1980: 175-81).
[41] On the distortion of facts in ancient literature through the perspective of the
conqueror, see Briant (1976) and B. Shaw (1984: 42-9). The latter (44 n. 123)
rightly stresses the novels' importance as 'a veritable storehouse of information on
popular perceptions of bandits, their motives, targets of attack, the structure of
brigand gangs, bandit behaviour and values and repression by the state'.
[42] θηρίων τῶν χαλεπωτάτων: Heliodorus 2. 24. 1.
[43] Winkler (1980: 179-81).
[44] Strabo 17. 1. 6.
[45] Yoyotte and Chuvin (1983: 60).
[46] B. Shaw (1984: 31), 'The equation "shepherd equals bandit" comes close to
being one that is true for all antiquity' and n. 79: 'Both in law (for example *CJ* 9.
2. 11 "id est pastorum latronumve", "that is of shepherds or brigands") or in general literature (cf. the ironic reversal of roles suggested by the shepherds in Fronto,
To Marcus Aurelius 2. 12 Naber p. 35; Loeb 1 pp. 150-3)'.
[47] 2. 17. 2; 5. 3. 2; 5. 7. 6.
[48] Cf. Scarcella (1977: 259 ff.).
[49] 2. 11. 11.   [50] 2. 13. 1-3.   [51] 4. 1. 1.

Egypt[52] sacked by bandits, who set fire to the houses and kill the population.

Longus might also be cited as an example where the country is being devastated through piracy, with the episode of the Tyrrhenian pirates plundering the harvest and taking the men to sell as slaves,[53] and through war, with the expedition of the Methymnians, who also carried off 'many sheep, a great deal of corn and wine . . . and a great number of people who were working there' (2. 20. 1). And it would indeed be worth recalling the words of those old countrymen who feast once the danger is over and remember previous attacks and pillaging they have escaped long ago.[54]

Land of choice for the brigands, the country is also a place of exile. In *The Ephesian Tale* a woman slave is punished by being sent to the country and married to 'a slave, one of the meanest at that, a goatherd' (2. 9. 2), and in *The Ethiopian Story* Cnemon's father decides to punish himself for his unjust treatment of his son by retiring to the country, presented as a 'remote place' (ἐσχατιά, 1. 14. 5). The country is also where unwanted children are exposed, as in Longus and Heliodorus.[55]

THE DELIGHTS OF SWEET RETREAT

This image of a dangerous countryside is contrasted by that of the sweet retreat, the villa with its park or, in Greek, its 'paradise', which for townsmen forms a charming change of scene. Take for instance the coast of Mytilene 'with its rich houses, its continuous row of bathing places, its parks and woods' (Longus 2. 12. 2): the rich Methymnian youths and the landowner's son go there to enjoy an 'exotic' pleasure, as the author himself puts it.[56] Chariton's and Longus' novels often depict sumptuous processions of townsmen travelling by land and by sea to their villas together with their slaves, their freedman and their *philoi*.[57] These descriptions may easily be compared to Philostratus' accounts of the travels of a great figure of the Roman Empire, the sophist Polemon

---

[52] 5. 2. 4-7.   [53] 1. 28. 1-2.   [54] 2. 32. 3.
[55] Longus 4. 21. 3; 35. 3-4; Heliodorus 2. 31. 2.
[56] 2. 12. 1 ἐν ξενικῇ τέρψει; 4. 11. 1 ξένης ἡδονῆς.
[57] Chariton, 2. 3. 3-4; 3. 2. 10; 3. 8. 3; Longus 4. 14. 1; 4. 33. 2.

of Laodicea.[58] Such processions appear to have been the norm for any member of the élite, as can be seen in *The Ethiopian Story* from the reaction of a fisherman who offers to put up Calasiris: 'unless he is one of those people who insist on grand houses and bring a huge crowd of servants with them' (5. 18. 6).

This positive countryside is above all a world of hunting: the sumptuous hunts organized by the Persian King in Chariton,[59] the tragic hunts of Cleinias' and Menelaus' lovers in Achilles Tatius,[60] and above all the hunting of the idle townsmen in *Daphnis and Chloe*. The latter opens indeed with the description of the narrator hunting on Lesbos.[61] The son of the owner of the estate where most of the action takes place also devotes himself to hunting 'as you would expect of a rich young man who spent all his time amusing himself' (4. 11. 1). The rich Methymnian youths also go to the countryside in order to indulge in 'various sports' (2. 12. 3) like hunting and fishing and to act a comic return to nature, eating what they collect, 'so their sport (τέρψις) also provided for their table' (καὶ τραπέζης ὠφέλειαν παρεῖχεν, 2. 12. 4).

More often, in the Greek novel, the idea of the country is associated with the gardens surrounding a villa. Most descriptions of nature are concerned with gardens, and even, as in Achilles Tatius, with urban gardens. The 'grove' (ἄλσος, I. 2. 3) at Sidon, the scene of the narration which merges with the novel, presents all the elements of the classical *locus amoenus*, that is, shade and fresh water. It is worthwhile recalling the description of the 'paradise' surrounding the hero's house in Tyre. It shows that the countryside is mainly considered as a landscape built for its 'pleasant aspect' (I. 15. 1), a pleasure doubled by the play of reflections in the central pool. This spectacle can only be understood from the perspective of a 'detached' observer, very different from a farmer's view of the land as a piece of work and a source of income.[62] The countryside is pleasant only when carefully separated from the outside world by a protecting wall,[63] when meeting with requirements

[58] Philostratus, *Lives of the Sophists* I. 25 (532).
[59] 6. 4. 1-9.   [60] I. 12; 2. 34.   [61] I. I. I.
[62] In his study of the town/country antithesis in English culture, R. Williams (1973: 120-6) rightly points out, in the chapter devoted to 'pleasing prospects, the characteristic eighteenth-century phase', that 'a working country is hardly ever a landscape. The very idea of landscape implies separation and observation.'
[63] I. 15. I. On the garden as an area closed by a wall in the novel, cf. Littlewood (1977) 34-6.

of order and symmetry[64] and establishing a close link between
nature and art, wilderness and civilization.[65] In short, the pleasant
country is always a picture, and it is certainly no coincidence that
this novel's pastoral evocations are mostly descriptions of paintings
or of other works of art, like the meadow where Europa was
abducted (strangely enough described as a closed garden with a
central fountain[66]) and the vine sculptured on the crystal bowl.[67]
Nature's wilderness is even transformed into an object of pleasure
when it is used as a setting for mythological scenes, like the
representations of Andromeda and Prometheus.[68]

In Heliodorus the description of the country is no less surprising
than in Achilles Tatius. For it has the appearance of the land of
Cockaigne, depicting an Egyptian landscape with meadows 'growing by themselves', as in the Golden Age,[69] and a wonderful
Ethiopia where palm trees and reeds are enormous, where cereals
grow as high as a man on a horse and have a productivity of three
hundred to one.[70]

In the Greek novels, then, as well as in the *progymnasmata* of the
orators, the country is a pleasant picture or a Golden Age ready to
be enjoyed. Later texts, reflecting an ancient rhetorical tradition,[71]
like Libanius' *Praise of Farming, Comparison of Sailing and Farming,*
or *Comparison of Town and Country*, do indeed transmit the same
images of a countryside as a place of leisure for townsmen, allow-
ing them to 'breathe'.[72] One may 'lie down ($\kappa\epsilon\hat{\iota}\sigma\theta\alpha\iota$) at midday, in
the shade of pine and plane trees'[73] and be charmed by the *sight*[74]

[64] Littlewood (1977: 34–6); 'The descriptions in the romance tend to emphasize
a scrupulously neat and orderly garden, with plant-life, though blooming, strictly
under control.'
[65] Achilles Tatius I. 15. 7–8 juxtaposes 'tamed' birds and wild ones.
[66] I. I. 3–6.
[67] 2. 3.
[68] 3. 6. 4–7. 9. See also in Heliodorus 5. 14. 2 the description of the intaglio
offered to Nausicles by Calasiris.
[69] 8. 14. 3. νομὴν ἀπαυτοματίζοντα, cf. Hesiod, *Erga* 117–18 καρπὸν δ' ἔφερε
ζείδωρος ἄρουρα αὐτομάτη.
[70] Heliodorus 10. 5. 2.
[71] Cairns (1975: 79–86) has even used these texts to explain the praise of the
country in the second *Epode*, for the conservative nature of rhetorical education in
Antiquity suggests that the themes developed by Libanios in his *progymnasmata* were
not very different from those learned by Horace.
[72] *Comparison of Town and Country* 13, ed. Förster, VIII 358 ll. 8–11.
[73] *Praise of Farming* 11, ed. Förster, VIII 2661 l. 1ff.
[74] Ibid. ὁρᾶν . . . ἰδεῖν . . . θέαμα; *Comparison of Sailing and Farming* 5, ed. Förster,
VIII 351 I. 3 θεαμάτων μὲν ἥδιστον ἀγρός . . .

of vineyards, harvest, and cattle, and also by the *sound*[75] of moo-
ing cows and bleating sheep. It is certainly no coincidence that the
pleasures a townsman takes from the country when contemplating
it as a detached spectator are double those charms offered in town
by theatres and paintings.[76]

THE REALITY OF LABOUR AND THE EXPLOITATION OF THE COUNTRY

In the novels, descriptions always lack the element of men at work.
This absence is significant and shows through even in the detail of
the vocabulary used. The verb γεωργεῖν 'to cultivate the land' is
never attested in Xenophon of Ephesus, which does not mean that
it was no longer in use at the time of the novel,[77] but, quite simply,
that it did not exist *in the eyes of the author*.[78]

In Chariton, that same verb occurs only *once*, at the end of the
novel, when Hermocrates of Syracuse, like a Roman general
offering land to his veterans, rewards the Egyptians who followed
Chaereas in Sicily with land 'for them to farm' (ὥστε ἔχειν αὐτοὺς
γεωργεῖν, 8. 8. 14).

In Achilles Tatius γεωργεῖν *never* describes a real farmer's ordinary work. It appears only in metaphors,[79] in fables,[80] or in descriptions of works of art,[81] as well as in the exotic excursus on the Nile
as being river, sea, earth and marsh all at once.[82] At the end of a
series of odd antitheses juxtaposing ship and hoe,[83] oar and
plough,[84] rudder and scythe,[85] the two activities of agriculture and
sailing,[86] usually opposed, end up coinciding: with a significant

---

[75] *Praise of Farming* 11, ed. Förster, VIII 266 l. 3 ἀκοῦσαι.
[76] Ibid. 12, VIII 266 ll. 5-7 ἐμοὶ μὲν γὰρ δοκεῖν μηδὲν εἶναι τὰ ἐν τοῖς θεάτροις
δεικνύμενα πρὸς τὴν ἀπ᾽ ἐκείνων ἡδονήν; *Comparison of Town and Country* 17-18, ed.
Förster, VIII 359 ll. 4-14.
[77] Scarcella (1977: 249 ff.).   [78] Bowie (1977: 95).
[79] Achilles Tatius 1. 8. 9.   [80] Ibid. 1. 17. 4 and 2. 14. 5.
[81] Ibid. 2. 3. 2.   [82] Ibid. 4. 12. 1.
[83] 'Hoe' (δίκελλα) is found only in the *painting* of Europa's abduction (1. 1. 6) and
in the hand of the heroine, Leucippe, whose degradation is symbolized by it (5. 17.
3; 18. 4). It is never held by a real farmer.
[84] The only occurence of this word in Achilles Tatius.
[85] 'Scythe' (δρέπανον) occurs only one more time; however, it is not an agricultural tool, but a weapon held by Perseus in a painting (3. 7. 8).
[86] As Libanius' *Comparison of Sailing and Farming* clearly shows.

ellipsis of the agent the author mentions the cultivation of the surface on which one sails and of the sea.[87]

An examination of the use of this verb in Heliodorus is just as conclusive. Γεωργεῖν is *never* used of agricultural work. Twice it has a metaphorical value and is used to describe a lover's servitude[88] or to refer paradoxically to the profession of merchant 'cultivated' by Nausicles.[89] Finally it is used for the Nile, said to 'cultivate the fields' (γεωργεῖ τὰς ἀρούρας, 2. 28. 4) in Egypt.

This absence of agricultural work, and of the verb to describe it, is not surprising since in the Greek novel the viewpoint is always that of the élite for which it is written and the lords it puts on stage. It is the perspective of the 'consumer city'[90] draining the resources of the country,[91] and of the landowner considering the land as a source of income.

In relation to this, one detail in Chariton's novel seems quite revealing to me. Since the action is supposed to take place in Asia Minor at a time when it was under Persian rule and governed by the Great King in Babylon, one would expect riches to be sent as tribute from the coastal cities to the capital. But in the Ionia described by the author 'there are princely fortunes pouring down from the Asian continent' (1. 11. 7). This anachronism may well reflect a reality contemporary to the author and a time when the inner country was being exploited by the coastal cities. It could be either the Hellenistic period or the Roman Empire. Therefore I shall refrain from drawing any conclusions about the (disputed) date of Chariton.

Moreover the Greek novel very often presents us with the figure who in my view controls the genre's outlook, the notable who lives in town and spends there the money he draws from his estates.[92]

The first and most accomplished embodiment of this figure is

[87] Achilles Tatius 4. 11. 5 πλεῖται . . . καὶ γεωργεῖται, and 4. 12. 1 ὅ φυτεύεις, τοῦτο πέλαγος γεωργούμενον.

[88] Heliodorus 4. 3. 2.

[89] Ibid. 6. 6. 3 ταύτην γεωργῶ τὴν τέχνην.

[90] On the concept of 'consumer city' attributed to Sombart and Max Weber and its applicability to ancient towns, see Finley (1975: 167 ff.), and Leveau (1983: 275 ff.), with Goudineau's reply (ibid.); Bruhns (1985).

[91] The image of the country as supporting the town is also found in Libanius' *Praise of Farming* 9, ed. Förster, VIII 265 ll. 4–8, and *Comparison of Town and Country* 14, ed. Förster, VIII 358 ll. 11–14.

[92] On the importance of this figure in the social reality of the Empire, see MacMullen (1974a; 5 ff., 20 ff.).

Chariton's Dionysios. This citizen of Miletus, described as 'the
wealthiest, noblest, and most cultured man in Ionia' (I. 12. 6),
besides his main residence in town, owns a second home about
fifteen kilometres out of town. It is modestly called ἔπαυλις,
'cottage', but is in fact 'richly' furnished.[93] The surrounding estate
is managed by a 'bailiff' who controls the whole of Dionysios'
wealth.[94] Under the latter's command is a 'steward' who lives on
the property.[95] A phrase of Dionysios even suggests that there was
a specialized administration. When he learns that his bailiff has
bought a slave, he tells him to call on a certain Adrastes, a 'very
experienced lawyer',[96] for the drafting of the contract. The landowner merely supervises the management by visiting his estate,
especially at harvest time.[97] When the bailiff wants to prompt his
master to go to the country, he tells him: 'Sir, you haven't been
on your estate by the sea for a long time now [this suggests that
he has other properties]. You're needed there. You have the herds
and the crops to inspect and it will soon be harvest time' (2. 3. 1).
Indeed, once arrived, for reasons that have nothing to do with eco-
nomics, Dionysios makes a very finicky inspection and expresses
his discontent to the steward.[98]

The same reality is found in Ephesus with Achilles Tatius'
Melitte, who is also 'very rich' (5. 11. 5). In town she owns a
house 'crowded with servants and richly furnished' (5. 17. 1). But
she also has a house in the country, where she goes as soon as she
comes back (from her four-months stay in Alexandria) in order to
'dispose of certain matters about the estate' (5. 17. 10). Here too,
the estate is managed by a 'bailiff' who is dismissed by the mistress
because of his bad treatment of a slave girl.[99]

One might also mention Longus' Dionysophanes, who again
lives in town, in Mytilene, but owns at about thirty-five kilometres
from there the 'very fine property' (I. 1. 2) where the novel's
narrative takes place. The property is a model of the type, since it

[93] πολυτελῶς I. 13. 5; 2. 3. 2.
[94] Chariton I. 12. 8 διοικετής . . . τῶν ὅλων. Similarly Mithridates, the Satrap of
Caria, has a διοικετής τῆς ὅλης οὐσίας (4. 5. 1).
[95] οἰκόνομος 2. 1. 1.
[96] ὁ ἐμπειρότατος τῶν νόμων 2. 1. 6.
[97] Cf. MacMullen (1974b: 254), 'Every July for the grain harvest, every
September for the vintage, public business in Rome was suspended, allowing the
aristocracy to go out to the supervison of their estates.' Cf. Beaujeu (1967: 124,
127-30).   [98] Cf. Chariton 2. 7. 2
[99] διοικετής; 7. 7. 3; διοίκησας, 5. 17. 10; 6. 3. 3.

combines the useful (fertile wheat fields, hills covered in vineyards and pasture for the cattle) with the pleasant (heights abounding in game and a long beach of fine sand).[100] Parallels in inscriptions[101] and in Dio of Prusa's *Euboicos*[102] seem to indicate that this is the typical estate of an ἀνὴρ εὐδαίμων (blessed man) with cattle, fields and mountains for hunting. This property is the main source of Dionysophanes' wealth.[103] It comes indeed in first place when he enumerates his possessions in 4. 24. 3-4. Here again the role of the landowner is restricted to occasional visits, normally at vintage time.[104] A master working himself on his estate is simply unthinkable, as can be seen from the laughter raised when Daphnis wants to carry on looking after his goats even though he has just been recognized as the landowner's son.[105]

These are the three most complete illustrations of a way of life exactly matching that of the local aristocracies of the Empire.[106] Other examples could be given. In *The Ephesian Tale* the leader of the Phoenician pirates is not only a merchant. He also owns a rural estate,[107] whose management is left to a steward.[108] This property is close to his main residence in Tyre,[109] and he travels between one another.[110] The Syrian to whom he marries his daughter, beside his house in Antioch,[111] also has a property in the country, where he goes quite often.[112] In Achilles Tatius the wealth of the hero's uncle is also in land. The latter is said to have come to live in Byzantium because the property he had inherited from his mother was there.[113] Still in the same novel the Egyptian Menelas, established in Alexandria,[114] has most of his estates near one of the Delta villages inhabited by 'herdsmen', therefore he is acquainted with all the notables.[115] In Heliodorus the Athenian Aristippos, a moderately wealthy man and a member of the Areopagos,[116] owns a property in the country where he can retire.[117]

[100] Cf. Longus I. I. 2.

[101] Bowie (1977: 93), 'Dionysophanes is an ἀνὴρ εὐδαίμων with an estate whose mixed farming corresponds to that shown on late 3rd century inscriptions (*IG* XII. ii. 76f.)'. [102] *Euboicos* 12.

[103] On land as main source of wealth in the Empire, see MacMullen (1974a: 48-51) and P. Leveau (ed.), *L'Origine des richesses dépensées dans les villes antiques* (Aix-en-Provence, 1985). [104] Longus 3. 31. 4; 4. I. I.

[105] Longus 4. 25. 2. [106] Gagé (1971: 390). [107] I. 14. 7; 2. 2. I.
[108] 2. 10. 2-4. [109] 2. 2. I. [110] 2. 2. I-3.
[111] 2. 9. I. [112] 2. II. I; 2. 12. I. [113] I. 3. I.
[114] 5. 15. I. [115] 3. 19. I. [116] I. 9. I.
[117] I. 12. I.

Besides, in the Greek novel the pretext most frequently used when someone wants to hide his absence, or on the contrary pretends to be absent in order to surprise an adulterer *in flagrante delicto*, is a journey to the country.[118]

As well-to-do and educated townsmen, the novels' protagonists and their readers (and probably also their authors) only feel contempt for countrymen, regarded as inferior. Again the vocabulary used is significant: ἄγροικος and ἀγροικία are pejorative words, and the Greek novels point out several times that people belonging to that category are neither handsome[119] nor have any sense of beauty,[120] that they are naïve, vulgar, and stupid,[121] that their brute force is easily overcome by urban smartness.[122] The novels offer the arguments commonly used by townsmen when they renounce the conventional praise of rural life.[123]

The reason for this strong contempt for the rural population is the fact that the difference is not only based on social class, but also on *race* and on *status*: townsmen are always *Greeks*, by culture if not by origin, and *free men*, whereas peasants are *Barbarians* and *slaves*.

Hellenization had indeed reached only the cities,[124] and the Greek novels, though usually ignoring differences of language, attest it at least once. In *The Ephesian Tale*, when the hero and his brigand friend leave Cilicia for *Mazacus*, 'a fine big town in Cappadocia' (3. I. I), the author tells us that the two companions get everything in plenty in the 'villages' (κῶμαι) they pass because the brigand 'was able to speak Cappadocian' (3. I. 2).

As a Barbarian, the peasant in the Greek novel is first and foremost a slave. Epigraphic and archaeological evidence certainly suggests, as MacMullen has shown,[125] that this image of the country in imperial times is too uniform and that the great estates should not be seen as having been run exclusively by slaves. However, this image is dominant in writings of landowners such

---

[118] Chariton 1. 4. 3; Achilles Tatius 5. 10. 2; Heliodorus 1. 12. 1.
[119] Chariton 2. 1. 5; Achilles Tatius 6. 7. 1.
[120] Heliodorus 7. 10. 3.
[121] They are easy to deceive (Heliodorus 1. 26. 3); they lack education (Heliodorus 4. 16. 5), and are incapable of inventing stories (Achilles Tatius 1. 17. 3).
[122] Heliodorus 10. 31. 5.
[123] Cf. MacMullen (1974*a*: 30–2).
[124] Cf. ibid. 45–7, with bibliography, 45 n. 53.
[125] MacMullen (1974*b*: 254–6).

as Pliny the Younger and is indisputably valid for the Greek novel, where the peasant is often represented as a type of slave.

In Chariton, for instance, the 'countrywomen' (αἱ ἄγροικοι γυναῖκες, 2. 2. 1) who gather around Callirhoe are not only naïve—they take this woman to be a goddess[126]—but also servile: they immediately start to flatter her as a future mistress.[127] Plangon, the steward's wife on Dionysios' estate, is also described as a mixture of cunning and baseness characteristic of the inferior. But minor details show even better to what extent the picture of the rural slave is drawn from the perspective of the urban master: the highest praise for a slave is to be called φιλοδέσποτος (loving his master),[128] and it is never called into question that the master's life is more valuable to a slave than his own freedom.[129]

Most revealing, too, is an episode in *The Ephesian Tale*, a lightly disguised transcription of a passage in Euripides' *Electra*. In both examples a poor but honest countryman shows respect for a young girl of noble birth who has come into his care through the meanness of others. But by substituting a goatherd,[130] i.e. a slave, for Euripides' owner,[131] Xenophon of Ephesus introduces a number of significant changes in the psychology and behaviour of this character, who is mainly following his thoroughly servile fear.[132]

As for the poverty of the rural world and the hard reality of peasant exploitation, these are matters which are hardly ever mentioned directly in the novels. The most notable exception is certainly in Heliodorus when he describes the home of the fisherman who accommodates the heroes in Book 5.[133] One might also recall another detail in this novel, suggesting that country products were sold at a price so low that people did not even care to bargain.[134] But one should above all consider passages revealing the misery of rural slaves, even though they are only indirectly concerned with them. This misery is indeed described only when it falls upon those who should normally have escaped it, the heroes. I shall restrict myself to one example in Chariton, but similar

---

[126] 14. 1.   [127] 2. 2. 1.   [128] 3. 9. 12.   [129] 2. 8. 2.   [130] 2. 9. 1.
[131] *Electra* 37 ff., 382.
[132] When Manto's husband falls in love with the heroine and seeks the complicity of her 'husband', the latter pretends to agree, but tells everything to Manto 'out of fear' (2. 12. 2), and then feigns to obey her orders by getting rid of Anthia 'for he was sorry for the girl, but feared Manto' (2. 11. 4).
[133] 18. 8–9.
[134] Heliodorus 5. 27. 9.

passages can be found in Xenophon of Ephesus[135] and in Achilles Tatius.[136] In *Chaereas and Callirhoe* the hero and his faithful companion are sold as slaves in Caria. We see them chained up when working on the landowner's estate and compelled, under the threat of whips, to dig the earth to the point of exhaustion.[137] The work is organized in brigades by an *ergostolos* who assigns everyone his daily work.[138] The picture is certainly blackened in order to move the reader to pity by representing the hero in the worst of hardships, and it would be naïve to believe that this was the fate of all rural slaves throughout the Empire. However, the conclusion drawn from this episode is certainly of interest for the historian of mentalities, for it is revelatory of the novel's viewpoint. Such an outrageous exploitation indeed ends in a revolt: the slaves kill the ἐπιστάτης (manager) and run away. But in a sense the outcome is moral: the guilty slaves are caught, and, to make an example, all inhabitants of the barrack are to be crucified, even those who have not taken part in the revolt at all, the hero and his friend. The indignation of the author and of the reader come from the fact that two innocent people, moreover young people of noble birth, are being condemned. But not a word is said to criticize the punishment of the slaves, and even later, in the speech to the Satrap owner of the estate, one of the two friends shows that he has always shared the masters' attitude. He is indeed the first to criticize conduct which lacks the *sophrosyne* one may expect from inferiors.[139]

RURAL SOCIETY IN LONGUS

The novels of Chariton, Xenophon of Ephesus, Achilles Tatius and Heliodorus, which make what are merely excursions into the country, may be contrasted with the novel by Longus, which reverses the quantitative relation between town and country. This 'herdsmen's tale' (ποιμενικά) is indeed entirely set in the country, apart from the heroes' short stay in town near the end of Book 4, before their definitive return to the fields 'because they were not

---

[135] 5. 8. 2–5 the hero Habrocomes works in a quarry in *Nuceria*.
[136] 5. 17. 3–6; 18. 3 Leucippe is a slave on the estate of Melitte, she has to work in the fields and endure the steward's insults.
[137] 3. 7. 3; 4. 2. 1 and 4. 2. 15–16.
[138] 4. 2. 2–3.
[139] 4. 3. 3.

able to bear life in town' (μὴ φέροντες τὴν ἐν ἄστει διατριβήν, 4. 37. 1). The town, however, is more present than it seems: in Book 2, in the trip of the young Methymnians (who are townsmen); in Book 3, in the episode of the 'urban' Lycaenion; and especially in Book 4, with the arrival of the landowners and their family, who normally live in town. In fact the novel is constantly opposing town and country.[140] This confrontation is the essence of bucolic poetry and is also found, at the time of the Second Sophistic, in works such as Dio of Prusa's *Euboicos*, the first part of which (1–80) tells the story of the forced journey of a *townsman* to the Euboean *countryside* and of his encounter with a hunter-*peasant* who eagerly tells him of his sole visit to *town*, and Philostratus' *Heroicos*, which describes a vine-grower from the Chersonese, not to mention Alciphron's *Letters of Farmers*.

The country certainly occupies a greater space in *Daphnis and Chloe*. But should one therefore believe that the adopted perspective is a different one and admit that, for some members of the educated élite at least, rural life as described in the novel was indeed an acceptable substitute? Are values being transformed, signs reversed, and the country changed into a positive concept? Should one even go as far as talking of a radical change of perspective, since the town would then be the object seen through the eyes of the rural population? I do not think so and I should now like to try and show that Longus' novel is only a variation of well-known themes and that it still represents the countryside seen through the eyes of urban people. In this regard, the beginning of the novel has a programmatic value. This herdsmen's tale opens indeed with the word 'city' (πόλις . . .) and with a description of the city of Mytilene, before moving to the country and to Dionysophanes' estate.

The country folk in Longus are still described in a rather negative way. The beauty of the two heroes should not put us under any illusion. These two peasants are beautiful not because they come from the country, but because they are born to rich townspeople. Their beauty does not call into question the theme of the ugliness of country people; on the contrary, it confirms it explicitly because it is κρεῖττον ἀγροικίας ('too good for the country', 1. 7. 1). Even if their urban origin were not established by the luxurious recognition objects accompanying them,[141] it would only be too

[140] As rightly stressed by Chalk (1960: 48–51) and Effe (1982a: 76–8).
[141] I. 2. 3; 5. 3.

obvious in a world where townsmen and countrymen alike assume
a priori that peasants are ugly. When Dionysophanes readily
believes that Daphnis is an exposed child, as claimed by the shepherd Lamon, it is because, as he says, 'it was incredible (ἄπιστον)
from the start that such a handsome son could have been produced
by an old man of that sort and his shabby (εὐτελούς) wife' (4. 20.
2). These kinds of thoughts even come to countrymen themselves:
the shepherd Dryas, wondering about Daphnis' origin, reflects that
he might not be his parents' son: 'he is handsome and quite unlike
that snub-nosed old man and his balding wife' (3. 32. 1). In the
same way Chloe's beauty proves that she cannot be Dryas' and
Nape's daughter: for when she is all dressed, 'even without the
tokens anyone would have sworn that Dryas was not the father of
a girl like that' (4. 32. 2).

Ugliness, then, is an exclusive characteristic of country people,
as is stupidity (their only recognized quality being physical
strength).[142] Several times[143] the heroes' unbelievable naïvety in
matters of love is explained by their having been raised in the
country. But the postulate of rural stupidity comes out most clearly
in Book 4. Indeed, when the urban Dionysophanes believes what
the peasant Lamon tells him, it is not because he credits him with
natural frankness as opposed to urban hypocrisy, but because he
considers him too stupid to be capable of inventing such a plausible
lie.[144]

Sometimes the action itself seems constructed to bring out the
characteristic stupidity of countrymen. This point is worth while
stressing, because *Daphnis and Chloe* has too often been read in a
Rousseau-ist perspective as the image of a world where the arrival
of evil is simultaneous with the intrusion of townsmen. However,
in the two episodes likely to have dramatic consequences for the
heroes, the prime cause of evil is nothing other than a countryman's idiocy. The wolf trap in which Daphnis nearly gets killed is
an invention of the peasants: they had dug pits in order to capture
the she-wolf that was ravaging the country and decimating their
cattle. But the result of this collective effort was, as the author
ironically puts it, that 'they didn't succeed in catching the she-wolf
(a wolf can tell when ground has been meddled with), but they did
kill a number of goats and sheep—and almost killed Daphnis too'
(1. 11. 2). Similarly, the incident which provoked the young

[142] 2. 14. 4.   [143] 1. 13. 5, 32. 4; 3. 18. 1 and 3.   [144] 4. 20. 2.

Methymnians' anger and the subsequent war is caused by the fool-
ishness of a peasant who needed a rope and stole the line holding
the Methymnians' ship;[145] they used a wicker rope instead, but it
was soon to be eaten by Daphnis' goats.

This incident also shows that there is no systematic moral idealization of the peasants. The novel is sometimes closer in spirit to
Maupassant than to Rousseau. The peasant who stole the rope has
done it secretly and is careful not to confess his deed.[146] It is even
questionable if this idealization is at all present in *Daphnis and
Chloe*. This has often been claimed, and the virtuous countrymen
who take up and raise exposed children as if they were their own—
and even better[147]—have often been opposed to the heartless rich
townsmen who expose their own offspring. But Longus' peasants
ought not to be confused with Victor Hugo's *Pauvres Gens*. Lamon's
first reaction, when he finds the baby and the rich objects, is to
leave the baby and take the objects. He is finally stopped by human
respect (αἰδεσθείς, I. 3. I) and by the feeling of shame for not imitating the philanthropy of the goat which had fed the child. Similarly
Dryas takes pity on Chloe because he has been 'instructed'
(διδασκόμενος, I. 6. I) by the example set by the sheep. In the
same way as the behaviour of Chloe's parents, as soon as their
'daughter' is wooed by local peasants, the goatherd's attitude in
The Ephesian Tale perfectly illustrates the servile mentality readily
ascribable to country folk—it should not be overlooked that
Longus' peasants, with the sole exception of Chromis 'who farmed
his own land',[148] are all slaves at the mercy of their masters[149] and
powerless against the townsmen's brutal behaviour.[150] When Dryas
refuses to marry Chloe to the rich peasants who seek her, it is
because of his fear to see Chloe's origin uncovered and to find himself in great difficulties.[151] When he is not led by fear, Dryas is
driven by greed: he finds the strength to decline the propositions
made to him and the gifts 'greater than one would expect for a
shepherd girl' (3. 25. 3) because he believes that the girl is going
to make him a rich man.[152] Therefore he gives delaying answers,

---

[145] 2. 13. 1.   [146] 2. 13. 2.
[147] I. 8. I 'They had brought the children up rather delicately, teaching them to
read and write and to do everything that was regarded as elegant in the country.'
[148] 3. 15. 1.
[149] As can be seen from the reactions of Lamon, Daphnis and Chloe after the garden has been devastated (4. 8. 1–9. 1).
[150] 2. 14. 3.   [151] I. 19. 3.   [152] 3. 25. 3.

which also allow him to benefit from the presents he keeps receiving.[153] But he immediately yields to Daphnis' three thousand drachmas.[154] The reactions of the other adoptive father, Lamon, are similar, for he too uses cunning in order to delay a marriage he finds beneath Daphnis.[155]

In such a context, it is no surprise that ἄγροικος and ἀγροικία keep this negative meaning in Longus. This is obvious when the words are used by townsmen, who only feel contempt for peasants. So, for instance, the landowner's son is astonished to see that a townsman like the parasite Gnathon should fall in love with a goatherd like Daphnis and should not be disgusted by the stink of the billy goat.[156] But before Daphnis' beauty he acknowledges that he 'was too good for the country' (ἀγροικίας κρείττων, 4. 19. 1). However, these words are used with the same negative meaning in passages giving the viewpoint of the author himself,[157] or, even more significantly in my opinion, of 'real' peasants like the children's adoptive fathers (not that they should have adopted urban values, but because they are creations of an author who knows no other). For Lamon and Dryas are both upset by the dream which enjoins them to make shepherds of their children,[158] and they agree in thinking that marriage with peasants would be misalliance for children most certainly born to rich parents.[159]

Rural inferiority contrasts with urban superiority, which is acknowledged even by countrymen. If it were not for Gnathon's depraved sexuality, Daphnis' father would indeed consider it as a advancement for his son to move from the country to the town;[160] this is also the master's feeling when he comes to announce what he thinks is good news for Lamon.[161] This episode, then, confirms *a contrario* what is found in *The Ephesian Tale*, where sending an urban slave to the country is seen as a form of punishment.[162]

Daphnis' and Chloe's obvious pleasure in the 'taste of urban cuisine' (ἀστυκὴ ὀψαρτυσία, 4. 15. 4) and in the meal sent to them by the master further illustrates the superiority of urban refinement over rural simplicity.

The end of the novel is even more significant. For Longus, even though he keeps praising Chloe's beauty, is far from exalting

---

[153] 3. 25. 3.
[154] 3. 30. 1.
[155] 3. 30. 5–31. 4.
[156] 4. 17. 2.
[157] 1. 7. 1; 3. 15. 1.
[158] 1. 8. 1.
[159] 3. 26. 3, 30. 5; 31. 4.
[160] 4. 19. 5.
[161] 4. 19. 2.
[162] 3. 9. 2–4. 12. 1.

nature's superiority, as represented by the countrywomen, over the
devices used by the townswomen. On the contrary, the narration
points out that the heroine's beauty is fully evident only once ornaments (κόσμος, 4. 32. 1) have been added. Chloe gains so much
beauty that even Daphnis hardly recognizes her. Here again, we
deal with an *a contrario* confirmation of what is found elsewhere in
the Greek novel. This episode is the reversal of the one in Achilles
Tatius, where the hero does not recognize his mistress when she
substitutes her urban ornaments for a slave costume: her hair has
been cut and she is wearing an ugly tunic.[163]

The distance thus created between the town and the country
reflects the gap separating the rich (= the townsmen) from the poor
(= the peasants). For the 'distinction' is made between a rural
world globally poor and a town globally rich, as represented by the
young Methymnians, Astylos and his father Dionysophanes,
Megacles, the rich townsmen to whom the fishermen sell their fish
and the rich townswomen who wish they had given birth to a girl
as beautiful as Chloe.[164] Admittedly the novel also speaks of rich
'peasants'[165] as opposed to poor ones, but this distinction is almost
meaningless, as can be seen from the conversation opposing
Dorcon, one of the 'rich country dwellers' (ἀγροίκων πλουσίων, 1.
16. 4), and Daphnis, 'so poor that he can't keep a dog' (1. 16. 2):
both share the same type of food.[166] The adjective 'rich', used twice
to describe Chloe's parents,[167] has hardly more meaning, for in the
entire novel their way of life differs in no wise from that of Daphnis'
'poor' parents. The opposition is but a device used to impede the
protagonists' marriage.

As presented in Longus the countryside remains a world of
misery. One episode is particularly significant in this respect. When
Dryas finds Lamon and Myrtale measuring the barley they have
just been winnowing and despairing because the quantity they
have gained is almost less than what they have sown, Dryas tries
to console them 'agreeing that the shortage was the same everywhere' (3. 30. 3).

I shall rather insist, however, on an element in the novel which
helps us to appreciate in a very concrete way the difference of scale

---

[163] 5. 17. 9, 19. 1.
[164] 2. 12. 1; 4. 11. 1; 4. 13. 2; 4. 35. 4; 3. 21. 1; 4. 33. 4.
[165] 1. 16. 4; 3. 25. 4; 3. 26. 4; 3. 27. 1.
[166] 1. 16. 4.
[167] 3. 26. 2, 4.

between wealth in town and country (this explains why relative differences between countrymen may be seen as negligible): the story of the purse of three thousand drachmas.[168] For the young Methymnians who carry it with them, it is but a comfortable amount of money aimed at covering all the expenses of their trip to the country. But once they have lost it, they can reasonably claim that 'it could have bought up all the fields' (2. 15. 3). There is much rhetorical exaggeration in their words, for their interest is of course to exaggerate the importance of the loss. But this appreciation seems to be confirmed by the subsequent misfortunes of the purse. For when the 'peasant' Daphnis finds it, he immediately considers himself as 'the richest, not only of the farmers there, but of all mankind' (3. 29. 1). All the wealth and all the presents countrymen could offer for Chloe's hand suddenly appear pathetic: 'goats and sheep and a couple of mangy oxen and corn that couldn't even keep farmyard fowls alive' (3. 29. 4). This judgement is shared by Chloe's parents. Whereas till then they had refused all the offers from rich peasants, beginning with those of Dorcon in Book 1, 'a pair of oxen for ploughing, four hives of bees, fifty apple trees, a bull's hide for cutting up into sandals, and, every year, a weaned calf' (19. 2), they immediately yield to Daphnis' offer 'when they saw all that money, far more than expected' (3. 30. 1). But whereas for peasants this sum of money represents fabulous wealth, for townsmen it is a present they can make without really touching their fortune: Dryas will later get another three thousand drachmas from Daphnis' parents,[169] and a gift from Megacles, Chloe's father, will ensure him ten thousand drachmas.[170]

This difference in scale explains why in Longus and in other novels people never engage in bargaining for the price of rural products, whose value is rated at best by the obol (⅙ of a drachma): the young Methymnians buy room and board from the countrymen 'paying several obols more than it was worth' (2. 12. 4). Understandably, raiding pirates lose interest in agricultural products when they find such a tall and handsome boy, 'worth more than the plunder from the fields' (1. 28. 2).

Thus Longus' picture of rural society is in accordance with that

---

[168] 3. 27. 4, 28. 1, 29. 1, 29. 4, 30. 5, 32. 1.
[169] 4. 33. 2.
[170] 4. 37. 2.

of the other Greek novels. Everywhere we find the same deprecia-
tion (and the word may also be understood in its strict financial
meaning) of the country and of those living there.

THE IMAGE OF THE COUNTRY IN LONGUS

The image of the land in Longus is as slanted as his picture of rural
society; it is dominated by an urban perspective and constructed
according to an ideal of pure pleasure. Once again, the beginning
of the novel is revealing. The prologue is a progressive introduction
to the pastoral novel through a gradation of beauty and delight.
It opens with a description of *beautiful* nature and of the wood
where the narrator is hunting, with all the components of the
classical *locus amoenus*, also found at the start of Achilles Tatius'
novel: trees, flowers and water running abundantly (καλὸν μὲν καὶ
τὸ ἄλσος, πολύδενδρον, ἀνθηρὸν, κατάρρυτον, 1). But the representation of nature in the painting is said to surpass the charms of this
beautiful nature (ἀλλ' ἡ γραφὴ τερπνοτέρα, 1), and the subsequent
narration, whose claim it is to compete with the painting (ἀντι-
γράψαι τῇ γραφῇ, 2), presents itself as 'something for mankind . . .
to enjoy' (κτῆμα . . . τερπνὸν πᾶσιν ἀνθρώποις, 3).

For the country as described by Longus is first of all a source of
pleasure. Apart from general evocations of the seasons which are
not localized, Longus' most elaborate descriptions are devoted to
gardens: the one of Philetas in Book 2 and the one of Dionysophanes in Book 4. Mention is certainly made of producers and the
effort of those who take care of these gardens does not pass in
silence. Philetas himself speaks of the trouble he has had (ἐξεπονη-
σάμην, 2. 3. 3) and Lamon is shown 'caring for' his master's
garden.[171] But the description is usually made from the perspective
of the consumer: Love who 'enjoys (τέρπομαι) flowers and trees'
(2. 5. 4) in Philetas' garden, and Dionysophanes who enjoys these
'delights' (τρυφή) at every season.[172] Longus' gardens, as those of
Achilles Tatius, are 'ready to please the eye in every respect' (εἰς
πᾶσαν θέας ἡδονήν, 4. 1. 2) and looked after 'so that they could be
seen in all their beauty' (ὡς ὀφθείη καλός, 4. 1. 3). In the sophisticated world of the pastoral novel, they are also sited in order to
offer a view. Dionysophanes' garden is situated on a hill from

---

[171] 4. 1. 3; 4. 4. 1.   [172] 4. 2. 6; 4. 3. 1.

where the rural world is seen as a spectacle: 'From there the plain was clearly visible, so you could see people grazing their flocks; the sea was visible too, and people sailing past were open to view' (4. 3. 1). Besides offering a view and a spectacle, the sweet country is also a place of comfort because it is carefully closed off (as opposed to the insecure 'real' country).[173] Dionysophanes' garden is even doubly closed, first by a small stone wall, but also by trees.[174]

The garden is a place of order and symmetry: 'everything was divided and separate' (4. 2. 5) and the temple of Dionysos stands 'at the midpoint of the length and breadth of the garden' (4. 3. 1).

Finally, it is also a place where the wild and the civilized, where nature and art mix together. 'Cultivated' ($\H{\eta}\mu\epsilon\rho\alpha$, 4. 2. 3) trees are associated with other species which are not. Beside wild flowers 'produced by the earth itself' grow flowers which are 'created by art' (4. 2. 6). Supreme sophistication is reached when nature appears artificial (trees 'without fruit' form 'a man-made wall', 4. 2. 4; their branches intertwine so well that 'they seem to be a work of art', 4. 2. 5), and when the natural becomes an artistic effect and a *trompe-l'œil* (ivy berries which 'looked just like bunches of grapes', 4. 2. 3).

Nature is thus reorganized in order to eliminate everything which could disturb the harmony of the spectacle, i.e. all the elements of real nature which interfere with it. Lamon starts by removing the dung from the courtyard 'so that it wouldn't annoy them with its smell' (4. 1. 3). An artificial countryside is created, matching exactly the townsmen's conception of it, as Longus points out ironically: Daphnis not only doubles the number of his goats and fattens them, but also takes care of their appearance 'putting oil on their horns and combing their hair' (4. 4. 4). The real vintage is substituted by a staged vintage of greater perfection than nature itself. The best grapes are fixed on the vines 'so that even the people coming from the city could have the pleasure of picking the grapes and seeing what the harvest was like' (4. 5. 2). However, Longus is perfectly aware of the trompe-l'œil effects, as he shows at the end with 'the pastoral wedding' (4. 37. 1) of the two heroes: people lie down on 'beds of green leaves' (4. 38. 1), but actually to eat 'lavishly',[175] and when real goats burst in, the

---

[173] 2. 3. 5 about Philetas' garden.
[174] 4. 2. 4.
[175] 4. 37. 2 λαμπρῶς; 4. 38. 1 πολυτελῶς.

townsmen, who find it not to their taste, take it as 'a disagreeble
intrusion' (τοῦτο τοῖς μὲν ἀστικοῖς οὐ πάνυ τερπνὸν ἦν, 4. 38. 4).

Admittedly the above themes occur mainly in Book 4. But it
would not be difficult to show in the whole novel that the two
heroes display towards nature an attitude which is closer to that of
townsmen out for pleasure than of peasants at work. In this respect
the description of summer in Book 1 is exemplary. The stress is
indeed on 'pleasure' (ἡδύς), 'sweetness' (γλυκύς), and above all on
the 'delight' (τερπνός) experienced by the two young people,[176] who
spend the winter 'remembering the pleasures they had left behind'
(3. 4. 2). They are opposed to the real peasants, 'enjoyed the short
holiday from their work and liked having meals in the morning as
well as the evening and sleeping late, so that winter seemed to
them sweeter (γλυκύτερον) than summer, autumn, and even spring'
(3. 4. 1).

This contrast is not surprising, for Daphnis and Chloe stand as
much apart from the work of the fields as the author or the readers
of the novel. Even before they are recognized as such, they see the
rural world with the eyes of landowners and derive an aesthetic
pleasure from the work usually done by others. Of the fishermen's
tiring work they catch only the pleasing sight of a passing boat and
the charming sound of their singing.[177] Admittedly, in Book 3,
Daphnis adopts the manners of a peasant in order to please Chloe's
father Dryas: 'I know how to reap well and to prune the vine and
plant trees; I also know how to plough a field and winnow the
grain in the wind' (29. 2). However, this fine programme finds
hardly any concrete applications in the novel. The sole agricultural
activity which gets a long and precise description is the vintage:[178]
it coincides (and certainly not by chance) with the time when
the landowners are present on the estate. When activities like
'planting trees', 'harvesting' or 'winnowing' are mentioned, which
is exceptional, they are always undertaken by 'real' peasants,
Dryas and Lamon.[179] Ploughing appears only in the peasants' songs
at the protagonists' wedding, with peasants 'singing with harsh,

---

[176] I. 23. I ἡδεῖα μὲν . . . γλυκεῖα δὲ . . . τερπνὴ δέ . . .; I. 27. I, ἔτερψεν . . .;
I. 28. I τοιάσδε τέρψεις αὐτοῖς τὸ θέρος παρεῖχει; 3. 24. I καιναὶ τέρψεις.

[177] 3. 21. 4 καὶ ἐγίνετο ἄκουσμα τέρπνον, and 22. I ἐτέρπετο τῇ νηὶ . . .

[178] 2. I. 1–2. 4.

[179] I. 19. I τὸν Δρύαντα φυτὸν κατορύττοντα; 4. 33. 2 ἔδωκαν . . . τῷ Λάμωνι τὴν
ἡμίσειαν μοῖραν τῶν ἀγρῶν θερίζειν; 3. 30. 3 κριθία μετροῦντας (Lamon and Myrtale)
οὐ πρὸ πολλοῦ λελικμημένα.

rough voices, as though they were breaking up the earth with forks' (4. 40. 2). At the end of the novel, when the heroes are definitively settled on their land, the question of work is also omitted. For the Greek text does not say, as G. Dalmeyda has it in the standard French translation, that Daphnis and Chloe were engaged in pastoral *activities*, but that they lived a pastoral *life* (τὸν πλεῖστον χρόνον βίον ποιμενικὸν εἶχον, 4. 39. 1) from which labour has totally disappeared: they may be defined as shepherds only because of their cult for pastoral deities ('they worshipped as their gods the Nymphs, Pan, and Love', 4. 39. 1) and their food ('they thought that fruit and milk were the sweetest kind of food', 4. 39. 1). As cattle-owners they only transfer to the country the life of ease which is usually found in town. The place and the type of consumption have changed: they consume *directly* and *on the spot*. But the essential point, i.e. the actual consumption by non-producers, remains the same.

Conclusion

Two conclusions may be drawn from this very incomplete analysis. The first is that the urban perspective is absolutely dominant in the Greek novel. Longus' originality is not that he substitutes the countryman's point of view, but on the contrary that he highlights at times the distortions caused by this purely urban perspective and that he introduces a critical distance which is not found elsewhere. The second conclusion is methodological. It seems to me that a study like the present one reveals how interesting these texts can be for the historian of mentalities, provided that he situates them in their own context and takes into account the characteristics that go with the genre.

5

The Role of Women in the Greek Novel: Woman as Heroine and Reader

BRIGITTE EGGER

The most recent monographs on the ancient novel put forward the interesting supposition that there is a woman concealed behind the pseudonym of one or other of the Greek authors.[1] This hypothesis, which might cause some astonishment in view of the lack of reliable biographical information on authorship, tries to acquire plausibility by citing the prominent role of women in these novels. In fact it merely represents an elaboration of a view taken by interpreters of this genre for centuries on the grounds that the Greek love- and adventure-novel appealed as well or particularly to a female readership.

For that reason, George Thornley in 1657 called Longus' novel 'a most sweet and pleasant pastoral romance for ladies';[2] and Gottfried August Bürger, in the preface to his German translation of 1775, described the novel by Xenophon of Ephesus as an 'albernes Romänlein . . . aber hin und wieder ganz lieblich, süß und artig' ('a silly little romance, but now and then quite lovely, sweet, and pretty'), and by comparing it with the 'Anecdotes intéressantes, die auf den Nachttischen herumpoltern' ('interesting stories which litter bedside tables'), he refers to female reading preferences.[3]

Whereas these two eminent translators obviously have in mind the female readers of their own times in the seventeenth and eighteenth centuries, philologists with the same tendencies refer

---

[1] Cf. Hägg (1983: 96); Holzberg (1986/1994: 42). Similarly Davies (1980).
[2] In the preface to his translation, London 1657, reprinted in the 1955 Loeb edition.
[3] In the first edition of his translation (Leipzig 25/9/1775).

expressly to the reception of the novel in antiquity. In 1876 Erwin Rohde declared that Hellenistic narrative erotic poetry, from which he believed the novel had developed, was 'ganz vorzüglich für Frauen bestimmt' ('especially suited to women', (67 = 72), and explains the 'moralischen Vorrang' ('moral predominance') of its female characters as a subconscious reflection of the intellectual, as well as moral, preponderance of the female sex in real life (356 = 383). Franz Altheim wrote in 1948: 'Die Weiblichkeit stellt die Hauptmasse der Leser. Und wo dies zahlenmäßig sich nicht beweisen lassen sollte, bestimmen doch weibliche Neigungen und weiblicher Geschmack die Haltung des Romans' ('The readership consists mainly of women. And if this cannot be proved in terms of figures, yet female predilections and female taste determine the attitude of the novel', 42). In 1957 Albin Lesky held: 'Stärker als je mag die Frau die Wünsche des Lesepublikums mitbestimmt haben. Wir können uns die Gorgo oder Praxinoa der *Adoniazusen* Theokrits nur schwer vor einer Tragödie des Sophokles vorstellen, einen der griechischen Romane geben wir ihr gern in die Hand' ('Women may have taken part in determining the audience's wishes to a greater extent than ever before. We can hardly envisage the Gorgo or Praxinoa of Theocritus' *Adoniazousai* watching a Sophoclean tragedy, but we happily supply them with one of the Greek novels', 1963: 917 and unchanged 1971: 961).

Modern interpreters also apply the new methods of comparative studies or reception aesthetics. Alexander Scobie, for example, compared the Greek novels, with reference to the uniform schemata of their stories and the invariability of their idealistic conventions, to the 'stories in women's magazines' (1973: 5), and Gerald Neill Sandy concluded from the much discussed 'elevation of women' in the transmitted texts 'that the authors anticipated a substantial female readership' (1982a: 61). This chain of quotations might be continued at will.

On the whole, modern scholarship seems to have agreed on a largely 'bourgeois' or 'middle-class' circle of readers, whose social boundaries are less open below than above.[4] The problem of a potential female reader is treated rather peripherally, while the

---

[4] Following the death of that harsh and depreciatory criticism, which esp. in Germany was heavily moralizing, the tendentiously negative assessment of the Greek novels (esp. Chariton's), which has influenced scholarship for a long time, e.g. Perry (1967) who considered the novels 'juvenile literature' (98) and their circle of addressees 'unacademic readers' (100) or 'uncultivated or frivolous people' (5), also

argument rests almost topically on two aspects: first on the
anachronistic translation of modern female reading habits into
antiquity, and secondly on the interpretation of the text along the
lines of a 'requirement' theory of literature—because of interests
which appeal to their identity,[5] women read novels by choice,
namely 'love'-stories and even 'women's' novels.[6]

Hand in hand with this goes literary evaluation, which has
long moved in a mostly contemptuous direction. This tendency
developed its adherents after Erwin Rohde's dismissal of the novel
as a literary form of decline. Rohde had especially associated his
key words 'dekadent', 'schwülstig', 'platt', 'spät', 'Unterhaltung'
('decadent', 'pompous', 'trivial', 'late', 'entertainment') with the
predominance of a—to his mind suspicious—femininity in story,
content, and audience. His connection of these two aspects mutu-

finally seems to have been overcome in several recent studies: cf. Schmeling (1974:
32 f.) 'middle-class audience'; Schmeling (1980: 133) 'a sentimental group', (138)
'sophisticated readers'; Hägg (1983: 4) 'Novels were most probably also read
in highbrow circles'; Müller (1981: 392) 'Ebenso wie die Autoren läßt das
"Publikum" keine schichtenspezifische Ausgrenzung nach "oben" erkennen';
Reardon (1976: 130) 'There can be no question now of the novel's being "popular"
by contrast with "educated".' He suspects 'Were they, perhaps, the relaxation of the
literate?' (ibid.). I most approve of Reardon's (1974) excellent representation of the
novel in its contemporary literary and social spectrum.

[5] Perhaps the nicest example of all: Schmeling (1980: 62) on the effect of the
Psammis episode, X. Eph. 3.11 (the heroine Anthia is under the possession and
power of an Indian maharaja): 'The episode is intended to appeal to the reader who
knows of Alexandria and India only as exotic fairytale places. And among
Xenophon's readers or listeners are probably young girls who will lie awake at night
out of fear (or hope) of finding themselves one day alone in Alexandria with an
Indian prince.' More seriously Altheim (1942/1948: 41 f.): 'Liebe ist die Domäne
des Weibes. Liebe erfüllt sie in einem Maß, das bei dem Mann unmöglich wäre.
Liebe bestimmt das Schicksal des Weibes. Die Herrschaft der Liebe besagt, daß das
Weib beginnt, Mittelpunkt zu werden. Eine weibliche Sicht bahnt sich an . . . Die
Weiblichkeit stellt die Hauptmasse der Leser.' Closer still García Gual (1969: 44):
'La importancia de la mujer . . . como lectora de novelas—ya hemos hablado de
la aspiración de un público femenino—es una de las razones sociológicas de la
predilección por el tema amoroso . . . por la "romantización" del amor . . . El amor
. . . presenta los rasgos de una estilización del tema.' It will hardly be surprising
that both authors do not rate the novel very highly.

[6] Literary sociology and reader psychology have proved this sufficiently for the
18th to the 20th c. During the 18th and 19th c. the link between novel-reading
and female readership was a locus communis; the often moralizing criticism of genre
and content besides the warning against the danger to the female readership were
equally topical (Flaubert's Emma Bovary!). The disregard of the novel as a genre on
the whole and the reproaches against it finally became attached to the 'women's
novel' of the 19th and 20th c., which is characterized by the female protagonist
and the dominating love theme. Cf. Beaujean (1964), Angress (1974), Kreuzer
(1977), Sauder (1977).

ally reinforced the disparagement.[7] Subsequently, the association of
subject and addressee became traditional in the concept of the so-
called 'Trivialroman', and the term 'Roman'—worse even than
English 'romance' in comparison to 'novel'—bore the stigma of
'unclassical' among philologists for a very long time. The triviality
of the themes—of endangered and finally triumphant love, a
merely private business portrayed at too little distance—and the
central role of women in the text seemed to correspond to the
banality of the experiences of the audience (presumably) appealed
to: that is to say, the semi-educated and women.[8]

This model of interpretation, in my opinion, fundamentally mis-

[7] Of course there was a long tradition of extremely negative evaluations of the
Greek novel among philologists before Rohde's devastating judgement. The actual
connection of the flaws of the 'Verfallsform' with the 'bedeutenden Übergewicht des
weiblichen Geschlechts in geistigen und sittlichen Verhältnissen' (354–5 = 386)
was, however, as far as I know, for the first time made by Rohde, who was
certainly influenced by contemporary topical opinions on modern novels and their
female readers: 'Es läßt sich allerdings von vornherein annehmen, daß in diesen
Zeiten eines reißenden Verfalls nicht gerade der Sittlichkeit, aber der moralischen
und geistigen Energie der alten Kulturvölker die Herrschaftsverhältnisse, wie es
unter solchen Zuständen zu gehen pflegt, sich zugunsten der Weiber einigermaßen
verschoben haben' (354 = 380–1). In the novels the 'überall bemerkbare Vorrang
der weiblichen Charaktere vor den, meist sehr schwächlich gehaltenen, männlichen
[mag] wie ein unbewußtes Eingeständnis des tatsächlich eingetretenen Verhältnisses
erscheinen' (356 = 383). In spite of this attempt at a psychological interpretation,
Rohde denies in the same passage that an actual change or improvement of
women's social status occured during the Hellenistic era (355 = 381)!

[8] 'Trivial literature' is a term which cannot be defined in a scientifically objective way by aesthetic criteria (i.e. content, style, or form), and which by no means
has any ahistorical validity. This is already proved by the fact that the appreciation
of several Greek novels has experienced considerable fluctuation during the history
of their reception. They enjoyed great popularity esp. among the educated public of
the Byzantine, Renaissance, and Baroque ages as 'high literature' (even with model
characters), before they fell victim to the depreciatory verdicts of the 18th-20th-c.
philologists. In the literary and extra-literary context of their time of origin, the
Greek novels can be judged as 'trivial literature' only according to the sociological
definition of Kreuzer (1967: 184 f.): as a 'Bezeichnung des Literaturkomplexes, den
die dominierenden Geschmacksträger einer Zeitgenossenschaft ästhetisch diskrim-
inieren'. By historicizing the term, trivial literature and its aesthetic-moralizing
devaluation become the phenomenon of a certain epoch. This explains ancient
literary theory's silence on the novel, its non-appearance in the ancient literary system, the missing name of the genre and even Philostratus' (*Letter* 66) or Persius'
(1. 134, see below) scorn; for this cf. already Perry (1930: 95–7 with nn. 5, 7) and
Perry (1967: 99), as well as Reardon (1974). This sober sociological concept of
'triviality', which no longer rests on irrational criteria of literary evaluation alone,
for the first time liberates the Greek novels' ancient and modern readers alike from
the stigma of banality. The dilemma of scholars in view of their disdain for their
subject—which they nevertheless treat in voluminous books—is illustrated again
and again: from Ch. D. Beck's dictum about Chariton 'qui non meretur, nisi semel,

places the actual problems which are raised by assuming a potential female readership for the Greek novel. I consider historical analogies can only be justified, when social conditions are demonstrably as comparable as literary forms and contents.

If the hypothesis of a female Greek novel reader is to be maintained, two separate questions seem important to me:

1. What do we know about the real historical female reader in the Greek-speaking half of the Roman Empire? From which social level does she come? What kind of education can be presumed for her?

2. Which models of imagined womanhood are there within the texts themselves? Which roles and schemata of behaviour serve to constitute the female image in the novels? What ensemble of *imagines* emerges?

Only after these questions have been answered can one investigate the relationship between fiction and reality: and whether the novels supply models of identification and whether their concepts of femininity are likely to correspond with social-historical facts.

In view of our scant knowledge about social reality in the time in question—a gap which strengthens the general phenomenon of the lack of female history—emphasis must be laid on the second complex of questions: the investigation of structures immanent in the texts; but the problem of real female readers should also be raised.[9]

---

legi' (in the preface to the 2nd edition of D'Orville's edition, Leipzig 1783), to Erwin Rohde's excuse for his lengthy representation of topics 'in welche selbst sich tiefer zu versetzen der Verfasser seinen Lesern keineswegs zumuten möchte' (xvif.), and finally to J. Helms' (1966: 13) ambivalence towards 'a literary genre [that] contains little to commend it . . . [whose] perusal will cause the modern reader to turn away from them'. To my knowledge, Beck's justification draws the earliest explicit comparison (from a philologist's point of view) between the ancient and the 18th-c. erotic novel, 'cum certum sit, multa nunc ex hoc amatoriarum fabularum genere, etiam longe ineptiora, verum vernacula lingua scripta, cupidissime non legi, sed devorari' (loc. cit.—the addiction to reading!). The aesthetic-social exoneration of the ancient readers implies the recognition that both 'highly literary' and critically/ aesthetically disparaged literature can be intended for the same educated upper-class audience: cf. Wesseling (1988). Ultimately, this historicized concept of triviality also draws attention to the fact that literary evaluation cannot be separated from the choice of topics. I shall treat the history of the philological evaluation of the Greek novel in more detail in my dissertation 'Rezeptionsästhetische Studien zum griechischen Roman: Die Frau als Heldin und Leserin'.

[9] This aspect will be treated more thoroughly in my dissertation (see n. 8).

THE REAL FEMALE READER: AN ATTEMPT TO SECURE
THE CLUES

The results of historical sociology and papyrology demonstrate a progressive increase in educational opportunities for women from the third century BC.[10] At least for Hellenistic and early imperial Egypt, a certain amount of women's education can not only be assumed but also proved in connection with the improved economic and legal status of upper-class women—and during the relatively prosperous first two centuries AD this term comprises wider circles than ever before or for centuries afterwards.[11] Hundreds of papyri are written by or addressed to women; that the girls acquired the ability to read and write by going to school is also proved by such documents.[12] Many other scattered reports

[10] Cf. Ziebarth (1914: 39f., 93f., 141f.); Marrou (1957: 149); Pomeroy (1975: 131f.; 1977); Cole (1981). The standard works on education in the period in question, Marrou and Nilsson, show little interest in the topic of girls' education: it is only touched in passing by Nilsson (1955: 145-7). Marrou basically speaks only of the 'child'—and means only 'boys'; at 212 and 328 he briefly mentions girls' education in the Hellenistic period, at 341f., 361f. and 401 among the Roman nobility. Those few sentences in a grand opus of more than 500 pages demonstrate the need for research into women's history.

[11] Pomeroy (1977; 1981: 309f.); Calderini (1956); Cole (1981: 230f.; in some cases too cautious).

[12] References already in Ziebarth (1914: 39f.) and the literature mentioned above in nn. 10 and 11. Lewis (1983: 62) says of the citizens of Egyptian provincial towns, 'The metropolitan class as a whole sent its sons to school. With regard to daughters the decision to educate or not appears to have been a personal one resting with the parents, rather than a social dictate. Half a dozen of letters of the early second century tell us about the daughters of a nome strategos who was at school away from home. But at the opposite extreme we find, in a document of AD 151, a member of the "colonist" élite signing for her sister, who is illiterate.'
The most famous historical reference for girls' education in Egypt is the case (also quoted by Lewis (1983)) of little Heraidous, daughter of the strategos of Apollinopolis (discussed in detail for the first time by Préaux (1929: 772f.)): study materials are to be provided for her (τὰ ἐπιτήδεια τῇ σχολῇ οἷον βυβλίον εἰς ἀναγινώσκειν, Pap.Giss. 85. 13-15); the mother arranges for a present to be sent to her teacher, ἵνα φιλοπονήσῃ εἰς αὐτήν (Pap.Giss. 78. 2).
In the novel girls' attendance at school is first alluded to in Apuleius' *Metamorphoses* (Areten meam condiscipulam memoras, 9. 17: 215. 16f.) and then in more detail in the *Historia Apollonii* (29 RA 1-5; 30 RA 6-7; 31 RA 22 and 31: with the terms *auditorium, studia, scola*). In my view—in contrast to Kortekaas' opinion (1984: 232, n. 556)—this is not an expression of the same attitude towards *paideia* which is predominant in the five Greek novels under discussion here (in which is never mentioned any formal and institutionalized education for girls), and on no account evidence for a Greek original from which the *Historia Apollonii* may have derived. Cf. for this below n. 30 with text.

derived from pictorial arts, epigraphy,[13] and various texts about women's literacy,[14] show that an—at least tendentious—transfer of the Egyptian data to other Hellenized areas is quite possible.

Our ancient sources are often silent about women, and in addition to that our difficulties are increased by the great indifference of scholars to collecting the scattered evidence. A standard work about the situation in the eastern Roman Empire or generally about the social history of this region during the first two centuries AD remains a desideratum.[15]

Although the literacy of Greek-speaking women of a certain social class is attested for Egypt, and is at least probable for other provinces, information about their reading preferences is almost completely lacking.[16] The ancient testimonies, very sparse on the novel anyway, are as a rule silent on the problem of a female readership.[17] Where any recipients are mentioned, they are mostly male.

The earliest reference—if it may be interpreted as such—in the Neronian satirist Persius assigns the *Callirhoe* as post-prandial reading to persons who had been occupied with the *edictum* (i.e. the forum or lawsuits) in the morning—that is, to men.[18] The emperor

[13] Some epigraphical texts relevant to women's social status are collected in Pleket (1969).

[14] It is not surprising that in different attempts to calculate the numbers and percentages of ancient illiterates statistically (Youtie (1975), Calderini (1956), Duncan-Jones (1977)), the number of illiterate women is always higher than that of illiterate men. Also in those economic classes, in which sufficient literacy for reading and enjoying books can be assumed, girls have access to education (as to all other rights and goods of civilization) to a lower degree in an invariably patriarchal society. For these reasons, earlier scholarship considered the educational possibilities for girls during the period in question to be generally few (e.g. Préaux (1959: 171f.)). However, what is important is not an illusory equivalence of the sexes, but the fact that for the first time ever in the Hellenistic or imperial period women actually come into question as a mass reading public—whether they read themselves, or literature is being read to them, which thus forces the author to take them into his consideration as an important recipient group with special interests.

[15] Cf. Lefkowitz (1986: 28). Pomeroy (1985) remains an exception.

[16] Consult Pack (1965) and Montevecchi (1973: 360-94, esp. 391), for the general popularity of Greek novel-reading. The novel (incl. adespota) seems to be the most prominent genre of the literature produced during the first three centuries AD, which was in fact not promoted by the educational and literary system and in terms of numbers remained far behind the classical and Hellenistic authors.

[17] Of course the group of female recipients contains readers as well as listeners—a group with an indirect access to literature.

[18] Pers. I. 131: *his mane edictum, post prandia Callirhoen do.* During the whole poem, a programmatic satire, the derided circle of 'literates' seems to consist only of male participants. Cf. Wesseling (1988: 67).

Julian's warning against ἐρωτικαὶ ὑποθέσεις (erotic themes) in his 89th *Letter* is directed to the pagan priesthood in the East;[19] the physician Theodorus Priscianus' approximately contemporary recommendation[20] of *fabulae amatoriae* as an antidote to impotence is also clearly intended for male patients.[21]

As regards other ancient testimonies which mention only male addressees of the Greek novel, the usual grammatical (as a mirror of cultural) subordination of the feminine under the masculine gender is a probable explanation. For example, in the 'Praise of Leucippe' by the so called philosopher Leon, one reads after six verses praising this girl's virtue and courage, εἴπερ δὲ καὶ σὺ σωφρονεῖν θέλῃς, φίλος, 'If you, too, want to live a pure life, friend,' look at the ending: chaste, matrimonial love.[22]

The same is true for the reader implicit in the text of the novels. Thus in Chariton's famous direct address to his readers (8.1)—a passage which can supply the starting point for the whole poetics of the genre. As is well known, the narrator here holds the view that after all these dangers and entanglements the last book will be the one loved best by his 'readers', τοῖς ἀναγιγνώσκουσιν, because of its happy ending, namely, ἔρωτες δίκαιοι and νόμιμοι γάμοι (that is 'lawful love' and 'legal marriage'). Here, as in many other passages, one may assume that because of grammatical usage ταῖς ἀναγιγνωσκούσαις are included.[23] Consequently, women often

---

[19] 300 C–301 D, in connection with the ideal of chastity, Julian discusses litera-ture recommended or not permitted for priests; 301 B, he distinguishes strictly between (permitted) historiography of facts ἱστορίαις . . . ὁπόσαι συνεγράφησαν ἐπὶ ποιημένοις τοῖς ἔργοις and (prohibited) fictional texts: ὅσα δέ ἐστιν ἐν ἱστορίας εἴδει . . . ἀπηγγέλματα πλάσματα παραιτέον ἐρωτικὰς ὑποθέσεις καὶ πάντα ἁπλῶς τὰ τοιαῦτα—a division Lucian and Antonius Diogenes had made fun of already cen-turies before him.

[20] 2. 11. 34, 'uti sane lectionibus animum ad delicias pertrahentibus, ut sunt . . . aut Herodiani aut Syrii Jamblichi, vel ceteris suaviter amatorias fabulas describentibus'. Compare the intended effect of an erotic novel here with Pantagruel's reading of Heliodorus as a remedy for insomnia in Rabelais!

[21] Both witnesses conceive reading matter—esp. fiction—to have a very direct effect on the readers' physical and psychical disposition—a main argument of moral censorship since Plato, which was to affect the novel (and by no means only the ancient novel) until far into the 20th c. In modern times, not only the distance from reality, but also the demoralizing effect of novel-reading on women in particular was feared again and again; cf. Berger (1984: 186), Kreuzer (1977), Sauder (1977).

[22] *Anthol. Palat.* 9. 203. 7f. (also printed in Vilborg's edition of Achilles Tatius, 163).

[23] In his anticipation of the happy ending and the readers' expectations, the nar-rator here describes a circle of (male and female) recipients which is interested in stable, legally composed eroticism and stable family environment, whose (literary)

disappear from our written testimonies simply because of grammatical rules.[24] Only one female novel reader, presumably of the first century AD, is known to us by name, Isidora, Antonius Diogenes' sister, to whom he dedicates his work: τῇ ἀδελφῇ Ἰσιδώρᾳ φιλομαθῶς ἐχούσῃ τὰ δράματα προσφωνεῖ, 'he dedicates the novel to his sister Isidora, who is very interested in it'. Here even her special predilection for such reading matter seems to be expressed! Unfortunately we do not have any further information about Isidora.[25] The next reference to female novel-reading is not made until a thousand years later. In his Neoplatonic, allegorizing, and moralizing interpretation of Heliodorus, the so-called Philippos Philosophos or Theophanes Cerameus (tenth to twelfth century) includes a list of Heliodorus' didactic qualities.[26] With regard to women these reside, in his opinion, especially in the deterrent fate of the negative protagonist Arsace—female readers are to recognize the dangers of attempted adultery: τοὺς ἔρωτας εἰς ἀγχόνην ἄτιμον κατλήξαντας, 'that such illegitimate love-affairs end with an ignoble rope' (70f.). This Byzantine author thus understands the novel very didactically as a training in actual power relations and gender-specific behaviour,[27] and consequently also presupposes

fantasies of happiness require such an ending, and indeed even stipulate it. For the function of this passage *inter alia* as a poetological differentiation from historiography and subsequent thoughts on theories of genre cf. C.-W. Müller (1976; esp. 134 f.).

[24] This phenomenon of grammatical incorporation and subordination of the feminine under the masculine gender is familiar to every philologist and identified as an ideological problem by modern feminist linguistics. Besides, it becomes a subject also of ancient juridical literature, where unambiguous definitions and identities are indispensable. For example, Servius *Dig.* 32. 62 says: 'semper sexus masculinus etiam femininum sexum continet'. Cf. Treggiari (1979: 185 f.) with further examples.

[25] Photios, *Bibl.* 111a-b. For the problem of a female readership it is of no importance whether the dedication to Isidora is only fictitious (for this opinion cf. e.g C.-W. Müller (1981: 395); it is important, however, that a woman with reading interests relevant to the subject is a potential addressee.

[26] The text follows Colonna's edition of Heliodorus, 366 f. Theophanes Cerameus was bishop of Rossano, 1130-40. The attribution, however, is not unambiguous. The fictitious situation: 'Many philologists' read [?recite] Heliodorus' novel in the temple precinct and ridicule it (9 f., 31 f.). It is now to be defended against this attack as παιδαγωγική . . . ἡ βίβλος καὶ ἠθικῆς φιλοσοφίας διδάσκαλος (35 f.). Its readers may learn *eusebeia* and the justified use of lies and deception from Calasiris, manly continence from Theagenes, *sophrosyne* of the highest kind from Charicleia (45 f.).

[27] Immediately afterwards there follows a further interpretation of the novel as a text for training in personal obedience: if someone wants to rebel against his master, he will be set right by Achaemenes' fate.

female readers. As, however, apart from Isidora's interest in novel-reading, further real testimonies for female reading behaviour are lacking, a study of female readers has to start from the signals in the text which control its reading. As a transition to the problem of the image of women in the novels themselves, discussion is first required of the importance of reading, especially of female readers within our texts. How lucky would we consider ourselves, if a Leucippe or Anthia, like a young lady in Jane Austen's *Northanger Abbey* caught reading, answered the question 'And what are you reading, Miss?' with 'Oh—it is only a novel!', and by this reply gave evidence both for female reading behaviour and the slightly deprecatory evaluation of her reading material.[28]

The women in Greek novels, as far as we know, do not read for entertainment. Whereas the main theme of the genre is merely private and emotional, precisely the private, everyday sphere with its occupations is hardly represented. The domestic, domesticated—and thus traditionally feminine—sphere is also unsuitable for literary representation in so-called bourgeois Hellenistic and imperial literature. This sphere is admittedly the object of the lovers' wanderings and conceptions of happiness, but never itself the subject.[29]

A certain amount of education is taken for granted among all members of the economic class, women as well, from which the protagonists are drawn. Their concept of *paideia*, which connotes social self-confidence rather than intellectual activity,[30] so includes

[28] Vol. I, ch. 5, end. The sequel of this ironical passage is interesting for the literary-sociological evaluation of novel-reading (as a disregarded genre with a chiefly female readership), too: "'Oh—it is only a novel!' replies the young lady, while she lays down her book with affected indifference, or momentary shame. "It is only *Cecilia*, or *Camilla*, or *Belinda*" . . . Now, had the same young lady been engaged with a volume of the Spectator, instead of such a work, how proudly would she have produced the book, and told its name!' The narrator, at any rate, considers this to be very unlikely, because the contents of the latter (entirely in contrast to novels!) are far too distant from the young lady's interests in life and reading.

[29] Only in Achilles Tatius do longer parts of the action take place at home (Bks. 1 and 2): here we are told e.g. about a girl of the top family's (daily?) evening walks (2. 10. 1) and cithara playing (2. 1. 1)—but both episodes serve as an erotically piquant motif rather than as a description of the domestic sphere.

[30] Above all in Chariton, where πεπαιδευμένος/η ('educated, cultured'), often in connection with the idea of Greeks behaving according to their rank, stresses the opposition to barbarity, e.g. 2. 4. 1; 6. 5. 8; 7. 5. 6; cf. also X. Eph. 1. 1. 2 (the observation that Abrocomes παιδείαν τε γὰρ πᾶσαν ἐμελέτα καὶ μουσικὴν ποικίλην ἤσκει ('acquired culture of all kinds and practised a variety of arts'), follows immediately after the mention of his parental home's distinguished social status—and includes hunting, riding, and armed combat), and Heliod. 7. 14. 2.

the ability to read and write. In Longus' novel, for example, the
foster-parents have both foundlings taught to write, as is proper for
their supposed higher status and contrasts with the 'normal' shepherd boys and girls: γράμματα ἐπαίδευον (1. 8. 1).[31] In the extant
texts up to Heliodorus, this provision of culture never becomes a
subject for its own sake—it is always subordinate to another (erotic
or action-centred) plot motif. Letters of love, recognition, and
farewell are written and read in the action novel only to move the
plot forward or to convey psychological insights.[32]

Also the only reader of a *book* who appears in the Greek novel,
Achilles Tatius' Clitophon, does not read for reading's sake or for
the sake of prestige or pleasure connected with it. He is only looking for a seemingly harmless opportunity to catch, as if by accident, the eyes of his Leucippe, with whom he has fallen in love,
and for that purpose he paces the room near her, feigning to be
absorbed in reading a book—ἐβάδιζον . . . κατὰ πρόσωπον τῆς
κόρης, βιβλίον ἅμα κρατῶν, καὶ ἐγκεκυφὼς ἀνεγίνωσκον—in order to
cast a quick glance at her whenever he turns at her door (1. 6. 6).

Only the heroine of our last Greek novel, Charicleia, καλὴ καὶ
σοφή (3. 4. 1), a self-confident and, to a certain extent, emancipated intellectual, exercises her academic interests for their own
sake or for the sake of theological-philosophical knowledge. However, it can hardly be imagined that she reads an adventure or
erotic novel for her own edification or even entertainment. Hers are
serious ambitions and she will not hear of love.[33]

On the other hand, the author rather obviously draws an ironic
picture of the naïve reader, who devours exactly this kind of novel,
in the character of Cnemon, who devotedly, without ever getting
enough of it, identifying himself fully with the romantic interest,
listens to the love story of Charicleia and Theagenes, as it is told

[31] Where, how and by whom is unfortunately not indicated. As further *bona* of
social differentiation, Daphnis and Chloe receive education in everything which is
καλὰ ἦν ἐπ' ἀγροικίας ('elegant in the country')—one can hear the city-dweller's
slight ironical distance—and daintier food!

[32] e.g. X. Eph. 2. 5. 1, 12. 1; Chariton 8. 4. 5; Ach. Tat. 5. 18. 3; Heliod. 2.
10. 1, 9. 2. 11.

[33] Her obstinate and offensive, even aggressive virginity is the reverse side of her
'masculine' public life in the circle of priests and philosophers in Delphi. Her denial
of her 'true' physis and feminine destination in life (2. 33. 6 τὴν ἑαυτῆς φύσιν καὶ
ὅτι γυνὴ γέγονεν εἰδέναι), which drives her fathers to despair (2. 33. 8), is its basic
requirement. On this subject cf. Lefkowitz (1981: 41 f.).

by Calasiris in the first books of the work.[34] By doing this, Heliodorus distances himself in a remarkable way from the traditional
expectations of the genre, which are indeed described here—in
order to meet them himself in the end, too, but with an ingenious
arpeggio.

THE FEMALE IMAGE IN THE TEXTS: SOME ASPECTS

What do the positive and negative images of femininity look like in
the Greek novels, our first fictional prose literature with a relatively
large circulation? Especially for a genre in which the relationship
between the sexes plays such a central part, and in which the private sphere of life appears to be the actual subject, even the vital
question,[35] the exact analysis of the female image, of its types and
stagings, in all kinds of aspects amounts to more than peripheral
research into motifs.[36] In the following I will have to concentrate

---

[34] 2. 23-5. 3. Sympathetic listener (reader!) identification with the narrative or
the protagonists: 3. 2. 3; 4. 3. 4, 4. 2; strong build up of illusion: e.g. 3. 4. 7; naïve
wish to hear everything in detail, insatiability for stories: 4. 4. 2 f.; 5. 1. 3 f. etc.;
even the addiction to reading is alluded to 4. 4. 3; 5. 1. 4: ἀκόρεστος, σειρήνιον.
Calasiris' intricate narrative as a 'novel within the novel' and the listener/reader
pose taken up by Cnemon in the role of the 'aggressively romantic reader . . . who
is eager to be treated to the full spectacle of what we would nowadays call a
widescreen technicolor romance' and the 'explicit reader' (in an inversion of Iser's
term) as well as the 'lector non scrupulosus' is brilliantly discussed by Winkler
(1982: 138 f.).
[35] For this cf. Reardon's explanation of the novel as the myth of the individual
and private life (1969: 307, 1971: 401).
[36] It used to be considered as such in the traditional study of literature, in which
it bore the same marginality and stigma as the 'triviality' of the novels' themes and
female readers mentioned above. I want to draw attention to the fact that the female
roles of the Greek novels—partly via indirect lines of tradition—represent an essential foundation for the imagination of femininity in fictional narrative prose since
the 17th and esp. the 18th c. This derives its literary models last but not least from
the texts in question here, e.g. 'innocence' (and its deviations) as the ideal form for
the later bourgeois literary idea of femininity: spiritualized innocence, the 'beautiful
soul' (one is reminded of Heliodorus' Charicleia), innocence gone astray (traces of
which can be found in Achilles Tatius' Leucippe), or, as a contrast to it, the guilty,
or sinful, woman, who violates the sexual codex, like Xenophon's and Heliodorus'
negative examples. Whereas the Greek novels' *Nachleben* has meanwhile given rise
to much interest in research, as far as I know no study yet examines the literary
impact of its specific presentation of femininity—undoubtedly one of its most
influential features—or the progress and the adaptations of this line of tradition up
to the 18th c. (and after!). Several basic approaches (from a structuralist point of
view, though) in Nolting-Hauff (1974).

on a few essential characteristics only. A study of female characters' behavioural roles in the novels shows—in contrast to the far
greater variety of male characters' roles—a restriction to four
categories only: the heroine, the antagonist, the confidante, the
mother (a few other minor characters like the priestess or the old
woman in the tavern can be passed over).

These four types do appear in the five extant representatives of
the genre, but each with a different valuation and importance. The
central focus, towards which the reader's attention and sympathy
are directed with the aid of various narratological means,[37] is of
course always held by the protagonist; the other three roles are
defined by their relation to her: as a relative, as a helper figure,
or as a (not always negative) antagonist.[38] Mothers, when they
happen not to be in standard situations (such as the wedding or
the leave-taking) or enter only briefly, always appear to have a
strained relationship with their children, especially with their
daughters. Separation, not affection, is associated with motherliness in the novel. They expose their children (Longus, Heliodorus),
abandon them (Chariton), or drive them away from home (Achilles
Tatius).[39] As confidante in her stead (so Chariton 1. 1. 14) figures
the nurse. The ambivalent structure of the ideology of motherliness
can be shown in all four fully extant novels (with the exception
of Xenophon's epitome[40]). Chariton's Callirhoe, to be sure, enters
into an unwelcome marriage far from home in order to save her
unborn child (3. 1. 13), but after that has to leave him behind
without complaining (8. 4. 5). In Longus, Nape, Chloe's foster-
mother, for example, is allowed immediately to experience 'natural'
motherly feelings as soon as she catches sight of the exposed

[37] Such means are: authorial commentary, different points of view, inner
thoughts. Hägg's detailed study of the narrative technique of the Greek novel only
treats the methods used to control readers' sympathies in a cursory way (1971a:
112f.).

[38] This is also true for Melite, the 'other woman' in Achilles Tatius' novel, compared with whom, as has often been observed, the heroine Leucippe seems so
colourless that Melite can displace her in the reader's interest for prolonged stretches
of the book.

[39] All this they do, to be sure, not of their own arbitrary decision, but because
they are forced to do so by repressive sexual moral and/or both social and economic
necessity. This is stated in a particularly blunt way in Persinna's letter to her
exposed daughter (Heliod. 4. 8).

[40] Which I take this text to be because of the arguments presented by Bürger
(1892b) and M. D. Reeve (1971), inter alia against Hägg (1966 and 1983: 21).
Xenophon's mothers only occur in topical contexts and stereotyped situations.

baby (1. 6. 3), and Myrtale's erroneous maternal happiness is
stressed (4. 19. 4). On the other hand, it is taken for granted that
women unresistingly abandon their newborn babies in order to
have them killed according to their husbands' wish (4. 21. 3; 4.
24. 1)—which logically negates the principle of 'natural' motherly
love.

Heliodorus' Charicleia, the girl with three fathers,[41] is veritably
motherless. In this novel, too, the mother's rights to cherish her
long-desired and only child have to be surrendered without com-
plaint to the patriarchal laws of chastity: a white daughter is not
easily explained to her black father and consequently has to be
exposed (2. 31. 1; 4. 8). During the *anagnorisis*, however,
Charicleia puts her trust in the μητρῷα φύσις, the 'natural' motherliness (9. 24. 8), which indeed soon causes a bond to arise between
Persinna and her child (10. 7. 3f.; similarly Longus 4. 23. 1). The
separation of a woman from her newborn child is a sacrifice
demonstrably demanded in contemporary reality by a father's
power to dispose of the life of his offspring.[42] This sacrifice is evoked
as a theme, but without offering the women any possibility of
digesting the experience from their point of view,[43] and represents
an ambivalent contradiction of the emotional appeal to the power
of the mother-tie. A true mother–daughter conflict is represented
in Achilles Tatius, who arranges for his Leucippe to be caught in
bed by her mother Panthia during her first night with Cleitophon
(2. 24. 4f.). During the following serious quarrel the mother's
furious aggression towards her erotically active daughter shows
her to be a vehement representative of patriarchal and restrictive
norms and the repressive authority who causes the sulking girl to

[41] Or four, if her natural father Hydaspes is added (whom she only finds again
at the end of the novel). I am thinking of her two foster-fathers Sisimithres and
Charicles as well as Calasiris, who is often described as her 'father' and characteristically even assumes some attributes of motherliness (2. 22. 4, 23. 2). Winkler
(1982: 116f.) does not go far enough by explaining Charicleia's dependency on all
these fathers only through reference to the contemporary reality of female dependency on male protectors.

[42] Cf. Vatin (1970: 234f.), Krenkel (1971), Dickison (1973), Adam (1977: 94f.)
Pomeroy (1983) and Eyben (1980) (all with further literature) on child exposure
and the *patria potestas*: a contribution to this topic by F. Kudlien (1989) appears in
Groningen Colloquia on the Novel, 2. The letter of Ilarion to his wife dating from the
1st c. BC is a real historical document, P.Oxy 4. 774: ἐὰν . . . τέκῃς ἐὰν ἦν ἄρσενον
ἄφες, ἐὰν ἦν θήλεα, ἔκβαλε (9f.). Cf. also Apul. *Met.* 10. 23.

[43] Which I take to be present in Euripides' *Ion*, where the feelings of the mother,
Kreousa, esp. her fear and suffering while she exposes her child, are described.

elope from home. The author directs his reader's sympathies towards Leucippe; the mother embodies a negative principle.[44]

Several mother figures in Xenophon's and Heliodorus' novels represent terrifying pictures even more clearly, like, for example, the witch-like old hag, hatefully cursed by her dead son's spirit (Heliod. 6. 15. 1f.)—a misogynistic motif dispensable for the story's continuation; as well as the special case of the evil 'stepmothers', the Phaedra-motif, for example Cyno in Xenophon (3. 12. 3), or Demainete in Heliod. 1. 10f. Here mother substitutes carry as connotations the phobic features of female erotic aggression.[45] Analysing the second female role, that of the confidante makes it plain, to begin with, how isolated the female protagonists in the travel novels are—not only at home, where no closer acquaintances or bonds with girls are described, but also during their wanderings, which they (when they are separated from their lovers) must endure mostly without a female friend or a helper.[46]

---

[44] The girl quickly regains her composure and cold-bloodedly invents excuses, even takes up the offensive (2. 25), and clearly is inwardly but little impressed by her parents' moral laws. She even feels her mother's treatment of her to be disgraceful, insulting and infuriating (ἤχθετο, ἠσχύνετο, ὠργίζετο) to such a degree that she decides to take revenge on her (2. 29. 4): the only φάρμακον against this humiliation, which is described in a long psychological digression, is ἀμύνασθαι τὸν βαλόντα τοῖς βλήμασι, to shoot back with the same missiles. This, however, is not granted to her as the weaker party. Quite clearly the relation between mother and daughter is characterized as a struggle for power (2. 29. 5). Out of helpless fury, from an onrush of emotions, Leucippe decides on running away out of her mother's sight (τῶν τῆς μητρὸς ὀφθαλμῶν) as a revenge for her humiliation (the alternative being suicide, which is also considered as a punishment for her mother: a typical infantile revenge fantasy).

The lengthy inner thoughts and the intervening 'scientific' psychological explanations from an authorial perspective direct the reader's sympathies to Leucippe, whose reactions and feelings are meticulously exposed; the mother's point of view and feelings are, in contrast to Leucippe's, only briefly shown in an outside view and are not described in greater detail. A further motive for Leucippe's elopement, obviously, is her wish to find erotic self-determination without parental restrictions. Of course Panthia only plays such an important part because Leucippe's father is not present; at any rate, this circumstance provides us with an exhaustive scene of a generational conflict between mother and daughter. The novel does not present a reconciliation between these two, only the reunion with and pardon by her father are described, who brings the girl back home and sanctions her union with Cleitophon (7. 16f.).

[45] Cyno's husband has adopted Abrocomes (3. 12. 4). She murders her husband, ὡς ἄνδρα ἔχουσα τὸν Ἀβροκόμην—her 'son'. Heliodorus' Demainete really is Cnemon's young stepmother, of the classic type crazed with love; here it almost comes to murdering the father, too (1. 12).

[46] This lack of friendships, to begin with, is explained by the literary topos that well-shielded (upper-class) young ladies hardly ever leave the house, e.g. Chariton

In contrast to this, the male characters are not only well integrated into the social net of private and public friendships and
acquaintances in their home town,[47] but are also often accompa-
nied by a companion during their travels, who is willing to share
their joys and sorrows—just think of the ever faithful Polycharmus
in Chariton or cousin Cleinias in Achilles Tatius.[48] Only Chariton
develops the starting point of a friendship between women a little
further by describing Callirhoe's first strained, then solidary relationship with the Persians Stateira and Rhodogune (8. 3. 6) and
her relationship of personal trust with her slave Plangon, which is
given some room (2. 8. 6f.; 3. 10. 3).[49]

The second striking point is the confidantes' social status. These
friends, nurses, matchmakers all are—with the sole exception mentioned above—slaves.[50] This implies a limitation of the women's

1. 1. 5; Heliod. 6. 11. 1; and if they do, it is only for cultic reasons and for the sake
of attending religious festivals—traditionally the only opportunity for an erotic
meeting (which is already long since shown to be an archaizing and conservative
fiction by the more realistic Latin novels). Considering this lack of worldly experience, the female protagonists on leaving this shielded sphere prove themselves to be
remarkably skilful and equal to all kinds of assaults. It is significant that the Greek
novel knows no word for 'female friend' or friendship between women (in contrast
to sufficiently differentiated terms for male associations). φίλη ('dear'), φιλτάτη
('dearest') only occurs as a formula of address between women. Only Heliod. 6. 11.
1 φίλτρον περὶ τὴν Χαρίκλεαν may be an exception.

[47] Chaereas is well liked among the young men in the gymnasium, νεολαία
(Chariton 1. 1. 10), he has συνέφηβοι and συγγυμνασταί (8. 6. 11); so has Cnemon
(Heliod. 1. 14. 3). Abrocomes, too, is being educated in the usual gymnasium (X.
Eph. 1. 1. 2). Clitophon associates closely with Cleinias (Ach. Tat. 1. 7f.), cf. Longus
4. 17 (Astylus and Gnathon) and 3. 12. 1 (the hunting party of the jeunesse dorée
from town). Only Daphnis and Chloe appear to be of equal rank concerning their
friendships on account of belonging to a different social class.

[48] Furthermore, Clitophon has Satyrus and Menelaus for his travel companions.
The young men moreover easily make new acquaintances or friends on the way:
with Menelaus or the strategos in Achilles, with Thyamis or Cnemon in Heliodorus,
with Hippothous or Aegialeus in Xenophon, with the King of Egypt in Chariton, etc.
Of course literary tradition offered many models of male friendships and only a few
of friendship between women, and surely contemporary reality offered girls only limited possibilities to socialize and communicate, but both phenomena appear to be
only a part of the explanation for this limited view of the novelistic female world of
experience.

[49] Of course the intimate servant's/nurse's solidarity and help substituting a child
or matchmaking—originally a motif from tragedy and comedy later taken over into
many other genres—is a literary convention; cf. Oeri (1948: 53f., 67f.); Ahlers
(1911: 66f.) This facilitated the portrayal of this kind of relationship. The motif of
confidence between Plangon and Callirhoe, however, goes beyond this by its continuation to the end of the novel (8. 4. 5).

[50] This has the remarkable consequence that the female slave—though easily

social contact to the *oikos* and at the same time a social devaluation of 'women's' friendship.

Achilles Tatius depicts his Leucippe as isolated from female society to a very high degree.[51] It is typical of the predominant male perspective and male company in this novel that the girl's sole confidante, her slave Clio, unaccountably disappears from the story after her escape from Leucippe's parental home and does not appear again. The narrator has simply forgotten her (2. 27. 1).[52]

Solidarity among women is evoked only rarely and in conventional situations. For example, in Achilles Tatius (5. 22) Melite by her request for help in her unhappy love affair appeals to Leucippe 'woman to woman', γυναικὸς γυνή. (The scene is lent a sarcastic tone from the fact that Leucippe is her most serious rival precisely in this love story.) Heliodorus even shows this kind of solidarity to be impossible. Whenever his female characters trust each other, treachery follows soon after.[53] Nowhere, with the exception of the oldest extant work, Chariton's, is friendship between women part of the presentation of reality.[54] These brief remarks already make it clear that the range of relationships experienced by women in the novels appears to be very limited. Public activity is out of the ques-

overlooked as a minor character—represents the female type with the most functions in the plot of the novel. The versatility of this type can be explained by the novel's postulated restriction of the female radius of action, and the necessity to unite several action-centred and emotional roles in the slave's character: the role of the mother as nurse or foster-mother; the role of the matchmaker/teacher of love; the role of the friend/confidante/companion (sometimes almost sister). Some examples apart from Chariton's Plangon may suffice: Heliodorus' Thisbe and Cybele, Achilles' Clio, Xenophon's Rhode. (Cf. the terms ἄβρα, σύντροφος, συμπαίστρια, συνόμιλος).

[51] e.g. 4. 1f. Leucippe seems to be the only woman in the Egyptian army camp; even during her serious illness she remains without female help and nursing (4. 10).

[52] Clio, being the accessory of her mistress's love-adventure, has to be removed (ὑπεξαγαγεῖν) from the house secretly because of imminent torture (in connection with Leucippe's mother's investigation of her daughter's nocturnal guest). Cleinias has a slave bring her on board a ship—and thus she leaves both the scene and the novel. The slave Satyrus, however, the other insider, becomes Clitophon's faithful companion during all the ensuing adventures.

[53] For example Thisbe's malicious behaviour towards Demainete (and vice versa) after initial intimacy (1. 15f.), or, more amply described, the fluctuating relationship between Arsace and Cybele which ends in the latter's breach of loyalty (8. 6); similarly the grave rivalry and intrigue between the courtesans Thisbe and Arsinoe (2. 8f.). The impossibility of reliable relations between women is illustrated by the novel's negative characters—Charicleia herself has no female friend (except Nausicleia, see below)—and it thus becomes part of the novel's misogynistic features.

[54] An exception at best is Heliodorus' Nausicleia (6. 6; 6. 11); her friendship with Charicleia, however, is not at all elaborately described.

tion anyway[55] (and, by the way, is only of secondary importance for the male characters, too[56]); family ties are always treated summarily, topically, or are considered to be negatively charged; friendship with other women does not take place or recedes into the background—whereas comradeship and solidarity (partly also charged with erotic connotations) between the male protagonists and their companions and confidants represent an important topic which takes up a considerable amount of the narrative.[57]

Community and communication between women are not objects of our authors' interest. Omitting the female range of experience from the novels' world, of course, goes back in a long literary tradition, but it throws a peculiar light on the often-observed fact that women were at the centre of action and sympathy.[58] Nearly all the contacts and emotions of the novels' female characters are seen in relation to men. In the first place, with a positive connotation, to their respective lovers or husbands, or, in the second place, with a negative connotation, to all the others: those pursuing her virtue.[59]

[55] With the exception of taking over cultic functions, because these belong to the natural duties of the female protagonists as members of the town's upper class. (Chloe as a girl of low social, even slave status remains an exceptional case where a public dimension is concerned. In the other novels, too, the 'common women' move more freely than the middle-class daughters.) Regular service in the temple is performed by Anthia (X. Eph. 5. 1f.) and of course by the priestess of Artemis, Charicleia. On women's real contemporary activities in public, as holders of (not only cultic) posts, cf. A. H. M. Jones (1940: 175), Pleket (1969), van Bremen (1981).

[56] The sons/youthful lovers seem, like the girls, to hold cultic posts only; more frequent are references to their fathers or other older local dignitaries assuming public or political tasks; but these aspects always remain subordinate to the importance of the private sphere and the love story.

[57] See above nn. 47, 48. Homosexual friendship between men is described rather attentively in Achilles Tatius and Xenophon—esp. in the sub-plots; but also Abrocomes' meeting with Hippothous, the 'noble robber' in the latter work, has been interpreted as a passing homoerotic relationship (Schmeling (1980: 52)). Only Daphnis and Chloe appear to be of equal status in their opportunities for friendship: they share all their friends. This, again, can be explained by their lower social rank, which makes it necessary for the girl to leave the *oikos* and allows her greater freedom.

[58] See above p. 111 and below n. 65. The advocates of the theory that the Greek novels can be read as mystery texts are able to explain the predominance of women in the novels as a reflex of their important position in the mystery religions, esp. in the cult of Isis: 'Und das Wort vom Ewig-Weiblichen, stimmt es eben für die Isisreligion nicht auch? Der griechische Roman . . . stottert dasselbe' (Kerényi (1927/1962: 229f.)).

[59] Other, not erotically determined, encounters of girls with men are very rare: only Charicleia shares Cnemon as a mutual friend with Theagenes; Anthia is only

More important than the confidantes are the representatives of
the third type, the antagonists. The theme of rivalry between
women is still treated with charm by Chariton in the form of a
beauty contest between the prettiest women of Asia and Europe,
ending amicably and to nobody's surprise with the Greek winning
without effort (5. 3). The other authors use the antagonist character more pointedly to represent a concept of femininity opposed
to that of the central character. The main distinguishing criterion
is—which is little surprise—the women's sexual praxis. Whereas
the heroine, according to the conventions of the genre, remains
chaste at all costs and faithful to her lover until the story's happy
ending (with the well-known exception of Callirhoe), the 'other
woman' is erotically active.[60] Apart from Achilles Tatius' Leucippe,
who at about the middle of the novel suddenly switches these two
roles—in my opinion a deliberate comic move of the author's and
no unintentional blunder[61]—the separation of the two types is
carefully maintained: viz. Leucippe and Melite in Achilles, Anthia
and Cyno or Manto in Xenophon, Chloe and Lycaenion in Longus,
Charicleia and Arsace, Demainete or Rhodopis in Heliodorus.[62]
Although virginity or continence are quite obviously always
represented as the positive principle and absolutely necessary for
a middle-class bride,[63] the contrasting image is not necessarily

safe from Hippothous' pursuit of her after he has recognized her as his best friend's
wife (X. Eph. 5. 9); Leucippe does not seem to be included in her Clitophon's circle
of travel companions and is at best object of their friendship and attention (Ach.
Tat. 2. 35; 1. 4. 6f.).

[60] Segal's explanation of the 'two sisters of the female archetype, the sensual and
the virtuous woman' (1984: 87) and 'the dual aspects of the archetype feminine'
(91), unfortunately fails to engage with historicity.

[61] 'Achilles Tatius makes grimaces in the direction of the naively romantic conception of love found in earlier novels' (Reardon (1969: 300 n. 26)). Cf. also G.
Anderson (1982: 23) and already Durham (1938). This parodic element corresponds with the farcical chastity tests at the end of the novel.

[62] Also, Heliodorus' Nausicleia is Charicleia's antagonist in an erotic sense: she
represents the erotically adjusted, 'normal' young woman, whose story ends with
her wedding (here with Cnemon, 6. 8).

[63] During the development of the genre, the protagonists' virginity becomes a
problem of historically increasing explosiveness. Whereas Callirhoe's σωφροσύνη is
overcome by her motherly love (μητρὸς φιλοστοργία, Chariton 2. 9. 1), it is the other
way round with Persinna (Heliod. 4. 8): Charicleia's virtue becomes the central
theme, around which the action evolves. But even Longus, whose Chloe grows up
freely to such a degree that only because of her ignorance do her sexual experiences
end shortly before coitus, has her father-in-law—after her social advancement to a
middle-class lady—ascertain her virginity before the wedding (4. 31. 3). The
embarrassing situation of the bride Leucippe confronted with her father, who after

defamed: Lycaenion is represented as really likable,[64] while Melite has often been felt by scholars to be one of the most engaging and successful persons in the novelistic world.[65] Melite, though, as an 'Ephesian Widow' is allowed to take certain liberties; and Lycaenion, a γύναιον or 'little woman' from town, very probably lives with her husband in a state of concubinage only (3. 15. 1).[66] Extra-matrimonial sexuality of lawful-wedded wives is not tolerated in any other novel (with the exception of the Hellenistic Chariton, who has his Callirhoe live in bigamy for the sake of her child[67]).

all her adventures is not able to believe in her virginity (Ach. Tat. 8. 7), looks substantially more serious than preceding arguments about her chastity (see n. 61). Only the Christian novels surpass the fuss about Charicleia's virginity, esp. during the ordeals at the end of the narrative (Heliod. 10. 8 f.). Here for the first time in the extant novels the man's virginity also becomes an ideal. 'Three brides are virgins; of the other two one is a chaste wife, the last a virtuous bigamist. But the use of the chastity standard is again a matter for the individual author. For Xenophon and Heliodorus the Heroine's chastity is virtuous, even aggressively so; that of Achilles' heroine is negotiable, of Longus' accidental' (Anderson (1984: 108 f.)).

[64] She even—in the generally conciliatory atmosphere of this novel—takes part in the wedding (4. 38. 1). For Lycaenion's character cf. Levin (1977) and Scarcella (1972b).

[65] e.g. Cresci (1978), Perry (1967: 106), Plepelits (1980: 35 f.), Vilborg (1962: 11). Philistine interpretations like Scobie's (1973: 94) 'sultry seductress' (Melite and Lycaenion) have become rare. The advocates of the mystery-texts theory explain these two characters as representatives of the goddess, or as mystagogues in the ritual of the *hieros gamos* during initiation (e.g. Merkelbach (1962: 144 and 213 f.); similarly Chalk (1960: 144)). In the same way they can interpret Anthia's clearly active erotic role during her wedding night (X. Eph. 1. 9) towards her passive bridegroom as an imitation of the goddess Isis during her union with the dead Osiris, or again the cultic staging of this *hieros gamos* (Kerényi (1927: 44, 223); Merkelbach (1962: 94 f.), Witt (1971: 249)).

[66] τούτῳ (sc. the neighbour Chromis) γύναιον ἦν ἐπακτὸν ἐξ ἄστεος, νέον καὶ ὡραῖον καὶ ἀγροικίας ἁβρότερον ('He had imported a wife from town who was young, pretty, and rather sophisticated for the countryside'). This was first pointed out by Scarcella (1972b: 65 f.) The term γυνή (in the sense of 'wife') in the Greek novel gives no evidence for the legal-juridical aspect of cohabitation; where the latter is stressed, it has to be specified—e.g. γαμετὴ κατὰ νόμους (Chariton 3. 1. 6), ἡ . . . νόμῳ τὸν συνοικοῦντα ἔχουσα (Heliod. 1. 11. 4). γύναιον has a disparaging overtone in Chariton and Heliodorus; in Longus the term reappears in another passage, however not in a negative, but a quite neutral sense (3. 6. 2).

[67] After wavering between σωφροσύνη (chastity) and τέκνον (child), a αἵρεσις περὶ τῶν μεγίστων for a woman (2. 10. 7), she decides against abortion and for marrying Dionysius in order not to give birth to a slave child: τὸ τέκνον με προδίδωσον ἀκούσης ἐμοῦ (2. 11. 5). (A child's legal status always depended on the mother's: 'partus sequitur matrem'; Mitteis (1891: 128). The slave child devolved upon the master of the slave mother and had no legal relationship to his father; Kaser (1971–5: I. 284).) The passage is discussed in detail e.g. in Schmeling (1974: 98 f.), G. Anderson (1982: 13 f.); but cf. p. 120 above and n. 39.

The contrast between the *imago* of the fair, chaste and the dark, sexually dangerous woman is morally critical only in Xenophon and Heliodorus: on the one side there is the erotically passive, chaste, faithful, 'good' protagonist, the Greek—on the other side there is the erotically active, scheming, unrestrainedly raving antagonist, the Barbarian.

This splitting up of womanhood into two designs, the white and the scarlet woman, displays almost pathological features in the last representative of the genre, Heliodorus: his anti-heroines become veritable visions of terror. Their unbridled sexuality results in a catalogue of fatal qualities, which are represented as necessarily attendant phenomena of their dangerous voluptuousness: they are double-dealing, vindictive, cruel murderesses, even ἀρχέκακον (I. 9. I), evil itself; even the expression 'animal' is used (θηρίον, 7. 24. 5). This demonization of female eroticism corresponds to the increasing prudery and almost aggressive virginity of the main character who represents positive femininity. Charicleia finally directs—and this is new to the genre—chastity speeches and measures even against her own fiancé—*ad nauseam* for today's reader, but with the full consent, as the reception history shows, of the early Christian, Byzantine, and Baroque eras.[68] Although the anti-heroines' perspectives, especially their dark desires, are followed up for long passages with great interest, thus vividly describing the fantasies of fear which are caused by female eroticism,[69] the increasingly didactic tendency ensures that there remains no uncertainty whatsoever as to which model of femininity is recommended, especially to the female reader.

[68] G. Anderson (1982: 38) discovers (consciously) comic features in Heliodorus' chastity theme and pruderies; I consider their humour—from our late 20th-c. point of view—to be in fact involuntary. The references under consideration here prove at any rate that what was appreciated was precisely the seriousness of the novel's sexual mores. By early Christian reception I mean esp. the apocryphal Acts of the Apostles, which are full of this kind of chastity speech; cf. already Söder (1932: 119f.). For further discussion of the *Nachleben* cf. Gärtner (1969) and Sandy (1982a: 95f.).

[69] This threat is still piquantly amusing in Achilles Tatius, sinister in Xenophon, and deadly in Heliodorus. Besides his great picture of fatal, untamed female passion in the person of Arsace, who follows the long tradition of Euripides' Phaedra, the Rhodopis episode (2. 25) becomes almost pathological (and esp. close to the opinions of several early Church Fathers) with the concentration of Calasiris' erotic feelings on this woman's almost demonic (and demonized) sexuality alone. As an ascetic self-punishment for his desire, the prophet gives up his position and homeland.

The Byzantine critic Philippos quoted at the beginning probably did not misread these signals in the texts after all, when he stresses the deterrent effect, which the ever-terrible ending of the passionate anti-heroine is supposed to evoke. He accounts for the fact that Heliodorus features more corrupt female than bad male persons with the explanation that κακία (evil) is simply 'implanted more deeply' (ἐνέσπαρται) in the female sex—a fair Christian interpretation. Here the reader's attention is to be called at least in passing to the entirely parallel bipolarization of the female image and the very similar negative views on 'demonic' female eroticism found in at least two pagan novels (those of Xenophon and Heliodorus) and early Christian literature—not only in the Acts of the Apostles, which follow the literary tradition of the Greek novel anyway—but especially in patristic literature.

HEROINE AND READER: AN ATTEMPT AT COMPARISON

To return to the initial question: What actually does constitute our female protagonists' oft-mentioned 'superiority'? Where does their strength come from? Their 'moral predominance' stated since Erwin Rohde appears mainly to have been justified in reception history by an erotic faithfulness which is superior to that of the men and by a more unswerving constancy when their virginity is subject to temptation. In addition to that, several heroines—especially Chariton's Callirhoe and Heliodorus' Charicleia—distinguish themselves by greater beauty, moral strength, wisdom and power of judgement—or additionally by a greater personal ability to force their point.[70] Indeed, in private and public spheres alike the women

[70] Critics have often commented negatively on the contrastingly relative weakness or 'sentimentality' found in the male protagonists, e.g. Sandy (1982a: 60), 'The portrayal of Theagenes is most disappointing'; Helms (1966: 28) on Chaereas' characterization: 'The result, though doubtless appealing to the reader of that day, now conveys the impression of extreme weakness'; Reardon (1969: 303) on Heliodorus: 'It may be that after all the psychology of the heroine offers more interest. For her intended mate Theagenes, athletic though he may be . . . has no more influence on this strong-minded and not very lovable young woman than has the tanist of fertility ritual on the queen of the matriarchal tribe', or G. Anderson (1984: 64): 'Chaereas and Theagenes do indeed tend to emerge as puppets, without any profile other than as consorts of the beloved'. I quote only the most recent statements: earlier interpreters' criticisms of the novels' heroes, who corresponded little with those scholars' ideal of masculinity, is far severer.

of the novels display remarkable strength of mind and a strongly marked personality. But it is basically only their erotic aura and sexual attractiveness which grants them their power over other people, mostly of course over men, and which they use in order to control their surroundings.[71] It is their power to fascinate as women that on its own provides them with any influence in life and the opportunity to manipulate those with real power. Other possibilities of asserting their interests or of taking up action on their own are granted to them only to a small extent, at any rate to a substantially lesser degree than they were granted in contemporary reality. This may be made clear by briefly contrasting several aspects of marriage law, on the one hand as known from papyri from Hellenistic and imperial Egypt,[72] on the other hand as expressed in the Greek novels. This provides us with the possibility of comparing literary description with contemporary reality, using the method of reception aesthetics.[73]

[71] For Chariton Reardon (1982a: 8f.) sees in the rivals' actions, which are motivated by Callirhoe's beauty, the underlying structure of the level of action: 'The central structure . . . , the body of what happens, is a series of agones: Chaereas' rivals . . . This central problem, this central rivalry, arises from Callirhoe's beauty.' At the same time he states that on another, affective level, Callirhoe is 'the emotional centre of the story' (12). By this he aptly describes the constellation which forms the foundation of the ideology of the feminine, and not only in this novel. The female protagonist is the emotional centre; on the other hand she is portrayed as virtually powerless and unable to act.

[72] A standard modern work on the Greek private law of this period, which embraces the results of research in papyrology and the history of law, is still a desideratum—though promised long ago by H. J. Wolff (1978: xi), it still does not exist and might recede still further following his death in 1983. Juridical practice in matters to do with women and families has, however, been the subject of considerable interest in both sciences: e.g. Modrzejewski (1970 and 1981), H. J. Wolff (1952, 1957, 1965, and 1973), Taubenschlag (1955 and 1959), Häge (1968), Vatin (1970), Kaser (1971–5), Mitteis (1891). These studies have been utilized in the following. I shall treat this problem more thoroughly in my dissertation (see n. 8).

[73] Scarcella (1976) compares marriage laws and customs in Heliodorus only with the (in reality long since obsolete) law of classical Athens, or else with sources from pre-Hellenistic times. By so doing, he admittedly explains the literary background of this novel's juridical conceptions and its author's historical knowledge, but not the references to the contemporary reality of the novels and their ancient audience, which I am interested in. Deviations from classical legal practice and theory are only labelled tersely by Scarcella as 'anachronisms' in a historical novel which aims to 'ricostruire il paesaggio socio-culturale dell'età attica' (95). Hardly helpful and factually incorrect is Calderini (1959), who also draws only on Attic law as a background for both novels and papyri.

Legal facts are only rarely the concerns of our Greek love stories. The legal foundations of the unions of the two protagonists or of the minor characters are, as is

In real life, the situation where women lacked personal rights, so notorious in the classical Athens of the fifth and fourth centuries, had long since become obsolete.[74] The marriage documents of the time in which our novels were written and read illustrate women's considerable independence and juridical autonomy, especially where marriage was concerned. Brides sign their marriage contracts themselves—with their father or mother as adviser—but also on their own. They give themselves into marriage, following the principle of so-called *autoekdosis*: occasionally they even bring along their own dowry, their personal property, sometimes even earned by themselves.[75]

In the novels' literary presentation, however, it is entirely up to the fathers to give their children, especially their daughters, in marriage; nor do they ask for their mothers' opinion on the matter.[76] This patriarchal power over marriage may certainly be

suitable for the genre, of secondary importance only compared with the description of their feelings and the romantic aspects. The sentimental aspects are at the centre of interest—despite the pleasure the authors take in depicting court scenes with their rhetoric and their juridical sophisms. Typically, oaths of faithfulness and protestations of love are described, but hardly ever a concrete marriage contract; one speaks of the magnificence of the wedding celebrations, only rarely of the dowry. The carefree wealth of the central characters' families is a *topos*, the actual circumstances of property and inheritance remain unmentioned. Socio-historical realism is in most cases not intended by the Greek novels (the one still most productive in this regard is Longus, cf. Scarcella (1970 and 1977)). Occasionally, relevant hints in the texts, in addition to the observation of implicitly presupposed legal conditions, allow a comparison with the historical reality of Graeco-Roman Egypt. In the following the different aspects of marriage law are exemplified only by the practice of giving away in marriage.

[74] This needs to be stressed, as the dependent and degraded position of the Greek middle-class females in Attic law, in the way it is represented esp. in the 4th-c. orators, is often generalized as the common Greek 'female condition'. But esp. in the sphere of private and family law great changes had occurred: a woman appears as a juridical subject with the legal capacity to contract business and own property, and her subjection to a family guardianship is now purely formal. One can, I think, agree with H. J. Wolff (1952: 164f., 180 and 1957: 168), that the historical background to the emancipation of the Greek woman in family law and the law of property is the loosening of the *oikos*-structure, which went hand in hand with the ending of democratic *polis*-organization and the new formations of society during the Hellenistic monarchies, and resulted in a weakening of the classical *patria potestas* and a strengthening of the rights of individuals including those of female family members.

[75] A list of papyri with marriage contracts is given in Montevecchi (1936), supplemented in ead. (1973: 204f.). Reviews in Modrzejewski (1981: 248f.); Taubenschlag (1955: 120f.); Vatin (1970: 165f., 200f.); Häge (1968: 24f., 132); Préaux (1959: 147f.).

[76] e.g. Chariton 1. 1. 11; Longus 1. 19. 1, 3. 26. 1, 4. 36. 2; X. Eph. 2. 5. 6

opposed to the genre's need for and finally always victorious ideal of a love match, and can thus form the first motif of the perils of love and the reason for conflict between the generations leading to an elopement from the parental home;[77] but it is never questioned as a matter of principle. The nupturients' consent does not appear to be juridically necessary in the novel. The girl's opinion is not obtained—the most blatant example is the case of Callirhoe (the parents show the bridegroom in—and she does not know who he is, 1. 1. 14) or of Leucippe (the father even engages her by letter, *in absentia*, 5. 10. 4). It is part of the requirements of the happy ending that the protagonists finally do get their lovers for their husbands—from the point of view of the ignorant girls this disposition is a happy accident and a passive experience.[78]

Only when marrying away from home does the bride encounter the custom of *autoekdosis*, for example Callirhoe's wedding in Miletus (Chariton 3. 2), Anthia's in Tarsus (Xenophon 2. 13. 8)—but these marriages are enforced by physical and psychological pressure. These emergency marriages, into which the daughter was not given by her father, are inevitably doomed to failure—they are not considered valid by the novels' ethos.[79] Heliodorus'

(otherwise mostly 'οἱ πατέρες'); Ach. Tat. 1. 3. 2, 2. 13. 2; Heliod. 5. 19. 1, 6. 8. 1. The mothers sometimes have mediating functions—e.g. in Longus 3. 25. 2f., 26. 2; Heliod. 10. 30—but no authority. Only Heliodorus preserves rudimentary traces of the ethical law principle: εἰ δὲ γάμος τὸ γινόμενον (here lawful marriage in contrast to rape in accordance with the martial law of booty) τὸ παρ' ἀμφωτέρων βούλημα συννεύειν ἀναγκαῖον ('But in the case of marriage the consent of both parties is needed', 1. 21. 2)—here he makes the mistake of an 'anachronism'; apart from that he is very ambivalent concerning *patria potestas* in marriage matters; cf. Scarcella (1976). Only in the *Historia Apollonii* does a father allow his daughter to choose her husband absolutely freely: 'illa sibi eligat, quem voluerit habere maritum' (RA 19); after she has decided he says: 'quod filia mea cupit, hoc est et meum votum' (RA 21) and 'ego tibi vere consentio' (22).

[77] In Achilles Tatius and Heliodorus (the escape from Delphi).

[78] The fathers choose their sons- and daughters-in-law because of political considerations (Chariton), an oracle (Xenophon), family connections (Heliodorus, Achilles Tatius), high social status (Achilles Tatius, Longus). Only Charicleia—twice—opposes her fathers' wishes: the marriage with her first cousin in Delphi (Heliod. 2. 33), and the one with her second cousin in Meroe (10. 24f.). The first marriage is even avoided by her eloping with Theagenes—though only from her foster-father's power; her natural father Hydaspes' *patria potestas* remains untouched. The discussion in which she has to answer to her parents for her self-chosen bridegroom becomes very embarrassing and difficult (10. 29f.). Cf. Winkler (1982: 132).

[79] All marriages in the novels involving *autoekdosis* also happen to be the second marriage for the bride (in addition to the two cases already mentioned: Melite, Ach. Tat. 5. 14. 2 and Charicleia, Heliod. 1. 21—though she is not yet married *de facto*, she is already 'married' ideally). This facilitates the circumvention of the father's

Charicleia travels half the world in order to marry with her true parents' consent (and, by doing this, to find her home, identity, and 'female destiny').[80] Literary imagination, as these aspects of marriage law already show, falls behind contemporary reality. The lack of juridical self-determination and actual economic independence which characterizes the women of the novels is actually a return to conditions which had long since been part of history. The real female readers' lives were far more emancipated than those of the novels' heroines.[81]

The archaizing tendency of the female image is in part explained by literary tradition, because its images of women (which themselves of course are projections too) surely had some influence on the design of the characters in the novels. Besides, the novels present themselves as more or less historical,[82] which may help to explain additional anachronistic features of the sexual stereotypes. Our question, however, concerns the function of these archaizing women's roles for the readers.

In this regard it is relevant to enquire into the particular connection in the image of the woman between on the one hand the actual, concrete inability to act and the lack of self-determination,

consent. In a brilliant tragicomic court scene, which allows Chariton to display all his rhetorical, dramatic, and ironical skills, and at the climax of which (5. 8. 1 f.) both husbands of Callirhoe, Chaereas and Dionysius, collide stichomythically, the two forms of marriage—the father's giving away in marriage and the bride's giving away of herself—confront one other: πατὴρ ἐξέδωκεν ('her father married her to me'), cries Chaereas, ἐμοὶ δὲ ἑαυτήν ('she married me herself'), answers Dionysius— each one of the two rivals believes his own marriage to be the only valid one. The two forms may count as juridical equivalents in reality, otherwise the narrator, who is doubtless well versed in legal practice, would have made one of the opponents profit by such an advantage (Callirhoe, by the way, remains a dumb object in this scene)—but they may not count as equivalents in the novels' morality.

[80] 4. 13. 13 γένος μὲν καὶ πατρίδα καὶ τοὺς φύντας κομίζεσθαι Θεαγένει δὲ ἀνδρὶ συνεῖναι. At 4. 18. 5 she has Theagenes swear ὡς οὔτε ὁμιλήσει τὰ Ἀφροδίτης πρότερον ἢ γένος τε καὶ οἶκον τὸν ἡμέτερον ἀπολαβεῖν ('that he will have no carnal knowledge of me before I regain my home and people'). On the absolute respect for paternal authority as the basic requirement of a legal marriage and thus the sanction of daughters' sexual praxis in the novel cf. e.g. Ach. Tat. 8. 5. 8 (Leucippe) and 8. 18 (Calligone and Callisthenes) or the wedding night in Longus 4. 37, 40.

[81] I use the term 'emancipation' first in a juridical-economic, following that in a social and emotional sense. It must not be confused with the girls' isolation after losing their native land, their parental home, their male relatives' protection (which does not allow them any capacity for action), or with their emotional and personal equality or even superiority over the men in the novels.

[82] On the generally retrospective character of the literature of the time under discussion cf. van Groningen (1965), Bowie (1970), Reardon (1971).

and on the other hand her strong personal charisma and especially her immense erotic power. The woman who is able to control
the actual rulers with her sensuous personality, and thus
(apparently) turns the real relations of government upside down,
never—as long as she is a positive type—becomes a real danger;
she remains virginal and effectively powerless. Callirhoe, it is true,
has the four mightiest men of the eastern Persian Empire, including the Great King himself, worshipping at her feet. All their
actions and desires are directed at getting their hands on her;
because of her they even risk their position and power, their own
lives, wars—but she is not even allowed to decide for herself her
place of abode (Chariton 4. 8. 9) or to be informed about the
reason for the voyage to Babylon (4. 7. 8), not to mention choosing which of her husbands she wants to live with (6. 1. 1). It never
occurs to anybody to ask her.[83]

In order to exculpate or relieve the female reader in view of this
sexual omnipotence, it is stressed again and again that the beautiful protagonist is naïvely unconscious of her destructive abilities, or
else that she rejects or fears them.[84] If this effect is desired or sought
after, or if a woman in the novel possesses actual, not simply emotional and sexual, superiority, she necessarily has to be the female
antitype[85]—most prominent is Heliodorus' Arsace.

A further, specifically female, fantasy of wishful thinking and
omnipotence which is spread throughout the Greek novels is the
idea that men have nothing else to think about or do but adjust
their whole lives to their erotic interest in the heroine, and that
romantic life and love is absolutely central for them, too: 'The men

---

[83] 5. 9. 7 Queen Stateira asks her ὁπότερον ἄνδρα βούλοιτο μᾶλλον ('which man
she wanted as her husband'): Callirhoe only cries instead of giving an answer,
because she is conscious of how powerless she is during the decision of whose 'prize'
she is. Stateira's comfort (5. 9. 3) and the other women's pieces of advice (6. 1. 4)
are well meant, but in fact useless.

[84] e.g. Chariton 2. 7; 6. 6. 4; X. Eph. 5. 5. 5. Only Xenophon's Anthia attempts
to win erotic interest from Abrocomes (1. 3. 2)—who, to be sure, becomes her
husband, and the female protagonists before Charicleia are allowed to develop
sensuous feelings for their husbands (cf. also n. 65 for a quasi-religious interpretation of Anthia's erotic initiative). The splitting in two of female sexuality within one
protagonist—Leucippe—instead of the usual division between a protagonist and an
antagonist is analysed by Segal (1984: 84f.). On the influence on the readers cf.
Modleski (1982: 52f.)

[85] The bait of these fantasies of female power, esp. typical for the novels, is taken
even by modern critics, who mistake them for 'emancipation' or even 'symmetry of
the sexes'.

spend their full time plotting the seduction';[86] the woman's importance is stressed and enhanced.

The fundamental 'sexual politics' of the Greek novel can thus be interpreted in the following way. The real limitations of female life are confirmed in literature and drawn even more strictly than in contemporary reality (*inter alia* by an archaizing return to a past with stricter rules for the roles of the sexes); at the same time, the wish for influence and power of decision-making is deflected and pacified by the illusion of the women's invincible emotional and sexual fascination. Real claims to decide for themselves or others are missing or denounced by the most appalling concomitant circumstances. This image of the feminine which typifies the genre, on the one hand idealizing and elevating, on the other hand archaizing and restrictive, was obviously approved of by ancient readers. The imaginary presentation of the roles of the sexes so described formed, we may suppose, a major ingredient in the genre's success—among its male and female readers. With reference to the female reader it has to be stressed that the background role of the other female characters, mentioned above, and their devaluation in comparison to the protagonist, together with other narrative techniques, promote a strong sense of identification during reading of the novels. A few conjectures on the sort of identification engendered by a reading of the last novel about the fair and prudent Charicleia may serve as a conclusion.

I have already called her a—to some extent—emancipated intellectual and the girl with three fathers. She is a priestess of Artemis in Delphi, studies and discusses with the philosophers and theologians of this town, lives alone—not in her father's house—and enjoys her public position.[87] This 'masculine' life has the price of virginity. Charicleia thus obstinately rejects love and marriage. Despite the pleadings of her father, who wants to have descendants, she rejects her 'female nature'; she beats him with his own weapons: her superior education and rhetoric.[88] Motherless, raised

[86] Modleski (1982: 18). Also think of the Callisthenes episode in Achilles Tatius ('a reformed-rake plot', ibid.) or of Chariton's potentates.

[87] Heliod. 3. 6. 2f.; 2. 33. 7 οὔτε γὰρ ἀπρόσμικτος ἐκείνη πρὸς τοὺς λογίους τῶν ἀνδρῶν ἀλλὰ τὸ πλεῖστον τούτοις συνόμιλος ἐπαρθενεύθη καὶ οἴκησιν οἰκεῖ . . . ἐνταῦθα, ἐντός φημι τοῦ περιβόλου καὶ περὶ τὸν νεών.

[88] 2. 33. 6; 2. 33. 5. This refusal deeply wounds her father (2. 33. 4), who wants to have grandchildren (2. 33. 7)—her Artemisian enthusiasm and rigid determination finally drive him into using Egyptian magic as the ultimate means against her opposition (2. 33. 6). Cf. n. 33.

among men only, she despises the social role of a wife and wants
to remain a priestess for ever. And then she falls in love after
all, with the equally beautiful Theagenes—and after some inner
struggle gives up all her gains, and submits to the female 'destiny'
(4. 11).[89]

If we grant the ancient female reader a sense of identification
when she reads this novel, the following picture emerges: Heliodorus complies well with his female recipients' fantasies of escapism
and power by stressing his heroine's unusual life in Delphi as well
as the extraordinary success of her beauty in the manner described.
But he already regulates this effect by the narrative trick of telling
her story through Calasiris' evaluative narratival viewpoint, and
eventually deflects, and finally blunts, these fantasies by the turn
he gives to Charicleia's fate.[90]

[89] 2. 33. 6 γνωρίσαι τὴν ἑαυτῆς φύσιν καὶ ὅτι γυνὴ γέγονεν εἰδέναι ('to acknowledge
her own nature and realize that she is a woman').

[90] I want to thank Barbara von Reibnitz and Peter Habermehl for all their
encouragement and improvements during discussion of this paper.

6

Callirhoe and *Parthenope*: The Beginnings of the Historical Novel

TOMAS HÄGG

The aim of the present paper is to discuss whether, or in what sense, we are entitled to describe as historical novels two of the Greek novels of antiquity, Chariton's *Chaereas and Callirhoe*, which survives in full, and the only fragmentarily (and anonymously) preserved novel of *Metiochus and Parthenope*, both possibly to be placed as early as the first century BC (hereafter *Callirhoe* and *Parthenope*, respectively).[1] Applying the term *historical novel* to these two works means questioning two common assumptions, one generally held by historians of modern literature and the other by classical scholars. Literary historians almost unanimously state that the historical novel is a creation of the early nineteenth century, or, more precisely, of Sir Walter Scott, whose *Waverley* was first published in 1814.[2] Classicists, on the other hand, do sometimes use the term

A shorter version of this paper was presented at a King's College London (KQC) symposium on 'The Greek Novel, AD 1-1985,' 24-6 March 1986, and appeared in a book of that title. [*Editor's note*: See Beaton (1988).] My thanks are due to the organizers and participants of the symposium; to Bryan Reardon, who was unable to take part in person in the symposium, for reading and commenting on the paper afterward; and to the anonymous referees of *Classical Antiquity*.

[1] *Callirhoe*, simply, may in fact have been the original title of Chariton's novel; see Plepelits (1976: 28f.) and Lucke and Schäfer (1985: 181) and cf. Reardon (1982*a*: 13 n. 22), and the analogous title *Parthenope* would well suit the anonymous novel with its apparent emphasis on the heroine and obvious play on her 'speaking name.' There is at least—*pace* Weinreich (1950/1962: 28) and Treu (1984: 457f.)—no evidence for these two 'historical' novels having originally had titles like historical or geographical works, such as *Sicelica*, *Samiaca*. This type was probably introduced later (*Ephesiaca*, *Aethiopica*), as were the double names (*Leucippe and Clitophon*, etc.). Cf. n. 60 below.

[2] 'To all intents and purposes the historical novel sprang to life, fully accoutred and mature, with the appearance of *Waverley* in 1814': thus Sanders (1978: ix), expressing the *communis opinio*; already Manzoni (1953: 1061) called Scott 'l'Omero del romanzo storico.' Cf., for the same sentiment, Lukács (1962: 19 and

historical novel/romance (*historischer Roman, roman historique*, etc.)
for ancient literary compositions, but then mostly with reference to
such works as Xenophon's *Cyropaedia* or the *Alexander Romance* of
Pseudo-Callisthenes, so calling them in order to distinguish them
from the so-called ideal Greek novel; I have followed that practice
myself earlier.[3] My present contention, however, is that, if we
speak at all of historical novels in antiquity, the ones that best
qualify for that description are *Callirhoe* and *Parthenope*.[4] To demonstrate this, I will first discuss terminology, definitions, and criteria
for the historical novel, as the term is used today. However, I hope
it will be clear that this is not just a theoretical exercise—nor, for
that matter, a naive attempt to vindicate another literary genre or
subgenre for antiquity—but that the discussion is meant to shed
some light on the character and purpose of the two ancient works
themselves.

Now, what *is* a historical novel? How is the term generally
defined by modern theorists and historians of literature, and what
criteria can we employ to decide whether a given novel is also a
historical novel? My concern is not, primarily, to distinguish
between *historical novel* and *historiography*, though that much-
debated question cannot be eschewed altogether,[5] but precisely to
distinguish between *novel* in general and *historical novel* in particular. Unfortunately, a look through the standard works on literary
theory and genre theory yields surprisingly few and disappointingly
vague answers to these questions. The term *historical novel* (etc.)
is used not infrequently, but is almost never defined—except
implicitly, in that it is mostly made to refer to works by Scott himself or some of his nineteenth-century followers: to Manzoni's *I pro-*

---

passim), Fleishman (1971: 25; cf. 23), and Hook (1985: 9f.); less categorically,
H. Shaw (1983: 31). See also the illuminating remarks of C. Lamont (1986: xivf.),
in substance identical with Lamont's large edn. (Oxford, 1981), xvi f.; my references
to *Waverley* will be to the paperback World's Classics edn. of 1986, which reproduces the 1814 text of the novel but also appends Scott's later prefaces and notes.

    [3] Hägg (1983: 125).
    [4] I find this view expressed earlier only by H. Maehler (1976: 19) (similarly
Maehler in Reardon (1977: 50f.) and by A. Dihle (1978: 54f.).
    [5] See, with regard to ancient literature, in particular B. E. Perry (1967: 32ff.),
and the penetrating remarks of Morgan (1982: 223–5). Cf. also Reardon (1969:
295 with n. 12; 1971: 315) and Treu (1984: 456–9). For a professional historian's
mixed feelings towards the genre 'historical fiction' exemplified by the *Historia
Augusta*, Yourcenar's *Mémoires d'Hadrien* and some modern historians (!), see now
Sir Ronald Syme's amusing essay *Fictional History Old and New* (1986); cf. also, in
quite another spirit, Helen Cam's *Historical Novels* (1961).

messi sposi or Hugo's *Notre-Dame de Paris*, to Dickens' *A Tale of Two Cities*, Tolstoi's *War and Peace*, Sienkiewicz's *Quo Vadis?* and so on. As Avrom Fleishman remarks: 'Everyone knows what a historical novel is; perhaps that is why few have volunteered to define it in print.'[6] Joseph Turner speaks of 'the morass of defining historical fiction'; his own contribution, an article with the promising title 'The Kinds of Historical Fiction: An Essay in Definition and Methodology' (1979), is successful in criticizing others but unfortunately not of much help for our present purpose, his attempt at classification being based only on a handful of twentieth-century American novels.[7] A recent authoritative study by Alastair Fowler, which heralds a renaissance of critical interest in literary genres, acknowledges the historical novel as a distinct and 'true' subgenre of the novel but still does not attempt any definition of the term.[8]

In the absence of an authoritative definition, the best procedure will be first to assemble a number of criteria for the typical (modern) historical novel, by looking at the novels commonly and intuitively so called and drawing on the critical work done on them. Besides Georg Lukács' seminal but rather idiosyncratic monograph of 1937, *The Historical Novel*,[9] the critical studies that I have found most useful are the book by Avrom Fleishman already mentioned[10] and Harry Shaw's *The Forms of Historical Fiction*.[11] I have also profited from the more general reflections on the genre in Harry Henderson's and Andrew Sanders' works on the American

[6] Fleishman (1971: 3).

[7] J. W. Turner (1979: 333). Turner distinguishes between 'documented,', 'disguised,' and 'invented' historical novels, the three representing 'distinct stages along the continuum' (341). A kindred tripartition was attempted by M. Wehrli (1942: 89-109): 'historische Bellettristik (Reportage), kulturhistorischer Roman, sittlich-religiöse Geschichtsdichtung' (108), a typology based on and as much determined by *his* particular material, the German 'historical novel' of the last 150 years, as Turner's by his. P. Green (1962: 37), in turn, suggests the categories 'Propaganda, Education, and Escapism.'

[8] A. Fowler (1982: esp. 121f., 153f., 168). The important point is that Fowler admits of the historical novel as a more distinct 'kind' than others, such as factory novel or university novel, which are grouped together exclusively according to subject matter and setting (122); cf. H. Shaw (1983: 20). Wellek and Warren (1949/1963: 232f.) also dismiss 'a grouping based only on subject-matter, a purely sociological classification' (e.g. the ecclesiastical novel), but admit the historical novel 'because of [its] ties to the Romantic movement and to nationalism—because of the new feeling about, attitude towards, the past which it implies.'

[9] Lukács (1962).

[10] Fleishman (1971), esp. ch. 1, 'Towards a Theory of Historical Fiction' and ch. 2, 'Origins: The Historical Novel in the Age of History.' Cf. also Fleishman (1978).

[11] H. E. Shaw (1983), esp. ch. 1, 'An Approach to the Historical Novel.'

and the Victorian historical novel, respectively.[12] The highly read-
able essay by Herbert Butterfield, *The Historical Novel*, has less
to offer in this connection, since its main concern is the relation
between the historical novel and history proper.[13] Something can
also be gathered from prefaces or postscripts to historical novels,
in which their authors, from Scott to Mary Renault,[14] have contributed to the critical elucidation of the genre; special mention
should be made of Alessandro Manzoni's essay 'Del romanzo storico
e, in genere, de' componimenti misti di storia e d'invenzione.'[15]
Finally, it is possible to check the more popular or intuitive concept
of the historical novel in a work like Daniel McGarry and Sarah
Harriman White's *Historical Fiction Guide*, an 'annotated chronological, geographical and topical list of five thousand selected historical novels,' compiled to meet the needs of librarians, teachers,
and readers of this vast popular literature.[16] It provides a healthy
counterbalance to the severe exclusiveness of a Lukács, in whose
eyes not many novels qualify as truly historical, whatever their
authors may have intended or the general reader may think he is
reading.

Time. Though it may be argued, and indeed not seldom is
argued, that 'all novels are historical novels, since they are set in
historical time and social reality,'[17] normal usage reserves the term
for novels set at least one or two generations back; it is customary
to refer to Scott's subtitle to *Waverley*, ''Tis Sixty Years Since,' as
indicating something of an ideal, or of a minimum.[18] Others,
then, are 'novels of the recent past'[19] or 'contemporary novels.'
Another essential criterion would be that the historical constituents

---

[12] Henderson (1974); Sanders (1978).

[13] Butterfield (1924). P. Green (1962) is another stimulating, but not too systematic, discussion of the subject.

[14] For Mary Renault's 'Notes on *The King Must Die*,' see McCormack (1969:
80-7).

[15] *c*.1851; repr. in Manzoni (1953: 1055-1114), now also in Eng. trans., with
a useful introduction by S. Bermann. The most recent detailed statement is that of
Umberto Eco (1983: esp. 73-7).

[16] McGarry and White (1963); quotation is the subtitle.

[17] Quoted from Fleishman (1971: 15 n. 9), who does not himself accept this
view. Cf. also Henderson (1974: xvif.), Turner (1979: 339f.), and H. Shaw (1983:
29 with n. 16), who advances as a criterion the 'desire to depict history.'

[18] For Scott's own comment, see *Waverley*, I. 1 (Lamont 1986: 4). Cf. Fleishman
(1971: 3, 24) and Sanders (1978: x, 11).

[19] Cf. Fleishman (1971: 3, 146) and H. Shaw (1988: 38), both referring for the
term to Tillotson (1954: 92f.). An example is Thackeray's *Vanity Fair*.

of the novel are 'researched rather than remembered,'[20] i.e., that the author has not himself experienced them but has had to rely mostly on written or oral sources.[21] There is, in principle, no corresponding limit backwards in time, although novels set in a dim prehistoric or mythological past may have difficulties with one or two other criteria to be mentioned below.

What matters, apparently, is only the span of time between the events narrated and the composition of the novel, not that between the events and the *reading*. A contemporary novel does not, technically, become a historical novel with the passage of time, even if it is true, for instance, that 'the novels of Trollope were read primarily as romances [i.e., historical novels] during the Second World War,' as Northrop Frye notes.[22] The convention may be studied in applied form in McGarry and White's selection of 5,000 historical novels. According to their definition, 'fiction is historical if it includes reference to customs, conditions, identifiable persons, or events *in the past*' (my italics).[23] In spite of the book's practical and pedagogical purpose of listing works from which the reader can learn about different periods of history, 'in the past' is obviously seen just in relation to the author. For instance, among the books listed as illustrating the history of the United States 1865–1900,[24] the vast majority were written in the twentieth century; a contemporary novel of the period does not qualify, however much history it may teach *us*. In Herbert Butterfield's words, 'a true "historical novel" is one that is historical in its intention and not simply by accident, one that comes from a mind steeped in the past.'[25]

Characters. The typical historical novel deals with fictitious characters—that is, after all, what makes it a novel—in a historical setting: the focus of attention is the personal experiences and

[20] Sanders (1978: 11; cf. ix); cf. Henderson (1974: xvi): '"set" in the unexperienced past, in the world that existed before the author was born.'
[21] On Scott's mixture of oral and written sources, see Lamont (1986: xv–xix; 1981: xvii–xxi) and cf. Scott's own comments in the last ch. of *Waverley* (Lamont 1986: 340 ff.) and in the various prefatory materials added in 1829 (pp. 348, 352 f., 388).
[22] Frye (1957: 307).
[23] McGarry and White (1963: [4]).
[24] Ibid. 417–45.
[25] Butterfield (1924: 4 f.); cf. H. Shaw (1983: 30): 'they [sc. standard historical novels] are also united, in a minimal way, by incorporating within their systems of fictional probability *a sense of the past as past*' (my italics).

concerns of private individuals.[26] As Wolfgang Kayser observes, while the epic has Odysseus as the main character, the novel features a certain Tom Jones or Ivanhoe.[27] But to make the novel historical, we expect real historical figures to appear as well,[28] ideally mixing with the fictitious ones so as to create a 'mixture of the real and the imaginary on the same plane of representation.'[29] For instance, in *Waverley* Prince Charles Edward and Colonel Gardiner are historical, but all the main characters fictitious.[30] The depth of characterization of the historical and fictional characters alike—whether historical verisimilitude is achieved, individually or generally—is another matter, to be dealt with under 'Truth,' below.

Setting. According to Avrom Fleishman, 'there is an unspoken assumption that the plot must include a number of "historical" events, particularly those in the public sphere (war, politics, economic change, etc.), mingled with and affecting the personal fortunes of the characters.'[31] Thus, a general historical background is not enough, unless specific events and figures are identified and brought into relationship with the fictitious characters. This is what makes novels set in a prehistoric milieu, or whenever written documentation of persons and events is lacking, less typically historical: they lack the peculiar appeal deriving from the juxtaposition of the real and the imaginary. At the other end of the scale we meet works that are too seriously documentary to allow the fictitious elements really to mingle with the historical ones: while *War and Peace* of course admirably mixes fact with fiction,

[26] Cf. Butterfield (1924: 67, 79) and H. Shaw (1983: 49). Scott says in *Waverley*, I.I (Lamont 1986: 4f.): 'my tale is more a description of men than manners,' and speaks of 'throwing the force of my narrative upon the characters and passions of the actors.'

[27] Kayser (1948: 360f.).

[28] Cf. Fleishman (1971: 3): 'it is necessary to include at least one such figure in a novel if it is to qualify as historical'; Turner (1979: 336) rightly modifies this saying that it 'may not be a necessary condition . . . but it comes very close to being a sufficient one'. To McGarry and White (1963: [4]), depiction of 'the everyday way of life, outlook, mores, and living conditions' is enough.

[29] Fleishman (1978: 53). For the problems involved, cf. Manzoni (1953: 1061f.) and Riikonen (1978: 24f.).

[30] See Lamont (1986: xif.; 1981: xiiif.), who adds: 'This is a formula for characterization which has proved favourable to the historical novel.' Similarly, but with reference already to the Greek novels, Treu (1984: 458): 'Das Rezept war von überzeitlicher Effizienz.'

[31] Fleishman (1971: 3); cf. his application of this criterion to novels by Hardy, Golding, and Thackeray (1971: 179 and 257 with n. 18; 1978: 53).

Solzhenitsyn's *August 1914* would probably not qualify as a typical historical novel for this very reason.[32]

The setting necessarily includes not only a certain period and certain historical events, but also the physical milieu. 'History is rooted in geography,' says Herbert Butterfield, 'and the historical novel, which is a novel that seeks to be rooted in some ways in actuality, finds one of its roots in geography.'[33] The author's research, mentioned above under 'Time,' thus applies to both history and geography (topography, ethnography, etc.), and so does the issue of accuracy, or 'Truth,' to be discussed next.

'Truth,' or historical probability. In one way or another, the reader of a historical novel is apt to demand some kind of truth, as far as the historical (or geographical, etc.) elements are concerned.[34] The naive reader expects that the dates will be correct, the important historical events correctly described, the historical places and figures depicted true to life. The sophisticated reader may look for a deeper kind of truth, 'an artistically faithful image of a concrete historical epoch,' to quote Georg Lukács.[35] He distinguishes between 'novels with historical themes,' of which there are many, and the genuinely historical novel, created by Scott but not achieved by many of his followers. Whereas the naive reader expects the historical figures to be 'true,' a Lukács lets this demand apply as much to the purely fictitious ones: a crucial criterion for the historical novel is the 'derivation of the individuality of characters from the historical peculiarity of their age.'[36] 'What makes a historical novel historical is the active presence of a concept of history as a shaping force,' says Fleishman.[37] To these critics, history as costume or masquerade is not enough to make a novel historical, however accurate the costume may be; the characters behind the masks must not be the contemporaries of the author but should as far as possible appear as being historically true. On the other hand, the propagators of this sophisticated approach tend to pay less attention to mistakes in the external

[32] I owe the example of *August 1914* to Jonas Palm. Cf. C. Moody's *Solzhenitsyn* (1976: 172 ff.), developing the comparison with *War and Peace* (and noting that Solzhenitsyn himself is anxious not to call *August 1914* a novel).

[33] Butterfield (1924: 41); cf. Fleishman (1971: xv) and H. Shaw (1983: 25 f.).

[34] Cf. Fleishman (1971: 4).

[35] Lukács (1962: 19).

[36] Ibid.; similarly Fleishman (1971: 10-12). Contrast Mary Renault's penetrating remarks (McCormack 1969: 84 f.).

[37] Fleishman (1971: 15, and cf. 25).

historical frame—anachronisms—so long as the historical verisimilitude is preserved. Few would deny that Scott's *Redgauntlet*,
though describing a third, purely imaginary Jacobite rebellion
and combining historical facts from three different decades of the
eighteenth century, nevertheless is a historical novel.[38]

As far as 'truth' is concerned, it is evident that no single,
generally applicable criterion can be formulated; there is too great
a gap between the popular, or intuitive, and the sophisticated, or
scholarly, view. An interesting middle way, however, is indicated
by Harry Shaw, who (against Lukács, Fleishman, and others)
argues that 'no single quality of historical insight defines historical
fiction,' merely demanding from the author 'the recognition of "the
past as past,"' 'the realization that history is comprised of ages and
societies that are significantly different from our own.'[39] (There will
be occasion to return to this discussion below in dealing with the
Greek potentially historical novels.) In the end, however, the lack
of agreement on this crucial point, which of course affects the other
groups of criteria as well, is just a reflection of the more general
issue of how to define or delimit literature as an object of scholarly
study. When distinguishing between genres, for instance, are we
then concerned only with 'serious' literature, perhaps only with
acknowledged works of art, or with the whole spectrum of literature? Probably most of the 5,000 historical novels of the list
referred to above, though still constituting a selection according to
quality,[40] do not belong within the domains of traditional history
or theory of literature. Harry Henderson symptomatically speaks of
'the vulgarity of the genre,' branding it as (periodically at least)
'the dominant middle-brow reading entertainment.'[41] Thus a definition of the historical novel based on 'serious' literature only is
bound to leave homeless the largest part of the fiction generally
referred to as historical.

One way to avoid this difficulty is to take as the starting point a
definition of the novel itself which largely evades the question of

[38] See K. Sutherland in her World's Classics edn. of *Redgauntlet* (1985: vii–ix),
and cf. Lascelles (1980: 114–19), in the ch. called 'the Historical Event that Never
Happened.' On historical accuracy and historical probability in Scott generally, see
J. Anderson (1981: 89–92; cf. 33–5) and, starting from the problems raised by
Redgauntlet, Brown (1979: 151–94).

[39] H. Shaw (1983: 24, 26).

[40] McGarry and White (1963: [4]): 'only *better* works of historical fiction.'

[41] Henderson (1974: xv). Cf., on contempt for the genre, Fleishman (1971: xivf.,
36) and H. Shaw (1983: 9).

artistic quality. The *Concise Oxford Dictionary* (7th ed., 1982)
defines a *novel* as a 'fictitious prose narrative of book length por-
traying characters and actions credibly representative of real life in
continuous plot.' Add, after 'life,' 'of a certain historical period,'
and we have a general definition of our object of study, 'credibly'
smoothing over the difference between the naive and the sophisticated reader, or between the inclusive and the exclusive attitude.
For the present purpose, however, and on the basis of the groups
of criteria discussed above, I would venture a more elaborate (and
admittedly more arbitrary) definition of what I would call the
'typical historical novel': it is set in a period at least one or two
generations anterior to that of the author, communicating a sense
of the past as past; it is centered on fictitious characters, but puts
on stage as well, mingling with these, one or several figures known
from history; enacted in a realistic geographical setting, it describes
the effects upon the fortunes of the characters of (a succession of)
real historical events; it is—or gives the impression of being—true,
as far as the historical framework is concerned. It may also aim at
achieving an artistically true reconstruction of the historical period
in question and its way of life, making the characters typical representatives of their age and social milieu. Such an aim, or success
in achieving it, is not a prerequisite, however, for the classification;
as Harry Shaw pertinently remarks, 'it is more useful to discrimi-
nate between great and mediocre historical novels than to exclude
imperfect works from the group.'[42]

With this tentative definition in mind we proceed to the ancient
works which classical scholars are wont to call historical novels:
Xenophon's *Cyropaedia*, the *Alexander Romance*, Philostratus's *Life of
Apollonius*, to mention just the most obvious candidates. It is true
that there is no consensus regarding which works to include under
the generic heading *novel*, or how to divide the genre into subgenres; Heinrich Kuch in a recent article clearly demonstrates the
prevailing diversity of classification.[43] Some, like Ben Edwin Perry,
prefer to reserve the term *novel* (or *romance*) for the Roman 'comic'
and Greek 'ideal' types.[44] But insofar as the term *historical novel* is

---

[42] H. Shaw (1983: 28). Cf. 49: '*In the greatest historical fiction*, characters and
narrative sequences elucidate historical process' (my italics).

[43] Kuch (1985: 3–19). See also Scarcella (1981: 342 n. 4).

[44] Perry (1967: 34 f., 40 f., 84–7, 168); similarly C.-W. Müller (1981: 392) and,
in practice, Bowie (1985*a*: 683–99 [= this volume, ch. 2], 877–86). Scobie (1973:
84 f.) likewise excludes from his classification of the various types of romance 'fiction

used at all, it constantly refers to one or other of the works mentioned, and in particular to the *Alexander Romance*.[45] Kuch himself
is more cautious than most, as regards the appropriateness of the
designation: he regularly speaks of 'der sog. "historische" Roman';
while admitting it (under this name) as a subgenre, he notes that
every ancient novel refers, more or less, to historical conditions and
events; and he remarks that it was no genuine (*echt*) historical
novel in the modern sense.[46] But he gives no explanation for this
verdict, nor does he present any alternative, better-qualified candidates for the designation.

The *Alexander Romance* of Pseudo-Callisthenes easily qualifies
according to our 'Time' and 'Setting' criteria. Irrespective of which
stage we choose, the postulated Hellenistic sources or the final late-
antique compilation, the action is firmly placed in the past. I pick
out just one detail in the last chapter of the oldest extant version
(Rec. A, 3. 35):[47] it is stated there that the thirteen cities founded
by Alexander 'are still [μέχρι τοῦ νῦν] inhabited and peaceful,'
which implies a distant past. The basis is not, even fictitiously
(as in the *Troy Romances* of Dictys and Dares), the author's own
recollections, but, apparently, mostly written sources of a legendary character. The setting is historical, no matter how fancifully
transformed: we are made to follow a succession of historical
events, though in a peculiar order and freely mingled with purely
imaginary (or legendary) ones, and all is set in a factual Mediterranean and Oriental milieu, with the important exception of the
fantastic travel adventures in the Far East. The main characters
are all historical: Alexander the Great, King Philip of Macedon
and Queen Olympias, King Darius of Persia, Alexander's teacher
Aristotle, his friends and generals, and so on. The 'Truth' criterion
causes greater difficulties, even in its crudest sense. The overtly and
topically fantastic ingredients apart, there are in the more strictly
historical parts gross anachronisms and geographical blunders; but
it is uncertain to what extent the author himself or the popular

---

masquerading as history or biography'; and so does N. Holzberg (1994/1986) in
his recent survey (1986: 22–6): 'Romanhaft-fiktionale Biographie.'

[45] See e.g. Helm (1956: 8–19), 'Historische Romane' (e.g. *Cyr.*, *Alex.*, *Ninus*);
Mazal (1962–3), 'Der historische Roman (e.g. *Cyr*, *Alex.*, *Vita Ap.*); Grabar'-Passek
(1969; quoted from Kuch 1985; 3f.), 'der historische Roman' (e.g. *Alex.*); and
Loicq-Berger (1980: 26), 'le roman "historique"' (e.g. *Alex.*, *Vita Ap.*).

[46] Kuch (1985: 8, 16).

[47] Kroll (1926); Haight (1955).

audience to whom he obviously addressed himself noticed or cared about them. The unequivocal historicity of the central figure and his overall achievement probably satisfied most readers' demands in this respect, securing a kind of historical probability for the story at large.

The point at which the *Alexander Romance* clearly fails to be a typical historical novel belongs under 'Characters': this is not about the private experiences of fictitious characters in a historical setting, but the account, however romanticized, of the public life and exploits of a world-historical figure himself.[48] As Avrom Fleishman remarks, such figures are not generally likely to be selected by a novelist, being 'by definition exceptional,' while the novelist seeks 'the typical man . . . whose life is shaped by world-historical figures.'[49] Even if Fleishman, following Lukács, naturally refers to literary works on quite a different level of intention from the *Alexander Romance*, nevertheless the private individual as protagonist seems to be the normal choice for a historical novelist, at any level. Of course there are exceptions—one need only mention, among more recent works, Marguerite Yourcenar's *Mémoires d'Hadrien* and Robert Graves' *Claudius* books—but then the emphasis is still on the private or inner life of the world-historical figure. In the *Romance*, Alexander speaks much and writes letters, but mostly in direct relation to his official activities; his inner life is scarcely revealed (nor is he granted any sex life).

Yet the main generic problem with the *Alexander Romance* is not whether it should be classified as a historical novel, but whether it is a novel at all. Once we admit it as a novel, by necessity we have to call it historical, however untypical it may be for this subgenre. The same is true for the *Cyropaedia*, Xenophon's ideal image of a ruler, and, if we quickly move some six hundred years forward, for the *Life of Apollonius of Tyana* by Philostratus who, much more soberly than Pseudo-Callisthenes, draws up the historical framework for his story and even ostentatiously refers to written documentary sources.[50] The easiest way out, no doubt, is to refer to all

---

[48] A similar remark is to be found in E. Schwartz (1896/1943: 83; cf. 26), explicitly referring to Scott for the modern historical novel. Cf. Reardon (1971: 329) on *Nectanebus* and *Alex.*

[49] Fleishman (1971: 10f.).

[50] G. Anderson (1986: 232) characterizes the *Vita Ap.* as 'a sort of Alexander-romance with the elegance of the *Cyropaedia*.' He addresses the issue of novel versus romanticized biography on pp. 229–32. Palm (1976: 40) aptly suggests the

three and their cognates as *lives* (βίοι, *vitae*)[51] or, rather, as *romanticized biographies*, to mark the difference from the Plutarchian *life*. These works are highly relevant in any discussion of the borderline between historiography and historical fiction; but for the present purpose it will be enough just to state that the term *historical novel* does not very adequately cover the nature of any of them.

As is already foreshadowed in the title and introduction of the paper, a couple of the 'ideal' Greek novels are in my view better candidates for that label. It should at once be made clear, however, that it is not a question of substituting *historical* for *ideal*. A classification into genres, or subgenres, can be made from several different perspectives, such as outer form (prose, prosimetrum, verse; different kinds of verse), subject matter (historical, contemporary; love, adventure, travels, politics, etc.), attitude (ideal, sentimental, comic, realistic), and so on. The failure to realize this elementary truth has marred some of the earlier attempts to define subgenres of the Greek novel.[52] Now, from one point of view, the five extant 'ideal' novels and a number of fragments form a coherent group; from another, it is more meaningful to group at least one of them, Achilles Tatius' *Leucippe and Clitophon*, together with the Roman novels of Petronius and Apuleius as being contemporary, while Chariton's *Callirhoe* and the *Parthenope* are historical. Again, in that respect, though not in others, these two go together with the *Chion Novel*, which is a political and philosophical novel-in-letters.[53] All three do so, but less closely, with the group of romanticized biographies, if we allow them novel status, and with the pseudo-documentary war chronicles of Dictys and Dares.

Chariton's attachment to history is well known and has been the subject of much comment, though mostly regarding either his relation to historiography[54] or the historicity of his characters and events.[55] His attitude, as expressed in his choice of a historical set-

modern designation *documentary novel*; according to one's assessment of the authenticity of the documents cited by Philostratus, one may prefer *pseudo-documentary*.

[51] There is MS authority for the term βίος only in the case of the *Alexander Romance*, however; the so-called '*Vita*' *Apollonii* goes under the Greek title τὰ εἰς τὸν Τυανέα Ἀπολλώνιον.
[52] e.g. those of Scobie (1973) and Loicq-Berger (1980).
[53] See the introduction to Chion of Heraclea by Düring (1951) for the documentary sources on which this novel is based and a discussion of its purpose.
[54] See, in particular, W. Bartsch (1934: 6–34), and cf. Reardon (1982a: 15 n. 26).
[55] Perry (1930: 100–4 with n. 11) and additions in Perry (1967: 353 n. 25);

ting, has attracted less attention.[56] The first sentences of the novel
are of crucial importance:[57] 'I, Chariton of Aphrodisias, clerk to the
rhetor Athenagoras, am going to tell you the story of a love affair
which took place in Syracuse [πάθος ἐρωτικὸν ἐν Συρακούσαις
γενόμενον διηγήσομαι]. Hermocrates, the Syracusan general, the
man who defeated the Athenians, had a daughter by the name of
Callirhoe . . .' (1. 1. 1). The author firmly places himself in contemporary society and the plot of the novel in a distant heroic past.
By modeling his introductory sentence on those of the classical
historians he is not trying to pass as a historian[58]—contemporary
historiography did not use this formula—but to communicate,
right from the start, the spirit of the very age in which the plot is
set. And that plot, he hastens to say, is a love story: again not the
posture of a historian, but that of a deliberate and unconcealed
novelist. He plays on the same contrast between fact and fiction
when he ends his novel with the words τοσάδε περὶ Καλλιρόης συνέγραψα, 'This is my account of Callirhoe' (8. 8. 16), συγγράφειν
being the word used by authors of factual accounts in prose,
notably by the historians,[59] while the reference to the heroine's
name suggests, rather, love elegy.[60]

Our first criterion, 'Time,' is satisfied: writing in late Hellenistic
or early imperial times, Chariton sets his action in the classical
period, more precisely some time after 413 BC, the date of the
defeat of the Athenian naval expedition to Sicily. Next comes the
criterion of 'Characters.' Hermocrates, the father of the heroine,
is a historical figure known from Thucydides and Xenophon. His

W. Bartsch (1934: 3–6); Zimmermann (1961: 329–45); Reardon (1971: 5–8);
Molinié (1979/1989: 5–8); and Scarcella (1981: 344–52, 363–5).

[56] But cf. the important remarks of P. Grimal (1967: 842f.) and of C.-W. Müller
(1976: 132f.; 1981: 379, 383, 387).

[57] For an excellent detailed analysis, see Müller (1976: 123–5).

[58] For such a view has often been expressed, e.g. by Plepelits (1976: 11): 'Das
Werk soll den Eindruck erwecken, als sei es im 5. oder 4. Jh. v. Chr. verfasst
worden'—a view hardly reconcilable with the acceptance (also by Plepelits) of
Chariton's self-introduction as to be taken at face value.

[59] On συγγράφω (Char. 8. 8. 16) and σύγγραμμα (Char. 8. 1. 4), see Bartsch
(1934: 3), Zimmermann (1961: 330), Plepelits (1976: 10), and Müller (1976: 120
n. 29). All except Müller, however, seem to overstate the case: συγγράφω is in no
way exclusively used for 'Geschichte schreiben'; cf. Xen. *Eq.* 1. 1, Pl. *Min.* 316D (on
medical writers) etc. (LSJ *s.v.* II. 1). The same of course goes for διηγέομαι (Char. 1.
1. 1), to which Bartsch and Plepelits refer, and for συντάσσω, σύνταγμα (Hld. 10. 41.
4) referred to by Weinreich (1950/1962: 28).

[60] Cf. the titles of Parthenius' Ἐρωτικὰ παθήματα, many of which (e.g. 10, 11)
mention the girl's name only. Cf. n. 1 above.

great historical achievement, the victory over the Athenians, already lies in the past—the allusion to it is kind of a leitmotif in the novel[61]—but as an individual he takes some direct part in the action in connection with his daughter's wedding, burial, disappearance, and homecoming. The Persian king Artaxerxes is the second unequivocally historical figure; he is involved with Callirhoe both in his public capacity of supreme judge and privately, falling in love with her. While Hermocrates may best be described as a background figure, Artaxerxes is one of the main agents of the story, and fully characterized. His queen, Stateira, takes part personally in the action as well, though less prominently. Some other figures, notably the Ionian nobleman Dionysius, may have received their names and some traits from historical persons,[62] but in any case they are not put on stage in their known historical roles. Of overall importance, from our point of view, are the facts that the hero and heroine are purely fictitious characters (even if a daughter of Hermocrates is known to have existed),[63] whose private experiences are at the center of the story, and that they are brought into direct relationship to historical figures. The criterion by which the *Alexander Romance* and its cognates failed to be typically historical novels is here almost programmatically fulfilled.

As regards 'Setting,' geographical and historical, the whole plot is enacted in a concretely depicted Mediterranean and Near Eastern world. There is elaborate description of traveling on land and sea, from Syracuse in the west via Miletus in Ionia to Babylon in the east, with mention of well-known cities, islands, rivers, etc., on the way. The administrative structure of the Achaemenid empire is there, with three satrapies specified and a couple of (probably imaginary) satraps taking part in the action. The consequences of Dionysius, the Ionian nobleman, being a Persian subject are well set out: he is summoned to trial before the Great King at Babylon

[61] Hermocrates' name appears more than fifty times in the text of the novel: see the Thesaurus Linguae Graecae (1979) *s.v.* Hermocrates, and cf. Molinié's useful analytical index (1979: 223); Zimmermann (1961; 336f.); and Scarcella (1981: 344).

[62] See Perry (1930: 100f. n. 11); Zimmermann (1961: 337f.); and Scarcella (1981: 345f.).

[63] See Perry (1930: 101 n. 11; 1967: 137-9); Zimmermann (1961: 337); and Scarcella (1981: 346f.). Perry's thesis that the whole plot is based on legend or 'a pre-existing popular or historiographical tradition' (1967: 138) can hardly be upheld; cf. Reardon (1971: 851f. n. 97; Müller (1976: 133 n. 87; and Plepelits (1976: 30-2).

and later has to take an active part in the war on the Persian side. The war itself, caused by a rebellion in Egypt and described with a fair amount of specific detail from the mobilization of the Persian army onward, deeply affects the fortunes of the hero and heroine, at the end bringing about their reunion. The mainly private first part of the novel is thus (6. 8) followed by a shorter part—about one-fourth of the whole—in which public affairs come to the fore.

Some obvious anachronisms appear in the historical framework. The most blatant one is letting the lifetime of Hermocrates (died 407) coincide with the reign of Artaxerxes II Mnemon (404-363/ 57). Furthermore, Miletus in fact was not again under Persian dominion until after 387,[64] and the Egyptian rebellion, the leader of which is cautiously kept anonymous, appears to be still more violently backdated, insofar as it is at all meant to describe an actual historical event.[65] But all this is hardly more than Scott allowed himself in *Redgauntlet*, taking similar temporal liberties and staging a purely fictitious rebellion. No doubt the general reader's demand for historical probability was more than satisfied by Chariton's drawing of the contours of a classical milieu, in combination with his occasional pastiche on the manner of the classical historians (culminating in a number of hidden quotations from Xenophon and others).[66] Accuracy and authenticity in historical fiction is of course to be seen in relation not to historical reality, but to the picture of an age which writer and reader share from reading the same history books. For instance, Chariton's image of the Great King and his court, colored as it is by his Greek spectacles, will have impressed his contemporary readers as authentic as long as it did not manifestly depart from the image given by Herodotus, Xenophon, and Ctesias. It is completely irrelevant that *we* happen to know better.

Admitting the general probability of the historical background for the love story, different readers will have judged differently

---

[64] See Scarcella (1981: 349).

[65] There are three different options regarding which rebellion or capture of Tyre was Chariton's model: Salmon (1961); Zimmermann (1961: 342f.) (Alexander's capture of Tyre in 332; the Alexander historians); Molinié (1979: 7f.) (Amalgam of actual events of 405, 389-387, 360, and 332); Scarcella (1981: 349). P. Grimal (1958/1980: 382) instead points at a 5th-c. event, the Egyptian rebellion in *c*.460-454 under Artaxerxes I.

[66] For an annotated list of Chariton's 'Entlehnungen aus klassischen Autoren' see Papanikolaou (1973*b*: 13-24); see also Perry (1930: 104-8) and Zimmermann (1961: 330f.).

where the line is drawn between fact and fiction, exactly as is the case with modern historical novels and modern readers.[67] No doubt some believed the whole story to be authentic.[68] That, however, was not the fault of the author, who certainly knew he was not writing history and never pretended he was.[69] In this as in other important respects, he appears to differ from the author of the *Alexander Romance*, but to side with most modern writers of historical fiction. It is commonly maintained that Chariton chose the historiographical form in order to make the novel seem less 'novel' to his readership, or that (in John Morgan's words) 'he saw his fiction as still sheltering under the wing of historiography.'[70] Viewing him against the background of modern practitioners of the same trade, I am more inclined to think that his aim was precisely to create that titillating sensation peculiar to historical fiction, which is the effect of openly mixing fictitious characters and events with historical ones.[71] This is not to try to pass the novel off as something else, but, rather, to make the most of the contrast; in his first and last sentences, Chariton shows that he is well aware of the possibilities.

If Chariton meets the general reader's demand for 'truth,' he certainly fails according to the severer norms of such critics as Lukács and Fleishman. His historical milieu is, precisely, contours, costumes, masks: historical persons and places named, historical events alluded to and customs described, and in addition the classical atmosphere created through stylistic means. But the characters themselves, who act against this background, are hardly conceived of as individuals of an age different from that of the author, let alone as typical representatives of that past age. Instead, as has

---

[67] Cf. Fleishman's discussion (1978: 4–7), starting from Sigrid Undset's *Kristin Lavransdatter*.

[68] Cf. C.-W. Müller (1976: 126).

[69] Bowie (1977: 91–6) tries to distinguish between intention and effect: 'the author *can*, even if he clearly does not expect to be, be taken to be treating the real world of γενόμενα' (92); 'the reader can treat the story as one which *might* have happened but eluded the classical historians' (93). Cf. also Bowie (1985a: 685).

[70] Morgan (1982: 225). Cf., with different emphasis, Perry (1967: 139, 168); Schmeling (1974: 55f.); and Hägg (1983: 16f.). More to the point, Stark (1984: 258).

[71] Treu (1984: 458) makes much the same observation but still seems to think that the purpose is to make the (naive) reader believe that if the secondary characters are historical, the protagonists are so too. Maehler, in Reardon (1977: 50f.) misses the point in a similar way, saying that '*all* [the] main characters are historical persons' (my italics).

been stressed by Bryan Reardon in particular,[72] it is late Hellenistic man who speaks and acts, late Hellenistic life that is really depicted, against the classical décor.[73] Chaereas' apolitical behavior, says Reardon, is the greatest among Chariton's anachronisms. We cannot claim that all this is deliberate strategy on the part of the author, that, like some modern writers, he chose a historical milieu in order to make his contemporary topic and characters stand out all the more effectively against that background. The kind of historical consciousness needed to recreate a historical past, or to realize the problem at all, simply was not at his disposal.

For *Parthenope* the picture is much the same, as far as it is possible to judge from the fragments, but with some interesting new nuances. Our main source for the Greek text is a comparatively extensive papyrus fragment (some seventy lines in all);[74] in addition, there are some Greek literary testimonia[75] and the fragments of an eleventh-century Persian verse-romance, *Vāmiq and ʿAdhrā*, ultimately based on the Greek novel.[76] Just as Chariton relies mainly on Thucydides for the historical connections of his main characters, the unknown author of *Parthenope* relies on Herodotus. Parthenope herself is the daughter of Polycrates, the tyrant of Samos; she appears, though anonymously, in Herodotus (3. 124). Her lover Metiochus (Hdt. 6. 39–41) is the son of Miltiades, the victor at Marathon. By bringing these two together as young lovers at the court of Polycrates, the author backdates Metiochus by some twenty or thirty years, and he creates an imaginary blood-relationship between Polycrates and Miltiades, making them both descend from Aeacus, the son of Zeus; in Herodotus, only Miltiades claims such a descent, whereas Polycrates' father is an ordinary mortal with a very similar name, Aeaces. Furthermore, on the basis of the historical fact that, during his rule of the Chersonese, Miltiades remarried (with a Thracian princess, Hegesipyle), the author invents an unhistorical, typically novelistic motive for

---

[72] See Reardon (1971: 341), and cf. Plepelits (1976: 14f.); Bowie (1977: 93f.); and Reardon (1982a: 19-26 [= this volume, below, 180-8]).

[73] Cf. Bompaire (1977), displaying the use in Chariton and Aelius Aristides of a kind of 'Syracusan myth.' Bompaire uses *décor* in a more positive way—as part of the novelist's legitimate means of creating a historical atmosphere—than do modern literary critics of the historical novel.

[74] See Maehler (1976) and cf. Scarcella (1981: 363 n. 97).

[75] See Maehler (1976) and Hägg (1984: 76f.).

[76] See Hägg (1985) and Utas (1984-6).

young Metiochus to leave the Chersonese: he flees from his step-mother's machinations.[77]

These are indeed the kind of manipulations we may expect from any author of a historical novel, modern or ancient, and there can be no doubt that the love story itself and the further adventures of the young couple are purely fictitious. The author of *Parthenope*, however, seems to have put rather more effort than Chariton did into the creation of a coherent historical background to his fiction. His Polycrates seems to have come more to the fore than Chariton's Hermocrates: together with his wife—who is possibly a daughter of King Croesus of Lydia (!)—he welcomes his fugitive relative Metiochus to his Samian court, entertains him in the evening, and shows an active interest in the young man. To create an authentic-looking environment the author introduces other historical figures as well and lets them mingle with the fictitious ones: Anaximenes of Miletus, the philosopher, serves as kind of toast-master at the symposium on the first night, Eros being the topic of discussion, and a well-known poet, who is probably none other than Ibycus of Rhegium, sings of the beauty of the young couple, both these prominent figures illustrating the cultural activities traditionally associated with Polycrates' court.

While Chariton is content to let Hermocrates' historical achievement belong to the prehistory of the plot, making his public activities in the novel itself depend on the fictitious intrigue rather than the reverse, *Parthenope* appears to have had a less static historical setting: it also included the death of Polycrates, the ascension to power of his former secretary Maeandrius, and finally at least the beginning of the reign of Polycrates' brother Syloson. Maeandrius apparently tries to win Parthenope for himself, is rebuffed, and takes his revenge by selling her as a slave. Syloson, on the other hand, is referred to in positive terms in one of the fragments and may well have had a hand in the final reunion of the lovers. Incidentally, the characterization of Maeandrius as bad and Syloson as good conforms to the picture of the two rulers given by Herodotus. To all appearances, then, the fictitious love-story is enacted—as envisaged by our criterion 'Setting'—against the background of a succession of historical events, each of which affects the fortunes of the lovers.

[77] For detailed documentation of the historicity of this novel, see Hägg (1985: 92–8).

If *Callirhoe,* and even more so *Parthenope,* thus fulfill several of the basic criteria for the typical historical novel, the same does not apply, as far as I can see, to the other surviving 'ideal' novels,[78] even when set in the past. Achilles Tatius makes a point of having himself met the protagonist and heard the story from his lips. The only reference to a potentially verifiable public event, a war between Byzantium and the Thracians, is probably just part of the fiction.[79] The mention of a 'satrap' of Egypt (4. 11. 1; cf. 4. 13. 4) does not, as some have believed, refer to the Persian dominion,[80] but is an Atticist way of saying 'prefect';[81] and the Egyptian robbers operating in the Delta, the *boukoloi,* who in the novel capture the lovers, are a phenomenon recorded by the historian Dio Cassius as late as AD 172[82]—i.e., not long before Achilles Tatius must have written his novel. His is consequently a contemporary novel.

Xenophon of Ephesus begins his story in a way reminiscent of the folktale's 'once upon a time': ἦν ἐν Ἐφέσῳ ἀνήρ . . ., 'There was a man in Ephesus . . .' (1. 1. 1); and he ends in a similar vein, but is content with leaving it at that vaguely preterite impression. He never specifies the period by referring to any identifiable public event or naming any historical person. There is some quite specific geographical information, especially regarding the route of the brigands in Egypt (4. 1. 1-4), but it is probably more or less contemporary,[83] as is the author's dose of 'social realism.'[84] Nothing

---

[78] Reservation must be made for the *Ninus* and *Sesonchosis* novels; the fragmentary state of preservation does not allow an assessment of what part history (or myth) may have played in their structure. On *Ninus,* see Perry (1967: 153 ff.); on *Sesonchosis* as close in type to the *Alexander Romance,* see O'Sullivan (1984: 44). Anyway, as Dihle (1978: 55) points out, 'Erzählungen aus grauer Vorzeit in exotischem Milieu' like these two cannot have had the same kind of appeal to a Greek reader as *Callirhoe* and *Parthenope.* For the view that they too are the products of a romantic nationalism, but in this case in Hellenistic Syria and Egypt, respectively, see Braun (1938: 6-18) and cf. Grimal (1967: 842f.).

[79] Ach. Tat. 1. 3. 6, 7. 12. 4, 8. 18. 1; cf. Bowie (1985a: 694f. [= this volume, above, 52]).

[80] Thus Gaslee (1917: 378 n. 2); *contra* Vilborg (1962: 11, 85).

[81] Cf. Philostr. *VS* 1. 22. 3 (p. 31. 1 Kayser), on which see Schmid (1896 [vol. iv]: 423) and Bowersock (1969: 52).

[82] Ach. Tat. 3. 9. 2 ff., 4. 12; Dio Cass. 71. 4. 1-2. See Altheim (1948: i. 121-4), and, on the role of the *boukoloi* in the novels generally, Scarcella (1981: 352-64); cf. also J. Schwartz (1976).

[83] See Henne (1936), who corrects E. Rohde's and G. Dalmeyda's judgment of Xenophon's Egypt as pure fantasy.

[84] See Morgan (1982: 235), with further refs.

else in the décor invokes the classical period; on the contrary, the
mention of Alexandria and Antioch sets the action in post-classical
times, that of the Prefect of Egypt (a public figure, but anonymous)[85]
makes it post-Hellenistic, and that of the Eirenarch of Cilicia in fact
probably even post-Trajan.[86] These might conceivably all be anachronisms on the part of this not very sophisticated author, but the
absence of any deliberate counterstroke must decide the question:
this is no historical novel according to our definition, either in
intent or in effect. The same is true for Longus, who likewise begins
in a past tense—the author interprets a painting describing a love
story that took place in the past (*praef.*; cf. 1. 1. 2 ἦν and 4. 39)—
but never makes any attempt to anchor his story in any particular
period[87] or puts on stage any historical figure.

Heliodorus' novel has greater claims to being counted as
historical; in fact, it has often been put on an equal footing with
Chariton's for setting its action in a historical past.[88] There are,
however, important differences between the two. It is true that
Heliodorus deliberately sketches a pre-Hellenistic background for
his story: his Egypt is under Persian dominion (which means ca.
525-330 BC), and Alexandria does not occur. It does not matter
much, from our point of view, how consistently this Persian Egypt
is described or how historically accurate are his classical Delphi[89]
and early-Meroitic Meroë;[90] all these are certainly amalgams of
facts from different historical periods with a strong admixture
of pure invention,[91] creating the general atmosphere of a distant
historical past.[92] What does matter, however, is the total absence
of identifiable historical figures or events. The Persian satrap

---

[85] Cf. Hägg (1971*b*: 30 f.).

[86] Cf. Gärtner (1967: cols. 2086 f.).

[87] Geographical realism in Longus is discussed by H. J. Mason (1979); P. M.
Green (1982); and E. L. Bowie (1985*b*: 86-91).

[88] Even C. W. Müller (1981: 391) speaks of 'allenfalls Gradunterschiede,' while
Dihle (1978: 54) acutely points to the differences.

[89] Pouilloux (1983) finds a surprising amount of authenticity in this description,
but the realism concerns Delphi of the imperial period, not the classical in which
the action is set.

[90] Cf. Morgan (1982: 237-50), who finds more of the Meroë of Herodotus than
that of later periods in Heliodorus' description.

[91] Cf. J. Maillon, in Rattenbury and Lumb (1935: lxxxviii f.), and Weinreich
(1950/1962: 41). Iamblichus' *Babyloniaca* probably presents a similar amalgam: cf.
U. Schneider-Menzel, in Altheim (1948: i. 77-84), on the personal names, and
(1948: i. 89-92), finding traces from the pre-Persian to the Parthian period; similarly Weinreich (1950/1962: 15).

[92] Morgan (1982: 236 n. 46) lists some of the obvious anachronisms.

Oroondates and his wife Arsace, the sister of the Great King, have simply been given typical names[93] (as have the satraps Mithridates and Pharnaces in Chariton); the Great King of the period is not specified, and King Hydaspes and Queen Persinna of Aethiopia, the parents of the heroine, are invented characters. No authentic figure like Hermocrates or Polycrates mingles with the fictitious characters at Delphi; the flying visit in the tale (2. 25. 1) of the Greek courtesan Rhodopis, known from Herodotus (2. 134; cf. Strabo 17. 1. 33), is a poor substitute. Any dependence on factual happenings, like the description of the siege of Syene (Book 9), which may have been inspired by the siege of Nisibis in AD 350,[94] is concealed rather than utilized to create an impression of authenticity. It goes without saying that nothing in the fortunes of the protagonists is imagined as affected by events outside the universe created by the novelist for the occasion.

The kind of historical probability the *Ethiopica* still undoubtedly achieves relies on other means: as John Morgan has shown, it is by dressing the story in narrative devices typical of historiography—expressing uncertainty, offering alternative explanations for events, providing authentic geographical and ethnographical information, etc.—that Heliodorus lends plausibility and an air of realism to his account.[95] By writing like a historian, or assuming 'the historiographical pose,' he wants his love-and-adventure story to appear as 'history' (which, as Morgan explains, is not quite the same as 'fact').[96] We may thus well choose to call the *Ethiopica* a historical novel, but bearing in mind that it has far less in common with the typical modern works of that designation than have *Callirhoe* and *Parthenope*. Of our criteria, it satisfies that of 'Time' and, to a reasonable extent, that of 'Truth,'[97] while essential traits are missing as regards 'Characters' and 'Setting.'

Discussing the modern historical novel, Harry Shaw asks why, in this very extensive genre, there have been so comparatively few acknowledged masterpieces; even great writers have failed when

[93] Cf. the notes on Hld. 2. 24. 2, 7. 1. 4, and 7. 14. 3 in Rattenbury and Lumb (1935), and see Morgan (1982: 247).

[94] See, most recently, Morgan (1982: 226 n. 15) and Sandy (1982*a*: 4 f.; with further refs.), who are both inclined to accept a late 4th-c. date for the novel. New arguments for Heliodorus' priority, however, have been advanced by M. Maróth (1979).

[95] Morgan (1982). For a different approach, see Winkler (1982) [= this volume, ch. 12].   [96] Morgan (1982: 223-6, 261 f.).

[97] Cf. ibid. 148.

venturing on a historical novel.[98] He finds what looks like an
insoluble dilemma inherent in the genre: novels are built up
around protagonists who are private individuals, and 'milieu,
minor characters, and plotted action are there to illuminate them.'
In historical novels, by contrast, the characters are ideally expected
to represent, at the same time, 'salient aspects of a historical
milieu,' and even to 'elucidate historical process.'[99] Succeeding in
conveying the spirit of the age, the author is apt to fail in individual characterization, and vice versa. Returning from ideals to
everyday practice, from the missing masterpieces to the flourishing
popular genre of the historical novel, we may ask the analogous
question: why is the genre so popular?—and seek the answer in
roughly the same direction. It is precisely at the point of intersec-
tion between the historical and the private sphere, I believe, that
the particular attraction of the typical historical novel lies. Or, at
least, one of its attractions, for plain interest in history is of course
a major part of the explanation too. Once we have relaxed from the
demand for historical 'truth' in the more profound sense, the
'dilemma' can be turned into a strength. The author introduces
private individuals with whom the reader can identify (they are
'timeless' human beings rather than 'representative' for a different
age) and makes them personally witness and experience great historical events and figures. This is why the best-known periods and
figures—a Napoleon, a Polycrates—are the favorites with writers
of popular historical fiction: the more familiar the historical décor,
the more titillating the reader's sense of taking part in the events
through the medium of the fictitious characters, breaking time
barriers as well as the barrier between the public and the private.

This is what Chariton and the author of *Parthenope* had discovered. They did not, like the writers of romanticized biographies,
put a historical figure at the center of their fantasies, nor did they
as conscientiously as Heliodorus pose as historians, giving to their
love stories a feeling of being historical accounts. Rather, they were
deliberately playing on the reader's naive delight in recognizing the
great figures of history and at the same time viewing them from
a new perspective.[100] But a touch was enough, a sketched back-

---

[98] H. Shaw (1983: 30 (top) and 30-50, 'The Problem with Historical Novels').
Cf. Henderson (1974: xvf.).   [99] H. Shaw (1983: 49).
[100] Cf. Bowie (1985a: 685 [= this volume, above, 42]): 'The reader can fancy
that he is enjoying a sentimental sidelight on conventional political history.'

ground to what was after all the main thing, the love story itself. Again, it was not just any period and place that they chose for its setting; it was the Golden Age of Greece, and the climate of incipient classicism in which they lived[101] gave them a convenient opportunity of appealing to a sense of nostalgia for that heroic past—incidentally, another point of contact with Scott and the Romantic period in which the modern historical novel arose.[102] To all appearances writing before classicism had yet become a commonplace, our two authors will have had a chance to convey, with the fresh charm of novelty, the 'classical feel'[103] to their late Hellenistic readers.

Finally, to return to the generic considerations discussed at the beginning of this paper: can we legitimately speak of a subgenre, the 'historical novel,' of which *Callirhoe* and *Parthenope* represent an early form, *Waverley* and *Ivanhoe* a modern.[104] The best way to address the problem is probably to follow Lukács and Shaw in

---

[101] See the illuminating remarks of Dihle (1978: 54 f.), who argues for a mid-1st-c. BC date. For a useful review of earlier attempts to date Chariton and the interesting (though not compelling) suggestions that Chariton's Athenagoras is identical with the rhetor Athenagoras (*Ant. Pal.* 11. 150), active in the first decades of the 2nd c. AD, see Ruiz-Montero (1980). The present argument is of course not dependent on as early a date as suggested above.

[102] See Fleishman (1971: 16 f.) and Sanders (1978: 1 f.). Other incentives for historical fiction than nostalgia are of course possible, e.g. a moralistic interest; that goes some way toward explaining why comparatively few modern authors have chosen the classical periods of antiquity as setting and so many the late antique period of decline. Cf. Riikonen (1978: 34-9, 203-5), and the comments of E. J. Kenney (1981: 282 f.). Needless to say, our two ancient novels have a deeper spiritual kinship with the Waverley novels of Scott (or, for that matter, with the *Iliad*) than with most modern historical novels set in antiquity. The parallel between the Homeric epic and 'le roman historique à la Walter Scott' was drawn in an interesting article by P. van Tieghem as an example of 'ces genres non formels, mais psychologiques, qui mettent en jeu les mêmes goûts du public' (1938: 99).

[103] The expression is borrowed from Reardon (1982a: 19), in a slightly different context.

[104] I am of course not suggesting any influence from Chariton on Scott; but it is interesting to note that Scott apparently was influenced by Heliodorus, probably indirectly through Sidney's *Arcadia*: 'Banquet turns to Battle' Hld. I. I, [*New*] *Arcadia* II. 27. 5 (*Old Arcadia*, p. 128. 7, Robertson), *Ivanhoe*, ch. 41. See S. L. Wolff (1912: 366, 463), and Kerlin (1907). Cf. Scott himself on his early reading, which at least included Madeleine de Scudéry's *Cyrus*: Lamont (1986: 13 f.), 'Waverley's' reading, and (1986: 350), General Preface to *Waverley*, 1829. Whether the *Ethiopica* in Underdowne's or any later translation ever came in his hands is impossible to say, but the early unpublished 'fragment of a romance' (Lamont 1986: 361—Appendix I) begins in a way strikingly similar to Heliodorus' novel: 'The sun was nearly set behind the distant mountains of Liddesdale, when a few of the scattered and terrified inhabitants of the village of Hersildoun . . .'

regarding the historical novel as just a temporary tributary of the great stream of the novel: it branches off for a while, then rejoins the main stream. The first novel we possess happens to be historical, the next three are not, and then, with the *Ethiopica*, history (of a kind) is there again; but Heliodorus has less in common with Chariton than with his immediate predecessors. The historical novel has no history of its own, but all the way it 'depends on the formal techniques and cultural assumptions of the main tradition.'[105] Setting the novel in a historical milieu, the writer achieves different results, depending both on the stage of development the novel as genre has reached and on the level of sophistication of the writer and his intended audience.

The stage that contemporary historiography has reached is an essential factor too. Historiography and historical novel can be shown often to go hand in hand; Scott's novels, for example, are unthinkable without the developments in historiography of the preceding decades.[106] It would be as absurd to demand from an ancient historical novelist like Chariton a sense of 'history as a shaping force,'[107] which we do not find in the historians or biographers of his age—in fact, perhaps not until after the French Revolution[108]—as it would be to demand of him any other special quality of the advanced modern novel, for instance the psychological insights of a Dostoevski. It is all the more remarkable that still, as we have seen, a number of basic characteristics of the typical historical novel of our time are already to be distinguished in the first Greek novels of antiquity.

[105] H. Shaw (1983: 23; cf. 30). Cf., for a similar viewpoint, van Tieghem (1938) as quoted in n. 102 above.
[106] See Fleishman (1971: 16-36) and, from a different viewpoint, Braudy (1970).
[107] Fleishman (1971: 15).
[108] Cf. Lukács (1962: 23).

PART III
Specific Studies

7

Theme, Structure and Narrative in Chariton

B. P. REARDON

A hundred years ago Chariton's romance *Chaereas and Callirhoe* seemed a poor thing. It seemed so, certainly, to Rohde,[1] who found plot and characters tame, and did not veil his contempt for the sentimentality of the story, for its unheroic and passive hero and heroine, for the cheapness of its general effect; at the same time he did grant that there was something not unpleasing about its simplicity. Two decades later, papyrological discoveries began to be made which were to lead, if not to a revolution in our estimation of the literary form of the romance, at any rate to such a reversal in our dating of the extant texts as enabled the form to be seen for the first time in a comprehensible literary context and line of development.[2] Chariton profited particularly: from Rohde's date of around AD 500 he was brought forward perhaps 400 years—nowadays some would put him a hundred years, or even two hundred, earlier than that; and there is general though not universal agreement that his is the earliest of the extant romance texts.[3] Furthermore, the fact that several papyri of Chariton were found suggests that his story was popular. This advance in knowledge enabled Ben

---

[1] E. Rohde (1876).

[2] See particularly Lesky (1971: 957-72); older histories of literature, such as Schmid's, are badly out of date. For a discussion of this topic see my forthcoming article in *Aufstieg und Niedergang der römischen Welt* 11 (*ANRW infra* [*Editor's note*: this has not yet appeared]); and my *Courants littéraires grecs des IIe et IIIe siècles après J.-C.*: Reardon (1971: 309-403), to which general reference may be made at this point for the bibliography on the subject. For the period 1950-70, see also Sandy (1974: 321-59).

[3] The evidence is conveniently summarized in the introduction to a recent German translation: Plepelits (1976: 4-9) for the exceptional view that would place the novel around AD 200, see n. 5 below. My own guess at the date of the work would be about AD 50; perhaps earlier—a date BC is not impossible—but not much later.

Edwin Perry, fifty years ago, to make of Chariton's story the basis
of an already fairly well-developed theory of the origins of the form
romance and its place in cultural history, a theory fully set out
in 1967 in his *magnum opus The Ancient Romances*.[4] *Chaereas and
Callirhoe*, Perry maintained, was a ripe specimen of the Hellenistic
romance, and on that score alone has considerable interest as
evidence for a critical stage in literary history; but in addition,
Perry, showing early the independence and pugnaciousness which
characterizes his work, stoutly maintained that the story, though
of a cheap type, had substantial merit in itself.

By that period there was beginning a reassessment of the
romances, or novels, that has been pursued, subsequently, with
increasing business. Literary merit has been emphasized, in Longus
and Heliodorus for instance; fragments have been edited seriously,
if not always well; relationships between romance and the age
which produced it began to be considered; it was even proposed
that these texts were a manifestation of the religious development
of post-classical antiquity.[5] For Chariton himself, associated questions have been studied: the relationship of his story with historiography and with contemporary social usage, its date, its language,[6]
in short, the literary provenance and cultural context of a work
apparently marking the critical stage of social development that
has been mentioned—rather, that is, than the story itself, its
literary characteristics.

But more recently *Chaereas and Callirhoe* has attracted specifically
literary criticism. Karl-Heinz Gerschmann offers a sustained commentary on the composition of the story; Carl-Werner Müller
approaches the basic question of the aesthetic nature of the work;
it is seen by others, variously, as the story of Chaereas or as the
story of Callirhoe.[7] The most searching analysis by far is the technical study of Tomas Hägg, in the relevant parts of his 1971 study

[4] Perry (1930: 93-134); *The Ancient Romances: a Literary-Historical Account of
their Origins*: Perry (1967).
[5] Kerényi (1927); Merkelbach (1962). Merkelbach's thesis (it is not Kerényi's)
requires a later date for Chariton; see Reardon (1971: 393 ff. and 338 n. 61).
[6] Reardon (1971: 340 ff., nn.); add, particularly, Zimmermann (1957: 72-81);
Papanikolaou (1973b; language, date); and see *ANRW*. Plepelits (1976) discusses
the 'historiographical' aspect of Chariton. Add, now, the introduction of G. Molinié
to his Budé edition of Chariton (1979).
[7] Gerschmann (1975); C.-W. Müller (1976); Schmeling (1974); Heiserman,
(1977, ch. 6), 'Aphrodisian Chastity'. Cf. also Molinié (1979/1989: 22-41).

Narrative Technique in Ancient Greek Romances.[8] Hägg finds in Chariton's novel much more technical skill even than Perry had suggested. Where Perry offered traditional, as it were 'instinctive' literary criticism, Hägg's is scientific, clinical, so to speak 'professional', operating—as does one kind of criticism of modern literature, whose approach he uses—with percentages, statistics and graphs, concerned with tempo and phrases of narrative, scene and summary, narrative time and dramatic time, point of view, internal reference system.[9] It is consequently not Hägg's primary purpose to evaluate, or to discern his author's 'subject' or 'aim', still less any 'message' that he might have. In fact, however, conclusions similar to Perry's do emerge, suggesting that Chariton does know what he is doing, and does it well on the whole—given, of course, certain basic assumptions about the nature of his story.

This paper proposes to pursue such topics as these: to consider the story of *Chaereas and Callirhoe* principally in its literary-critical rather than its literary-historical aspects; to examine what the story is about, how it is put together, how it is told—its theme, structure, narrative method; and to discuss some other aspects of it arising from these considerations. In doing so I shall be referring to things that have already been said, particularly in the last decade or so, and shall try to take account of the most useful of these contributions. There will be nothing revolutionary in what is said here; much has been at least adumbrated by Perry and others; and the rest is a matter of emphasis, of fashion perhaps. We do not really have enough evidence to assert categorically that this story marks a turning-point in literary history. But we do have enough to justify us in treating it, less ambitiously, as an early point of reference for the Greek romance, or novel—extended fictitious narrative in prose. Our knowledge of the range of that form has been increased in very recent years by yet more fragments, variously lurid, scabrous, or less spectacular.[10] They are by no means fully explained, of course. But it is worthwhile to look at Chariton again, in a context slightly fuller, and more fully considered, than it once was; to examine with some care the nature and not just the fact of this reference-point. The hinge is worth examining; and

---

[8] Hägg (1971*a*).
[9] Cf. e.g. Wellek and Warren (1949).
[10] Notably Henrichs (1972); Parsons (1971); Maehler (1976). There have been numerous less remarkable fragments as well.

Hägg in particular has given us a microscope, to examine it with, that we shall find useful.

Perhaps it will be well to sketch the story. It is not very well known, the text itself has not always been readily available until very recently, and even translations are few and far between.[11] The situation has, however, been to some extent remedied by the appearance of a Budé edition; and this fact, together with the recent work just described, gives some reason for hoping that the time is past when this story and its congeners could be simply disregarded because they were unfamiliar to scholars.

The devastatingly beautiful Callirhoe is the daughter of the famous Hermocrates of Syracuse; Chaereas is the son of an only less prominent Syracusan who is Hermocrates' bitter enemy. The pair fall in love, on the occasion of a festival of Aphrodite. Opposition from their families is overcome by the enthusiastic urgings of the whole town, and Chaereas and Callirhoe are married. But Callirhoe had had other suitors; in their anger they mount a plot which leads Chaereas, out of jealousy, to kick his wife, who falls apparently dead. She is buried richly. The pirate Theron sees the costly funeral, and that night he robs Callirhoe's tomb—just as Callirhoe is recovering from what was really a coma. Theron carries her off to Miletus, sells her to the seigneur of the region, Dionysius, and makes off hastily. Dionysius at once falls in love with her. At this point Callirhoe discovers that she is pregnant by her husband; reluctantly, thinking herself separated for ever from Chaereas, she decides to marry Dionysius for the sake of her child.

Meanwhile the tomb-robbery has been discovered, and Chaereas, grief-stricken, has set out in search of Callirhoe, dead though he believes her to be. By good fortune he comes across Theron drifting helplessly, his ship disabled by storms and his crew dead. Theron tells all, and is executed. Chaereas sails to Miletus; there he learns of Callirhoe's marriage to Dionysius; but his ship is attacked and he himself taken prisoner and sold as a slave to Mithridates, the satrap of Caria and neighbour of Dionysius.

In due course Callirhoe bears her child, whom she passes off as

[11] The text used in this paper is that of W. E. Blake (1938); for the new Budé, see my review: Reardon (1982*b*). A projected Loeb edition has been postponed indefinitely [*Editor's note*: see now Goold (1995)]. Translations: W. E. Blake (1939); a new version will appear in a volume I am currently assembling [= Reardon (1989)]. In other languages: P. Grimal (1958); add the Budé; and K. Plepelits (1976).

Dionysius'. She has by now heard of the arrival and destruction of the Syracusan ship, and is in her turn grief-stricken for Chaereas, whom she thinks now dead. In an attempt to lay his ghost, Dionysius builds a cenotaph for Chaereas. At the dedication ceremony Mithridates is present. As soon as he sees Callirhoe he falls in love with her; returning to Caria, he mounts an intrigue to win her, using for the purpose his prisoner Chaereas, whose identity he has by chance discovered. This intrigue is discovered by Dionysius, who charges Mithridates with malpractice; and the whole situation is reported to the King of Persia, who summons all the parties to Babylon, so that Mithridates can be put on trial.

Here Chariton elaborately mounts a full-dress debate between the rivals Dionysius and Mithridates, over who is, or who is to be, Callirhoe's husband. By now, however, the matter is complicated by the fact that the King, as soon as he catches sight of Callirhoe, inevitably falls in love with her himself. And it is still further complicated by the dramatic appearance, at the critical point of the trial, of none other than Chaereas—to the utter astonishment of all but Mithridates, who has stage-managed the apparition. Chariton here (5. 8. 2) pulls out all the stops: 'who could describe adequately that scene in court? What dramatist ever staged so sensational a story? You would have thought you were in a theatre crowded with passions all tumbling over each other—πάντα ἦν ὁμοῦ, δάκρυα, χαρά, θάμβος, ἔλεος, ἀπιστία, εὐχαί. Χαιρέαν ἐμακάριζον, Μιθριδάτῃ συνέχαιρον, συνελυποῦντο Διονυσίῳ, περὶ Καλλιρόης ἠπόρουν—weeping and rejoicing, astonishment and pity, disbelief and prayers. How happy all were for Chaereas! How glad for Mithridates! For Dionysius how sorrowful! As for Callirhoe, they did not know *what* to think about her.' And well they might not. They didn't know what to think about Callirhoe; and the King doesn't know what to do about her. This climactic scene issues in a welter of emotions: profound heart-searching in the King, despair in Dionysius, relief in Mithridates; and in the still-separated Chaereas and Callirhoe themselves, heart-rending anguish. But as far as the plot is concerned, it issues in an impasse: the King cannot decide what to do. The impugned pretendant Mithridates has abandoned his hopes, but Dionysius remains and Chaereas remains; and the King, even though in his head he knows he cannot replace his Queen with Callirhoe, or sully his dignity by acting more arbitrarily, cannot bring himself to adjudge Callirhoe to either of her husbands. The author solves the problem by having a sudden rebellion in Egypt, which demands the King's instant attention—much to the King's relief; and which sends Chaereas flying in despair to the rebel side, in order at least to achieve a glorious death and damage his enemies if he can—it is the most whole-hearted of several attempts he has made at suicide. But *tyche* has not exhausted her quiver of *paradoxa*: Chaereas proves so brilliant a soldier and admiral that he defeats the King. In doing so, he recovers his Callirhoe; and they return to Syracuse, where they live happily ever after.

The conventions that operate here are as clear as those of a Victorian melodrama, and for immediate purposes we need do little more than observe rapidly their principal features. Melodrama, precisely, is the most prominent of them; and with melodrama, sentiment, pathos and simplicity of attitude—these make up the principal characters, those to whom the events happen; the events themselves are spectacular, coincidental, of capital import. Having said this, we should look beyond these features of the story. Such stories stand in a clear relationship with their society and culture— other examples of the kind may be more sophisticated (Longus' story, notably), but do not differ in substance from Chariton's. All offer, in a general way, a spiritual photograph of their time, their Hellenistic-imperial time: isolated individuals seeking, in a wide world and an open society, security and very identity, in love of their fellows—or, in other texts, in love of God.[12]

So much should be said here, and can be said briefly. The purpose of the present remarks is less general, and concerns this particular story. What is it about? Is it about Chaereas? or about Callirhoe? or about Chaereas and Callirhoe? Or is it really about something wider: about love, or about life, or about people? I shall suggest that this is a matter of perspective, of illusion even; and that is what can lead to different answers to that question. I shall discuss the story in three aspects: first, its overall structure—that is, its plot and the disposition of its major elements; second, its narrative technique—that is, the way in which that plot and those elements are presented to the consumer; and lastly, its theme, as that theme emerges from the plot, narrative, and the writer's attitude to his story and characters.

---

[12] I have developed this interpretation in Reardon (1971), and more briefly in Reardon (1969); see also Reardon (1971: 321 n. 31), for other studies in general interpretation of the form.

If we analyse the story into its elements, what are those elements? That will depend on the criterion we adopt: dramatic effect, or mechanical disposition of matter, or logical structure. Perry, following Reitzenstein, saw in the story a Hellenistic drama in five acts:[13] Callirhoe's marriage to Chaereas and to Dionysius; Chaereas' enslavement; the trial; the war; the reunion. The effect of using a dramatic criterion is to turn the spotlight rather on Callirhoe than on Chaereas. A mechanical analysis following the book-divisions—which are Chariton's own[14]—would suggest four stages of development, each given roughly equal time in two books: the adventures of Callirhoe; the adventures of Chaereas; Chaereas and Callirhoe together (in Babylon); and Chaereas again; and although this division cannot be very different from Perry's, Chaereas here seems more important.

But what is the overall impression the story makes on its reader? What is its logical structure, what is its emotional effect? What, that is, is its total aesthetic impact? Here, we shall have to adopt a less mechanical criterion; we shall have to examine both the events of the story and its emotional content, and the relation between them. And this is the first point at which Hägg's statistical critical tool will have interest for us: the modern theoretical division between 'summary' and 'scene'—between the reporting of what happens and the representation, the mimetic representation, of what happens.

What are the events, then? And what place does Chariton give them? Considered as *what happens*, the story can be analysed as follows:

1. A brief introduction—the marriage of Chaereas and Callirhoe.
2. Separation, beginning with Callirhoe's coma; the fact of this separation is structurally important, since it is the basis of the subsequent plot.
3. The main events—the main things that happen—are the relationships of Callirhoe with Dionysius, Mithridates, and the King. These can be seen as a series of *agones*: the *agon* with Dionysius includes the marriage and the trial; that with Mithridates

[13] Perry (1967: 140 ff.)

[14] Müller, C.-W. (1976) suggests that the eight books constituted two papyrus rolls, and that the résumé at the beginning of 5 of the contents of 1–4 may indicate later publication of 'Part II'. Chariton probably had compositional reasons for placing this résumé and many others where he did place them, but certainly the résumé at 5 *init.* is unique in covering the previous action comprehensively.

includes the intrigue and the trial; that with the King includes the trial and the war.

4. Reunion: this, although long, is in itself *structurally* unimportant.

The central structure, then, the body of what happens, is a series of *agones*: Chaereas' rivals.

But is this the aesthetic effect on the reader? Not without qualification. Unquestionably the 'best' part of the story, in the sense of the most striking, memorable, and 'successful', is the trial in Babylon: Dionysius and Mithridates, rivals for Callirhoe's hand, arguing fast and furiously, before a King of Persia who is himself another rival, while all the time Chaereas, her original husband, is sitting helplessly on the sidelines. Chariton puts his best efforts into the scene—I have indicated the nature of the writing at this point: dramatic, spectacular, pathetic. This looks like the climax of the work; and in Perry's discussion, for instance, we read that 'the trial of Dionysius vs. Mithridates overshadows in interest and importance everything that has preceded, and what follows consists in the unravelling of the situation thereby developed . . . It is the culminating point of a suspense which has been gathering momentum for the space of an entire book . . . everything converges towards this climax.'[15]

In fact, this is where the principal illusion lies: an illusion created by the relative fullness with which 'scene', dramatic spectacle, is described by Chariton, and the brevity with which critical events are narrated, with which what actually critically happens is set out. The structure of the story deserves further examination.

The critical events are the *agones*; and what happens 'about' them, as it were, is that (a) they begin—after the separation that creates a vacuum, or a vacancy; (b) they take place, *and the issue of all of them is the same*—they are causally linked the one to the next, and they all issue in the *same result*, namely that *no decision is made*; and (c) they end, when Chaereas recovers Callirhoe *by force*. The trial in Babylon is structurally no different from the other *agones*: as Hägg says, it is a parenthesis.[16] The main problem after the trial, from Callirhoe's point of view, is precisely what the main problem was before the trial: Chaereas versus Dionysius: will Callirhoe have definitively to pass from her first husband to her second? For the earlier stages of the Mithridates episode are merely

[15] Perry (1930: 113).   [16] Hägg (1971a: 265).

another parenthesis. After the trial the King has to decide between Chaereas and Dionysius. But the matter of decision between Chaereas and Dionysius could perfectly well have arisen, and in fact in embryo did arise, in Miletus, before anyone ever set foot on the road to Babylon. Structurally, the parentheses, the detours, alter nothing; Mithridates and the King are merely doublets of Dionysius; the only real *agon* is that of Chaereas versus Dionysius, and in respect of it the mounting of the trial is a piece of illusion. The trial, indeed, is the climax of a yet longer series of *agones*, which really begins at the very beginning of the story, with the intrigues of Callirhoe's other suitors—who are Chaereas' earliest rivals. There is a clear progression in the series of rivals, the last of whom is none less than the King of Persia, and this point will have its importance later. For the moment, however, the fact remains that structurally *all* of these *agones* are the same *agon*: Chaereas versus a rival.

This central problem, this central rivalry, arises from Callirhoe's beauty, which engenders love: divine beauty is the motor of the initial movement, and of its complications. The complications are that beauty and love lead to one marriage and consequently (because of Callirhoe's pregnancy) to another. And the problem is only settled by force; war is the real arbiter. Dionysius and Chaereas are involved as associates of the powers of Persia and Egypt, and the state quarrel settles the personal issue; the personal issue rises to the level of an affair of state, and is settled *thereby*.[17]

The problem, then, arises from beauty, consists of rivalry for beauty, and is settled by force. The line of events is simple; complications are only apparent. The structural or dynamic function of the whole Babylon episode is not to create a situation but to renew the initial situation, to renew but not to change the movement of the plot; to raise the stakes, as Callirhoe's beauty captivates the highest in the land. And it is precisely because the Babylon episode is inconclusive—a parenthesis—that it can give way to new action, in the shape of *tyche*.

---

[17] We may observe that Chaereas, in recovering Callirhoe by force, has become a man of action—no longer passive, ineffective and suicidal, although this is paradoxical since his action began as an attempt at suicide. I exclude this point from my text as not being directly relevant to my argument at this point; but it is worth observing that Chariton has thus observed also the structural weakness which lies in Chaereas' passivity. It is after all the hero—helped, certainly, by *tyche*—who solves the problem, and in so doing regains happiness for himself and the heroine.

But this is only events; and the story consists also of reactions to events. The other pole of the story is emotion. And in this respect, in respect of the emotions that it is the story's whole purpose to generate, Babylon *is* a turning-point. In Babylon, and not till then, Chaereas and Callirhoe are 'reunited' in the sense that they have found each other, have seen each other; each knows the other is alive. Chaereas has long known that Callirhoe is alive; but she has been irrecoverable; Babylon, representing his first real hope of recovering her, is, thus, crucial emotionally for him. As for Callirhoe: she has been quite unsure whether Chaereas is alive, and he has been unobtainable anyway; for her, Babylon represents her first real assurance that he is alive, and the first point at which she can hope—as she does, on leaving Babylon in the King's train, hope that things will take a turn for the better. Babylon is thus emotionally crucial for her too. Thus emotionally Babylon *is* the culmination of the series of *agones*. The weight of the emotion has lain on Callirhoe's side, because it is her side of the story that Chariton shows us more of; and he shows us more of it because it is the more emotionally-charged—she is the one who has the series of lovers, she is the one who has the baby. And she is the emotional centre of the story also in that the *male* emotional life in it is distributed over several different men. Here we return to our structural analysis of the series of lovers and *agones*; but this time it is to observe, not an illusion, but a very positive value in the structure. One of the story's major themes is the power of love, and that is seen very clearly in love's power over a series of men, in successively higher place. Political power and status become as nothing when the man, however highly placed, falls in love; he is reduced to the common lot of humanity. And it is Callirhoe in whom the power of this emotion is concentrated—*in* her, and also, by means of the progression of lovers, *on* her.

What Chariton has done, that is, in the overall structure of the story, is to play events against emotion. The story is 'about' both; it has a double focus of interest.

And here we may turn to the analysis made by Hägg, not of the overall structure, but of the manner in which the story is unfolded—its narrative technique.[18] Characteristically, it proceeds by means, first, of rapid narrative summarizing a sequence of events; then, by degrees, the tempo slows; and finally a 'scene' material-

---

[18] Hägg (1971*a*: esp. chs. 1, 2).

izes, displaying the actions, thoughts, utterances of an important character at an important juncture of events—Callirhoe, for instance, deliberating whether or not to marry Dionysius. Then the story proceeds—perhaps the subject is changed—and the process is repeated. Events in sequence are played against the crises, in particular the emotional crises, that arise from them. Fundamentally it is the same aesthetic process as we have just observed in respect of the story's overall structure. And here we may note the statistics: practically 90% of Chariton's text is 'scene', and half of that is direct speech; only 10% is 'summary'.[19] So marked is the perspective, the illusion; by so much do the critical moments, and notably their emotional content, predominate over narrative of action. Of course all novelists use such a technique, such illusion, in greater or less degree, with more or less conscious purpose; I am suggesting that conscious purpose is very clear in the case of Chariton, and that the simplicity that Rohde admired is not as artless as he no doubt thought.

The illusion is the more marked in that, for all the rapidity with which he narrates them, Chariton none the less organizes his events with great care. That he does give them a very important place is shown by, among other things, the conscious demonstrations he offers us of his line of events, in the form of a long series of recapitulations: no fewer than 20 of them, some very full and carefully placed at crucial points in the action—just after the trial in Babylon, for instance, or at the beginning of the final book.[20] But the changing of focus is what emerges from Hägg's analysis as the paramount feature of the author's technique. For much of the time Chariton gives Callirhoe centre stage. And stage, scene, is what it is, as he represents ($\mu\iota\mu\epsilon\hat{\iota}\tau\alpha\iota$) her situation and reactions in detail and dramatically, often in monologue, as time after time she comes to a crisis in her affairs. This is indeed a further factor contributing to the emotional predominance, noted above, of Callirhoe in the story. Time and again Chariton uses *her* as his vehicle for discussing the situation, for bringing out its emotional content.[21]

---

[19] I am here compressing a very full and detailed examination (and rounding off figures), but I hope not misrepresenting it (or Chariton). The most useful single reference, here, to Hägg's book would be to the 'Syncrisis' on 'Tempo and Phases of Narrative', pp. 82 ff. (with diagrams); but Hägg's summaries cannot dispense the reader from following in detail the exacting analysis conducted in his chapters.

[20] Hägg (1971a: 264 ff.).

[21] At 1. 3. 6 she offers a shrewd guess when she sees the traces of revelling; this

Chaereas' side of things is altogether more scantly treated, even
when he does something as spectacular as capturing Tyre (like
Alexander). Events are played down in the narrative, so they tend
to look rather threadbare. But they *are organized*; and when it suits
his purpose Chariton demonstrates their *line* with care, and perhaps even (as Hägg suggests) with pride—precisely because it is
not events that in his story are made conspicuous.

In this sense, then, 'theme' and 'structure' are not the same
thing. Chaereas is as necessary to the *structure* as Callirhoe is, and
in this sense the story is about both of them. But the *theme* is
really the emotional situation; and in that respect it is Callirhoe
who predominates. Τοσάδε, says Chariton at the very end of his
story, περὶ Καλλιρόης συνέγραψα ('this is my story about Callirhoe').
Possibly Plepelits is right in thinking that Chariton's title for his
story was simply *Callirhoe*.[22]

Let us change our own critical focus, here, and look for a
moment at what the story may be 'about' in a broader, less concrete sense. Is it 'about' life, or love, or people—as great novels
are?

Clearly there is a 'spiritual content', in that what is readily
visible to the reader is adventure and emotion—that is, what
happens to people, or at any rate these people, and how they feel
about what happens to them. And there is a whole gallery of
dramatis personae—perhaps one should say a whole stageful of

heightens the tension. At 1. 9. 3 (quoted below, p. 178), when she guesses the truth
(already known to the reader) on waking up in the tomb, Chariton again uses her
to step up the emotional charge of the situation. At 1. 11. 1-2 and 1. 13. 10 she
knows the pirates are lying to her—and this makes things even more grim. There
are many other occasions where her perception of the state of things brings her
close to the reader, in an almost confidential relationship, and thus makes him see
the story through her eyes.

[22] Plepelits (1976, introduction, 28 ff.) The usual title *Chaereas and Callirhoe* rests
only on the evidence of the unique (late Byzantine) MS. *Callirhoe* is found in a
papyrus (but see Crawford, (1951: 1); this title could be an abbreviation). But this
is a matter of fashion: the form *Jack and Jill* is apparently imperial, but romances
were also called e.g. *Ephesiaca*. In pre-romance times plays, for example, were called
Hippolytus, or *Medea*; Heliodorus' novel was commonly known as *Charicleia* in the
Byzantine period. Certainly no interpretation can be built on a title. For the substance of the matter: Schmeling (1974: 130-41), discusses Chaereas as 'a new kind
of hero' undergoing a 'marvellous journey' and *rites de passage* to expiate his guilt.
Heiserman (1977), on the other hand, sees the story as being concerned entirely
with Callirhoe (whose name he misspells): 'a fantasy of erotic power' is 'in conflict
with, and therefore sanctioned by, a fantasy of moral power', and Chariton's story
'reconciles our desire to be Aphrodisian with our desire to be good'.

them. But events viewed as emanations of character are really rather bleak; Rohde's word for the plot was *armselig*, wretched. The reason is that of the *dramatis personae* nobody who is important enough is nasty enough. Again, Rohde pointed that out long ago; what I would observe here is that Dionysius and the King, notably, are too *civilized* to set the world, or this story, on fire. This is in very striking contrast with the vigour, indeed brutality, of much of older Greek literature (*Agamemnon, Oedipus Tyrannus*). Only the minor characters, and not all of them, have enough punch in their personality to interfere effectively with events—Theron the pirate, Plangon, Phocas, Leonas, Artaxates, the servants of Dionysius and the King. And they cannot *direct* events—when they try to, things end badly; they are not clever New Comedy slaves who can resolve situations successfully. And if Dionysius and the King are too civilized, Chaereas and Callirhoe themselves are even less effective; they are really attitudes, sensitized personality-matter rather than people with real emotions. It is true that they choose the 'big things': Callirhoe chooses maternity, Chaereas war, and these αἱρέσεις ('choices') do determine the main lines of the story, its events and emotions. But otherwise they are pale, and even these choices are really 'attitudes' which precipitate action, rather than themselves action—Callirhoe and Chaereas are such people as, faced with such circumstances, will inevitably make a 'pathetic' choice. Chariton is not principally concerned with people's characters, although what he does with some of them—Theron, Artaxates the King's eunuch, and the King himself are good examples— shows ability with people.[23] Events, then, are melodramatic; emotion is really sentiment; the principal people are only half-alive. Perhaps we cannot really maintain that Chariton has, consciously, profound things to say about life, or love, or people, in universal terms.

But he does say something in more limited terms: about life, love (perhaps), people in his Hellenistic world; and he says so in a Hellenistic way, a Hellenistic form. Two things stand out about

[23] Perry (1930: 115 ff.) discusses some of these—notably Theron—in some detail, but is pursuing a topic of limited profitability; it is followed further, and given some theoretical basis, by Helms (1966). What transpires from these studies is that Chariton depicts character dramatically—as could be expected. This topic is brought within the scope of Hägg's study in an addendum by that scholar (1972: 545-56); as in other aspects of his narrative, there is, on examination, considerable but unobtrusive technical subtlety in Chariton's presentation of his characters.

Chaereas and Callirhoe: its technique, and the report it gives us of some aspects, at least, of its author's society. I have already touched on both of these topics—they are closely connected—and here return to them, to develop them further; first, to the matter of Chariton's narrative technique.

The principal technical problem Chariton has to face, as we have seen, is the problem of relating events to scene, to character (in the sense of the *personae* presented in the drama). That is to say that Chariton, or his generation, has in effect to invent narrative fiction—at least, extended narrative fiction, as opposed to the oral *conte*. It has of course some relationship to epic, which is extended and narrative and largely fictitious. But if he is doing an old thing, he is doing it in a new form, the form of prose. Narrative prose has some, but not all, of the characteristics of heroic epic. It is extensible, it is receptive, it can narrate—all of this as opposed to drama, which does not have these characteristics. But it has no fixed constructional base, such as the formulaic hexameter provides. This is a function of its diffusion: it is hard to think that romances were usually purveyed orally to fairly large groups. There may well have been small reading-circles, but presumably a work like *Chaereas and Callirhoe* was essentially a written thing aimed at literate individuals. This, along with social diffusion, would affect its reception, and hence its creation: the result is a freer form, whose narrative conventions had to be shaped. Perry rightly describes the form as 'latter-day epic for Everyman'.[24]

Chariton is writing, however, in the cultural context of the most familiar popular medium of his day, namely dramatic spectacle of one kind or another: Hellenistic drama, or excerpts from the classics, or mime. Hence Perry's further description of the form as Hellenistic drama in prose.[25] There is in fact a fair resemblance, in *Chaereas and Callirhoe*, to 'Scenes from Shakespeare': a monologue by Callirhoe strongly resembles a soliloquy by Lady Macbeth, or a speech like 'The quality of mercy is not strained'; and it is not difficult to imagine a famous actress 'playing' Callirhoe. Only, Chariton insists on the logical thread of events, on the *mythos*. Besides affecting scenes, his story has structure, logical backbone.

---

[24] Perry (1967: 48). Müller (1976) goes so far as to suggest that Chariton's frequent quotations of Homer are not just decoration but part of the very fabric of a story which its author thought of as epic; this is exaggerated.
[25] Perry (1967: 72 ff.).

The question is, the mix. And the illusion of 'subject' and 'treatment', of theme and narrative method, is an aspect of this technical problem; that is why the two cannot be clinically separated; it is a matter of selection and representation.[26]

Chariton selects and represents, as we have seen, by what is essentially a dramatic technique, the changing of focus; it is perhaps his principal technical device. To continue to report Hägg's examination, this changing of focus, in its turn, is characteristically achieved by 'gliding': 'what we see is a continual gliding motion on a scale extending from great distance and general narrative over medium distance and individualized narrative to a nearness which involves quoting the "exact" words of the persons talking, and, at times, even going a step further to reporting the simultaneous inner mental processes, using more time in the narration than the material narrated "actually" took'; or, *aliter*, Chariton uses 'a continuous time sequence, combined with quick and frequent changes in tempo'.[27] The example that Hägg analyses in detail is the episode (1. 12. 5–1. 13. 6) of the sale of Callirhoe by Theron the pirate to Leonas, Dionysius' steward: we see all of Theron's actions over 24 hours, but much of this time is covered in rapid narrative, while certain small parts of it—the discussions between Theron and Leonas—are reported in detail, in direct speech, as it were in close-up.

Another example will serve other purposes as well, here: the episode of the tomb-robbing (1. 7–1. 9). We are shown, in sequence, Theron, Callirhoe, and Theron again. First, Theron is introduced into the story: his previous career as a brigand is rapidly sketched, in a very few lines; then we see him observing the funeral; and immediately after this his thoughts are brought before us as, that night, he forms the project of robbery: 'why should I risk my life

---

[26] Epic and drama are of course the real aesthetic sources of romance, they are what narrative fiction is 'like' aesthetically. The *form* is that of historiography; this is the most important literary ancestor formally, in that it offers a prose antecedent. But, as Eduard Schwartz said long ago (1896/1943), *degenerate* historiography; the nearer romance is to historiography, the worse for the historiography it is near to. The real problems of historiography—use of sources, narrative method, criteria for analysis, selection of material—are different from the problems of narrative fiction, and the overlap is only partial. It is of course true—the observation is again Perry's—that a historiographical façade can offer to such a story the dimension of academic respectability. To the literature on Chariton's pseudo-historical setting, add now Plepelits (1976: 15 ff.), and Molinié, Budé edition (1989: 5 ff.).

[27] Hägg (1971*a*: 38).

battling with the sea and killing living people and not getting much out of it, when I can get rich from one dead body? Let the die be cast; I won't miss a chance like that of making money. Now, whom shall I recruit for the job? Think, Theron; who would be suitable, of the men you know?' The next day's action consists of his rounding up a suitable gang; again, this is described rapidly, and is at once followed by a detailed representation in direct speech of the colloquy of the assembled villains, who are instructed by Theron to gather that night for the enterprise. The narrative then passes to Callirhoe, who on that night, in her funeral vault, begins to awaken from her coma.

Her respiration had stopped, but lack of food started it again; with difficulty, and gradually, she began to breathe. Then she began to move her body, limb by limb. Then she opened her eyes and came to her senses like someone waking up from sleep; and thinking Chaereas was sleeping beside her, she called to him. But since neither husband nor maids paid any attention, and everything was lonely and dark, the girl began to shiver and tremble with fear; she could not piece things together. As she stirred into consciousness she happened to touch wreaths and ribbons and make gold and silver objects rattle; and there was a strong smell of spices. So then she remembered the kick, and how it had knocked her down; and reluctantly and fearfully she recognized the funeral vault.

The narrative now glides quickly to the thoughts and reactions of the girl as she realizes that she has been buried alive; and that realization is as it were actualized in the direct speech of her terrified monologue. Then we pass immediately to Theron again; he and his gang are approaching the tomb as Callirhoe has just become aware of the horror of her position; the approach is described rapidly, and once more we pass quickly to a close-up, a long, detailed, animated, dramatic representation of the encounter of the now awakened Callirhoe and the astonished robbers:

When they began to use crowbars and hammer heavily to open the vault, Callirhoe was gripped by a variety of emotions—fear, joy, grief, surprise, hope, disbelief. 'Where is this noise coming from? Is some divinity coming for me—poor creature—as always happens when people are dying? Or is it not a noise but a voice—the voice of the gods below calling me to them? It is more likely that it is tomb-robbers; there, there is an additional mis-fortune; wealth is of no use to a corpse.' While these thoughts were still passing through her mind, a robber put his head through and came a little way into the vault. Callirhoe, intending to implore his help, threw herself

at his knees; he was terrified and jumped back. Shaking with fear, he cried
to his fellows 'Let's get out of here! There's some sort of spirit on guard in
there who won't let us come in!' Theron laughed scornfully at him and
called him a coward and deader than the dead girl. Then he told another
man to go in; and when nobody had the courage to do so, he went in
himself, holding his sword before him. At the gleam of the metal Callirhoe
was afraid she was going to be murdered; she shrank back into the corner
of the vault and from there begged him in a small voice 'Have pity on
me, whoever you are—I have had no pity from husband or parents! Do
not kill me now you have saved me!' Theron took courage, and being an
intelligent man realized the truth of the matter.[28]

I have used the term 'close-up'; and indeed what Hägg calls
'gliding' a film director would call 'zooming'; from the panoramic
view of the deserted street, the camera zooms in on the lonely and
frightened sheriff in *High Noon*. Perhaps the more intimate television is an even better parallel: from events in causal sequence we
can pass, in television as in Chariton's novel, to close and intimate
examination of the emotions they arouse.

The episode of the tomb-robbery will illustrate also two other
characteristic features of Chariton's narrative: the connection of
successive episodes by thought—not by mechanical time-sequence
—and the distribution of the action among several characters. The
passage from Theron to Callirhoe to Theron is a passage determined by a criterion of intellectual continuity: we need to see both
aspects of the event to understand it. If we have already observed
the Aristotelian feature of *mythos*, we observe here something very
close to the Aristotelian feature of *dianoia*: intellectual content,
coherent sequence of thought. We see too that the line of events
can be distributed, in its narration, among the characters who act
out its several elements: Theron does his plotting, Callirhoe subsequently does her awakening, Theron subsequently does his tomb-

---

[28] This passage raises the question of how seriously Chariton is treating his story.
To modern taste it seems almost farcical; and there are other occasions when we
may wonder whether the author's tongue is in his cheek. But overall Chariton
seems 'serious' enough—this is not to deny that he is capable of seeing humour as
well as pathos in his scenes at times. The whole question of humour in these
romances is worth pursuing. My own view of Achilles Tatius' *Leucippe and Clitophon*
(?late second century) is that he is certainly in places guying the form, grotesque-
ly. And Longus is overtly detached enough from his story to make us smile at his
heroes. But the question is not a simple one: the taste of the period is not altogether
ours. A full discussion may be expected in a forthcoming study by Graham
Anderson [= G. Anderson (1982)].

entering—and that is all we are shown: we are not told what
Theron did between his plotting and his tomb-entering, because the
knowledge of that is not needed. The action is passed, that is, from
one character to another: Hägg happily characterizes the technique
as a 'relay-race'.[29] It is of course *dianoia* in another aspect; it also
helps to economize narrative, and thus contributes substantially to
the preponderance of 'scene' in the story.

Let us here 'glide'—imitating Chariton again—to another aspect
of his romance, which I will call its 'general characteristics'. In so
doing we shall, I believe, discover more fully its 'theme'. We shall,
however, see that the movement from its narrative technique is
not a very abrupt movement. It will be convenient to start from
another of Perry's *dicta*: Chariton, he said, 'writes Greek romance
as it should be written'.[30] This looks like one of those intuitive and
forthright statements that characterize Perry's work. What did he
mean?

Perry liked the *classical* feel of Chariton (perhaps his instinct was
not so very different from Rohde's). We have seen *mythos* and
dianoia, which, while no doubt not exclusively classical literary
features, are certainly commonly visible in classical literature, for
instance Sophocles; we have seen also that their existence in the
story can be attributed to, and expressed in terms of, identifiable
and even measurable techniques—recapitulation, scene and summary, relay-race. While we are at it, we should here recall, with
Perry, the major classical characteristic of *Chaereas and Callirhoe*:
namely, the dramatic irony that the author really does use very
effectively (we have just seen that too in the tomb-robbery). It
can likewise be pinned down: it is achieved by the convention
of authorial omniscience.[31] These features are what Perry was
referring to in praising the manner of Chariton's writing. But we
should look also at the matter, at the nature of 'Greek romance'.
We should consider with imaginative sympathy, if necessary with
a temporary disengagement of our 'classical' judgment, another
aspect of the story: its Hellenistic-ness, its Hellenistic aspect, and
setting, and assumptions.

We may observe, first, that the very action of the story is set
squarely in the Hellenistic world, in that it shows the rivalry of two
Greeks, Chaereas and Dionysius, resolved (as we have seen) by

---

[29] Hägg (1971*a*: 151).   [30] Perry (1930: 129).
[31] Hägg (1971*a*: 118-19).

their involvement in the state affairs of two Oriental empires. But some might say that *Chaereas and Callirhoe* is most notably Hellenistic in displaying a technique more substantial than the content it is meant to carry. There is yet more skill, however, than has yet been pointed out, and to dismiss it as 'mere technique' is to do the story serious injustice. The use of illusion, for instance, extends beyond the *trompe l'œil* of subject and perspective; it extends to the passage of time in the story, for Chariton offers very little indication of the 'real' chronological framework—the calendar time taken by events.[32] Deprived, thus, of a firm objective 'handrail' to guide us through events, we turn the more readily to what the author wants to present as important, namely his characters' psychological reactions as set in the emotional *sequence* of events—this is of course an aspect of the gliding-and-close-up technique discussed above. The very basis of the plot—the essential plot-element of separation of hero and heroine—is matter of illusion, for that separation is not as marked as it appears to be (I return to this point below). The relay-race technique does more than economize narrative; it also peoples the story—Chaereas and Callirhoe may be insubstantial, but the characters through whom we learn what happens to them are much less so: their rivals, their rivals' servants. Much of the story is carried by such people, not by the hero and heroine: the tomb-robbery, the sale of Callirhoe, the intrigue which leads to Mithridates' inculpation; and to estimate the effect of this we have only to imagine how baldly these incidents would have been narrated by Xenophon Ephesius. The care for causation is not limited to the major events, the succession of marriages and intrigues, but extends to lesser articulations: Theron is represented as selling Callirhoe extremely hurriedly, and it is this very haste which makes Dionysius realize that she is not a slave and that in consequence he can marry her.[33] If the transitions, the 'glidings' are smoothly managed, so are the changes of subject—by a subordination, a participle, an element of vocabulary.[34] Not only such narrative bridges, but structural bridges too, are built with care:

---

[32] Hägg (1971*a*: 26–7); but in fact all time is accounted for, p. 44. Hägg remarks (p. 210) that Chariton seems not to have paid special attention to temporal structure. This is perhaps instinctive avoidance of realistic precision; or it may be conscious omission (see p. 22 and n. 36).

[33] Gerschmann (1975: 31 ff.).

[34] Hägg (1971*a*: esp. 141 ff.).

Theron both restores Callirhoe to life and restores Chaereas to the plot[35]—after which he is promptly executed to avoid too easy a solution (similarly Shakespeare executes Mercutio to keep him in his place).

There is illusion, then, in all directions: illusion in respect of subject, of theme and climax, of perspective. These several forms of technical skill could without difficulty be documented more fully. Hägg's pages indeed do so document them, and are required reading for any serious student of Chariton; they reveal, dispassionately, what can easily be obscured to the prejudice of a Rohde, or even to the relative enthusiasm of a Perry. The reader who is disposed to notice such skill will find it. It is not, however, the primary intention of this paper to expound such matters systematically, as Hägg does, but rather to take due note of their importance—and having done so, to observe that the presence of marked technical skill is itself one of the distinctive general characteristics of *Chaereas and Callirhoe*, one that itself contributes to its Hellenistic-ness.

Not that technique is exclusively a Hellenistic phenomenon. But some elements of Chariton's do contribute to a typically Hellenistic intention. The geographical separation of hero and heroine is illusory, it has just been suggested. They are close enough, in Miletus and Caria, for the author to maintain a contact between them—in the shape of a shrine of Aphrodite which both can visit, a satrap whose involvement is justified by his proximity, and later a war in which hero and heroine are on contiguous sea and land; Chariton calculates his distances. But some distance is vital to the separation of the pair; and the purpose of this separation is not, as in other such works, separate adventures, but the emotional isolation of each of the principals. And this, with the emotional stop-pulling that it gives rise to, is Hellenistic.

In respect of the manipulation of the emotions, Chariton is indeed at one point as explicit as it is possible to be. At the beginning of the last book, he advertises its contents: 'you will like this book', he tells his readers, 'because it contains nice things, ἔρωτες δίκαιοι, νόμιμοι γάμοι "lawful love and sanctioned marriage": no more brigands or slavery or trials or wars—it will clear out the memory of all those nasty things, καθάρσιον . . . ἐστι τῶν ἐν τοῖς πρώτοις σκυθρωπῶν' (8. 1. 4). It is hard not to think that he is

<hr>

[35] Hägg (1971a: 141 ff.); Phocas similarly provides a bridge between hero and heroine, 3. 7. 1-2.

referring to Aristotle (and thus classicizing consciously). But it is
not necessarily what Aristotle meant—whatever it is that Aristotle
did mean. Chariton seems to mean that the good will replace the
bad, will make you forget it. Whether he had Aristotle in mind or
not, the quality and nature of the sensibility he posits is not what
we think of as classical: it is sentimental, and it is Hellenistic.
Sentimental, and not reticent. Not that classical tragedy is reticent.
It is often strident enough. But this whipping-up of emotions for the
sake of emotions is not what Sophocles is *about*, in the *Oedipus*, or
Euripides in the *Medea*; it *is* what Chariton is about.

I do not want to suggest that Chariton's technique is flawless,
or always felicitous. It is not; there are defects in plot and narrative. Some of them merely represent the cost to Chariton of some
advantage or another. The execution of Theron, for instance: *ben
trovato!*, yes—but how likely is it that Hermocrates would destroy
the only lead he has to his lost daughter? Some, again, are mere
carelessnesses, and relatively trivial. When Chaereas first sets out
from Syracuse to hunt at random for Callirhoe (3. 3. 8), there
appears to be no difficulty in setting out to sea in mid-winter; but
when, a few pages later (3. 5. 1), he runs into Theron's ship,
brings it to Syracuse, screws the truth out of the brigand, and sets
sail again—then the enterprise is represented as utterly unthinkable, ἀδυνατόν.[36] Yet others are instances of waste, simply. The
Montagu and Capulet theme is a very damp squib in this story.

But some of the very shortcomings of the story are distinctively
Hellenistic. Some of the causation, and in major matters, Chariton
motivates by attributing it to *tyche*: the finding of Theron's ship,
the outbreak of the Egyptian rebellion which alone enables the
author to find a dénouement for his story. To do him justice,
Chariton seems acutely conscious of the operation of *tyche* in his
story, and one suspects that he is embarrassed by it;[37] none the
less, he does use this Hellenistic device. Another embarrassment—
or such it seems to be—is the disposition of Callirhoe's child, who

[36] It may be noted (Hägg 1971a: 26) that this latter occasion is one of the very
few specifications of time in the story.
[37] Some examples besides those quoted (3. 3. 8 Theron, 6. 8. 1 the rebellion): 1.
13. 4 it is *tyche* who brings Theron to Dionysius' estate; 2. 8. 3 though Callirhoe's
pregnancy is explicable enough, *tyche* uses it to overcome her fidelity to Chaereas—
and thus sets up the series of *agones* that constitute the action; 4. 5. 3 Chaereas'
letter to Callirhoe miscarries (in the last two instances the natural motivation is in
fact perfectly adequate); 8. 1. 2 *tyche* is about to separate Chaereas and Callirhoe,
at Arados, but is overruled for once.

is left at the end of the story with Dionysius. This may be, as Perry suggested, the vestige of a legend: there are hints enough that when the boy grows up he will return to Sicily to take his place as the descendant of Hermocrates, which seems appropriate enough to a son of a Dionysius.[38] But if this is legend, it coincides conveniently with the fact that Chariton is embarrassed by his treatment of Dionysius; he has represented him throughout as a noble soul, and as *sympathique*, and cannot bear to leave him out in the cold altogether. Sophocles could have borne it. But in this story, everyone must have a prize (except Theron). Dionysius gets a whole clutch of consolation prizes: military glory, a pre-eminent position in the King's entourage—and a son. 'And they all go down to the beach and have a lovely time.' It doesn't seem very cathartic to us.

But if Dionysius gets the child, Callirhoe abandons it; and that seems rather ignoble—does her duty, and affection, end with seeing that the child is born, and is properly looked after? There is indeed a good deal of ignobility, to our kind of romantic taste; all of the principal characters do things which hardly fit heroic standards, or even the standards of Victorian melodrama. Dionysius wants Chaereas to die, but is relieved when *his steward* takes the responsibility of attacking his ship (3. 9. 12). The King of Persia is restrained in his desire for Callirhoe not by any μεγαλοψυχία ('magnanimity'), but only by the thought of his own position, and of what the Queen would say (6. 1. 8-12). Callirhoe is quite prepared to consider abortion, and to pass off Chaereas' child as Dionysius'. Chaereas takes Tyre by deceit (7. 4. 3ff.), and misleads his naval crews when the Egyptian land army is defeated (8. 2. 5). All of this so clearly forms a pattern that one cannot call these cases 'loose ends' in the story. They are part of the morality of Chariton's world. If the story is epic, its setting is hardly heroic.

This suggests a whole topic, the world-outlook of this Hellenistic world. If it has its own sentiments, it also has its own philosophy, its own theology; and that is far from being clear-cut. Apparently Aphrodite is behind the whole action, as she is behind that of the *Hippolytus*, but her purposes are here altogether less clear—certainly less frank and brutal and uncompromising. She wants to teach Chaereas a lesson, evidently—but Chaereas survives to profit from it. We are told, late in the day, that Chaereas' fault is ingrati-

[38] e.g. 2. 11. 2; 3. 8. 8; 8. 7. 12. But see Plepelits (1976: 30ff.) for arguments against Perry.

tude to Aphrodite, shown in his initial jealousy and paid for by his tribulations.[39] We can suppose also that his (and Callirhoe's) redeeming virtue is loyalty to love.[40] That is to say, Aphrodite is thoroughly on the side of the bourgeoisie: stern, but ultimately cosy. And this fits with the characters. There is not even a glimpse of tragedy, not even as much as in the figure of Malvolio in a similarly cosy world; only melodrama.

Whether all this amounts to a 'theology' is another matter. The theology of *Chaereas and Callirhoe* is as vague as much of the theology of the period—that of Isis, for example, who would be all things to all men, a comforter; not so much a perception of forces in life as a projection of wishes. Aphrodite is Love-who-makes-the-world-go-round, and love, beauty and marriage are umbilically linked. Another magazine-convention, another attitude: love and marriage, in the words of a once-popular modern song, go together like a horse and carriage. Aphrodite has underlings: Eros and *tyche*; *tyche* has to be kept in line when at the beginning of the last book she aims to keep our couple separated—this seems too much to Aphrodite. But this hardly amounts to a firm theological system.[41] It is not clearer than Homer's problem about the precedence of Fate over Zeus. *Tyche* is nothing more than a convention: human plans go wrong; and Eros is virtually a doublet of Aphrodite, for the most part. There *is* a divine machinery, of a kind; and Chariton does underline Aphrodite;[42] but he is not underlining anything very substantial. It is not clear that Aphrodite's—that is, Chariton's—intentions did not develop in the course of the story's construction. At the very beginning (1. 1. 3–4) Eros, stimulated by the difficulty of the Montagu–Capulet situation, resolves to unite the young people; possibly (but not probably) he instructs Callirhoe to worship Aphrodite (1. 1. 5);[43] and an unnamed deity, ὁ θεός

---

[39] ἤδη γὰρ αὐτῷ διηλάττετο, πρότερον ὀργισθεῖσα χαλεπῶς διὰ τὴν ἄκαιρον ζηλοτυπίαν, ὅτι δῶρον παρ' αὐτῆς λαβὼν τὸ κάλλιστον, οἷον οὐδὲ Ἀλέξανδρος ὁ Πάρις, ὕβρισεν εἰς τὴν χάριν. ἐπεὶ δὲ καλῶς ἀπελογήσατο τῷ Ἔρωτι Χαιρέας ἀπὸ δύσεως εἰς ἀνατολὰς διὰ μυρίων παθῶν πλανηθείς, ἠλέησεν αὐτὸν Ἀφροδίτη (8. 1. 3).

[40] e.g. (Chaereas) 4. 2. 1–3; (Callirhoe) 4. 7. 8; 5. 8. 6; 6. 7. 12.

[41] As Gerschmann suggests (1975: 93 ff.)

[42] Blake, *Index nominum propriorum s.v.* 'Venus', lists over 30 references to her. Helms 1966; 115 ff. sorts them into groups: she is frequently held responsible by Callirhoe for her misfortunes; her aid is invoked by Callirhoe; Callirhoe is compared to her in point of beauty. But there is no more 'theology' than is indicated in the present text.

[43] At 1. 1. 5. 2 Gerschmann (1975: 3, 131) proposes Ἔρωτος (τοῦ πατρὸς Blake) κελεύσαντος προσκυνῆσαι τὴν θεόν. This is palaeographically tempting (see Blake's

(who could be Aphrodite) contrives that Chaereas and Callirhoe should see each other (1. 1. 6). At 2. 2. 8 Aphrodite plans another marriage for Callirhoe, but does not intend it to last. At 2. 4. 5 Eros is at odds with Dionysius for his σωφροσύνη ('restraint'). At 7. 5. 3 Callirhoe thinks Aphrodite is offended by her beauty (νεμεσητόν . . . τὸ κάλλος), at 8. 3, as we have seen, we learn that Aphrodite has been angered by Chaereas' jealousy. All of this may be reconcilable; but it is hardly an explanation of how the world works. It is a reflection, rather, of not very comprehending popular attitudes; an aspect of this story's cultural and social context, not of its intellectual content.

A Hellenistic story in a Hellenistic context: a society of ordinary people. They like cosiness; they are romantic, sentimental, passive, mediocre—Perry has no difficulty in finding suitable adjectives; I should like to recall the adjective 'civilized', not necessarily as a term of praise, but to adjust our angle of vision—civilized, social. The story is full of indications of people's attitudes, of their 'civilization' in the sense that they live in society and reflect the values accepted by that society. They are—that is, Chariton is— thoroughly provincial: he feels the need to show that he knows Athens, and an equal need to affect to despise it[44]—it is the attitude of the provincial Frenchman to Paris. He provides captions from his ordered world: Theron is ὁ πανοῦργος, ὁ κακοήθης, the big bad wolf (e.g. 3. 3. 12, 17). He is impressed by barbarians as well as scornful of them—the Euphrates is the outer limit of the acceptable world, but at least there is no nonsense about who is boss in Persia (although Chariton does suppose that the δῆμος, 'people', has a voice there).[45] Chariton's little man knows a seigneur when he sees one: Dionysius is a βασιλικὸς ἀνήρ ('true aristocrat' 2. 1. 5), and φύσει γίνονται βασιλεῖς ('royalty is born in people' 2. 3. 10); just as he knows that slaves always have an eye to the main chance (6. 5. 5). And Chariton is sententious with the accumulated wisdom of the world: φύσει εὔελπις ὁ Ἔρως.[46]

apparatus), and it is true that Eros has already, early as it is, appeared twice. But Callirhoe is represented as being taken to the festival by her mother, on her first public appearance, and it is not clear how Eros could intrude into this family occasion. The reading would have merit only as an element in a more coherent theological structure than can be found in the story.

[44] The pirates think of selling Callirhoe there, but recoil before its litigiousness, 1. 11. 5-7.   [45] 5. 1. 3; 5. 4. 1; 6. 7. 3.

[46] 2. 6. 4: see Blake's *Index sententiarum*.

Here an important qualification needs to be made. I have described the tone of this romance as 'Hellenistic'; but that is not intended as a derogatory evaluation. It has long been conventional to admire the literary achievements of the 'classical' world, and to be rather condescending towards those of the succeeding period—although much of the philosophy and science, and many of the social mechanisms, that we admire in the ancient world are post-classical. If its literature, in this specimen, seems to reflect a world less elevated than that of a Sophoclean hero, the reason is not necessarily that the Hellenistic world was in all respects of that quality; it is rather that popular attitudes are reflected in such literature much more fully than they commonly are reflected in what has survived of 'classical' literature. If Chariton's world seems undistinguished, we should remember that most people in most societies *are* undistinguished. The realities of life for the inhabitants of fifth-century Athens were surely not very different from the realities observed by Chariton's 'little people'. Their theology was no less vague and confused; we have no reason to suppose that their morality was any more lofty. Aristophanes' heroes would probably recognize Chariton's characters readily enough. And it is no bad thing that a writer should reflect his world. On the contrary, to reflect it as clearly as Chariton does is an achievement worthy of more recognition than it has yet received in the canonical histories of literature.

The scene, then, is Hellenistic; indeed, Chariton's concentration on scene is itself Hellenistic; his interest in personal psychology and its expression recalls Hellenistic statues. He is a photographer of this society; a better one than Xenophon Ephesius, because his art is more flexible; a less sophisticated one than Achilles Tatius, but clearly his audience is less sophisticated too. Plutarch would surely have recognized the feel of literature like this; he is more educated than Chariton, but just as comfortable.

This *is* new; and it did have success; and it merited success; because Chariton shows artistic genius in perceiving the plasticity of this new form. 'Greek romance as it should be written': *Chaereas and Callirhoe* is not merely a romantic—non-classical—story written with classical craftsmanship. The formula, attractively simple, is too simple. There is more to it than that: Chariton uses his medium with something of the fluidity of film or television; and he knows very well what he is doing. His technique in this new narrative medium is equal to the task of carrying a story that he conceives essentially in dramatic terms. Others, later—Achilles Tatius, Heliodorus—were to use the form for more specifically narrative purposes.

What Chariton uses medium and technique for is to represent his world rather than to create a new one. And this, at the end, is what his story is 'about': it is about the sentiment of a mass civilization. It is about the situation of his Chaereas and (particularly) Callirhoe. Not about their characters, or their actions, but above all their situation: isolation, and grief—and reunion. Life can bring isolation and grief; but if Fortune is kind, they can be overcome; let us, for our comfort, suppose that Fortune is kind. This is the salient thing, it is what Chariton has to say.[47] Philostratus is very snobbish about Chariton: 'Do you really suppose', he says in an 'Imaginary Letter' (*Ep.* 66) to him, 'that civilized people are going to remember your story when you are gone? You are a nobody even now you're alive; you'll be less than a nobody when you're dead.' The word that I have here translated as 'civilized people' is Ἕλληνες—for that is what Philostratus means by it: cultured people, civilized in his sense. But the Hellenistic, imperial world did not share Philostratus' contempt. And we need not share Rohde's.[48]

---

[47] Hägg (1971*a*: 119) comments that 'Chariton's interest does not lie exclusively in the two particular persons whom he has chosen as the hero and heroine of the romance' (he is discussing the effect of Chariton's authorial point of view). Not exclusively—but primarily. Other characters ('every single character is . . . seen from inside') exist to serve the story of the lovers. Their world, it is true, is peopled with characters often more 'real', or realistically drawn, than they themselves are; and we are certainly invited to feel with Dionysius and Artaxates, for example. But the point of the *mythos* which is so carefully underlined is the situation that Chaereas and Callirhoe find themselves in, as the dominant exemplars of their civilization's emotional physiognomy.

[48] Versions of this paper have been read at Berkeley and at the Hellenic Society; I am grateful for comments made on those occasions. And I wish here to offer particular thanks to the editor of the present volume, Mr J. J. Winkler, for his remarks on the original version of the paper; he will recognize, and I wish to record, that I owe much to his thoughtful and detailed remarks.

8
Longus: Towards a History of Bucolic and its Function in the Roman Empire

BERND EFFE

Longus' pastoral novel—apparently written during the second half of the second century AD[1]—presents remarkable testimony of the Greek fiction of the Roman Empire, and in two respects in particular. On the one hand we conceive this novel to be the last representative (within the limits of Greek antiquity) of the literary bucolic which began with the works of Theocritus. This, as it were, automatically poses questions about both the history of the genre and the history of its function: What position does Longus occupy in the bucolic tradition? What is the function of bucolic in Longus with respect to his contemporary audience? On the other hand, the novel poses questions of a different kind, too. It is, as it were, the result of a bold experiment in genre: the attempt to combine two strands of tradition by mixing two genres to create a new synthesis, the hexameter genre of the bucolic idyll and the prose genre of the so-called ideal erotic novel.[2] In their evolution since the

---

* The following paper developed from a lecture given at the Mommsen-Gesellschaft in Würzburg in May 1980.

[1] It is still impossible to establish with certainty an exact date for the novel. A series of clues, esp. its interactions with the literature and art of the 2nd and 3rd c., enable us to make Longus a younger contemporary of Lucian. On this cf. Reich (1894), Dalmeyda (1932), Carugno (1955: 153ff.), Weinreich (1950/1962: 18f.); the arguments are collected by Schönberger (1970/1980: 9ff.). Incidentally, there seems to be a relationship between Longus and Achilles Tatius (who cannot be safely dated either): ecphrastic introduction; Syrinx story (2. 34: A. T. 8. 6); παράδεισος-ecphrasis (4.2ff.: A. T. 1. 15); cf. also below, n. 10. This would form another starting point for a relative dating. It cannot, however, be pursued here.

[2] In addition to these two subsystems, other genres enter into the system of this particular novel, too (anagnorismos-structure; stock characters with speaking names; the scenery of the last book).

Hellenistic era, both literary forms were determined by their own set of artistic procedures and elements of content and motif, and each of these had its own specifically structured system of norms and conventions, which controlled both the production and the reception of the text.[3] By keeping both lines of tradition present throughout his hybrid synthesis, Longus continually evokes for his reader two literary horizons of expectation and thus enables his book to be read in two different ways. The text can be read against the background of the erotic novel as well as that of the pastoral idyll. The reader, however, only fully experiences the aesthetic pleasure intended by the author when he becomes aware of the innovative momentum of this mixing of genres, that is, the mutual permeation of the two levels of genre. For this reason alone—and for many others, too[4]—it is evident that this novel is intended for an aesthetically sensitive, i.e. urbane and cultivated, audience well versed in literature.

It would be rewarding to investigate the procedure through which the genres were mixed as such by, to begin with, tracing how the bucolization of the novel, or rather the epicization of the bucolic, functions in concrete terms, and then by using the result of this as a starting point for general theoretical considerations regarding the genre. This, however, will not be done here. Instead, the following study focuses on those problems of genre and functional history mentioned above and accordingly in the first place illustrates the direction of the bucolic tradition as it is represented in the novel. This rather one-sided restriction of the perspective—apart from the fact that reflectively selecting the formulation of the question is a principal form of legitimate scholarly method—may be accepted in good conscience, particularly as Longus by no means aims at a harmonious balance between the two systems of genre, but rather concedes a clearly dominant position to one of them. The meaning is primarily carried by the bucolic elements. The conventional novelistic motifs, in so far as they are perceived

[3] For the concepts of literary genre and genre-history used in this paper cf. Jauss (1972) (based on the genre-theory developed by the Russian formalists; cf. in this connection esp. the papers by Tynjanov (1971)); see also Vosskamp (1977), Effe (1977: 10 ff.).

[4] In this context, two singularities of the text need to be pointed out: firstly the ambitious, intricate style (cf. E. Rohde (1914: 550 ff.), Castiglioni (1928), Dalmeyda (1934: xxxviii ff.)), secondly the extraordinarily sophisticated allusive technique, esp. with reference to the bucolic tradition (cf. Scarcella (1971); also cf. the literature listed in n. 13).

at all, appear as a rule in bucolic transformation; they do not acquire any significant meaning and weight of their own.[5] Longus, as it were, quotes one schema of genre and evokes it in his readers' consciousness in order to direct their attention to the bucolic transformation. A few examples may be used to illustrate this fact at the outset.

One stereotypical motif of the erotic novel is the erotic intrigue. The hero's or heroine's beauty rouses the desire of the persons into whose power they have come, and this threatens the lovers' innocence or faithfulness. This schema, with several bucolic variations, occurs also in Longus. For example, when the cowherd Dorcon is trying to lay hands on Chloe by force, contrary to novelistic tradition the attack ends in a harmless, funny way, eventually even allowing a reconciliation,[6] the reason being that Dorcon (as a cowherd) on principle belongs to the 'safe' world which is represented above all by Daphnis and Chloe.[7] (The meaning of the bucolic as a positive counterpart of given reality will be discussed in detail below.) Another, again bucolic, variation of the motif is represented by the famous Lycaenion-scene (3. 15ff.). In contrast to the harmlessly naïve Dorcon, Lycaenion as a woman whose character is moulded by the experience of urban life has the neccessary intriguer's knowledge and erotic abilities to employ deliberate scheming successfully in her assault on Daphnis' innocence. Here the author uses this worn-out motif in order to bring out the (to him important) opposition between his 'pure' fool's rural naïvety and the erotic shrewdness of his urban seductress.[8] One further example. When the happiness of the two young shepherds is endangered by Tyrian pirates attacking and abducting Daphnis, and when this evil intermezzo is at once brought to a

[5] This has been repeatedly stressed with good reason; cf. e.g. Dalmeyda (1934; xx ff., Mittelstadt (1970; esp. 220 ff.).

[6] 1. 20 f. Dorcon, dressed up in a wolf-skin, waylays Chloe—and becomes the victim of the shepherds' dogs who discover and dishevel him badly. The 'wrong-doer' is soon given the opportunity to 'rehabilitate' himself by helping to save Daphnis from the hands of the pirates (1. 29 f.). This re-establishes the harmony among the shepherds that had been temporarily disturbed.

[7] The intrigue of another hapless rival for Chloe's favour may be compared, that of the 'audacious' cowherd Lampis (4. 7 and 28 f.). His assaults, too, are, as it were, neutralized by forgivingly including this troublemaker in the harmonizing wedding feast at the end of the novel (4. 38).

[8] This scene is paralleled in the fourth book, too: in the urban parasite Gnathon's (faltering) attempts to make Daphnis obey his sexual desires (4. 11 f.; cf. below, pp. 201 f.).

happy ending in a miraculous way—the pirates suffer shipwreck
and perish, but Daphnis is saved—Longus on the one hand 'quotes'
a whole bundle of motifs which had long been automatic in the
novel (pirates, abduction, shipwreck), but on the other hand gives
them a simultaneously bucolic twist by turning this episode into an
obvious expression of a central thematic idea: the shepherds' world
enjoys the protection of wonder-working divine powers.[9]

Finally, one has to draw attention to an element essential for the
whole structure of the plot of the novel. A stereotypical, hardly
ever violated, convention of the erotic novels requires that the two
lovers' innocence and faithfulness, despite all tribulations, remain
intact right up to the happy ending.[10] By this rule of the genre
Chloe keeps her virginity until the last chapter, her wedding night
with Daphnis. But the motivation has shifted significantly. What
the traditional novel presents as the result of an ever-triumphant
morality, in Longus arises from a consistently retained bucolic trait
of his heroes' character: their naïvety. Chloe simply does not have
the relevant knowledge about sexual practice at her disposal; even
if she wanted to lose her virginity, she would not know how;
and Daphnis, though he possesses this knowledge as a result of
Lycaenion's erotic lessons, is still naïve enough to allow his fear of
inflicting a bloody wound upon Chloe during the act of love to prevent him from applying it (3. 20. 24). Thus this by now empty
novelistic motif is given a new, bucolic meaning.

Apart from the tendency, which has only been sketched here
briefly, of continually bucolizing the novelistic schema, Longus at
every step effects in his new synthesis of genres a natural integration of the traditional bucolic idyll's elements of motif and form.[11]

---

[9] 1. 28 ff. the 'cow miracle'—the stolen cows hear the syrinx's sound, plunge
into the sea because of it and thus cause the ship to capsize—finds a parallel in
Pan's miraculous intervention and rescue in the course of the Methymnean-episode
(see below, p. 201).

[10] When an offence against this norm is found—as in Achilles Tatius (5. 27)—
it is a matter of a spectacular innovation, of a calculated game with the models of
the genre; cf. for this Reardon (1969: 300). A game of this kind can also be found
in Longus in the Lycaenion-scene, in which Daphnis' naïvety succumbs to urban
charm. It is possible that Longus refers to the corresponding passage in Achilles'
novel (cf. above, n. 1).

[11] A small selection under the keywords (cf. the literature cited in n. 13 below):
motif—the shepherds' presents (1. 15; 3. 18; etc.), competition between two shepherds (1. 16), description of places and seasons (passim), sympathetic animals (1.
31 f.), Eros as a boy (2. 3 ff.); form—translation of the βουκολιασμός-form into prose
(1. 16 parallelisms, 2. 15 shepherd as arbitrator).

In addition to this, he intersperses the text with a large number of obvious allusions to the poems of Theocritus and the later bucolic poets[12]—signals which again and again remind the reader of Longus' claim to continue, or revitalize, the tradition of the genre inaugurated by Theocritus. Longus represents himself as *Theocritus alter*, and wants to be understood primarily as a bucolic writer.[13]

2. This fact raises two problems, which will be investigated in the following. (i) What is the *meaning* of the bucolic in Longus' novel, that is, what is the author's *intention* when he has recourse to the bucolic genre? What message does the bucolic transmit to his contemporary audience? (ii) What is the relation between authorial intention and the actual *function* of his bucolic, its *meaning* as it is understood by his readers? Does the meaning of the bucolic as intended by Longus coincide with the impact it had really developed in contemporary communication, or is there a discrepancy between them?—a discrepancy that is in essence always possible in literary communication, that is, between planned and actual effect, between intended meaning and the realized function of a text.[14] A definite answer to both questions is of course extremely difficult, if not impossible, because of the considerable temporal distance between the text and its modern interpreter and the lack of explicit authorial statements or positively documented reception. At any rate, an attempt at answering these questions can only work by incorporating perspectives relevant to the genre's history.

For a long time scholars have been concerned with the problems of meaning and function in Longian bucolic, without being able to produce a reliable, generally accepted answer. On the contrary, we are dealing with an extremely controversial problem. If the relevant literature is surveyed, apart from mere modulations, three strands of interpretation emerge.[15] The beginning of modern discussion is

[12] Cf. among other passages 1. 10. 2: Th. 1. 52 ἀκριδοθήρα; 1. 23. 1 f.: Th. 1. 1 ff.; 7. 139 ff. (summer image); 2. 3 ff.: Bion fr. 13 (hunting the boy Eros); 2. 7: Th. 3; 11. 1 ff. (disappointed love for Amaryllis; no remedy against Eros); 2. 33. 3: Th. 1. 23 ff. (Sicilian goatherd sings for a promised gift); 3. 13: Th. 1. 87 f. (the animals' mating game as a stimulant); 3. 33. 3: Th. 7. 143 ff. (abundance of fruit); 4. 38. 3 f.: Th. 6. 44 ff. (bucolic scene). Further and more detailed material can be found in the studies cited in the following note.

[13] This claim is properly investigated by G. Rohde (1937); cf. also Valley (1926: 79 ff.), McCulloh (1970: 56 ff.), Mittelstadt (1970), Christie (1972).

[14] On the categories used here and their fundamental importance for an adequate interpretation cf. Hirsch (1972) and, based on it, Effe (1977).

[15] The following survey tries to characterize the basic positions of modern Longus

marked by the position taken by E. Rohde in his epoch-making
study of the Greek novel.[16] He asserted that the story of Daphnis
and Chloe was the literary product of a sentimental, i.e. self-
contradictory, longing for rural simplicity, which was expressed
again and again in imperial literature. The bucolic element was
there to gratify this longing, but without the author ever seriously
intending to involve himself in the alternative way of life developed
in the novel. The affected and mannered style, and especially the
erotic scenes, showed that Longus remained rooted in the perspective of urban refinement and 'daß alle Naïvität dieses Idyllikers nur
eine künstlich präparierte, daß er selbst eben doch nichts anderes
als ein Sophist [sei]' ('that all the naïvety this writer of idylls displayed was only an artificial pose, that he himself was nothing but
a sophist after all', 1914: 549). Almost all more recent studies
have come out in a more or less pronounced manner against this
position, which interprets the bucolic element in the light of a
fundamental opposition between town and countryside and stresses
the sentimental contradictions in the author's attitude, resulting in
the work's internal fracture. It was G. Rohde who, in a paper of
importance in the history of scholarship, began the debate on
E. Rohde's interpretation.[17] According to him the bucolic element
arises from Longus' individual, genuine experience of Nature. The
novel is even considered as the expression of a seriously practised,
religiously determined worship of Nature. This, he believes, had
nothing in common with a town-dweller's sentimental love for the
country, someone who looked on a stay in the country simply
as a continuation of his usual luxurious way of life in another
environment. 'Für Longus aber ist die Natur etwas Göttliches, sein
Naturerlebnis stellt sich ihm als ein Mysterium dar und saugt
gleichsam mythische und religiöse Züge in sich ein' ('For Longus,
however, nature is a divine power, he experiences nature as a
mystery which, as it were, absorbs mythical and religious features';
1937: 48f.). While stressing his author's quasi-religious intention,
G. Rohde also contemplated a relationship between the novel and
mystery religions, but abandoned the idea as inappropriate. Yet

---

research by a rudimentary sketch of the history of scholarship. As fundamental
differences are to be illustrated, certain simplifications may be tolerated.

[16] E. Rohde (1914: 531ff.).

[17] G. Rohde (1937). This interpretation is in outline followed—divergencies of
detail notwithstanding—esp. by Mittelstadt (1966 and 1970).

this line of interpretation was the precise starting-point for those studies which explicitly establish a connection between bucolic and the mystery religions, and which take the actual meaning of the novel, hidden beneath an apparently entertaining, pastoral surface, to be the propagation of Dionysiac rites (Merkelbach), or the religious doctrine of Eros' power as an omnipotent natural force and initiation into his mysteries (Chalk).[18]

The bucolic element is, then, on the one hand viewed as an expression of urban-sentimental longing for rural simplicity, on the other hand as the reflex of an individual, quasi-religious worship of Nature, and finally as bearing a mystic-religious doctrine which must be traced with the help of symbolic meanings.[19] This state of research might give the impression that bringing up the controversial problem again would be fairly unrewarding. But perhaps after all it is possible to reach, if not a once and for all binding solution (indeed such a claim would hardly be justifiable in the present state of affairs), at least a certain basic consensus. Based on this consensus, a plausible hypothesis can be constructed, if on the one hand one distinguishes, in the way explained above, between the intended meaning and the realized function of a text and keeps in mind the discrepancy which may possibly reveal itself here—in this previous scholarship has been deficient—and if on the other hand one as closely as possible reconstructs the contemporary horizon of expectation and takes it into consideration during interpretation.[20]

The horizon of expectation,[21] the preconceived disposition of the consciousness which controls text production and reception alike, possesses two essential dimensions with respect to our problem.[22]

[18] Merkelbach (1962: 192 ff.) (Wojaczek (1969: 5 ff.) tries to support Merkelbach's thesis); Chalk (1960) (a very influential paper: McCulloh (1970: 79 ff.), Reardon (1971: 374 ff.), Heiserman (1977: 130 ff.). A detailed criticism of this interpretation is found in Berti (1967) and Geyer (1977) (in my opinion a conclusive refutation which makes any further discussion within the scope of this paper unnecessary); cf. also Mittelstadt (1966: 163 ff.).

[19] Extreme representative of this interpretation: Forehand (1976).

[20] This has not yet been done to a sufficient extent, either; attempts can best be found in E. Rohde (1914: 537 ff.).

[21] On this hermeneutic category as the basic concept of a literary history based on reception aesthetics cf. Jauss (1970: esp. 171 ff.) and the further discussion in Mandelkow (1970). The concept used here is an equivalent of Mandelkow's stronger 'Epochenerwartung'.

[22] On the double aspect of the horizon of expectation cf. Jauss (1970: *passim*, esp. 177), where he stresses 'daß der Leser ein neues Werk sowohl im engeren Horizont seiner literarischen Erwartung als auch im weiteren Horizont seiner Lebenserfahrung wahrnehmen kann.'

In the first place there is a dimension relating to the literary genre, the extent to which the author's and his readers' consciousness is prejudiced by the system of norms and conventions which in the course of the evolution of the bucolic genre had constituted itself as genre-specific. In this dimension the horizon of expectation is determined in a diachronic way as a result of the genre-historical process which the author embarks on with his work. In addition to this, the horizon of expectation possesses a synchronic, a particularly extra-literary dimension centred in worldly experience. It is determined by that kind of contemporary reality which moulds the author's and his audience's thought and action, or, to be exact, the current attitudes and behaviour patterns assimilated in the text, on the basis of which the text is read. In the following I shall first attempt to reconstruct the two dimensions in the selection relevant to our problem, and then come back to the two main questions posed above.

The literary horizon of expectation deals in the first place with the question of what kind of expectations were associated with the bucolic genre in Longus' time, i.e. in particular, which communicative function had the bucolic taken up in the course of its history as a genre. The Hellenistic, post-Theocritean evolution of the genre is determined amongst other things by two essential tendencies, which had established themselves as countermovements to the original intentions of the Alexandrian archegete of the genre.[23] One tendency consists of a playful, but also sentimental-pathetic representation of erotic (and other) affairs. Here Longus was able to fasten onto the erotic components of his novel. In view of our question, however, this does not have to be discussed in detail. The other tendency concerns a central part of our problem. Theocritus had focused on the pastoral world as a part of the 'common' people's life experience and, from an ironic distance, had exposed the shepherds' limited simplicity to his urban audience's superior smile. These shepherds, however, acquire in the course of the Hellenistic Theocritus-reception an as it were positive connotation. Their world is understood as a counterpart to a reality which is felt to be unsatisfactory, i.e. it offers a form of identification. This view has its source in a mood which can be found increasingly from the beginning of the Hellenistic era: a feeling of uneasiness and weari-

---

[23] In the following I summarize what I discuss and substantiate elsewhere in more detail (Effe (1977); cf. also Effe (1982*b*)).

ness with urban life, a new appreciation of simple and natural living, an attitude which all too easily could lead one towards finding
in the shepherds' life everything one had been desperately looking
for. This genre-historical circumstance in all probability also affects
Longus' and his audience's horizon of expectation.[24] The bucolic
becomes associated with a connotation field which can be outlined
as a 'positive appreciation of rural simplicity from the point of view
of urban civilization'.

This genre-specific expectation coincides very closely with certain
attitudes and behaviour models which seem particularly common
during the second century AD. In reconstructing this dimension of
the horizon of expectation, attention has to be drawn to begin
with to the urban classes' seemingly growing interest in the lived
experience of the rural population. This at any rate can be
construed from the fictitious farmer- and fisherman-letters by
Alciphron and Aelian.[25] However, because of its atticistic-romantic
orientation towards the past and especially towards the motif
repertoire of Attic comedy, which flourished centuries before, and
because of its affected artificiality, this literary genre is far from taking a serious interest in or mirroring the 'common' people's real
contemporary patterns of work.[26] Nevertheless one has to start
from the supposition that this genre is intended for an urban

---

[24] This is true despite a problem which can hardly be resolved with certainty—
the question of whether one must assume an unbroken tradition in the genre
between Theocritus and Longus, or whether one has to reckon with the occasional
break in continuity: approximately between the end of the 1st c. BC and the beginning of the 2nd c. AD, when an increasing interest in Theocritus seems to become
apparent (see below, p. 199 with n. 31). The transmitted bucolic corpus does not
permit a definite answer in one direction or other, nor does its 'sideline'—the bucolic landscape epigram in the tradition of the early Hellenistic poetess Anyte. Though
this literary form provides reliable testimonies only for the period between
Theocritus and the end of the first century BC (Leonidas of Tarentum, *AP* 7. 657,
9. 326, 16. 230; Myrinus 7. 703; Thyillus 6. 170; Meleager 7. 196; Crinagoras 6.
253, 7. 636; anonymous 9. 374, 10. 12, 16. 227), the evidence is insufficient to
allow us to conclude that the bucolic genre in the narrower sense suffered a break
in tradition.

[25] As is the case with Longus, the date of Alciphron is dependent on more or less
reliable clues. The most probable period is between Lucian and Aelian: Alciphron is
likely to have been a contemporary of Longus; cf. the literature cited in n. 1 and
Benner and Fobes (1949: 6 ff.).

[26] Cf. Carugno (1960), Reardon (1971: 180 ff.). The anachronistic concentration
on the world of the 'classics' (extending to early Hellenistic Greece) is in general a
well-known tendency which determines the course of second-century literature
(including Longus' novel: its setting is the time of the autonomous Greek *poleis*); cf.
for this Bowie (1970) (with a plausible hypothesis on the origin of the trend).

audience which has a specific sentimental interest in the largely
'realistic', but sometimes also idealized, representation of this world
of experience including its characteristic way of thinking and feeling.[27] In this connection, moreover, mention must be made of Dio
of Prusa's *Euboikos* (written during the reign of Trajan). This treatise, in which real experience and fictitious elaboration have
become almost indissoluble,[28] sketches with great sympathy an
idyllic picture of a happy and harmonious existence in rural solitude and simplicity and uses it as a paradigm of a self-sufficient
way of life. The positive estimation of the rural idyll, which the
author is obviously able to assume in his audience, serves as a
starting point for a Cynic-Stoic *parainesis* of a life in blissful absence
of need.[29] Furthermore it is remarkable that the painting and architecture of this time also show an appreciation of the rural and of
nature, which closely corresponds to the horizon of expectation in
the bucolic genre.[30] In view of this all-pervasive 'bucolic' mood, it

[27] The focus of Alciphron's fishermen's and farmers' letters is on the poverty of
these classes and the economic, moral, and erotic problems resulting from it. They
are portrayed from a sympathetic, sometimes also ironic, point of view, but as a rule
without any intention to idealize and transfigure their way of life. Such a view
(which is reminiscent of Longus) appears only occasionally (2. 8, 9 and 15).
Normally Alciphron's fishermen and farmers are only too willing to exchange their
arduous life for the amenities of the town. The contrast between Alciphron's
approach and Longus' continual idealization of rural life is discussed by Scarcella
(1970: 127 ff.).
[28] Sceptical on Dio's realism: Day (1951: 209 ff.), C. P. Jones (1978: 56 ff.).
Relations with the novel: Jouan (1977: 38 ff.).
[29] The paradigmatic character of the 'Euboean Idyll' with regard to the philosophical theory it supports is already well stressed by its late-antique interpreter
Synesius (cf. *Dion* 2); cf. also Vischer (1965: 157 ff.). When Hommel (1958: 749 ff.)
interprets the speech as the expression of an attitude of escape from the urban way
of life, carried by a 'bucolic' mood, he fails to see that Dio is primarily interested in
proving the value of poverty for a life 'in accordance with nature,' cf. esp. Vischer
(1965: 81 f. and 103). In so far as, according to Dio, town life is not exactly con-
ducive to this aim, the argumentation becomes on a secondary level 'an indirect
laudation of country life' (C. P. Jones (1978: 56)).
[30] On the 'bucolic' mood of painting around the middle of the 2nd c. cf. Wirth
(1934: 83 ff.), further Dawson (1944: 199 f.), Weinreich (1950/1962: 18 f.) The
testimonies, however, are not numerous and in addition to that their dates are not
undisputed: Rumpf (1953: 175 f.). Mittelstadt (1967) tries to explore the relations
between Longus and contemporary cyclic-narrative painting (as he finds it mirrored
in, among other examples, Philostratus' *Imagines*). On architecture cf. the interpretation of the relevant letters of Pliny in Lefèvre (1977) (who stresses the 'senti-
mentalischen Naturauffassung'); further Grimal (1969: 219 ff., 334 and 415 ff.).
   Here also a curious passage of Herodes Atticus' biography deserves mention.
When this well-known 'sophist', who in view of his prominent cultural and
financial-social status must be seen as an esp. typical representative of contempo-

is hardly accidental that during the second century AD a renewed
and increased interest in Theocritus' works is apparent.[31] Presumably the urban classes' specific attitude to country life and
nature was also the cause of their rediscovery of the archegete of
literary bucolic.

Especially illuminating for our problem is finally the fact that certain texts of this time offer exact proof of this positive appreciation
of rural simplicity, which I have shown to be an essential element
in the literary horizon of expectation and in actual behaviour. For
example, one of Alciphron's letters describes how rich urban young
people rent a fishing boat and are rowed out to sea in order to take
part for once in fisherman's work—an entertainment of a special
kind, during which the young people by no means intend to do
without the usual urban luxuries (1. 15). Another letter by the
same author describes a group of courtesans on an excursion into
the country, who take this temporary shift of their activities to an
idyllic *locus amoenus* as a pleasant change from routine.[32] In both
cases the same sentimentality is expressed. Rural life is not considered as a serious alternative to the urban way of living, but only
as its continuation by a different means, as an opportunity for a
new kind of enjoyment within the scale of urban values, which as
such are never really questioned. And this contemporary attitude
is reflected exactly in certain scenes of Longus' novel, for example
the Methymnean *jeunesse dorée*'s excursion to the country, looking
for a ξενικὴ τέρψις ('pleasure trip away from home'), and fishing
and hunting as a pastime (2. 12 ff.), or the scene towards the end
of the novel, where the rich town-dwellers take a special delight in
arranging Daphnis' and Chloe's wedding in the country—with of
course all the outlay which is at their disposal (4. 37f.).

These two dimensions of the horizon of expectation, the literary
dimension and the dimension of life experience, show clearly by

rary urban civilization (cf. Bowersock (1969: *passim*)), of all people becomes friends
with an eccentric countryman from Attica, whose explicitly simple, 'alternative'
way of life displays decidedly anti-urban characteristics (Philostr., *Lives of the
Sophists* 552 ff.), this significantly illustrates the sentimental tendencies of the time;
cf. Bowie (1970: esp. 30); further Graindor (1930: 158 ff.).

[31] Indicated by papyrus finds and a newly established interest in commenting on
Theocritus (material in Gow (1952: i. xlviii ff. and lxxxii ff.)).

[32] 4. 13; cf. esp. § 6 ff. (charms of rural life and description of the idyllic place).
Letters to Farmers 2. 9 is permeated by a similar mood. Aelian's description of the
Tempe valley may also be compared (*Var. hist.* 3. 1): this passage also stresses the
recreational value of the idyllic landscape.

converging the fundamental consciousness which controls the genesis and the reception of the novel alike.[33] Taking this as a basis for our considerations, the following initially global hypothesis offers itself as the answer to the question of the meaning of the bucolic in Longus. The pastoral world of Daphnis and Chloe fulfils the function of a positive counterpart to an urban reality of life which is felt to be deficient and thus fundamentally (at least for the time being) negative in value.[34] This hypothesis can indeed be verified as far as possible by analysing some important scenes from the novel, and at the same time it can be differentiated in the light of concrete details.

3. Right at the beginning of the novel Longus uses this conception to emphasize in two different ways the central thematic idea outlined above. When he stresses the $\phi\iota\lambda\alpha\nu\theta\rho\omega\pi\iota\alpha$ ('humanity') of the animals (a goat and a sheep) who look after and feed the children exposed by their parents, and when he has corresponding to it the compassion and affection of the shepherds who accept the foundlings into their families, he implicitly shows their rich, town-dwelling parents to be quite inhuman, since they had handed over their own children to a certain death.[35] The reader may conclude that these human values, which had already been lost long ago in the town, evidently still count in the country among the simple people. The opposition between real life and its rural counterpart becomes even more evident in two sequences already mentioned above. When the Tyrian pirates brutally invade the countryside with its harmony and happiness (1. 28ff.), both violence and wickedness appear strikingly as extremely negative items of urban reality. The author even enhances the suggestive power of the opposition by allowing the raid's victim, the cowherd Dorcon,

---

[33] On the productive role of the horizon of expectation, on the 'Komplementarität von Erwartungen und Werkreaktionen' cf. Vosskamp (1977: esp. 31), 'Konstante Erwartungen gegenüber den Gattungsmodellen [bestimmen] in entscheidendem Maße die Werkproduktion.'

[34] Insufficient attention paid to the horizon of expectation has resulted in an increasing minimalization of the contrast between countryside and town (which was still considered as central by E. Rohde; see above, p. 194); cf. e.g. Chalk (1960: 48ff.), Mittelstadt (1966: 162f.).

[35] The animals' $\phi\iota\lambda\alpha\nu\theta\rho\omega\pi\iota\alpha$: 1. 3. 1. A remarkable parallel to Longus' idea is represented by a scene in the novel of Xenophon of Ephesus, who probably flourished around the same time as Longus. There the simple goatherds' unselfish behaviour towards Anthia when she is being pursued contrasts sharply with that of the other characters who keep only their own interests in mind (2. 9ff.).

a touching death scene, thus bringing the readers' sympathies
irresistibly over to the side of the country. This is also the side
taken by the gods; because here—as is demonstrated last but
not least by the behaviour of the two young shepherds—they are
still worshipped with unadulterated piety. This aspect becomes
especially prominent in the continuation of the Methymnean
episode (2. 12ff.). The rich young town-dwellers' excursion to the
sea and country at first seems to be quite harmless. But as soon as
they lose their ship and part of their fortune with it because of their
own thoughtlessness, their generous carelessness, which the reader
may at first not even have considered unsympathetic, is completely
inverted into sheer violence: they lay their hands on Daphnis
as the alleged guilty person, but have to submit before the rural
solidarity opposing them. At this point Longus could have let the
episode end. However, he is interested in bringing out the thematic
opposition even more thoroughly. Once they return to their native
town, the young men obscure the actual facts out of vanity,[36] and
bring forward false accusations against Mytilene instead. Thus from
futile grounds, from urban carelessness and pleasure hunting, war
comes upon the shepherds with all possible brutality. Chloe falls
into the hands of enemies who significantly show only contempt
and scorn to the statues of the deities before which the girl had
taken refuge (2. 20. 3). But then it becomes apparent that the
countryside is under the protection of the gods.[37] Because of Pan's
miraculous intervention, Chloe is freed and the shepherds' peaceful and happy world is reinstated.

Another urban element is on show in the Lycaenion-scene (3.
15ff.). Lycaenion is town-bred and married to a farmer; she stands,
at it were, at the meeting of two worlds. As a woman, however,
who is called ἀγροικίας ἁβρότερον ('rather sophisticated for the

---

[36] 2. 19. 2: τῶν μὲν ἀληθῶν λέγοντες οὐδὲ ἕν, μὴ καὶ πρὸς καταγέλαστοι γένοιντο
τοιαῦτα καὶ τοσαῦτα παθόντες ὑπὸ ποιμένων ('they didn't tell the truth about a single
thing. Apart from anything else, they didn't want to appear ridiculous at having
suffered so badly and so much at the hands of shepherds').

[37] Cf. esp. Pan's words to the leader of the Methymneans: Ὦ πάντων ἀνοσιώτατοι
καὶ ἀσεβέστατοι, τί ταῦτα μαινομέναις φρεσὶν ἐτολμήσατε; πολέμου μὲν τὴν ἀγροικίαν
ἐνεπλήσατε τὴν ἐμοὶ φίλην . . . ἀπεσπάσατε δὲ βωμῶν παρθένον . . . καὶ οὔτε τὰς Νύμφας
ᾐδέσθητε βλεπούσας οὔτε τὸν Πᾶνα ἐμέ ('Most unholy and impious of men, what madness has driven you to act so recklessly? You've filled the countryside I love with
war . . . you have dragged from the altars a girl . . . and you showed no shame
before the Nymphs when they watched what you did, or before me—Pan', 2. 27.
1f.).

countryside', 15. 1), she represents an urban eroticism which is
seeking pleasure beyond the matrimonial bounds. Thus she allows
her appetite to be aroused by the beautiful Daphnis and is
sufficiently cunning and erotically experienced to achieve what she
desires. As the shepherd's mental and erotic naïvety and innocence
surrender to Lycaenion's cleverly contrived intrigue and seductive
art, a further aspect of the opposition between town and countryside presents itself. This aspect becomes even more apparent in
another passage. The character of the parasite Gnathon, who
infests the rural world as a companion of his young urban master,
gives the author many opportunities to demonstrate the extreme
excesses of urban reprehensibility and perversion (4. 11ff.). As the
profligate product of a life of urban luxury,[38] Gnathon represents a
perverse, homosexual, eroticism, and its abnormal unnaturalness
also finds expression in his pretence that it is a cultural tradition of
urban civilization.[39] Gnathon's advances, however, fail because of
the naïve—and at the same time natural—attitude of Daphnis,
who refuses his homoerotic overtures with references to animal
behaviour, and when the parasite tries to use force, the shepherd
can easily keep the drunken lecher off. But guileless Daphnis can
only escape from Gnathon's ensuing clever intrigue because his
true origin is revealed.[40]

This fundamental thematic opposition is stressed once again at
the end of the novel. After Daphnis and Chloe have found their real
parents, it is possible for them to live a life in riches and luxury,
but nevertheless the couple feel the urge to go back to the countryside. They cannot bear the urban way of life. Thus the wedding
is arranged in the country (4. 37f.). And whereas the town-
dwellers take their specific pleasure in it—the sojourn in the
country offers a welcome interruption to their usual life—they are
not at all pleased when the goats happen to get too close to them,

---

[38] 4. 11. 2: ὁ δὲ Γνάθων, οἷα μαθὼν ἐσθίειν ἄνθρωπος καὶ πίνειν εἰς μέθην καὶ
λαγνεύειν μετὰ τὴν μέθην καὶ οὐδὲν ἄλλο ὢν ἢ γνάθος καὶ γαστὴρ καὶ τὰ ὑπὸ γαστέρα
('But all Gnathon knew how to do was to eat and to drink till he was drunk and
to have sex when he was drunk. He was nothing but a mouth and a stomach and
what lies beneath the stomach').
[39] Cf. esp. 4. 17. The gallantly dallying eroticism displayed in this conversation
between the young master and his parasite is in sharp contrast to the naïve and
innocent love represented by Daphnis and Chloe.
[40] Gnathon, too—like Dorcon (cf. above, n. 6)—eventually gets the opportunity
to 'rehabilitate' himself: by rescuing Chloe from the hands of Lampis (above, n. 7).
Thus he is able to be included in the harmonious ending (4. 29).

because their love for the country is only sentimental. Daphnis
even chooses to be close to his goats—he takes them by their horns
and kisses them. From this time on, as the author stresses, Daphnis
and Chloe led their pastoral life honouring the gods and 'considering fruit and milk to be the most delicious of foods' (39. 1).

In view of the passages cited the question about the authorially
intended meaning of the bucolic can be answered quite confidently
as follows. Longus is interested in an evaluative confrontation of
two worlds. Urban reality, which is felt to be deficient, is contrasted
with its positive counterpart, a rural, naïvely innocent world of
peaceful harmony protected by the gods. These two worlds are
related to each other as ideal and reality. The author uses the
attraction of his bucolic ideal to propagate a new way of life which
is radically opposed to the urban experience.

4. This result seems to bring us very close to the position of
G. Rohde that was referred to at the beginning.[41] Our analysis,
however, is not yet finished. Thus far we have only been interested
in working out the author's main intention; the question of the
function, that is, of the meaning of bucolic as it was actually realized by the author's audience, is yet unanswered. In trying to find
a relatively plausible answer to this complementary and, as things
stand, not definitively resolvable problem, it is advisable to look
thoroughly at several aspects of the text, whose *Tendenz* is in some
ways at variance with the main intention as set forth. They allow
the display of just that urban mentality the author turns against
when he establishes his bucolic counterworld.

In the following this urban orientation of the text, which
counteracts the author's intention, will be demonstrated with the
help of some instructive passages. To begin with, some remarks
on the complex of eroticism. Longus treats this theme in close connection with the children's naïvety, the main bucolic element

[41] See p. 194 above; cf. esp. Rohde's final remarks: Longus' feeling for nature
'hat nichts mit der sentimentalen Landliebe des Städters gemein; wie aus den
Städten in unserem Roman alles Unfromme und Lasterhafte kommt . . . so ist auch
die Landliebe der Städter nichts als eine Form von Schwelgerei, τρυφή, also selbst
etwas an das Laster Grenzendes . . . Nur auf dem Lande wirken die Götter noch
. . . Die Stadt hingegen ist gottlos . . . die Natur und die Götter lassen [das Land]
nicht zugrunde gehen, sondern in unverdorbener Schönheit emporwachsen, ja sie
erstatten es den Verdorbenen zurück und mahnen sie damit zugleich an ihre
Verkehrtheit. Für Daphnis und Chloe aber hat die Stadt keine Reize, weil sie ein
höheres und reineres, den Göttern nahes . . . Leben kennen' (1937: 48 f.).

which determines the protagonists' characters throughout the novel. A significant ambivalence develops out of this naïvety in so far as this quality, which constitutes a basic element in the positive counterworld at the level of the intentional opposition of country and town,[42] is at the same time in the erotic context presented as the object of sensual enjoyment from the viewpoint of urban superiority.[43] An instructive illustration of this comes in the cicada episode in Book 1 (25f.). Chloe has fallen asleep and thus offers Daphnis a good opportunity to watch his beloved 'with insatiable looks and without reserve.' A cicada strays into Chloe's dress. She starts from her sleep, and Daphnis uses this pretext to let his hands glide inside her dress and down her breasts in order to produce the intruder. On the one hand, this episode illustrates the naïve innocence of the two children's love games. At the same time, however, this scene is presented in such a way that a reader with erotic interests can slip into Daphnis' role and enjoy the situation from his advanced position, as it were, as a voyeur. This is even truer for two other scenes. Longus turns to the two lovers' erotic problem. They have in the meantime been instructed in the three 'remedies' to Eros (kissing, embraces, lying close to each other with naked bodies), but are still ignorant of the precise modalities of the last φάρμακον, and Longus describes in detail their activities to achieve the desired satisfaction which, however, always fails (2. 8ff.). This display of sexual inexperience and helplessness serves the reader's erotic pleasure as well as the Spring scene, in which Daphnis, excited by the mating activities of the animals around him, asks his beloved to grant him everything he desires and to let him do 'what the rams do to the ewes and the billy-goats to the nannies' (3. 13f.)—a bold attempt, in the end resulting again in failure, because both adolescents lack the relevant 'know-how'. Author and reader smirk as they enjoy the naïvety of actors who are desperate enough to try imitating the animals; an erotic-voyeurist amusement is derived from the open presentation of a sexual technique, as may be characteristic of a sophisticated urban

[42] To give one example of many: the Lycaenion-episode, the nub of which is the confrontation between urban erotic refinement and rural naïve simplicity (cf. above, pp. 201f.), is followed by a love scene between the two adolescent shepherds, which in its charming naïvety emphasizes the contrast with eroticism à la Lycaenion (3. 20).
[43] Cf. Chalk's (1960: 48ff.) apposite remarks on the ambivalent role of this naïvety.

eroticism. This is precisely not a picture of simple and natural love, but of clumsy and frustrated sexual practices.

Scenes of this kind obviously serve to satisfy a specific need for erotic entertainment—a need which was also taken into consideration by other contemporary authors,[44] and was presumably already envisaged by Longus in the prooemion, when he promises his reader an ἱστορία ἔρωτος ('story of love') and further on a κτῆμα τέρπνον ('something to possess and enjoy').[45] Given this aspect, the Lycaenion-episode requires further analysis. In view of the very concrete and detailed description of Daphnis' seduction and erotic 'initiation' (3. 18) it becomes all too apparent that the author is not only interested in exhibiting the opposition of countryside and town (cf. above pp. 201 f.), but also in developing the sexual side as such. Scenes of this kind have led some scholars to accuse him of pornographic lasciviousness.[46] A moralizing evaluation, problematic as it may be, nevertheless contributes to an adequate interpretation of the novel in so far as it draws attention to aspects of the text which have often enough been left out or minimalized by other scholars.[47]

We have seen that, in carrying out his intention of establishing the countryside as a positive counterworld, Longus occasionally disassociates himself from some urban circles' sentimental love for the country, which I have shown to be the real world dimension

[44] Several texts by Lucian may be mentioned in this context (*Loves*; *Dialogues of the Courtesans*), also Achilles Tatius' novel, the *Lucius or Ass*, Alciphron's erotic letters, Philostratus and Aelian, furthermore Rufinus' and Straton's epigrams which are full of drastic eroticism, and finally the fact that the development of late Hellenistic and early imperial bucolic is apparently also determined by a tendency to display stronger sensual and erotic effects, cf. Arland (1937: 78 ff.). The possibility cannot be ruled out that texts like ps.-Bion 2 and ps.-Theocritus *Id.* 27 were written about Longus' time.

[45] This explicit statement in the prooemion naturally causes some difficulties to scholars who ascribe the novel a serious and didactic function in the sense of the symbolic meaning characterized above; cf. e.g. Chalk (1960: 48).

[46] E. Rohde (1914: 549): 'Man mag es auch gelten lassen, wenn die Liebe dieses jugendlichen Hirtenpaares sich wenig von dem Boden eines süßen sinnlichen Begehrens entfernt. Aber die Art, in welcher der Dichter dieses Begehren anstachelt und durch lüsterne Versuche stets nur bis an die Grenze der Befriedigung führt, zeigt ein abscheuliches muckerhaftes Raffinement.' Schmid (1924: 824) speaks of a 'dem Rokoko geistesverwandten Mischung von dezenter Süßlichkeit und derber Sinnlichkeit' and stresses the 'pornographischen Reiz, den dieser Roman trotz aller vorgeblichen Unschuld und Reinheit immer ausgeübt hat und ausüben will'. Similarly Helm (1956: 51), 'schwüle Schlüpfrigkeit'.

[47] This is esp. true for G. Rohde, but also for Chalk and other interpretations of this kind.

of the contemporary horizon of expectation (above pp. 197 ff.). Now
it is extraordinarily significant that just this kind of attitude nevertheless controls long stretches of Longus' text: the novel's use of
bucolic is itself at least in part an expression of the sentimental
mood of the time.[48] This is already apparent in the insertion of idyllic topographies or seasonal images, which plainly enough display
the spirit of evasion-centred longing for country life.[49] It appears
still more clearly in the following scenes. To begin with, back once
again to the Methymnean episode. Here the negative value of the
jeunesse dorée's behaviour only gradually becomes apparent as the
action develops (above p. 201); at the beginning every sign of a
critical evaluation is missing. The author obviously takes up the
town-dwellers' point of view—which is also his audience's—and,
like them, sees that the charm of such an excursion at sea and to
the country consists of enjoying the beautiful landscape and hunting (2. 12). Nature as ξενικὴ τέρψις, as a change or recreation area
for an urban way of life,[50] but not as an alternative to it: this view
is especially prominent at the beginning of the last book. There
much space is given to a description of the garden laid out by the
shepherds for their urban masters' pleasure before they arrive. In
its position and arrangement this garden is typical of the kind of
rusticity looked for by rich town-dwellers.[51] The luxuriant exuberance of the flowers, plants and trees, the refined interaction of
nature and art, the beautiful view of the spreading landscape and
out to the sea,[52] a temple with manifold pictures at its centre: all

---

[48] Though G. Rohde adequately stresses the author's critical attitude towards
urban love of the countryside (cf. above, n. 41), he completely misses the aspects of
the text which let this very urban mentality shine through. Chalk in contrast
is right to point out that the tension between town and country, as one between
reality and ideality, does allow intermediate steps: 'We must not sentimentally
imagine that Longos did not feel sympathy for the town-dwellers' (1960: 49).

[49] Cf. e.g. the description of the *nympheion* (1. 4) and the summer image
(1. 23): both passages offer models of identification for an urban readership in a
'bucolic' mood.

[50] A parallel to the young Methymneans' behaviour is found in young master
Astylus' excursion to the country. He, too, goes hunting for a pastime: οἷα πλούσιος
νεανίσκος καὶ τρυφῶν ἀεὶ καὶ ἀφιγμένος εἰς τὸ ἀγρὸν εἰς ἀπόλαυσιν ξένης ἡδονῆς ('as
you'd expect of a rich young man who spent all his time amusing himself and had
come to the country to find a new type of pleasure', 4. 11. 1).

[51] A very similar garden ecphrasis is found in Achilles Tatius (cf. above n. 1). On
the mentality behind this kind of cultivated landscape, cf. E. Rohde (1914: 544 ff.),
Elliger (1975: 413 ff.), Lefèvre (1977).

[52] Sentimental enjoyment of a landscape is already important at the beginning
of Hellenistic Theocritus-reception: ps.-Theocritus, *Id.* 8. 53 ff.; cf. Effe (1977: 24 ff.).

this serves as an enjoyable interruption (in truth: continuation) of the urban way of life, which would be considerably spoiled by elements of rural reality such as dirt or smell. This also accounts for the shepherds' careful removal of these ingredients of their world before their masters' arrival (4. 1. 3). Here, too, the author, far from criticizing, fully adjusts himself to the urban point of view, which he allows increasing influence during the course of the last book, without the slightest embarrassment. The author, as it were, 'forgets' his actual intention and gets carried away by the usual viewpoint of his contemporaries.

When the farmers leave some of the most beautiful grapes hanging on the vines during the grape harvest, to give their urban masters the possibility of staging a small-scale vintage on their own for their own pleasure—without of course any trouble or exertion (4. 5)—Longus completely omits any criticism of this sentimental and make-believe way of enjoying rusticity. In another passage he describes how the urban visitors, after enjoying a rural performance, retire for breakfast and how Daphnis and Chloe delight in the fine urban food which has been sent to them (4. 15)—and thus establishes a contradiction to the final bucolic tone of the novel, where it is stressed that the two lovers would in future consider fruit and milk to be the most delicious of foods (above, p. 203). This positive judgement of urban τρυφή,[53] intruding, as it were, against one's will, goes together with a changing attitude to wealth. On the basis of the author's intended main opposition, wealth actually belongs to the negative urban side, but appears without question— especially at the end of the novel—to be a desirable and in no way problematic good.[54] Thus the nymphs promise Daphnis that he will one day be a rich man (3. 27). And just as the qualities of 'rich' and 'good' unite without difficulty in Daphnis' father Dionysophanes,[55] for Daphnis himself it is not an unimportant part of the happiness he finally achieves that he inherits from his father a large fortune (4. 24). Corresponding to the progressive domination of the urban point of view, the reader is prepared for the fact that

---

[53] In this context it is also remarkable that the urban masters return to Mytilene 'in great luxury' (τρυφῇ πολλῇ, 4. 33). The author describes this and the dinner on the following day as a culinary feast beyond compare (4. 34), but only in a matter-of-fact way and without any critical undertones.

[54] The countrymen, by the way, are not at all free from material interests either: 3. 25 ff.

[55] 4. 13. 2 καὶ πλούσιος ἐν ὀλίγοις καὶ χρηστὸς ὡς οὐδεὶς ἕτερος.

Daphnis never even thinks of continuing his previous life unchanged, though a lot of sentimentality is on display when he takes his leave of the pastoral world after his true identity has been disclosed.[56] Or to cite a last, perhaps even more telling detail: when Chloe as the bride of Daphnis, who has meanwhile become rich, puts on clothing becoming her new status and when the author comments upon this with the words ἦν οὖν μαθεῖν οἷόν ἐστι τὸ κάλλος, ὅταν κόσμον προσλάβῃ ('then you could learn what beauty is like, when it is properly presented', 4. 32. 1), he inadvertently denies all the other claims of appreciating rural simplicity.

5. To summarize the above analysis. The result in its central points confirms, or rather re-establishes, the truth of E. Rohde's position which today is generally held to be obsolete. Longus' novel is determined by the intertwining of two tendencies running in opposite directions. Whereas the author's dominant basic intention is to oppose to the given urban reality a positive counterpicture of an ideal world of rural, pious happiness, again and again, especially towards the novel's end, this intention conflicts with attitudes and points of view which result from the urban way of life and its normative horizon as familiar to both author and audience. In the end Longus remains deeply rooted in these. The opposition of the two tendencies results in the inner fracture and self-contradiction of the text—particularly when one takes into account the real-life dimension of the contemporary horizon of expectation shown above (pp. 197 ff.). This allows the following hypothesis about the actual function of the bucolic in Longus. It obviously does not serve to establish an alternative to given reality, but rather offers a temporary, pleasurable evasion from a world of living whose values and standards as such are never seriously questioned. The novel enables its reader to take part in the amusement of an, as it were, literary excursion to the country.

In view of the basically self-contradictory, sentimental attitude to rusticity and nature,[57] the novel, as has been shown, is a typical

---

[56] The same is true of Chloe's farewell to the countryside (4. 32).

[57] It should be noted that Goethe's famous and oft-quoted judgement alludes exactly to this basic characteristic of the novel and takes it as the opportunity for praise of the highest kind—in sharp contrast to the attitudes of later generations: Longus' novel displayed 'Verstand, Kunst und Geschmack auf ihrem höchsten Gipfel'. The composition was 'so schön, daß man den Eindruck davon, bey den schlechten Zuständen in denen man lebt, nicht in sich behalten kann' and 'verräth

representative of its time. In addition to that it embodies a characteristic feature of the bucolic genre on the whole as it developed
after Theocritus. The genre to a large extent displays the same
sentimental desire of urban circles for escape as Longus' novel,
or to put it differently: with respect to its functional context the
novel continues the course which was determined by the post-
Theocritean, Hellenistic evolution of the genre (above, pp. 196 f.).
By limiting the author's innovation only to the formal element of
a synthesis of genres which does not affect the traditional bucolic
clichés as such, by thus in the end merely 'putting old wine in new
bottles', this novel of the imperial age, too, only confirms the image
of the town-dwellers' love of the country that Theocritus had
already drawn and passed on, as it were, so prophetically. In his
famous Seventh Idyll, still the subject of controversial debate,[58]
Theocritus uses the town-dweller Simichidas' determinedly bucolic
behaviour to characterize and ironize exactly this kind of pseudo-
bucolic sentimentality and urban desire for rural simplicity, of
which Longus' novel has now been shown to be the last representative in the course of the ancient history of the genre.

die höchste Kunst und Cultur'. The novel proved 'Geschmack und eine
Vollkommenheit und Delicatesse der Empfindung, die sich dem Besten gleichstellt
das je gemacht worden' (quoted after Grumach (1949: 318 f.)).

[58] The interpretation adhered to here is principally based on the three following
works: Weingarth (1967), Giangrande (1968), F. Williams (1971); cf. also Effe
(1977: 23 f.).

9

The Novel of Longus the Sophist and the Pastoral Tradition

LIA RAFFAELLA CRESCI

Pastoral poetry is already distinguished in its origins by the ability to fuse in a new mixture structural elements and contents which are specific to other kinds of literature. In Theocritus' *Idylls* it is easy to grasp the combined influence of epic and mime, the alternation of bucolic and erotic themes, the predominance at times of lyric, singing or the *agōn*.[1] If the variety of the themes and forms in which the poetry of Theocritus and that of his imitators is articulated has led to a very complex definition of what is meant by the term 'pastoral', it has undoubtedly also been one of the reasons that explain the vastness and depth of the influence it has exercised on other literary genres, from elegy to epigram. To these pastoral poetry brings glimpses of landscapes, pictures of pastoral life, and the portrait of a poet-shepherd like Daphnis with whose unhappy loves one may identify one's own agony.[2] But the strength of the penetration of bucolic also manifested itself in another field, giving life in Longus the Sophist's *Daphnis and Chloe* to the only pastoral novel of antiquity.

In it dependence on the pastoral tradition, already evident from the title, is explicitly reaffirmed thanks to some very obvious allusions which allow the identification of the models upon which Longus based himself: Philitas and Theocritus. In the novel, in fact, it is the herdsman master of singing and expert in the things of love, the one who instructs Daphnis and Chloe (2. 3),[3] who is called Philitas, even though, in the choice of the name, we ought

[1] Legrand (1898: 413–36); Kroll (1924: 202–8).
[2] It is enough to think of the elegies of Cornelius Gallus: cf. Kroll (1924: 205).
[3] The observation was made for the first time by Reitzenstein (1893: 260 n. 1) and then repeated by Legrand (1898: 154–6); Bignone (1934: 30); Schönberger (1970/1973: 18); Mittelstadt (1970) 214.

not to underestimate the etymological meaning of a form which is particularly suitable for a character whose duty it is to reveal to the two youths the existence and the power of Eros. Longus could thus well attribute to Philitas the role of the initiator of bucolic poetry, providing us with an insight that must be assessed with much care and caution in the light of current critical trends.[4]

To refer to Philitas, however, is not something irrelevant: it means being part of a specific literary tradition, accepting its schemes, laws, and conventions. Even if Reitzenstein's theory of a clique of βουκόλοι/herdsman-poets on Cos appears to have been superseded,[5] and interpretations which want to see *Idyll* VII of Theocritus as a pastoral masquerade appear debatable,[6] it is beyond doubt that the reference to Philitas sets Longus in the midst of a tradition, a genre, that surely does not provide a realistic representation of pastoral life. The very presentation of the character of Philitas follows, in Longus, a quite precise model: the shepherd, capable συρικτής, who also knows the laws of Eros and reveals them to Daphnis and Chloe, recalls the Lycidas of *Idyll* VII of Theocritus, as the contrast between the rural clothing and the level of knowledge shows.[7] The designation of Daphnis as the successor

---

[4] ll. 39–41 of *Idyll* VII of Theocritus have also recently been interpreted as recognizing Philitas as ἀρχηγέτης of pastoral poetry; cf. Puelma (1960: 158), against whom Lohse (1966: 420) and Serrao (1971: 30–2 and 39–68) argue with reason.

[5] Reitzenstein (1893: 193–263, particularly 200); his theory was accepted by G. F. Knaack, in *RE* 3/1 (1899: 998–1012), s.v. Bukolik; Legrand (1898: 154–6); Bignone (1934: 34–5); Wojaczek (1969: 41). The theory of the pastoral masquerade was overturned by Wilamowitz (1906: 165 ff.).

[6] The first to see a true shepherd in Lycidas was Cataudella (1955: 159–69), followed by Sanchez-Wilderger (1955: 62 ff.); Kühn (1958: 66 ff.); and partially Puelma (1960: 145); Serrao (1971: 17–21).

[7] Longus 2. 3 Τερπομένοις δὲ αὐτοῖς ἐφίσταται πρεσβύτης σισύραν ἐδεδυμένος καρβατίνας ὑποδεδεμένος, πήραν ἐξηρτημένος καὶ τὴν πήραν παλαιάν ('While they were enjoying themselves, an old man came up to them. He was dressed in a goat's-hair cloak and had rawhide sandals on his feet and had a bag hanging on his shoulder, a very old one'). Theocritus VII. 15–19 ἐκ μὲν γὰρ λασίοιο δασύτριχος εἶχε τράγοιο | κνακὸν δέρμ' ὤμοισι νέας ταμίσοιο ποτόσδον, | ἀμφὶ δὲ οἱ στήθεσσι γέρων ἐσφίγγετο πέπλος | ζωστῆρι πλακερῷ, ῥοικὰν δ' ἔχεν ἀγριελαίῳ δεξιτερᾷ κορύναν ('On his shoulders he had the fawny skin of a | Shaggy, coarse-haired goat, smelling of new rennet, | Over his breast an ancient smock was tightened with a | Broad belt, and in his right hand he held a crooked staff of wild olive'). Longus 2. 3 Φιλητᾶς, ὦ παῖδες, ὁ πρεσβύτης ἐγώ, ὃς πολλὰ μὲν ταῖσδε ταῖς Νύμφαις, πολλὰ δὲ τῷ Πανὶ ἐκείνῳ ἐσύρισα ('My children, I am old Philitas. I sang many songs to these nymphs here, I played many tunes on the pipe to that Pan over there'). Theocritus VII. 27–9 Λυκίδα φίλε, φαντί τυ πάντες | ἦμεν συρικτὰν μέγ' ὑπείροχον ἔν τε νομεῦσι | ἐν τ' ἀματήρεσσι ('Lycidas dear, they all say | You are the champion piper among the herders | And the harvesters').

of Philitas in the art of συρίζειν ('piping') is not absent from Longus, who closely follows the Theocritean precedent of Lycidas designating Simichidas as bucolic poet.[8]

In the context of the episode of the pastoral feast celebrating Pan and the Nymphs (2. 33), which is completely interwoven with reminiscences of Theocritus,[9] Longus puts in an explicit reference to his main model by making Lamon declare that he learned the myth of Syrinx from a Σικελὸς αἰπόλος ('Sicilian goatherd').

The complexity of the problems which emerge from the need to harmonize different genres is accentuated in the case of Longus' work, where such varied literary traditions as novel and pastoral come together. A first step towards reaching a definition of the links running between the two genres was the annotation of lexical parallels between Longus on the one side and Theocritus and his imitators on the other. The analysis carried out in this area by Valley was fairly exhaustive;[10] Schönberger has drawn on it in his commentary, as well as G. Rohde,[11] and later Mittelstadt,[12] in their attempts to broaden the study from the representation of single words to the identification of the process by which Longus inserts Theocritean ideas into the narrative fabric of his novel. It is thanks to these studies that the Theocritean ancestry of many of the aspects of pastoral life described by Longus has been identified. The participation of animals in events which involve the protagonists (1. 31-2), for example, surely goes back to Theocritus IV. 12-14, VI. 42-5; the characterization of the *aipolos* ('goatherd') in Longus I. 16 is derived from Theocritus V. 51-2, VII. 10. The customs and the seasons that order the work of Daphnis and Chloe also have a

---

[8] Longus 2.37 καὶ τὴν σύριγγα χαρίζεται φιλήσας καὶ εὔχεται καὶ Δάφνιν καταλιπεῖν αὐτὴν ὁμοίῳ διαδόχῳ ('and kissing him, he gave the pipes as a present and prayed that Daphnis too would leave them to a successor as good as himself'). Theocritus VII. 128-9 ὁ δέ μοι τὸ λαγωβόλον, ἁδὺ γελάσσας | ὡς πάρος ἐκ Μοισᾶν ζεινήιον ὤπασεν ἧμεν ('he gave me the crook, laughing sweetly | As before, to be the Muses' token of friendship'). Cf. Chalk (1960: 37).

[9] Longus 2. 31 καὶ κρατῆρα ἀπέσπεισε μεστὸν γλεύκους καὶ ἐκ φυλλάδος στιβάδας ὑποστορέσας ('and poured out a mixing bowl full of sweet new wine as a libation. He spread out beds of leaves'). Theocritus VII. 65-8; Longus 2. 32 ἄλλος ὡς μόνου τοῦ Πανὸς δεύτερα συρίσας ('another that he had played the pipes better than any-one except Pan'). Theocritus I. 3 μετὰ Πᾶνα τὸ δεύτερον ἆθλον ἀποισῇ ('After Pan you shall take second prize').

[10] Valley (1926: 80 ff.).

[11] Schönberger (1970/1973).

[12] G. Rohde (1937); some of his conclusions were anticipated by Vaccarello (1935); cf. Mittelstadt (1970).

precedent in Theocritus: the harvesting of grass for the kids, 1. 21 and 2. 20—Theocritus XI. 656; the habit of shepherds in love of throwing apples at one another, 1. 24—Theocritus V. 88, VI. 6; the typical pastoral-erotic situation which sees the woman contemplate the shepherd who guides the flock to pasture 3. 15— Theocritus V. 89. Even for the gifts that Longus' characters exchange we can compare Theocritus: Longus 1. 28—Theocritus V. 8, VI. 43; Longus 3. 18—Theocritus I. 10, 57. The research of G. Rohde and Mittelstadt, though, has moved almost exclusively within the comparative limits set by Valley and has thus remained anchored to the investigation of passages where Longus literally, or almost literally, imitates Theocritus. An analysis that is limited to this type of comparison between the two authors runs the risk, in my view, of failing to pick up the full significance and complexity of Longus' dependence on Theocritus. The lexical reminiscence is not in itself of much relevance in a writer who draws so abundantly on Homer, Sappho, and Aristophanes.[13] Placing various reminders of Theocritus into the narrative fabric of the novel constituted only one, and surely not the most thorny, of the problems posed for Longus by the conjunction of two literary genres. What he needed to do was to resolve the difficulty of widening within the frame of a whole novel that landscape which in an idyll often exists in outline only. He was required to use other ideas to enrich the pastoral-fictional element as a whole without then running into sudden hiatuses. Furthermore, to which technique should one resort to transform the unchanging genres of pastoral in order to introduce them into the plain narrative flow of Longian prose? How should one adapt the typical themes of the pastoral tradition to the requirements of novelistic content and structure?

The aim of the following analysis is to identify some of the solutions devised and to attempt an evaluation of Longus' answers to the problems that the composition of a pastoral novel inevitably presented.

---

[13] Cf. Scarcella (1971).

THE PASTORAL LANDSCAPE IN LONGUS

In evaluating the picture of Lesbos as outlined by Longus there is one primary consideration: the total absence of any pretence of realistic description, which is excluded by the literary nature of Longus' base plan, even before the usual comparison is made between the novel and information on the island provided by ancient sources.[14] Lacking any pretence of descriptive truth, Longus could only appeal to pastoral poetry to extrapolate elements of the landscape and use them to compose the backdrop to Daphnis and Chloe's amorous adventures. But even in this field, it is necessary to make a preliminary distinction: although Longus explicitly resorts only to Philitas and Theocritus in his novel, the novel reflects the whole pastoral tradition which we can, in fragmented fashion, pick up in the *corpus Theocriteum*, the collection of non-epigrammatic Hellenistic poetry compiled by Artemidorus in the first century BC, the epigrams of the *Anthologia Palatina*, reliefs of the Hellenistic period, and paintings at Pompeii based on Greek models.[15]

The pastoral genre, in which Longus should clearly be placed, underwent an evolution after Theocritus which saw, on the one hand, the insertion and development of new themes and, on the other, a progressive rigidity in the invention and combination of specific motifs. The landscape, which in Theocritus is born from a fusion between the re-working of Homeric settings and the capacity to pick up detail realistically, becomes clarified and crystallized in the pastoral tradition.

Already *Idylls* VIII and IX bring about, as regards Theocritus, a change that is more perceptible in atmosphere than in the insertion of real and characteristic novelties of content.[16] In *Idyll* VIII the shepherds, both very young,[17] directly involve the landscape and their flocks in the melancholy and amorous yearnings and the sentimental feelings of their song.[18] The goat becomes a messenger

---

[14] Cf. Scarcella (1968a).

[15] Rizzo (1929: 72–80); Schefold (1952: 73–81).

[16] Wörmann (1871: 76); Arland (1937).

[17] The youth of the protagonists in *Idyll* VIII was noted by Bignone (1934: 82); in it Arland (1937: 12) saw a rather unrealistic feature in contrast with the dominant role played in the idyll by the erotic.

[18] Arland (1937: 13).

of love for Milon, ll. 49-52, the wolf is begged not to attack the
flock of so young a shepherd as Menalcas, ll. 63-4. Out of fantasy
is born a landscape, a literary 'place', which gradually loses any
contact with reality,[19] while the space given to the erotic element
is widened.

In the epigrams the schemes of composition reveal themselves as
having little flexibility and the choice of names, of objects, and of
the elements in the landscape, shows itself to be more and more
restricted: the tree under the shadow of which the shepherd sits to
play the σῦριγξ ('pipes') and to oversee the flock, the cave, the
stream of icy water, the meadows, the woods, the flowers, all
become fixed elements which assemble the picture of the pastoral
landscape. A similar inflexibility is to be found in the description of
the habits of life and work of the shepherds: the emphasis is persistently placed on repeated gestures, on lucky and not so lucky
love affairs, on the passion for singing, on a very limited sequence
of objects: the staff now called κορύνη,[20] now λαγωβόλον,[21] the
γαυλός ('pail'),[22] the knapsack.[23]

The fundamental lines upon which Longus bases his pastoral
world appear to follow the stereotypes of the genre very closely.
The essential and canonical elements of the landscape are rapidly
outlined: meadows, mountains, gorges, and woods (I. 9), inhabited by bleating flocks (I. 23), delighted by birdsong and by the
buzzing of bees (I. 9). Daphnis and Chloe pause for quite a while,
particularly at midday, under an oak to watch the animals or play
the σῦριγξ (I. 12, 13, 25; 2. 11, 21, 30; 3. 12, 16). Further, the
objects which surround them are the ones accredited by the
pastoral tradition: the καλαύροψ (crook: I. 12; 3. 17), the γαυλοί
(I. 23; 3. 33), the knapsack (I. 13; 2. 18; 3. 20; 4. 14). The
stylization in comparison to the Theocritean model, though this is
present, is immediately perceptible: in Theocritus, beside the oak
and the pine, there appear tamarisks (I. 130), elms (I. 21; VII. 8),
reeds (I. 106), olives (IV. 44), oleander (V. 32), poplars (VII. 8,
136), laurels (XI. 45), and cypresses (XI. 45). Beside the staff
and the γαυλός, the ταρσοί ('cheese-racks': XI. 37), the στιβάς

[19] Ibid. 18; Latte (1954: 157).
[20] Leonidas of Tarentum *AP* 6. 35; Macedonius the Consul *AP* 6. 73;
Eratosthenes Scholasticus *AP* 6. 78; Julian the Prefect *AP* 9. 797.
[21] *AP* 6. 177.
[22] Leonidas of Tarentum *AP* 6. 35.
[23] *AP* 6. 177; *AP* 14. 104.

('straw bed': VII. 67–8), the κισσύβιον ('drinking cup of ivy wood':
I. 27), the τάλαρος ('cheese basket': V. 86), the winnowing-shovel
(VII. 156) are all mentioned. In Longus we find that same reduction in the variety of the Theocritean world which, together with
the obsessive repetition of certain details, is typical of pastoral
epigram and is reflected in paintings from Pompeii with a bucolic
theme.[24]

Direct references to Theocritus are not missing within this
general setting: in the description of spring (Longus 1. 9) and the
luxuriance of summer (1. 23 and 3. 33), for example, the dependence on Theocritus XVI. 94–6, I. 1–2, VII. 143–7 is direct and
the imitation takes the form of verbal echoes.

Longus has therefore designed the rural frame of his novel
according to the data and reference points provided for him by later
bucolic, aiming to enliven the picture with some references to
Theocritus; but the freshness and vitality of the landscapes of that
poet are not to be compared with the flat conventionality of
Longian scenery. The requirements of movement, of adventure,
and of right places for lovers' trysts, which are characteristic of the
novel, impose the presence of the sea and a type of setting which
responds to the requirements of erotic literature. Longus therefore
finds himself needing to accommodate these elements to the
pastoral picture without introducing cracks in its unity and he
extracts himself from this awkwardness with some elegance.

Needing to square the description of the life of the shepherds
with the proximity of the sea, he turns to the bucolic-marine landscapes present in the pastoral and figurative tradition.[25] The theme
of the relationship between the *aipolos* and the sea, seen as an
adynaton, had been developed by Theocritus in *Idylls* VI and XI,
based on the figure of Polyphemus, and it had found space in the
sentimental landscape of *Idyll* VIII:[26] ll. 55–6 ἀλλ' ὑπὸ τᾷ πέτρᾳ τᾷδ'
ᾀσομαι ἀγκὰς ἔχων τυ, | σύννομα μῆλ' ἐσορῶν Σικελικάν τ' ἐς ἅλα ('but
beneath this rock I shall sing with you in my arms, | Gazing on my
partner flocks and the sea of Sicily'). It is exactly to this passage

---

[24] For an analysis of every detail of the landscape in *Idyll* VII cf. Schönbeck
(1962: 123–5). Also Scarcella (1968a: 24) observes that Longus mentions few
varieties of trees and from that infers that Lesbos had very little woodland. I would
say that Longus chooses only the trees highlighted by the pastoral tradition. For the
Pompeian paintings cf. Schefold (1952: 73–5).

[25] Mnasalcas *AP* 9. 333.

[26] Wörmann (1871: 74); Bignone (1934: 84); Arland (1937: 14).

that Longus goes for the construction of a whole episode: 3. 20–1.
The elements which build the picture are the same as in the *Idyll*:
the shepherd watches the flock together with the loved one and in
the background is delineated the marine landscape. The one diver-
gence between the brief mention in the *Idyll* and the elaborate
episode of the novel is in the song that Menalcas means to
sing; but, in Longus' work, the exposition of the myth of Echo
carries out a role largely similar to that developed by song in the
Idylls. In Longus the sea in the background is not, as in *Idyll* VIII,
a detail, however relevant, but the new element which allows him
to vary the typical and already widely exploited picture of Daphnis
and Chloe grazing their flocks, seated in the shadow of a tree. By
taking advantage of just this element, Longus constructs a complex
scene in which a place is found first for the astonishment of Chloe
as she hears clearly and nearby the song of the fishermen whose
ship she descries in the distance, second for the interest of Daphnis
in new tunes to play on his pipe, and third for the amused
indulgence with which he explains to Chloe, in the form of a myth,
the phenomenon of the echo.[27]

The problem of harmoniously inserting an erotic landscape into
a pastoral one is also resolved happily. If one of the most successful scenes of the novel, that of hunting with mistletoe in a wintry
setting,[28] is broken up into its component parts,[29] it becomes apparent that the scene is the result of an inlaying, of a careful combination of elements pre-existing in the pastoral tradition and of
commonplaces of erotic literature. The winter hunt with mistletoe
finds a parallel in a letter by Alciphron (2. 27), who, in another
passage (4. 13 = fr. 6), describes a place sacred to love, the usual
meeting place of two lovers: ὀλίγη δὲ παρὰ τὴν ἔπαυλιν ἀνεῖται
σπόριμος τὰ δὲ λοιπὰ κυπαρίττια καὶ μυρρίνη, ἐρωτικοῦ, φίλη,
κτημάτιον ὄντως, οὐ γεωργοῦ . . . [§4] μικρὸν δὲ ἄπωθεν τῶν ἐπαυλίων
πέτρα τις ἦν συνηρεφὴς κατὰ κορυφὴν δάφναις καὶ πλατανίστοις,
ἑκατέρωθεν δὲ μυρρίνης εἰσὶ θάμνοι, καί πως ἐξ ἐπιπλοκῆς αὐτὴν
περιθεῖ κιττὸς ἐν χρῷ τῇ λίθῳ προσπεφυκώς ('But spreading out at

---

[27] Elliger (1975: 407–508) discusses the function played by the landscape in the
story of Echo. On the role of the seashore in this novel see the acute observations
of Longo (1978: 105–6).

[28] From a realistic idea the theme of winter hunting very soon becomes a literary
inheritance: cf. Callimachus *AP* 12. 102; Horace *Odes* I. 37. 19, *Sat.* I. 2. 105,
and perhaps Pliny the Younger *Ep.* 5. 6.

[29] Mittelstadt (1966: 171–2).

the side of the villa is a little land fit for planting, and the rest is
cypresses and myrtle—really the seat of a man of pleasure, my
dear, not of a farmer . . . [§4] A little way off from the villa was a
rock, its summit shaded by laurels and plane trees; on either side
of it are myrtle thickets; and ivy runs around it as though it were
interwoven, attaching itself closely to the stone', trans. Benner and
Fobes). The resonance with Longus 3. 5 is evident: πρὸ τῆς αὐλῆς
τοῦ Δρύαντος ὑπ' αὐτῇ τῇ αὐλῇ μυρρίναι μεγάλαι δύο καὶ κιττὸς
ἐπεφύκει, αἱ μυρρίναι πλησίον ἀλλήλων, ὁ κιττὸς ἀμφοτέρων μέσος·
ὥστε ἐφ' ἑκατέραν διαθεὶς τοὺς ἀκρέμονας ὡς ἄμπελος ἄντρου σχῆμα
διὰ τῶν φύλλων ἐπαλλαττόντων ἐποίει καθ' οὗ κόρυμβος πολὺς καὶ
μέγας ὡς βότρυς κλημάτων ἐξεκρέματο ('In front of Dryas' farm, right
next to the farmyard itself, two big myrtles and some ivy had
grown up; the myrtles were near each other, and the ivy lay
between the two of them. The ivy spread its tendrils into each of
the myrtles, like a vine, and made a kind of cave with the interwoven leaves, while the clusters of ivy berries hung down, as
numerous and as big as grapes on vine shoots').

Myrtles, ivy, the trees that join their branches are the fixed elements in scenes of this type.[30] Longus, however, is able to harmonize this *topos* with the pastoral setting which frames the whole
event: myrtle and ivy shape a kind of cave from which Daphnis
hopes—in vain—to see Chloe appear. The situation retraces in
some aspects the one described in Theocritus' *kōmos*: the *aipolos*
would like to be a bee so he can penetrate the ivy which covers
the entrance of Amaryllis' cave: III. 13-14 αἴθε γενοίμαν | ἁ
βομβεῦσα μέλισσα καὶ ἐς τεὸν ἄντρον ἱκοίμαν, | τὸν κισσὸν διαδὺς καὶ
τὰν πτέριν ἅ τυ πυκάσδει ('I wish I were | The humming bee to pass
into your cave through the ivy and the fern that covers you').
The cross-reference to Theocritus performs the task of fusing the
components of the erotic landscape with a situation that is already
documented in the pastoral tradition.

---

[30] Cf. Menander, *On Epideictic*, 3. 403 Spengel. The dispute about the relationship between Longus and Alciphron goes back to Rohde and Reich (1894), the
latter stating the priority of Longus, followed by Dalmeyda (1932: 277-87) and
Carugno (1955: 153-9). E. Rohde (1960: 534-5 nn. 2-3), maintained that Longus
imitates Alciphron. The hypothesis of an independent utilization of the *topoi* of the
pastoral genre is presented, in my view rightly, by Bonner (1909: 276-90).

THE LINK FUNCTION OF THEOCRITEAN IMITATION

The use of Theocritus III. 13–14 provides a clear example of one of the functions of taking up a Theocritean motif, the harmonious insertion into pastoral romance of a theme that does not belong to the pastoral genre.

The influence of Sappho in one episode of the novel had already been noted by Rohde;[31] Valley and Mittelstadt have identified some passages in which it is possible to discern imitation of the poetess.[32] Sappho's χλωροτέρα δὲ ποίας ἔμμι ('I am greener than grass') (fr. 31 Voigt) is the clear model of Longus I. 17 χλωρότερον τὸ πρόσωπον ἦν πόας θερινῆς ('his face was paler than the grass in summer'), which describes the amorous sickness of Daphnis. But between Sappho and Longus intervenes the mediation of Theocritus: the typically Hellenistic taste for scientific precision is reflected in the καί μὲυ χρὼς μὲν ὁμοῖος ἐγίνετο πολλάκι θάψῳ ('and many a time I turned the same colour as yellow fustic'; II. 87). If one accepts Courier's very convincing conjecture (θερινῆς), it is possible to observe Longus imitating Theocritus in his attention to detail, the desire to make more specific the second term of Sappho's comparison, but, not liking the too exact term, he prefers a more generic πόας θερινῆς ('grass in summer') to the Theocritean θάψῳ ('fustic').

This is not the only instance in which Longus draws on Sappho by elaboration and in accordance with Theocritean sensibilities. A similar example is presented in this same chapter 17, where Longus describes the astonishment of Daphnis when he appreciates the beauty of Chloe for the first time: καὶ τὸ πρόσωπον ὅτι λευκότερον ἀληθῶς καὶ τοῦ τῶν αἰγῶν γάλακτος ('her face was really even whiter than the goats' milk'). Gregory of Corinth (Rhetores Graeci 7, 1236, 10 ff. Walz) testifies to the presence in Sappho and Anacreon of expressions like γάλακτος λευκοτέρα. Even if there is no lack of studies tending to show that Gregory followed Sappho exclusively,[33] Mittelstadt is rash in attributing γάλακτος λευκοτέρα to Sappho alone;[34] however, it is perhaps against generic and abused images of this kind that the ironic revival of Theocritus XI 20 λευκοτέρα

---

[31] E. Rohde (1960: 552).
[32] Valley (1926: 29); Mittelstadt (1970: 224–5).
[33] M. Treu (1955: 183 ff.).
[34] More cautiously Valley (1926: 99) does not attribute γάλακτος λευκοτέρα solely to Sappho.

πακτᾶς ποτιδεῖν ('whiter to behold than curds') is directed. I would say that in Longus more than ironic intent is at stake in his attempt to typify the *aipolos* in love. But, yet again, although he follows in the path of Theocritus' elaboration in the phrase λευκοτέρα πακτᾶς, Longus has substituted for the 'technical' πακτᾶς ('curds')[35] the vaguer τοῦ τῶν αἰγῶν γάλακτος ('goat's milk').

If the citations of Gregory of Corinth do not offer incontrovertible proof of the influence of Sappho on Longus for λευκότερον ἀληθῶς καὶ τοῦ τῶν αἰγῶν γάλακτος, I believe that Mittelstadt's hypothesis, which links the ἀλλ' ἄκαν μὲν γλῶσσα πέπαγεν ('my tongue froze') of Sappho fr. 31 Voigt to Longus 1. 17 πολλάκις ἐψύχετο ('he shivered repeatedly'), is to be rejected. Mittelstadt bases this combination on Cobet's already outmoded conjecture, πέπαγεν. Furthermore the symptom to which Sappho alludes, the inability to utter a word, does not coincide with that described by Longus: the cold, the shiver, as a sign of amorous passion does appear in Theocritus II. 106 πᾶσα μὲν ἐψύχθην χίονος πλέον ('I was colder than snow all over') and is taken up in the context of the erotic epigram by Meleager *AP* 12. 132,[36] and by Paul the Silentiary *AP* 5. 239.[37]

Another sign of loving passion consists in the listlessness of the person in love towards his own work: Sappho fr. 102 Voigt,

> γλύκηα μᾶτερ, οὔτοι δύναμαι κρέκην τὸν ἴστον
> πόθῳ δάμεισα παῖδος βραδίναν δι' Ἀφροδίταν
>
> ('Truly, sweet mother, I cannot weave my web
> for I am overcome with desire for a boy because of
> slender Aphrodite', trans. Campbell)

The motif is repeated four times in Theocritus: with reference to Simaetha taken from Delphis II. 83 οὔκετι πομπᾶς | τήνας ἐφρασάμην ('I no longer noticed the procession'), of Heracles in love with Hylas XIII. 67 τὰ δ' Ἰάσονος ὕστερα πάντ' ἦς ('the voyage with Jason was in second place'); in a pastoral context for the negligence admitted by Bucaeus X. 14 τοιγὰρ τὰ πρὸ θυρᾶν μοι ἀπὸ σπόρω ἄσκαλα πάντα ('the ground before my very door is not hoed since

[35] The Theocritean comparison will be recalled by Rufinus *AP* 5. 10 γαλακτοπαγεῖ χρώντι, in which παγής seems to me to be the complete opposite of lack of strength, as maintained by Page (1978: 91).
[36] *AP* 12. 132 ἀναψύχεις.
[37] *AP* 5. 239 ψυχόμενος Παφίῃ· ψύχεται αὐτομάτως.

sowing') and observed by Milon X. 1-4, and in a more appropriate comparison in the apathy shown by the Cyclops in love XI. 11
ἀγεῖτο δὲ πάντα πάρεργα ('everything else was irrelevant').[38]
Daphnis and Chloe in love also suffer from a sudden listlessness in
their work: Chloe 1. 13 τῆς ἀγέλης κατέφρονει ('she disregarded her
flock'), Daphnis 1. 17 ἠμέλητο καὶ ἡ ἀγέλη ('even the flock was
neglected').

A motif that appears for the first time in Sappho comes to Longus
through the mediation of Theocritus, who had inserted it into the
pastoral thematic. Obviously Longus perceived as too abrupt the
direct introduction of a reminiscence of Sappho into the narrative
context of the novel and he found in the constant references to
Theocritus a linking point between the erotic thematic present in
Sappho and the pastoral setting of the loves of Daphnis and Chloe.
The imitation of Theocritus in these cases, far from presenting itself
as a lifeless revival, has the role that we might define as that of
stylistic filter.

RE-WORKING THE BUCOLIC TRADITION

Some of the scenes in the novel have their roots in the codified
themes of the post-Theocritean pastoral tradition. Often Longus
does not limit himself to imitation but makes interventions and
modifications, sometimes profound ones. I intend to illustrate some
aspects of this relationship between Longus and the pastoral tradition, from the simple revival of a *topos* to its overturning.

Idyll VIII of the *corpus*, with its stress on the very young age
of Daphnis and Menalcas and the slightly languid sentimentality of
their song, is a rich source of ideas for Longus. The conclusion of
the episode of the goat's escape from Daphnis' flock sees the two
shepherds giving the animal to the cowherd as a gift, but then
finding themselves in difficulty: 1. 12. 5 τοῦτον μὲν δὴ τυθήσομενον
χαρίζονται σῶστρα τῷ βουκόλῳ, καὶ ἔμελλον ψεύδεσθαι πρὸς τοὺς οἴκοι
λύκων ἐπιδρομήν, εἴ τις αὐτὸν ποθήσειεν ('As a reward for helping to
save Daphnis' life, they gave the cowherd the goat to be sacrificed.
If anyone at home missed the goat, they planned to make up a
story about an attack by wolves'). That the two shepherds have to
answer for the flock entrusted to them and therefore cannot freely

[38] Serrao (1971: 147-9 and n. 66).

dispose of even one goat is not, in my view, a realistic feature that
bears witness to Longus' efforts to bring his literary countryside
close to the real one, because in other moments of the novel
Daphnis and Chloe sacrifice animals to Pan and to the Nymphs
with total confidence.[39] I would say rather that in 1. 12 Longus
has in mind a passage of Theocritus *Idyll* VIII, where the young
shepherd Menalcas confesses to Daphnis that he may not offer as
a prize an ἀμνός ('lamb') so as to avoid the wrath of his parents
when they proceed to check the flock at night, ll.14-16 *ΔΑ*:
μόσχον ἐγὼ θήσω, τὺ δὲ θὲς ἰσομάτορα ἀμνόν. | *ΜΕ* οὐ θησῶ ποκα
ἀμνόν, ἐπεὶ χαλεπὸς ὁ πατήρ μευ | χἀ μάτηρ, τὰ δὲ μῆλα ποθέσπερα
πάντ᾽ ἀριθμεῦντι ('Daphnis: I'll put in a calf; you put in a lamb like
its mother. | Menalcas: I shall not put in a lamb—my father | And
mother are difficult and count the whole flock every night').

To attribute fault to the wolf for the disappearence of something
or someone is perhaps a commonplace, maybe a proverbial expression, which is present also in Ps-Lucian *Lucius or Ass* 33 καὶ ἢν
ἔρηται, πῶς οὗτος ἀπέθανε, λύκου τοῦτο καταψεύσασθε ('and if the
question comes up as to how he died, blame it on the wolf'). The
wolf, however, is one of the chief elements of the literary genre: it
plays the part of the shepherd's most fearsome enemy, of a constant threat. To it Menalcas' song is directed to beg it to spare his
flock: *Idyll* VIII. 63-4 φείδευ τᾶν ἐρίφων, φείδευ, λύκε, τᾶν τοκάδων
μευ | μηδ᾽ ἀδίκει μ᾽ ὅτι μικκός ἐὼν πολλαῖσιν ὁμαρτέω ('Spare the
kids, wolf, spare their mothers | Don't harm me because I'm puny
but my flock is many').

Longus redevelops this *topos* until he overturns it: irritated with
the goats whose fighting disturbs Chloe's afternoon sleep, Daphnis
rails against the wolf for not attacking them: 1. 25 ἀλλὰ καὶ
οἱ τράγοι τοῖς κέρασι παταγοῦσι μαχόμενοι· ὦ λύκων ἀλωπέκων
δειλοτέρων, οἱ τούτους οὐχ ἥρπασαν ('And the he-goats are fighting,
with crashing horns! Oh, you wolves—more cowardly than foxes—
why haven't you carried them off?'). To give room to the erotic-
sentimental component, Longus ends up by overturning a traditional motif of the pastoral genre; or rather I would say that the
topos recovers a certain expressive ability only when it is used with
an opposite intent.

Longus offers other examples of overturning in his use of a *topos*.
The description of the life of the shepherds during winter is directed

[39] Longus 2. 30, 31.

so as to to juxtapose the joy of all the shepherds in idleness and
rest with the desperation of Daphnis and Chloe forced to be separate: 3. 4. Longus concludes the picture of the lazy winter days of
the shepherds with one observation: ὥστε αὐτοῖς τὸν χειμῶνα δοκεῖν
καὶ θέρους καὶ μετοπώρου καὶ ἦρος αὐτοῦ γλυκύτερον ('so that winter
seemed to them sweeter than summer, autumn, and even spring'),
the sense of which is grasped only when it is realized that here he
overturns the *topos* of spring as the season shepherds prefer: cf.
Bion fr. 2. Another motif attested in the pastoral tradition is the
dislike the *aipolos* has of the sea. The opposition between land and
sea is articulated in every possible way in the song of Polyphemus
in love with Galatea in *Idyll* XI; fr. 1 of Moschus is further proof
of the recurrence of this theme.[40] Daphnis, following directions provided by the Nymphs in a dream, finds on the seashore a chest
filled with gold that will allow him to gain superiority over his
rivals and obtain Chloe's hand from her adoptive parents. Longus'
annotation 3. 28 καίπερ γὰρ αἰπόλος ὤν, ἤδη καὶ τὴν θάλατταν
ἐνόμιζε τῆς γῆς γλυκυτέραν, ὡς εἰς τὸν γάμον αὐτῷ τὸν Χλόης συλ-
λαμβάνουσαν ('Goatherd though he was, he now thought the sea
was sweeter than the land, because it was helping him to marry
Chloe') is based on a reference to a motif of pastoral poetry that he
himself here contradicts.

At other times Longus can accept, within a *topos* of the pastoral
tradition, the original note, the variation brought about by
Theocritus. A number of epigrams[41] state that a shepherd despairing over the loss of his flock may commit suicide by hanging himself on a tree. Lamon's fear[42] of being hanged with Daphnis for not
having been able to prevent damage to the garden shows that
Longus knows this topic as a motif. But for the amorous anguish
of the protagonist he turns to a Theocritean precedent. In *Idyll* III
the *aipolos*, desperate because of the obstinate indifference of
Amaryllis, thinks of putting an end to his suffering by throwing
himself into the sea and threatens to kill himself without leaving
out any details: III 25–26 τὰν βαίταν ἀποδὺς ἐς κύματα τηνῶ

[40] The motif has deep roots outside the pastoral genre, as can be deduced from
the title of a mime by Sophron Ὡλιεὺς τὸν ἀγροιώταν and by a comedy of Epicharmus
Γᾶ καὶ θάλασσα: cf. Wilamowitz (1905: 169). The theme of the shepherd and the
sea is also reflected at a proverbial level: cf. Σικελὸς τὴν θάλασσαν Zenobios 5. 51,
Corpus Paroemiographorum graecorum, ed. Sentzel-Schneidewin (1899: 141–2).
[41] Antipater of Thessalonica *AP* 9. 149, 150; Philip *AP* 9. 255.
[42] Recalled by Chloe: 4. 8.

ἀλεῦμαι, | ὥπερ τὼς θύννως σκοπιάζεται Ὄλπις ὁ γριπεύς ('I'll strip
off my skins and leap into the waves | Where Olpis the fisherman
watches for the tuna'). Theocritus turns to an *adynaton* in order to
describe the amorous madness of the κωμαστής ('reveller') Daphnis
also thinks of suicide when he sees Astylus running towards him,
fearing that he will be given to Gnathon as his servant: 4. 22 ῥίψας
τὴν πήραν καὶ τὴν σύριγγα πρὸς τὴν θάλατταν ἐφέρετο ῥίψων ἑαυτὸν
ἀπὸ τῆς μεγάλης πέτρας ('he threw down his bag and his pipes and
rushed to the sea to throw himself off the big rock'). In Theocritus
the clarifications put into the mouth of the *aipolos* as to the how
and where of his imminent suicide produce a comic effect and
contribute to the characterization of the ingenuity of the naïve
kōmastēs. The same elements of the text, transposed in Longus onto
the descriptive plane, lose a great part of their ironic finesse: the
subtlety and expressive meaningfulness of Theocritus, then, are
reflected in a lifeless and dampened manner in Longus' imitation.

The examination of these cases shows that the pastoral tradition
is the backdrop, the base, upon which Longus moves. His adher-
ence to the rules and compositional schemes of the genre is total
and the variations, his original development, can be verified only
in the difference, in the separation, duly underlined, from the more
usual form in which a *topos* is presented. The knowledge and the
acceptance of the pastoral tradition are so deeply rooted in Longus
as to influence also the more marginal aspects, the most hidden
creases, of the narrative structure.

It appears that Longus might have taken on board one peculiarity of the pastoral genre: the ability to draw briskly landscapes,
ambiences, scenes, in the form of very short excursuses. In the
description of the strategem devised by Dorcon Longus does not fail
to indicate the origin of the wolf's skin with which the cowherd
covers himself: 1. 20 λύκου δέρμα μεγάλου λαβών, ὃν ταῦρος ποτὲ πρὸ
τῶν βοῶν μαχόμενος τοῖς κέρασι διέφθειρε ('He took the hide of a big
wolf that a bull had gored to death once fighting for its cows'). This
precision of detail is part of a tendency to make of the pastoral
environment a world closed in on itself: the pastoral origin of
almost every object is pointed out.[43] I would not exclude, however,
the possibility that Longus might have profoundly modified a
passage in *Idyll* IX where Daphnis recalls the incident in which the

[43] Cf. Scarcella (1970: 117-18).

beasts whose skins made up his στιβάς had died, ll. 9–11 ἔστι δέ μοι
πάρ᾽ ὕδωρ ψυχρὸν στιβάς, ἐν δὲ νένασται, | λευκᾶν ἐκ δαμαλᾶν καλὰ
δέρματα τάς μοι ἁπάσας, | λὶψ κόμαρον τρωγοίσας ἀπὸ σκοπιᾶς ἐτίναξε
('there is a bed for me beside the cool brook, piled high | With fine
skins from white heifers, all of which | The south wind dashed off
the cliff while they grazed the arbute'). Rather than conclude that
Daphnis might have killed the animals of his herd to obtain skins,[44]
ll. 9–11 seem to introduce a quick sketch of pastoral life, a picture
of nature that is not serene or idyllic. Longus too in the short
digression on the wolf's skin allows the insertion of a small episode
which enriches the essentially literary picture of pastoral life with
new detail.

TECHNIQUES OF TRANSFORMING PASTORAL CONSTANTS

One of the distinctive features of Theocritus' style and, albeit to a
lesser extent, that of his successors is the vitality of the dialogue,
the cleverness of the comments, the speed of the sketches, the
allusive strength of the most fleeting hints. The novel, with the
need to motivate every detail, to frame with precision every element, to create plain links between the different events, is the least
suitable genre to take up the brilliant tone of pastoral poetry.
Longus's style, then, slow, diffuse, careful to note even the particular, makes the gap even wider. In order to overcome this difficulty
Longus must interfere with the pastoral constants, transforming
them according to criteria and diverse rhetorical techniques that
are often combined among themselves.

Amplification

The simplest procedure consists of widening and expanding into a
whole episode something which Theocritus simply mentions.

In one of the most lively scenes of the novel two goats are fighting and Daphnis, having grasped a stick, chases in anger the goat
that had injured the other animal: 1. 11. Since all are engrossed
in the attempt to capture the fugitive, Daphnis does not see the
trap set by the κωμῆται for the she-wolf and falls into it with the

---

[44] Legrand (1925: 29 n. 7). IX. 9–11 appear incredible if referred to heifers,
according to Brinker (1884: 34) and Kettein (1901: 76).

goat; rescued by Dorcon, he cleans himself in the Nymphs' grotto, rekindling the admiration and love of Chloe. The chase of the animal and the subsequent injury to the shepherd are already present in Theocritus IV. 44–57: Battos and Corydon have to stop their conversation to prevent heifers from eating the shoots of an olive and are forced to climb on a λόφος ('rise') thick with vegetation to chase Cymaetha; here Battos hurts his naked foot with a thorn. Longus follows closely the sequence present in Theocritus' *Idyll*: the flight of the animal, the chase, the injury to the shepherd, but he widens the few remarks of Theocritus to the point of constructing a complex episode in which space is found for the fight between the animals, the rage of Daphnis, the chase, the fall into the trap, the despair of Chloe, and the help given by Dorcon the cowherd, who does not fail to show his love for Chloe straightaway.

In Theocritus' first *Idyll* Pan sarcastically hints at the clumsiness in the field of love of the *aipolos* who looks longingly at the animals in love: ll. 85–8 ἆ δύσερώς τις ἄγαν καὶ ἀμήχανος ἐσσί. | βούτας μὲν ἐλέγευ, νῦν δ' αἰπόλῳ ἀνδρὶ ἔοικας. | ὡπόλος ὅκκ' ἐσορῇ τὰς μηκάδας οἷα βατεῦνται, | τάκεται ὀφθαλμὼς ὅτι οὐ τράγος αὐτὸς ἔγεντο ('A fool for love and weak you are. | They said you were a cowherd, but you look like a goatherd—| The goatherd who watches the she-goats when they're mounted, | His eye pines because he can't be a billy'). The erotic inexperience of the goatherds must have been a widespread *topos*: it appears once more in Theocritus VI. 7 δυσέρωτα καὶ αἰπόλον ἄνδρα καλεῦσα ('calling him a goatherd, a fool for love') and it is picked up again by Longus himself at 3. 18 ἀλλ' ἄτε ἄγροικος καὶ αἰπόλος καὶ ἐρῶν καὶ νέος ('Being a rustic, a goatherd, in love and young').[45] The quick, playful hint of Theocritus is expanded in Longus' novel into a long section devoted to the meticulous description of the awakening of nature and men in spring. The narrative rhythm is relaxed: from the review of the luxuriance of the blossom and the vitality of the animals it moves to the description of the amorous anxieties of Daphnis who, after long debate, decides to imitate his goats in everything: 3. 13 οἳ δὲ καὶ νέοι καὶ σφριγῶντες, καὶ πολὺν ἤδη χρόνον ἔρωτα ζητοῦντες ἐξεκάοντο πρὸς τὰ ἀκούσματα καὶ ἐτήκοντο πρὸς τὰ θεάματα . . . [3. 14] ἀνίστησιν αὐτὴν καὶ κατόπιν περιεφύετο μιμούμενος τοὺς τράγους ('Daphnis and Chloe, blooming with youthful energy, who had

[45] On the *topos* of the erotic clumsiness of the αἰπόλος cf. Gow (1952: ii. 20).

long since been searching for love, were inflamed by what they heard and felt faint at what they saw . . . [3. 14] he made her stand up and clung to her from behind, copying the he-goats'). The discouragement of Daphnis in the face of failure and his disconsolate confession of ignorance πολὺ δὲ μᾶλλον ἀπορηθείς, καθίσας ἔκλαεν εἰ καὶ κριῶν ἀμαθέστερος εἰς τὰ ἔρωτος ἔργα ('he felt more puzzled and sat down and wept at the thought that he was more stupid than the rams at making love') reflect Theocritus' ἆ δύσερώς τις ἄγαν καὶ ἀμήχανος ἐσσί.

From a playful remark in Theocritus Longus has drawn an entire episode and one that is surely not illuminated by irony: the amplification and extension of every possible development of Theocritus' trouvée have led him to give explicit reasons for all that was implicit in Theocritus, resulting, as a consequence, in an inevitable flattening of tone.

'Steigerung'

As an antidote to the triteness that pastoral themes suffer once they are introduced into the narrative structure of the novel, Longus has recourse to intensification.

The tendency to exaggerate a *topos* can be seen at 3.24 ὁ μὲν ἐσύριζεν ἁμιλλώμενος πρὸς τὰς πίτυς, ἡ δὲ ᾖδε ταῖς ἀηδόσιν ἐρίζουσα ('On his pipes he competed with the whistling of the pines, while she sang in contest with the nightingales'). As he had already done at 1. 23,[46] Longus imitates the beginning of *Idyll* I of Theocritus,[47] showing that he had not understood the stylistic planning. Theocritus with his ἁδύ . . . ἁδὺ δὲ καί constructs a priamel which prepares Thyrsis' invitation to the *aipolos* to sing. Longus, instead, focuses his interest only on the connection between the pine and the pipe and tries to instil in the motif a new vigour, making Daphnis compete with the pine. A like *Steigerung* has been applied also in relation to the traditional motif of human song compared to that of the nightingale.[48]

[46] Longus 1. 23 ἡδεῖα μὲν τεττίγων ἠχή, γλυκεῖα δὲ ὀπώρας ὀδμή, τερπνή . . . βληχή ('The chirping of the cicadas was pleasant; the smell of the fruit was sweet; the bleating of the sheep was delightful').

[47] Theocritus I. 1–3 ἁδύ τι τὸ ψιθύρισμα καὶ ἁ πίτυς, αἰπόλε, τήνα | ἁ ποτὶ ταῖς παγαῖσι μελίσδεται, ἁδὺ δὲ καὶ τύ | συρίσδες ('Something sweet is the whisper of the pine, goatherd | That makes her song by the springs, and sweet no less do you | Play your pipe').

[48] *Idyll* VIII. 37–38 αἴπερ ὁμοῖον | μουσίσδει Δάφνις ταῖσιν ἀηδονίσι ('If Daphnis makes | Music like the nightingales').

With a similar technique Longus produces an enjoyable epilogue
to the day spent by Daphnis in Chloe's home at 3. 9 (Δάφνις δὲ
κενὴν τέρψιν ἐτέρπετο· τερπνὸν γὰρ ἐνόμιζε καὶ πατρὶ συγκοιμηθῆναι
Χλόης· ὥστε περιέβαλλεν αὐτὸν καὶ κατέφιλει πολλάκις, ταῦτα πάντα
ποιεῖν Χλόην ὀνειροπολούμενος, 'But Daphnis enjoyed an empty
pleasure: he thought it pleasant to sleep even with Chloe's father,
so he embraced him and kissed him often and dreamed he was
doing all this to Chloe') from a sentence Theocritus had put in the
mouth of his aipolos at III. 20 (ἔστι καὶ ἐν κενεοῖσι φιλήμασιν ἀδέα
τέρψις, 'even in empty kisses there is sweet delight').[49] The kisses,
according to Theocritus, are only the first and surely not the most
intense among love's delights, although it is possible to obtain joy
from them. Longus 'intensifies' the gnome of Theocritus (Daphnis
cannot even approach Chloe and the kiss too is imaginary) and he
attempts to intellectualize it by inventing the variation of the hugs
and kisses for Dryas as a meagre comfort for Daphnis' distance
from Chloe, with the result that he completely loses the elegant
irony of the Theocritean passage.

Rationalistic Motivation

The limited tendency of the novel, and of Longus in particular,
towards the cleverness and the sudden winks and hints that are so
typical of Theocritus is fully reflected in the process of rationaliza-
tion that is undergone by some of the most lively recurrent motifs
of the pastoral tradition.

The combination, in sarcastic key, of the sexual behaviour of the
animals and of the shepherd is an invention of Theocritus when in
Idyll V Comatas casts Lacon's past up in his face: 41-2 ἁνίκ'
ἐπύγιζόν τυ, τὺ δ' ἄλγεες· αἱ δὲ χίμαιραι | αἴδε κατεβληχῶντο, καὶ ὁ
τράγος αὐτὰς ἐτρύπη ('When I buggered you, you moaned; and the
nannies | Bleated too when the billy pushed it in them'): the
chiastic position brings Lacon close to and assimilates him with the
goats and Comatas with the τράγος. The motif had proved lucky:
there are resonances of it, in a more faded form, in Virgil Ecl. 3. 8
and, with more bluntness, in the epigram at AP 9. 317. 3-4
αἰπόλε, τοῦτον ἐγὼ τρὶς ἐπύγισα, τοὶ δὲ τραγίσκοι | εἰς ἐμὲ δερκόμενοι
τὰς χιμάρας ἔβλεπον ('Goatherd, I buggered him three times, while
the billy-goats were looking at me and eyeing the nannies').[50]

---

[49] The verse is taken up again at Idyll XXVII. 4.
[50] Cf. Gow and Page (1965: 586).

Longus refers to this *topos* in order to set upon it the skirmish between Daphnis and the homosexual Gnathon. With this constant he makes another come into play, that of the *aipolos* as a person who is not particularly fussy in matters of sex.[51] The townsman Gnathon thinks that he has easily gained the upper hand over Daphnis and turns to images and arguments that in his judgement are nearer the experience and mentality of an *aipolos*: 4. 12 εἶτα ⟨ἐδεῖτο⟩ ὄπισθεν παρασχεῖν τοιοῦτον οἷον αἱ αἶγες τοῖς τράγοις ('then he tried to talk him into letting himself be used as he-goats use the she-goats'). To his arguments Daphnis has no difficulty in answering: ὡς αἶγας μὲν βαίνειν τράγους καλόν, τράγον δὲ οὐπώποτε εἶδέ τις βαίνοντα τράγον, οὐδὲ κριὸν ἀντὶ τῶν οἰῶν κριόν ('he said that it was all right for he-goats to mount she-goats, but that nobody had ever seen a he-goat mounting a he-goat or a ram mounting a ram instead of a ewe'). In the novel, however, the sarcasm of Comatas' remark disappears and in Daphnis' answer is perceivable that rationalistic note and that absence of irony that mark the Theocritean echoes in Longus.

In *Idyll* XXVII Daphnis, in the course of his rapid courting of the girl, does not limit himself to persuasive words and experiences a reprimand: I. 49 τὶ ῥέζεις, σατυρίσκε; τί δ᾽ ἔνδοθεν ἅψαο μαζῶν ('What are you doing, satyr boy? Why is your hand inside my bosom?'). The motif returns in Longus too, but sweetened and diluted in a long narrative section which sees Chloe's sleep interrupted by a cicada that, pursued by a swallow, has hidden in her bosom: I. 26 ὁ δὲ Δάφνις ἐγέλασε, καὶ προφάσεως λαβόμενος καθῆκεν αὐτῆς εἰς τὰ στέρνα τὰς χεῖρας καὶ ἐξάγει τὸν βέλτιστον τέττιγα μηδὲ ἐν τῇ δεξιᾷ σιωπῶντα ('Daphnis laughed. Taking this opportunity, he put his hands between her breasts and took out that obliging cicada, which did not go quiet even when it was in his hand'). Longus accords the episode a wide pastoral frame and takes care to motivate (and to justify) Daphnis' gesture through a complex series of circumstances.

One of the scenes which decorate the κισσύβιον offered to Thyrsis depicts a boy who, completely engrossed in building a trap for crickets, lets foxes enter the vineyard which he is guarding: Theocritus I. 52–3 αὐτὰρ ὅγ᾽ ἀνθερίκοισι καλὰν πλέκει ἀκριδοθήραν |

---

[51] Cf. Antipater of Thessalonica *AP* II. 327 and *AP* 12. 41, and the reflections of van Groningen (1958: 314–15 n. 6 and 317).

σχοίνῳ ἐφαρμόσδων ('he's weaving a fine cage for the crickets from asphodel | And plaiting it with rushes'). Longus interweaves the motif of the boy engrossed in building an ἀκριδοθήρα with a second *topos*, that of the offer by one shepherd to watch the flock of another, while the latter sings or plays.[52] Daphnis and Chloe take turns in caring for the flock, but only to provide the other with the opportunity to sing: I. 10 ἤδη δέ τις καὶ τὰς ἀγέλας ἀμφοτέρας ἐφρούρησε θατέρου προσλιπαρήσαντος ἀθύρματι, ἀθύρματα δὲ ἦν αὐτοῖς ποιμενικὰ καὶ παιδικά. ἡ μὲν ἀνθερίκους ἀνελομένη ποθὲν ἐξελθοῦσα ἀκριδοθήραν ἔπλεκε καὶ περὶ τοῦτο πονουμένη τῶν ποιμνίων ἠμέλησεν ('Sometimes one of them looked after both the flocks, while the other was absorbed in some toy. Their toys were of a pastoral and childish type. She picked stalks of asphodel from here and there and wove a trap for grasshoppers, and while she was working on this, she paid no attention to her sheep'). All the grace and the naturalness of the Theocritean boy have disappeared in Longus, who is careful to give pedestrian reasons for introducing the theme of the ἀκριδοθήρα with ἀθύρματα δὲ ἦν αὐτοῖς ποιμενικὰ καὶ παιδικά. In this case, over and above motivation and rationalization, we need to speak of intellectualization: Longus observes from the outside at some distance the theme of pastoral play that in Theocritus is well encompassed in the mime; to define the ἀθύρματα ('toys') of Daphnis and Chloe as ποιμενικά ('pastoral') and παιδικά ('childish') is to let the reader know, to provide him with a clue that makes it easier to decipher the literary imitation.

Visualization

A procedure that we might define as 'visualization' has determined the transformation of the motif of the watchdog of the flock who growls at Galatea when she is in love with Polyphemus and threatens to bite her flesh (Theocritus VI. 9-14). Longus has profoundly redeveloped this theme, setting it within a complex episode, that of the ambush of Chloe by Dorcon disguised as a wolf. The dogs of Daphnis and Chloe will hurl themselves against the cowherd, reducing him to desperate straits: I. 21 οἵ τε κύνες περισπῶντες τὸ δέρμα τοῦ σώματος ἥπτοντο αὐτοῦ ('and the dogs dragged the hide off and got their teeth into Dorcon's own body'). It is worth noting the different justification the two authors give for the dogs' attack. In Theocritus VI. 9 it is Galatea who provokes the

---

[52] Theocritus I. 14; III. 1; VII. 89-90.

beast, throwing some apples at it: πάλιν ἄδ᾽, ἴδε, τὰν κύνα βάλλει, |
ἅ τοι τὰν οἴων ἔπεται σκοπός ('she flings them at the dog | Which
guards your sheep'), in Longus it is the wolfskin clothing of Dorcon
that attracts the dogs: I. 2I καὶ οἱ κύνες, οἱ τῶν προβάτων ἐπιφύλακες
καὶ τῶν αἰγῶν ἑπόμενοι, οἷα δὴ κυνῶν ἐν ῥινηλασίαις περιεργία,
κινούμενον τὸν Δόρκωνα πρὸς τὴν ἐπίθεσιν τῆς κόρης φωράσαντες,
πικρὸν μάλα ὑλακτήσαντες ὥρμησαν ὡς ἐπὶ λύκον ('The dogs who
went out to guard the sheep and the goats were busy sniffing
things out, as dogs usually are, and they caught Dorcon moving
to attack the girl. They pounced on him, barking shrilly, taking
him for a wolf'). Besides the tendency to unfold in a whole episode
what Theocritus suggests only fleetingly, it is evident that Longus
translates into an event, described in its minute details, what in
Theocritus is merely a note: ll. I3–I4 φράζεο μὴ τᾶς παιδὸς ἐπὶ
κνάμαισιν ὀρούσῃ | ἐξ ἁλὸς ἐρχομένας, κατὰ δὲ χρόα καλὸν ἀμύξῃ ('see
it doesn't rush at the girl's legs | As she comes from the sea, and
tear her fine skin').

A similar visualization is found in the episode that Longus builds
out of fr. I05 Voigt of Sappho:

οἶον τὸ γλυκύμαλον ἐρεύθεται ἄκρῳ ἐπ᾽ ὔσδῳ
ἄκρον ἐπ᾽ ἀκροτάτῳ· λελάθοντο δὲ μαλοδρόπηες·
οὐ μὰν ἐκλελάθοντ᾽, ἀλλ᾽ οὐκ ἐδύναντ᾽ ἐπίκεσθαι,

('As the sweet-apple reddens on the bough-top
On the top of the topmost bough; the apple-gatherers
  have forgotten it—
No they have not forgotten it entirely, but they could
  not reach it',

trans. Campbell).

This would enjoy some favour among the Hellenistic poets.[53] What
in the poetess appears as a comparison, an image, is in Longus
3. 33 translated into reality. Naturally in the transposition into
Longus' calm prose the gentle irony that characterized Sappho's
fragment is lost. We must note how Longus recalls the playful cor-
rection of the poetess λελάθοντο δὲ μαλοδρόπηες· | οὐ μὰν ἐκλελάθοντ᾽,
resolving it with a precise annotation that is flat and pedantic:
ἔδεισεν ὁ τρυγῶν ἀνελθεῖν, ἠμέλησε καθελεῖν ('the apple picker must

[53] Callimachus, *Hymn to Demeter* 28 ἐν δὲ καλὰ γλυκύμαλα; Theocritus VII. II7
ὢ μάλοισιν Ἔρωτες ἐρευθομένοισιν ὁμοῖοι ('Oh Loves like the reddening apples'), XI.
39 τὸ φίλον γλυκύμαλον ('the dear sweet-apple'). Cf. Voigt (I97I: II9).

have been frightened to climb up there and failed to take it down').
As already in the verbal recollections, so in this case too the relationship between Sappho and Longus is not direct: the erotic theme
of the γλυκύμαλον is inserted into the frame of the novel thanks
to the angry resentment of Chloe. In *Idyll* III of Theocritus the
aipolos, in order to ingratiate himself with Amaryllis, offers her ten
apples, specifying that he had picked them up where she wanted:
ll. 10–11 ἠνίδε τοι δέκα μᾶλα φέρω· τηνῶθε καθεῖλον | ὧ μ' ἐκέλευ
καθελεῖν τύ, καὶ αὔριον ἄλλα τοι οἰσῶ ('See I've brought you ten
apples; I plucked them | From where you told me to, and tomorrow
I'll bring you more again'), but even so he is unable to win over
her surliness. In Longus the *topos* is inverted: Chloe will get angry
because Daphnis wants to pick apples exactly on that tree, at the
top.

Sometimes the technique of 'visualization' produces results that
are very debatable. Philitas, in describing the apparition of Eros,
records that the latter hopped from one branch to the next, like a
small nightingale, only to disappear suddenly: 2. 6 ταῦτα εἰπὼν
ἀνήλατο καθάπερ ἀηδόνος νεοττὸς ἐπὶ τὰς μυρρίνας, καὶ κλάδον ἀμείβων
ἐκ κλάδου διὰ τῶν φύλλων ἀνεῖρπεν εἰς ἄκρον ('He said this and then
hopped like a young nightingale into the myrtles and, moving from
branch to branch, worked his way through the leaves to the top').
Evidently Longus has in mind here a passage in the ecphrasis of
Theocritus *Idyll* XV,[54] ll. 120–2 οἱ δέ τε κῶροι ὑπερπωτῶνται Ἔρωτες,
| οἷοι ἀηδονιδῆες ἀεξομενᾶν ἐπὶ δένδρῳ | πωτῶνται πτερύγων πειρώμενοι
ὄζον ἀπ' ὄζω ('the Love-babes spread their wings | Like nightingales
flitting from bough to bough | In the tree as they try their grow-
ing wings'), where a comparison is made between the flight of the
cupids and that of the little nightingales that, still unsure of themselves, flutter from one branch to the next. The attempt to transform the imagery of Theocritus into narrative reality has given rise
in Longus to the strange depiction of an Eros who, without reason,
flies between the branches and suddenly disappears. To transfer to
the behaviour of Eros the features that characterize in their simile
the flight of the nightingales has created a clumsy and gratuitous
representation of the god. Perhaps woven into the imitation of the
Theocritean passage there is a memory of fr. 13 of Bion, in which
a young hunter seeks in vain to capture Eros in a net: ll. 1–6
Ἰξευτὰς ἔτι κῶρος ἐν ἄλσεϊ δενδράεντι | ὄρνεα θηρεύων τὸν ἀπότροπον

εἶδεν Ἔρωτα | ἑσδόμενον πύξοιο ποτὶ κλάδον· ὡς δὲ νόησε, | χαίρων
ὤνεκα δὴ μέγα φαίνετο τὤρνεον αὐτῷ, | τὼς καλάμως ἅμα πάντας ἐπ'
ἀλλάλοισι συνάπτων | τᾷ καὶ τᾷ τὸν Ἔρωτα μετάλμενον ἀμφεδόκευε
('Once a fowler-boy in a wooded grove | Was hunting birds and
saw retiring Love | Perching on a box-wood bough; when he saw,
| He rejoiced at what seemed a bird so large. | Fitting all his rods
together | He lay in wait for Love hopping back and forth'). Here
the flight from one branch to the other is justified by the necessity
of fleeing from the nets, whereas in Longus Eros, having revealed
his real identity to Philitas, surely need not fear being captured.

ADAPTING BUCOLIC MOTIFS TO THE ROMANTIC FRAME

In a novel adventure, improvisation, and movement constitute
a base element, a fundamental ingredient, which is difficult to
reconcile with the by-and-large serene picture of the life of the
shepherds. Longus needed to find the link between the novelistic
element and the pastoral one in such a way that the themes
specific to the pastoral tradition would not exercise a limiting effect,
but, on the contrary, would insert themselves deep into the narrative structure of the novel.

This operation is, at times, accomplished successfully. At 1. 30
Daphnis is able to survive the wreck of the ship of the pirates who
had kidnapped him because he is dressed in light clothes, as a shepherd always is when leading his flock to pasture in the plain: ὁ δὲ
Δάφνις ἀνυπόδητος ὡς ἐν πεδίῳ νέμων ('But Daphnis had bare feet—
as you'd expect of someone grazing on the plain'). There is evidently here a recollection of Theocritus IV. 56 εἰς ὄρος ὅκχ' ἕρπῃς,
μὴ νήλιπος ἔρχεο Βάττε ('When you go up the hill, don't go without your shoes, Battos'), in which Corydon reprimands Battos for
having gone barefoot into the mountains. The heavily armed
pirates of Longus I. 28 ἐκβάντες σὺν μαχαίραις καὶ ἡμιθωρακίοις
('they disembarked with cutlasses and breastplates') drown and
Daphnis, the only survivor, can easily get back to the shore.

A very common topos is seen in the often threatening calls that
the shepherd makes to animals that have gone to browse where
they should not have done: Theocritus IV. 44–9 ΒΑ. θαρσέω, βάλλε
κάτωθε τὰ μοσχία· τὰς γὰρ ἐλαίας | τὸν θαλλὸν τρώγοντι, τὰ δύσσοα.

234 L. Cresci

*KO. σιτθ' ὁ Λέπαργος, | σίτθ', ἁ Κυμαίθα, ποτὶ τὸν λόφον. οὐκ
ἐσακούεις; | ἠξῶ, ναὶ τὸν Πᾶνα, κακὸν τέλος αὐτίκα δωσῶν | εἰ μὴ ἄπει
τουτῶθεν. ἴδ' αὖ πάλιν ἄδε ποθέρπει. | αἴθ' ἦς μοι ῥοικόν τι λαγωβόλον
ὥς τυ πάταξα* ('Battos: It's o.k. Drive your calves up—they're eat-
ing | The olive shoots, the good-for-nothings. Corydon: Come on
Lepargus, | Come on Cymaetha, up the rise. Will you not obey? |
I'll come, by Pan, and make it bad | Unless you move from here.
Look—she's turning back again. | I wish I had a crooked stick to
hit you with'), cf. V. 100-3 *KO. σίττ' ἀπὸ τᾶς κοτίνω, ταὶ μηκάδες·
ὧδε νέμεσθε | ὡς τὸ κατάντες τοῦτο γεώλοφον αἵ τε μυρῖκαι. | ΛΑ. οὐκ
ἀπὸ τᾶς δρυός, οὗτος ὁ Κώναρος ἅ τε Κιναίθα* ('Comatas: Move, you
nannies, from the wild olive: your grazing's | With the tamarisks
on the hillside slope. Lacon: Out of the oak, Conarus, Cinaetha!').
The same scene reappears on a relief of which there remains a
drawing by L. Ghezzi,[55] and on an engraved silver plate.[56] Longus
ingeniously re-works the theme, making it the pivot of the complex
episode which sees the tranquil life of Daphnis and Chloe disturbed
by the sudden arrival of the young hunters of Methymna: 2. 12.
The rope that secures to the land the boat in which they move
along the coast is stolen by a peasant and the Methymneans weave
one from vegetable fibre: 2. 13 *σχοῖνον μὲν οὖν οὐκ εἶχον ὥστε
ἐκδήσασθαι πεῖσμα· λύγον δὲ χλωρὰν μακρὰν στρέψαντες ὡς σχοῖνον
ταύτῃ τὴν ναῦν ἐκ τῆς πρύμνης ἄκρας εἰς τὴν γῆν ἔδησαν* ('they didn't
have a rope to tie up as a mooring cable, so they twisted a long,
green willow shoot into a rope, and with that they secured the
boat, by its stern end, to the land'), and then disperse across the
plain to hunt. Their dogs frighten Daphnis' goats who, pushed
toward the seashore, *ἔχουσαι δὲ οὐδὲν ἐν ψάμμῳ τρώξιμον, ἐλθοῦσαι
πρὸς τὴν ναῦν αἱ θρασύτεραι αὐτῶν τὴν λύγον τὴν χλωράν, ᾗ δέδετο ἡ
ναῦς, ἀπέφαγον* ('Having nothing to gnaw at in the sand, the more
adventurous ones went to the boat and ate up the green willow
shoot the boat had been moored with'). The ship, no longer
anchored, moves off and Daphnis is beaten by the Methymneans
as they hold him responsible for the damage caused by the goats:
only the energetic intervention of the peasants and shepherds
will save him. In this case Longus has been able to link skilfully a
traditional motif of the pastoral with the lively vicissitudes required
by the novel.

[55] Schreiber (1894a: pl. LXXVII).
[56] Schreiber (1894b: 469). Cf. Nicosia (1968: 86-8).

At other times, however, the fusion does not come off and a certain clumsiness is perceivable in the writing. In the two episodes that see Chloe threatened by Dorcon (1. 21) and kidnapped by the Methymneans (2. 20) Daphnis is prevented from intervening to aid her because in both cases he is busy cutting grass for the kids.[57] We are dealing with a canonical pastime of pastoral living, as seen in Theocritus XI. 73-4, but the mechanical repetition in two different contexts shows the difficulty in articulating motifs of the pastoral genre in a way that merges them—without overly obvious stitching—with the needs and narrative rhythms of the novel.

The pastoral constants, besides being inserted into the novel more or less successfully, also had to undergo necessary adaptations and alterations which would take into account the structural requirements of the new literary genre.

The first elaboration concerns the name and the pastoral role of the protagonist. The name of Daphnis is always associated with a *boukolos* and to assign it to an *aipolos* forms a not inconsiderable novelty, given that a precise hierarchy exists among the different types of herders.[58] Longus had to reconcile two different needs; that of assigning to his protagonist a 'renowned' name within the pastoral tradition,[59] and that of assigning him a role that allows for the continuous, daily proximity of life and work with Chloe. The solution consisted in making Daphnis an *aipolos*: flocks of sheep and goats can graze together, offering the shepherd and goatherd

[57] Longus 1. 21 Χρόνος ὀλίγος διαγίνεται καὶ Χλόη κατήλαυνε τὰς ἀγέλας εἰς τὴν πηγὴν καταλιποῦσα τὸν Δάφνιν φυλλάδα χλωρὰν κόπτοντα τοῖς ἐρίφοις τροφὴν μετὰ τὴν νομήν ('A little time went by, and then Chloe drove the flocks to the spring, leaving Daphnis cutting green leaves as fodder for the kids after they had finished grazing'). Longus 2. 20 ὁ μὲν Δάφνις οὐκ ἔνεμε τὰς αἶγας, ἀλλὰ εἰς τὴν ὕλην ἀνελθὼν φυλλάδα χλωρὰν ἔκοπτεν, ὡς ἔχοι τοῦ χειμῶνος παρέχειν τοῖς ἐρίφοις τροφήν ('Daphnis was not grazing his goats but had gone up to the wood and was cutting green leaves so that he would have fodder for the kids in winter').

[58] Aelius Donatus, *Vita Verg.* 49 (pp. 22 ff. Diehl): 'tria genera pastorum sunt, qui dignitatem in bucolicis habent, quorum minimi sunt qui αἰπόλοι dicuntur a Graecis, a nobis caprarii; paulo honoratiores qui μηλονόμοι ποιμένες id est opiliones dicuntur; honoratissimi et maximi qui βουκόλοι, quos bubulcos dicimus', 'the bucolic poets rank the three types of herders as follows: the least important are called *aipoloi* by the Greeks, *caprarii* ("goatherds") by us; those with a little more status are *mēlonomoi poimenes*, "flock-grazing shepherds", whom we call *opiliones* ("shepherds"); the greatest and most honourable are the *boukoloi*, whom we call *bubulci* ("cowherds").'

[59] Longus 1. 3 ὡς δ' ἂν καὶ τὸ ὄνομα τοῦ παιδίου ποιμενικὸν δοκοίη, Δάφνιν αὐτὸν ἔγνωσαν καλεῖν ('To make sure the child's name sounded pastoral, they decided to call him Daphnis').

every chance of life together. This shifting of roles, if it has borne fruit in the invention of so many little idyllic vignettes, has created difficulties for Longus in the episode of the quarrel between Daphnis and Dorcon, for which the precedent of Theocritus' *Idyll* VI, and particularly that of *Idyll* V, though a source of ideas and individual phrases, could not be followed exactly. In Theocritus a *boukolos* and an *aipolos* never come to quarrel. Longus obviates this problem with skill, resorting to the erotic-sentimental element: Dorcon the cowherd is a dangerous suitor for Chloe's hand and his relative prosperity should easily get the better of the more limited resources of the goatherd Daphnis. The latter's victory will be the proof of Chloe's love and of her unselfishness.

During the quarrel, however, some Theocritean conceits do appear, the transformation of which in Longus' novel indicates the difficulty of adapting to a disagreement between βουκόλος and αἰπόλος ('herdsman' and 'goatherd') cutting remarks and controversial arguments born in the context of a rivalry among equals or those who are almost so. A topical moment of the ἀγών is created by the boast of a shepherd whose rival answers in a way that recalls his words in a parodic form. In *Idyll* V of Theocritus to Lacon's invitation in ll. 50–51 ἦ μὰν ἀρνακίδας τε καὶ εἴρια τεῖδε πατησεῖς, | αἴ κ' ἔνθῃς, ὕπνω μαλακώτερα ('You'll tread on lambskin fleeces, | If you come here, that are softer than sleep'), Comatas answers ll. 55–7 αἰ δέ κε καὶ τὺ μόλῃς, ἀπαλὰν πτέριν ὧδε πατησεῖς | καὶ γλάχων' ἀνθεῦσαν· ὑπεσσεῖται δὲ χιμαιρᾶν | δέρματα τᾶν παρὰ τὶν μαλακώτερα τετράκις ἀρνᾶν ('And if you come here, you'll tread on delicate fern | And pennyroyal in bloom. Goatskins are laid | Down four-times softer than the lambskins you have there'). This scheme of cut-and-thrust finds an application in Longus 1. 16, where to the scornful evaluation of Dorcon Ἐγώ, παρθένε, μείζων εἰμὶ Δάφνιδος, καὶ ἐγὼ μὲν βουκόλος, ὁ δ' αἰπόλος τοσοῦτον ⟨ἐγὼ⟩ κρείττων ὅσον αἰγῶν βόες ('I am bigger than Daphnis, my girl, and I'm a cowherd, while he's a goatherd; so just as cows are better than goats, I'm better than him'), Daphnis reacts: νέμω δὲ τράγους τῶν τούτου βοῶν μείζονας ('I look after goats that are bigger than his cows').

The disproportion in the contrast between the herd of the cowherd and the flock of goats belonging to Daphnis makes the statements of the latter look ridiculous. G. Rohde and Mittelstadt have already observed that Longus transforms the singing contest among shepherds, typical of the pastoral genre, into a competition that has Chloe as the prize, that is, into something that comes close to the compositional schemata of the novel, in which the lover must beat many rivals in order to conquer the beloved.[60] However, I would say that Longus, even in this case, does not invent, but rather has recourse to the re-working of a motif that the pastoral tradition is already familiar with: in *Idyll* VIII of the *corpus* Daphnis, winner of the singing competition with Menalcas, marries Nais.[61] The two themes of the poetic contest and Daphnis' wedding are not, however, linked in this idyll, because Nais is not the reason for the contest and she is not its prize.[62] The scholia to *Idyll* VIII inform us that Daphnis' singing contest with a rival for the love of a Nymph called Thalia was the subject of Sositheus' *Lityerses*.[63] The hint in *Idyll* VIII was, perhaps, developed and modified by Sositheus, whom Longus had probably taken as the model for his contest between Dorcon and Daphnis. Already from this example it is possible to extract some indication as to the method followed by Longus in order to reconcile and merge *topoi* from two different literary genres. He chooses, in the context of the pastoral tradition, those motifs which appear more susceptible to the elaborations and adaptations required to set them in the frame of the novel.

Even in the field of the representation of the love that binds the two protagonists the novel imposes very precise laws. One of them consists of the chastity and inexperience of the lovers. Longus transforms this into something that is closer to that which can be found in the patrimony of the pastoral genre, that is, the roughness of the goatherd and his proverbial inability to make love. Another obligatory motif is found in the hidden dangers and the temptations that both lovers must endure: if Daphnis does not

[60] G. Rohde (1937/1963: 102–3); Mittelstadt (1970: 222–3).
[61] Longus knows the end of *Idyll* VIII as is shown by the description of the clothing of the defeated Dorcon, I. 17 Δόρκων μὲν οὖν ἀλγήσας ἀπέδραμε ζητῶν ἄλλην ὁδὸν ἔρωτος ('Dorcon was hurt and ran off, looking for another route to love'), recalling the similar reaction of Menalcas: VIII. 90–1 ὡς δὲ κατεσμύχθη καὶ ἀνετράπετο φρένα λύπᾳ | ὥτερος ('the other was all but extinguished, his heart turned upside down | In grief').
[62] Menalcas, in fact, will tell of his love for Milon: l. 47.
[63] Σωσίθεος δὲ Δάφνιν γενομένον, ὑφ' οὗ νικηθῆναι Μενάλκαν ᾄδοντα Πανὸς κρίναντος, γαμηθῆναι δὲ αὐτῷ καὶ Νύμφην Θάλειαν (Wendel 1914: 203–4), 'there is a Daphnis in Sositheus who beats Menalcas in a singing competition judged by Pan; the nymph Thaleia becomes his wife'.

certainly put up a strong resistance to the explicit offers of Lycaenion, his refusal of the advances of the homosexual Gnathon is quite clear.

If it is true that Theocritus reveals himself as a rich source for the characterization of the erotic inexperience of the *aipolos*, a direct imitation would have had less profitable results for the description of the reciprocal and happy love of Daphnis and Chloe. For this reason Longus had to turn to later pastoral writers in whom the erotic element emerges in the foreground in comparison to the pastoral one.

Some reminders of Moschus are evident in the whole of the episode in which Eros is the protagonist: his restless gaiety and cheek, 2. 4-5, make him closer to Moschus' Eros Δραπέτης, and the solemn revelation of his identity to Philitas at 2. 5 οὔτοι παῖς ἐγὼ καὶ εἰ δοκῶ παῖς, ἀλλὰ καὶ τοῦ Κρόνου πρεσβύτερος καὶ αὐτοῦ τοῦ παντὸς χρόνου ('I'm not really a boy, even though I look like one, but I'm even older than Cronus and the whole of time itself') closely follows the end of the *Europa*, where the girl discovers that the bull is Zeus: ll. 155-6 αὐτός τοι Ζεύς εἰμι, κεἰ ἐγγύθεν εἴδομαι εἶναι | ταῦρος ('I am Zeus himself, though I just seem to be a | Bull').[64] In the astonished questions that Daphnis and Chloe ask themselves while they are still unable to recognize love as the cause of their anxiety (1. 14 and 17) it is perhaps possible to trace an echo of Europa's dismay after the dream, ll. 21-7.

In the post-Theocritean pastoral tradition, however, the erotic element shows an exuberance and is tinged with a passionate nature that must be dampened so as not to violate the rigorous rules of chastity that the novel imposes on its protagonists.

The example of the complex justification devised by Longus for the advances of Daphnis, 1. 26, is revealing in this context.[65] One of the moments of more languid pathos in the *Lament for Adonis* is marked by Aphrodite's kiss to her by now dying lover: ll. 45-6 ἔγρεο τυτθόν, Ἄδωνι, τὸ δ' αὖ πύματόν με φίλησον, | τοσσοῦτόν με φίλησον ὅσον ζώει τὸ φίλημα ('Awake for a while, Adonis, give me one last kiss, | Kiss me as long as your kiss lives'). Longus inserted this motif into the scene of the death of Dorcon, who, injured by the pirates, reveals to Chloe how to save Daphnis and asks her for

---

[64] Cf. Bühler (1960: 193).
[65] Cf. above p. 229.

a final kiss: I. 29 σὺ δὲ ἀντὶ τῶνδε καὶ ζῶντα ἔτι φίλησον ('in return, kiss me while I live') and I. 30 Δόρκων μὲν τοσαῦτα εἰπὼν καὶ φίλημα φιλήσας ὕστατον ἀφῆκεν ἅμα τῷ φιλήματι καὶ τῇ φωνῇ τὴν ψυχήν ('Dorcon said this and kissed his last kiss; with that kiss and those words he let out his final breath'). The circumstances in the novel are, however, very different from those taken up as a model: Dorcon and Chloe are not lovers and Dorcon's request (which comes unexpectedly and is not well motivated) has nothing of the consuming sentimentalism of the desperate Aphrodite. Longus' imitation is thus a bit cold and forced, even if it assists in enlivening for a moment the otherwise very colourless figure of Chloe, who, moved to pity Dorcon, will grant a kiss that she will later have to conceal from Daphnis.

From the analysis of the imitations of Theocritus and, more generally, those of the pastoral *corpus*, and of the reconditionings that these revivals imposed on the novel, I believe some conclusions can be drawn. Longus works within literary genres which allow a very narrow margin for invention, for the personal *trouvée*. The pastoral tradition offers a very limited series of *topoi* that Longus is able to widen thanks to direct recollections of the pastoral world of Theocritus, who presents a greater wealth and articulation of motifs. The novel, in turn, dictates very rigid laws that impose interferences of all kinds on the love of the protagonists: kidnappings, assaults by pirates, material difficulties, advances by rivals, *anagnorismoi*. In the attempt to link two orders of *topoi* which are fairly inelastic the fluidity of the narrative rhythm, the irony, the sarcasm, the vitality of Theocritus' style, have all inevitably been sacrificed. Even in the sections that more specifically belong to the novel it is possible to pick up a certain clumsiness in the invention of the episodes and in the links between the adventures and the disturbances brought by the pirates, by the youths, and then by the soldiers from Methymna, and the peaceful frame of pastoral life. Even in scenes better motivated and supported by some vitality in the narrative it is possible to perceive that Longus' centre of interest is somewhere else, in the more specifically pastoral episodes. The novelistic, then, is an element that sometime interferes and that the author tries to reabsorb into the pastoral.

At any rate we have to acknowledge that Longus was undoubtedly able to reconcile the contrasting needs of the two literary genres and to succeed, in some cases, in inserting the pastoral element deeply into the narrative plot of the novel.

* * *

With Longus' Lesbos a new kind of Arcadia is born: within a landscape built according to the stereotypes of the pastoral genre move
figures of naïve little shepherds, busily playing the syrinx and
weaving talks of love in the shadow of the oak. Their day is marked
by the codified rituals of the literary tradition: the visit to the
Nymphs' grotto, the dedication of their musical instruments to
Pan, the exchange of gifts, the loving care of the flock. It is an
idealized countryside in which hard work does not exist and work
is transformed into play; but also in the composition of the pastoral
picture, the novel has imposed a radical change on some fundamental features. The process of imitating one Theocritean passage
is the clearest exemplification of this. In Philitas' advice to Daphnis
and Chloe 2. 7 Ἔρωτος γὰρ οὐδὲν φάρμακον, οὐ πινόμενον, οὐκ
ἐσθιόμενον, οὐκ ἐκ ᾠδαῖς λαλούμενον, ὅτι μὴ φίλημα καὶ περιβολὴ καὶ
συγκατακλιθῆναι γυμνοῖς σώμασι ('There is no medicine for Love, no
potion, no drug, no spell to mutter, except a kiss and an embrace
and lying down together with naked bodies') we can immediately
recognize the recollection of Theocritus XI. 1–3 Οὐδὲν ποττὸν ἔρωτα
πεφύκει φάρμακον ἄλλο, | Νικία, οὔτ' ἔγχριστον, ἐμὶν δοκεῖ οὔτ'
ἐπίπαστον, | ἢ ταὶ Πιερίδες ('There's no medicine against love, |
Nicias, no lotion, no plaster known to me, | But the Muses'). But I
would not see in Longus a controversial correction of Theocritus,[66]
rather the answer to a structural requirement of the novel. Longus
could not, of course, adapt Theocritus' version of the οὐδὲν ποττὸν
ἔρωτα πεφύκει φάρμακον . . . ἢ ταὶ Πιερίδες. In pastoral poetry a
primary role is taken by singing. In Theocritus the shepherds are
always singing, either alone or in a contest: the landscape, the
animals, the objects and events of their daily lives can find a place
in the song, through hints that are broad or not so broad, but they
remain a function of the song and they are always set within it.[67]
In the novel these elements, which are relevant in Theocritus, but
marginal in comparison to the singing, are in the foreground, making up the plot of the story and leaving the singing element in the

---

[66] G. Rohde (1937/1963: 99); Mittelstadt (1970: 217).
[67] Cf. Snell (1963: 394 ff.); Klinger (1962: 296–8).

background. Obviously Longus underlines the fact that Daphnis is συρικτής and episodes like that of the celebration of Pan and the Nymphs (2. 30-7), where song and dance take a primary role, are not neglected. But sometimes it is possible to detect the strain that results from this change in perspective. The substitution of a *mythos* (that of the Syrinx) for the song that would be imposed by tradition creates a lack of harmony noted by Longus himself, who skilfully tries to muffle it: 2. 35 Ἄρτι πέπαυτο τοῦ μυθολογήματος ὁ Λάμων καὶ ἐπήνει Φιλητᾶς αὐτὸν ὡς εἰπόντα μῦθον ᾠδῆς γλυκύτερον ('Lamon had just finished his story-telling, and Philetas was praising him for telling a story sweeter than any song').

Another problem is presented by the animals: in the *Idylls* of Theocritus they enjoy some attention.[68] Often the shepherd interrupts his train of thought to turn to them, with love or anger, to give orders or to formulate threats: that is, because they are inserted directly into the monologue or the exchange of remarks between shepherds, they have a very different effect from that which is given by the descriptive course of the novel. Longus describes their movements, the behaviour modified by the alternation of the seasons, he lingers on the care that Daphnis and Chloe bestow on the flock; but, if he had stopped at these details, their presence would inevitably have been colourless. Longus is too refined a connoisseur of pastoral poetry to give up one of the elements that typifies it and he turns to the common folk tale of Orpheus in which singing and his effect on animals are fused. The flocks of Daphnis and Chloe are *mousikai*: the shepherds with singing or with the sound of the syrinx direct their movements and determine their behaviour. The song, the music, and the presence of the flocks, two topical themes of the pastoral tradition, have found in Longus a fusion at the level of magic.[69]

The theme of the flocks guided by music is another sign of the idealization and stylization that bucolic representation attains in Longus. But Longus' Arcadia knows many limitations. The naïvety of the young shepherds is observed, judged, and underlined from the outside with such frequency and precision as to exclude any sentimental identification by the author.[70] Furthermore the

[68] On the role of animals in Theocritus see the good observations of T. G. Rosenmeyer (1969: 131-4).

[69] Cf. Longus 1. 22, 27, 29; 2. 3, 28, 29, 38; 4. 15. On the αἶγες μουσικαί and the Virgilian precedent of *Ecl.* 7. 1-4 see Bonner (1909: 279).

[70] Longus 1. 31, 32; 2. 39; 3. 19. Cf. Longo (1978: 108).

exaltation of the countryside and the idealization of pastoral life are
limited to Daphnis and Chloe, whose non-farming origin is often
recalled: their beauty, for example, qualifies them as different from
and superior to the other shepherds,[71] who are not spared physical
defects.[72] Just as those who better personify the ideal of pastoral life
belong by birth to another environment,[73] the city, in fact it is precisely in contrast to urban life that there takes place the discovery
of the beauty and simplicity of the countryside.[74]

The stylization in an Arcadian sense finds another obstacle in the
disturbances brought about by pirates, young spoilt citizens, venal
parents who aspire to weddings of the right social rank for their
offspring, shepherds in love with Chloe who resort to attacks,
cunning, and kidnapping: it is the need for adventure, of narrative
plot, of unforeseen events characteristic of the novel that drastically
reshapes the perspective of the Longian Arcadia. In this context
too, then, are the laws of the different literary genres that condition Longus' approach. Beyond the judgement of his merits and
defects, both evident, in his imitative technique, it is more important to stress how profoundly the *topoi* of the pastoral tradition
influence the invention, the linking, and the internal structure of
the episodes of the novel and how Longus found himself working
within the context of a very rigid tradition. On these grounds I
believe that it is possible to base an evaluation of Longus' personality that is more precise in terms of literature and more correct in
terms of methodology.

[71] Longus 1. 7, 20; 3. 25; 4. 30. Cf. the observations of Longo (1978: 106-9).
[72] Longus 3. 32.
[73] In Shakespeare's *The Winter's Tale* the idyllic atmosphere of the dialogues
between Perdita (daughter of the king of Sicily) and Florizel (son of the king of
Bohemia) contrast with the realism of the peasant and of Autolycus.
[74] Pasquali (1966: 521-53).

Achilles Tatius and Ego-Narrative

B. P. REARDON

Of the three so-called 'sophistic' Greek novels, that of Achilles Tatius has probably been the least generally read and admired.[1] Whereas Longus and Heliodorus have seemed more immediately accessible, Achilles has often puzzled and troubled readers and scholars by the mixture that *Leucippe and Clitophon* offers: sensational melodrama side by side with sophisticated psychology and complex intrigue, simplistic novelistic convention along with a difficult narrative technique and elaborate rhetoric. Reactions have been varied. On the one hand, various degrees of dislike, from the moral disapproval of Photius in the ninth century to the contempt of Rohde in the nineteenth and the critical strictures of the early twentieth; later, a gleam of understanding, mixed with puzzlement and irritation; most recently, re-evaluation as some form of comic narrative, though hard to situate—parody, comedy, sick humour?[2] None of these judgements is altogether without foundation. No doubt because of this uncertainty about how to approach the story, it has not often been the object of sustained analysis, compared to its fellows.[3] The present paper will try to find a standpoint that will allow the various ingredients of *Leucippe and Clitophon* to come into proper perspective, and allow us to align our reactions with Achilles' intentions. Although no unchallenged interpretation exists, there is a degree of common ground in our own day; to the taste of the late twentieth century, the story is some form of comedy. What is offered here, then, is a reconsideration of some

---

[1] Modern editions: Garnaud (1991); Vilborg (1955/1962); Gaselee (1917; 2nd edn. 1969). Translations: English, Winkler, in Reardon (1989: 170-284), Gaselee (1917); French, Garnaud (1991), Grimal (1958); German, Plepelits (1980); Italian, Cataudella (1958).

[2] Photius, *Bibliotheca* 87 and 94; for the other reactions, see later.

[3] Besides the works mentioned in later notes, there are useful sections in Fusillo (1989/1991: esp. 97-108), and Plepelits (1980: introduction).

ideas by now familiar enough in themselves, in the hope that it
may be useful to reshuffle them.

The features of the story that merit attention here have been
touched on; they are:

1 the technique of ego-narrative;
2 psychological realism;
3 sensational adventures and melodrama;
4 the use of standard novel conventions;
5 sophistication of manner and style;
6 variety of content.

The most profitable approach will be to consider how these features
are interrelated. The general questions that need to be answered
are, how serious is Achilles? Is this melodrama or comedy—or, if
it is both, what is the relation between them? What is the place of
this novel in its genre? One preliminary comment should be made.
It is virtually certain that Achilles wrote in the latter part of the
second century, and therefore is a near-contemporary of several
other writers of fiction whose dates are fixed firmly enough for
present purposes: certainly Apuleius (*Metamorphoses*), Lucian (*True
Story, Philopseudes, Toxaris*, perhaps a version of the *Asinus*-story),
Iamblichus (*Babyloniaca*), and very probably others including
Longus (*Daphnis and Chloe*) and the authors of several stories of
which we possess fragments of varying tone. Working in this
creative age, Achilles assuredly had every incentive to experiment,
as did his contemporaries, with the form of this fashionable genre,
and in fact several of the qualities of his writing can be found in
the above works. A priori, therefore, we may reasonably expect to
find in him originality and ingenuity in the treatment of familiar
themes.

The most notable formal feature of *Leucippe and Clitophon* is that
it is cast as ego-narrative.[4] Why has Achilles chosen this form?
What does he gain by abandoning the more obvious and easier

[4] Technically, as reported ego-narrative, since the main story is told in the first
person by Clitophon to the ostensible narrator, who himself is represented as now
recounting it to the reader. That is to say that initially the story is in double ego-
narrative—initially, because this 'reporting frame' is not closed at the end. On the
ego-narrative mechanism in this novel, see Fusillo (1989/1991: 166–78). The
modern distinction between an ego-narrator who himself participates in the action
(like Clitophon) and one who does not (like Clitophon's interlocutor in the opening
chapter) may be noted, since it is Clitophon's personal participation that is the basis
of Achilles' narrative strategy.

omniscient authorial narrative method of earlier fiction of this kind, such as *Ninus* and *Chaereas and Callirhoe?* What difficulties does it entail, and how does he deal with them? This complex of questions will be seen to lead to a number of important aspects of the structure and content of the story.

One thing that ego-narrative notoriously can do is to make it impossible, if the writer so wishes, for narrator (and hence reader) to 'see' some of the action. The reader, in this convention, can learn only what the narrator learns as events unfold, without benefit of any knowledge acquired subsequently by the narrator. Alternatively, the narrator can be represented as learning part of the story subsequently to his own participation in the events it contains, and as being therefore in a position, at the time of his narration, to tell the listener (= reader) not only what he knows from his own participation, but also what he found out later. That is to say, the writer can have it both ways. He can let the reader learn the whole story of a given incident the first time that incident occurs in the ego-narrator's account of events; in that case the ego-narrative is being used not to keep the reader ignorant but for some other purpose. Or he can deliberately hide some of the story from the reader; in which case the ego-narrative form is being used *in order* to mystify, or produce some comparable effect on, the reader.

If we examine what Achilles does in this respect, we find that his practice varies.[5] In the first part of the story he conscientiously represents Clitophon as narrating only what he himself knew at the time of the action in question, namely the arrival of Leucippe in Tyre, the death of Charicles, the flirtation with Leucippe and its immediate sequel in the lovers' journey to Egypt—all of which we see through his eyes, as it happened at the time to his own knowledge. But at 2. 13-18 comes the story of how Callisthenes abducted Calligone, mistaking her for Leucippe, and at this point in his story Clitophon could not know about some of this—for instance, about Callisthenes' desire to marry Leucippe, and his request to Sostratus in Byzantium for her hand. He got to know about all of this later (8. 17. 2); so he is here, at 2. 13, introducing subsequent knowledge into his account of events. That is to say that Achilles has moved from one mode of ego-narration to another, in

---

[5] Hägg (1971*a*: 124-36), 'Points of view: Achilles Tatius'; this meticulous examination is fundamental to the present study.

order to put the reader in possession of the necessary knowledge
and relevant explanations.

All very well so far; this can be considered a legitimate version
of ego-narrative. It certainly simplifies matters for the author, since
it can add greatly to the coherence of the action, from the reader's
point of view—although it can, of course, tend to turn the narrator into an 'omniscient author', and thus spoil the specific ego-
narrative effect. Achilles, at any rate, seems after this point to
prefer to stay consistently on this less uncompromising level. At
two major points, however, he reverts to the stricter technique,
and they are significant points indeed. First, at 3. 15 Clitophon tells
us about the 'sacrifice' of Leucippe, and once more describes events
as he saw them *at the time they happened*, including the gruesome
details about how Leucippe's belly was slit open and her entrails
spilled out, only to be seized, cooked and eaten. That is to say that
we, the readers, are deliberately prevented from knowing what
has really happened, as we should have known with omniscient
narrative or with ego-narrative with hindsight. Obviously this is for
the sake of sensational effect. And that is the point of making this
observation: having tacitly dispensed himself from respecting his
own original narrative practice, Achilles chooses to return to it
here—for what purpose? In order to give himself the opportunity
to invent a singularly lurid incident of human sacrifice and
cannibalism. There was, after all, no need whatever to concoct so
grotesque an episode. But Achilles has stacked the cards ruthless-
ly: he invents the rhapsode's theatrical equipment, conjured up
handily by a pirate attack on a ship, and he invents also the
requirement that Menelaus and Satyrus perform human sacrifice as
an initiation rite for entry into the robber band. This point should
be stressed: he is not simply taking advantage of a situation that
the story has thrown up of its own accord, so to speak, he has
deliberately fixed the whole scene, gone out of his way to set it up,
expecting his audience to enjoy the kitsch,[6] to relish the *frisson*
such an incident would induce. It is one of the vicissitudes of the
tyche attaching to the survival of the Greek novel that in our day
a papyrus has come to our knowledge describing in even more
revolting detail an episode of startling similarity from another novel

---

[6] *Webster's Dictionary* defines kitsch as 'gaudy trash . . . writing of a pretentious
but shallow kind, calculated to have popular appeal'. The element of self-
consciousness is strong in this specimen.

of the period, the *Phoenicica* of Lollianus.[7] Together with the Grand Guignol of Iamblichus' *Babyloniaca*, with its ghosts, suicides, mutilation, poison, murder, magic practices and other entertaining features, these episodes demonstrate that there was undoubtedly a taste for fiction as sensational in its methods as any modern ghost or science fiction story.

The reader, duly mystified, naturally wants to know what happened. But before his curiosity is satisfied a few pages later (3. 20-2), Achilles takes advantage of the situation he has set up to attribute to Clitophon a soliloquy that revels in the nauseating details of the incident, in the fact that Leucippe's entrails have been eaten by human beings. Winkler's translation nicely catches the tone and a crucial antithesis: 'Your body is laid out here, but where will I find your vitals? Oh, far less devastating had the fire devoured them, but no—your insides are inside the outlaws, victuals in the vitals of bandits' (3. 16. 4).[8] Gaselee's version of 1917 just as nicely catches the tone not of Achilles Tatius but of so much scholarship on him; translating the passage lamely—'now has the burial of them been at the same time the robbers' sustenance'—he comments that 'the appalling ill taste of this rhetorical outburst prevents the English translation from being anything but ludicrous'.[9] It is of course exactly that—a question of taste—and one may of course deplore it; kitsch is not to everyone's liking. But the point is that the episode is very evidently constructed precisely in order to set up this appalling ill taste. It is deliberate, and it is the point of the whole episode. Far from being crude sensationalism, this is, for better or for worse, highly sophisticated sensationalism.

Having milked his resuscitated device of strict ego-narrative, Achilles repeats the trick once, at 5. 7, where apparently Leucippe is decapitated. This time, however, no doubt aware that he cannot expect to deceive his reader a second time in the same way, Achilles varies the recipe. Instead of being enlightened almost at once, the reader is explicitly fended off at 5. 20, where Satyrus tells Clitophon 'you will hear in due course', and has to wait almost beyond patience for the explanation, until virtually the end of the whole novel (8. 15-16); at which point Achilles himself archly

---

[7] Henrichs (1972); preliminary publication Henrichs (1969).
[8] Winkler (1989: 217).
[9] Gaselee (1917: 168-9).

says 'this is the only episode left incomplete in the whole story'. But again we have had an aria from Clitophon, though a short one (5. 7). The central antithesis this time is between the useless bulk of the surviving trunk and the smallness of the dominant but lost head; a perfect specimen of the contorted rhetoric of the Second Sophistic—and again, the last thing we should do is take it seriously.[10] Had these two episodes occurred in Xenophon's *Ephesiaca* or Iamblichus' *Babyloniaca* they would indeed have been 'serious', in the sense of being part of the real fabric of the story. In Achilles they are isolated and special episodes, staged for their effect in their own right, for which the author has chosen to revert to an uncomfortably severe form of ego-narrative that he has in principle already abandoned.[11]

More commonly Achilles allows his narrator to tell us not only what he saw happening at the time it happened, but also what he came to know subsequently; this is in fact his normal procedure after the watershed of 2. 13. Occasionally there is a passage where the stricter form interplays with the looser, and this can lead to irony. At 7. 1. 3, for example, we hear the story of Leucippe's third 'apparent death' (her alleged murder by the agents of Melite), which Clitophon recounts as he heard it at the time; but by then we as readers know what Clitophon at the time of the incident did not know, namely that Leucippe is alive; the narrative has by now become complex. In some cases, where we might wonder how Clitophon learned what had really happened, Achilles will throw in a brief justificatory remark.[12] As the story proceeds, however, the conventions are observed more and more loosely, until in the final two books the ego-narrator in effect turns into an omniscient narrator, for all the world like an omniscient author. For even given

[10] 'No translation can make this laboured rhetoric anything but ridiculous'— Gaselee (1917: 253).

[11] A third scene picked out by Hägg (1971a: 133) is 5. 17. 3 ff., where Clitophon describes meeting 'Lacaena' without saying that she was actually Leucippe (as he obviously knew at the time of narration); here, however, the effect of surprise is spoiled by Clitophon's comment that she reminded him of Leucippe. Here Achilles is doing his best to get out of a patently absurd situation in which his hero would not in any way recognize his heroine; that is, Achilles is not in this case exploiting the situation (he is in fact trying to disentangle himself from his own plot).

[12] To take one case of a number listed by Hägg (1971a: 132 ff.), already at 2. 30 Clitophon, reporting Leucippe's reaction to her mother's irruption into her room (which had caused Clitophon to escape unseen, so that he could not himself have witnessed Leucippe's reaction), retails what she said to his servant Satyrus with the phrase 'When I heard about this'.

the fullest information after the event, Clitophon could never have come to know some of the things Achilles represents him as telling us on his own authority. From the point at which Thersander enters the plot (5. 23) to the end of the story we are repeatedly told not only what Thersander did but also what went on in his mind. For instance, at 6. 11 (an interview between Thersander and Melite), and again at 6. 18 (Thersander and Leucippe), feelings are attributed by Clitophon to Thersander that Clitophon could not possibly learn about subsequently from the only conceivable source, namely Thersander himself; Thersander was his bitterest enemy, and cannot be imagined as communicating such intimate matters to Clitophon, and in any case Thersander disappears abruptly from Ephesus and from the novel at 8. 14. Sometimes Achilles tries to explain away this apparent omniscience—notably at 8. 15, where we are told that Sosthenes (Melite's steward, who abets Thersander), when threatened with torture, described Thersander's machinations in detail; Sosthenes cannot however be credibly represented as reporting Thersander's unspoken thoughts. There are other instances of such justification, sometimes encapsulated in a single phrase.[13] But Achilles is fighting a losing battle. The root of the matter is that he has set himself a task that is difficult enough from the very beginning, and by the final movement of his story he cannot credibly maintain the fiction of watertight ego-narrative—particularly if he wants to get inside Thersander's mind at this point as he has earlier got inside Clitophon's, Leucippe's and Melite's, all of them via his only channel, namely his narrator Clitophon. The longer his story goes on, the more complex it becomes, and the less strictly can he observe his own narratorial convention. It is the story that wins; the convention suffers. Wolff was not exaggerating very much when he said long ago that Clitophon 'assumes omniscience wherever Achilles finds it con-venient'.[14] It is not that he is without conscience in the matter; on the contrary, he tries very hard to clear up loose ends where he can, notably the story of Callisthenes and Calligone. But there are limits to what he can do. In practice, Clitophon is used increasingly as the voice of the omniscient author.[15]

---

[13] See Hägg (1971a: 132).

[14] S. L. Wolff (1912: 199f.), quoted with approval by Hägg (1971a: 134 n. 2).

[15] We may note here in passing that the frame of Clitophon's story is never closed. This has worried scholars, who have sometimes accused Achilles of forget-fulness or incompetence. Neither is a very likely explanation, given so much evi-

All of which brings us to the question of why Achilles embarked on ego-narrative in the first place. How does this structure serve his aim, and what does it tell us about it? What kind of story did he want to write?

Fundamentally *Leucippe and Clitophon* is a 'standard' Greek novel. It contains all the ingredients one would expect: lovers, travel and adventures, separation and tribulations, rivals and fidelity, divine intervention and *tyche*. We have already seen some of the adventures, and have seen that they are distorted; and we shall see distortion or at least modification of other elements as well. This does not necessarily mean that the whole story flouts the generic conventions; it is, however, the distortions that give it its special flavour, and we should examine them. In doing so we shall find the feature of ego-narrative recurring frequently as a major factor contributing to that distortion and that flavour.

First, the lovers, and the element of love. In the less sophisticated specimens of the genre, *Chaereas and Callirhoe* and the *Ephesiaca*, love is simply a given, born in a moment, totally simplistic and unexamined throughout the story. In Achilles' story the picture is different; neither Clitophon nor Leucippe is naïve or sentimental. Clitophon, it is true, falls in love at first sight, but what he aims at in the first place is not ideal marriage but simply sexual satisfaction; his approach to it is highly sophisticated, based as it is on realistic psychology rather than romantic convention, and Chariton's or Xenophon's few lines of bare assertion of love become two books of quite unideal courtship. Leucippe does not fall in love at first sight; she has clearly read her Ovid and knows the rules, and she unideally yields to seduction—that it does not come to

dence of care in construction in general. More probably he thought that a logically satisfactory closure would be pedantic and would detract from the ending of the real story, thus creating worse problems than it solved; and as has been pointed out before now, he had the precedent of Plato's *Republic* and other dialogues to justify him—the best possible precedent for so literary an author. See Hägg (1971*a*: 125): the opening frame launches the whole story—and that is all Achilles wants it to do. Most (1989) attributes this 'weakness' to a 'taboo against excessive self-disclosure' and a convention whereby autobiography in Greek literature has to be a tale of woe, which does not suit a Greek romance with its happy ending; this, it is claimed, explains both Clitophon's otherwise inexplicable sadness at the beginning of the story and the omission, at its end, of reference to the autobiographical nature of this ultimately happy story. This seems specious; it is hardly likely that Achilles would go to so much trouble in order to end up painting himself into a corner. In setting out his position Most defends the complete integrity of the ego-narrative, but he does not meet adequately the evidence adduced by Hägg.

completion is not her fault. This is the first instance of another of Achilles' devices, which one may call brinkmanship: he very nearly abandons the convention, in order to produce a thrill in the reader. But thereafter Leucippe turns into a conventionally virtuous virgin heroine; when, at 41, at the first opportunity since the couple's flight from home, Clitophon again seeks satisfaction, Leucippe refuses it. The real reason for this refusal is that Achilles wants to change tack. He has used the modified love-motif to get his story off to a convincing start: the departure of the lovers is motivated not by some melodramatic intervention of the gods (as in Xenophon) or of *tyche* (the apparent death of Callirhoe in Chariton), but by the realistic indignation of Leucippe at being unjustly disbelieved by her mother when she protests that she has not lost her honour—a very Achillean irony. Having thus put this particular departure from convention to effective use, he needs now to get back again to the main structural beam of such a story, namely the impregnable virtue of the heroine; and in order to do so he is quite ready to resort to another convention, divine intervention, in the shape of a dream sent to Leucippe by Artemis, enjoining her to remain a virgin until she is married to Clitophon. Having begun his story by standing conventional love on its head, Achilles now retreats into conventional love.

During this first stage the strict ego-narrative technique has been put to use in the realistic representation of Clitophon's—that is, the narrator's—psychology, which sets the tone for the whole novel; and we have already seen that in the subsequent stage of the action, the adventures of the couple in Egypt, the technique is used to produce sensational effects. In the third stage—Clitophon's entanglement with Melite—it is used quite simply to get Leucippe out of the way. Since Clitophon thinks Leucippe is dead, his narrative will naturally leave her out of account; it will concentrate, and therefore we shall concentrate, on Melite. We may here turn to the standard ingredient of rivals and fidelity; and here too Achilles has stood novel-convention on its head. As the heroine's rival, Melite could be expected to be cast as a female villain, anything from the black-and-white caricatures Manto and Cyno of Xenophon to the impressive predatory *femme fatale* Arsace of Heliodorus. In fact she becomes something close to a secondary, or even simply a second, heroine. The female interest is now transferred to Melite, and once more Achilles embarks on an

impressively realistic piece of psychology in presenting this substitute lover; if there is one character in the story who has regularly
attracted readers' sympathy, it is Melite.[16]

And once more Achilles indulges in a piece of brinkmanship,
comparable to the episode of Leucippe's near-capitulation in Book
2. This time, of course, it is Clitophon whom we half-expect to give
in; Leucippe's mother appeared just in time to save her daughter
from the wrong kind of love, we remember, but will Leucippe herself appear (or reappear) in time to save Clitophon from another
version of it? As Ephesus comes closer and closer we wonder how
long Clitophon can hold out. How is this crisis to be dealt with? Of
course Leucippe does reappear in time—just; and because she does,
Melite can unconsciously assure her of Clitophon's fidelity precisely
by enlisting her, ironically, in a final attempt to subvert it by
employing Leucippe's alleged magical abilities as a 'Thessalian' to
conjure Clitophon's affections. Brinkmanship . . . but this time,
having only just pulled his hero back from the brink, Achilles
trumps his own ace by suddenly throwing him over the brink after
all, as after all Clitophon suddenly does give way to Melite—when,
and precisely because, the situation has been saved and he is no
longer in danger. Yet a further piece of realism: 'I felt as any man
would', says Clitophon (5. 27). Yet again Achilles had disconcerted
us with the unexpected, and made of it his masterstroke. Here we
revert to the situation in Books 1–2, in that we are made to see
the operation of love through Clitophon's eyes; in the degree in
which this is (after all) a love-story, the verisimilitude accruing
from the use of ego-narrative in both cases in itself adds to the realism of the emotions thus treated, and makes of the story something
more than a generic exercise.

Yet structurally the function of even this realistic episode is not
to make Melite central to the story, but on the contrary to get rid
of her so as to bring the story to its expected conclusion. Clitophon
pays his dues to passion and passion bows out. We return to novel-
convention; this time, to reunion. Yet again, however, it is
convention distorted. For this double reunion—Leucippe and Clitophon, Melite and Thersander—is precisely what prevents the standard reunion of lovers, through the agency of Thersander, who
becomes the other rival and the obstacle to that reunion. And once
more the story changes key; we have seen that variety of episode

[16] Rojas Álvarez (1989).

is one of its main features. Parallel adventures now become intrigue, a veritable amatory fugue—or perhaps a better analogy would be musical chairs: who will be left out when the music stops—Clitophon, Leucippe, Melite, Thersander? Of course we know who will *not* be left out; but the process has to be visible, credible, 'natural'—if the word can be applied to such a product of artifice. And we should recall now that all this is too much for Achilles' ego-narrative framework, which will not sustain the complications of action and motive that characterize this final movement. *Leucippe and Clitophon* becomes simply a different kind of story, much closer to New Comedy than is, say, the *Ephesiaca*.

Thus, one thing the device of ego-narrative has been used for is to create suspense in the reader in regard to the unexpected and sometimes grotesque turns of the plot; and another is the pursuit of psychological realism. One of the principal effects of ego-narrative, in fact, is to induce credibility: the actor in events is telling you himself what happened, and he ought to know. But with Achilles it is primarily psychological realism that is achieved, and that is one of his most marked features. Careful attention to the nature and sources of human behaviour is, we have seen, built into the structure of the story; the actions of the characters, at any rate the principal characters, arise from their personalities, in a way that is not true of Chariton or Xenophon. This is true of Clitophon's pursuit of Leucippe, of Leucippe's own reactions in the early part of the story,[17] and certainly true of the passionate Melite. Admittedly, other elements of the action are motivated by *tyche* (which is sometimes guyed), and some characters are drawn largely in black-and-white (Thersander) or are purely functional (Menelaus, Satyrus) in a plot whose main lines are determined by other causes.

Other elements on our initial list of Achillean features have already been touched on in the perspective of ego-narrative, but may warrant some further comment. The adventures of Books 1-2 are grotesque, certainly, but not more so than those of the

[17] One might well think it is true of the later, obstinately virginal Leucippe too; now that the stage of flirtation and capture is over, and she and Clitophon are committed (as English says, 'engaged') to each other, Leucippe—not Achilles—retreats, at 4. 1, into convention; perhaps Artemis' injunction that she remain virgin until marriage is merely a cover (conscious or unconscious) on her part for what she intends to do anyway? Compare the (understandably) proprietorial tone of her letter to Clitophon at 5. 18. Leucippe cannot be accused of lacking personality.

Ephesiaca or *Babyloniaca* or *Phoenicica*, or even Apuleius' *Meta-morphoses*; there is no need to take them more seriously in themselves. The point about their appearance in Achilles is not the fact that they appear, but the purpose for which they are used—suspense—and the mixture of so lurid an element with realism and with a developed love-interest, neither of which figures in Xenophon or Iamblichus. Clearly such episodes constituted 'popular entertainment'; but this entertainment is sophisticated.

To continue with the catalogue of novel-conventions as used by Achilles Tatius, one notorious problem for a writer of such stories is how to handle the separation of the lovers and the parallel story-lines it entails. Xenophon and Chariton find it difficult; their solution is to pass alternately from one to the other, which involves either a not very satisfactory ping-pong effect or losing sight of one lover for a long time for no very positive reason. Heliodorus and Longus separate their lovers only marginally, so do not really have to solve the problem. Achilles has contrived a very good reason for losing sight of one lover: he makes his ego-narrator lose sight of Leucippe himself, to the point of thinking her dead. It is of course true that by the time of her 'deaths' Clitophon has broken the strictest ego-narrative rule, as we have also seen, by reporting that what he had come subsequently to learn, in the case of Callisthenes and Calligone; but as he tells his dramatic story we as readers hardly expect him to know what was really happening to Leucippe, so caught up are we in the melodrama. As far as the narrative is concerned, Leucippe can credibly disappear from it, and be brought back into play when convenient to the author; not only that, but her adventures during her absence from the narrative can all be apparent deaths, and the *frissons* multiplied. Here too, then, Achilles uses standard conventions with a wry twist.

It may also be noted that whereas the 'primitive' Chariton and Xenophon use the separation of their lovers to underline the isolation of each of them, Achilles uses it rather for the purpose of mounting a complex intrigue: each of the two is beset by an importunate rival. The topic of parallel action is in fact inseparable from that of another novel-convention, the theme of the rival, the 'other man' or 'other woman'. All of the novels make play with this kind of danger to ideal love; if in Xenophon the theme is represented by brief and crude passing incidents (Manto, Cyno), in Chariton it is the basis of the whole plot, which is built not on the simple opposition of good guy (or girl)/bad guy (or girl), but on the very nobility of Chaereas' rival Dionysius. The eternal triangle is of course a—perhaps *the*—fundamental romantic narrative situation. Achilles plays all his cards here: psychological realism (Melite and Clitophon), melodrama fit for the Victorian stage as Leucippe cries to Thersander, in effect, 'Unhand me, villain!', and above all complication. Not only does the plot produce rich possibilities of misunderstanding and reproach between the two basic couples, but there are cross-currents: Melite/Clitophon and Leucippe/ Thersander, obviously, but also jealousy between the males Clitophon and Thersander and ironic misprision between Leucippe and Melite. The eternal triangle becomes a quadrilateral, and an irregular one at that. Achilles, that is, develops intrigue more fully, and in so doing comes closer to New Comedy, than any of the other novelists. It is another of his major characteristics, and another aspect, along with realism and melodrama, of his mixture of fictional styles, of the disparate ingredients that constitute his story. But we have seen that he does so at the cost of effectively abandoning ego-narrative. It breaks under the strain—but at this point he has no further real use for it.

To close the account of Achilles' treatment of novel-conventions, we may glance at the reverse side of the theme of rivalry, namely the theme of fidelity, and its concomitant chastity. Again, what we find is an Achillean grimace at a romantic cliché; for in one way or another all of the principal characters offend against the rules. Clitophon and Melite offend by commission, however excusably; if Leucippe does not, it is not her fault. This is an unromantic view of sexual purity. But ultimately Achilles does just stay within the convention, in that his heroine does recover her virginal stability; as for Clitophon, he is at any rate no more blameworthy, or not much, than Longus' Daphnis—and is there not a margin accorded to men? By another irony, the striking example of observance of the romantic code comes not from a major actor, but from one of the extras—Callisthenes, who, initially moved by romantic passion for a Leucippe he has never seen, ends up romantically falling in love with her understudy Calligone and respecting her honour with the utmost rigour. Callisthenes and Calligone, we may note, are in no way necessary to the plot; they simply serve as a backdrop of normality in a story which throughout distorts the romantic norms.

The present analysis started from Achilles' technique of ego-

narrative, and may at this concluding stage return to it as a point
of entry into the central question posed at the beginning, namely
how 'serious' is Achilles, and what is the nature of his story?
Ego-narrative is a common device of comedy (Petronius, Apuleius'
Metamorphoses, *Moll Flanders*), for a reason already adduced: it
authenticates the narrative, and in particular the realistic detail
that is the stuff of comedy. There is a strong link, furthermore, with
psychological realism, in that we are inside the narrating character. Now, the tendency of realism is to abandon the moral high
ground, the level of tragedy and of ideal behaviour. People 'as they
really are' are not ideal, and representation of their behaviour
turns readily to comedy. This moral migration is what characterizes this version of the ideal romance. Realism is the distinguishing
feature of *Leucippe and Clitophon*. The most scathing assessment of
it came from Rohde, who asserts that Achilles' realistic psychology
consists in debasing his characters, all of whom are worthless—as
if novels should be manuals of high-minded behaviour (which is
assuredly what Rohde did think).[18] A more temperate and just view
was expressed by Perry, for whom in Achilles

the comic or picaresque tradition of epic narrative has been grafted onto
the ideal, thereby greatly widening the scope of the genre romance and its
capacity as an artistic medium for the criticism or interpretation of life in
all its aspects.[19]

But this point had already been made by Rattenbury; 'Achilles
Tatius seems to have been to Greek Romance what Euripides was
to Greek Tragedy. He broke down the conventions.'[20] This judgement has been taken farther. Some years after Rattenbury's formulation of Achilles' place in the history of the genre, Durham went
so far as to suggest that *Leucippe and Clitophon* was in effect a
parody of the form.[21] More recently Heiserman saw it as quite
simply a comic novel, and Anderson as 'carefully calculated sick

[18] E. Rohde (1876: 511). For Rohde's attitudes see Cancik (1985).
[19] Perry (1967: 115).
[20] Rattenbury (1933: 256-7). It is true that Rattenbury was making the point
to argue that Achilles was later than Heliodorus, which was disproved by the later
publication of papyri; but although this complicated the literary history of the form,
it does not affect the essential point made by Rattenbury.
[21] Durham (1938); specifically, of Heliodorus' *Ethiopica*. His article was another
contribution to the debate about chronology; ironically, it was in the same year that
the first of the more recently published papyri appeared. As with Rattenbury's
article, the point at issue here is not fundamentally invalidated.

humour'.[22] This battery of comments highlights the relation between the novel and the New Comedy tradition which is one of its principal ancestors, and illustrates the problems that this example of the form has created for scholars.

The shape of the answer, already adumbrated in the 1930s, is easier to discern today. In recent decades it has become more apparent (partly as a result of papyrological discoveries and partly through the serious attention increasingly accorded to the genre) that these texts are not the simplistic things they were once thought to be, all formed on the same simple pattern and written by solemn, unsophisticated writers. We are now armed with enough knowledge of the chronology and cultural context of these stories to be able to see them in better perspective than was possible in the nineteenth century, or even in the early twentieth. We are also, thanks to shifts in our own attitudes, more free than were earlier scholars to see late Greece as by no means simply a tired leftover from classical Hellenism, but on the contrary a highly sophisticated society. It is this note of sophistication that is important for the immediate purpose of placing Achilles Tatius. We can allow ourselves, as earlier periods had difficulty in doing, to see various qualities and merits in the novel. In particular, we can accept the possibility of humour in the ideal romance,[23] and can see Achilles' story as essentially an amused comment on its own genre. It is above all a sophisticated work, whose sophistication lies partly in its narrative structure, partly in its realism and partly also in the way it juxtaposes romantic elements: it plays the lurid off against the refined, melodrama against realism.[24] The mixture of

[22] Heiserman (1977); G. Anderson (1982: 32).

[23] G. Anderson (1982) devotes a whole book to this theme, though with unequal results.

[24] There is also another feature that is 'sophisticated' in the very strict sense of reflecting the literary culture of the Second Sophistic. It is to be found in the elaborate stylistic and rhetorical devices used throughout by Achilles: the digressions and ecphrases, couched invariably in very complex language (unlike the narrative, which employs a quite straightforward style), the carefully mounted and polished monologues and debates, the numerous references both overt and covert to Greek cultural tradition. Some of this can be studied with profit in S. Bartsch (1989), a most perceptive study. Bartsch perhaps overstates her case, namely that the descriptions in Heliodorus and Achilles Tatius are integral in the conception of these novels and should be integral in their interpretation; but her basic contention is not unjust, in that the rhetorical elaboration of the story is very much of a piece with the approach visible in its structure, as considered in the present study. It would be somewhat difficult, however, to develop this theme in the present context, that is to say without reference to the original Greek.

ingredients, far from being a problem for scholars, should be seen as the point of the work. It is not yet exactly parody; a parody would be concerned exclusively with making fun of its genre, whereas Achilles does have a story to tell of the conventional kind, and carries it through to its end conscientiously. That story is a version of the familiar pattern, not a sustained send-up of it; it is written for its value as a story, not for its value as parody. Nor is it yet altogether a 'comic novel'. The romantic conventions ultimately hold; they are strained, but they hold. Achilles takes too much trouble over the story for us not to take it seriously as a genuine if offbeat specimen of its genre.

But serious is not solemn. Achilles is markedly unsolemn, irreverent. He deflates the very romantic conventions he uses, pushes them to the limit: decapitation, forsooth! One may perhaps think of it as a 'comedized' version of the standard novel plot—if one can properly talk of that hypothetical creation. It is at once inventive, self-conscious and critical; it employs alike ego-narrative and falsetto voice. But it does have a serious side to it. It explores, convincingly, real human psychology, and in particular, like most of the novels, feminine psychology; the pathos of Callirhoe, the melodrama of Anthia, give way to the more recognizable, more accessible behaviour of Leucippe and Melite. Rattenbury's comment is as close to the mark as any.

I I

The Story of Knemon in Heliodoros' *Aithiopika*

J. R. MORGAN

Heliodoros' *Aithiopika* is the story of Theagenes and Charikleia: of
their falling in love, their elopement from Delphi where Charikleia
lives as the adopted daughter of the priest of Apollo, their encounters with pirates, bandits and unwanted suitors, and finally of their
arrival in Ethiopia, land of Charikleia's birth, where she is recognised as the daughter of the king and queen, and the lovers' union
is sanctioned, sanctified and implicitly consummated after the conclusion of the narrative. It is a commonplace of discussion of the
novel to draw attention to the artfulness with which the story is
presented,[1] to the temporal dislocations occasioned by beginning
the plot (or narration) in the middle of the story,[2] and to the
consequent shift which the author has been able to effect from the
straightforward, linear, proairetic mode of simple storytelling to a
hermeneutic mode[3] which draws the reader into a quest, shared
with the characters of the novel, for true understanding of facts of
which he is already in possession.

Near the beginning of the novel, however, is inserted a novella
on an apparently unconnected subject: the experiences of a young
Athenian, Knemon, with whom Theagenes and Charikleia share

---

[1] *Cf.* esp. Hefti (1950: 1 ff., 98 ff.); Keyes (1922: 42–51); Reardon (1971: 381 ff.).
[2] This antithesis between 'plot' (or 'narration') and 'story' is as close as one can
get in English to the distinction made by the Russian Formalists between *sjužet* (the
sequence of events as presented in the narrative) and *fabula* (the sequence of events
as they 'really' happened), and taken up by French structuralists in the terms *récit*
and *histoire*.
[3] These rather nasty terms 'proairetic' and 'hermeneutic' are taken from the
'codes' of reading analysed by R. Barthes (1970). The 'proairetic' code directs the
way the reader follows and integrates the plot, step by step according to the logic
of the action; the 'hermeneutic' the solution of enigmas. In redeploying the terms
to denote types of narrative I am following the precedent of P. Brooks (1984: 18 ff.).

captivity among the Boukoloi, Egyptian outlaws who infest the marshes of the Nile Delta. This subsidiary narration, which takes up a sizeable proportion of the first book, would be a surprising, not to say distracting, excursus in an ordinary proairetic text; but in one like Heliodoros', whose beginnings are so full of enigmas and uncertainties, it runs the risk of throwing the reader into deep confusion. It is difficult enough to identify and integrate the fragmentary lines of the main narrative, whose hero and heroine—if they are even recognised as such[4]—are at this stage little more than names to the reader, without the intrusion of a secondary (or *is* it secondary?) narrative whose relationship to the main plot will remain for some time problematic and undefined.

Thus Knemon's story invites questioning at two levels: from the first-time reader seeking to locate and connect the two narratives with which he is being compelled to juggle; and from a reader looking back from the end of the text, or reading the novel for a second time, trying to account for and legitimate the prominent position of the novella in the structure of the novel as a whole. Whatever one's final view of Heliodoros' literary stature, whether or not the *Aithiopika* is anything more than just a story told superlatively well, it is obvious that it is a skilfully engineered text in which things do not happen at random. We are entitled, then, invited, even obliged, to assume that there is reason, and hence meaning, in the author's decision to arrange and present his material in the way he does. The purpose of this paper is to set out some possible approaches to the problem posed by Knemon's novella, and then to propose a reading of it as a perhaps loosely connected but nonetheless germane component of the whole work.

[4] Some MSS of the *Aithiopika* (BPZ) include the names of heroine and hero in the title given at the beginning of the first book; and the Byzantines in general seem to have referred to the novel simply as Χαρίκλεια (cf. the citations given as Testimonia nos. x, xii, xv, xvii, xix, xx in the edition of the novel by A. Colonna (1938)). A reader of such a copy would find little difficulty in locating the main characters. But other MSS (CVM) are headed simply Ἡλιοδώρου Αἰθιοπικῶν βιβλίον πρῶτον (*vel sim.*), and our earliest reference to the work (Sokr. *Hist. ekkl.* 5. 22 [= Colonna Test. i]) seems to confirm that this was the novel's original title. Anyone reading a MS of this kind would have to wait until the course of the narrative itself cast Theagenes and Charikleia as hero and heroine. It is tempting to read this as a deliberate manoeuvre to prolong the reader's uncertainty and sense of disorientation, an effect typical of the author, but one spoiled by the alternative title.

I

Firstly, a summary of Knemon's story:

(*a*) 1. 9. 1-14. 2: Knemon's father, Aristippos, marries a second wife, Demainete, with whom he is infatuated. She, however, conceives a passion for her stepson, and one night when he returns from participating in the procession of the Great Panathenaia she attempts to seduce him while Aristippos is out of the house. She is rebuffed, and next morning accuses Knemon of having assaulted her, resulting in his receiving a beating from his father. Not satisfied with that, Demainete then sets a slave-girl, Thisbe, on to Knemon. Thisbe becomes intimate with him, and offers to show him his stepmother in bed with a lover. Sword in hand he goes to her room, only to discover that the man with her is his own father, who indicts him before the *demos* on a charge of attempted parricide. Escaping execution only on a technicality, Knemon is exiled and goes to his mother's relatives on Aigina.

(*b*) 1. 14. 3-17. 6: the sequel is presented in a doubly inset narrative by Knemon's friend Charias, who is also intimate with Thisbe and thus able to use information obtained from her. Demainete continues to hanker for Knemon, and Thisbe, afraid that her resentment at his loss might lead to reprisals against herself, decides to strike first. She deceives her mistress into believing that Knemon is still in Athens, at the house of Arsinoe the flute-girl, whose lover he is. Thisbe offers to arrange for Demainete to take Arsinoe's place in Knemon's bed, and simultaneously informs Aristippos that he has an opportunity to take his wife in adultery. With further lies to Arsinoe about her purpose in borrowing the house, Thisbe duly instals Demainete in bed, and then leads in Aristippos. The non-existent lover supposedly escapes but Demainete is arrested. On her way to the assembly, however, she hurls herself into the *bothros* in the Akademia and dies. Aristippos begins to canvass for Knemon's return.

(*c*) 1. 18. 1-2. 8. 3: at this point Knemon breaks off his narrative, and we revert to the story of Theagenes and Charikleia, in which Knemon is now an actor. In the course of this section the village of the Boukoloi is attacked by a rival gang of bandits, and Charikleia, with whom the robber-chieftain Thyamis has fallen in love, is concealed for safety in a secret, labyrinthine cave. However, despairing of his own safety, Thyamis steals back to the cave, and there kills a Greek-speaking woman whom he believes to be his beloved Charikleia. When Theagenes and Knemon return to release her, they discover the body, which turns out, after a scene of tragic irony, not to be Charikleia at all, but Thisbe, much to Knemon's shock.

(d) 2. 8. 4–10. 1: when Theagenes and Charikleia are reunited, Knemon resumes his narrative, this time using information from another friend, Antikles. After Demainete's death, Thisbe contracts a liaison with Nausikles, a merchant from Naukratis, previously the lover of Arsinoe. In jealousy, Arsinoe informs Demainete's family of Thisbe's machinations. Aristippos is brought to court and convicted not of murder but of being an accessory to Demainete's death: his property is confiscated and he is exiled. To escape interrogation under torture, Thisbe elopes with her merchant to Naukratis, whither Knemon pursues her in an effort to clear his father's name.

(e) 2. 10. 1–4: the mosaic is completed firstly by information from a tablet found on Thisbe's body, revealing that she had been held captive by Thyamis' *hypaspistēs*, and secondly by . . .

(f) 2. 12. 2–3: an authorial statement to the effect that this *hypaspistēs* had stolen her from Nausikles on the highway, and hidden her in the cave during the fighting, where Thyamis mistook her for Charikleia.

I have summarised the novella at length for two reasons. Firstly because the first stage in our discussion must be to examine its mechanical connection with the primary narrative;[5] and secondly because some of its details will turn out to have a significance beyond their immediate function.

Most obviously, then, the novella accounts for the presence in Egypt of Knemon, who, although he does not play a strictly indispensable role in the plot itself and eventually drops out of the story in Book Six, is nevertheless a prominent figure who plays the important bit-part of 'hero's friend', saving Theagenes from suicide just as Polycharmos saves Chaireas in Chariton's novel,[6] and most importantly acts as audience for Kalasiris' long narration of the early history of the love of Theagenes and Charikleia.

---

[5] Well treated by G. N. Sandy (1982a: 33 ff.).

[6] 2. 2. 1, 2. 3. 4; cf. Char. 1. 5. 2, 1. 6. 1, 5. 10. 10, 6. 2. 8 ff.

Scarcely less important is the figure of Thisbe, who has a significance extending beyond her function as a cog in the mechanism of the plot. At first she gives the impression of having been invented simply to provide a colourful and concrete motivation for Knemon's exile. Her reappearance in the narrative as a corpse is a stunning *coup de lecture*, almost as startling to the reader as it is to the unfortunate Knemon. There was of course no absolute necessity why the female killed in Charikleia's stead had to be anyone previously known to the reader, but it is undeniably more effective and economical that the solution to one enigma (the reader has been deluded into believing Charikleia dead, but it is unthinkable for a novel to lose its heroine with nine-tenths of the plot still to come; how can the apparent facts of the narrative be squared with the expectations inherent in the form?) should generate a new enigma (how did Thisbe come to be in the cave?) whose solution in its turn *is* functional to the plot: she was put there by the ὑπασπιστής, who on his return to claim her will harbour natural enough suspicions that those on the scene of the crime are those responsible for her death. He is liable to turn dangerous and Knemon is given the task of losing him. Thus Knemon is separated from Theagenes and Charikleia and set up to become Kalasiris' audience.

Similarly Thisbe, this time in combination with her Naukratite lover Nausikles, is an essential part of the process by which Charikleia is separated from Theagenes but reunited with Kalasiris. In order to recover Thisbe Nausikles procures a detachment of Persian troops under their phrourarch Mitranes to storm the Boukoloi's stronghold in the marshes. They arrive only after the destruction of the village by a rival gang of outlaws, and succeed only in capturing Theagenes and Charikleia. Nausikles, struck by Charikleia's beauty, identifies her as Thisbe—a deception in which she connives—while Theagenes is retained by Mitranes for the service of the Great King. The narration of this episode is characterised by its carefully controlled release of information: Kalasiris tells Knemon at 2. 24. 1 where Nausikles has gone, while Charikleia's experiences are filled in by a retrospective authorial narration running from 5. 4. 3 to 5. 9. 2, but only after Heliodoros has played with both Knemon's and the reader's puzzlement as to whether Nausikles might somehow be speaking the literal truth when he claims to have recovered 'a better Thisbe' (5. 1. 7 βελτίονα Θίσβην ἐκτησάμην).

Nausikles makes only an incidental appearance in the novella. At first he seems introduced merely as a convenience to get Thisbe to Egypt (2. 8. 5), but he is named at his first appearance—a sign of importance—and his name can therefore startle both Knemon and reader when we learn that this same man is Kalasiris' host at Chemmis (2. 23. 6). Although it is pure coincidence that Thisbe's lover is also owner of the house where Kalasiris tells Knemon the story of Theagenes and Charikleia, the coincidence is functional to the plot in the sense that, as we have seen, it allows for the interchange of Thisbe and Charikleia and the reunion, unexpected to Nausikles, of Charikleia and Kalasiris.

To draw these threads together, we can say then that part of the cast-list of the novella (Knemon, Thisbe, Nausikles) is firmly written into the central plot, and their relationships, established in the novella, on some occasions function as necessary causal links in the primary plot, and on others permit the author to contrive effective but essentially decorative scenes such as Knemon's comic panic at Thisbe's apparent resurrection (5. 2. 1 ff.). It is also clear, I think, that there is considerable aesthetic advantage in presenting the material in the way that Heliodoros does. Given that the past of the characters is active in the present of the narrative, the alternative would have been to insert explanatory authorial statements as and when needed. But that would have been to run the risk of deflating and dissipating dramatic moments, and, more important, it would have produced a less sophisticated mimesis. That is to say that an overt intrusion of the authorial voice would draw attention to the fact that there *is* an author, whereas the indirect method which predominates in the *Aithiopika* allows the author to recede and authority for statements to be located inside rather than outside the frame of the plot, so producing a novel which, for all its artfulness, gives the impression of having written itself, of being a transcription of reality.[7]

Nevertheless, it is equally the case that there is much in the novella which is *not* organically connected to the central plot.[8] In

---

[7] And so, of course, of being a transparent documentary record of 'real' events, rather than a self-referential text that constantly alludes to its own fictional status. The method of presentation is part of the realism of the *Aithiopika* which I analysed in my article 'History, Romance and Realism in the *Aithiopika* of Heliodoros', Morgan (1982: 221–65; see esp. 260 ff.).

[8] Although a certain 'realistic residue' of non-essential material is only to be expected in the causes of the mimesis just referred to; cf. ibid. 250 ff.

fact, the central parts of Knemon's story, his stepmother's attempts to seduce and destroy him, are, from the point of view of the novel-plot, no more than an elaborate apparatus to introduce the character of Thisbe. Aristippos and Demainete could be stripped away without leaving so much as a scar on the story of Theagenes and Charikleia. And yet it is precisely these elements which are thrown most into question and prominence through their problematic juxtaposition to the (as yet unintegrated) stump of the main plot; Thisbe's appearance is accounted for by her relation to Demainete in a way that Demainete's own entry is not by her sudden appearance at the head of an apparently unconnected sub-narrative. So, although during a first reading, when the reader's passions are directed forwards to the solution of the riddling opening scene of the whole novel and, beyond that, to discovering how the story ends, Demainete may be forgotten as the latter part of the novella meshes with and fuels the main plot, in retrospection or on a second reading the question of what exactly Demainete is doing in the text is liable to recur with redoubled force.

The mechanical approach to Knemon's narrative, then, offers an important but only partial answer to its problems. At this juncture we are faced with a choice: one might say that the elaboration of Knemon's novella at a length excessive for its strictly defined functional relevance is no more than an aesthetic miscalculation or self-indulgence on the author's part. There is nothing inherently implausible or unrespectable in such a view, and we must keep our minds open to it as a possibility. But before embracing a reductionist conclusion of this kind, we must explore other approaches in search of a convincing explanation.

II

We read a novel from a desire to know its ending, for it is only at the end of a novel that its meaning is complete.[9] Yet the pleasure that we derive from following a plot resides in the tensions, uncertainties and thrills that we are made to experience. The knowledge which the ending brings and towards which our reading is directed is thus the end of our pleasure in the senses of both goal and extinction. In the course of a long and complex novel the final

---

[9] Cf. Brooks (1984: 37 ff.)

discharge of tension may well be anticipated several times *in parvo* as individual facts are made sense of, or partial explanations and understandings become apparent. And an author can prolong the pleasure of his text by deferring the consummation of his plot. The next approach to Knemon's novella is to think of it as a retardation of the solution of the enigmatic opening tableau, and hence as a prolongation of the pleasurable uncertainty to which that solution must put an end.

A novelist usually achieves pleasurable prolongation by introducing complexity into his plot. To put it in its crudest terms, a 'happy ending' is a generic requirement of most types of fiction; even the occasional tragic ending[10] gains much of its effect by the shock it administers to the reader's conditioned expectations. Complications in a romantic plot are generally of such a kind as to seem to block the path of the story towards the ending that the generically experienced reader would both expect and desire. A frisson of fear is generated that the plot will somehow short-circuit, reach the end too quickly and in the wrong way (for instance by the premature death of the central figures), a fear played off, of course, against a security implied by generic rules that guarantee, but not with absolute certainty, a happy ending. This kind of complication is characteristic of the surviving Greek romances: in structural terms the threats posed by all those pirates, shipwrecks, lustful rivals, obstructive parents and so on are blocks potentially capable of precipitating the wrong ending rather than essential links in the narrative chain. Threatened short-circuits of this kind abound in the *Aithiopika*, even to its very last pages, when the unexpected arrival of Charikles and his accusations against Theagenes (10. 34ff.) seem set to derail the plot just as it reaches its terminus.

However, this is not quite the effect of Knemon's novella. If we are to explain it in terms of functioning to produce suspense by deferring the progress of the main plot, it will have to be in a somewhat cruder manner. The main plot is simply postponed by the insertion of extraneous material—although, as we have seen, a proportion of this material turns out, unexpectedly, to be not quite as extraneous as it appeared at first sight. However, even a device

---

[10] There is no surviving example of an ancient novel that does not end happily, but compare the remarks of B. E. Perry on the lost *Kypriaka* of Xenophon of Cyprus (1967: 120f.).

as crude as this is capable of Heliodorian subtleties, and the very
lack of connection has a positive point in that not only will the
reader's desire to know what happens next in the main story grow
more urgent in proportion to the length of the excursus, but so too
will his desire to find the connection—if indeed there is one—
between that excursus and the primary narrative. It is no accident
therefore that the first part of the novella, the attempted seduction
of Knemon by his stepmother, is the part least connected to the
main plot, and that we are kept waiting, in suspense, until Thisbe
reappears as a corpse before the mechanical meshing of the cogs
can become apparent.

However, the kinds of effect which I have sketched in the two
preceding paragraphs are really appropriate only to a straight-
forwardly proairetic narrative. But the impulse of the first half of
the *Aithiopika* is primarily hermeneutic. That is to say that the
reader, passionate for meaning, is less concerned with how the
story of Theagenes and Charikleia will end than with how it began,
or even who they are. His desires are attuned not to event but to
explication, and this enables Heliodoros to work some rather clever
tricks and conjure with a new and subtler form of suspense.

The novel opens with a macabre and memorable tableau: a
beach strewn with twitching corpses, an empty ship, the only
living figures a young woman of incomparable beauty tending a
young man who lies at her feet. Our bewilderment as to what it is
all about is intensified by the manner of the presentation: the scene
is viewed through the eyes of Egyptian bandits peering down at it
from the hilltops overlooking the Nile Delta and trying to interpret
what they see. By themselves they are unable to 'read' the scene,[11]
and the presumably omniscient author/narrator is keeping the
truth to himself. Information can only reach us through the limited
perceptions of the bandits, whose ignorance and puzzlement we
have to share. It seems that the enigma will only be resolved by
new information from within the narrative frame itself, and this
appears to be on its way when the girl breaks into speech at 1. 3.
1—but then our hopes of further enlightenment are brusquely
shattered by the announcement at 1. 3. 2 that the Egyptians cannot comprehend a word she says (οὐδὲν συνιέναι τῶν λεγομένων
ἔχοντες). Although we, the readers, can understand her words, or

---

[11] I. I. 7: οὐδὲ συνιέναι τὴν σκηνὴν ἐδύναντο; I. 2. 6: ἡ τῶν γινομένων ἄγνοια . . .
τὰ ὄντα δὲ οὔπω ἐγίνωσκον.

at least construe them grammatically, further revelations are
thwarted by the absence inside the narrative of an audience with
a similar level of comprehension. Heliodoros has arranged this
sequence to titillate. He arouses desire to know, seems about to
satisfy the desire, and then backs off at the last moment. He now
proceeds to repeat the flirtation: the first bandits are driven off by
a second group, who are also unable to make sense of the tableau,
though they do make an attempt to surmise its meaning, producing an answer that even we, with our minimal information, know
to be erroneous.[12] Their leader grabs the girl and tells her to come
with him. This time the anticipated sequence of revelation is cut
short even sooner, for *she* cannot understand what *he* is saying (1.
4. 1 τῶν . . . λεγομένων οὐδὲν συνιεῖσα), and thus any further utter-
ance (which might be informative to the reader if not to the
bandits) is forestalled. The motivic repetition, underlined by verbal
echo, makes it perfectly clear that any revelation *from* the couple
on the beach (and the narrator has already shown himself dis-
inclined to make any revelation *about* them) is going to be dependent on the presence of an audience capable of understanding
the Greek language. This audience is, apparently, duly arranged
when the young couple are entrusted to the care of another Greek
prisoner, specifically for the sake of conversation (1. 7. 3 τοῦ
διαλέγεσθαι ἕνεκεν). Knemon is thus set up to be the recipient inside
the narrative of the revelation that the reader, outside the narrative, wants to eavesdrop on; after two false starts, one feels, the
third approach must surely succeed. But what delicious frustration
as Knemon blithely misunderstands the obvious implications of τοῦ
διαλέγεσθαι ἕνεκεν and becomes narrator instead of audience! And,
of course, the irony is compounded when Knemon does eventually
become the audience he ought to have been earlier, but the audience of a new and unexpected narrator whose existence we had
not even been led to suppose.

This is all an extremely witty and effective exploitation of the
conventions of storytelling, and serves to illustrate the ludic elements implicit in the whole business of producing and consuming
fictional narrative. The central convention of the realistic novel is
precisely the pretence that there are *no* conventions, that the text

[12] 1. 3. 5: οἱ δὲ λῃσταί [the new group] . . . ὑπὸ τῆς τῶν ὁρωμένων ἀγνοίας ἅμα
καὶ ἐκπλήξεως τέως ἀνεστέλλοντο; 1. 3. 6: τοὺς μὲν γὰρ πολλοὺς φόνους ὑπὸ τῶν
προτέρων γεγενῆσθαι λῃστῶν εἴκαζον.

is a transparent and mimetic transcription of its own imagined 'reality'. But Heliodoros exploits generically determined expectations that derive from officially non-existent conventions, and so comes within an ace of breaking the mimetic illusion, like when a character in a film suddenly acknowledges the existence of a camera whose presence the conventions of the medium had hitherto suppressed.[13]

This group of readings, then, stresses the function of Knemon's novella as interruption, and seeks to explain its presence in terms of the effects (suspense, frustration, titillation) which it allows the author to produce in the reader. As with the mechanical approach, we have an answer here but not a whole one. We can go some way towards explaining why there should be *some* digression from the main plot, but not why it has to be *this* one.

III

The third approach to the novella is perhaps liable to the same general criticism. This is to stress the manner rather than the matter of Knemon's narrative, as done by John J. Winkler recently in a fine and provocative paper.[14] 'Knemon's tale is of special interest as a demonstration model of an alternative narrative strategy . . . the powerful narrative intellect which we can sense behind the opening tableau here enters a simpler persona and works within the narrower conventions of a naive raconteur in order to make clear what kind of story the *Aithiopika* is *not*.'[15] Winkler stresses the unproblematic nature of the novella's beginning, counterpointing the unintelligibility of the mysterious tableau at the start of the novel; and Knemon's straightforward chronological progression as opposed to the temporal inversions and convolutions of the primary narrative. We might summarise his conclusions—not I hope unfairly—by labelling Knemon's novella a proairetic narrative,

---

[13] I would not wish to argue that it was Heliodoros' *intention* to highlight the conventional aspects of fiction and hence the fictionality of his own discourse. It is more that, as a virtuoso, he plays the game at the limit of its rules, thus running the risk of *incidentally* making conscious conventional rules of which every reader was already subconsciously aware anyway.

[14] Winkler (1982) (= this volume, ch. 12).

[15] Ibid. 107 (= below, p. 299). I hope I am not distorting his sense by taking 'story' here to mean *sjužet* rather than *fabula*; cf. n. 2 above.

whose function in the economy of the novel as a whole is to establish a paradigm of normal narration for the hermeneutic narrative
of the novel itself to bounce off.

As a rhetorical device to allow Winkler to define with greater
precision the nature of the novel's narration this antithesis is unobjectionable. But as a literal statement of the author's intentions
it is much less attractive. Firstly, as Winkler himself admits,
Knemon's novella is by no means a simple narrative. Despite the
simplicity of its opening,[16] it possesses a luxuriance of style little
different from that of the author's own narration,[17] the third
sentence of Knemon's speech running to no fewer than seventy-
five words; verbally Knemon is not characterized as a different kind
of narrator from Heliodoros himself. Furthermore, his story is presented via a mechanism of multiple narrators, each with a limited
point of view (Knemon, Charias, who in part reports Thisbe,
Antikles), which demonstrates Heliodoros' concern for documentary realism (how does Knemon know what he tells?), but seems
to weaken the contention that Knemon's novella serves as a paradigm of 'normal', straightforward if artistic and intelligent story-
telling. Most importantly, it is not wholly accurate to suggest that
Knemon's story is chronologically ordered. At the point where
novella joins novel we know Thisbe's ending before we can understand what preceded it, and the final instalment of his narrative
(§ d in the summary above) is expressly intended as retrospective
explication of events (Thisbe's presence and death in Egypt, § c
in the summary) whose meaning is, to the reader, enigmatic. As
narrative strategy this approximates, admittedly in a less elaborated and prolonged form, to the answering of the riddle posed by
the opening tableau in Kalasiris' retrospective narration: another
indication perhaps that Knemon as narrator is not to be differentiated from his author.

Secondly, it is a rather lopsided view of the *Aithiopika* as a whole
to characterize it solely as a hermeneutic text. After the narration
of Kalasiris is concluded and the riddles of identity and causation
have been solved, the *Aithiopika* proceeds to its ending as a wholly
proairetic novel, though of a wonderfully sophisticated kind; and

[16] I. 9. I: Ἦν μοι πατὴρ Ἀρίστιππος, τὸ γένος Ἀθηναῖος κτλ.
[17] Heliodoros generally makes no attempt to characterize through style. Even the
eunuch Bagoas, whose Greek is, we are specifically informed (8. 15. 3), fractured,
is presented speaking in fluent periods, with even a Euripidean allusion.

the fixed moral certainties of character which Winkler detects in Knemon's novella[18] pertain equally, for instance, in the episode set in the satrap's palace at Memphis in Books Seven and Eight. It is unsatisfactory then to cast Knemon as 'naive raconteur' and set him in authorially intended opposition to the narration of the rest of the novel, when the narrative structure of the second and climactic half of the whole novel is, if anything, even more 'naive', in that omniscient third-person narrative is a simpler mode than documentary first-person. To pre-empt a somewhat larger argument, I would suggest that the simplification of narrative technique towards the climax of the novel betokens an overall emphasis on substance rather than manner, on story rather than narrative. Heliodoros, as a sophisticated storyteller, in other words, makes use of the hermeneutic mode for calculated effect, but in the last resort it is what the story is about rather than how it is told that really matters. It is perhaps typical of Winkler's concern with questions of narrative technique that he finds the structural complexities of the first half of the novel more compelling than the technically straightforward second half,[19] just as he poses the enigma of the opening scene in terms of narratorial authority rather than content (not 'what has happened?' but 'who is telling?').[20] Perhaps it is not too simple-minded to wonder whether these terms of reference are not anachronistic. Of course any text can be read as an ongoing commentary on its own strategies, but the conventions of the Greek romance, including the *Aithiopika*, seem to me to be representational rather than self-referential, and I find it hard to believe that the *Aithiopika* was written to be in essence a discourse about how to tell and read a story.

Thirdly, and very briefly, Winkler's characterisation of Knemon as a naive raconteur is of a piece with his interpretation of him as a naive and sensation-seeking listener, 'distanced from us by the broadly drawn comedy of his hyper-romantic sensibility',[21] and liable to miss or misunderstand the ironies and subtleties of Kalasiris' account.[22] But far from being distanced, Knemon is just one member of a whole series of audiences inside the fiction, starting with the bandits on the beach, who seem to serve as proxy

[18] Winkler (1982: 107 = below, p. 299).
[19] A perfectly valid judgment, of course, but patently not the author's own.
[20] Winkler (1982: 96f. = below, pp. 289f.)
[21] Ibid. 142 = below, p. 333.
[22] Ibid. 147 = below, p. 339.

for its real audience outside the fiction. A full understanding of Knemon's rôle as listener would entail an investigation of all these other audiences too, and falls outside the scope of this paper. But we must at least enter a query against the suggestion that Knemon is a naive audience, and hence, by extension, against the cognate suggestion that he is a naive narrator whose product is in some sense held at a distance from both author and reader.

IV

Winkler himself offers a reading that puts the story of Knemon in counterpoint to that of the main plot, firstly in that it moves from simplicity to complexity as the main plot proceeds in the opposite direction, secondly in that like Charikleia's story it deals in the themes of return from exile and vindication of a parent's honour.[23] The reading that I wish to offer in conclusion might also be phrased in terms of counterpoint, but in a motivic and thematic rather than a structural sense.

Let us begin, as Heliodoros would have liked, with something quite different. In Book Six, after Kalasiris has been reunited with Charikleia through the offices of Nausikles, he and Knemon set off with their host in search of Theagenes, whom they believe to be in the custody of Mitranes the phrourarch. On their way, however, they encounter an acquaintance of Nausikles, from whom they learn that Theagenes has been snatched from Mitranes by the Boukoloi of Bessa under the command of Thyamis (6. 3. 1–4). This is, as Sandy puts it,[24] 'Heliodorus's elaborate method of having Calasiris informed that Theagenes has passed from the hands of Oroondates' [the satrap's] agent to those of Thyamis'. We may add that it also serves to inform us that Thyamis, who disappeared from the narrative at the end of Book One, when he was captured alive by a rival gang of brigands,[25] has somehow—the details are never revealed—just become the leader of his captors.[26] The little scene then is an excellent example of the way that Heliodoros contrives to release information to his reader through the interaction

---

[23] Winkler (1982: 108 ff.).

[24] Sandy (1982a: 31).

[25] A state of affairs recalled as recently as 5. 4 3: ἐπειδὴ γὰρ ὁ μὲν Θύαμις ἁλοὺς ἐξώγρητο καὶ εἴχετο αἰχμάλωτος . . .

[26] 6. 3. 4: ὁ τούτων ἔναγχος ἀποδειχθεὶς ἔξαρχος Θύαμις.

of his *dramatis personae* and without intruding his own voice as omniscient narrator into the action.

What concerns us more in the present context, however, is the way that the anonymous informant is characterised. There was, of course, no need to characterise him at all. His is just a walk-on part, his only function to deliver his information before disappearing from the plot for good. But Heliodoros has elaborated him into an amusing vignette. When Kalasiris and his companions encounter him, he is in urgent haste on an errand for his mistress, Isias of Chemmis, who has commanded him to fetch her a flamingo. His whole life is devoted to her service; he works his land for her and supplies her every need; she allows him no rest by night or day; and in return he receives nothing but mockery, unfounded accusations and ἀκκισμοί—playing hard to get.

It is quite clear that this apparently spontaneous little portrait is rather more than just a fleck of colour in the tapestry of entertainment. When the main narrative concerns a quest for Theagenes, whom Charikleia calls her soul and without whom she cannot live, it can be no accident that the vignette concerns a quest that is both trivial and futile, the whim of a cruel and capricious mistress. Equally it is no accident that the informant is presented as a man in love, but a love of a very different kind from that shared by Theagenes and Charikleia. He is a slave to his mistress, her ὑπηρέτης: his side of the relationship is figured by the word ὑπηρετοίμην (6. 3. 2), while hers is underlined by a series of repetitions: τὰ προσταττόμενα . . . ἐπιτάττῃ . . . ἐπίταγμα (6. 3. 2) . . . τὰ ἐπιτάγματα . . . ἐπέταξεν (6. 3. 3). We are dealing here with the erotic trope familiar to us from Latin love elegy as the *servitium amoris*, where it crystallises in the ambiguity of the word *domina*. The selfish and degrading materialism, the irresponsibility and absence of any basis for permanence in Isias' love are opposed to and illuminate the earnestness, the reciprocity, the spirituality, the life-long commitment and life-enhancing quality of the true love of Theagenes and Charikleia. Thus a minor figure whose function is merely that of a small component in a large and intricate mechanism is made the representative of an alternative and perverted style of loving: he forms one element of a moral polarity and so becomes part of an implicit statement of values.

What I want to suggest is that Knemon's novella works in much the same way, only on a much more comprehensive scale. It provides a prolonged portrait of perverted, immoral, simply bad love, which, by being placed programmatically at the start of the whole novel, will inform and structure by antithesis the reader's appreciation of the true love of the central characters, and at the same time provide positive points of reference for some of the hostile elements that threaten their love, notably the Persian princess Arsake. The novella is a paradigm, of an inverse kind, that provides a scale against which the significance of the central plot can emerge. Good and bad are two sides of the one coin: they cannot exist apart. Between them, the negative love of the novella and the positive love of the novel form a framework of moral values, the expression and reinforcement of which is the fundamental *raison d'être* of the *Aithiopika*. This may be best articulated in a series of polarities between the novel and the novella.

(a) The love of Theagenes and Charikleia is mutual. Thus, in describing how they fell in love at first sight, Kalasiris stresses that they were both equally affected (3. 5. 4-6), and later he reassures Charikleia that Theagenes' feelings are as deep as her own and of the same kind (4. 11. 2: ἀπὸ τῶν ὁμοίων); at 4. 18. 2 the lovers throw themselves at Kalasiris' feet and proclaim that they have forfeited everything ἵν᾽ ἐκ πάντων μόνους ἀλλήλους κερδήσωσι ('to win one another, the only thing in the world that we desire'); at 5. 5. 2 their mutual love is a guarantee of recognition; and Charikleia's most secret prayer is that she and Theagenes will be preserved for one another (5. 15. 3). There is hardly any need to list declarations of love on both sides. The reciprocity of their passion is, of course, tightly laced into the whole structure of their story: it is a bond that draws them together when events conspire to pull them apart. Love in Knemon's Athens, on the other hand, is unreciprocated. Aristippos is infatuated with Demainete, virtually her slave (once again the *servitium amoris* figures the archetypal one-sided passion); Demainete for her part is obsessed with Knemon, who, for the most laudable of motives, shuns her advances; his sexual attentions are directed at Thisbe, but she is only acting under orders from her mistress, and feels nothing for him.

(b) Athenian love is egocentric. Demainete is interested only in her own gratification and is indifferent to Knemon's welfare; she sets in motion a scheme which she hopes will lead to his death, and at 1. 15. 3 regrets the clemency of the court, which by sparing his life has also kept her passion alive. Thisbe's actions throughout are motivated by self-interest. This applies even to Knemon himself, who sees in Thisbe's behaviour only an index of his own increased attractiveness (1. 11. 3), and has no further regard for her feelings. The love of Theagenes and Charikleia, on the other hand, involves the merging of self with another. So for Charikleia separation from Theagenes is tantamount to the loss of her own life (1. 29. 3: ὥσπερ ψυχῆς τοῦ Θεαγένους ἀφῃρημένην); their embraces seem to fuse their very beings (2. 6. 3: ὥσπερ ἡνωμένοι; 5. 4. 5: οἱονεὶ συμπεφυκότες); when Theagenes runs his race at Delphi, Charikleia's soul runs beside him (4. 3. 3; cf. her reaction to his bull-chase at 10. 29. 2); when she has lost Theagenes, Charikleia's only reason for continuing to live is the hope of reunion (5. 2. 9, cf. 5. 33. 1). Both Theagenes and Charikleia persistently refer to the other as their ψυχή,[27] an erotic commonplace founded on the metaphorical premise that lover and beloved between them constitute a single identity.[28] In fact the interests of the beloved often outweigh the lover's own: Charikleia on the beach at the start of the novel is more concerned for Theagenes' wounds than for her own dangers (1. 3. 6); Kalasiris recalls Charikleia from her manic excess of grief by reminding her that Theagenes depends on her life (6. 9. 3); and even Arsake knows that a lover feels his beloved's pain more deeply than his own (8. 9. 21). Repeatedly they express a preference for dying together rather than living apart.[29]

(c) Athenian love is promiscuous and ephemeral, an appetite to be satisfied and abandoned. Knemon feels no compunction about embarking on a casual sexual liaison with a slave-girl, and even says in a perfectly matter-of-fact sort of way that he had himself tried to initiate such a liaison on many occasions in the past (1. 11. 3: ἡ πολλάκις πειρῶντά με ἀπωσαμένη . . .); his father finds Demainete's allegation that Knemon spends all his time drinking and whoring only too plausible (1. 10. 4). What Demainete feels for Knemon is nothing but a physical itch, with no sense of

---

[27] 1. 8. 4, 2. 5. 2, 5. 2. 10, 8. 6. 4, 10. 20. 2.

[28] Demainete does twice refer to Knemon as her ψυχή, but the first instance (1. 9. 4) is in a passage of obvious insincerity and is no more than a stratagem to wheedle him into her bed; the second (1. 14. 6) occurs after she has destroyed him, and is lamenting her loss, ostensibly as a mother but in reality as a lover: the irony is clear.

[29] 1. 2. 4, 1. 4. 1, 2. 1. 2f., 2. 4. 4, 5. 33. 1, 6. 8. 6, 6. 9. 3, 8. 8. 4, 8. 9. 8, 8. 13. 3, 10. 19. 2.

commitment or responsibility to him; and Thisbe convinces her
that even this will disappear with its gratification.[30] Even while
trying to seduce Knemon, Demainete continues to sleep with
Aristippos, who has himself forsaken the memory of Knemon's
mother to take a new wife. Thisbe in the course of the novella is
represented as having sexual relationships with Nausikles and
Charias as well as Knemon, and tricks Arsinoe into lending her
the use of her house with a fiction of a fourth liaison with the
boy Teledemos (1. 16. 1). Her 'professional' acquaintance with
the flute-girl Arsinoe[31] is, given their mutual connection with
Nausikles, no doubt as much sexual as musical. The clear implication is that the relationships actually mentioned in the text are
only the tip of Thisbe's sexual iceberg. Nausikles, who so casually
transfers his attentions from Arsinoe to Thisbe on the most superficial of pretexts (2. 8. 5: he does not like the way flute-playing dis-
tends her cheeks), is a family man with a daughter at home in
Chemmis, though nothing is said of a wife. On the other hand,
neither Theagenes nor Charikleia has any previous sexual experience: Charikleia deifies the virgin state, to the chagrin of her
foster-father (2. 33. 5), while Theagenes swears on oath to
Kalasiris that he has never had carnal contact with a woman
because he has never found a woman worthy of his love (3. 17.
4). Once they have fallen in love, however, their love is permanent
and lifelong;[32] each would rather die than be coerced into union
with anyone else.[33] It would violate the whole moral code of the
novel to imagine that one day they might grow tired of one
another. Their sufferings can only make sense if a lifetime of happiness together awaits them at the end.

(d) Besides being reciprocal, the love of Theagenes and Charikleia

---

[30] 1. 15. 8: εἰ δὲ τύχοις ὧν βούλει, μάλιστα μὲν εἰκὸς σχολάσαι τὸν ἔρωτα, πολλαῖς
γὰρ κατὰ τὴν πρώτην πεῖραν ἐναπεσβέσθη τὰ τῆς ἐπιθυμίας· κόρος γὰρ ἔρωτος τῶν ἔργων
τὸ τέλος.

[31] 1. 15. 7: τὴν Ἀρσινόην, οὖσαν μοι πάλαι γνωρίμην ἀπὸ τῆς τέχνης . . .

[32] e.g. 5. 5. 2: οὐδένα γὰρ χρόνον εἶναι ὅσος ἀμαυρῶσαι αὐτοῖς τῶν ψυχῶν τὰ ἐρωτικὰ
γνωρίσματα; 5. 2. 7: βιώσεσθαι . . . τὸ λειπόμενον ἅμα τῷ φιλτάτῳ.

[33] 1. 8. 3, 1. 26. 1, 2. 4. 2, 4. 13. 4, 5. 29. 4, 7. 21. 5, 7. 25. 5, 7. 26. 3, 10.
33. 2. At 4. 11. 3, after Charikles has expressed a wish that Charikleia should
marry her cousin Alkamenes, she exclaims: Ἀλκαμένει μὲν . . . τάφον πρότερον ἢ
γάμον τὸν ἐμὸν εὐτρεπιζέτω, ἐμὲ γὰρ ἢ Θεαγένης ἄξεται ἢ τὸ τῆς εἱμαρμένης διαδέξε-
ται. This has been misunderstood by translators: she is not wishing Alkamenes dead
but praying for her own death, as the second clause makes clear; τὸν ἐμὸν agrees
with τάφον as well as γάμον (for the word order cf. 4. 14. 1: σὺν τέχνῃ πολλῇ καὶ
σοφίᾳ τῇ ἐμῇ, and 4. 18. 5: γένος τε καὶ οἶκον τὸν ἡμέτερον).

is spontaneous and—once initial feelings of shame are overcome—given freely and joyfully. To continue to love one another despite all the obstacles and all the temptations to the contrary is the supreme choice that gives their lives meaning. Athenian love on the other hand deals in seduction, deception and, in the last resort, coercion. Demainete tries to seduce Knemon with false displays of maternal love (1. 9. 3), just as she traps the doting Aristippos with insincere exhibitions of devotion (1. 9. 2). When Knemon refuses to be seduced, she concocts a scheme, equally deceptive, to punish him.[34] Demainete then herself falls victim to a deceptive ruse. Falsehood lies close to the heart of the Athenian ethos as manifested in the novella; it is a close cousin of infidelity, and antithetical to the close, open, pure and true love of Theagenes and Charikleia.

(e) The power to seduce and coerce depends on a disparity of age and status which marks all the Athenian relationships, though this is to an extent counterbalanced by the seductive power of the Athenian female. In her dealings with Knemon, Demainete uniquely combines social authority (in the status of stepmother, which gives her quasi-parental power over Knemon and also makes her an honorary member of his father's generation and so entitled to his deference) with the female power of seduction. She exploits the latter alone against Aristippos, who is her senior,[35] as does Thisbe against Knemon, who is her social superior. At Athens seduction and female τέχνη can reverse hierarchies of age and station, but the point is that we are always left with relationships in which the two participants meet as in some sense superior and inferior. Athenian love is, among other things, about power and domination. Theagenes and Charikleia meet as equals: they are of an age[36] and have similar social backgrounds in the very top echelons of Greek society.

(f) We have just mentioned the skill at seduction displayed by the Athenian women. This is their τέχνη, a necessary part of their

---

[34] Possibly, on the basis of the parallels between Demainete and Arsake, we should read this punishment as an attempt to coerce him into complying with her desire; if so, it is implied rather than stated; cf., however, 1. 15. 5: ὥσπερ οὐκ ἐρῶσα τινος ἀλλ' ἄρχουσα δεινὸν ὅτι μὴ ἐξ ἐπιτάγματος ὑπήκουσεν ἐποιησάμην.

[35] This, I take it, is the point of the diminutive, γύναιον, with which she is characterised on her first appearance (1. 9. 1); cf. 1. 9. 2: τῇ τε ὥρᾳ τὸν πρεσβύτην ἐπαγομένη.

[36] Charikleia is seventeen (10. 14. 4); Theagenes' age is not specified, but he is introduced as an ἔφηβος (1. 2. 2).

armament as sexual predators. So, Demainete is described as δεινή εἴπερ τις γυναικῶν ἐφ᾽ ἑαυτὴν ἐκμῆναι καὶ τέχνην τὴν ἐπαγωγὸν ἐκτόπως ἠκριβωμένη ('if ever a woman knew how to drive a man mad with passion, she did, so extraordinarily well versed was she in the arts of allurement', 1. 9. 2), and Thisbe shares a suggestive τέχνη with Arsinoe (1. 15. 7). Their skill leads them, unnaturally, to take the sexual initiative. Demainete tries to seduce Knemon, Thisbe comes to him in the night; it is easy to forget how abnormal it must have been for a slave-woman to take the initiative in a sexual liaison with her master—though no doubt the episode embodies a fantasy of a kind widespread among the novel's predominantly male readership. Athenian women are blatant and forward. Charikleia on the other hand is all modesty and innocence. What attracts men to her is her peerless beauty, an entirely natural beauty that owes nothing to human artifice. She already possesses it at the age of seven when Charikles sees her for the first time (2. 30. 6), and in the opening scene of the whole work, when she is in a sticky situation, surrounded by twitching corpses and with her lover expiring at her feet, her physical beauty retains its power to stun the Egyptian bandits (1. 2. 5). This is the opposite of Demainete, who is introduced as a γύναιον ἀστεῖον (1. 9. 1) and employs the allurements of dress and cosmetics,[37] a specific aspect of the polarity between τέχνη and nature.

(g) Charikleia will not allow her love to be consummated outside marriage. She has fended off even Theagenes until the day their union can be legally solemnized[38] and makes her unfortunate lover swear an oath to have no carnal knowledge of her until she is reunited with her parents.[39] The whole novel ends with a ceremony of betrothal and the departure of the entire cast into the city of Meroe to celebrate τὰ ἐπὶ τῷ γάμῳ μυστικώτερα ('the more mystic parts of the wedding ritual', 10. 41. 3, the very last words of the text apart from a colophon in which the author identifies himself).

---

[37] So, for example, Thisbe says to her (1. 17. 1): κόσμει σαυτήν· ἁβρότερον ἔχουσαν ἥκειν προσήκει.

[38] 1. 25. 4: εἰς δεῦρο διετέλεσα καθαρὰν ἐμαυτὴν καὶ ἀπὸ σῆς ὁμιλίας φυλάττουσα, πολλάκις μὲν ἐπιχειροῦντα διωσαμένη, τὸν δὲ ἐξ ἀρχῆς ἡμῖν συγκείμενόν τε καὶ ἐνώμοτον ἐπὶ πᾶσι γάμον ἔνθεσμον εἴ πῃ γένοιτο περισκοποῦσα.

[39] 4. 18. 5: καὶ ἔτι μᾶλλον τῶν μελλόντων ὅρκῳ πρὸς Θεαγένην τὸ ἀσφαλὲς ἐμπεδωθείη ὡς οὔτε ὁμιλήσει τὰ Ἀφροδίτης πρότερον ἢ γένος τε καὶ οἶκον τὸν ἡμέτερον ἀπολαβεῖν ἤ, εἴπερ τοῦτο κωλύει δαίμων, ἀλλ᾽ οὖν γε πάντως βουλομένην γυναῖκα ποιεῖσθαι ἢ μηδαμῶς. Cf. also 4. 10. 6; 6. 9. 4; even in her dreams he must respect her chastity (6. 8. 6).

Athenian marriage is unloving, and love is extra-marital. It recog-
nises social prohibitions on and punishments for adultery only to
disregard them (1. 11. 4).

(h) Charikleia is a paradigm of chastity. Chastity was enjoined on
her by her mother in the ταινία ('band') left beside her when she
was exposed as a baby (4. 8.7), and dominates her thoughts
throughout the novel,[40] until the theme culminates with the radiant and triumphant vindication of her virginity on the Ethiopian
gridiron, an icon of luminous purity shared with Theagenes (10.
9). But, despite a tempting biographical tradition identifying
Heliodoros as a Thessalian bishop who enforced celibacy among his
clergy,[41] the *Aithiopika* is not an anti-sexual text. Love's consummation is the end to which the experiences of hero and heroine are
directed. It is also the end of their novel. It is to achieve union that
they endure the whims of destiny. Neither they nor their creator
seems inclined to think beyond the consummation of their love: it
is an act that nothing can follow, a true *telos*. Charikleia's chastity
is what imparts meaning to her ultimate surrender of herself to
Theagenes: that she considers her virginity worth preserving at
such cost makes it a gift of infinite value to the man to whom she
chooses to yield it. Her chastity, then, is not a value in itself (as
she had mistakenly believed it to be before she met Theagenes),[42]
but part of the high seriousness with which a love of such profundity must be enacted. She and Theagenes are untypical ideals,
as the Ethiopian chastity-test makes clear, and again they stand at
the opposite pole to the morality of Athens: Athenian love is not
meaningful because it is not chaste. Here love is devalued by its
ready availability (in the case of Thisbe at least) into a meaningless physical act which can serve as a means to other ends. So
Thisbe seduces Knemon to further Demainete's schemes of revenge;
she and Arsinoe both sleep with Nausikles for pecuniary gain, and
also, in Thisbe's case, to facilitate escape from justice; Demainete
herself uses sex as a means to obtain what she wants from
Aristippos—status and wealth. Athenian morality involves an
inversion of means and ends, and so desecrates what should be the
culmination of human life.

[40] 1. 3. 1, 1. 8. 3, 2. 33. 4f., 4. 18. 4ff., 5. 4. 5, 6. 8. 6, 8. 13. 2, etc.
[41] Sokr. *Hist. ekkl.* 5. 22 (Colonna [n. 4 above] Test. i); cf. Rattenbury (1927:
168ff.), C. Lacombrade (1970: 70ff.).
[42] 2. 33. 4–5: ἀπηγόρευται . . . αὐτῇ γάμος καὶ παρθενεύειν τὸν πάντα βίον
διατείνεται . . . ἐκθειάζουσα παρθενίαν καὶ ἐγγὺς ἀθανάτων ἀποφαίνουσα.

(i) The love of Theagenes and Charikleia is a sacrament. Its whole course is of concern to the gods, who are acknowledged at the end as the authors of its successful conclusion (10. 40. 1: θεῶν νεύματι τούτων οὕτω διαπεπραγμένων; cf. 10. 41. 1). Their first encounter is resonant with Platonic allusions and takes place under the sanction of a religious festival, the performance of an ἐναγισμός for the Thessalian hero Neoptolemos at the Pythian Games. Their story reaches its culmination, as it began, at a religious ceremony, to which the announcement of their marriage forms the climax. There is an important motivic link here with Knemon's story. It is when he returns from the Great Panathenaia, still in his ephebic uniform, that Demainete's lust becomes uncontrollable. Her advances profane the sacrament of his piety. The juxtaposition is one of significant irony and heightens the sense of shock engendered by her shamelessness. Thus the repeated motif of religious pageant locates Athenian and Charikleian love at opposite ends of a scale running from blasphemy to sacrament.

(j) Finally we may contrast the outcome of Athenian love with that of the ideal. Love leads Demainete to humiliation, judicial arrest and death in a pit, the *bothros* where sacrifices were made to chthonic heroes. It leads Thisbe to the threat of judicial torture and then to death under ground, in an Egyptian cave at the hands of Thyamis. It leads Knemon to judicial conviction for attempted parricide, to a narrow escape from execution by being hurled into the βάραθρον near the Akropolis, then to exile. It leads Aristippos to judicial confiscation of his property, then to exile. But Charikleia's love leads her home from exile to a final pageant of light and joy. Her story ends not with death but with a recognition couched in judicial terms (10. 10. 1: δίκη . . . καὶ κρίσις), reunion with her parents, presented as like a second birth (9. 25. 1, 10. 3. 1, 10. 16. 2, 10. 16. 6, 10. 16. 10, 10. 18. 3), and finally in marriage to the man she loves for the procreation of children, θεσμῷ παιδογονίας (10. 40. 2). The mirroring is obvious: instead of conviction and condemnation, recognition and reprieve; instead of exile, return; instead of death, new life. The striking parallels between the death of Demainete and Thisbe (and the execution so narrowly escaped by Knemon) form part of the pattern. The darkness of death under ground, of the Underworld almost, coheres with the darkness that shrouds Knemon's novella (which is told at night, and most of whose action takes place at night), but contrasts with the radiance surrounding Charikleia on the Ethiopian grid-iron,[43] with the torchlight accompanying the final procession into Meroe, with the whiteness of the priestly insignia and of the animals pulling the ceremonial carriages (10. 41. 3), and, most important, with the light-giving deities Helios and Selene, whose ministers Theagenes and Charikleia have become. Polarities of light and dark, white and black, are a fundamental part of the novel's image-system,[44] but here they are made to underpin, by the close parallel of theme and motif, a somewhat larger and ethically meant antithesis between Athenian and Charikleian love.

This antithesis is embodied in the persons of Charikleia and Thisbe, who seems deliberately written up as a sort of *Doppelgänger* to the heroine. She is mistaken for Charikleia in the cave first by Thyamis, who kills her, secondly by Theagenes, who mourns over her body. Both Thisbe and Charikleia were secreted in the cave by their brigand admirers, who themselves form a contrasting pair of noble outlaw, who respects his female captives and leads his men like a king, against simple ruffian. Later, Charikleia is made to adopt the name and identity of Thisbe after being captured by Nausikles, and is once again mistaken for Thisbe, by Knemon as she laments (5. 3. 1). This last example is partly just a spooky effect, of course, but the persistence of the pairing is suggestive of something more than a simple thrill, and confirms that we should read Thisbe as an anti-Charikleia. One of Heliodoros' imaginative strengths is his ability to construct icons, profoundly memorable, of the issues and significations of his text. One such icon encapsulates the meaning of Thisbe and Charikleia. Charikleia is hidden in a labyrinthine cave on an island surrounded by labyrinthine reed-beds (1. 29. 1, cf. 1. 6. 2). Knemon stations her at the very heart of the double labyrinth, where a certain, dim light penetrates (1. 29. 2), but Thisbe is hidden away from the centre, in total dark-ness. Is it too fanciful to see here a cypher for the novel itself, whose multiple narrations are like concentric mazes? At the centre of the maze/text stand heroine and her antitype, differentiated by light and darkness, one to live, one to die. If we can grasp what

---

[43] 10. 9. 3 ff., a passage verbally and thematically connected to the scene at Arsake's stake (8. 9. 13 f.), when after a judicial process expected death makes way for a salvation saturated with light.

[44] The prominence of the sun in the novel is part of this image-system, not (as argued by F. Altheim (1948: 93–124)) a declaration of faith by a devotee of the Emesan sun-cult.

the juxtaposition of these two figures means, we are very close to understanding the values that the *Aithiopika* expresses.

So we have a whole series of interlocked and overlapping polarities between the action of the novella and that of the novel. To demarcate and enumerate them as I have done is, of course, an artificial exercise, alien to the experience of actually reading the text, but its justification is that it articulates into manageable segments a large antithesis that is meant to be felt as a whole, and illustrates just how comprehensive and basic that antithesis is. Ideal love is defined, motif by motif, by the illustration of its polar opposite, and the grid of values provided by the juxtaposition of novel and novella enables us to locate morally the other amatory situations that confront the hero and heroine: the sensual carnality of the Persian court, the unreciprocated desires of certain males for Charikleia, the convenient and conventional but unloving marriages to her cousins Alkamenes and Meroebos into which her adoptive and natural fathers try to dragoon her, the activities of merchants who cannot see beyond financial values. Read in this way the greater part of the novel can be seen as following on from Knemon's novella in exploring the antithesis between true love and various corrupt or otherwise unsatisfactory alternatives.

This is a romantic view which places love uncontested at the centre of human experience. We can perhaps understand the conception more fully if we compare it with the erotic system of, for example, Roman elegy. In elegy the basic polarity is one of loving or not loving. The life of love stands in opposition to the social norm of civic and military duty, and the literary norm of public, specifically epic, poetry. Love represents a rejection of social convention. In romance, on the other hand, the possibility of not loving is hardly countenanced. Even the potentially ascetic priestly characters of the *Aithiopika* act willingly to promote the love of Theagenes and Charikleia and rejoice at its happy ending. The underlying polarity that informs the episodes of the plot is one of loving well or loving badly.

Of all the episodes of the main plot, the one that most concretely embodies loving badly, and also that which is most precisely prefigured by Knemon's novella, is that of the Persian princess Arsake. She poses the same kind of seductive threat to Theagenes as Demainete posed to Knemon. Like Demainete, she is a predatory female, sexually promiscuous,[45] a slave to illicit and perverted pleasure.[46] She pursues Theagenes but is concerned only with her own gratification; when she fails to obtain it immediately, her passion, like Demainete's, becomes destructive and degenerates into madness (7. 9. 3 cf. 1. 14. 6). If her advances are rebuffed, she resorts to punishment and coercion, or vengeance, as in her previous attempt on Thyamis (7. 2. 1ff.). If Demainete regretted acting like a tyrant instead of a lover (1. 15. 5), Arsake has no such qualms and rejoices when the course of events allows her to proclaim Theagenes literally her slave (7. 24. 4)—though he demonstrates his superiority to the average human male by continuing to defy her, a telling inversion of the familiar trope which makes the lover his mistress's willing slave. She even has a female servant who corresponds roughly to Thisbe: her old nurse Kybele, whose function it is to act as procuress for her mistress, and whose Lesbian origins are surely intended to define her morally (7. 12. 6). Like Demainete, Arsake ends by taking her own life, after her adulterous conduct has been revealed—or, rather, is on the point of being revealed—to her husband. Demainete and Arsake have much in common, then, both in their characterization and in the overall shape of their stories. But Heliodoros has employed a clever device to ensure that we link them. It is no original observation to point out the similarity of the story of Demainete and Knemon to that of Phaidra and Hippolytos, a similarity to which Demainete herself draws attention when she calls Knemon ὁ νέος Ἱππόλυτος.[47] It is interesting and suggestive that the one important facet of Euripides' Phaidra omitted from the tale of Demainete, the relationship of the heroine to her nurse and the rôle of the latter as go-between, seems to be resumed in the episode of Arsake. Most crucially, however, Arsake is also linked to Phaidra by means of unmistakable verbal allusion to Euripides' play.[48] So Demainete and Arsake are connected through the mythical figure of Phaidra and are intended to stand jointly as the antitype of the sexual morality of the central pair.

[45] Cf. Achaimenes' reaction to the arrival of Theagenes in the palace (7. 16. 1): σύνηθές τι καὶ ἀφροδίσιον διακόνημα τῇ Ἀρσάκῃ τὸν Θεαγένην ὑποτοπήσας.

[46] 7. 2. 1, 7. 9. 2.

[47] 1. 10. 2. A reference to Theseus follows in the MSS, but is impenetrable as the text stands; it should perhaps be excised, as argued by P. Neimke (1889: 15 n. 1), anticipating Rattenbury's note in the apparatus of his Budé text. For discussion of the novella as variant of the Phaidra story, see Donnini (1981).

[48] 8. 15. 2: τέθνηκεν Ἀρσάκη βρόχον ἀγχόνης ἀψαμένη, echoing E. Hipp. 802: βρόχον κρεμαστὸν ἀγχόνης ἀνήψατο.

This patterning is not gratuitous. We have already touched on the idea that narrative satisfaction depends on the story reaching the right end at the proper time; excitement and suspense arise when intrusions threaten to short-circuit that process and bring the story too soon to the wrong end. Now clearly the right ending to the story of Theagenes and Charikleia is the consummation of their chaste love in Ethiopia, and so the complications of the narrative tend to involve threats to their lives or their virtue. If either of them were to die, or were to prove inadequate, to yield to temptation or circumstance and compromise on the essential nature of their love, the plot would short-circuit and fail to reach the conclusion which we desire it to reach, and which, as practised readers of the genre, we know it *must* reach. The episode in Arsake's palace deals with the subtler of the two potential short-circuits: temptation. The hedonistic, dominating princess is a male fantasy-figure: we are encouraged to imagine the sensual delights that await Theagenes should he accede to her desires. And yet the consequences of compromised virtue have already been rehearsed through the novella of Knemon, which has implanted in our minds the autodestructive nature of profane love of the kind offered by Arsake. The issues at stake in the palace and the threat to the course of the story are activated in a way that would have been impossible without the programmatic novella. In this Heliodoros anticipates the use of the double plot in much modern drama and fiction, where a subplot is exploited to demonstrate a different solution to the problems worked through by the main plot. The *Aithiopika* then is a real artistic unity.

We are now in a position to state some summary conclusions. Knemon's novella is, by reason of its programmatic position and its contents, a vital part of the moral economy of the whole novel. At one level it can be read as guaranteeing the 'truth' of the central experience offered by the *Aithiopika* by pre-empting any suggestion that Charikleia's virtue is no more than the product of her author's naive idealism. The subplot demonstrates that he knows and understands the negative as well as the positive potential of human nature.[49] At a second level, the novella rehearses and primes the threat of short-circuit posed not just by Arsake, but by other amatory encounters also. At the third and deepest level it forms part of a statement of values, of an examination and taxonomy of

---

[49] This use of the double plot is outlined by W. Empson (1950: 53).

different kinds of love: giving and taking, spiritual and physical, sacred and profane, serious and trivial, selfless and selfish, meaningful and meaningless. The values themselves may strike us as bourgeois, conventional, sentimental, merely comfortable. They are certainly the kind of thing that a readership in an increasingly fragmented and depoliticised world would like to hear. But they are real values none the less, not so very different from the ethics that made Christianity such an attractive belief in that same uncertain world, and still potent even today. The function of Knemon's novella as I see it is to focus the work on the sexual and social values that romance in general takes for granted. It allows the *Aithiopika* a dimension beyond being simply an exciting fiction well told (though it remains the supreme ancient example of that, too), a philosophical dimension that gives a serious answer to the question of how and why one should love. The conclusion is paradoxically obvious: Heliodoros wrote a novel about love, but, thanks to the inclusion of Knemon's story, it is a novel *about* love in a new and deeper sense.

12

The Mendacity of Kalasiris and the Narrative Strategy of Heliodoros' *Aithiopika*

JOHN J. WINKLER

Two persistent problems which otherwise enthusiastic readers of the *Aithiopika* have raised are the apparent contradictions, first in Kalasiris' character, and second in his narrative. The troubling aspect of Kalasiris' character, as some readers feel it, is the tension between his oft-alleged wisdom, piety, virtual sanctity on the one hand, and his outrageous mendacity on the other. Kalasiris is boldly and repeatedly deceitful, cozening anyone—and there are many—who might stand in the way of his success in getting Charikleia and her lover to Aithiopia. The second problem could be said to stem from the first: one particular lie which Kalasiris seems to tell in his long narrative to Knemon is that after exiling himself from Memphis he happened to arrive in Delphi and while there happened to discover that Charikleia was actually the princess of Aithiopia. But he later mentions that he had in fact already visited Aithiopia and undertaken at the queen's request to search for her long-lost daughter. This inconsistency, fundamental to his entire story and motivation, is usually regarded as a simple contradiction in the narrative which Heliodoros should have avoided.[1] I want to suggest that this contradiction is not a mere oversight or poorly planned effect but more like a deliberate narrative strategy on Kalasiris' part, and hence an aspect of the larger problem of his honorable mendacity.

---

[1] The 'contradiction' was first discovered by V. Hefti (1950; diss. Basel) and is reported in Bryan Reardon (1971: 390–2). Reardon's is the basic work to consult on the Greek novels and cites the standard bibliography, which will be omitted here. On Kalasiris, see Sandy (1982*b*). On matters of more remote background (love literature and story telling in general) E. Rohde (1876: chs. 1–2), has still not been superseded.

My focus then is on Kalasiris the crafty narrator, who fools various audiences, and yet seems in some sense to maintain his integrity and lofty morality in the service of divine providence. I take these two problems to be important ones because Kalasiris, who is the narrator (with some interruption) of Books 2. 24 through 5. 33, employs the same sophistication and narrative skills as Heliodoros does in his role as narrator of the rest of the novel, and the analysis of Kalasiris' religiosity and craftiness is simply a test case for our understanding of Heliodoros' religious and narrative strategies in general.

Heliodoros' principal narrative excellence (in the judgment of enthusiastic critics since the Renaissance) is his disposition of material so as to arouse interest in the careful reader by the giving or withholding of information.[2] The two kinds of effect which depend on the careful manipulation of information from author to reader are surprise and suspense, which are differentiated precisely by the degree of information given the reader. Suspense is an effect of knowledge, surprise of ignorance. What creates suspense in a narrative is the foreknowledge of a perilous event that may be averted; the simple closing of a library door on time can be an incredibly tense event when the audience is fully aware, as the clock ticks away, that the event (ominous in context) is scheduled to happen.[3] Surprise on the other hand is an effect dependent upon ignorance, such as the unexpected appearance of a murderer in the bathroom while the heroine is taking her shower. To revert from modern popular entertainment to ancient, we may compare the parental recognitions in *Daphnis and Chloe*, which are surprising because unforeseen, with those in Heliodoros, which are suspense-

---

[2] The views of Amyot, Tasso, and Scaliger are reported in Forcione (1970). Amyot in his preface to his translation says that Heliodoros 'maintains [the audience's] attention through the ingenious relating of his story, for they do not understand what they have read at the beginning of Book 1 until they see the end of the fifth; and when they have arrived at that point they find themselves even more eager to see the end than they have been to see the beginning. Thus the reader's mind remains constantly in suspense until he comes to the conclusion.' The extraordinary menace and power of the opening scene is described by Michael Psellos as like the head of a serpent so coiled that it is lying in the center of its own windings, ready to spring forth with great force. (Psellos, and other pre-Renaissance testimony, is accessible in A. Colonna's edition of the *Aithiopika*.) Norbert Miller (1968) well analyzes the respectful attention paid to Heliodoros by eighteenth-century novelists.

[3] Hitchcock's *Shadow of a Doubt* (Universal, 1943).

ful, having been carefully planned from the moment in Book 4 when we learn the truth of Charikleia's parentage.[4]

Generally speaking, whereas the other Greek novelists do contrive some surprises, though very little suspense, Heliodoros regularly manipulates points of view so as to contrast and highlight states of relative knowledge and ignorance. These are calculated to produce neither pure suspense nor pure surprise, but rather states of partial knowledge: provocative uncertainties, riddling oracles, puzzles and ambiguities. All these forms of relative knowledge and ignorance are cases of *incomplete cognition*, a phrase which I will use to analyze several conscious strategies of the author, and which I regard as the fundamental principle of Heliodoros' narrative technique. The focal point in this game of knowledge and ignorance must always be the reader, who is by turns puzzled and enlightened in a shifting chiaroscuro of irony, half-truths and recognitions. If it were true that the reader at any point in the narrative were pointlessly puzzled, that would be a serious charge against the author. But I maintain that this is not the case in the *Aithiopika*, and that the novel's plotting not only withstands close scrutiny but invites it. I will show this by analyzing the general principles of Heliodoros' narrative technique, mainly from examples in Book 1 (section I), his use of duplicity as an intellectual and moral theme (section II), and finally Kalasiris' narrative strategy (section III).

I. OMNISCIENCE, IRRELEVANCE, AND DETECTION

We have a name for the narrative format of novels which begin as Heliodoros' *Aithiopika* does: they are called 'omniscient author' novels. The term implies that the narrator of the story knows all there is to know about the characters and events. This may broadly and roughly be contrasted with the 'documentary' format, in which some pretence is made that the narrator has discovered

---

[4] Criticisms of Heliodoros for 'revealing the secret' too soon are quite off the mark (as in Dunlop (1816: 22)). Our knowledge of Queen Persinna's exposure of her white child makes possible many situations of suspense and irony. Further, it gives us a firm grasp on the essence of Heliodoros' plotting, *viz.*, that adventures and locales do not succeed each other randomly (as in the novels of Xenophon of Ephesos and Achilles Tatius) but are organized in a linear and irreversible progression to a unique goal, represented by the land of Aithiopia.

what really happened, whether by personal observation of the events, by interviewing characters who took part in the story, by finding a document which sets down the tale, or a combination of these reportorial methods.

Nowadays we are so used to the omniscient author as a familiar narrator's voice that we may fail to appreciate just how unusual it was for a novel to begin, 'The day began to smile, and the sun had gilded the summits of the mountains, when certain men armed like thieves were peering over the ridge of a hill, near one of the many mouths—this one the Herakleotic—where the Nile flows at last into the ocean.'[5] By ancient conventions this prologue-less beginning is startlingly abrupt, an opening which could well prompt the reader to wonder, 'Who is speaking, and from what point of view?' The novels of Longos, Achilles Tatius, Chariton, and Antonius Diogenes begin (like most literary compositions) by identifying the author and the circumstances of discovery (Diogenes, A. T.) or composition (Longos, Chariton) of the story.[6] But with the *Aithiopika* we have to deal with a narrator who is not only omniscient but by ancient standards quite peculiarly and provocatively absent. Yet in a sense we learn to identify that narrator as a certain kind of mind, one characterized by three principles or habits of organizing and presenting the story. I will present these three principles in this first section as a general sketch of Heliodoros' narrative technique. They are (1) the aporetic measuring of characters' ignorance ('Little did they know . . .'), (2) the dis-

---

[5] The translations in this paper are my revisions of either the anonymous 1717 translation published in London or Walter Lamb's (1961). The Greek text is that edited by R. M. Rattenbury and T. W. Lumb (1960).

[6] The one known exception—Xenophon of Ephesos—confirms the principle in an indirect way. His simple introduction ('There was in Ephesos a man among the most prominent citizens whose name was Lykomedes') is modelled on the opening of Xenophon's *Anabasis*—a *faux-naïf* suppression of the writer's usual statement of identity and point of view. As Lucian remarks of later writers who aped the opening of the *Anabasis* but without Xenophon's real sophistication, akephalous histories (which skip the preface and go right to the events, ἀπροοιμίαστα καὶ εὐθὺς ἐπὶ τῶν πραγμάτων, *De hist. conscrib.* 23) ought somehow to imply all that would ordinarily be made explicit in a conventional proem (οὐκ εἰδότες ὡς δυνάμει τινὰ προοίμιά ἐστι λεληθότα τοὺς πολλούς, ibid.). The opening of Xenophon of Ephesos' *Ephesiaka* is a 'virtual proem' inasmuch as he provides us with a cast of characters, the dramatis personae, suitably described and commented on, and a set of simple motivating forces (pride, love, jealousy, divine anger) which will keep the plot rolling. The story is so clearly in the author's control—and modelled upon classic precedent—that no uneasiness is felt in the absence of a personal statement by 'Xenophon'.

covered relevance of seemingly incidental details or digressions ('So *that* was why . . .'), and (3) the postponement of wanted information ('But the answer to that would have to wait for . . .').

It is the narrator himself who provokes us to wonder from what point of view the opening tableau is narrated, not only by the absence of a conventional prologue, but by the aporetic style of his exposition. The formula for these *aporiai* is a binary one: sense data, usually visual,[7] followed by the brigands' conjecture or bafflement. Thus, looking out to sea they spy nothing that might be preyed upon, but closer to shore they notice a moored cargo ship. They infer that it is heavily laden because they can see—even at a distance, καὶ τοῖς πόρρωθεν—that the water is lapping up to her third line. Yet they are nonplussed by the absence of any men on board, sailors or passengers. They see corpses littered in various attitudes all over the beach and overturned banquet tables; from this they draw the limited conclusion that there had been an unexpected fight, but beyond that they are deeply puzzled. The fact that 'some are in the last throes of death and their limbs still twitching was a plain indication that the bloody action was only lately over'; but the vanquished have no victors, a defeat was plain but no spoils taken away. The meaning and correct interpretation of this theatrical tableau eludes them (οὐδὲ συνιέναι τὴν σκηνὴν ἐδύναντο).[8] Throughout the scene the narrator tells us what the bandits saw, what they inferred, and what left them confused.[9]

---

[7] Bühler (1976: 177–85). The pretense of a strictly visual, impersonal camera-eye view of things gives way, of course, to the unsuppressible sense of a narrator-in-charge, particularly in the gnomic comments (1. 2. 9, 4. 3, etc.) and in the occasional οἶμαι (1. 8. 1, 2. 22. 1, 5. 5. 3, 7. 8. 2, 9. 9. 5, 10. 6. 5), but the ἐγώ implied in that οἶμαι is never exposed.

[8] Walden (1894).

[9] The scene is well-lit, fully visible, quite clear to see, but the mind looking on is in the dark. At the risk of sounding Pythagorean, I will list the key elements of this scene in two opposing categories, references to optical phenomena and references to interpretive responses of the characters:

Vision: 1. 1, καταυγάζοντος, ὀφθαλμοῖς, ὄψεις, θέᾳ; 1. 2, τοῖς πόρρωθεν; 1. 4, τὰ φαινόμενα σύμβολα; 1. 7, θεωρούς; 2. 1, θέαμα; 2. 3, κατεφαίνετο, ἀντέλαμπεν, ὀφθαλμοῖς, ὄψις, ὁρᾶν, ἑώρων; 2. 5, ὄψεως ὥσπερ πρηστῆρος, ἔδοξε (a trick of perspective); πρὸς τὸν ἥλιον ἀνταυγαζούσης; 2. 6, ὁρώμενον; 2. 7, ὁρῶντες; 2. 8, σκιὰς τοῖς ὀφθαλμοῖς παρεμπεσούσης, ἀνένευσε καὶ ἰδοῦσα ἐπένευσε, ὄψεως; 3. 1, κατὰ πρόσωπον, ἀνένευσε, ἰδοῦσα, ὄψιν; 3. 6, ὁρῶντες; 4. 3, ἐφαίνετο, ὄψις. Interpretive reaction: 1. 2, συμβάλλειν; 1. 3, κατηγορούντων; 1. 7, οὐδὲ συνιέναι; 1. 8, ἀποροῦντες; 2. 1, ἀπορώτερον, ἀναπείθουσα; 2. 4, Theagenes' query; 2. 6, ἡ τῶν γινομένων ἄγνοια, ταῦτα ἐγίνωσκον, τὰ ὄντα δὲ οὔπω ἐγίνωσκον; 2. 7, πρὸς ἑτέρας ἐννοίας τὴν γνώμην μετέβαλλον, τὴν τῶν ἀληθῶν γνῶσιν; 3. 1, ἑῴκεσαν, ὡς ἔοικεν;

The process of careful detection, including decipherment and reading small signs as tokens of a larger pattern, is one of Heliodoros' favorite modes of presentation. Helm compares this technique to that of a modern *Kriminalroman*:[10] there are *corpora delicti* (so to speak) but no murderer. The brigands, from whose limited perspective the reader takes in the scene, are only second-rate detectives. They can figure out that since the tables on the beach were still full of food the attack must have been a sudden one in the middle of a meal. From the position of one of the bodies half-hidden under an overturned table they surmise that he had tried to take cover and had thought himself secure from view but was wrong in that belief.

The scene of the crime is even more like a detective story than the audience at first reading can guess, for one sentence is a Clue. After the survey of methods of death (bludgeoning with cups, cleavers, rocks and shells snatched from the beach, firebrands, etc.), the narrator remarks, speaking from the bandits' observation, 'But most were killed by some archer's arrows' (οἱ δὲ πλεῖστοι βελῶν ἔργον καὶ τοξείας γεγενημένοι). I have intensified the clue-quality of the sentence by the ominous 'some archer'; the Greek is more general and impersonal—'most deaths had been the work of missiles and archery'. It is not until the 'solution' (5. 32) that we learn the meaning of this phrase—Charikleia, dressed in her robes as priestess of Artemis, had been shooting into the melee from the safety of the ship's deck. If she is thus identified as the murderer of most (οἱ πλεῖστοι), it is ironic that the bandits treat her as the least likely suspect: they plunder the cargo and pay no attention to the woman and the wounded man she is nursing, leaving them 'under no other guard but their own weakness' (ἰσχυρὰν αὐτοῖς φυλακὴν τὴν ἀσθένειαν αὐτῶν ἐπιστήσαντες). And yet, in detective story fashion, they had actually noticed that she was still carrying an unstrung bow and a quiver on her shoulder and had even con-

---

3. 2, οὐδὲν συνιέναι ἔχοντες; 3. 5, ὑπὸ τῆς τῶν ὁρωμένων ἀγνοίας; 3. 6, εἴκαζον; 4. 1, οὐδὲν συνιεῖσα, συμβαλοῦσα; 4. 2, συνείς, προσδοκήσας.
The contrasts between the two groups include light/dark, knowledge/uncertainty, and picture/explanation. Perhaps the most basic contrast underlying this scene is the definiteness of spatial location and time of the day as opposed to the indefiniteness of 'location' in the plot. It is a beginning which has all the signs of being an end, and the reader is very far from being able to place the scene in the novel's spatio-temporal framework, that is, to know just where it is in the middle.

[10] Helm, (1956: 40).

jectured, in a moment of panic when she leaped up from the rock where she was sitting, that she might be a goddess or a frenzied priestess 'inspired with divine fury to execute that great slaughter plain to see' (οἱ δὲ ἱέρειαν ὑπό του θεῶν ἐκμεμηνυῖαν καὶ τὸν ὁρώμενον πολὺν φόνον ἐργασαμένην).[11] Though the brigands suspect her of the deed as long as she seems to be a goddess or priestess, they abandon the hypothesis that she might be the guilty party. And so do we. Interestingly enough, it is only at this moment in the scene that the narrator utters a sentence which might be read as an intrusive 'Little did they know': καὶ οἱ μὲν ταῦτα ἐγίνωσκον, τὰ ὄντα δὲ οὔπω ἐγίνωσκον. Even this phrase may be read in two ways—either as the narrator's personal intrusion, commenting on the bandits' ignorance, or as a more sophisticated indirect statement of what the brigands were thinking, 'So much we know, but the truth we do not yet know.' This sleight of hand directs our attention away from the truth (that Charikleia is the murderous archer). It is almost as if, in order to achieve this, Heliodoros is willing to *seem* to abandon his very objective, self-effacing tone and speak instead as the popular story-teller, rather like a Chariton, who chats with the reader as the plot moves along. All the other references of the narrator to the incomplete cognition of the characters in this scene are quite relentless reports of what their eyes and mind were objectively able to comprehend.

We must revise, then, our understanding of the term 'omniscient author' as applied to Heliodoros, for the contrast between omniscient author and documentary author does not hold in his case. Heliodoros combines the superior authority of an omniscient narrator, who has immediate access to all relevant knowledge, with the critical discrimination of a documentary narrator, who verifies the reliable accuracy of every sentence, every observation. What interests Heliodoros most in the opening tableau is the *process of interpretation*, particularly in the forms of misapprehension and failed understanding. Though we must think of the

[11] There might be a parallelism between the three elements of Charikleia's appearance which the brigands notice and the three conjectures they make: (a) clang of arrows—Artemis; (b) gold clothes gleaming—native Isis; (c) flowing, unbound hair—frenzied priestess. It is the second element which seems uncertain. This reference to 'native Isis' is one of the signs that the novel is written from and for a Hellenocentric point of view: a reference by name to Neith, the arrow goddess whose home city was Sais near Naukratis, would have had to be glossed. Of course this does not prevent Heliodoros from contriving non-Hellenic viewpoints, as when Kalasiris refers to 'someone or other named Lykourgos' (2. 27. 1).

narrator as one who knows 'the truth' which the bandits fail to grasp, yet he does not advertize his knowledge or even his presence but conceals himself behind the splendid bafflement of that panorama and its tiny predators, whose failure to understand it is the clearest fact of all.

We must ask now what are the limits of Heliodoros' ruthless objectivity. We could imagine a yet more radical isolation of the pure perceptual field apart from all mental constructs, but that would be the technique of the *nouveau roman*, not of the ancient. Heliodoros, on the contrary, assumes that the ordinary principles of common sense and empirical truths are still valid, as when the brigands conclude that the ship is fully loaded because the water laps up to the third line. This is important: Heliodoros does not require us to suspend judgment or bracket all empirical knowledge, and particularly not the expectation that this is a romance. In solving this scene not only the laws of nature but the conventions of the genre will hold good. Yet he is requiring that we hold on to those expectations in a more conscious and critical way, perceiving them for what they are—not data of the text but patterns of probable foreknowledge brought to the text by the literate reader. These generic expectations of what the limits are within which the problem will be resolved are analogous to Kant's categories of the mind 'operating' on sense data, literally making sense of them. Generic expectations are, according to a familiar modern comparison, like the rules of a game,[12] which tell us what range of moves is possible and meaningful but not which move will be made in any particular situation. The opening tableau leaves us both certain *that* this is a romance and quite uncertain as to *how*. My thesis will be that Heliodoros' techniques of displaying incomplete cognition are designed to heighten our awareness of the game-like structure of intelligibility involved in reading a romance, and that Kalasiris is the major representative of one who knows how to play this game.

The second principle of the Heliodoran narrator's mind or style is his demand that every item be significant. The opening chapters are in many ways very pictorial,[13] but it would be wrong to call

---

[12] Neatly qualified by Greenberg (1971: 330-52). 'In a chess game we know the rules. . . . But language is more like a game in which we are trying to deduce the rules by watching the games' (p. 344).
[13] Indeed one of the closest analogs to the Heliodoran tone is the voice often

them an *ekphrasis*, insofar as that term often connotes the elaboration of a descriptive passage for its own sake rather than to provide information, plot development or any functional connection.
Heliodoros utterly eschews irrelevance, though he sometimes
allows the deceptive appearance of irrelevance. It may be that he
intends us to be tempted to understand the opening scene of the
Aithiopika as a novel kind of *ekphrasis*, in contrast with the novels
of Longos and Achilles Tatius, which begin by describing paintings
which are only tenuously and obliquely related to the general
thematics of the ensuing stories. Heliodoros' opening tableau looks
like one of those paintings, but so far from being marginal it is a
critical scene from the very center of the *Aithiopika*'s plot. Another
intended contrast may be the occurrence of a crocodile at Achilles
Tatius 4. 19 and Heliodoros 6. 1. Achilles Tatius, master of the
inconsequential filigree, had described the crocodile at length in a
manner which as usual had nothing to do with the plot ('And I
saw another creature of the Nile . . .'), but in Heliodoros the beast
slips like a shadow along the ground, hardly visible much less
described at length, and more importantly its passage is functional.
Knemon's fright at barely glimpsing it starts a conversation about
an earlier show of cowardice and leads to the revelation of the
name Thisbe. I think it likely that the pattern of describing exotic
beasts in some detail was so well established that any reader would
have noticed the absence of *ekphrasis* at this point.[14] A variation
occurs at 10. 27 where the marvellous appearance of giraffe is
described. This seems at first to be a typical irrelevant digression
such as romances allowed and even cultivated. However what
seems to be a digression becomes functional when the animals
assembled for sacrifice are frightened by the strange giraffe and
give Theagenes an opportunity to perform an impressive rodeo
stunt which wins the hearts of his captors. Heliodoros particularly

adopted by Philostratos describing a painting, raising questions, musing on the
possible meanings of the visible details. One of his paintings, the murder of
Kassandra (2. 10), closely resembles the banquet-turned-battle in Heliodoros' opening tableau (bodies everywhere, blood mixed with wine, men still breathing, tables
filled with food, cups fallen from the hands of drinkers, various manners of death,
a maiden in the midst of it looking at a weapon poised to bring her death—as
Charikleia has her dagger ready for suicide). Certainly Philostratos' interrogation of
the meaning of what he sees is closer to Heliodoros than is the unproblematic
descriptions of temple art which open the novels of Longos and Achilles Tatius.

[14] Rommel (1923).

likes to present casual conversations which unexpectedly lead to important revelations (1. 8. 5–6; 2. 10. 4–5, 23. 6–24. 3; 6. 3. 1–4).[15] Perhaps the most significant instance is 4. 16: Kalasiris is hastening to the Delphic oracle to seek a solution to a problem when an accidental encounter with a Phoenician merchant answers his prayer before he had even uttered it. 'God is very sharp-witted', remarks Kalasiris at that point (4. 16. 3).

The asides between Kalasiris and Knemon which retard the long flashback to Delphi are sometimes thought to be irrelevant digressions, but consider what is probably the chief candidate for such a charge—the tale of Egyptian Homer's birth (3. 14). In form it is a digression on a digression, explaining why Kalasiris, when he explained the marks by which a true god is recognized in human form, called Homer 'Egyptian'. Knemon makes a demand which we may make our own for the entire novel: that not a single word slip by without scrutiny for its precise meaning (μὴ παραδραμεῖν σε τοῦ λόγου τὴν ἀκρίβειαν), and he compels Kalasiris to tell the hitherto unheard story that Homer was an Egyptian by birth. The ensuing tale of Hermes fathering Homer by the wife of a Hermetic prophet might seem irrelevant to the *Aithiopika*, but the pattern of a genetic fluke (his hairy thigh, like that other son of Hermes, Pan) bringing on charges of bastardy and resulting in exile and wandering is in fact a neat parallel for Charikleia's own story. As Heliodoros continually draws on Homeric material for his novel, so his heroine, by a witty conceit, is living out a destiny essentially like Homer's own. We may even say of this double digression what Charikles says of his own digression: 'So there, my friend, you have the explanation of my traveling thither, but there is something parenthetical to my tale, or rather, to speak more truly, the principal point of it, which I would have you know' (. . . ἦν δέ σε βούλομαι παρενθήκην γνῶναι τοῦ διηγήματος, μᾶλλον δὲ ἀληθέστερον εἰπεῖν, αὐτὸ δὴ τὸ κεφάλαιον . . . , 2. 30. 1). This technique of significant displacement, which makes the incidental necessary and the random relevant, is fundamental to Heliodoros' style of thinking, and we will see it deployed even more strikingly in section II below.

---

[15] And casually introduced persons who become significant actors: the brigand chief and his henchman (1. 3. 4), the Naukratite merchant Nausikles (2. 8. 5), a daring pirate (5. 25. 1), a soldier of Mitranes (7. 1. 2). At first mention these all seem to be forgettable walk-on parts.

A third basic feature of Heliodoros' narrative technique, which is evident in the opening scene and carried through the rest of the book, is postponement. I will here analyze only its use in the first book. If we consider Book 1 in the light of the conventions of narrative information—the initial identification of characters, relations and motives—we can say that the book is structured around four major postponements of that information. Each of these postponements is so timed as to provoke the reader to a greater awareness of the conventions of reading fiction, which are (1) an intelligible language shared by author, reader and characters, (2) a plot, (3) a smattering of conventional motifs and familiar themes, and (4) a certain identification with the fortunes of the heroes.

(1) Part of the mystery of the opening tableau is that the reader has questions ('Who are these characters?', 'What is their story?') which would normally be answered when the actors begin to speak. We can tolerate a certain amount of preliminary scene-setting whose meaning is not entirely perspicuous, but we expect the characters' speeches at least to provide the information which is necessary for us to situate ourselves in the story. The first conversation does not do this (1. 2. 4); it is an intimate exchange between the seated maiden and the wounded young man (both as yet unnamed) which tells us that they are devoted to each other unto death, and therefore probably romance heroes. We have more justified hopes of being informed about the situation when the bandits advance upon the maiden, for they are strangers like ourselves and stand in the same need of explanation. Her speech to them displays a courageous character,[16] but it is not particularly informative. This would normally be followed by questions and answers, but just as we are ready to learn who she is the narrator tells us that they understood not a word she said (1. 3. 2) but instead rushed past her to gather booty. And so the novel remains a curious dumb show until the protagonists are assigned a translator (1. 8. 5). Heliodoros' Greek is hard even by ancient standards, which means that the brigands' noncomprehension of Greek is simply the extreme case of what every reader is experiencing, that

---

[16] More specifically, that melodramatic display of resolve which was often exhibited in tragedy, hence the verb for her speaking is ἐπετραγῴδει. If Euripides is the grandfather of the Greek romance, Heliodoros is his favorite grandchild, and Koraes rightly calls him φιλευριπίδης.

is, a certain struggle to comprehend and sort out not only the plot but the very *language* of the plot.

I believe Heliodoros is unique in ancient literature for his continual attention to problems of language and communication.[17] He repeatedly describes situations in which ignorance of a language blocks communication (1. 4. 1f., 2. 33. 1) or in which knowing a foreign language makes communication possible (2. 21. 5; 10. 31. 1, 39. 1, 40. 1). To navigate one's way through this conspicuously polyglot world it is very helpful to know at least two languages, and several characters do: Knemon (1. 7. 3, 19. 3, 21. 3; 2. 18. 3), Kalasiris (6. 12. 3, 14. 1), Hydaspes (9. 25. 3). Professional interpreters are essential (7. 19. 3, 8. 17. 2, 9. 1. 5). One can use another person's ignorance of a language to avoid being understood (5. 8. 4, 10. 9. 6). The point of this constant awareness might be simply a striving for naturalism if it were not for two facts: Heliodoros uses knowledge and ignorance of a language in a dramatic and significant way to underscore the cross-purposes, complications and dénouements of his plot. To this end, the references to linguistic knowledge and ignorance are particularly frequent in the first and last books. The best example occurs at the conclusion of Book 1: Thyamis, shouting in Egyptian, is led through the darkness of the cave by following the voice of a woman speaking in Greek. Of course we are not told what they were saying since her identity must not be revealed to the reader. But had they understood each other's language in this striking bilingual duet of voices seeking each other out, the murder which is its culmination would have been averted (1. 30. 7). Secondly, Heliodoros not only describes a world like the real one in which many languages are actually spoken, but cultivates scenes in which a dim and partial awareness of a foreign language is displayed, ranging from the minimal knowledge of a foreign name (2. 12. 4)[18] to quasi-competence (2. 30. 1; 8. 13. 5, 15. 3; 10. 15.

[17] Hippothoos knows the Cappadocian language (Xen. Eph. 3. 1. 2). Chariton's Persians and Egyptians all speak Greek to each other, even though at one point the author notices that this is not to be assumed (7. 2. 2). References to translators and knowledge of foreign languages crop up everywhere in ancient literature from Homer on (cf. Allen, Halladay and Sikes (1936: *ad Ven.* 113) but I think nowhere with such sustained attention as in Heliodoros.

[18] Thermouthis falls asleep, grieving for his murdered mistress Thisbe, and muttering her name: 'He went back to the mouth of the cave and coming to the body of the slain woman he knelt down and placed his head on her breast, saying "Oh Thisbe"—repeating the word often and nothing more, until shortening the

1, 35. 2, 38. 2). This purblind consciousness of what a language, a speech, or a text means is another form of incomplete cognition and rightly takes its place in the Heliodoran universe of steadily expanding meaning. In the same category come other scenes of failed communication, not because the language is foreign, but because one character is partly deaf (5. 18. 4–6) or totally absorbed in his thoughts (2. 21. 3). These two motifs are combined at 5. 1. 5, where Kalasiris does not notice the entry of Nausikles: 'I didn't notice (says Kalasiris), perhaps because I've become a bit hard of hearing at my age; old age, you see, especially affects the ears; or perhaps I was just concentrating on my narrative.' This remark closes the long session of story-telling which extends from 2. 24 to 5. 1. with an ambiguous double explanation. (Heliodoros uses this 'either/or' construction to mark significant transitions in his narrative; they are the subject of section II below.)

To return to Charikleia's tragic speech at 1. 3. 1, the news that this speech is just so much garbled gibberish to the brigands who hear it is a special kind of literary shock. Heliodoros associates our disappointment at not learning more of the truth with the brigands' ignorance of the language in which the novel is written. This is an effect of defamiliarization: our ordinary comprehension of the language of the text becomes suddenly a thing of some wonder rather than an unquestioned habit. Our natural assumption is that, because we understand the language which the author and his first speaking character use, so will all the characters automatically have the same faculty, inasmuch as they have their literary being, their mode of existence, in a Greek novel. But from now on, knowing Greek must be felt as an achievement rather than a premise, and our comprehension of Greek characterizes us from that moment on as readers, and the brigands as non-readers, of this novel.

(2) Later, alone in a tent (1. 8), Charikleia and Theagenes speak vaguely of their past sufferings and Apollo's persecution. The interpreter assigned to protect them, Knemon, is the first stranger who can communicate with them in the same language. However, for the next ten chapters they listen to his story and then fall asleep without telling him their own. This is a second major postpone-

name bit by bit and gradually losing consciousness he fell insensibly asleep' (2. 14. 5). We had earlier been told that the name 'Thisbe' is the one word of Greek which Thermouthis has learned (2. 12. 4).

ment, and it reveals much about Heliodoros' ideas of narrative, both in itself and in relation to the still-postponed plot of Charikleia.

The tale of Knemon which thwarts our desire is a complex one with multiple narrators, hidden motives, betrayal and double-dealing, false accusations and shocking revelations. It is almost as if the protagonists of the *Aithiopika* were taking time out from their adventures to read a different novel. The balance at this point may be precarious for the reader who is still trying to locate the basic terms of this narrative: who are the central and who the inciden-tal characters?[19] But even the reader who knows that Charikleia is indeed the heroine should wonder why the author delays her story while she listens to a completely unconnected novella. In fact, however, Knemon's tale is of special interest as a demonstration model of an alternate narrative strategy. We may even say that the importance of Knemon's novella lies principally in the fact that the powerful narrative intellect which we can sense behind the open-ing tableau here enters a simpler persona and works within the narrower conventions of a naive raconteur in order to make clear what kind of story the *Aithiopika* is *not*.

The distinctive feature about the conventions of Knemon's tale is that they are instantly intelligible. There is no Heliodoran irony about the meaning of this narrative event. In fact Knemon sounds rather like Xenophon of Ephesos: ἦν μοι πατὴρ Ἀρίστιππος, τὸ γένος Ἀθηναῖος . . . , 'My father was Aristippos, an Athenian by birth . . .', though by the third sentence he has noticeably reverted to Heliodoros' characteristic luxuriousness of language (a sentence of 75 words, exquisite compounds such as ὑπερθεραπεύουσα, clausular balance, expressions which are by turn sententious and prolix). The characters are not only clearly named and put into relation to each other (father, stepmother, maid, etc.) but assigned fixed moral characters, particularly the insidiously wicked Demainete (1. 9. 2). This is a narrative shorthand which allows the quick development of plots; Knemon says as much—καὶ τὰ μὲν ἄλλα τί δεῖ μηκύνοντα

---

[19] We may even ask a question which many readers have probably forgotten: how soon is the reader of the *Aithiopika* sure that Charikleia and Theagenes are in fact the protagonists? In the time when the novel was referred to by the title *Charikleia*, the reader would have known at 1. 8. 3-4, when the names Theagenes and Charikleia are first used. But if a reader came upon the book under the title *Aithiopika* and before its reputation was established, he or she might continue to wonder (as I did on first reading) how to distinguish the main characters from the minor ones.

ἐνοχλεῖν; 'And as for the other (signs by which she showed her true character), what need for me to tire you with a lengthy recital?' (I. 9. 4). This ploy serves to accommodate the coexistence of two opposite narrative structures, allowing Knemon to speak both as an omniscient narrator who declares at once the inner reality of his characters (Demainete's wickedness), and as a documentary narrator who relates only what he experienced. These two structures are effectively combined so that we follow Knemon's story both as a well-made tale by an author who has designed the plot and also as a personal account by the man who lived it. Knemon's references to what happened outside his immediate knowledge (Demainete's plotting) are easily integrated with the documentary stance; the implicit qualification accompanying all such information is, 'as I later learned'. The narrator exploits the best features of both narrative stances: he communicates a masterly sense of control over the story by references which alert the audience to transitions and remind us of the beginning and end: 'in the end it came to this: . . .' (I. 10. 1); 'She, for she was not yet sated, devised a second plot against me, as follows: . . .' (I. 11. 2); 'But Demainete, hateful to heaven, did not continue to escape punishment. The manner thereof you shall hear anon' (I. 14. 1–2). And on the other hand the narrator in his role as experiencing-I recaptures the immediacy of dramatic moments as if they were happening now, in a way no third-person narrator could (I. 12. 2–3) without straining credulity.

The relation of Knemon's tale to the major plot is much more than mere retardation or postponement—important as that is:

(a) Insofar as it is a tale with a perfectly intelligible beginning, an unproblematic narrative from its very first words, it has been designed and positioned to emphasize the ambiguity and unanswered questions of the opening tableau. Knemon's tale shows that Heliodoros is perfectly capable of writing an old-fashioned novel in a direct narrative mode, one which tells a story from the beginning, and that in the *Aithiopika* he is writing against that mode.

(b) Knemon's tale is a model of the ordinary *chronological* intelligibility of all plotted stories, no matter what form they may take. No matter what point in the plot the narrator chooses to begin from, he must sooner or later assemble the parts so that meaningful chronological order is understood. Knemon's tale is, particularly at the beginning, an instance of this ideal narrative intelligibility, what every narrative must in some sense be reducible to. Photius' report of the *Aithiopika* (*Bibl.* cod. 73) re-assembles the plot in chronological order, so that in his words it sounds like a straight-forward series of adventures rather than the epistemologically self-conscious work it is. Knemon's tale represents not only what pre-Heliodoran novels were or happened to be, but an inherent demand for meaningfulness which any fiction, including his own, must somehow obey.

(c) Knemon's narrative moves in counterpoint to the main plot of the *Aithiopika*, for whereas the novel as a whole begins in cunning obscurity and gradually moves (by means of 'discovering' a narrator, namely, Kalasiris) to a unified and reasonably straight-forward pattern, Knemon's novella begins with ingenuous sim-plicity but becomes more and more complex in narrative structure, and then does not end cleanly and clearly but has a number of partial endings and unexpected resumptions.[20]

(d) Knemon's particular story also reproduces the problem of Charikleia's story. He is exiled from his native land by a move to vindicate a mother's chastity, just as Charikleia was. The over-arching question of the *Aithiopika* turns out to be whether (and how) Charikleia will return to her homeland. This question very slowly and sinuously winds toward its answer in the final book. The same question governs Knemon's plot. He has come to Egypt to find Thisbe because only she can explain what really happened, and only with her evidence can he bring about the restoration of

---

[20] Complexity: In the second phase of the novella, Demainete's maid Thisbe the clever arranger of intrigues in which each character has a different notion of the truth. As arch-manipulator she successfully tells different lies to Demainete, Arsinoe and Aristippos and contrives a double bed-trick: Demainete taking the place of Thisbe, who is taking the place of Arsinoe. Thisbe is also the source of the story, the ultimate narrator. The reader gets so wrapped up in her involuted but carefully planned web that it comes as a small shock when Charias, the intermediate narra-tor, says 'you' to Knemon (1. 17. 2)—so completely do we forget the framing narrative situation. When the story comes to an end we experience in a rush the multiple transition from Thisbe to Charias to Knemon to Heliodoros, a Chinese box of narrators.
Incomplete endings: 1. 14. 2, Knemon tries to stop for sleep; 1. 18. 1, Knemon actually stops for sleep; 2. 11, 'the rest I am unable to recount'; 6. 2-3, Knemon repeats his entire story, Nausikles refrains from filling in his part of it; 6. 1. 8, Nausikles reveals himself as Thisbe's lover and Knemon agrees to return with him to Athens. We never learn whether Nausikles' testimony, in place of Thisbe's, was sufficient to clear Aristippos.

his father's property and citizenship (2. 9. 3-4). So it is the same question of the child's return from exile to its parent and homeland and the ensuing vindication of the parent's honor which is fully and luxuriously answered in the case of Charikleia but left hanging in the case of Knemon. Knemon's story is a variation of Charikleia's, just as Homer's invented etymological biography is patterned on Charikleia's history.

(e) Finally, Heliodoros places the two narratives in an explicit relation of equivalence, as in the two pans of a balance scale. Knemon's tale and Charikleia's are *exchanged* in a bargain struck between Kalasiris and Knemon. They enter an agreement to tell each other their histories (2. 21. 5-7), an agreement which they treat from the start as a binding contract of reciprocal exchange (ἐν μέρει, 2. 21. 7). This mutual obligation requires that the first to ask is the first to be answered, and that Kalasiris must therefore tell his complete story before Knemon is required even to reveal his name.[21] These terms become clear when several times they are nearly violated (2. 21. 5, 26. 3; 3. 1. 1-2; 5. 2. 3). This series of postponements comes to an end at 6. 2. 2 when Knemon has both occasion (the name of Thisbe again) and opportunity (a journey) to tell his story. 'It is your turn now, Knemon, to give us the story which you have so often promised to relate to me, and which will acquaint us with your own adventures, but which you have hitherto put off each time with various dodges' (σὸς ὁ λόγος, ὦ Κνήμων, ὃν πολλάκις μοι διελθεῖν γνῶσίν τε τῶν κατὰ σεαυτὸν παρασχεῖν ἐπαγγειλάμενος εἰς δεῦρο τε ποικίλαις ἀεὶ διαδύσεσιν ὑπερθέμενος ἐν καιρῷ λέγοις ἂν τὸ παρόν). This is followed by a synopsis of Knemon's tale as we already know it from the first, well-framed narrative situation (1. 9-17) and the later additions (Knemon's further narrative, 2. 8. 4-9; Thisbe's letter, 2. 10). Knemon's fulfillment of his part of the bargain comes late and, as far as we the readers of the *Aithiopika* are concerned, is perfunctory; but this should not conceal the structural relation which is posited between the two narratives. The histories of Kalasiris and of Knemon are contractually bound to each other as an equivalent exchange.[22]

---

[21] The same contract, without self-conscious testing of the convention, at Xen. Eph. 3. 1. 4f., 2. 15.

[22] The metaphor of mercantile value assigned to the transaction is made explicit at 2. 23. 3-4. The most valuable object which Kalasiris can give to Knemon in

(3) The third major postponement encountered in Book 1 is another narrative. Summoned before the brigands' council, Charikleia accepts an offer of marriage from their captain (himself a priest's son in exile) and in doing so tells them the story of her birth and the recent events which led to the puzzling banquet-and-battle scene on the beach (1. 22). Part of her story is that she is still within, but near the end of, a year's service to Artemis, and she asks that her marriage wait upon her official retirement from that office in a ceremony which must take place at any established altar or temple of Apollo. Her story thus serves immediately to postpone (εἰς ὑπερβολήν, 1. 25. 6) the proposed marriage, and a few chapters later we realize that it has also postponed our learning who Charikleia really is. The tale was a lie—told in the service of chastity, or as Charikleia puts it 'an account adjusted to the occasion and serving a useful purpose' (λόγων ἐπικαιρίων καὶ πρός τι χρειῶδες εἰρημένων, 1. 25. 3). Theagenes understands that her calling him her brother has saved his life and that her tale of wanderings (πλάνη) has led them astray (πλάνην τῷ ὄντι τοῖς ἀκούουσιν ἐπάγοντα, 1. 25. 6); thus Heliodoros informs us that those parts of her story were not true. She then recommends that in view of the dangers which surround them they hold to his lie (πλάσμα) as a sort of jiu-jitsu feint or wrestling trick (πάλαισμα) and not trust even Knemon with the truth. The effect of her cunning and caution is that we will be given no opportunity to learn what we want to know in order to begin appreciating her situation as part of an intelligible plot.

Her account is not only a lie, it is nearly a parody of the Greek romance as a genre, conflating typical motifs from several novels, as a sort of least common denominator of what such a story could

return for the appearance of Theagenes and Charikleia in person is his tale of their romance. This second bargain struck is not identical with the first, and it will make a difference (see below, pp. 338–9) whether Kalasiris is thought of as telling his own story (the original contract) or Charikleia's (the second request).

A scene which duplicates the theme of exchange is Kalasiris' payment of a precious engraved ring to Nausikles for the return of Charikleia (5. 12–15). In both cases the receiver is in some sense duped, appreciating the superficial glamor of the gem/tale but not fathoming how it was produced; and in both cases the object exchanged for the heroine is one whose boundaries are cleverly blended with its content and whose most marvelous quality is not the material itself but the interaction of container and content (5. 14. 4). Kalasiris' religious charade is performed in the name of Hermes, the presiding genius of the *Aithiopika* (see nn. 25 and 51).

be expected to be.[23] It is as if for Heliodoros the measure of the brigands' gullibility is their willingness to believe in the plot of a Greek romance. A reader who like the brigands accepted her word at face value or like Thyamis was 'enchanted as if he had been listening to a Seiren' (1. 23. 2) should feel a little put out when Charikleia not only admits she was lying but remarks on the rustic simplicity of persons like Thyamis who are easily misled and mollified by words complaisant to their desire (1. 26. 3). The parallel is a designed one—Thyamis the easily beguiled lover is to Charikleia's lie as the fond and romantic reader is to the conventional Greek romance. The plot of her lie presents no thoughtful difference, no challenge of any kind to the reader who knows Xenophon, Chariton and Achilles Tatius. It is a 'compliant story, one which matches pace with the expectations' of the reader, as Charikleia says of her strategy in spinning a fiction for Thyamis (λόγος εἴκων καὶ πρὸς τὸ βούλημα συντρέχων, 1. 26. 3).

Each of the three major postponements so far in Book 1 which prevent our getting a grasp on this plot defines one of the three fundamental parameters within which Heliodoros is composing his novel: language, narrative sequence, and conventional romantic motifs. These three obstacles are paradoxically the three premises which the reader would bring to the text: that it makes sense in Greek, that it tells a story, that it is in the tradition of the romance. All of these turn out to be true, but only after Heliodoros has made us conscious that they are assumptions which we employ in making sense of the text.

(4) The conclusion of Book 1 is in a sense another postponement, and a drastic one. The death of the heroine is the end of her story, and cuts short the better part of our curiosity as to her identity and history. This is designed to shock (or, if we don't believe that she died, at least to make explicit) another one of our fundamental operational principles, namely, our identification with the fortunes of the protagonists. The mysterious emptiness of the conclusion to Book 1 is increased by its formal balance with the opening scene, which was designedly paradoxical and puzzling.

---

[23] γένος μέν ἐσμεν Ἴωνες, Ἐφεσίων δὲ τὰ πρῶτα γεγονότες ~ ἦν ἐν Ἐφέσῳ ἀνὴρ τῶν τὰ πρῶτα ἐκεῖ δυναμένων, Xen. Eph. 1. 1. 1; ὁλκὰς οὖν ἐπληροῦτο χρυσοῦ τε καὶ ἀργύρου καὶ ἐσθῆτων ~ ναῦς μεγάλη . . . πολλὴ μὲν ἐσθὴς καὶ ποικίλη, πολὺς δὲ ἄργυρος καὶ χρυσός, Xen. Eph. 1. 10. 4; γήρᾳ τε προηκόντων ~ ἐσχάτῳ γήρᾳ, Chariton, 3. 5. 4; the crowd of citizens is frequent throughout Xen. Eph. and Chariton; the storm at sea ~ Achilles Tatius 3. 1–3.

The same band of brigands are again looting and again bypassing Charikleia. The lighting has changed—from dawn to dusk—and the lovers have reversed roles, Theagenes from apparently dead to inactive, Charikleia from inactive to apparently dead. All this, however, is action without a narrative context within which it makes sense. If it makes sense at all, it does so as some kind of closure—death, sunset and captivity all promoting the sense of an ending. It is as if we had been reading a book rather casually while half our mind was engaged elsewhere and we suddenly realize that it is over before we know what is happening.

To summarize the argument so far: the three principles of Heliodoros' narrative technique are (1) the precise, often aporetic, measurement of degrees of incomplete cognition, (2) the insistence that every part of the text have a relevance to the whole, sometimes discovered after the fact; and (3) the suspension of attention by postponement of expected information, which occurs four times in Book 1, each time so arranged as to provoke the reader to a greater awareness of one of the conventions of reading fiction, which are (3a) an intelligible language, (3b) a sequential plot, (3c) familiar motifs, and (3d) identification with the heroes. Of these, (3b) receives very elaborate illustration in the long interpolated tale of Knemon, which has a complex relation of contrast and equivalence with Kalasiris' narrative and with the *Aithiopika* as a whole.

One answer to the question of what kind of meaning is to be found in the *Aithiopika* is—sentential. The three principles of narrative technique which we have isolated as significant in this novel are exactly the categories which guide our comprehension of any complex, periodic sentence. Heliodoros' sentences are often mobiles of intricately articulated and well-balanced cola, such as test and refine our powers of attention. A random example:

Πετόσιρις ἀδελφὸς ἦν αὐτῷ κατὰ τὴν Μέμφιν· οὗτος ἐπιβουλῇ τὴν ἱερωσύνην τῆς προφητείας παρὰ τὸ πάτριον τὸν Θύαμιν παρελόμενος νεώτερος αὐτὸς ὤν, τὸν προγενέστερον ἐξάρχειν ληστρικοῦ πυνθανόμενος, δεδιὼς μὴ καιροῦ λαβόμενος ἐπέλθοι ποτὲ ἢ καὶ χρόνος τὴν ἐπιβουλὴν φωράσειεν, ἅμα δὲ καὶ δι' ὑποψίας εἶναι παρὰ τοῖς πολλοῖς αἰσθανόμενος ὡς ἀνῃρηκὼς τὸν Θύαμιν οὐ φαινόμενον, χρήματα πάμπολλα καὶ βοσκήματα τοῖς ζῶντα προσκομίσασιν εἰς τὰς κώμας τὰς ληστρικὰς διαπέμπων ἐπεκήρυξεν. (I. 33. 2)

He had a younger brother, Petosiris, at Memphis, who had treacherously and in defiance of ancestral usage usurped the office of high priest from

Thyamis. Petosiris' inquiries had revealed to him that his elder brother was the leader of a band of outlaws, and he was afraid that Thyamis might one day seize an opportunity to take action against him; besides, he could see that he was generally suspected of having murdered the missing Thyamis. And so he had sent word round the bandit villages, offering cattle and large sums of money as a reward for anyone who brought his brother to him alive.

Simply to read such a sentence is already to employ the mind in making assessments of the relevance, subordination, and completeness of each phrase as it contributes to the intelligible unity of the whole. If the narrative structure of the *Aithiopika* be compared to a long sentence, Book 1 is like an introductory clause about whose meaning we must suspend judgment until much more of the sentence is uttered. Heliodoros has given his novel a narrative movement of discovered coherence analogous to that of reading any sentence.[24] The *Aithiopika* belongs to that class of literature which does not naively assume the conventions of some genre but pricks us to the highest awareness of literature as self-referential, as an act of language whose limits and whose accomplishments are those of language itself.[25] Heliodoros plays with the fundamental features of language so as to make us aware that literature is (among other things) a textual game, and is like a sentence in that within its structure our foreknowledge of admissible possibilities is being continually refined and particularized. This is the deepest sense in which the narrative technique of Heliodoros is one of

[24] It is interesting to see this critical insight expressed not only among the avant-garde ('. . . the fundamental premise that a homologous relation exists between the sentence and extended narrative discourse . . .', Barthes, (1966: 3)) but also in traditional philological journals: Mazal (1958: 116-31) speaks of the *Gestaltungs-wille* of an author being apparent not only in the overarching design of the work but in each well-constructed period.

[25] The accomplishments of language are catalogued by Plato at *Kratylos* 407e-408d, and it reads like a list of the major themes in the *Aithiopika*. Hermogenes, who is charged (like Kalasiris' Egyptian Homer) with being or not being a son of Hermes, asks the etymological riddle of the name of Hermes, to which Socrates in a series of puns replies that Hermes stands for translation, communication, theft, verbal deceit, and sharp business practices, in short all the functions of λόγος, and that Pan too is an emblem of language's essential duplicity in that he has two natures (διφυής)—smooth/hairy, divine/mortal, true/false. Language here means any system of signs which can be used to tell a lie; if something cannot be used to tell a lie, it cannot be used to tell the truth, it cannot in fact be used to tell at all.

Ironically, the Gymnosophists, who are forbidden to lie (10. 14. 1), dwell in the temple of Pan (10. 4. 1).

incomplete cognition: the passage to a solution that is *predictable within certain limits* is the same as the movement of any sentence from subject through dependent clauses to a concluding verb. So it is that in each of my own sentences the reader knows within ever tighter limits as the thought progresses what words can bring this sentence to a successful and meaningful

II. DUPLICITY, AMPHIBOLY, AND THE NEED FOR INTERPRETATION

In this section I will address the issue of Kalasiris' mendacity and morality, but the approach to that central topic will necessarily be gradual because the issues of interpretation are complex. This is the point—that interpretation itself is a complex and difficult process, and Heliodoros often describes the problems which characters have in interpreting what they see or read. He constructs several scenes as debates about the meaning of a dream or oracle and elsewhere exploits to great effect amphibolies (either/or's) which pose alternative explanations for a single event. It is by way of these interpretative scenes and amphibolies that we will set up the terms to make plausible the claim that Kalasiris' duplicity is morally good.

I begin with Charikleia's dream of losing her right eye (2. 16), which most commentators have thought is an otiose premonition of danger, one which has either no fulfillment or a trivial one.[26] However, as we have seen, loose ends and irrelevancies are fundamentally antithetical to Heliodoros' technique. Charikleia's mysterious dream is unsolved at the time, but it points forward to a significant turn in the plot, namely, the death of the narrator, Kalasiris.

Asleep in the treasure cave, Charikleia sees a violent man approach her with a sword and cut out her right eye (2. 16). She wakes with a scream; her first response is to feel her face and realize that the dream was not literally true. Her next thought is the wish that it had been literally true (ὕπαρ) rather than symbolically true (ὄναρ), 'for I greatly fear that this dream points to you (Theagenes) whom I regard as my eye, my soul, my all' (2. 16).

---

[26] No meaning: Goethals (1959: 187f.), Morgan (1978: 228), 'a red herring'. Trivial: Kerényi (1927/1962: 51-3), Weinstock (1934: 46) both take the dream to refer to the next day's capture of the pair and their separation.

Knemon quiets that romantic alarm by providing an alternative explanation: since eyes refer to parents, loss to death, and the right side to males, the total dream must mean that Charikleia's father will die.[27] But since neither Theagenes nor the king of Aithiopia dies, and the dream is not mentioned again in the novel, critics have concluded that the episode is a meaningless scare.

There is however a solution to the dream, one which is clearly marked by every sign *except* a tediously explicit 'So *this* was the meaning of that dream in the cave!' Charikleia has many 'fathers' in this novel: an Ephesian aristocrat, according to her early lie (1. 22); Charikles, 'her supposed father' (ὁ νομιζόμενος πατήρ, 3. 6. 1, 4. 11. 2); Hydaspes, her natural father; and the man who is most often called her father during the course of this novel, Kalasiris. Of these the only one who dies is Kalasiris, and it is his death which her dream foretells. The evidence for this is extensive and I will cite only a few of the key passages in which the equation is established. Kalasiris is introduced to us as a father bereft of his children (2. 22. 4); these children are identified as Charikleia and Theagenes (2. 23. 1–2); it comes as a surprise that the two children whom Kalasiris mentions at 2. 24. 6 are Thyamis and Petosiris rather than Charikleia and Theagenes. Throughout their adventures Kalasiris acts as and is regarded as their father.[28] When he dies the relationship is dwelt on at length, the word 'father' being repeated again and again.

The sacristan consoles them, 'However, you may be pardoned, since you have been bereft, as you say, of your father, your protector and your only hope' (7. 11), Kybele similarly speaks to them of Kalasiris 'who had been in the place of a father to you' (ἐν πατρὸς ὑμῖν χώρᾳ γεγονώς, 7. 12). Theagenes emphasizes the reality of the relationship when he says, 'We have lost not only our natural parents but Kalasiris, our reputed *and actual* father' (τὸν δοκοῦντα καὶ ὄντα πατέρα μετὰ τῶν ἄλλων προσαπολωλεκότες, 7. 13). Left alone Charikleia and Theagenes lament their new

---

[27] This is standard oneirocritical symbolism, found for instance in Artemidoros' *Dream Analysis* 1. 26. In the same chapter Artemidoros discusses dreams of blindness as signifying that travellers will not return to their homeland (33. 5 f. Pack).

[28] He cares for Theagenes as for a child (ἅτε μοι λοιπὸν ὡς παιδὸς ὑπερφροντίζειν προῃρημένος, 4. 3. 4) and takes the place of Charikles as Charikleia's guardian and father (οὐχὶ πατήρ εἰμί σοι . . . ; 4. 5. 7, σῷζε πατέρ, 4. 18. 1). The characters they meet on their journey all regard Kalasiris as the lovers' father (e.g. 5. 20. 2, 26. 3 f., 28. 1; 5. 15. 1, which is evidently the background to the mention of information withheld at 5. 16. 5). Details on this and other verbal questions may now be explored much more conveniently by using Thesaurus Linguae Graecae (1979).

misfortunes and the loss of Kalasiris their father, emphasizing the word (τὸ γὰρ χρηστότατον ὄνομα καλεῖν ἀπεστέρημαι πατέρα, τοῦ δαίμονος πανταχόθεν μοι τὴν τοῦ πατρὸς προσηγορίαν περικόψαι φιλονεικήσαντος, 'No more may I call anyone Father, the best of names, for heaven has made it its sport at every turn to deny me the right to address anyone as my father', 7. 14). Then Charikleia lists all three of her 'fathers'—Hydaspes, τὸν μὲν φύσει γεννήσαντα οὐκ ἔγνωκα ('My natural father I have never seen'), Charikles, τὸν δὲ θέμενον Χαρικλέα, οἴμοι, προδέδωκα ('my adoptive father, Charikles, alas, I have betrayed'), and finally Kalasiris, τὸν δὲ διαδεξάμενον καὶ τρέφοντα καὶ περισῴζοντα ἀπολώλεκα ('I have lost the man who took me into his care, cherished me, and saved my life') whom she asserts she will call 'father' even against the will of fate, ἀλλ' ἰδού σοι, τροφεῦ καὶ σῶτερ, προσθήσω δὲ καὶ πάτερ, κἂν ὁ δαίμων μὴ βούληται ('But come now, my guardian and saviour—and I shall add the name of Father even though heaven denies it me'), 7. 14.

As if these indications of the dream's fulfillment were not enough, Heliodoros adds a few references to blindness (7. 12. 2) and to impaired sight (7. 14. 3).

To understand the deeper significance of Charikleia's dream and its fulfillment we must remind ourselves how important a fact it was for a maiden to have a father. In the course of her life Charikleia, like every maiden, was socially defined by reference to a male protector: Sisimithres (from her birth to the age of seven), Charikles (from seven to sixteen), and Kalasiris (her seventeenth year).[29] This group of protecting men, her *kyrioi*, occupy in turn that necessary role of maiden's sponsor and safeguard which would ordinarily be exercised by her natural father.[30] With the

[29] Our society has lost now a good deal of that extraordinary pressure which once dictated an unmarried woman's total symbolic dependence on a male figure, whether a father or some other man *in loco patris*. Charikleia, for instance, is represented as deeply reluctant to speak in the presence of a group of strange men (1. 21. 3). The less insightful characters all assume that this is a valuable social practice (e.g., Knemon at 6. 7. 7). But the logical outcome of such protective practices is spiritual annihilation of the protected, a sort of foot-binding of the free will, and in the case of choosing a husband (a father's right, as Charikles and Hydaspes think) what feels to Charikleia like rape. See further the end of section II, pp. 323f., 328f.

[30] In a sense the whole novel is built around the birth rite whereby a mother presents her newborn child to its father for approval and recognition. Because Persinna hesitated at that moment, out of fear that she would be considered adulterous and her child killed or dishonored, a series of intermediaries—foster-fathers—is required to conduct Charikleia away from Aithiopia to Greece and then in the fullness of time back again to the motherland (ἡ ἐνεγκοῦσα, as Heliodoros so often and strikingly calls it), so that she may be recognized by her father as his

death of Kalasiris she has lost not merely one of her fathers but any father at all; heretofore she had merely changed fathers, one taking up where his predecessor left off. When no other protecting father immediately replaces Kalasiris in Charikleia's life, her dream has very significantly been fulfilled.

Consider next Thyamis' dream (1. 18), which is also debated immediately on waking. He sees in his dream the temple of Isis at Memphis, altars streaming with blood and crowds clamoring in the porches, and the goddess herself presents Charikleia to him with the words 'You will have her and not have her; you will do her wrong and you will slay the foreign woman but she will not be slain.' Thyamis ponders the text and image, turning them one way and another to grasp at their significance. Eventually he decides that the goddess' sentence must be interpreted as both elliptical and metaphorical: he supplements the first part ('You will have her *as a wife* and you will no longer have her *as a maiden*') and understands 'slaying' as a metaphor for sexual penetration, a 'wound' from which she will not die.

His dream however has a true fulfillment which is different from the interpretation he reached. At the end of Book 1 Thyamis is surrounded by flowing blood and corpses in flickering light and recognizes the scene from his last night's dream. He then makes up his mind that no one else will have Charikleia and rushes off to the underground cave where she has been placed and there kills a woman in the dark. His dream-oracle turns out to have that Delphic quality of not only eluding interpretation but actually inducing the horror it hints at. The horror in this case is an illusion (he kills the maid Thisbe, not the heroine Charikleia), and this illusion is the real fulfillment of the prophecy: 'You will do her (Charikleia) wrong (by intending to kill her), and you will slay the foreign woman (Thisbe) and she (Charikleia) will not be slain.'

Now Heliodoros quite carefully notes Thyamis' inadequacy in producing a satisfactory meaning for the dream: 'Tiring at length of this (perplexity and interpretive effort), he forced the solution to suit his own wish . . . This was the sense in which he construed

new-born child, and at the same time as a newly-wed wife and a newly-installed priestess. Interestingly, these three foster-fathers are themselves chaste priests, two are widowers and well on in years, one is young and celibate, and this gives them a certain absolution from sexual suspicion which as unrelated men they would certainly have come under—at least this is Heliodoros' point of view, 4. 18. 4 f., 5. 4. 5. Kalasiris in particular is quite maternal, like a mother bird at 2. 22. 4.

his dream, according to the exegesis of his own desire.' (ἤδη δὲ ἀπειρηκὼς ἕλκει πρὸς τὴν ἑαυτοῦ βούλησιν τὴν ἐπίλυσιν. ... τὸ μὲν ὄναρ τοῦτον ἔφραζε τὸν τρόπον, οὕτως αὐτῷ τῆς ἐπιθυμίας ἐξηγουμένης, 1. 18.) Thyamis' exegetical shortcomings are serious; he does violence to the text (ἕλκει), he lets his need and desire for a particular meaning project that meaning onto the dream, and above all lacks the patient attentiveness and the ability to suspend the demand for immediate completion which every reader of a long and sophisticated novel must have.

A similar remark on inadequate exegesis is made by Kalasiris at the end of Book 2:

When the god had thus pronounced his oracle, a deep perplexity possessed the company gathered there, who were at a loss to construe what was the meaning of it. Each of them strained (ἔσπα) the message to a different sense, making some conjecture to suit his own will; but none at that time could apprehend the truth of it, for oracles and dreams in general are decided (interpreted, κρίνονται) by their outcomes. And besides, the Delphians were in a flutter of excitement to see the procession, which had been magnificently equipped, and they would not trouble themselves to search out the exact meaning of the oracle (πρὸς τὸ ἀκριβὲς ἀνιχνεύειν). (2. 36)[31]

The Greek allows a pun to connect 'meaning' and 'desire': the people are unable to explain what the oracle *means* (ὅ τι βούλοιτο), so they force it in various directions according to individual *will* (ὡς ἕκαστος εἶχε βουλήσεως).[32]

Why does Heliodoros pay attention to various kinds of misinterpretation, failed communication, and especially the role of private desire in forcing a text to mean what the interpreter wants rather than what it wants? The answer is that the originating event, Charikleia's conception and birth, is a marvel which cannot adequately and plausibly be conveyed in ordinary terms. Hence it

---

[31] 'Following the tracks of accuracy' is one of Heliodoros' best metaphors for thinking carefully and drawing conclusions from the signs and tokens which the truth leaves in its trail: he uses it to describe Hydaspes' missing the point (10. 33. 1), and plays with the idea in a misreading of Homer concerning the traces left by the feet and shins of the gods: the real oddity of that Homeric passage is not the pretended ambiguity of ῥεῖ' but rather the sense in which shins (κνημάων) can be said to leave tracks. I suspect that a pun is intended on the name of Knemon, who is supposedly being taught to read such traces more accurately and 'from a more mystical point of view' (3. 13. 1).

[32] This ordinary Greek idiom expresses the intentionality of a speaker aiming at an idea, trying to communicate a thought, as in our expression 'I mean to say'.

requires a web of international intrigue, multiple agents with cross-purposes shuttling back and forth over several countries for seventeen years, to create at last a context in which the king of Aithiopia (and his people) can accept with full understanding the sentence that Persinna wanted to say to him at the moment of Charikleia's birth, 'This child, though white, is your daughter.' Charikleia herself is the message or communication of the queen to the king, at the time a failed communication,[33] wrapped in her own story and sent away as a challenge to the higher powers to make the child's birth believable. The problem posed by Persinna to the higher divinities (and to Heliodoros) is whether they can construct a plot which will satisfyingly lead a sophisticated reader of normal resistance to take a profound enjoyment in an incredible romance. As Persinna puts it in her embroidered message, 'for no one would believe me if I told them this extraordinary turn of events' (οὐ γὰρ πιστεύσειν οὐδένα λεγούσῃ τὴν περιπέτειαν, 4. 8).[34]

The deepest anxiety which informs this novel is the fear of *misinterpretation*. Persinna's case is exemplary and of course central. The entire revelation of Charikleia's conception is a story of acts of knowledge which are at the same time acts of desire, culminating in a decision to postpone uttering a simple but astonishing sentence and to commit the child and the thought instead to writing. Charikleia's conception began with Hydaspes' dream (ὄναρ), which commands him to have sex with his wife while they are taking a noon-day rest. It is a full ten years since Hydaspes first knew (ἐγνώρισεν) Persinna as wife. At the moment of climax Persinna instantly perceives that she is pregnant (ᾐσθόμην τε παραχρῆμα κυοφορήσασα τὴν καταβολήν). When Charikleia is born white Persinna understands the cause (τὴν αἰτίαν ἐγνώριζον) but feels equally sure that she will not be understood and so consigns her daughter/message to fine needlepoint, hoping that the ministering letters will not remain mute and unread/unfulfilled (τὸ γράμμα διάκονον . . . τάχα μὲν κωφὰ καὶ ἀνήνυτα). Fear of misinterpretation is Persinna's motive for withholding her daughter/knowledge from Hydaspes and for launching her child/text rather into the uncer-

---

[33] When Sisimithres passes Charikleia on into the protection of Charikles he is prevented from completing the account of her birth (2. 31. 5), an interruption which reproduces the relation of Persinna to Hydaspes.

[34] Heliodoros seems to know his Aristotelian poetics, as noted by Kerényi (1927/1962: 22) and Heiserman (1977: 197f.) Heiserman's chapter on Heliodoros is excellent.

tain world of coincidence and happenstance where ignorance and ambiguity are the rule (τὸ γὰρ ἄδηλον τῆς τύχης ἀνθρώποις ἄγνω-στον, 4. 8).

This tale of desire, knowledge, and fear of misinterpretation lies hidden for seventeen years until at last Charikleia is recognized and her swathe read by the first person crafty and knowing enough to do so—Kalasiris. The success of Charikleia's return to her beginning and of the novel to its end depends on maintaining a level of intelligence equal to Kalasiris', particularly in the ability to recognize what is missing, to wait for what could complete an incompletely understood oracle or dream or event. Therefore Heliodoros deliberately presents characters like Thyamis who are significantly unable to comprehend such messages, whose desire in one fashion or another intervenes as exegete of the text. Poised somewhere between the perfect interpreter (Kalasiris) and the inadequate interpreter (Thyamis, the Delphians, *et alii*) stands the actual reader, who must be taught how to read the *Aithiopika*.

As a recurrent reminder of the difficulty of reading and interpreting any signs, be they oracles, events, or letters on a page, Heliodoros inserts explicit questions about the ambiguous nature of various events. The first of these amphibolies occurs just at the moment of Thyamis' dream:

Meanwhile Thyamis (for so was the captain of the thieves called), having slept soundly the greatest part of the night, was waked of a sudden by an odd sort of dream, that employed his thoughts some hours in considering its solution. For about the time that cocks begin to crow (whatever the cause of that act may be, whether—as some say—the bird by natural perception of the sun's return is moved to proclaim the god's welcome to our hemisphere, or whether, because of the day's warmth and an eager desire to feed and be officious, he cries aloud a message peculiar to himself, to rouse his fellow domestics for work), I say about the time of cockcrowing the captain had from the gods a vision of this nature. . . . (1. 18)

The contrasting explanations are roughly those of spiritual providence and material desire. Cock-crowing is in either case a meaningful song, but it makes a great difference whether the message be interpreted as a religious hymn to the sunrise or as a command to eat and work.[35] The occurrence side by side of this

---

[35] The cock is an appropriate token of the amphiboly which Heliodoros will so often exploit between natural and supernatural explanations, for on the naturalistic side its crowing at sunrise was traditionally and commonsensically said to be the

amphiboly and Thyamis' effort to interpret his dream, both raising an opposition between impatient mortal desire (ἐπιθυμίας, 1. 18. 3, 19. 1) and divinely providential meaning, must be ascribed to the author's πρόνοια and not to τύχη.

The same is true of the amphibolous interpretation provided for Kalasiris' death:

He laid himself down to sleep, and—whether it was that through the greatness of his joy his pores of respiration were excessively stretched and slackened and so his aged body of a sudden was unstrung, or that in fact (εἴτε καί) the gods granted this as a thing he asked for—at the crowing of the cocks he was known to be dead. (7. 11. 4)

This ambiguity is couched in the same general terms as that preceding Thyamis' dream—material causes or providential explanation. Both Charikleia's dream and Thyamis' are placed early in the novel as prominent examples of the kind of image or text which is incomplete and requires interpretation. Thyamis' dream, forcefully and passionately misconstrued by him, soon finds its real meaning. Charikleia's, however, is drastically postponed. When its solution does occur the scene is marked as a companion to Thyamis' dream: the temple of Isis at Memphis, clamoring crowds and torchlight, cock-crows—these are the contents and circumstance of Thyamis' dream and they are the very scene of Kalasiris' death.

I take the narrator's digression on cock-crowing to be significantly placed, but how shall we describe its effect? Does it suggest that there is a philosophical or religious underpinning to the melodrama? And—a far more important question—if there be such an ideological framework is it philosophically or religiously *meant*? A good approach to these questions, which will lead on to Kalasiris' duplicity, is to consider the amphibolies which Heliodoros has scattered through the *Aithiopika*. To anticipate the results of that survey, the answer I would give to the former question is that in the *Aithiopika* the only theology to be found is a vague and shifting set of contrasts between provident/malevolent or provident/indifferent. The answer to the latter is that these references are not meant philosophically or religiously but rather as reflexive allusions

---

effect of warmth and dryness (Theophrastos, *ap*. Ailian *NA* 3. 38) and on the supernatural side its foreknowledge of the sun's rise made it (to believers) not only Helios' special creature (Proklos, περὶ ἀγωγῆς ed. Kroll, quoted by Hopfner in *RE* Suppl. 4 (1924: 14) but a living ouija board—a grain of corn was laid on each letter of the alphabet in the sand and a cock allowed to peck at will (Riess, *RE* I (1894: 1363).

to the novel's own structure of progressive and problematic intelligibility.

The eighteen amphibolies in the novel, which I will label by the
letters (a) through (r), fall into four groups. The first group contains those which leave the question open or (more often) seem to
weight the scales in favor of the more supernatural alternative, by
placing it second and adding an intensive καί. I have already
quoted (a) the cock-crow at Thyamis' dream (1. 18), and (b) the
death of Kalasiris (7. 11. 4). (c) Theagenes decides to try to stop a
runaway bull, 'whether moved by his own masculine spirit or in
fact (εἴτε καί) by an impulse from some one of the gods' (10. 28.
4). (d) At Charikleia's arraignment for murder a maid cries out that
she is innocent, 'whether she felt a pang of kindness towards
Charikleia bred of their companionship and shared routine or in
fact (εἴτε καί) it was the will of heaven' (8. 9. 2). (e) Thermouthis
dies in his sleep—'by the bite of an asp, possibly by the will of fate'
(2. 20. 2). (f) Hydaspes regards Charikleia either as possessed by
some god or simply out of her wits through excess of joy (10. 22.
4, similar to the effects of excessive joy on Kalasiris, 7. 11. 4, and
also on the Aithiopian populace, 10. 39. 1). (g) At twilight the sea
grew suddenly rough, 'possibly it took this turn from the time of
day, or perhaps in fact (τάχα δέ που καί) it was transformed by the
will of some Tyche' (5. 27. 1). (h) The wind dies down, 'as though
it were setting with the sun, or to speak more truly were bent on
serving the purposes of our pursuers' (5. 23. 2). These elegant
touches of uncertainty put the narrator at an enigmatic distance.
We might translate their force into the clichés of popular, intrusive
narrative style as follows: 'But what guiding hand was at work in
these events, dear Reader? Is Charikleia a plaything of sportive
fortune, or merely a mortal body in a world of natural law, or is
she in fact a favored child of providence? Read on!'

Charikleia and Theagenes themselves spend a good deal of time putting
this very question to themselves, most extensively at 7. 10f. Theagenes
assumes that providence has just done them a good turn, but Charikleia
(who is as usual—ἔστι γὰρ χρῆμα σοφώτατον, 5. 26. 2—more clever
than her lover) tries to keep an open mind (ἀμφιβάλλειν 7. 10. 2): either
the gods favor them, as the recent rescue might show, or the gods hate
them, as their persistent run of bad luck indicates, or possibly (putting
those two points of view together) god is a professional magician per-
forming impossible feats with their lives. This last possibility is both

blasphemous (says Theagenes immediately, 8. 11. 1) and true (compare
θαυματοποιία τίς ἐστι δαίμονος 'the divinity's way of working miracles',
8. 10. 2, with αἰσθανώμεθα τοῦ θείου θαυματουργήματος, 10. 39. 3).
Depending on one's views of discipline and love one might place 4. 1. 2
either with this group of amphibolies or the next.

   The second group of interpretive dilemmas contains those which
are so phrased as to suggest that a providential explanation is
unlikely or even foolish. (i) Two very long and complex physical
explanations are given of why the dike around Syene collapsed,
followed by the laconic 'or one might attribute the deed to divine
assistance' (9. 8. 2). (j) After explaining that Homer kept his native
land a secret out of shame at his exile and rejection from the priesthood, Kalasiris adds, 'or else it was a clever trick whereby Homer
in concealing his real country might woo every city to take him as
their own' (3. 14. 4).[36] (k) A similarly cynical note is struck in the
double explanation of the name Hypata: 'a metropolis with a
glorious name—as the citizens themselves would have it—derived
from its ruling and being exalted (ὑπατεύειν) over the rest, but as
others think from its mere (περ) position at the base of Mt Oita (ὑπὸ
τῇ Οἴτῃ)' (2. 34. 2). Like Thyamis, the Hypatans interpret an
ambiguous (and minimal) text in a sense favorable to their
interests, and Kalasiris (who relates this) implies that they are
deceiving themselves, that they are precisely reading an exalted
meaning into an ordinary word with a plain physical meaning.[37]

[36] This motif is also employed at 2. 34. 5, where Charikles explains the claim of
Theagenes to be a descendant of Achilles. Other tribes than the Ainianes falsely
claimed Achilles as their ancestor to add his glory to themselves. The connection of
this passage with the Hermetic Homer story is very close: Homer is here first called
Egyptian, and the claim of Theagenes involves a quibble on the Homeric text
(similar to 3. 13. 3) as to the meaning of Phthia then and now. Notice how
Heliodoros is not content simply to make Theagenes a Phthian and so justify his
descent from Achilles without any further ado but makes an issue of it, basing
romantic heroism (Theagenes looks Achillean, 2. 34. 4) on a scholarly dubiety. The
claim's thematic connection with the Homer joke at 3. 14. 4 and proximity to the
Hypatans' equally dubious (and cynically treated) claim to interpret the name of
their own city (see the next amphiboly) casts the whole Achilles comparison in a
profound shadow of skepticism; the rite too of Neoptolemos, which is what formally
brings the lovers into first contact, then takes on a certain High Anglican quality
of protested antiquity. Some of Heliodoros' characters seem to have that viewpoint
which W. Levitan describes, in a brilliant article (1979), as 'the sensibility of the
near miss'.
[37] The brigands have the same sensitivity to nice points of usage which may
affect their honor and self-esteem: Thyamis summons his men to divide the booty,
'which he called by the more dignified name "spoils of war"' (λάφυρα τὰ σκῦλα

This amphiboly comes just before the Delphians' significant non-comprehension of the oracle at 2. 36. (1) Most cynical of all are Heliodoros' alternatives for Thyamis' attempted murder of Charikleia in the treasure-cave. Heliodoros remarks that barbarians in desperate straits always kill their beloved ones 'either falsely believing (ἀπατώμενον) that they will rejoin their loved ones after death, or wishing to rescue them from an enemy's violence' (1. 30. 6). The supernatural motive is expressly labelled an empty hope and those who act on it are deceived. The hint here of a metaphysical opinion—denial of personal survival after death—is the opposite of the implication at 3. 5. 4-5 where Charikleia and Theagenes fall in love at first glance, in such a way as to

confirm belief in the soul's divinity and its kinship with the powers on high. For at the moment of meeting the young pair looked and loved, as though the soul of each at the first encounter recognized its fellow and leaped towards that which deserved to belong to it . . . as if they had had some previous knowledge or sight which they were recalling to memory.

The hint of Platonic *anamnesis* is muted but unmistakable. The specific contrast of these two passages simply brings into sharper focus the general problem of a text which alternately raises and twits our hopes that a superstructure of providence—Someone up there who likes Charikleia—will be meaningful in this book.[38]

(m) The positive and negative terminals of this alternating current are nearly brought into contact during the description of the siege of Syene. Egyptian theology with its deification of the Nile is outlined in two passages (9. 9 and 22). The former passage contains its own ambiguities (several levels of esoteric and mystical meaning involving physics, mythology, and Deeper Significance) but seems at the time to be treated seriously. At least the narrator refuses out of holy reverence to dwell on the mysteries any further (9. 10. 1). The subject is resumed at 9. 22 where the priests of Syene show Hydaspes the Nilometer and explain the numerological equation of the Nile with the year. Hydaspes' reply is fairly

σεμνότερον ὀνομάζων, 1. 19. 1), in the very sentence which describes how he construed his dream to fit his own desire.

[38] The theology of the *Aithiopika* is not a coherent system, as J. Morgan has shown (APA panel on the novels as *Mysterientexte*, Vancouver 1978). The same could be done for Heliodoros' references to an afterlife, which are strictly designed to fit the occasion (in addition to those cited in the text see 2. 24. 6, 7. 11. 9, 8. 11. 10).

terse, reminding them that all they have said of the Nile's favor to
them applies first to the Aithiopians, and he refers to the Nile as
'this river, or god according to you'. This flippant dismissal is
another example of the cynical bent which Heliodoros gives to *some*
of his alternatives, and so flatly contradicts his 'own' attitude at 9.
10. 1 ('Thus far may our account of this matter meet with divine
approval; but the deeper secrets of the mysteries must be paid the
respect of strict silence') that we must ask whether the author has
failed to make a connection or have we.

The answer, I will argue, is that both groups of alternatives—
those weighted toward the supernatural and those weighted
toward the natural—are meaningful and have complementary
functions in the context of a melodramatic narrative whose
characteristic feature is the alternation between hope and despair.
When the narrator pauses to reflect on the significance of an event,
on the larger interpretative scheme within which it will make
sense, he poses both an optimistic view and a pessimistic view,
inclining now to one, now to the other. That the real meaning of
these ambiguous alternatives is to express the nature of the novel
itself as melodrama is supported by two further groups of such
amphibolies which pertain to aesthetics and to Kalasiris.

Three amphibolies are employed to celebrate what we might call
an aesthetic of Mind-Boggling Variety. (n) At 7. 6. 4 'whatever
divinity or whatever tyche oversees human affairs' is invoked as
responsible for the stage-entrance of Kalasiris into an already
complex tableau. This entire scene (7. 6–8) is a culminating show-
piece of conflicting emotions, of pain and joy, concluding with the
death of Kalasiris. (o) Knemon overhears the voice of a woman
who identifies herself as Thisbe, his dead mistress (5. 3–4). As the
cocks crow, he stumbles to his room and swoons. Heliodoros then
remarks on the two explanations of Knemon's situation: some
divinity makes jest and sport of human affairs, mingling pain into
what ere long will bring us joy, or else it is simply a fact of human
nature itself that joy in its purity cannot be experienced. Reflections
such as these on the crazy-quilt of Life and whether a friendly
designer or a brute force is behind it have the value of self-
advertizements for the author, since the novelist will be most
successful on his own terms if we regard his story as one of
impossible odds and plausible resolutions, that is, an elegant mediation between the hopelessness of a world governed by malevolent

or indifferent tyche and the confidence of a world mysteriously orchestrated by providence.

(p) At the close of the novel (10. 38. 3-4) the entire Aithiopian audience applaud the dénouement, even though it has been conducted in a language foreign to them, namely Greek: 'The spoken words, on the whole, they could not comprehend, but they conjectured the facts from what had previously transpired concerning Charikleia; or else it might be that they were led to surmise the truth by the influence of some divine power that had designed the whole of this dramatic scene, and by whose means extreme contraries were now composed into a harmony, etc.' This final amphiboly in the *Aithiopika* is about how to explain the audience's appreciation of a scene they ought not to be able to understand. It corresponds to the opening scene of failed communication between the black brigands and the white maiden.

The double explanation offered for the Aithiopians' transcendence of the language barrier is very ironic—either they guessed the right answer correctly and *en masse* by a natural process of the mind, or they were enlightened by God the Author of this novel. In either case what is being explained is the Aithiopians' role as audience to a Romance, and that from a cognitive point of view. The central aesthetic structure is described as a hard-won balance between centrifugal Variety and centripetal Unity: '. . . by whose means extreme contraries were now composed into a harmony. Joy and grief were intertwined, tears were mingled with laughter, and the most baleful proceedings were converted into festivity' (10. 38. 4). This is the same response which Kalasiris feels when he reads Persinna's embroidered message, a mini-novel. I have explained above how that message is a tale of partial recognitions and incomplete communication; the capstone of that series is the reader's (Kalasiris') understanding and recognition of its meaning: 'When I had read these words, Knemon, I recognized (ὡς ἀνέγνων ἐγνώριζον) and admired the wise dispensation of the gods. Filled with mingled feelings of pleasure and pain, I went through the singular experience of weeping and rejoicing at the same moment' (4. 9. 1). The singular experience of this novel for us is its analysis, through romance-readers like Kalasiris, of comprehending a romance. Heliodoros' sophistication lies not merely in his mastery as a narrator but in his presentation of narrators and audiences caught in the fact of understanding or missing the romantic pattern.

This third group of amphibolies, centering on the aesthetics of the romance, explains the underlying compatibility of the first two groups—the sublime and the cynical. Our epistemological progress through the labyrinthine ways of this plot takes us along stretches where the light at the end of the tunnel disappears and then again glimmers closer than we thought. By reminding us both of providential and of naturalistic hypotheses, Heliodoros keeps alive the questions of how and on what terms the plot will resolve itself. Particularly effective are the *detailed material explanations* of what in other romances might be simple miracles or wondrous but unexplained coincidences. The very suggestion that the protagonists' escapes and successes may be the result not of divine protection but of the laws of physical nature—analyzed in close detail in a few instances—calls into question the naive but fundamental pretense which is the presupposition of the other novels, namely, that an identifiable god has inaugurated and throughout controls the varying fortunes of the protagonists. The *Aithiopika* is a palimpsest, written on the tablet of naive romance, and one of its fascinating reinterpretations of the underlying conventions is the tentative exploration of a naturalistic explanation of the romantic plot. Heliodoros has raised the question of supernatural control and, like a devil's advocate, has provided counter-evidence against such a belief by interpreting various events in terms of physical law or naturalistic psychology.

The most extended example of such naturalism is found in the fourth group of amphibolies, those uttered by Kalasiris. (q) When Charikles asks Kalasiris to diagnose his daughter's indisposition, which Kalasiris has just vividly described to Knemon and us as Love-at-first-sight, he replies that it must be the evil eye. Charikles tries to reject this as popular superstition, and Kalasiris launches into a quite long scientific analysis of the evil-eye phenomenon in the human and animal realms (3. 7–8). His explanation combines physics and psychology, pores and passions, in a display piece of anti-romantic analysis.[39] Kalasiris then is the spokesperson for both views—the lovers' souls share in the divine nature at the moment of mutual recognition *or* Charikleia's orifices were infiltrated by an effluence which popular lore calls the evil eye. Both views make sense in their respective contexts, the romantic extravaganza for

---

[39] Ironically Kalasiris adduces love-at-first-sight as an analogy to confirm his hypothesis of the evil eye.

the sentimental Knemon, the learned disquisition for the father to be fooled. Kalasiris quite naturally adopts both tones which Heliodoros employs in his other amphibolies, the sublime and the naturalistic. What ought to be a contradiction on the level of serious ideology is perfectly normal practice for a narrator: Kalasiris is simply the best single representative of the mind of the author himself.

(r) Kalasiris, at the point in his narrative when Theagenes comes to consult him as a love-magician (3. 16), expounds to Knemon the true meaning of Egyptian lore. It is a double knowledge, or rather two quite different cognitive practices which have the same name— a legitimate astral foreknowledge of things to come, which is beneficial to mankind and a prerogative of the priestly class, and a bastard sciolism which confusedly and ineffectually tries to raise spirits of the dead and use herbs and spells as love-magic. Of the several contrasts drawn between the two knowledges—aristocratic/ plebeian, celestial/earthly, male/female, divine/pseudo-demonic— the most important for our analysis is that of pander to unbridled pleasure (ἡδονῶν ἀκολάστων ὑπηρέτις) vs unworldly mystic, for Theagenes and Charikles consult him as if he were the former and he accommodates his outward behavior to their expectations.

Kalasiris' explanation of the two cognitive systems which pass under the same name of 'Egyptian wisdom' (ἡ Αἰγυπτίων σοφία) is in effect a presentation of two views or interpretations of his own activity at Delphi covering Books 2. 24 through 4. 21 (recurring at 10. 36. 4). Heliodoros traces the precise path of misconception: 'When Theagenes heard mention of "Egyptian" and "prophet", he was at once filled with delight . . .' (3. 11. 3); 'I surmised that, having heard at the banquet that I was an Egyptian and a prophet, he had come to obtain my assistance in his love-affair' (3. 16. 2). If Theagenes or Charikles had been as crafty about the exact meaning and implication of words as Heliodoros (mainly through Kalasiris) is teaching us to be, they would not have leaped to the conclusion that 'Egyptian prophet' means 'erotic pharmacologist'. As it is, both approach him with a *preconception* of his role and express to him their desire that he make Charikleia fall in love (Charikles: καὶ γάρ σε καὶ διά τι χρήσιμον ἐμὸν ἀκροατὴν γενέσθαι τῶν συμβεβηκότων πάλαι ἐβουλόμην, 'Actually for some time I have wanted to tell you the story of my past, because I think you may be able to help me', 2. 29. 2; πρὸς ταῦτα δὴ σὲ βοηθὸν ἐπικαλοῦμαι.

. . . σοφίαν τινὰ καὶ ἴυγγα κίνησον ἐπ᾽ αὐτὴν Αἰγυπτίαν, 'This is the
problem on which I am seeking your advice . . . Use your magic
and cast an Egyptian spell on her', 2. 33. 6; οἶσθα ὡς ἐπὶ τοῦτό σε
καὶ παρεκάλεσα, 'You know that it was to achieve precisely that
that I enlisted your aid', 3. 9; veiled at 3. 19. 3 and 4. 6. 2;
Theagenes: συνεργὸν πρὸς τὸν ἔρωτα ληψόμενος, 'he had come to
enlist my help with his love', 3. 16. 2; οὐκ ἐσφαλμένος . . . ὧν
προσεδόκησε, 'his hopes . . . had not been disappointed', 3. 17. 3).

Kalasiris' role throughout is not that of meddler or manipulator
but of observer, waiting for his partial knowledge to be completed
in the gods' own good time. The gods make various things fall into
Kalasiris' hands: 'I was glad that the young man was at my door
and bade him enter, with the thought that a beginning for my
plans in hand was presenting itself to me of its own accord
(ταὐτόματον),' 3. 16. 2; 'I was making my way towards the
temple of Apollo, intending to entreat the god for an oracle to guide
my escape with the young couple. But in truth divinity is sharper
than any mind and comes to the aid, all unbidden, of those who
are acting according to his will, often anticipating a request of his
own benevolence,' 4. 16. 2-3. Kalasiris sums up his approach
when he finally reveals his mind to Charikleia: 'for a long time
now, as you know, I have been dwelling here, and from the beginning paying all proper attention to you, keeping the facts silent,
waiting to seize the right moment . . . ,' 4. 13. 1. If we read the
whole of Kalasiris' narrative, the general impression is that of a
shrewd but very passive observer, one who knows a good deal
more than those he is watching and who uses opportunities that
are presented to him, but not one who *makes* things happen. One
of the opportunities thrust on him is the pressing requests of
Charikles to arouse his daughter's dormant sexuality and when she
is sick to cure her. (These two requests are nearly the same thing
for Charikles: 'May Charikleia too feel one day a lover's longing!
Then I should be satisfied that she was in good health and not sick'
3. 9.) In all the scenes where Kalasiris describes how he complied
with these requests there is a clear consciousness of playing not
just *a* role but *their* role, living up to their presuppositions about
his knowledge and power, and an equally clear sense that behind
his masked performance the integrity of his knowledge and purpose
is intact. In the play-acting scenes of witchcraft (3. 17. 1, 18. 3;
4. 5. 2-4, 6. 3-5, 7. 1-2, 7. 12-13, 10. 1-12. 1, 14. 1, 15. 2-3)

Kalasiris is improvising with the material which the gods have put in his way, quite uncertain of how it will turn out, waiting for the kairotic moment when knowledge will be fully clear and action appropriate. 'I realized then that it was the right time (καιρόν) to play the magician for him and to seem to divine what I already knew' 3. 17. 1.

> When I was left alone with her I began what you might call a piece of play-acting business. I burnt the incense and, after muttering some pretended prayers with my lips, I shook the laurel briskly over Charikleia, up and down, from head to foot; then, letting my mouth gape in a sleepy sort of way—really like an old crone—I finally came to a slow halt, having deluged the both of us with a great deal of nonsense. She kept shaking her head, with a wry sort of smile, to signify that I was hopelessly adrift, with no inkling of her sickness. (4. 5. 3-4)

What Kalasiris actually does know through all this—both by inspiration and by observation—will be examined in the next section. For the moment let us conclude the discussion of Kalasiris as love-magician with the main point of contrast. The lower Egyptian magic works by violence, forcing unwilling persons to experience desire, forcing the reluctant dead to return (6. 15), whereas the higher wisdom seeks to accommodate itself to the divine will wherever possible. Charikles, and to a much lesser extent Theagenes, want to force Charikleia to feel a love she does not (in Theagenes' case, may not) want. The standard vocabulary for the effects of love-magic is couched in terms of compelling, overmastering, conquering: 'She is indeed somewhat austere and stubbornly resists subjection to the sway of love . . . but art can find a way to force (βιάζεσθαι) even nature', 3. 17. 5. 'You must cease insulting me and my art, by which she has already been captured and compelled (ἤλωκεν καὶ κατηνάγκασται) to love you and prays that, like some god, you might come before her eyes', 4. 6. 4. 'It was clear enough that she would not withstand even my first onset, without any harassing action by my stronger forces', 4. 7. 2.[40]

---

[40] I cannot resist referring the reader to the story of that very Charikleian heroine, Sosipatra, in Eunapios 466 ff. Boissonade (400 ff. Wright). She was a radiant and beautiful child who was trained from the age of five by two mysterious old men ('her truer guardians and parents'), after which she was prescient and telepathic. She chose her own husband, and later dealt with a kinsman who tried to use love-magic on her. This is a bout of spells and counter-spells from which she emerges victorious. She also surpassed her husband in wisdom, as Charikleia does Theagenes.

Kalasiris however is in fact acting in precisely the opposite way—
so far from doing any violence to Charikleia, his negotiations with
her are characterized by the gentlest tact and understanding, allowing her full freedom at every stage (3. 7. 1, 19; 4. 5. 4–6. 2, 7. 8,
10. 1–13. 5). Though her supposed father Charikles is concerned
for her and treats her tenderly, he nurtures a fixed plan to wed her
to his nephew and will in time force the issue (πρὸς βίαν, 4. 13. 2)
whereas Kalasiris offers her an opportunity to make her own choice
(4. 11. 1, 13. 2). The contrast then between the higher and lower
Egyptian lores is a basic structuring principle behind Kalasiris'
Delphic narrative, and it characterizes him as a passive observer
who appears to comply with the will of others who want to force
Charikleia to experience *eros*. His role is to protect her from this
rape of her will.

This contrast between Charikleia's free choice to accept a love because she
feels it and judges it honorable and the selection of a spouse for her by her
fathers (Charikles, Hydaspes) carries through to the final book, where even
her mother assumes that Charikleia will of course submit to the parental
decision in this matter (10. 21. 3). The candidate is at hand (10. 24. 1 f.,
33. 2). The extraordinary pressure laid on young women not to affirm and
declare their own sexual feelings or choices shapes the action of the last
book from the recognition of Charikleia (ending at 10. 17). The question
from there on is 'Who is that man you were travelling with, whom you
said was your brother?' (10. 18. 1 f.). Charikleia tries to answer the
question, blushing—ὅστις δέ ἐστιν ἀληθῶς αὐτὸς ἂν λέγοι βέλτιον, ἀνήρ
τε γάρ ἐστιν ἐμοῦ τε τῆς γυναικὸς εὐθαρσέστερον ἐξαγορεύειν οὐκ αἰσ-
χυνθήσεται, 'Truly he could better answer the question, who he is, for he
is a man/husband and will not be disgraced to speak out more boldly than
me a woman/his wife' (10. 18. 2). This remarkable sentence is both an
answer to the question, and a statement of the principle (woman's silence,
as in 1. 21. 3–22. 1) which leads to its misinterpretation. Hydaspes 'does
not grasp the sense of what she said', that is, does not see the forbidden
answer in the modest self-denigration. She tries to tell him again at 10.
19. 2 and 20. 2 (the latter, I think, a hint at suicide, like the tale at Paus.
7. 21), with the same results. The force of convention is stated most
clearly at 10. 22. 1, which Charikleia experiences as a condemnation of
her sexuality. When pressed by circumstances to acknowledge explicitly
that she has run away with a lover she uses metaphors of nakedness and
unveiling (10. 29. 5). At 10. 33. 4 she finally does so, but the shamefaced
author allows it to be private. The shock is alleviated by the dramaturgy,
for when it is announced (by Persinna) that Theagenes is her bridegroom
(νυμφίος, 10. 38. 2), the people raise such a shout of approval that the

king has no time to wonder about the proprieties. Sisimithres immediately turns this fact into the final flourish of proof that the gods designed this melodrama for their own good purposes (τὸν νυμφίον τῆς κόρης τουτονὶ τὸν ξένον νεανίαν ἀναφήναντες, 10. 39. 2), and the pageant sweeps on to its stately conclusion.

Another interpretation of Heliodoros' amphibolies has been advanced by John Morgan,[41] who maintains that they are a well-known literary device by which historians generate the impression that they are telling the strict truth. In a display of detailed factual information an historian's occasional admission of ignorance on one point lends credence to the accuracy of the rest. It is not only historians who may do this but any narrator speaking in what I called the documentary, as opposed to the omniscient, mode—e.g. *Od.* 9. 237-9, Lucian, *Tox.* 17. The pose in question is that of any realistic narrator of actual facts in contrast to the story-teller who is free to make things up as he goes along. Heliodoros aims for this sense of historiographic or documentary verisimilitude in order to make our experience of the *Aithiopika* more intense than that of Chariton's *Kallirhoe*. His motto is, Truth is stronger than fiction.

This is quite true as far as it goes, but there are two points which must be made to sharpen and extend Morgan's insight. First, we must note the distinct effects of two different classes of expression— expressions of uncertainty, including amphibolies as one form, and supernatural/natural alternatives. Some amphibolies are simply documentary (Herodotos 1. 61. 2; Heliodoros 8. 9. 3) and are virtu-ally equivalent to the phrase ταῦτα οὐκ ἔχω ἀτρεκέως διακρῖναι, 'I cannot rightly determine' (Hdt. 7. 54. 13 *et saepe*). The set of issues raised by such expressions of uncertainty are indeed part of the historiographic pose which Morgan has in mind. A whole different set of issues however is raised by competing explanations when one of them is supernatural, issues such as rationalism, belief, tradition, criteria of probability, theories of divinity and its operation in human affairs. All these, which we may call the rationalistic problem, are also found expressed as double explanations in many genres besides historiography: epic—*Od.* 7. 263, A.R. 1.804*, Vergil, *Aen.* 9. 243-6, Q.S. 11. 184f.; mock-epic—*Culex* 193; tragedy—Eur., *Hek.* 488-91, *Helen* 137-42; philosophy—Pl., *Rep.* 330e, *Phaidros* 229 b-230 a; fiction—A.T. 8. 6. 13, *Herpyllis* 55-60. Historians naturally have many occasions to deal with

[41] Morgan (1978; lxi-lxxix, 69, 73, 95f., 470f., 596), and Morgan (1982).

conflicting accounts of extraordinary events, but when they contrast supernatural and natural explanations it is not *qua* historian
that they do so but as intelligent narrators of events to which some
persons have attached a theological meaning.[42] They share this role
with geographers, antiquarians, philosophers, and people in the
street.[43] To take an extreme example, the issues of interpretation
central to Heliodoros have more in common with Petronius, *Sat.*
137 (mantic hocus-pocus with an observer's detection of a natural
explanation)[44] than with Herodotos 2. 103. 2 (alternative motives
for Egyptian soldiers settling in Kolchis).

Secondly, we must make a distinction between merely using a
phrase and meaning it. Literature composed on the shoulders of a
great tradition is capable of being mindless repetition or highly
mindful rethinking. It is one thing, for instance, to write in Ionic
after the manner of Herodotos by culling phrases from his *Histories*;
it is quite another to try to think and perceive as Herodotos did
(see Lucian, *Herod.* I, *Syria dea*). Heliodoros to be sure employs his
share of borrowed phrases used for ornament alone—ὀλλύντων καὶ
ὀλλυμένων 'as each side slew and was slain' of a fierce battle (1. 22.
5, 30. 3); Thucydidean neuter participles, τοῦ θυμοῦ τὸ φλεγμαῖνον,
7. 21. 4, τὸ πεπτωκὸς τοῦ τείχους, 9. 8. 1—but in the case of the
amphibolies *with rationalizing content* he is not just using a well-
known device of realistic narration but posing a problem, setting
up terms with which we may think about this particular literary
construct. The sort of thought provoked by the rationalizing
amphibolies is not merely 'Perhaps these events really happened,
since the narrator does not know all the answers', but even more
'What does this novelist have up his sleeve when he goes out of
his way to cast doubt on the providential control of his plot?' (see
pp. 319-20 above).

[42] I find one lonely example of a Heliodoran amphiboly, spectacular and mutedly
cynical, at Polyb. 10. 11 and 14. Scipio promises his men both handsome
remuneration and a sign from Poseidon, vouched for by the god himself in a dream,
to encourage them to fight bravely at New Carthage; he then times his attack to
coincide with the beginning of ebb-tide, which empties the lagoon with phenomenal
speed, and the soldiers walk through the shallow water, convinced that the god is
fighting on their side. Thucydides too is famously pungent on the divine meanings
read into things (2. 54, 7. 50. 4).

[43] Plutarch is perhaps a good example of a general enquirer rather than a
historian proper. His religious attitudes are excellently analyzed in Brenk (1977).

[44] Or Lucian, *Philops.* 13-15 (a Hyperborean magus casts a powerful love spell
on a woman whom the narrator thereafter identifies as a willing partner whose love
is readily available without any spell).

Heliodoros' irony and sophistication in the use of historiographic and rationalistic devices such as the amphiboly stands out clearly when we compare him with a 'real' historian of about the same time who merely juggles narrative clichés from the common stock available to all later writers. Herodian's *History* is an extensive repertoire of inherited tropes, and might indeed have been on Heliodoros' reading list, for they use very many of the same items—Thucydidean neuters,[45] the stage-management of jealous tyche,[46] the private grief motif,[47] the barbarian gnome,[48] *dual explanations,*[49] the slightly cynical verb ἐκθειάζω[50]—but uses them only randomly and decoratively, and never like Heliodoros to mark the structure of a systematic intellectual project.

If Heliodoros had really wanted to create an historiographic verisimilitude he would have spoken in the first person as Herodian, Polybios and Herodotos do. Notice in particular that Herodotos, the most fabulous and romantic narrator, as well as one of the most shrewd and intelligent, is quite intrusive, even when he is pointing out his suspension of judgment, and when he discusses contrasting versions (5. 85–7, for instance), he does not leave the reader in doubt about his own opinions. The provocative absence of this identifiable persona, however, is of the essence of

---

[45] τὸ πνιγῶδες τοῦ ἀέρος, 6. 6. 2. See Stein (1957); Kettler, (1882: 22f.)

[46] 1. 8. 3.

[47] ὠλοφύροντο κοινῇ μὲν πάντες τὰ δημόσια, ἕκαστος δὲ ἰδίᾳ τὰ αὑτοῦ, 1. 14. 3.

[48] φύσει γὰρ τὸ βάρβαρον φιλοχρήματον . . . , 1. 6. 9; ἐρᾷ δὲ τὸ βάρβαρον καὶ ἐπὶ ταῖς τυχούσαις ἀφορμαῖς ῥᾶστα κινεῖσθαι, 1. 3. 5, *et saepe*, cp. Hld. 1. 30. 6.

[49] Both of the 'historiographic' type which simply admits ignorance (6. 6. 1, 7. 10. 5) and the amphiboly which pits supernatural and natural explanations against each other (1. 9. 5, 8. 3. 9). A sort of link between the two is formed by the type in which Herodian wonders whether a proffered claim is truth or fiction (5. 3. 10, 4. 12. 5, 7. 1. 8).

[50] Sometimes the verb in Herodian means 'regard as divine' or 'give a divine explanation to' with no judgment implied on the truth of the belief (1. 14. 6 [ἐπιστώσατο does not imply Herodian's assent], 2. 4. 2, 4. 2), but the cases are more striking where he uses it with a touch of irony (Commodus' 'divine' beauty, 1. 7. 5, Ganymede's 'divine' dismemberment, torn apart in a struggle between his brother and his lover, 1. 11. 2). The attitude is most fully expressed in his discussion of the Emesan black conical rock in the temple of Helios: διοπετῆ τε αὐτὸν εἶναι σεμνολογοῦσιν, ἐξοχάς τέ τινας βραχείας καὶ τύπους δεικνύουσιν, εἰκόνα τε ἡλίου ἀνέργαστον εἶναι θέλουσιν, οὕτω βλέπειν ἐθέλοντες, 5. 3. 5. The language of interpretive desire is quite Heliodoran here. Heliodoros uses ἐκθειάζω of some characters' hyperboles (2. 33. 5 from Charikles' point of view, 8. 2. 1, 10. 29. 1). Its use at 9. 9. 4 is certainly colored by the preceding θεοπλαστοῦσι and σεμνηγοροῦντες, 9. 9. 3. I regard the effect of even a single cynical analysis in an otherwise pious text as infectious rather than inoculating. (The correlative concept, 'give a human explanation to divine things', is found at Plu., *de Isid.* 360a: ἐξανθρωπίζειν τὰ θεῖα.)

the *Aithiopika* as an impersonal, structured ascent of problematic language resolving itself.

Heliodoros presents events as texts, that is, as incomplete until read and interpreted, and as quite likely to be misread and misinterpreted by the reader with presuppositions. If the author intrudes too much he may spoil the reader's discovery that there are problems, the discovery that available categories are too narrow to enclose the richness and wonder of this plot, and the discovery that the exegete's desire must be chastely held in suspense or else the deepest beauty of the text will forever elude.

We have reached then a solution to the first of our problems, that of Kalasiris' moral duplicity. It is only by trying to fix him under a certain preconception of the priest and truth-teller that the problem arises. In fact Kalasiris in his very play-acting as love magus liberates Charikleia to make her own choice and saves her from the raping intentions of others. His hypocrisy is both a cover to conceal and a means to effect the most moral attitude in the book—his loving care for Charikleia. It is as an actor in the gods' complicated plot at Delphi that Kalasiris appears duplicitous, but the justification of his behavior is not that he acts basely in the service of a higher cause, rather *duplicity itself* is the proper moral attitude, duplicity in the sense of carefully weighing alternatives and respecting the volition of all the characters. In his incredible passivity and reluctance to intervene Kalasiris observes the conflict of interests, he actually furthers the unfortunate purposes of Charikles and the purblind purposes of Theagenes and uses them as a wrestler uses an opponent's weight (καθάπερ πάλαισμα τὸ πλάσμα, I. 26. 5) to enhance the options of his beloved Charikleia.[51] He is the best guardian, the protector most respectful of her person, and he is the reader whom *Charikleia* the novel and Charikleia the heroine require, for only an accurate and patient intelligence can both perceive alternative explanations and bide its time for the perfect moment when a delicate balance between them can be resolved. Against the others who read her symptoms and tell her story in ways accommodated to their own will, forcing her into someone else's plot, Kalasiris alone has the necessary double-

---

[51] The wrestling metaphor is finally played out at 10. 31 f.: Theagenes has a refined and exquisite knowledge of this Hermetic technique (τήν τε ἐναγώνιον Ἑρμοῦ τέχνην ἠκριβωκώς, 10. 31. 5) and he uses it craftily, feinting and pretending (κατασοφίσασθαι . . . ἐσκήπτετο . . . ἐσχηματίζετο, 10. 31. 5–6).

ness of mind to read the events around her, and so he alone can adequately cooperate in the slow emergence of an unexpected sense—her plot—which is complex and hard to fathom.

The *Aithiopika* is certainly a moral fiction, not just a novel about moral characters but a novel in which being morally perfect requires being an intelligent actor and reader. Kalasiris' duplicity needs no excuse, it simply needs careful analysis. I refer the reader again to the series of encounters between Kalasiris and Charikleia (3. 7. 1, 19; 4. 5. 4-6. 2, 7. 8, 10. 1-3. 5), in which her whole person—her mind, feelings, aspirations and choices—are accorded a respect no other character offers her. And it is exactly because he can suspend judgment about her identity and the meaning of the oracles around her that Kalasiris can eventually perceive who she really is. His suspension of judgment about her is the intellectual equivalent of his refusal to violate her will. In this sense the *Aithiopika* is a moral fiction, and Kalasiris is its duplicitous saint.

III. WHAT KALASIRIS KNEW

But some readers have asserted that Kalasiris does not suspend judgment: he knew all along that Charikleia was Persinna's daughter, that her homeland was Aithiopia, and that she would return there safely. For he had visited Aithiopia on his travels, had been told by Queen Persinna the story of her long-lost daughter and had been informed by the gods that she was living in Delphi (4. 12). We may focus the discussion of what Kalasiris knows on his claim that he only partially understands the important oracle (11.35.5) which is (apparently) a not-very-enigmatic summary of the plot:

> τὴν χάριν ἐν πρώτοις αὐτὰρ κλέος ὕστατ' ἔχουσαν
> φράζεσθ', ὦ Δελφοί, τόν τε θεᾶς γενέτην·
> οἳ νηὸν προλιπόντες ἐμὸν καὶ κῦμα τεμόντες
> ἵξοντ' ἠελίου πρὸς χθόνα κυανέην,
> τῇ περ ἀριστοβίων μέγ' ἀέθλιον ἐξάψονται
> λευκὸν ἐπὶ κροτάφων στέμμα μαλαινομένων.

Notice, O Delphians, her whose first is *charis* and whose last is *kleos*, and also him born of a goddess (θεᾶς γενέτην); leaving my nave and cleaving the wave they will come to the dark land of the sun, and there they will

find the great prize for their virtuous lives—a white garland on brows
turned black.

The Delphians may be pardoned for being puzzled at this saying
since they do not know that this is a romance, but the reader has
no such excuse and certainly understands at least that Charikleia
and Theagenes will come successfully to Aithiopia, which is both
the land from which Charikleia's black guardian brought her
(already known from 2. 32. 1–2) and the title of the book, after an
adventurous but virtuous career. Yet thrice Kalasiris claims to
Knemon that that crucial oracle remained a puzzle to him (3. 5. 7,
11. 4; 4. 4. 5–5.1), one which required much thought and on
whose solution much depended. Our question, more exactly put,
will be 'Does Kalasiris really not understand (as he claims) that the
oracle refers to Charikleia's Aithiopian origin and destiny, an
understanding which every romance-loving reader reaches at once
and which Kalasiris ought to have had since he had come from
Aithiopia looking for Charikleia?' Is his claiming not to understand
the oracle a lie, or is it perhaps an innocent fraud like his hocus-
pocus with incense and laurel leaves (4. 5), or is it a slip on
Heliodoros' part, or is it the truth?

I shall argue in this section that Kalasiris' assertion that he is
puzzled as to the oracle's real meaning is a truthful statement, and
more importantly one which is meant to sharpen the option
between reading the *Aithiopika* in a naively romantic way *as
Knemon does* or in a subtler and more attentive way, which is the
pattern set by Kalasiris. Kalasiris' narrative to Knemon (2. 24–5.
3) is, on one level, about the way in which conventional assumptions, such as those which lead the reader to feel confident at once
of the meaning of that oracle, are short-sighted and misleading.
One of the discoveries which can and should be made by the
reader of Kalasiris' narrative is that the oracle's interpretation is a
problem. This discovery, I admit, is a difficult one, first, because the
obvious romance pattern imposes itself so easily (exile–trials–
reward), and second, because Kalasiris, though he says repeatedly
that he is somewhat puzzled by this and similar texts, does not
clearly say why. The reader therefore is left with the option either
of taking the oracle to mean what it obviously means (and
Kalasiris' claim of incomplete cognition to be decorative mystifica-
tion) or of reading Kalasiris' mind. The *Aithiopika* is still an impres-

sive novel if read in the former way, as it always has been. But Heliodoros has designed it with the latter reading in mind, a reading which is more difficult, not easily available to the reader who would rather drift with Xenophon than struggle to think with Thucydides.

A bare summary of the points in the following argument runs thus: (1) the narrative of Kalasiris to Knemon is a model, partly ironic, of how authors and readers play the game of literature together; (2) Knemon is an aggressively romantic reader and as such adequate only to the conventional elements in the plot; (3) Kalasiris is a very subtle narrator of *two* complex plots—(a) the love story of Charikleia and Theagenes and (b) his own discoveries both that Charikleia is the Aithiopian princess whom he is incidentally looking for, and that the gods intend her to reach the dark land of Aithiopia rather than the dark land of Hades (the ambiguous image of blacks); (4) three minor motives support Kalasiris' mysteriosophic pose: (a) his vow of silence, (b) his teasing of Knemon, and (c) his use of Odyssean duplicity as one of the ordinary excellences of literary discourse; (5) in the final pages of the novel (10. 39-41) Heliodoros reformulates (in a new language) what the whole plot means, in a way which corresponds to Kalasiris' primary quest for divine wisdom (of which (3b) is a byproduct) rather than to Knemon's desire for a smashing romance (which is the understanding of (3a) parodied in (2)).

In Kalasiris' narrative to Knemon (2. 24-5. 3) Heliodoros gives us a view—I would say, partly a paradigm and partly a parody— of the literary event. The text of, say, a romance is not just a dead letter or inscribed memorial but a semantic performance in which both author and reader have active parts to play. They are contestants in a sort of 'game for two players', and Heliodoros here offers us a model, often ironic, of the correlative crafts of constructing and appreciating a novel. It is not sufficient to call Kalasiris' narrative a flashback, as if it were no more than the absent first stages of the plot into whose *medias res* we have been plunged. As Heliodoros presents it this is not just a romance but a romance-in-frame. The subject in the foreground is Kalasiris' act of 'romancing' in the presence of Knemon. Since both persons, speaking from their present (narrating) time, constantly interrupt the smooth course of the account taking place in past (narrated) time, the conventional impression of a thing-like plot, whose events are

independent of the listening audience and usually of the narrator
too, cannot gel. Our attention is continually being diverted from
the story to its teller and hearer, whether by substantial interrup-
tions or by the simple vocative ὦ Κνήμων. Kalasiris' narrative is at
least as much about the roles of narrator and audience (that is, by
an obvious extrapolation, author and reader) as it is about a
particular pair of lovers. And the question of Kalasiris' mendacity
can only be properly addressed if his role as romancer is understood.

Inasmuch as Kalasiris' narrative to Knemon is about the performance of literature, as well as being the narrative of a love
story, it is operating on two levels. There is a temptation for the
eagerly curious part of our own minds to regard only the plot of
Charikleia and Theagenes as of importance, the interchanges
between Kalasiris and Knemon being treated as humorous or sus-
penseful punctuation. But this attitude is exactly that of Knemon,
who is eager to be treated to the full spectacle of what we would
nowadays call a wide-screen, technicolor romance. The ironic
presentation of Knemon should be a major caution against dealing
with Kalasiris' narrative as if it were simply a flashback to the long-
awaited beginning of this great love story. Rather Kalasiris' narrative is essentially double, not to say duplicitous, in being both that
long-desired story of Charikleia and a series of readings, responses,
and interpretations of it by Knemon. One of the effects of his
interventions is to shape the narrative so that it becomes
Charikleia's story more than Kalasiris would have it be.

Let us look first at the character of Knemon. Kalasiris addresses
him shortly after he begins to narrate as ὦ ξένε (2. 25. 5) and ὦ
νεανία (2. 26. 1), for it is only at 2. 26. 3 that Knemon's interruption leads to the revelation of his own name. From then on he is
addressed by name frequently, so that the reader can never for long
lose awareness of the fact that Kalasiris is speaking to one particular listener, a listener who actively approves or disapproves,
questions, delays, shouts his excitement, and generally by his
unrestrained conduct makes a nuisance of himself. There are four
stretches in Kalasiris' narrative (each ranging from five to nine
Budé pages)[52] where the reader for a time might be lulled into

---

[52] From 2. 26. 3 (Kalasiris learns Knemon's name) to 2. 32. 3 (closure of the
triple-box of narrators); 3. 5. 7 to 10. 3 (followed by Kalasiris' double digression
and the characterization of Knemon as a simple reader, 3. 12. 1–15. 1); 3. 17 to

forgetting Knemon's presence; but each of these is followed by a rather more extensive or significant development of Knemon's character as listener.

Knemon is characterized in ways which have the effect, first, of identifying his response with our own as readers, and second, of parodying his over-eagerness and emotionalism in such a way that we disassociate ourselves from him. In the first category come Knemon's appreciative remarks on Kalasiris' performance (2. 26. 3, 3. 15. 1), his interested questions about points of detail (3. 12. 1, 14. 1 [referring back to 2. 34. 5 and 3. 13. 3]; 5. 17), his vexation, curtly expressed, at the elaborate triple-box of narrators leading up to the solution of Charikleia's real identity, a solution which is however postponed once again (2. 32. 3). Knemon's active participation in Kalasiris' narrating makes him what we might call, reversing Wolfgang Iser's term, *der explizite Leser*.[53] Most of all do we identify with Knemon when he recognizes the names which Kalasiris mentions from his past and present history— Nausikles and Thisbe (2. 24. 1), Theagenes and Charikleia (2. 23. 2), and Thyamis (2. 25. 7). For since we possess the same information as Knemon, his recognition of these names duplicates what we experience at each of those moments, and we might even call Knemon's startled reaction a sort of stage direction or rubric for the appropriate reader's response. Further, since Knemon's own story is known and, as far as we can tell, finished, he is able to be Kalasiris' audience (for the story which *we* want to hear) with almost no overlapping or confusion of his different roles as audience and as actor or narrator. Having been before both actor and narrator, he is now pure auditor; his knowledge and ignorance of the heroine and hero is identical with ours, and he will not surprise us by taking further part in their narrative as an actor. He is precisely as concerned and interested in them as are we (based on a similarly short acquaintance) and he listens to Kalasiris tell the story of their earlier adventures with a curiosity and romantic excitement such as we might bring to a work of this genre.

But Knemon is gradually distanced from us by the broadly drawn comedy of his hyper-romantic sensibility. There is a notice-

4. 3. 4 (followed by Knemon's alarm and relief at Theagenes' race, 4. 3. 4–4. 3); 4. 4. 4 to 8. 1 (the account of recovering the swathe). After this the game between Kalasiris and Knemon is essentially over.

[53] Iser (1972).

able escalation of enthusiasm from the opening passage, where he
is slightly impatient with Kalasiris' delay in launching at once
into his story (2. 22. 5, 23. 5, 24. 4), to his insistence on
an unabridged version of the Delphic procession in honor of
Neoptolemos, including a verbatim quotation of the complete
hymn to Thetis (3. 1. 1–3, 2. 3), to his acknowledgement that he
is indeed insatiable in his lust for love, whether physical or literary:
'I never found my appetite flag either in enjoying the act of
romance or in hearing stories about it. But when Theagenes and
Charikleia are the subject, who might be so hardy or iron-hearted
as not to be quite spellbound with the history of their amours,
though it held the year round. And therefore pray go on' (4. 4. 3).
At these moments Knemon is characterized by his contrast to
Kalasiris: first he is eager to begin the narrative at once, whereas
Kalasiris insists on ceremoniously arranging the place (2. 21. 6),
washing themselves and arranging comfortable couches (2. 22. 2),
food and libations (2. 22. 5); but while the story is in progress
Knemon finds postponements desirable and demands minute
elaboration of descriptive scenes when Kalasiris would prefer to
speak more pointedly (3. 1. 1–2). Knemon is magnetically drawn
to the luscious and spectacular, perhaps not in itself a fault were
he not also characterized as uncritical and self-indulgent in this
taste. The contrast with Kalasiris' orderliness in keeping his mind
always on the point of the story (διηγήσομαι δέ σοι τἀμαυτοῦ
πρότερον ἐπιτεμών, οὐ σοφιστεύων ὡς αὐτὸς οἴει τὴν ἀφήγησιν ἀλλ'
εὔτακτόν σοι καὶ προσεχῆ τῶν ἑξῆς παρασκευάζων τὴν ἀκρόασιν, 'But
first I shall tell you briefly about myself. This is not, as you think,
a sophist's trick to avoid telling the story, but the logical way to
present my narrative and an indispensable preliminary', 2. 24. 5)
is decisive in shaping our impression of Knemon as uncritically
absorbed in the moment rather than thoughtful about the design
of the whole. He enjoys riding the story like an emotional roller-
coaster: 'No wonder (said Knemon) that the spectators on the spot
were anxious when I am myself in fear now for Theagenes; so I
beg you to go on and tell me quickly whether he was declared the
winner' (4. 3. 4). 'You have brought me back to life (said Knemon)
by telling of his victory and his kiss; but what happened next?'
(4. 4. 2). Notice especially that his absorption in the narrative *as if
he were present at the events* is precisely an obliteration of the
difference between narrating time and narrated time. Knemon

reduces this necessary doubleness which every literary narrative maintains (that is, of two time streams: the events as they *happened* over a certain span of time and the events as they are *told* over another span of time, quite different usually in extent and tempo) to a singleness, as if it (the history) could be apprehended as a thing in itself rather than as a telling and recounting of things. Knemon, once his romantic desires are pricked by the names 'Theagenes and Charikleia' (2. 23. 2), forgets the present: Kalasiris reminds him of the passage of time from high noon to evening (3. 4. 9) and far into the night (4. 4. 2), time to which Knemon is oblivious. He lives in the narrative of Kalasiris as if it were a present reality, even exclaiming at one point about the vividness of the picture in his mind's eye as if it were immediately visible (3. 4. 7, an old comic gag, cf. Plautus, *Pseud.* 35f.).

In these respects Knemon seems to illustrate the comedy of misreading, rather like the bourgeois couple from the audience in *The Knight of the Burning Pestle* who are invited onto the stage to help construct the play. His role as *lector non scrupulosus* is consistent with his characterization throughout the novel: Charikleia suspects that he is untrustworthy and is glad when he will no longer accompany them (1. 26. 5–6, 6. 7. 8); Theagenes speaks scornfully of his easy fear of stage bogies (2. 7. 3), his feebleness of resolution (2. 18. 3), and his penchant for melodramatizing a situation (2. 11. 2–3). Even Nausikles and Kalasiris jeer at his cowardice (6. 1. 3), and Heliodoros supports these judgments by his description of Knemon as easily frightened (2. 13. 2–3, contrasted with Theagenes) and prone to emotional paroxysms (6. 7. 3). Indeed his own tale shows him in the role of victim and dupe, never a schemer. The connection between his general cowardice and his romantic misreading is very neatly drawn in the scene which follows Kalasiris' narrative (5. 2. 3), for here he is shown banging against objects in the darkness as he hurries frightenedly away from the room where he has just overheard 'Thisbe'. What Heliodoros earlier called 'the exegesis of desire' (1. 19. 1) is here presented as an exegesis based on fear: Knemon interprets the speaker's references to her slavery, to her imprisonment among brigands, and to the man she loves and depends on in light of his overriding fixation on Thisbe. His paranoia inserts Charikleia's references to Theagenes into the preconceived framework of Thisbe's relation to Knemon, and thus he systematically under-

stands everything she says in a way which expresses and heightens
his own fear. There is a fine cleverness in the final words of her
speech: ἀλλὰ σῴζοιό γε μόνον καὶ θεάσαιό ποτε Θίσβην τὴν σήν· τοῦτο
γάρ με καλέσεις καὶ μὴ βουλόμενος ('I pray only that you are alive
and that one day you will see your Thisbe; for by that name must
you call me, detest it as you may!', 5. 2. 10)—Charikleia means
that Theagenes will call her Θίσβη even though he would rather
call her 'Charikleia', Knemon takes her to mean that he (Knemon)
will call her τὴν ἐμήν even though he would rather run away! As
a sign that we are near one of the central nodes of Heliodoros'
complex web, the cocks crow (5. 3. 2), as they did for Thyamis'
dream (1. 18. 3) and Kalasiris' death (7. 11. 4) and nowhere else
in the book. Charikleia of course is acting out a role, and it is
Knemon's special failing to respond to literature as if it were life
(2. 11. 2-3). He cannot sustain the critical distance which drama
and novels require as representations of reality, rather than reality
itself, and without that ability to perceive and maintain an ongoing
duplicity Knemon will certainly never appreciate the crafty narrative of Kalasiris except as a romantic extravanganza.

That Kalasiris' narrative is, or rather becomes, a romantic
extravaganza is not in doubt. But it is another of Heliodoros'
duplicities that we are brought to regard the gorgeous pageantry
at Delphi, the long, lush description of Theagenes and Charikleia,
and the exquisite slow motion of their first love glance as decorative enhancements demanded by Knemon, somewhat off the point
as Kalasiris sees it, and for which he is therefore absolved of full
responsibility. One of the principal uses which Knemon's comic-
audience role serves is to allow Heliodoros to indulge a taste
(*our* taste) for sentimental scenes of elaborate beauty and yet to
maintain the fiction that the narrator's real *raison de raconter* is the
detection and discovery of how a divine plan is riddled in these
events. As long as we can think of the romantic and emotional
pyrotechnics as existing precisely for Knemon, as Kalasiris' indulgence to him rather than as the narrator's endorsed choice of
presentation, we can maintain our pose (with Kalasiris) of restraint
and wisdom. Effective sentimentality is surely one of the most
difficult literary effects to bring off, and it is significant that
Heliodoros has chosen to present the *beginning* of the plot—the
most treacherously romantic part of such a story (the love at first
sight of an incredibly beautiful hero and heroine)—in suspension

between two points of view, Knemon's naive taste for romantic
candy and the more crafty pose of Kalasiris. Kalasiris is caught in
the dilemma of every Serious Artist—he must pander to the taste
of the common folk if his more Significant Message is to find a
hearing.

For Kalasiris' lofty-mindedness is also a pose. It is not that only
Knemon's style of reading is treated ironically, Kalasiris too is a
poseur. His mysteriosophic attitude is delineated in a systematic
contrast with Knemon. Thus over against Knemon's eagerness to
plunge into the story (an eagerness trebled when he discovers that
it will concern his romantic idols, Theagenes and Charikleia) we
find Kalasiris' reluctance to speak readily, his Protean postponements (2. 24. 4), his insistence that the tale, though it must be told
(2. 21. 6), be told 'in order and with attention to the way things
follow and fit' (εὔτακτόν . . . καὶ προσεχῆ τῶν ἑξῆς, 2. 24. 5). What
is important to establish in the first place is not the reality of
Kalasiris' cryptic perceptions but the image of him as a careful and
scrupulously thoughtful narrator who weighs the relevance of each
item before including it in his tale. This restraint is twice the
ground for rejecting information that might otherwise have been
included—once ironically, when Kalasiris passes over the fact that
he had been to Aithiopia ('for it contributes nothing to the story
you asked for', συντελεῖ γὰρ οὐδὲν εἰς τὴν παρὰ σοῦ ζήτησιν, 2. 26.
1), and once unsuccessfully, when he gives in to Knemon's petu-
lant, Athenian lust for the spectacular ('I would rather keep you
on target, restricting you to the relevant parts of my narrative and
such as will answer the question you originally asked', ἐπὶ τὰ
καιριώτερά σε τῆς ἀφηγήσεως καὶ ὧν ἐπεζήτεις ἐξ ἀρχῆς συνελαύνων,
3. 1. 2). The essential contrast between this narrator's view of his
performance and this auditor's expectations is that Kalasiris comes
across as aware of the complexity and mystery of these events, as
if their real point and their actual coherence might be missed,
whereas Knemon appears as enthralled by the superficial glitter of
immediate delights, as one whose appreciation is without *appro-
fondissement*. To be sure he asks some questions, but these serve to
highlight Kalasiris' vast knowledge and lofty perspective (a pose,
remember) over against Knemon's viewpoint as one of οἱ πολλοί
(3. 12. 2–3). Knemon's questions here give him a diminished and
ironic participation in Kalasiris' major quest for exactitude (τοῦ
λόγου τὴν ἀκρίβειαν, 3. 14. 1, with Kalasiris' disclaimer ἀλλ' οὐδὲ

ἀκριβῶς οὐδὲν ἔτι τῶν ἑξῆς χρησθέντων συνέβαλλον, 3. 5. 7), just as
Kalasiris displays some of the romantic affection for the lovers
which so dominates Knemon's reaction to the tale.

Both in and out of his narrative Kalasiris is reluctant to bare his
thoughts ('many times Nausikles pressured me to disclose the
sacred secret of my tale but each time I found a new excuse to
thwart him', ὃν πολλάκις γε δι' ὄχλου γινόμενον μυηθῆναι τὴν
ἀφήγησιν ἄλλως ἄλλοτε διεκρουσάμην, 2. 23. 6, with 2. 35. 3); not
only does he keep his own counsel, the little information he does
give out is often duplicitous (the learned explanation of the evil
eye, 3. 7. 8, is a façade covering his knowledge of Charikleia's love,
3. 5). His duplicitous poses in the narrative are matched by the
tones of irony in his role as narrator: 'elevating his mind to a more
mystical perspective' (3. 13. 1), Kalasiris then explains that Homer
was either the child of Hermes by an Egyptian woman or he lied
about his birth in order to enhance his reputation and presumably
his income (another function of Hermes) (3. 14).

What is this priest-narrator's duplicity in the service of? Not just
the furtherance of Charikleia's and Theagenes' love-affair, not just
Queen Persinna's request to find her missing daughter, but his own
pursuit of wisdom, a goal which includes the other two as integral,
subordinate parts. His motive for leaving Memphis was double—to
avoid succumbing to the erotic power of the courtesan Rhodopis
(2. 25. 1–4) and to avoid the sight of his two sons fighting each
other (2. 25. 5–6). Both of these frightful events are *possibilities*
rather than actualities, possibilities which Kalasiris' reading of
the divine pattern in the stars and so forth has discovered
(προαγορευθέντων μοι πρὸς τοῦ θείου δυσχερῶν, 2. 25. 3, ἡ ἄρρητός
μοι πολλάκις ἐκ θεῶν σοφία . . . προηγόρευε, 2. 25. 5). His positive
motive for going to Meroe and Delphi rather than anywhere else is
also his divine wisdom (2. 26. 1, 4. 12. 1). Kalasiris is a man above
all obedient to the divine plan and devoted to ferreting out the
gods' intentions as they are disclosed to him in stages of ever
greater definiteness. When asked by Knemon to give an account of
himself, Kalasiris agrees to do so, and we may call this story which
he intends to tell 'My Priestly Life: Adventures in the Service of
Gradual Revelation'. But at the moment when Knemon realizes
that this tale will touch on Charikleia and her lover *he focuses his
attention* (and ours) *on the love-story alone*. This narrowed aspect of
Kalasiris' history is in a sense another story, which we may

entitle 'How Charikleia and Theagenes Fell in Love and Eloped to Points South'. Knemon originally asked for the former, then re-asked for the latter, and he continually construes all that Kalasiris has to say only within the framework of his desire for a sentimental romance. The reader of the *Aithiopika* watches Knemon following Kalasiris' narrative, accommodating it to his taste and misconstruing it. We are easily led (for reasons given above on p. 333) to identify with Knemon and to adopt his basic understanding of what Kalasiris' story is. But in doing so we miss, as Knemon does, the irony, the subtlety and the duplicity of Kalasiris' account of how he pursued divine wisdom, how he unraveled its tangled skein, and in the process furthered the love of Charikleia and Theagenes as a sort of interesting sub-plot.[54] This is not the view usually taken of Kalasiris' narrative, so I shall now retell the story 'from a more mystical perspective' (3. 13. 1) as a divine detective story, an adventure in unriddling the uncertain traces of god's intentions.

Kalasiris' σοφία, by which he has foreknowledge of important developments in the future, is not a clear and complete knowledge but an incomplete cognition. It allows both a latitude for eluding a possible future (Rhodopis) and a certain indeterminacy, of which oracular riddles are the best example. They do not unambiguously picture the future but hint at the general outline of things to come. The entire narrative of Kalasiris from 2. 35 to 4. 13. 3 is structured around the progressive certification of a Delphic prediction. By his wisdom Kalasiris learns from the gods, at Queen Persinna's request, that her long-lost daughter is still alive and is at Delphi. He does not learn her name, rank or more detailed history, only that she is living somewhere in Delphi. When he arrives there, in primary pursuit still of divine wisdom but secondarily (as he says

---

[54] There are three journeys made for the seeking out of wisdom which result in the seeker's association with Charikleia as a sort of 'bonus': Charikles' journey to Katadoupa (καθ' ἱστορίαν τῶν καταρρακτῶν τοῦ Νείλου, 2. 29. 5), Kalasiris' journey to Aithiopia (ἐπιθυμίᾳ τῆς παρ' ἐκείνοις σοφίας, 4. 12. 1), and Kalasiris' journey to Delphi, whose intellectual attractiveness, described at 2. 26. 1, is his *primary* reason for going there: 'And so I came to Delphi intending to accomplish the request she had vowed me to, though this was not the reason why I took my journey to these parts so seriously but rather by the supplement of the gods it has been the greatest profit I made on my wandering' (4. 13. 1). Charikles too made an unexpected profit, his free acquiring of the ambassador's jewels when he agreed to care for Charikleia (2. 30. 3f.). This secondary profit in gems, which a merchant like Nausikles will regard as primary, is analogous to the romance of Charikleia, which is both subordinate to the higher plans of wisdom and yet very distracting to readers whose hearts are set on a love story.

at 4. 13. 1) hoping that the gods will continue to guide him in locating the queen's daughter, he waits until some sign indicates which Delphian maiden is the white Aithiopian. The break comes when Charikles tells him that his foster daughter was given him in trust by an Aithiopian ambassador. This makes Charikleia the chief suspect, though the case for her identity is not yet airtight. At this point comes the oracle which links Charikleia to Theagenes and a voyage to a dark land. There are two aspects of this new clue which Kalasiris finds puzzling. First, why have the gods introduced a new character (Theagenes) into the plot of Charikleia's life, and second, is the dark land Aithiopia? The former is answered when by careful observation Kalasiris detects the love interest in the eyes of the young pair on first beholding each other:

These effects, naturally enough, escaped the notice of the multitude, since everyone was absorbed in one or another interest or consideration of his own; . . . but I was occupied solely with my observation of the young pair, ever since, Knemon, the oracle was chanted concerning Theagenes as he sacrificed in the temple; and I had been moved by hearing their names to speculate on what would befall them. But I could still not make out any accurate meaning for the succeeding lines. (3. 5. 7)

That night Apollo and Artemis entrust the young pair to Kalasiris' care on a voyage to Egypt and then to a land of the gods' choosing (3. 11. 5). Kalasiris then has his commission to escort *both* of them, though he is not perfectly sure that Charikleia is the young woman he is looking for and he is gravely suspicious that the land of the gods' choosing may be Hades.

This linkage of Aithiopia and Hades, quite clearly expressed elsewhere in the novel but significantly not made explicit by Kalasiris when it would illuminate his train of thought for Knemon and the reader, must be briefly documented.[55] The initial confrontation of Charikleia and the black Egyptian brigands takes place on a battlefield littered with corpses. The grisly possibility is raised that the brigands are ghosts haunting the scene of their untimely sorrow, and it is precisely their black and unkempt look which triggers this interpretation (1. 3. 1). The equation is virtually explicit at 4. 14.

---

[55] For further examples see Winkler (1980: 161–4). Other references to haunting or revenants in Heliodoros at 2. 5. 2, 11. 3; 6. 14f. The author's attitude to this superstition depends (as do all his 'beliefs') on the occasion: he can encourage us to view ghost-raising as either silly or wicked depending on the needs of the story at that moment.

2-15. 1, where Kalasiris presumably takes the dream of dusky and shadowy phantoms to whose land Charikleia is taken as referring to Aithiopia, while Charikles understands it to mean that she will soon die and go to Hades. The most explicit form of the equation is another dream interpretation in which ironically the *explanandum* is Aithiopia, Hades the *explanans* (8. 11. 3-5). Theagenes takes his perfectly literal dream message and gives to each term a translated significance.[56] As we saw in the case of Charikleia's dream of blindness, Heliodoros takes a special pleasure in playing with problems of interpretation and particularly in postponing solutions, which, when they come, are not announced *as* solutions. This displacement occurs also in Kalasiris' narrative, which is framed as a plot of detection but whose clues and deductions are not explained to us. The uncertainty which Kalasiris several times says he feels about the meaning of the oracle's final lines is a real one, which has been prepared from the opening scene, and which creates an undercurrent of abiding danger about Charikleia's destiny.

Though Kalasiris accepts the gods' new commission to bring Theagenes as well as Charikleia back to Egypt with him, he still does not understand the *point* of the love story, i.e., why the wisdom of the gods has ordained it, and neither do we until the final chapters. This is a real question. Romance readers will assume that a love story is what is expected, but Kalasiris represents a different point of view. To him the emergence of a love interest is a puzzling and unlooked-for development: 'I rejoiced at having found something which I had not expected' (3. 15. 3). Still, he is a patient and open-minded reader of events, able to revise and refine his understanding of what it is that the gods are having him do: he had originally left Memphis to avoid seeing the conflict of his sons, but the gods arranged this exile 'not more for that reason, it seems, than for the discovery of Charikleia' (3. 16. 5). By careful watching (ἐκ πολλοῦ παρατηρῶν, 4. 3. 2) and silent waiting (ἀλλ' ὅμως ἐσιώπων, τὸ μέλλον ἀπεκδεχόμενος, 2. 35. 3) Kalasiris reaches a point where he has guessed with virtually complete certainty that Charikleia is the white Aithiopian princess and must only confirm that by acquiring the baby clothes in which Charikleia was set out:

---

[56] Similarly Persinna interprets her dream metaphorically when its truth is literal (10. 3. 1).

But as to the problem of what land they were to be conducted to I could see but one solution—to get hold of, if somehow I could, the swathe which was exposed with Charikleia, and on which was embroidered the narrative (διήγημα) about her, as Charikles said he had been told; for it was probable (εἰκός) that both her fatherland and the maiden's parents, whose identity I had already begun to suspect, could be learned conclusively (ἐκμαθεῖν) from that source and perhaps it was to there that they were being conducted by destiny. (4. 5. 1)

Having gulled so many people for so long a time Kalasiris at least reveals 'everything as it was' to the one person who matters, Charikleia herself (4. 12. 1). He explains to her not only the story of her true birth but the choice she must make about whether to elope with Theagenes, since that is the course of action which the oracle and dream have indicated: 'And with that I reminded her of the oracle's words and explained to her their meaning: Charikleia was not ignorant of them, as they were sung and scrutinized by many' (παρὰ πολλῶν καὶ ᾀδόμενος καὶ ζητούμενος, 4. 13. 3).

At this moment Kalasiris learns that what had seemed to be two different divine plots were actually *two ways of saying the same thing*. His Aithiopian commission was to send back the lost princess, whoever she might turn out to be; his Apolline commission was to guard the young lovers on their way to a dark land, wherever that might be. These are now seen to be two incomplete descriptions of the same plot, though they came from opposite ends of the earth. What was indefinite in the one is definite in the other. This movement of revelation is parallel to the announcement that Apollo in Delphi and Helios in Aithiopia are the same divine force, which is the penultimate religious theme of the novel (10. 36. 3).

Incidental to this analysis of Kalasiris' discovery there are three other points which might be made to make the shape of his narrative fully intelligible. (1) When Kalasiris accepted his Aithiopian commission, the queen bound him to silence on solemn oath. 'She conjured me to compliance, repeatedly invoking the Sun, an oath no man of religion would dare to transgress' (4. 13. 1). While at Delphi Kalasiris maintained an air of innocence and casualness about what he was really looking for: he did not announce that he was seeking a white Aithiopian maiden to all and sundry. In narrating his story to Knemon, Kalasiris is not deviating from the way the events appeared at the time. It had then the form of a detective story, with the right interpretation of clues withheld from all but the investigator. (2) Knemon teases Kalasiris by not telling him straight out where Theagenes and Charikleia are, saying with an air of mystery that they will appear. This withholding of information is strictly according to narrative contract (as explained above, pp. 302). Kalasiris must first complete his part of the bargain, which was to tell the story of his adventures—not the story of Theagenes and Charikleia. The agreement was struck before Knemon knew that Kalasiris was involved with them. Technically speaking, Knemon's ζήτησις was just about Kalasiris' misfortunes. Perhaps this is why Kalasiris says, 'I will omit the events between Memphis and Delphi, young man, for they contribute nothing to your ζήτησις' (2. 26. 1). There is more razor-edged repartee between these two players at 2. 4-10. Since Knemon has checked Kalasiris' request to know where the lovers are, playing strictly by the rules, Kalasiris in return finesses Knemon by postponing the information about Charikleia's origin, again in strict accordance with what the rules allow, since his original enquiry did not concern her. (3) The Odyssean background of the *Aithiopika* may put us in mind of how subtle and necessary an art lying is. Verbal control by misdirection and half-truth are still a prominent part of Greek socialization. The lies of Odysseus even to Athena and Laertes illustrate that one of the excellences of speech is its use to conceal the speaker and play with the auditor. Kalasiris' tincture of hypocrisy is a bright, pleasing performance, authentically Hellenic in its craftiness and reluctance to trumpet the truth.[57]

There are hints of a deeper cosmic meaning underlying the romantic exile and return of the Aithiopian princess. The following calendrical coincidences are not fortuitous: (a) Charikleia was conceived by divine command on a summer's day at noon (τὸ μεσημβρινόν . . . ὕπνου θερινοῦ, 4. 8. 4) and her return coincides with the summer solstice (κατὰ τροπὰς τὰς θερινάς, 9. 9. 2). (b) The Nile's sources are at the Aithiopian–Libyan border, where east meets south (καθ' ὃ μέρος τὸ κλίμα τὸ ἀνατολικὸν ἀπολῆγον ἀρχὴν τῇ μεσημβρίᾳ δίδωσιν); according to its unique nature (ἡ ἰδιάζουσα φύσις) it increases in the summer because at the summer solstice the 'annual' winds drive clouds from north to south (ἐπὶ τὴν μεσημβρίαν) (2. 28. 1-3). (c) The annual changes in the Nile's movement are called its 'growth' (αὔξησις, 9. 9. 2, 22. 3, 5) and 'return' or 'subsidence' (ὑπονόστησις, 9. 22. 3, 5). (d) The unique diversion of the Nile around Syene features both a subtle increase of its waters at midnight (κατὰ μέσας που νύκτας . . . αὐξομένου . . . τοῦ ὕδατος, 9. 8. 2) and the revelation at daybreak that the water has returned to its natural bed (τὸ ἡμέρας φῶς . . . τοῦ ὕδατος ἀθρόον

[57] See Walcot (1977).

ὑπονοστήσαντος, 9. 8. 4). (e) This artificial 'return' of the river
allows the people of Syene more gladly to celebrate the Neiloa, the
summer solstice festival of the river's manifest increase (ὅτε ἀρχὴν
τῆς αὐξήσεως ὁ ποταμὸς ἐμφαίνει τελουμένην, 9. 9. 2), an event
to which they attach mystical significance (θεοπλαστοῦσι . . .
σεμνηγοροῦντες . . . ἐκθειάζουσιν, 9. 9. 3) on several mirroring
levels simultaneously—agricultural, scientific, mythically romantic,
and Something Deeper (9. 9. 3-10. 1). From these elements
the clever reader[58] can begin to conjecture cosmic patterns—
Charikleia's journey north and return south reproducing, in
harmony or counterpoint, the river's growing up (αὔξησις) and
returning home; significant turning points (τροπαί) of the day
(dawn, noon, sunset, midnight) and the year (the solstices) marking patterns of the sun's motion across the sky and Charikleia's
across the earth, and so forth. But these are only tantalizing hints,
a Jamesian figure in her carpet, which elude precise formulation.

The real religious message of the novel, though it is not religiously *meant*, is the declaration by Sisimithres at 10. 39 that the
gods have fashioned the entire plot of Charikleia's life *in order to*
convince the Aithiopian people to abolish their paternal rite of
human sacrifice (τὰ πάτρια, 10. 7. 1). Let me develop these two
points: that the novel concludes with a new religious significance
read into the romantic events, and that this religious significance
is not religiously meant.

The gods, it seems, wanted the otherwise blameless Aithiopians
to accept a fundamental change in religious custom and to this
end they could find no better means than a romance, one whose
beauty and intricacy would astonish, charm, and successfully
persuade them to abolish human sacrifice once and for all. This is
the interpretation which Sisimithres gives at 10. 39:

Hydaspes then enquired of Sisimithres: 'What is to be done, my wise
friend? To deny the gods their sacrifice is impious; to butcher those whom
they have bestowed on us is unholy: we must think carefully what is to be
done.' Sisimithres replied, speaking not now in Greek but in Aithiopian,
so as to be understood by everyone: 'O King, exceeding joy, it would seem,
overshadows the minds of even the most sagacious men. You at least
ought to have realized long ago that the gods are not welcoming this
sacrifice that is underway. For they have now manifested the fortunate

[58] Like the anonymous sophisticate (τις τῶν ἀστειοτέρων, 2. 28. 1) who provoked
the first discourse on the Nile.

Charikleia as your daughter, snatching her from the very altar, and they have sent here from midmost Greece her guardian Charikles, as if *ex machina*, and further they struck the horses and bulls held ready at the altars with that alarm and disorder, by which they meant us to understand that what is regarded as the highest ritual would be abruptly halted, and now, as the colophon (κορωνίς) of their good deeds and as it were a drama's torch, they have presented this foreign youth as the bridegroom of the maiden. Come, let us recognize the divine wonder-working and become collaborators in the gods' will: let us limit ourselves to the holier offerings, and proscribe the sacrifice of human beings unto all future ages.'

The many threads of the complex spiderweb in Book 10 have nearly converged when Hydaspes puts his simple question—what is to be done? Sisimithres' answer is not just a piece of advice but an interpretation, a reading, of the events in Book 10. Four astonishing developments (he could have listed more) are too many to attribute to random chance and merely human motivation, especially when each of them can be read as an omen opposing human sacrifice. He summarizes, that is, the course of Book 10, with its two movements (the recognition of Charikleia, 1–17, and the fortunes of Theagenes as he waits for Charikleia to announce that they are vowed to each other as man and wife, 18–38), but does so from a new point of view. The female victim was saved from sacrifice by the revelation that she was not a foreigner; the male victim is also protected from that fate by an auspicious reading of the animals' alarm. As if these two anti-sacrificial signs were not enough, both omens have been confirmed by a specifically theatrical turn—the appearance of Charikles *ex machina* and of Theagenes as the bridegroom escorted by torches in the finale of a play.[59] This pattern of omen/melodrama, omen/melodrama, says Sisimithres, is too novelistic, entirely too coincidental not to have been the result of, not merely divine planning (βούλημα), but divine play-writing (σκηνοποιία).

The reason intelligent observers did not detect the pattern is that their otherwise wise minds were overshadowed by excessive

---

[59] This perhaps answers Morgan's objection (1978 *ad loc.*) that we would expect the article with δράματος. Theagenes is revealed as the bridegroom in *a* drama, a general dramatic sort of effect, not as the bridegroom in this drama or any specific play. W. G. Arnott's argument (1965) is essentially correct on this passage, though I should emphasize that weddings are often the finale of a comedy and, given Sisimithres' equation of bridegroom and torch, the sort of dramatic prop in question must be thought of as a wedding torch.

emotion, which is to say they were following the events of Book 10 to see how Charikleia and Theagenes would be saved, as any reader of a naive romance would do. From 'a more mystical point of view', the rescue and happy final state of Theagenes and Charikleia are not the telos of this action. It is not the abolition of human sacrifice which makes possible the successful conclusion to the romance, it is the romance itself (complex plot, recognition, coincidences, tableaux and daring exploits) which facilitates the abolition of human sacrifice. The whole seventeen years of romantic incidents were contrived not for their own sake but to make a point. This is why the gods staged such a spectacle, this is the goal towards which even Kalasiris' directives from the gods were aimed, though he did not live to see it realized. If we had not been assuming that this was a romance we might have seen the point long ago (καὶ πάλαι).[60]

Sismithres represents that higher point of view on the action, much the same as Kalasiris' mysteriosophic pose. He has like Kalasiris intimations of what telos the gods seem to have in mind, but will not force their hand ahead of time by second-guessing them. His announcement that the story was all along designed for a different point altogether, which subtle minds unclouded by intense emotional involvement in the play could see, is both a sophisticated *jeu* with the conventions of reading a romance and a trick itself from popular melodrama. For it is a cliché, and an effective one, from the popular stage that 'the Real Truth was More Astonishing than we realized'.[61] The sophistication of Heliodoros' use of this cliché is that he makes it refer to the form itself of his novel, for what we learn at the end (or almost the end) is that where we thought Heliodoros was writing a romance, the Real Truth is that Heliodoros is telling the story of how the gods devised a romance. He is not a romancer but a mere scribe of the divine melodramatist.

The fact that all readers have continued to regard the *Aithiopika*

---

[60] There is an analogous moment in A. Christie, *Murder on the Orient Express* (London, 1934) when the detective points out that the presence of twelve people on the same train, all of whom had a perfectly good reason for killing the murdered man, is too great a coincidence. Indeed it is, but the reader had all along been assuming that that fact was part of the *form* of the mystery story rather than a fact to be questioned or explained. Sismithres' explanation that all the events of Book 10 are too theatrically satisfying, just a little too neat for merely human purposes to achieve, is of the same order as Hercule Poirot's.

[61] Apuleius, *Metamorphoses* 10. 11 f., analyzed as a mime by Wiemken (1972).

as a romance and Heliodoros as its author is explained by my
second point, that the religious re-signification of the plot is not
religiously meant, but is rather part of Heliodoros' playful exploration of popular narrative and its audience. As Knemon was the
ironic audience-figure in Kalasiris' narrative, so the Aithiopian
populace plays that role in Book 10. Most of the events are presented to them as a drama in a foreign language (Greek), which is
nonetheless clear enough for them to follow in the main. The
semantic entertainment of Book 10 consists in our watching the
Aithiopians as audience of the Charikleia-mime,[62] beginning
with the non-verbal message of Hydaspes' victory: 'The special
messengers . . . waved palm branches in their hands as they passed
on horseback through the more important parts of the city, publishing the victory by their appearance alone' (μόνῳ τῷ σχήματι
δημοσιεύοντες, 10. 3. 2). Each of the major scenes is not only
presented in Greek to us but is to be thought of as a pantomime
independent of words, performed for the Aithiopians: the brazier
(10. 9. 3–5, note the response of the crowd, βοὴν μίαν ἄσημον μὲν
καὶ ἄναρθρον, δηλωτικὴν δὲ τοῦ θαύματος ἐπήχησαν, 'in unison they
made the heavens resound with their cry, wordless and unmean-
ing, but expressive of their astonishment'), the picture (ἄλλων πρὸς
ἄλλους, ὅσοι καὶ κατὰ μικρὸν συνίεσαν τὰ λεγόμενα καὶ πραττόμενα,
διαδηλούντων καὶ πρὸς τὸ ἀπηκριβωμένον τῆς ὁμοιότητος σὺν περι-
χαρείᾳ ἐκπλαγέντων, 'those members of the crowd with the slightest
understanding of what was being said and done explained it to
their neighbours, and the exactitude of the likeness struck them
with delighted astonishment', 10. 15. 1), the reunion (τὸν δῆμον
. . . πρὸς τὴν σκηνοποιίαν τῆς τύχης . . . , 'the people . . . at destiny's
stage management', 10. 16. 3), the rodeo stunt (τὰ μὲν δὴ πρῶτα
φυγὴν εἶναι τοῦ Θεαγένους τὸ γινόμενον οἱ παρόντες ὑπελάμβανον . . .
προιόντος δὲ τοῦ ἐγχειρήματος ὅτι μὴ ἀποδειλίασις ἦν μηδὲ ἀπόδρασις
τοῦ σφαγιασθῆναι μετεδιδάσκοντο, 'At first the onlookers assumed
that Theagenes was attempting to escape . . . But as the exploit
proceeded, they saw that they had been wrong, that this was no
pusillanimous attempt to escape being sacrificed', 10. 28. 5), the
wrestling match (10. 32. 3), Charikles' hauling off Theagenes
(ἐσείσθησαν πρὸς τὰ γινόμενα σύμπαντες, τὰ μὲν ῥήματα οἱ συνιέντες,

---

[62] Admittedly more sophisticated than the Chariton-mime (*P. Oxy.* 413, D. L.
Page, *Greek Literary Papyri*, no. 76), but they share crowds of black foreigners
shouting a strange language, a great king, and a heroine in danger.

τὰ ὁρώμενα δὲ οἱ λοιποὶ θαυμάζοντες, 'The incident gave rise to general consternation: the few who could understand his words were no more astounded by what he said than were the rest by what they saw', 10. 35. 2), and the finale (10. 38. 3). We are audience to a scene which includes an audience who perceive and understand the action in a different mode. Just as in the long narrative of Kalasiris, we are once more treated not only to a romantic melodrama but to the attendant by-play of two minds interpreting the scene—a higher mysteriosophic point of view and a lower, demotic response to the mere thrill of it all. Heliodoros clearly loves both sophisticated self-consciousness in literary irony and popular literature in its most time-tested clichés. It is the interplay of these two interests which gives the Aithiopika its special character, and certainly not the particular content of its Religious Truths (sun worship, abolition of human sacrifice, the providence of the gods for beautiful people). It is not Heliodoros' religiously held belief, nor meant to be ours, that an occasional human sacrifice is contrary to the actual divine will. The gods might contrive a romance to prove this point but no human believer ever would. The religious beliefs in the Aithiopika are so unobjectionable (killing people is wrong) and so malleable (the sun is a high god) that it would be hard to imagine an average ancient reader who would need to be convinced. Indeed Heliodoros must place his action in a fabulous land at the earth's ends where utopia and dystopia ambiguously meet in order to provide us with an audience who are dead set on the heroine's death and whose conversion to her favor by the theatrical force of the romance itself we can somewhat ironically watch.[63]

The two commonest misinterpretations of the Aithiopika are that it is (simply) a romance and that it is meant to recommend some religious beliefs. The involution of its plot, however, is not just a difficulty in chronology to be sorted out but rather puts in question the perception and interpretation of the events, most notably by the addition of hyperintelligent (Kalasiris, Sisimithres) and subintelli-

[63] Ironically because human sacrifice is not the real danger but only the necessary stage villain for romance: 'The human sacrifice, usually of a virginal female, is astonishingly persistent as the crucial episode of romance: we meet it in the sixth book of The Faerie Queen, and it is still going strong in the late prose romances of William Morris', Frye (1976: 81). Hence the neatness of contriving that the populace renounce human sacrifice because they have been so thrilled at the performance of an excellent stage romance.

gent (Knemon, the Aithiopian mob) perspectives. The romantic plot is the raw material, the sense data, as it were, for these minds to operate on: each makes of it what his categories allow. It is mere convention, theatrical convention, that the 'higher' perspective is privileged and seems to prevail in the end. It is not that Heliodoros is any kind of believer but merely that he must employ beliefs to illustrate the comedy of composing a romance. There has to be some Noble Message or other at the end, any one will do.

I think I hear a laugh on the closing page, and I will close by mentioning what I think it is. In the midst of their desperate straits the lovers had agreed on a pair of code words to identify themselves—λαμπάς 'torch', and φοῖνιξ 'palm' (5. 5. 2). They have chosen these symbols from their own first meetings when Charikleia gave Theagenes a ceremonial torch (λαμπάδιον, 3. 4. 6, δᾴς, 3. 5. 3) at the games of Neoptolemos and a branch of palm (φοίνικος ἔρνος, 4. 1. 2, φοῖνιξ, 4. 4. 2) for winning the Pythian footrace (she was also carrying a ritual λαμπάδιον on the latter occasion, 4. 1. 2). No author plants code words unless he means to use them later, and in due course one of them serves its purpose: 'Oh Pythian', she said to him softly, 'have you not remembered the torch?' (7. 7. 7). The torch recurs as a wedding torch in Sisimithres' final revelation of the Meaning of it all (ὥσπερ λαμπάδιον δράματος, 10. 39. 2). Has the φοῖνιξ been forgotten entirely? Perhaps not. Theagenes in the same phrase is called the κορωνίς, the final flourish of the scribe's pen which closes the book, as well as a theatrical wedding torch, and it is in the author's own final flourish that he identifies himself as Φοῖνιξ, a Phoenician (10. 41. 4).[64]

τύχη or πρόνοια? There are many ways to play the game of literature, and a sophisticated player is now and then caught allud-

---

[64] This may in some part explain the order of the final words, 'a small masterpiece of style in the way it builds up to the statement of the author's name in the very last word', Morgan (1978: 627). ἀνὴρ Φοῖνιξ Ἐμισηνός, τῶν ἀφ' Ἡλίου γένος, Θεοδοσίου παῖς Ἡλιόδωρος. Φοῖνιξ and Ἡλιόδωρος are both given special prominence by their unusual position. The ordinary form of naming is personal name—name of father—name of city—name of people (in authors: Herodotos, Thucydides, Dionysios of Halikarnassos 1. 8. 4). Heliodoros' self-reference reverses that normal order so as gradually to unfold the secret of his identity, each phrase becoming more specific than the last. When 'Heliodoros' is finally named as the elusive individual who has been so long hidden behind this book, there is a curious satisfaction in the name, as if it were the solution to some larger riddle as well as the immediate paronomasia of Ἡλίου and Θεοδοσίου.

ing to his private sense of being an author ('Oh Jamesy let me up out of this', says Molly Bloom) and to the ironies of communication. This is an unavoidable dimension of an author's consciousness at least since the invention of writing, and we find it in writers from Aratos to Nabokov.[65] Heliodoros is such an author, and the *Aithiopika* is an act of pure play, yet a play which rehearses vital processes by which we must live in reality—interpretation, reading, and making a provisional sense of things.[66]

[65] See Levitan (1979). An example of Levitan's 'sensibility of the near miss' is perhaps the closing scene in which Charikles, watching the young couple leave the set crowned with white mitres, remembers (once again!) that oracle and quotes its closing lines, '. . . a white crown on brows turned black'. But does μελαινομένων, the final word, really mean anything? They both still look white; Charikleia has become black in the sense that her Aithiopian generation has been acknowledged, but this is inapplicable to Theagenes. It is at least odd not only that the word was used once (anything might be forgiven, even in a work consecrated to Detection and an image of accuracy), but that it should be so highlighted and actually quoted here strikes me as a palpable 'near miss', like the discord which closes Charles Ives' Second Symphony.

[66] This paper was first given as a talk at the International Conference on the Ancient Novel at Bangor, July 1976, and has been improved in its fuller form by comments from Gerald Sandy, Terry Comito, John Morgan.

13

The Mirror of the Moon:
Lucian's *A True Story*—
From Satire to Utopia

MASSIMO FUSILLO

A META-LITERARY PASTICHE

Lucian's *A True Story* is explicitly presented as a meta-literary work:

My readers will be attracted by . . . the humorous allusions (*ouk ako-moidetos einiktai*) in every part of my story to various poets, historians, and philosophers of former times who have concocted long, fantastic yarns—writers I should mention by name did I not think their identities would be obvious to you as you read. (I. 2)

This declaration is not to be taken too seriously, and this goes for the whole prologue, which is clearly a form of understatement. In fact, there are few cases where the narration unmistakenly 'alludes' to a particular author. This is partly to be explained by the insufficient evidence we have for ancient fantasy literature, and partly by the extreme nature of Lucian's satirical hyperboles, which have a narrative development all of their own.[1] Anyway, Lucian's authorial statement makes clear what the privileged object of his satire will be: not one author nor one literary genre in particular, but rather the entire classical tradition of fantasy

* This paper is the revised text of a lecture held in the University of Geneva. Beside André Hurst, I wish to thank A. Lukinovitch, G. Paduano, A. Roselli, and A. Schoysman (for the French version).
Note: all references to Lucian's text are based on Macleod's Oxford Classical Text vol. i (1972).

[1] Stengel (1911) tried to identify all the allusions contained in this work; although his study is the most complete commentary on *A True Story*, parallels and allusions are revealed clearly only in a few cases, while in the rest we are dealing with more generic matters of *langue*.

literature, including 'poets, historians, and philosophers'. This
tradition clearly goes back to the Homeric archetype of Odysseus'
tale of his exotic adventures, which he tells before the 'poor and
simple Phaeacians' (1. 3). This was considered as the paradigm of
lying narrative as early as Plato (*Republic* 10, 614d).

The account of the journey starts after the prologue. The ego-
narrator sails off with a group of loyal friends and, after a short
stop on an island where there are traces of visits by Heracles and
Dionysus, he is caught in a storm and carried off to the Moon.
There, he is welcomed with great kindness by King Endymion (the
Moon's lover in mythology), and takes part in the war against
Phaethon, the king of the Sun (though in Greek myth he is known
as the child of the Sun). Once peace is established, however, he
refuses to remain on the Moon to marry Endymion's son and
moves on to Lamptown. From there the protagonist and his
companions end up in the mouth of a giant whale, where they
become friends with an old man and take part in a war among the
inhabitants of this small world.

The second book opens with their perilous escape from the
whale's mouth. After adventures such as sailing on ice, stopping
on Cheeseland, and meeting the cork-footed people, they finally
arrive on the Island of the Blest. There they attend Rhadamanthus'
trials, speak to the soul of Homer, and participate in the war
against the Wicked. Later, they stop on the Island of Dreams and
at Ogygia, where they meet Calypso and give her a letter from
Odysseus. There follows a series of short episodes: the encounter
with the Pumpkin-pirates and the Nut-sailors; the enormous
halcyon's nest; sailing on top of the forest; the fight with the Ox-
heads; meeting the men who use their penises as masts for their
boats and those who sail on pieces of cork pulled by dolphins.
The last dangerous stop-over is on the Island of the Donkey-legs,
inhabitated by female cannibals. Finally, the circular composition
is closed and the *topos* of the storm brings them back to Earth.

Within the vast mine of fantasy Lucian works some important
distinctions in the course of his narrative. Whereas almost all of
classical culture follows the rule that invention belongs to poetry
and reference to prose, Lucian's satire is mainly targeted at the lies
of historians rather than those of poets. On the Island of the Blest,
Homer is held in a position of absolute prestige, and during his
conversation with the narrator he appears as a model poet defaced

by the pseudo-scientific activity of the grammarians (2. 20).[2] Aristophanes also gets a good press, as a wise and truthful poet (1. 29). Herodotus, on the other hand, appears together with Ctesias on the Island of the Wicked (which is described according to the conventions of the Underworld) as a punishment for not telling the truth (2. 31). Therefore, in absolute terms, it is not fantasy literature that is the target of Lucian's satire, but its travesty under the appearance of true experience, that is, all the extravagant descriptions of societies and codes of behaviour reported as true and personally experienced by ethnographers. *A True Story* echoes a thematic developed in a more scientific manner in *How to Write History*: the criticism that historiography was increasingly void of serious reference and close to works of poetry, replete with ornamental descriptions.[3] One particular aspect of this deviation from the objective truth is subjected to satire in the form of a fantasy tale: the journey to distant countries, in imitation of the peregrinations of Odysseus. This is the real focus of the satire, as is proved by the judgement passed on the utopianist Iambulus, who is cited in the prologue with Ctesias as the most important representative of this vein of literature: 'Iambulus, too, wrote a long account of the wonders of the great ocean; anybody can see it is fictitious, but it is quite entertaining none the less as a theme' (1. 3).

The vast spectrum of texts referred to in *A True Story* makes the definition of pastiche seem particularly appropriate for this work. In Genette's classification of hypertextual devices the fundamental opposition lies between transformation and imitation, between saying the same thing in different words and saying another thing in the same words. The former is usually concerned with isolated texts and their distinctive features, and parody is a part of it, whereas the latter works on the stereotypes and stylemes of a

[2] This privileged relation to Homer is esp. apparent at 2. 15 (his works are sung at symposia), 2. 22 (together with Hesiod he wins the poetic contest of the Games of the Dead), 2. 24 (he celebrates the victory over the Wicked in a poem); and also, for example, in the final part of *How to Write History*, where Homer is presented as a model even for historians, or indeed in the many citations of his poetry (on these cf. Householder's useful book (1941)); see Horn (1934: 24); Bouquiaux-Simon (1968: 358–63).

[3] See esp. 8, 20, 29 in the *pars destruens* of the text. On the opposition *historia/poietike*, see Avenarius (1956: 16–22) and his vast comparative material on the theory of ancient historiography; Canfora (1974: 14–32), esp. in relation to Thucydides; on the complementarity with *A True Story*, see Horn (1934: 6, 24–6). But this does not prevent *A True Story* from dissimulating a pleasure in the imaginary, as we shall see.

whole class of texts. Pastiche obviously belongs to it, and *A True Story* should doubtless to be put in this category since it is a satirical deformation of the conventions of one vast class of texts: the genre of the exotic journey. The structural distinction between transformation and imitation cuts across a classification based on the tonality used in second-degree elaboration, of which the three basic types are: ludic, satirical and serious, with intermediate levels. In our case, the prevailing tonality is certainly satirical, even though one also finds neutral playfulness and gentle irony, or, at the opposite pole, evident examples of aggressive polemic. The type to which Lucian's text belongs is therefore that of satirical pastiche (termed *charge* by Genette). This strikes at the norms of a genre by means of amplification and degradation (combined solutions are familiar too).[4]

A German dissertation of 1951 attempted to read *A True Story* as a parody of Antonius Diogenes' *Wonders beyond Thule*. Of this, as is well known, there remains only the summary by the patriarch Photius. The work has nevertheless been credited with some spectacular inventions in fantasy. In certain cases, a textual reference by Lucian can be proved from the summary, for instance, the episode of the Moon. It is, however, difficult to demonstrate, as also to believe, that the *Wonders*, which were so rich in imaginary journeys but also so full of erotic stories unheard of in Lucian, should have been the privileged model of a satire which was actually concerned with the whole vast topic of ethnographical accounts, from Aristaeus to Skylax and from Megasthenes to ps.-Callisthenes' account of the deeds of Alexander the Great.[5] The thesis is based on a notice in Photius in which the patriarch concludes his summary of the *Wonders* by defining them as 'the fount and root' of Lucian's *A True Story* and Lucius' *Metamorphoses*. He adds that they also constitute the 'model' for the fantastic accounts of Iamblichus, Achilles Tatius, and Heliodorus. Unlike us, Photius had direct access to the text, but this does not imply that all his

---

[4] See Genette (1982: 11-40) on these theoretical categories and 96-104 on textual examples of *charges*. Bompaire (1958: 599-655) examines the use of parody and pastiche as instruments of 'comic recreation' in Lucian's entire œuvre and distinguishes them by virtue of the greater critical power of the former.

[5] Reyhl (1969); against this thesis, see G. Anderson (1976a: 1-7), with well-documented arguments. On the tradition of ethnographic tales ('Reiseroman'), E. Rohde's work remains fundamental (1876: pt. 2, 204-9), esp. on Lucian's *Parodierung*.

critical assessments are to be taken very seriously, considering
amongst other things the moral aims of his works. The novels he
cites as directly influenced by Antonius Diogenes offer in fact a
totally different approach. *A True Story* deploys its irony only on the
side of the fantastic and the unreal, while in Lucius' *Metamorphoses*, as far as we can judge from the Greek epitome and
from Apuleius, the relationship is even less direct, since the only
common features between the two narratives are the theme of
magic and the picaresque tone. As for the erotic novel, a distinction also has to be made. If it is true that Antonius Diogenes introduced the element of love into the adventure story, but not within
the thematic of the thwarted couple, it is also true that the
supernatural element so prominent in the *Wonders* is not present
to the same extent in the authors cited by Photius. It seems that
Iamblichus did make considerable use of it, as Photius' summary
tells us, whereas Heliodorus takes it over and motivates it in
accordance with his Neoplatonic outlook. Finally, Achilles Tatius
not only introduces supernatural themes, but also manages to
parody the typical magical scenario of the resurrection of a dead
man (3. 15-22). His conception of reality is usually sceptical and
materialist.

Photius' short notice has given rise to the idea that *A True Story*
was a parody of the *Wonders beyond Thule* and of the entire Greek
erotic novel, associated in the broad with Antonius Diogenes.
However, the relation between Lucian and the Greek novel ought
to be reconsidered through a more detailed and balanced approach.
Graham Anderson's study has been a first step in that direction.[6]
To restrict ourselves to the text, it must be admitted that certain
passages seem to be a satire on novelistic elements, for instance
the meeting with the Pumpkin-pirates, a grotesque distortion of a
widespread narrative *topos*, or the false paradoxographic asides on
strange animals, referring to a vast pseudo-scientific literature, on
which Achilles Tatius and Heliodorus drew.[7] This does not exclude

[6] G. Anderson (1976a: 83-9); the parallels cited on 84-5 sometimes seem too
vague and out of context, but the author correctly evaluates the main difference,
the absence of the theme of love in Lucian, which makes it impossible to judge
whether the contact was direct or came through the influence of rhetorical culture.

[7] Bompaire (1958: 674-5) thinks of a common rhetorical stock used by Lucian
and the Greek novel. The earlier dating of the erotic novel on the basis of papyrological evidence allows a direct connection (except for Heliodorus, who is certainly
later), but it may not be a univocal one.

the possibility of finding positive points of contact, especially with
Achilles Tatius, the most disenchanted of the Greek novelists, who
comes very close to Lucian's rationalism. *Leucippe and Clitophon*
may indeed be seen as a pastiche of the Greek erotic novel, in a
purely ludic manner rather than aggressively satirical, but with the
strong meta-linguistic aspect that is characteristic of literary production in the period of the Second Sophistic, to which Lucian, all
in all, belongs as well.[8]

I hope to have established the literary matrix in which satirical
imitation operates in *A True Story*, and to have thrown some light
on its hypertextuality. It is basically a form of literature that ranges
over several genres—epic, historiography, philosophical prose,
novel: the imaginary journey, presented as personal experience by
an ego-narrator. This form based on the Homeric paradigm of
Odysseus' tales, has been used by ethnographers staking a claim to
authenticity as well as by utopianists as a fictional device. It was
also to know immense good fortune in Western literature, from
Dante to Voltaire, from Swift to Butler and Wells.[9]

THE NARRATOR AS EYEWITNESS

The satire of the imaginary voyage starts at the level Genette has
termed 'paratext', i.e. the level of all the secondary information (be
it the author's own or not), half-way between external comments
and text: preface and postface, title and sub-title, epigraph, table of
contents, illustrations, notes.[10] These elements are less well defined
in antique culture because of the differences in book production
and circulation. In the present case, the title is clearly an anti-
phrase—*A True Story*—used to describe a work full of paradoxical
fiction. This is even more explicit in what may be regarded as the
preface, although it is not clearly distinguished from the text. In
the first four paragraphs, the author pretends to have written his

[8] J. Schwartz (1976: 618-26) lists several parallels between the two authors,
but as G. Anderson (1976a: 87-9) points out, these are very common themes in
imperial rhetoric. A link can only remain on the most abstract level of literary forms
and of their axiologic corollaries. On Lucian's place in the neo-rhetorical context of
the Second Sophistic, see Bompaire (1958: pt. 1) and Reardon (1971: 155-80).

[9] On the fortune of this literary form in Western literature, see Gove (1961: pt.
1). However, the author overstresses the concept's taxonomic definition and the
history of criticism. On Lucian, see 18-19.

[10] Genette (1982: 9-10).

story out of mere vanity, from a wish to leave something behind
for posterity—so he would not be the only one who did not enjoy
the liberty to make up stories and so he might invent lies, though
nothing special had happened to him: 'Consequently I turned to
romancing myself. But I am much more sensible about it than
others are, for I will say one thing that is true, and that is that I
am a liar' (1. 4).[11]

Many narrative literatures use this *topos* of presenting the tale in
a preface as a personal experience of the protagonist, so as to
relieve the author of his responsibility (cf. Defoe's *Moll Flanders*).
Introductory frameworks may be established to give an impression
of real life, like the *topos* of the uncovered manuscript, Plato's
settings of his dialogues and letters, and the novella in the
Renaissance. In the Greek novel there is Achilles Tatius' introduction with the meeting between the author and the narrator-
protagonist, or Longus' description of the story of Daphnis and
Chloe as represented in a painting.[12] These are the devices used by
narrative fiction to make itself look authentic, for the pleasure of
story-telling is repressed by realist force: it is a phenomenon that is
particularly noticeable in texts where the imaginary predominates.
Ancient as well as modern utopias are always presented as
real travels, well documented and narrated by the protagonist
(Euhemerus, Iambulus, More, Campanella, Butler, but also the
anti-utopias of Orwell and Huxley). Lucian, however, by a clearly
marked satirical contrast, asserts the falsity of his tale (speaking
furthermore in the first person) and he concludes by saying, 'My
subject, then, is things I have neither seen nor experienced nor
heard tell of from anybody else: things, what is more, that do not
in fact exist and could not ever exist at all. So my readers must not
believe a word I say' (1. 4). Here we deal with the exceptional case
of an author professing the absolute unreliability of the chosen
narrator, who, moreover, declares himself to be identical with the
author, in the fashion of autobiographic narration, for instance in

---

[11] On the antiphrastic nature of this preface, see Bompaire (1958: 547). Stengel
(1911: 13) cites Ctesias' and Antonius Diogenes' claims to truth as striking
examples of this *usus*, which has roots of course in Herodotus (1. 52, 66; 2. 99).

[12] The form and function of these introductory frames in narrative texts are
analysed by Romberg (1962: pt. 1, ch. 2, esp. 33-8 and 68-81). On Achilles
Tatius' introduction—a typically 'epic situation', reused in the comic fashion of
everyday life and in a different manner from the historical travesties of the other
Greek novelists—see Hägg (1971a: 125). For the descriptive frame in Longus,
which creates a greater distance, see Kestner (1973: 166-71).

the Elysian Fields when the protagonist asks Homer to write an inscription: 'Lucian, befriended by the blessed gods, saw this land and returned to his own country' (2. 28).[13]

It is worth while focusing our attention on the figure of the narrator, who has a vital function in the making of satirical pastiche. The intense narratological debate of recent years has given us the means to distinguish between the various possible types of narrator. There are three main divisions: his involvement—or non-involvement—in the story (which often corrects the misleading opposition between first and third person); his position at the primary level of narrative or in a narrative framed by the principal narrative; and his relation to the characters' level of knowledge and to their ideology (a category which takes up the reflections of the Jamesian school in this area). The narrator of *A True Story* not only takes part in the story, but is its direct protagonist, placed at the primary level of narration and usually making his perspective as narrator identical to his perspective as actor. To use Genette's technical terminology, he is a homodiegetic and extradiegetic narrator with internal focalization. This is a narrative situation typical of the picaresque novel and of *Gil Blas*. It is also highly suited to giving the impression of an authentic and direct grasp on real life, inasmuch as it takes the form of an entry in a personal journal, no doubt in mediate terms (for if it were immediate, it would form what we call 'interior monologue') but in the least possible *a posteriori*.[14]

It is not just coincidence that the ego-narration in the ancient novel should be linked to the layer of narrative usually called 'comic-realist', to which belongs *Lucius or Ass*, Petronius, Apuleius, and partly also Achilles Tatius (the Greek erotic novelist who is closest to the world of Menippus).[15] In these texts, as in all ego-narrations, there is a tension between the I who narrates and the

[13] For a similar statement of falsity, see Theopompus in Strabo 1. 2. 35. The various degrees of credibility that are available to a narrator have been examined by Booth (1961: 155–7 and pt. 3). On the author–narrator–character dynamic in autobiography, see Lejeune (1978: pt. 1, esp. 22–31, on proper names).

[14] On this typology of narrative situations, see esp. Lintvelt (1981) and Genette (1981: 77–89), who draws his conclusions after a long discussion. On the various degrees of distance between narrator and characters, and particularly on the effect of direct control, see Rousset (1973: 25–7) and Pugliatti (1985: 8–26).

[15] On the comic use of ego-narration in ancient picaresque literature, see Perry (1967: 111–17) and Plepelits (1980: 29–31), who sets it in opposition to the third-person narration more typical of historiography or pseudo-historiography.

I who acts (*erzählendes Ich* and *erlebendes Ich* in Stanzel's terms[16]): in most cases the I who narrates makes use of the more extended information he has about himself as an actor-protagonist, and displays several signs of what we call the 'omniscient narrator'. This is true of Homer's Odysseus, who always retains a panoramic view with zero focalization which he never focuses on himself as character. This technique is sometimes used by the ancient novelists mentioned above,[17] and it is applied with extreme thoroughness by Lucian in *A True Story*.

The narrator's anticipation of future events in the story is in fact very rare and vague. After listing all the gifts he had received from Endymion, King of the Moon, he adds, 'All of which I left behind in the whale' (1. 27). At this stage in the story, the internal prolepsis is particularly charged with suspense. The other events are told without anticipating information given during the narrative and are seen through the eyes of the actors, in other words those of the protagonist-narrator who has undertaken this fantastic journey beyond the Pillars of Hercules with a group of his friends, driven by *curiositas* (just as the cosmic voyage in *Icaromenippus* 5-10 is born of a scientific urge to test philosophical theories about the Moon, with the obvious result of ridiculing and criticizing all of them).[18] After the heavy storm which lifted the ship three thousand stades above the earth for seven days,

On the eighth we saw a large tract of land suspended in the atmosphere like an island; it was bright and spherical, and bathed in strong light. We

---

[16] F. Stanzel (1979: 109-48). The distance between these two levels is exactly what prevents confusion between first-person usage and restricted perspective, a confusion that has a long history in literary theory and is still found in applied criticism. Cf. Genette (1972).

[17] The narrative technique of Homer's *Odyssey* has been correctly established by Suerbaum (1968), who stresses the *mise en abyme* between *aoidos* and character. For the internal focalization used by Petronius' ego-narrator in the *Cena Trimalchionis*, see Veyne (1964: 303-4). On the passages in Achilles Tatius (esp. Leucippe's first two apparent deaths, at 3. 15 and 5. 7), see Hägg (1971a: 131-4), Effe (1975: 150-1). The recent book by Winkler (1985) is entirely based on the operations of this dialectic in the *Asinus Aureus*.

[18] On the far-ranging *topos* of travels undertaken for the sake of knowledge, present for instance in Dante's Ulysses or Jules Verne, see Herodotus 1. 29-30 (Solon's travels) for historiography, and Antonius Diogenes 2 for adventure tales. So too Lucius, the protagonist of the *Asinus* attributed to Lucian, is driven by his curiosity to experience magic (9); this element is developed by Apuleius 2. 1. *Curiositas* in general and *navigatio* in particular are seen as constant features of the Menippean utopia by Koppenfels (1981: 32), from Lucian to More to Alice.

put in to it, anchored, and went ashore. On exploring the land, we found
it to be inhabited and cultivated. We could see nothing from it during the
daytime, but when night fell many other islands became visible near to it,
some larger, some smaller, the colour of fire. There was also another land
below us, with cities, rivers, seas, forests, and mountains; this we
supposed to be our earth. (1. 10)

The arrival on the Moon, it seems to me, clearly demonstrates how
the focalization is restricted to the ego-actor, not the ego-narrator.
That the place actually is the Moon comes to our knowledge
only when King Endymion says this to the characters. The
intrusion of the imaginary allows for a gradual introduction of
strange elements, thanks to the description of their very first sensa-
tions and perceptions, which are half-way between the real and the
fantastic.[19]

The real-life effect is also achieved by a constant and precise
indication of the origin of the narrator's information. This is
clearly a satire on the historians' habit of reporting the oral or
written sources of their accounts. With a chronology imitating an
historical narrative and created by the rhythmical opening of the
whale's mouth, we get the description of the battle between the
giants who sail on big islands and use huge trees as oars. The
characters watch this battle from in between the whale's teeth,
and later the names of the two leaders and the cause of the battle
are reported: 'to judge from the accusations they hurled at each
other as they called out their kings' names' (1. 42). The author
thus pays careful attention to the means and intermediaries used
by the narrator to perceive the events and to deduce his information.[20] This styleme even occurs negatively when the narrator
confesses his ignorance, as in this passage of the war between the
Moon and the Sun:

There were also supposed to be seventy thousand Sparrow-acorns and five
thousand Horse-cranes coming from the stars above Cappadocia. As they

[19] The arrival on the Island of the Blest (the parallel episode in Book 2) is fully
identical. The parallelism of the two main episodes in the two books, which correspond to two other works in the macrotext of Lucian, *Icaromenippus* and *Menippus*,
was highlighted by Hirzel (1895: 317). The principle of parallel composition in the
two books of *A True Story* is stressed by G. Anderson (1976*a*: 7–11), with perhaps
an excessive precision and some hypotheses on the hypotext. The same analysis is
applied to the whole of the Lucianic corpus in Anderson (1976*b*: ch. 9, esp. 140–1,
164), on the parallelism of the two works relating to Menippus.
[20] Bakhtin (1978: ch. 3) laid great stress on the value of this narrative feature
in his analysis of the Greek novel and of adventure time in general.

did not arrive, I did not see them; hence I have not presumed to describe them—report made them out wonderful creatures, too wonderful to be credible. (I. 13)[21]

Lucian has applied the principles of eyewitness narration with great thoroughness, by reporting only information that was actually known to the protagonist, and only at the time of action when it came to his knowledge. He does this by choosing a narrator who is involved in the story, with a focalization on himself as actor. The type of narrative technique adopted by Lucian, typical of ethnographic travel accounts, stands in striking contrast to his preliminary statement of absolute falsity—and this contrast is actually the starting point of the satirical attack. Indeed, the preface undermines the foundations of the narration which follows the parameters of authentic experience. Susanne Lanser has established a spectrum of possible ways in which the narrator presents his narration as real or fictional ('referential claim'): the pole of absolute historical reference ('report') is eyewitness narration, reporting a true story, as in the narrative body of Lucian's work, whereas the opposite pole of pure fiction is represented by parodic and parasitical literature. This is the category towards which the preface turns when it states the text's literarity, as we have seen.[22]

This is why all interventions made by the narrator to confirm the incredible truth of his tale have a strongly comic effect: 'I do not record the numbers of them, however, lest I be disbelieved, so many they were' (I. 18, on the Cloud-centaurs); 'I hesitate to mention the nature of their eyes; it sounds incredible; still, I will do so' (I. 25, on the Moonites); 'Anyone who does not believe this has only to go there himself someday to find out that I am telling the truth' (I. 26, on the mirror reflecting the earth's image); 'I know this is going to sound far-fetched, but I shall describe it nevertheless' (I. 40, a precaution before narrating the battle between the giants straddling the islands).[23] The final episode, summing up the tale and falsely announcing its continuation ('What happened on the continent I shall relate in the books to

---

[21] In Herodotus (I. 193), Thucydides (3. 113), Tacitus (*Germania* 46) there is a noticeable reluctance to report non-verifiable events. This feature is satirically reversed here: see Stengel (1911: 23–4).

[22] Lanser (1981: 163–4); intermediate levels are: 'formal realism', 'fictive truth', 'fantasy'.

[23] E. Rohde (1876: 205–6) on the value of the parody in passages aimed at historiographical usages.

follow', 2. 47), is a further element parodying phraseology which is typical of descriptions of voyages, i.e. the promise of continuation. This seems to have been common in Antiquity, to judge by Lucian's criticism in *How to Write History* (31); it was also found in philosophical prose (cf. the well-known announcement of continuation in the second book of Aristotle's *Poetics*).[24] The tendency persists in modern utopias, for instance Butler announcing a *Return to Erewhon* at the end of his *Erewhon*.

AMPLIFICATION

Some parts of the text, however, escape narrative organization. These are the excursuses on different lifestyles, which are narrated in the timeless-descriptive present tense and playfully rewrite the ethnographical digressions so typical of historiography (especially Herodotus) and not unknown to epic and novel (Apollonius Rhodius, Achilles Tatius, Heliodorus).[25] In terms of time these digressions are presented as a summary of observations made during the journey: 'I should like to describe the novel and unusual things I noticed during my stay on the Moon.' This is how the excursus is introduced in 1. 22, starting with physical characteristics, carrying on with matters of food (directly imitated in Cyrano's *Autre Monde*) and sexual habits, and ending with other strange bodily features, agricultural production, clothing, and finally with the most bizarre characteristic, the removable eyes (1. 22-6).[26]

[24] The scholion on the passage already held that this statement of continuation was the last of Lucian's lies, and the parallel with the theoretical work on history seems to remove any doubt about its satirical character: strangely enough Bompaire (1958: 673) believes it to be true. For an opposite view, see Ollier (1962) and G. Anderson (1976a: 11).

[25] The most recent study of ancient ethnography is K. Müller (1972). On Apollonius' excursuses, see Fusillo (1985: IC); and for the novel, Rommel (1923).

[26] The element of carrying a foetus in the calf of the leg certainly echoes and distorts the mythical birth of Dionysus, born from Zeus' thigh, something Lucian developed in his *Dialogues of the Gods* 9. Dietary habits—smoke from roasting frogs and moisture from compressed air—recall esp. Herodotus' accounts on the inhabitants of the islands in the Araxes and of the Scythians (1. 202 and 4. 75), who lived on the smell of burned fruit, and what Megasthenes tells us about India (717 F 30 Jacoby); the glass clothing is a satire of the priests' linen clothes in Euhemerus (63 F 3 [5. 46. 2]); the removable eye may be a reference to a mythical theme, the story of Lamia hiding her eyes (Diodorus 20. 41); for other comparative studies of these excursuses, esp. for Ctesias (the structure of the intestines, the size of the ears) and the Pythagoreans, cf. Stengel (1911: 34-8) and Ollier (1962).

Ancient ethnography had established a real 'rhetoric of the Other' (Hartog), entirely based on the *topos* of the reversed world and the figure of inversion in relation to standard Greek customs, according to a Hellenocentric perspective which is here falsified.[27] In this abstract scheme the operation consists only of an amplification of the strange. It is the typical feature of pastiche, called 'stylization' by the Russian formalists and 'saturation' by Genette, and is based on an accumulation of the literary model's stylistic hallmarks.[28]

The same technique is used in Book 2 for the excursus on the Island of the Blest. There the target of the satire is utopian writing, which finds its first really profound expression in Plato (especially in the *Critias*) and its most distinctive fantasy characteristics in the Hellenistic utopias, particularly Iambulus.[29] When the protagonists approach the Island, they breathe in a marvellous air. Lucian describes it by multiplying the topical element of floral scents: 'It was like the scent of roses, narcissi, hyacinths, lilies, and violets, and of myrrh and laurel and flowering vine too' (2. 5). The utopian city represents an accumulation of various typical elements, like scented air, glass baths filled with warm dew, people wearing clothes made of a kind of cobweb, eternal dawn, the extraordinary fertility of nature—taking up the *topos* of the Golden Age so frequent in Western literature from Hesiod onward.[30] Even

---

[27] The reversed world is systematically described by Herodotus with reference to the Egyptians (2. 35); Rosellini and Saïd (1978) base their reading of Herodotus' *History* on the following principle: the farther removed from Greekness, the more inverted the customs; this interpretation has been radicalized by Hartog (1980).

[28] Genette (1982: 94–5).

[29] A complete study of ancient utopias is to be found in Ferguson (1975): on Lucian's parody (Iambulus rather than Euhemerus), see 174–6; on the relation of ancient and modern utopias, see Kerényi (1963); and, for a more articulated structural view, Kytzler (1973: 57), on ancient anti-utopia and on Lucian; see also Trousson (1975: 13–28, 39–43).

[30] The inhabitants of Iambulus' utopian city (Diodorus 2. 59. 4) wear purple clothes. On the Golden Age, see Hesiod, *Works* 109–26, esp. 117–18 on the fertility of the earth (as already with Homer's Phaeacians: *Odyssey* 7. 117–20) together with the joyful songs of those feasting. These themes occur also in the utopia of Euhemerus (Diodorus 5. 43), Hecataeus of Abdera (264 F 7 [1] Jacoby), Theopompus (in Aelian, *Varia Historia* 3. 18), Iambulus' Island of the Blest (2. 56. 7), Dio Chrysostom (35. 19). The Homeric land of the Cimmerians is covered in perpetual mist (*Odyssey* 11. 14–15) and the land beyond Thule has very long nights (Antonius Diogenes 9); as for the veiled light of the Moon in Lucian, the parallels with Theopompus are even more striking (cf. Aelian, op. cit.) and Plutarch (*De facie in orbe lunae* 941d). For the element of scented air, cf. the Island of the Blest in Pindar (*Olynthiaca* 2. 130) and, with a more pronounced accumulation, Euhemerus (in Diodorus 5. 41. 4).

greater stress is put on the description of the banquet, with winds serving dishes, trees offering cups of wine, clouds drawing up perfume, and springs of Laughter and Pleasure,[31] the listing of the guests. Then there are the sexual habits based on the principle of absolute freedom (2. 11-19).[32] This whole passage is entirely based on amplification: ancient utopias and extra-terrestrial visions insisted in their representation of the world on elements such as spontaneous wealth, peaceful life amongst the pleasures of art, the happiness of fellow-diners, and of collectivity: all these are present here in a very dense enumeration.

As we have seen, ethnographic and utopian writings are treated satirically in the form of descriptive excursuses. The more properly historiographic style, on the other hand, is used for episodes of war. As soon as the protagonists arrive on the Moon, they are caught in the war between King Endymion and Phaethon, king of the Sun, caused by some colonial expedition. The account of the battle is absolutely canonical. It opens with a list of the allies' forces, especially of the stranger elements. The darkening of the Moon through the building of a wall—an image taken from Aristophanes' *Birds* (550-2)—brings Endymion to capitulate and to sign a treaty, the text of which is transcribed with great accuracy (in pseudo-juridical language) as also are the names of the sworn witnesses (1. 13-20).[33] In this episode and in other similar ones the rhetori-

[31] The invisible servant is a widely diffused folklore element: cf. Stengel (1911: 61), citing a parallel in Apuleius 5. 2. On trees which spontaneously offer food, cf. Dio Chrysostom 35. 21. The two springs are a clear reference to Theopompus' utopia with its springs of Pleasure and Pain (Aelian, *Varia Historia* 3. 18).

[32] The catalogue of guests in the Beyond is a reference to Plato's *Republic* (10. 620a-d), where one also finds the origins of sexual collectivism (5. 457d), limited by Plato to the class of warriors, but extended to pederasts by the radicalizing 'ultra-Platonists' of the Island of the Blest; the same sexual habits appear in Iambulus (Diodorus 2. 58. 1), as well as in Herodotean ethnography, where they are seen as a deviation from Greek morality, in various degrees: 1. 216 (the Massagetae, who retain the institution of marriage); 4. 104 (Agathyrsi), 180 (Machlyes and Ausees, without cohabitation); on public sex, see again Herodotus 1. 203 and 3. 101, Apollonius Rhodius 2. 1023-25, Megasthenes 715 F 27 Jacoby.

[33] The narrative of the battle is too often of a type to be a reference to a particular model: see however, as an example for the disposition of troops, Thucydides 4. 93-4 (Boeotians and Athenians). Likewise it is useless to seek for earlier models of the treaty: see Bompaire (1958: 640), in his very interesting analysis of the parody of official style (637-41); on the parody of decrees, see also the end of *Icaromenippus*, and Helm (1906); Ollier (1962), against Stengel (1911: 29-30), citing Thucydides 5. 18-19. On comic battles as constant features—with very many variations—see G. Anderson (1976a: 26-7, 36-8).

cal figure of amplification operates at the level of language through the accumulation of historiographical stylemes recalling those of Thucydides, especially at the level of narrative time. The various battles are told with rather unnatural rapidity, following a principle used by Lucian throughout his story. As early as the *Odyssey*, the characteristic feature of adventure tales was a rapid juxtaposition of episodes (Cyclopes, Laestrygonians, Aeolus), and a condensation of dead times (the stay with Calypso). Lucian radicalizes this feature (for instance in the episode of the whale, the peace interval between the internal and external battle is narrated within three lines), giving his narrative a frenetic pace without equal, except perhaps in Voltaire's *Candide*, which we known is a close relative of *A True Story*.[34] The rhythm of the narration is seen as *Candide*'s most fascinating feature by Italo Calvino; and it is well known that Calvino as a writer owes much to this rich source and its mixture of rationalistic irony, meta-literary reflection, and fantastic invention.[35]

To sum up, in the case of historiography as well as of ethnography and utopia, what we see in Lucian is not the parodic transformation of isolated texts (as on the contrary is the case with certain epic elements: Helen's abduction, the storm of the *Odyssey*, Calypso, and the Sirens), but a satirical re-working of a literary code, that is, the rhetorical amplification of topical ways of expression. The same technique is used for the pastiche of Herodotus in *On the Syrian Goddess*, and partly also in *Toxaris*.[36]

[34] Another battle inside the whale: 1. 35–9; on the tribute as cause of the war, see Thucydides 1. 99. 1; a trace of Thucydides can be found at the end of the episode of the erection of the trophy (1. 38/4. 134. 2), though this is quite unusual for Lucian. The fantastic battle of the giants is a tissue of verbal reminiscences of the battle between the Corinthians and the Corcyraeans in Thucydides 1. 48–54; cf. Stengel (1911: 44–5). Cf. also 2. 23–4.

[35] Calvino (1974: 'Introduction', 5–10).

[36] Stengel's work probably takes the preliminary statement too seriously, i.e. that each textual element alludes to one particular text (he thus earns G. Anderson's irony: 1976a: 10); but the vast number of parallels often adduced by Stengel for a single incident tends to prove that Lucian tried to base his pastiche in a rich vein of literature. Anderson (ch. 5) gives many parallels between *The Syrian Goddess* and *A True Story* in order to corroborate Lucian's authorship of the former, as already claimed by Bompaire (1958: 646–53); the parallelism with *Toxaris*, offering a broader spectrum of rhetorical and philosophical references, is esp. pertinent to the narrative structure: cf. ibid. 12–23.

MENIPPEAN DEGRADATION

Amplification is not the only technique upon which Lucian's pastiche is based. I have alluded to oscillations in the tone of expression, from the ludic to the polemic. The accumulation of ethnographic and utopian *topoi* already mentioned is no doubt an integral part of a mainly neutral meta-literary play: a subtle ironizing of the literary form which hides the telling of fantastic stories under the appearance of historical enquiry. However, a more tendenciously satirical attack is at work through a feature Freud considered an active constituent of the comic, degradation (*Herabsetzung*).[37] *A True Story* is indeed filled with low and grotesque elements. It has therefore been compared, like many of Lucian's writings, to Menippean satire, a literary genre which is notoriously difficult to delimit. Bakhtin's genial study has identified a tradition of underground dissemination and a persistently secular character, a kind of carnivalesque literature which starts with Aristophanes and goes all the way to Dostoevsky. Clearly the diachronic perspective cannot be as fluid as this. Otherwise Menippean satire would be in danger of becoming a universal archetype, as in Frye's criticism. A more thorough study of the genre's morphology and its ramifications is needed, but this goes far beyond the scope of this paper, even when restricted to the classical period in which Lucian, together with Petronius, Seneca, and Martianus Capella, represents a major turn.

It may be asserted, however, that the vulgar, the bodily, and the deformed are the thematic kernels of this literary vein. With his strong linguistic imagination (making use of Greek's facilities for creating compounds, which among the European languages is peculiar only to German), Lucian invents for his imaginary people all sorts of names which often strike a tone of burlesque devaluation.[38] This arises from paradoxical juxtapositions which are typically Menippean. In the battle between the Moon and the Sun the image of food prevails. The soldiers of the Moon ride on 'Vegetable-

---

[37] Freud (1905: ch. 7).

[38] Cf. esp. Bakhtin (1970: ch. 1); Frye (1969). A vast catalogue of Menippean texts arranged by chronology and themes has been compiled by Kirk (1980); Koppenfels (1981) offers good insight into some formal and thematic features of Menippean satire. On linguistic invention in Lucianic compositions, see Matteuzzi (1975: 225–9).

wings' (*Lachanopteroi*), gigantic birds with vegetable shoots instead of plumage, and 'quill feathers just like lettuce leaves'. The 'Millet-slingers' and the 'Flea-archers' (*Psyllotoxotai*) are also parts of Endymion's army (1. 13). The forces of the Sun comprise the 'Stalk-mushrooms' (*Kaylomyketes*), named so because they use mushrooms as shields and asparagus stalks as spears (1. 16). Ridiculous arms are common too in the lunar forces: 'helmets made of beans, which grow big and hard there, breastplates of overlapping lupin pods, stitched together, the pods being hard as horn' (1. 14; see also 1. 27). Even stronger is the image used for the 'Sky-dancers' (*Aerokordakes*), the light-armed foot soldiers of the Sun: 'They slung great radishes from long range, and whoever was struck by them could not last even a short time but died from the foul-smelling wounds they caused' (1. 16). This burlesque travesty clearly echoes the ancient heroic-comic masterpiece, the *Batrachomyomachia*, which is filled with bizarre types of armour (122-31, 160-5).[39] And, finally, the signal given for the start of the battle is quite odd: 'As soon as the standards were raised and the donkeys had brayed—they used donkeys as trumpeters—they began to fight' (1. 17, based on Herodotus 4. 129). The ass is indeed an anthropological symbol for the lower parts of the body, and, as is well known, is central to the *Lucius or Ass*, extant in an epitome attributed to Lucian (but its authorship is a matter of very complex debate).[40]

This continuous linguistic invention, of which only a few significant examples have been given (the episode of the whale has a more predictable marine imagery), highlights a logic latent in the text which, as we shall see, constantly blends in with the dominant logic of rationalist satire. The play with names expresses the pleasure of the absurd, reminding us of the strange characters

---

[39] Hermann (1949: 359-61) on the relation between Lucian and the *Batrachomyomachia*. On this ps.-Homeric poem as heroic-comic archetype and on the gap between grotesque content and aulic style, see Genette (1982: 147-9).

[40] The image of the ass is reused for the people living on Witchcraft Island (2. 46), called Donkey-legs because they had donkey hooves instead of feet; this episode seems to contaminate a reference to the Homeric sirens with a reference to Circe: cf. G. Anderson (1976*a*: 18). In chs. 3 and 4 of his book Anderson suggests, on the basis of thematic comparisons, that we attribute to Lucian both the lost original and the extant epitome of the *Asinus*; see his vast bibliography. For the image of the donkey-trumpeters, cf. also ps.-Eratosthenes, *Catasterismoi* 11; Stengel (1911: 48-9) also cites Lucian's *Bacchus* 4 in order to confirm that this *prolalia* introduces Book 2 of *A True Story*; but this point is highly debated.

Alice meets in Wonderland (which represent the conceptual dis-
integration of the Victorian world at the time of Lewis Carroll).

In addition to these elements of low-level comedy there come a
number of genital images. Among the Sun's army we find the
'Acorn-dogs' or 'Dog-nuts' (*Kunobalanoi*) (1. 16), 'men with dogs'
faces, fighting from winged acorns'. With perfect symmetry in Book
2, dominated by marine isotopy, the protagonists meet 'men
sailing in a novel manner, for they were both crew and ship as
well', that is, they used their enormous penises as masts by float-
ing on the water and operating the sails (2. 45).[41]

What is satirically degraded here, in fact, is the convention
stating that a voyage of adventure implies an encounter with paradoxical creatures. In his preface the author himself had claimed
that the writers he had read followed Ctesias and Iambulus on the
model of Odysseus, 'with his stories of winds enslaved and men
with one eye and cannibals and wild men, of many-headed beasts,
and of how his crew were drugged and transformed' (1. 3).

HYPERBOLIC SPACE

A further semantic feature of the Menippean world is its dynamism.
This attests its philosophical origins in the revolutionary school of
the Cynics. It is mainly found at the level of the form of expression,
for example in the periodical alternation of verse and prose, which
is present in *A True Story*, though to a lesser degree, and which
Lucian himself in *Double Indictment* (39) claims as a practice
which is intentionally hybrid and systematically Menippean. It is
also found in the ironic articulations of narrative voices, strongly
marked here, as we have seen, if one recalls the author's denial of
his own narrator. In our text this relativism is felt particularly at
the thematic level of space, the load-bearing axis of every utopian
text.[42] The fantastic journey in *A True Story* has the picaresque

---

[41] In the excursus on Libya Herodotus (4. 191) speaks of dog-headed men. In G.
Anderson's scheme (1976a: 8–9), the symmetry of the two books always
follows the syntagmatic order: this means that the people using sails are paralleled
by those using their cork feet in 2. 4; but the scheme is too rigid and excludes cross-
references on a paradigmatic level.

[42] On the mixture of verse and prose in classical literature, see Bartonkova
(1976: 65–92; on Lucian 70–5); also Householder (1941) and Bompaire (1958:
382–404). According to Koppenfels (1981), such mixing, the ironic presentation of

structure of continuous peregrinations, common also to Petronius and *Lucius or Ass,* and is articulated in three spaces, all in polar inversion to the real world. The journey starts at the Pillars of Hercules (I. 5), the canonical limits of the known world at the time. After a storm of twenty-four days (a hyperbolic amplification of the storms in the *Odyssey*),[43] the protagonists arrive on an island showing traces of the passage there of Heracles and Dionysus. Here, the satirical attack is mainly aimed at accounts of Alexander the Great's expedition (the favourite figure of the abhorred Stoics), the Macedonian king taking these two gods as his models (I. 6-8).[44] From this island the protagonists are carried off by the storm up to the Moon. This is the first space in which a good part of the action is passed. To it corresponds the mouth of the whale, still in Book I. These two spaces have a clearly marked, insular, restricted, and closed character and contrast symmetrically with the real world through their hyperbolic height and their hyperbolic depth. The third space, in which most of the narrative of Book 2 takes place, also has an insular nature. Its remoteness from earth is not only in space, but also in time; it is the pagan Beyond, located between the islands of the Blest and the Wicked, which form such a neat contrast. It is precisely this spatial-temporal paradox of the journey to Hades which has always attracted writers of the Menippean genre, from Aristophanes in the *Frogs* to Seneca in the *Apocolokynthosis.* Lucian uses it several times (especially in *Menippus*).[45]

fiction, and the eccentric spatiality are constituent elements of Menippean satire and its paradoxes; in its spatiality it crosses with utopian fiction through the use of strange and remote viewpoints (sky, Hades, Olympus, with an equipollence of high and low).

[43] According to Ollier (1962), Lucian's parody is aimed mainly at the storm in Iambulus, which lasted at least four months as told by Diodorus. Anyhow, it is a topical element of travel tales, following in the wake of the Homeric paradigm as a justification for its detachment from the everyday world; it is found also in Bacon's *Nova Atlantis* and in Swift.

[44] On divine prototypes in Alexander's propaganda, see Goukowsky (1981). The idea of an exotic place visited by Heracles and Dionysus is a satire of historiographic accounts of India in particular: cf. Megasthenes (in Diodorus 2. 38. 3–39. 4) for foundations of cities during Alexander's expedition. Zambrini (1982 and 1985) is an interesting reading of this aspect of Megasthenes: the work should be considered half-way between an ethnographic account and a utopian project. The detail of the physical sign (footsteps) attesting the presence of the gods, on the other hand, is a parody of Herodotus (4. 82; cf. also 2. 91).

[45] Koppenfels (1981: 33) stresses the relation of these three main spaces as a sign of the passage from a satirical duality to a plurality of worlds, largely echoed

These spaces are dominated by an absolute gigantism: the Sun forces are formed principally by 'Horse-ants', 'great beasts with wings, just like our ants except in size, for the biggest of them was two hundred feet long' (1. 16). The conflict between Moon and Sun is brought to an end thanks to the late intervention of the 'Cloud-centaurs', who were 'a very odd sight, a mixture of men and winged horses. The human part, from the middle up, was the size of the Colossus of Rhodes; the horse part as big as a cargo vessel' (1. 18); this creation originates in a passage of Aristophanes' *Clouds* (346).[46] Hyperbolic dimensions are also attributed to the whale. It is the biggest one encountered in the sea after the return from the Moon, 'not far short of two hundred miles long' (1. 30). It swallows the entire ship, which, however, remains intact and even manages to pass between its teeth. Once inside the protagonists see 'a great cavern, broad in every direction and high, big enough to hold a large city. It had fish large and small, and fragments of many and various animals were lying in the middle of it, as well as ships' masts, anchors, human bones, and merchandise, hills, even woods with trees of all kinds; the circumference of the land was thirty miles' (1. 30–31). They also discover the temple of Poseidon and meet an old man, who teaches them how he cultivates vines, fishes, swims, and takes a bath. It is an independent, self-sufficient microcosm. The animal's macroscopic dimensions appear very clearly when the protagonists decide to break out.[47] A real taste for hyper-

in modern utopias. Fauth (1979: 51–4), on the other hand, points out a fourfold correspondance between Moon and whale, Island of the Blest and Island of the Wicked; in the two books the contrast is between a paradisiacal space and an infernal space, the former being vertical and the latter horizontal. On the theme of Hades, cf. Bompaire (1958: 365–78), relativizing the relation to Menippus; also G. Anderson (1976a: 98–100) and his negative judgement at 175.

[46] Herodotus (3. 102) reports that in India ants were slightly smaller than dogs and bigger than foxes (so too Dio Chrysostom 35. 23): Lucian parodies the historian's bizarre zoological account by exaggerating it and transforming the ants into fantastical beings. Beside alluding to Aristophanes' model, the Cloud-centaurs concretize the myth of the birth of the Centaurs, born from the clouds with which Zeus protected Hera from Ixion's violence: on this technique, cf. below. On Lucian's numerical humour, see Bompaire (1958: 594–5): in this case, the satire's target is the historiographical habit of always giving figures, even to illustrate details of little credibility; cf. the parallels listed in Stengel (1911: 21–2), esp. Herodotus 1. 60, Theopompus in Aelian, *Varia Historia* 3. 18, Hecataeus of Abdera 264 F 12 Jacoby.

[47] The theme of a ship swallowed by a sea monster refers no doubt to the Homeric episode of Scylla and Charybdis (*Odyssey* 12. 429–46), as noted by Ollier (1962); Stengel (1911: 40) also indicates a possible geographic parallel: Dionysius

bole is also apparent in the brief episode in Book Two, where the satirical attack is aimed at the implausibilities of natural science. The protagonists see an enormous halcyon's nest measuring sixty stades in circumference. The bird almost capsizes their ship with its wings. The eggs it leaves behind in the nest are as big as wine barrels, and the chick they find is as big as twenty partridges (2. 40).[48]

The satirical meaning of this colossality is obvious. On the one hand it relativizes the human world by overturning its parameters and by representing as giantic living things of small or microscopic size on earth, such as ants, mosquitoes, radishes, crabs, lupins. The same relativism emanates from the inversion of customs, for example from considering bald as beautiful or growing beards on one's knees, two characteristics of the Moonites (1. 23). In modern utopias excursuses have a similar relativizing function. Cyrano's novel *L'Autre Monde, ou les États et les Empires de la Lune*, is particularly close to *A True Story* because the paradoxes of behaviour affect all forms of moral and cultural conventions. Besides, this grotesque deformation strikes at the real world, obliquely as often in satirical texts, by giving the fantastic worlds the same human vices: Moon and Sun fight for the privilege of sending a colony to the Morning Star (1. 12), the inhabitants of the whale are wild, unsociable, and ask for an annual tribute to be paid in oysters (1. 35), the giants with the fiery hair are at war with each other because Seadrinker had devastated Aeolocentaur's herds of dolphin (1. 42).

As a satirical device, the hyperbole of gigantic enlargement—a forerunner by contrast of Swift's Lilliput—is absolutely equivalent and symmetrical to the reduction of the earth's size seen from above in Lucian's *Icaromenippus* and *Charon*. In these two works, however, unlike in our text, the space occupied by criticism of contemporary reality is much greater than that given to fantastic invention. That this is the object on which the satire of imaginary

Periegetes 596–600; but Lucian's daring invention is to develop within this still insular space another world with towns, a sea and other islands; on the entanglement and on the resulting novelty in relation to the usual seriality, cf. Koppenfels (1981: 33), stressing once more the anticipative value of this work.

[48] Lucian appears to radicalize information found on this bird in Aristotle (*Historia Animalium* 9. 14, 542b 24–5 and 616a 14–26); detailed comparisons are to be found in Stengel (1911: 85); but Aristotle himself considered it to be a rare bird; cf. Fauth (1979: 46–7), also on the hyperbole of magnification in general.

worlds actually reflects can be seen from the nice, powerful narrative image used at the end of the excursus on lunar life, derived,
as so often in Lucian, from Aristophanes, the image of the Moon
as a mirror:

And I saw another marvelous thing in the palace. There is a huge mirror
there, suspended over a quite shallow well. If you go down the well, you
can hear everything that is said down here on earth; and if you look in
the mirror, you can see every city and nation just as if you were standing
over them. I actually saw my own people and country when I was there;
whether they saw me too I cannot say for sure. (1. 26)

This embryonic telescope, anticipating Traiano Boccalini's *lentes*
and Galileo's and Newton's real inventions, is the key to Lucian's
work: the inverse world of the Moon, amplified in a grotesque
manner, is the deforming mirror through which the author gnaws
away at the contemporary world.[49]

CONCRETIZATION

Concretization of metaphors and myths common in the classical
tradition is another technique used by Lucian in his satire. In this
respect, *A True Story* was probably influenced by another utopian
journey, that of Euhemerus, unfortunately lost, which gave an
entirely human interpretation to Greek mythology.[50] At the start of
their journey in Book 2, before reaching the Island of the Blest, the
actors find a sea of milk (which may be a parody of the
Pythagorean concept of the milky river leading to the Elysian
Fields),[51] with a white island (a space obsessively dominant in the

[49] The satirical value of the distance from earth is well analysed by Koppenfels
(1981: 30-1): the telescope is the symbol of Menippean satire's tendency to
examine the human world through the microscope. In *Icaromenippus* (23) Zeus
examines humans' prayers through little holes which strongly remind us of the well
on the Moon containing the mirror of the Earth. On the theme of long-distance
observation, see also *Charon* 2 and 6; *Apology for Essays in Portraiture* 12; G.
Anderson (1976a: 122).

[50] The work of Euhemerus has come down to us through extracts in Diodorus
(5. 41-46 = 63 F 3 Jacoby); on his concrete rationalism, cf. Ferguson (1975: ch:
12). On the relation between *A True Story* and Euhemerus, cf. Horn (1934: 18-22);
Ferguson (1975: 174-5) takes the description of the whale's inside world as a direct
parody of Euhemerus' utopia (1. 39/5. 42. 6ff.), whereas the stele of Heracles and
Dionysus (1. 7) is a reminiscence at the level of religious thought.

[51] For the ridiculing of the topical elements of the extraordinary river (of wine,
milk, perfume, etc.) see also 1. 7 and 2. 13, and the material collected by Stengel
(1911: 14-15); particularly useful is Dio Chrysostom 35. 18.

text, as always in utopias, as a physical projection of Otherness[52]) which is but an enormous cheese of twenty-five stades in circumference. Once on land, the protagonists find milk-producing vines, on which they feed as well as on the island's soil itself. They see a temple of the Nereid Galatea and learn that the Nymph Tyro reigns over the island—the word play is based on the etymology of Galatea, derived from milk (*gala*), and of Tyro, from cheese (*turos*) (2. 3). Paradoxically the episode is only a narrative materialization of the island's name, transforming in burlesque manner both the Pythagorean mystic and the traditional myth. To this tendency towards euhemerism can be added the human and bourgeois character which is given to these mythical figures. We may think of the war between Endymion and Phaethon (1. 12–21),[53] of the novella-like erotic intrigue woven by Helen to flee with the son of Scintharus (2. 25), of Odysseus' letter to Calypso, handed over to the protagonist, in which he expresses his nostalgia and his desire to escape (2. 29), of Calypso's joy when she hears bad things about Penelope (2. 35–36).[54]

In Book 2, during their journey, the protagonists suddenly see a very dense forest of pines and cypresses, paradoxically planted in the sea. Pulling their ship up with ropes to the top of the trees, they keep on sailing in the usual way and the narrator cites this verse of Antimachos: 'And as they journeyed, sailing through the wood' (2. 42, fr. 62 Kinkel). This technique, which is far more a part of comedy than satire, takes the poetic metaphor literally and turns

---

[52] Fauth (1979: 39–42) focuses on this point (he provides rich documentation). Insularity is a persistent feature of utopia, according to Trousson (1975: 19–20).

[53] The myths of Phaethon's fall from the solar chariot and of the Moon's love for Endymion are already treated in a very human tone by Lucian in *Dialogues of the Gods* (25 and 11); but here the bourgeois character is independent of mythical elements; cf. Bompaire (1958: 671–2), for whom these are the two most fascinating moments in Lucian's works. G. Anderson (1976a: 50–1) objects that the two episodes are full of both traditional and Lucianic themes: most of the latter, however, seem rather generic to me.

[54] Helen's abduction rewrites the mythical episode on which the *Iliad* is based, substituting for Paris the much lower figure of a young fisherman. The episode of Calypso is a comic degradation of the *Odyssey* and of the cyclic poems, since Odysseus narrates his adventures from Ogygia to his death in a letter which is clearly in the tradition of erotic epistolography: see Chariton 8. 4 where the letter has a similar function, though in a different register, i.e. to upset the couple's faithfulness. The tendency towards an eroticization of Odysseus' adventure goes back to Alexandrian elegy: cf. E. Rohde (1876: 79–80, 111), citing Philetas' *Hermes* (in Parthenius 2: the sojourn with Aeolus amplified by an erotic episode), Ovid, *Ars amatoria* 2. 123 ff., Propertius 1. 15. 19 ff. (Calypso).

it into a concrete event, always representing the absurd as a
natural element (the same technique is used with the Homeric
image of Zeus making a shower of blood for the death of his son
Sarpedon, 1. 17).[55]

RATIONALIST CRITICISM

The conjunction of all these techniques of expression which are
constantly overlapping in this very dense narrative—amplification
of ethnographical *topoi*, grotesque degradation, spatial hyperboles,
concretization of myths and metaphors—produces a materialist and
rationalist ideology. Indeed, *A True Story* was written at a time
when Lucian felt very close to Epicurean thought, even though he
constantly rejected professional philosophy, as is clear especially
from *Hermotimus*.[56] This ideology may very often turn into axi-
ology, when explicit literary and philosophical criticism is produced
and when the tonality of the writing reaches extreme levels of
polemic. This is particularly the case in the episode of the Beyond,
something that is structurally adapted to function as a narrative
travesty of speculative discourse, from Virgil to Dante to Milton.
On the Island of the Blest, beside the honours given to Homer
and other poets, all of them lyric (Eunomus, Arion, Anacreon,
Stesichorus: 2. 15), as we have seen, one notes especially the
ambiguous position of Socrates, present but constantly threatened

---

[55] For this passage of Homer, cf. *Iliad* 16. 459; besides the explicit Antimachian
ancestry, sailing on a forest may be a comic reminder of the forests on the sea
reported by Megasthenes in his work on India (715 F 25 Jacoby). On the technique
of literal reduction of metaphors, see Matteuzzi (1975).

[56] Lucian's attitude towards philosophy ranges from fierce satirical aggression, in
Philosophers for Sale, to radical agnosticism denying it any usefulness in
Icaromenippus and in *Hermotimus*, to a more cautious acknowlegement of past
thinkers as opposed to contemporary charlatans, in *The Fisherman or The Dead Come
to Life* and in *Runaways*, and even sympathy for the antidogmatic schools in
Alexander the False Prophet or *Zeus Rants*. Cf. Caster (1937: chs. 1-2); he concludes
that Lucian was closer to the Cynics and esp. to the Epicureans (84-112) as a result
of the fact that their philosophies involved the practice of civility and lucid
simplicity, even though there are profound differences (the life of retreat, use of
culture). Innocenti (1978: 30-53) stresses this positive contact, in regard to
Lucian's conversion to philosophy (Stengel (1911: 68), however, thinks that *A True
Story* is to a certain extent a satire on the Epicureans, despite their positive representation), whereas Barberis (1977: xxii-xxvii) wants to see the Cynic element of
negative destruction as the preponderant one; Reardon (1971: 151) denies any
trace of speculation in Lucian.

with exclusion by the judge Rhadamanthus because of his use of irony which spoils the pleasure of the banquet. In the *Menippus* too Menippus tells us that Socrates spends his time in Hades refuting every argument, together with Nestor, Palamedes, and Odysseus. The same company is found in *A True Story* and in *Dialogues of the Dead* 20 (a concretization of Plato's wish at *Apology* 41a), where Socratic philosophy mixes with rhetorical and dialectical skill, from which Lucian keeps his distance. This even leads him to pen a caustic satire on the celebrated death of Socrates (*Dialogues of the Dead* 21).[57] There are also other commonplaces of anti-Socratic criticism: attacks on his pederasty (2. 17 and 19) and on his military ineptitude (2. 23). One also notes the absence of Plato, relegated to his own invented city (2. 17; as in the Hades of *The Lovers of Lies* 24), of the Stoics, busy climbing the hill of Virtue, of the Academics, still uncertain about the existence of the island and rather scared by Rhadamanthus' judgement 'since they themselves had denied the possibility of proper judgement' (2. 18). Empedocles arrives just at this time, but is not let in (the same violent attack on suicide is found in *Dialogues of the Dead* 20, *Death of Peregrinus* 1, *Runaways* 2). Pythagoras is welcomed but not without some irony about his cyclical transformations (2. 21). Diogenes is mocked for his conversion from asceticism to unbridled hedonism. On the other hand, the most respected philosophers are the disciples of Aristippus and of Epicurus, precisely because they are pleasant company, as in the *Menippus* (2. 18). Literary polemic is developed especially in the conversation with Homer, which comes very close to Lucian's *Dialogues of the Dead* and Philostratus' *Heroicus*. The poet lays claim to the verses considered unauthentic by the Alexandrian grammarians, he professes that he started with Achilles' wrath out of mere caprice, and that he certainly wrote the *Iliad* first (2. 20).[58]

Theoretical studies have often stressed the close relation between utopia and satire. Representing a world different from the real one may have both the positive function of offering an alternative model and the negative function of criticizing the existing one in a

[57] On anti-Socratic criticism, see also *Philosophers for Sale* 15 (pederasty); *Dialogues of the Dead* 20; and Helm (1906: 35–6); Stengel (1911: 65–7).
[58] Seneca (*De Brevitate Vitae* 13. 2) tells us that the question of which of the two poems came first had become a collective illness (*morbus*)—which lasted a very long time, as we all know. The priority of the *Iliad* reaffirmed here is also found in *On the Sublime* (9. 12–13). On this occasion Lucian also denies the famous biographical tradition of Homer's blindness.

figurative mode. This is what is called 'dystopia'. It is very close to satire, which always has a concrete reference, unlike parody.[59] The negative and positive sides of utopian writing are not incompatible nor clearly distinguished. Their simultaneous presence has been noted as early as the *Odyssey* (Cyclopes/Phaeacians) and is still found in modern utopias, for instance in More, who takes up Lucian's twofold structure, the first book being the more satirical, the second the more utopian (and, to understand this author's huge success, one has to bear in mind that the people of *Utopia* read Lucian regularly). *A True Story* has indeed a predominantly sceptical momentum, be it in the light-hearted pastiche of adventure literature, the satire of war and customs, or in its criticism of all mysticism from the Platonists to the Stoics, the Pythagoreans, and even the grammarians. But between the lines of this ironic rewriting of the Island of the Blest in Book 2 one may see the ideal of a communal and peaceful life, a cautious hedonism highlighted by poetic activity. Herein precisely lies the main difference from Epicurean hedonism, which minimizes the arts in the name of rational naturalness, whereas Lucian's ideal is always a classical *paideia*, a lucid intellectual education dominated by a sense of measure (this is true also of his relationship with the other school he felt close to, the Cynics and their unbridled polemic).[60] In *A True Story* the most favourable judgement is on poetry, because it does not—and does not have to—seek absolute truth, unlike Herodotus' insufficiently appreciated work or Platonic idealism. On the contrary, it turns real experiences into fantastic inventions as, for instance, in the images of Aristophanes, the death of Sarpedon in Homer, or in any myth, always in the sense of a new, vivid elaboration of material events.

[59] On simultaneous presence of eutopia and dystopia (already in Homer) see Ferguson (1975: 13-15); on the relation between utopia and satire, see Trousson (1975: 33); Koppenfels (1981: 21-3), examining More's fusion of the two elements (much greater than in his Lucianic model).

[60] According to Caster (1937: 120-1), *paideia* is the key to Lucian's thought, not common sense, as some have claimed; for Barberis (1977: xxxii-xxxv) the true constructive value of Lucian's work is its Bakhtinian playfulness.

THE LATENT IMAGINARY

Until now our analysis has been focused on a sphere pertaining to the author's project, as explained in a preface which is itself far from being devoid of ironic fiction (the work of the real author under false pretences). His project is to write a satirical pastiche of the entire literary tradition of the fantastic in the topical form of the imaginary journey. We have seen how this operation is realized in the text through a series of techniques ranging from the most playful to the most overtly tendencious, all of them finalized according to an essentially Epicurean vision of the world. It is precisely these last observations on the relation between utopia and satire that allow us to put ourselves at a level which escapes this satirical intention. For someone convinced that literature is the privileged sphere of the ambiguous, the plan of an author's project and its realization do not entirely solve the question of the interpretation of the text (in some cases they even impede it). Francesco Orlando's Freudian rhetoric has shown how this polysemy in literary discourse may be read, following the logical model of the creation of compromise, and using as a key the contradictory tension between a repressive force and a repressed force, which blend together in a unitary semiotic manifestation. These two elements may be found in various typologies and with various intensities, but both are fundamental for the dialectic of the literary text. To privilege the 'repressed' force as the ultimate and deep truth of a work is a naïvety shown by many 'wild' literary psychoanalysts. Until now this model has been applied only to subjects of an ethical and affective nature, but its applicability to a rational type of repressed, and therefore to the subject of the supernatural, certainly cannot be excluded—Orlando himself has started to research in this direction.[61] From the above it will be quite clear that Lucian's *A True Story* is to be situated in a genre of texts where the power of repressive rationality, which gives no credit to the supernatural, is overwhelming, at least at a conscious level. This genre, dominated by the aim of ridiculing the fantastic,

---

[61] Cf. Orlando (1973) for the first formulation of this theory, which was then deepened following Matte Blanco's 1982 research on logical symmetry (see already Orlando (1980)). Recently this analysis of the rational-type 'repressed' has been applied to the supernatural and to its acceptance in literary texts. In this perspective, see also Serpieri (1986: pt. 1).

without doubt finds its purest representative in Voltaire. However, these texts can also channel a repressed pleasure in imaginary story-telling. In our case, this pleasure is hidden under the recreational goal which is stated in the preface in the metaphor about athletes' physical relaxation (I. I). This reminds us of a masterpiece of fantasy literature like Lewis Carroll's *Alice in Wonderland*, which is addressed to children. This contradictory tension could furnish a key for reading the entire work of Lucian, illuminist *avant la lettre*, but raised to a more profound level through magic, exoticism, superstition and irrational cults. The case of *The Lover of Lies* is symptomatic because the polemic, which is aimed at people's attraction to lies, hardly even veils the free and unconditional assertion of fiction.[62] And even in *How to Write History*, where polemic plays an overwhelming part, this repressed pleasure in the imaginary comes through: some of the examples given by Lucian in order to illustrate the rhetorical exaggerations of historiography should probably be seen as inventions or, at least, as amplifications of his own.[63]

Although it is hidden behind its image of a pastime reproducing pre-existing literature, the fantastic occupies a considerable space. It is not simply coincidence that *A True Story* should have been considered the first extant text of science-fiction.[64] For the first time, here as well as in *Icaromenippus*, we find the theme of travel to the Moon, which would become the favourite subject of utopian literature, from the visionary seventeenth century with Godwin and Cyrano, to Wells at the beginning of this century, before it ceased to be anything supernatural. In all these texts, the voyage to the Moon is dictated by deliberate choice, as in *Icaromenippus* but unlike *A True Story*. However, what links the latter with the rich

[62] Bompaire (1958: 657–73) reads *A True Story* as a pastiche where parody and pure fantasy are constantly mixing; Fauth (1979: 57–8) also admits the independence of a 'Lust zu Fabulieren' in addition to the moralizing aim. On the *Lovers of Lies* as an Epicurean critique of fantastic beliefs, but conceived as an assimilation of the criticized object, see Bompaire (1958: 694–8); and Caster (1937: ch. 9). The comparison with Voltaire is a *topos* of modern criticism: see Hewitt (1924–5), and Bompaire (1958: 499 n. 2, with further bibliography). Bompaire, however, relativizes Lucian's comprehension of the religious thought of his time (as developed by Caster); so Reardon (1971: 171–5), who tends to minimize the elements of criticism in Lucian even more (although in my opinion his comparison with Oscar Wilde in n. 35 is unacceptable).
[63] Cf. G. Anderson (1976a: 56–62, 77–80), suggesting that even named but otherwise unknown historians are as fictitious as a Lexiphanes.
[64] Cf. Fredericks (1976).

seam of the fantastic is the unfettered invention applied to the inhabitants of the Moon and their paradoxical ways of life, a constant which we find right down to the *First Men on the Moon*. We know that a voyage to the Moon was narrated in Antonius Diogenes' *Wonders beyond Thule*. Lucian certainly parodied it, but we are not able to determine how far he simply distorted his model or added something of his own. The episode of the 'star wars' seems to be a product of his imagination.[65] Even the stay in the whale's mouth is an element that totally favours the freedom of fantasy, and which may well derive from an unfortunately lost author, Antiphanes of Berge, and, strangely enough, would be taken up again many centuries later in Raspe-Bürger's *Der Baron von Münchhausen*, where a good deal is owed to Lucian, and in a fantasy work for children, Collodi's *Pinocchio*.[66]

To conclude I should like to alight for a while on certain passages where this repressed part of the imaginary gets the upper hand over the mocking rational, or to put it more schematically, where utopia gets the upper hand over satire. In Book 1 between the stay on the Moon and the episode of the whale, comes the stay in Lamptown (1. 29–30), a creation which reappears in Rabelais' *Gargantua* (5. 33–4). The travellers find only lamps, some poor, others rich and very bright. Welcomed with great hospitality, they learn that each night one of them is called by name by the king and is killed, i.e. put out, if it comes late. The protagonist recognizes his own lamp and asks about his family. Not surprisingly this very Ariostoesque episode is situated close to the visit to 'Cloudcuckooland', the city of Aristophanes' *Birds*, where our companions do not stop because of the wind, but which is the opportunity for paying tribute to the comic Athenian author, 'a wise and truthful man, whose works arouse undeserved disbelief'.[67]

[65] Nicolson (1960) runs through the rich tradition of this fantasy theme: she recognizes (14–16) the inaugural value of the story in Lucian and rightly points out the difference between the fortuitous origin of the voyage to the Moon in *A True Story* and Menippus' deliberate choice in the dialogue. On the relation to Antonius Diogenes, see Stengel (1911: 19); G. Anderson (1976a: 1–3) notes the distorting effect of taking the war episode back to the *Wonders*, as Reyhl does (1969: 39); Caster (1937: 289–92) observes how little this sojourn on the Moon owes to the Pythagoreans: only the inhabitants' death by dissolution is relevant (cf. Plutarch, *De facie in orbe lunae* 944e).

[66] For the biblical and folklore theme, cf. Coulter (1926: 41 ff.), Weinreich (1942: 16–23).

[67] Parallels cited for this episode are neither numerous nor obvious: Stengel

The episode of the stop at the Island of Dreams, on which the heroes never manage to land, occupies a symmetrical position in Book 2. The idea clearly derives from Homer. The description of the island is presented as an original creation: 'I am going to talk about the town first, because no-one has ever written about it except Homer, and what he says is not very accurate' (2. 32).[68] The description of the Palace of Sleep plays on the ambivalence of dream experiences, as is clearly the case with the temples of Deceit and Truth. The strongest creative moment is the representation of the dreams' appearances, ranging from the shabby to the resolute, the golden and the kingly. The protagonists recognize several dreams they have already experienced and are enraptured by others. The idea that dreams allay one's desires is dominant:

They came up and greeted us like old friends, took us in charge, put us to sleep, and showed us most excellent and ingenious entertainment. Their hospitality was splendid; among other things, they promised to make us kings and satraps. Some of them actually took us home and showed us our families and brought us back the same day. (2. 34)

This narrative invention reminds us of some light situations in Aristophanes, like the city in the *Birds*, where the satirical attack is cushioned by the transfiguration into fantasy in a poetically utopian dimension.[69]

The structure underlying *A True Story* is without doubt the satire of the imaginary voyage. Its aim is to convert into burlesque the

---

(1911: 39) refers to Lucian himself (*The Downward Journey, or the Tyrant* 27) for the personification of the lamps, and to Homer (*Odyssey* 11. 174–7) for the enquiry about the family, whereas Caster (1937: 289–90) cites Airstophanes' *Peace* (838 ff.) which reports a meeting between rich stars and poor lanterns. For G. Anderson (1976a: 23–4), beside Aristophanes' influence, we have a mosaic of themes from Lucian himself, but the parallels found in his other works are more satirical since their target is real life. On Rabelais' utopia, see Koppenfels (1981: 40–4; relation to Lucian, n. 43).

[68] In *The Dream or The Cock* 6 similar criticism of Homer is made regarding dreams. The parallelism between Lamptown and the Island of Dreams is pointed out by G. Anderson (1976a: 9–10). For Fauth (1979: 55–7), these two moments are characterized by an immateriality typical of utopian illusion. For Lucian's influence on Cyrano, see Koppenfels (1981: 58–9).

[69] Critics are unanimous in taking the *Birds* as the most constructive and utopian moment in Aristophanes' works—see for instance Kerényi (1963: 25–8); Koppenfels (1981: 29); nevertheless, there must also be parody of Hippodamus of Miletus' utopia (1005–9: see Kytzler (1973)), and, in general, by proposing an alternative world, Aristophanes ends up sliding, with a certain ambiguity, towards satirical criticism and conservative reaction: see Paduano (1973).

fantastic inventions of the historians, the ethnographers, and the utopians, by amplifying them in a narration which from the start professes its own falsity. However, into the cracks of this polemical discourse another meaning, a latent one, finds its way: a free, carnivalesque lucidity, a liking for paradox, play with language, a pressure towards fantasy stories. So, while satirical pastiche is based on rationalistic criticism in the name of absolute and natural truth, the second semantic level has, on the contrary, the profile of relativism. It demonstrates univocal ideologies, it creates multiple, dialogical perspectives, it invents possible worlds.[70] It is remarkable that the vast posterity of *A True Story* (Lucian's later fortunes begin in earnest in the sixteenth century, cf. Erasmus) should have privileged the hidden side of this dialectic: the imaginary rather than the polemic, utopia rather than satire.

[70] On this dynamic, 'revolutionary' value of the imaginary, see Jackson (1981); Serpieri (1986: pt. 1, ch. 1).

BIBLIOGRAPHY

Note: the Bibliography lists all works cited in the individual chapters together with some additional material on the Greek novel. For information on bibliographical aids see Introduction n. 119 with text.

ADAM, S. (1977), *Aspects juridiques et sociaux de la maternité dans la Grèce ancienne et l'Égypte gréco-romaine* (Paris).

ADRADOS, F. R. (1979), 'The "Life of Aesop" and the Origins of the Novel in Antiquity', *QUCC* 30: 93-112.

AHLERS, H. (1911), *Die Vertrautenrolle in der griechischen Tragödie* (Diss. Giessen).

ALLEN, T. W., HALLADAY, W. R., and SIKES, E. E. (1936), *The Homeric Hymns* (Oxford).

ALPERS, K. (1996), 'Zwischen Athen, Abdera und Samos. Fragmente eines unbekannten Romans aus der Zeit der Zweiten Sophistik', in M. Billerbeck and J. Schamp (eds.), *Kainotomia. Die Erneuerung der griechischen Tradition* (Fribourg), 19-55.

ALTHEIM, F. (1942), *Helios und Heliodoros von Emesa* (Nijmegen) = id., *Literatur und Gesellschaft im ausgehenden Altertum*, i (Halle/Saale, 1948), 93-124.

——(1951), *Roman und Dekadenz* (Tübingen) = id., *Literatur und Gesellschaft im ausgehenden Altertum*, i (Halle/Saale, 1948), 13-47.

ALVARES, J. (1997), 'Chariton's Erotic History', *AJP* 118: 613-29.

ANDERSON, G. (1976a), *Studies in Lucian's Comic Fiction* (Leiden).

——(1976b), *Lucian: Theme and Variation in the Second Sophistic* (Leiden).

——(1982), *Eros Sophistes: Ancient Novelists at Play* (Chico, Calif.).

——(1984), *Ancient Fiction: The Novel in the Graeco-Roman World* (London).

——(1986), *Philostratus* (London).

——(1993), *The Second Sophistic: A Cultural Phenomenon in the Roman Empire* (London).

——(1997), 'Perspectives on Achilles Tatius', *ANRW* II. 34. 3: 2278-99.

ANDERSON, J. (1981), *Sir Walter Scott and History* (Edinburgh).

ANGRESS, R. (1974), 'Sklavenmoral und Infantilismus in Frauen- und Familienromanen', in R. Grimm and J. Hermand (eds.), *Popularität und Trivialität* (Frankfurt), 121-9.

ARLAND, W. (1937), *Nachtheokritische Bukolik bis an die Schwelle der lateinischen Bukolik* (Diss. Leipzig).

Arnott, W. G. (1965), 'ΩΣΠΕΡ ΛΑΜΠΑΔΙΟΝ ΔΡΑΜΑΤΟΣ', Hermes, 93: 253-5.

Avenarius, G. (1956), Lukians Schrift zur Geschichtsschreibung (Meisenheim am Glan).

Bakhtin, M. (1970), L'Œuvre de Rabelais et la culture populaire au Moyen Âge et sous la Renaissance (French trans.) (Paris).

—— (1978), Esthétique et théorie du roman (French trans.) (Paris).

—— (1981), The Dialogic Imagination: Four Essays, trans. M. Holquist and C. Emerson (Austin, Tex.).

Barber, G. (1989), Daphnis and Chloe: The Markets and Metamorphoses of an Unknown Bestseller. The Panizzi Lectures 1988 (London).

Barberis, F. (1977), introduction to Luciano, Racconti fantastici (Milan).

Barns, J. W. B. (1956), 'Egypt and the Greek Romance', Akten des VIII Internat. Kongr. f. Papyrologie (Vienna), 29-36.

Barthes, R. (1966), 'Introduction à l'analyse structurale des récits', Communications, 8: 1-27.

—— (1970), S/Z (Paris; English trans. by R. Miller (London 1975)).

Bartonkova, D. (1976), 'Prosimetrum, the Mixed Style, in Ancient Literature', Eirene, 13: 65-92.

Bartsch, S. (1989), Decoding the Ancient Novel: The Reader and the Role of Description in Heliodorus and Achilles Tatius (Princeton).

Bartsch, W. (1934), Der Charitonroman und die Historiographie (Diss. Leipzig).

Barwick, K. (1928), 'Die Gliederung der narratio in der rhetorischen Theorie und ihre Bedeutung für die Geschichte des antiken Romans', Hermes, 63: 261-87 = Gärtner (1984), 41-67.

Baslez, M.-F. (1992), 'De l'histoire au roman: la Perse de Chariton', in Baslez-Hoffmann-Trédé (1992, 199-212).

—— Hoffmann, Ph., and Trédé, M. (1992) (eds.), Le Monde du roman grec (Paris).

Beaton, R. (1988) (ed.), The Greek Novel, A.D. 1-1985 (London).

—— (1996), The Medieval Greek Romance² (London).

Beaujean, M. (1964), Der Trivialroman in der zweiten Hälfte des 18. Jahrhunderts. Die Ursprünge des modernen Unterhaltungsromans (Bonn).

Beaujeu, J. (1967), 'Remarques sur la datation de l'Octavius. Vacances de la moisson et vacances de la vendange', Rev. Phil. 41: 121-34.

Beck, R. (1996), 'Mystery Religions, Aretalogy and the Ancient Novel', in Schmeling (1996), 131-50.

Behr, C. A. (1981) (trans.), P. Aelius Aristides. The Complete Works, ii (Leiden).

Benner, A. R., and Fobes, F. H. (1949) (eds., trans.), The Letters of Alciphron, Aelian and Philostratus (London/Cambridge, Mass.).

Berger, G. (1984), 'Legitimation und Modell: Die Aithiopika als Prototyp des französischen heroisch-galanten Romans', *A&A* 30: 177–89.

BERTI, M. (1967), 'Sulla interpretazione mistica del romanzo di Longo', *SCO* 16: 343–58.

BETA, S., DE CARLI, E., and ZANETTO, G. (1993), *Lessico dei romanzieri greci*, iii. (*K–O*) (Hildesheim/Zurich/New York). (For vols. i–ii see *s.v.* Conca.)

BIGNONE, E. (1934), *Teocrito* (Bari).

BILLAULT, A. (1981*a*), 'Aspects du roman de Chariton', *Information littéraire*, 33: 205–11.

——(1981*b*), 'Le Mythe de Persée et les *Éthiopiques* d'Héliodore. Légendes, représentations et fiction littéraire', *REG* 94: 63–75.

——(1989), 'De l'histoire au roman: Hermocrate de Syracuse', *REG* 102: 540–8.

——(1991*a*), *La Création romanesque dans la littérature grecque à l'époque impériale* (Paris).

——(1991*b*), 'Les Formes romanesques de l'héroisation dans la *Vie d'Apollonius de Tyane* de Philostrate', *Bull. Assoc. G. Budé*, 267–74.

——(1996*a*), 'La Nature dans *Daphnis et Chloé*', *REG* 109: 506–26.

——(1996*b*), 'Characterization in the Ancient Novel', in Schmeling (1996: 115–29).

BLAKE, W. E. (1938) (ed.), *Charitonis Aphrodisiensis de Chaerea et Callirhoe Libri Octo* (Oxford).

——(1939) (trans.), *Chariton's Chaereas and Callirhoe* (Oxford).

BOLL, F. (1907), 'Zum griechischen Roman', *Philologus*, 66: 1–15.

BOMPAIRE, J. (1958), *Lucien Écrivain: Imitation et création* (Paris).

——(1977), 'Le Décor sicilien dans le roman grec et dans la littérature contemporaine', *REG* 90: 55–68.

——(1988), 'Comment lire les *Histoires Vraies* de Lucien?', in D. Porte and J. Néraudau (eds.), *Hommages à Henri le Bonniec* (Brussels), 31–9.

BONNER, C. (1909), 'On Certain Supposed Literary Relationships', *CPh* 4: 276–90.

BOOTH, W. (1961), *The Rhetoric of Fiction* (Chicago/London).

BORGOGNA, A. (1971), 'Menandro in Caritone', *Riv. Fil.* 99: 257–63.

BORGOGNO, F. (1975*a*), 'Sui *Babyloniaca* di Giamblico', *Hermes* 103: 101–26.

——(1975*b*), 'Sulla struttura degli "Apista" di Antonio Diogene', *Prometheus*, 1: 49–64.

——(1979), 'Antonio Diogene e le trame dei romanzi greci', *Prometheus*, 5: 137–56.

BOUQUIAUX-SIMON, O. (1968), 'Les Lectures homériques de Lucien', *Mémoires de l'Académie royale de Belgique, Classe de Lettres*, 59: 358–63.

BOWERSOCK, G. W. (1969), *Greek Sophists in the Roman Empire* (Oxford).

——(1994), *Fiction as History: Nero to Julian*, Sather Class. Lectures 58 (Berkeley).

Bowie, E. L. (1974 (1970)), 'The Greeks and their Past in the Second Sophistic', in M. I. Finley, *Studies in Ancient Society* (London, 1974), 166-209 (rev. from *P&P* 46 (1970), 3-41).

—— (1977), 'The Novels and the Real World', in Reardon (1977: 91-6).

—— (1978), 'Apollonius of Tyana: Tradition and Reality', *ANRW* II. 16. 2: 1652-99.

—— (1985a), 'The Greek Novel', in P. E. Easterling and B. M. W. Knox (eds.), *The Cambridge History of Classical Literature*, i. *Greek Literature* (Cambridge), 683-99 (with an appendix of information on texts, translations, and studies at pp. 803-52).

—— (1985b), 'Theocritus' Seventh *Idyll*, Philetas and Longus', *CQ* NS 35: 67-91.

—— (1994), 'The Readership of Greek Novels in the Ancient World', in Tatum (1994), 435-59.

—— (1995), 'Names and a Gem: Aspects of Allusion in Heliodorus' *Aethiopica*', in D. Innes *et al.* (eds.), *Ethics and Rhetoric. Classical Essays for Donald Russell on his Seventy-Fifth Birthday* (Oxford), 269-80.

—— (1996), 'The Ancient Readers of the Greek Novels', in Schmeling (1996), 87-106.

—— and Harrison, S. J. (1993), 'The Romance of the Novel', *JRS* 83: 159-78.

Branham, R. B. (1989), *Unruly Eloquence: Lucian and the Comedy of Traditions* (Cambridge, Mass.).

Braudy, L. (1970), *Narrative Form in History and Fiction: Hume, Fielding and Gibbon* (Princeton).

Braun, M. (1934), *Griechischer Roman und hellenistische Geschichtschreibung* (Frankfurt).

—— (1938), *History and Romance in Graeco-Oriental Literature* (Oxford).

Brenk, F. E. (1977), *In Mist Apparelled: Religious Themes in Plutarch's Moralia and Lives* (Leiden).

Bretzigheimer, G. (1988), 'Die Komik in Longos' Hirtenroman "Daphnis und Chloe"', *Gymnasium*, 95: 515-55.

—— (1998), 'Die Persinna-Geschichte—eine Erfindung des Kalasiris? Ueberlegungen zu Heliodors Aithiopika 4.12.1-13.1', *WS* III: 93-118.

Briant, P. (1976), 'Brigandage, dissidence et conquête en Asie Achéménide et Hellénistique', *DHA* 2: 163-258.

Brinker, K. (1884), *De Theocriti vita carminibusque subditiciis* (Diss. Rostock).

Brooks, P. (1984), *Reading for the Plot* (Oxford).

Brown, D. (1979), *Walter Scott and the Historical Imagination* (London).

Bruhns, H. (1985), 'De Werner Sombart à Max Weber et M. I. Finley: La Typologie de la ville antique et la question de la ville de consommation', in P. Leveau (ed.), *L'Origine des richesses dépensées dans la ville antique* (Aix-en-Provence), 255-73.

BÜHLER, W. (1960), *Die Europa des Moschos* (Wiesbaden).

——(1976), 'Das Element des Visuellen in der Eingangsszene von Heliodors *Aithiopika*', *WS* 10/89: 177-85.

BÜRGER, K. (1892*a*), 'Der antike Roman vor Petronius', *Hermes*, 27: 345-58 = Gärtner (1984), 1-14.

——(1892*b*), 'Zu Xenophon von Ephesus', *Hermes*, 27: 36-67.

BUTTERFIELD, H. (1924), *The Historical Novel: An Essay* (Cambridge).

CAIRNS, F. (1975), 'Horace *Epode* 2, Tibullus I.1 and the Rhetorical Praise of the Countryside', *Mus. Philolog. Lond.* 1: 79-91.

CALDERINI, A. (1912), *Prolegomeni a 'Le avventure di Cherea e Calliroe'* (Turin).

——(1956), 'Gli ἀγράμματοι nell'Egitto Greco-Romano', *Aegyptus*, 30: 14-41.

——(1959), 'La ἐγγύησις matrimoniale nei romanzieri greci e nei papiri', *Aegyptus*, 39: 29-39.

CALVINO, I. (1974) (ed.), *Voltaire, Candido ovvero l'ottimismo* (Italian trans.) (Milan).

CAM, H. (1961), *Historical Novels* (Historical Association, London).

CANCIK, H. (1985), 'Erwin Rohde—ein Philologe der Bismarckzeit', in W. Doerr (ed.), *Semper Apertus. Sechshundert Jahre Ruprecht-Karls-Universität Heidelberg 1386-1986*, ii. *Das Neunzehnte Jahrhundert 1803-1918* (Berlin), 436-505 (abbreviated and trans. as 'Erwin Rohde', in W. W. Briggs and W. M. Calder (eds.), *Classical Scholarship: A Biographical Encyclopedia* (New York/London, 1990), 395-404).

CANFORA, L. (1974), *Teorie e tecniche della storiografia classica* (Bari).

CARUGNO, G. (1955), 'Alciphrone nei suoi rapporti con Longo e il mondo bucolico', *GIF* 8: 153-9.

——(1960), 'Intrighi familiari, inesperienza ed ignoranza dei contadini nelle Epistole rustiche di Alcifrone', *GIF* 13: 135-43.

CASTER, L. (1937), *Lucien et la pensée religieuse de son temps* (Paris).

CASTIGLIONI, L. (1928), 'Stile e testo del romanzo pastorale di Longo', *Rend. 1st. Lomb.* 61: 203 ff.

CATAUDELLA, Q. (1927), 'Riflessi virgiliani nel romanzo di Caritone', *Athenaeum* 5: 302-12.

——(1955), 'Lycidas', in *Studi in onore di U. E. Paoli* (Florence).

——(1958) (trans.), *Il romanzo classico* (Florence; 2nd edn. 1973).

CHALK, H. H. O. (1960), 'Eros and the Lesbian Pastorals of Longus', *JHS* 80: 32-51 = Gärtner (1984), 388-407 = Effe (1986), 402-38.

——(1963), review of Merkelbach (1962), in *CR* NS 13: 162-3.

CHASSANG, A. (1862), *Histoire du roman et ses rapports avec l'histoire dans l'antiquité grecque et latine*² (Paris).

CHRISTIE, F. C. (1972), 'Longus and the Development of the Pastoral Tradition', (Diss. Harvard; summary in HSCPh 77 (1973), 246 ff.).

COLE, S. G. (1981), 'Could Greek Women Read and Write?', in H. Foley (ed.), Reflections of Women in Antiquity (New York/London), 219-45.

COLONNA, A. (1938) (ed.), Heliodori Aethiopica (Rome).

——(1950), 'L'assedio di Nisibis del 350 D.C. e la cronologia di Eliodoro', Athenaeum, 38: 79-87.

CONCA, F., DE CARLI, E., and ZANETTO, G. (1983), Lessico dei romanzieri greci, i (A-Γ) (Milan).

——(1989), Lessico dei romanzieri greci, ii (Δ-Ι) (Hildesheim/Zurich/New York). (For vol. iii see s.v. Beta)

COULTER, C. C. (1926), 'The "Great Fish" in Ancient and Medieval Story', TAPA 57: 32-50.

CRAWFORD, D. S. (1951), Papyri Michaelidae (Aberdeen).

CRESCI, L. R. (1976), 'Citazioni Omeriche in Achille Tazio', Sileno, 2: 121-6.

——(1978), 'La figura di Melite in Achille Tazio', A&R 23: 74-82.

——(1981), 'Il romanzo di Longo Sofista e la tradizione bucolica', A&R 26: 1-25.

DÄLLENBACH, L. (1978), Le Récit spéculaire. Contribution à l'étude de la mise en abyme (Paris).

DALMEYDA, G. (1926) (ed.), Xénophon d'Éphèse. Les Éphésiaques (Budé) (Paris).

——(1932), 'Longus et Alciphron', in Mélanges G. Glotz, i (Paris), 277-87.

——(1934) (ed.), Longus. Pastorales (Budé) (Paris).

DAUDE, C. (1991), 'Le Roman de Daphnis et Chloé, ou comment ne pas être un "animal politique"', in N. Fick and J.-C. Carrière (eds.), Mélanges É. Bernard (Paris), 203-25.

DAVIES, S. (1980), The Revolt of the Widows: The Social World of the Apocryphal Acts (Chicago).

DAWSON, C. M. (1944), Romano-Campanian Mythological Landscape Painting (New York).

DAY, J. (1951), 'The Value of Dio Chrysostom's Euboean Discourse for the Economic Historian', in P. R. Coleman-Norton (ed.), Studies in Roman Economic and Social History in Honor of A. C. Robinson (Freeport), 209-35.

DENNISTON, J. D. (1965), Greek Prose Style² (Oxford).

DICKISON, S. (1973), 'Abortion in Antiquity', Arethusa, 6: 159-66.

DI GREGORIO, L. (1968), 'Sugli Ἄπιστα ὑπὲρ Θούλην di Antonio Diogene', Aevum, 42: 199-211.

DIHLE, A. (1978), 'Zur Datierung des Metiochus-Romans', WJA 4: 47-55.

——(1994), Greek and Latin Literature of the Roman Empire from Augustus to Justinian, trans. M. Malzahn (London).

DILKE, O. A. W. (1980), 'Heliodorus and the Colour Problem', *PP* 35: 264-71.

DÖRRIE, H. (1938), 'Die griechischen Romane und das Christentum', *Philologus*, 93: 273-6.

DONNINI, M. (1981), 'Apul. *Met.* X, 2-12: Analogie e Varianti di un Racconto', *Mater. Contr. Stor. Narrat. Greco-Latina*, 3: 145-60.

DOWDEN, K. (1996), 'Heliodoros: Serious Intentions?', *CQ* 46: 267-85.

DUNCAN-JONES, R. (1977), 'Age-Rounding, Illiteracy and Social Differentiation in the Roman Empire', *Chiron*, 7: 333-53.

DUNLOP, J. C. (1816), *The History of Fiction* (Edinburgh; rev. edn. 1888).

DURHAM, D. B. (1938), 'Parody in Achilles Tatius', *CPh* 33: 1-19.

DÖRING, I. (1951), *Chion of Heraclea: A Novel in Letters* (Göteborg; repr. New York 1979).

EAGLETON, T. (1981), *Walter Benjamin, or Towards a Revolutionary Criticism* (London).

ECO, U. (1983), *Postille a il nome della rosa* (Milan); = *Postscript to the Name of the Rose*, trans. W. Weaver (San Diego, Calif./New York, 1984).

EDWARDS, D. (1994), 'Defining the Web of Power in Asia Minor: The Novelist Chariton and his City of Aphrodisias', *Journ. Amer. Acad. Religion*, 62/3: 699-718.

EDWARDS, M. J. (1997), 'The Art of Love and the Love of Art in Longus', *AC* 66: 239-48.

EFFE, B. (1975), 'Entstehung und Funktion "personaler" Erzählweisen in der Erzählliteratur der Antike', *Poetica*, 7: 135-57.

——(1976), 'Der missglückte Selbstmord des Aristomenes (Apul. *Met.* I, 14-17). Zur Romanparodie im griechischen Eselroman', *Hermes*, 104: 362-75.

——(1977), *Die Genese einer literarischen Gattung: die Bukolik* (Constance).

——(1982a), 'Longos. Zur Funktionsgeschichte der Bukolik in der römischen Kaiserzeit', *Hermes*, 110: 65-84.

——(1982b), 'Theokrit und die hellenistische Bukolik', in id., R. R. Grimm, and K. Krautter (eds.), *Bukolik. Genese und Funktionswandel einer litterarischen Gattung* (Munich).

——(1986) (ed.), *Theokrit und die griechische Bukolik* (Darmstadt).

——(1987), 'Der griechische Liebesroman und die Homoerotik: Ursprung und Entwicklung einer epischen Gattungskonvention', *Philologus*, 131: 95-108.

EGGER, B. (1988), 'Zu den Frauenrollen im griechischen Roman. Die Frau als Heldin und Leserin', *GCN* 1: 33-66.

——(1994a), 'Women and Marriage in the Greek Novels: The Boundaries of Romance', in Tatum (1994), 260-80.

——(1994b), 'Looking at Chariton's Callirhoe', in Morgan and Stoneman (1994), 31-48.

ELLIGER, W. (1975), *Die Darstellung der Landschaft in der griechischen Dichtung* (Berlin/New York).

ELLMANN, M. (1994), *Psychoanalytic Literary Criticism* (Longman Critical Readers) (London).

ELSNER, J. (1997), 'Hagiographic Geography: Travel and Allegory in the *Life of Apollonius of Tyana*', *JHS* 117: 22–37.

ELSOM, H. E. (1992), 'Callirhoe: Displaying the Phallic Woman', in Richlin (1992*b*), 212–30.

EMPSON, W. (1950), *Some Versions of Pastoral* (London).

EYBEN, E. (1980), 'Family Planning in Graeco-Roman Antiquity', *Anc. Soc.* 11–12: 5–81.

FAUTH, W. (1979), 'Utopische Inseln in den *Wahren Geschichten* des Lukian', *Gymnasium*, 86: 39–58

FERGUSON, J. (1975), *Utopias of the Classical World* (London).

FEUILLÂTRE, E. (1966), *Études sur les Éthiopiques d'Héliodore. Contribution à la connaissance du roman grec* (Paris).

FINLEY, M. I. (1975), *L'Économie antique* (French trans.) (Paris).

FLEISHMAN, A. (1971), *The English Historical Novel: Walter Scott to Virginia Woolf* (Baltimore).

——(1978), *Fiction and the Ways of Knowing: Essays on British Novels* (Austin, Tex.).

FORCIONE, A. K. (1970), *Cervantes, Aristotle, and the Persiles* (Princeton).

FOREHAND, W. E. (1976), 'Symbolic Gardens in Longus' Daphnis and Chloe', *Eranos*, 74: 103–12.

FOUCAULT, M. (1986), *The History of Sexuality*, iii. *The Care of the Self*, trans. R. Hurley (New York).

FOWLER, A. (1982), *Kinds of Literature: An Introduction to the Theory of Genres and Modes* (Oxford).

FREDERICKS, S. C. (1976), 'Lucian's *True History* as Science Fiction', *Science Fiction Studies*, 3: 46–60.

FREUD, S. (1905), 'Der Witz und seine Beziehung zum Unbewussten', in id., *Gesammelte Werke*, xi (Frankfurt).

FRIEDLÄNDER, P. (1912), *Johannes von Gaza und Paulus Silentiarius. Kunstbeschreibungen justinianischer Zeit* (Leipzig/Berlin).

FRYE, N. (1957), *Anatomy of Criticism: Four Essays* (Princeton) = *Anatomie de la critique* (French trans.) (Paris, 1969).

——(1976), *The Secular Scripture: A Study of the Structures of Romance* (Cambridge, Mass/London).

FUSILLO, M. (1985), *Il tempo delle Argonautiche. Un'analisi del racconto in Apollonio Rodio* (Rome).

——(1988*a*), 'Le Miroir de la lune. L'"Histoire vraie" de Lucien, de la satire à l'utopie', *Poétique*, 19/73: 109–35.

FUSILLO, M. (1988b), 'Textual Patterns and Narrative Situations in the Greek Novel', GCN 1: 17–31.

——(1989), Il romanzo greco. Polifonia ed eros (= La Naissance du roman grec, trans. M. Abrioux (Paris 1991)).

——(1990a), 'Les Conflits des émotions: un topos du roman grec érotique', MH 47: 201–21.

——(1990b) (ed.), Antonio Diogene. Le incredibili avventure al di là di Tule (Palermo).

——(1990c), 'Il testo nel testo: la citazione nel romanzo greco', MD 25: 27–48.

——(1996a), 'Modern Critical Theories and the Ancient Novel', in Schmeling (1996), 277–305.

——(1996b), 'Il romanzo antico come paraletteratura? Il topos del racconto di ricapitolazione', in O. Pecere and A. Stramaglia (eds.), La letteratura di consumo nel mondo greco-latino (Cassino), 47–67.

FUTRE PINHEIRO, M. (1987), Estruturas técnico-narrativas nas Etiópicas de Heliodoro (Lisbon).

——(1998), 'Time and Narrative Technique in Heliodorus' Aethiopica', ANRW II. 34. 4: 3148–73.

GABBA, E. (1991), Dionysius and The History of Archaic Rome, Sather Class. Lectures 56 (Berkeley).

GAGÉ, J. (1971), Les Classes sociales dans l'Empire romain² (Paris).

GARCÍA GUAL, C. (1969), 'Apuntos sobre la novela griega', Emerita, 37: 29–53.

——(1988 (1970)), Los Orígines de la novela² (Madrid).

GARIN, F. (1909), 'Su i romanzi greci', SIFC 17: 423–29.

GARNAUD, J.-PH. (1991) (ed., trans.), Achille Tatius d'Alexandrie. Le roman de Leucippé et Clitophon (Budé) (Paris).

GARSON, R. W. (1978), 'Works of Art in Achilles Tatius' Leucippe and Clitophon', Acta Classica, 21: 83–6.

GÄRTNER, H. (1967), 'Xenophon von Ephesos', RE 2. ser. 9: 2055–89.

——(1969), 'Charikleia in Byzanz', A&A 15: 47–69.

——(1984) (ed.), Beiträge zum griechischen Liebesroman (Hildesheim).

GASELEE, S. (1917) (ed.), Achilles Tatius (Loeb Classical Library) (London; 2nd edn. 1969).

GENETTE, G. (1972), Figures III. Discours du récit (Paris).

——(1981), Nouveau Discours du récit (Paris).

——(1982), Palimpsestes. La littérature au second degré (Paris).

GERSCHMANN, K. H. (1975), Chariton-Interpretation (Diss. Münster).

GESNER, L. (1970), Shakespeare and the Greek Romance: A Study of Origins (Lexington, Ky.).

GEYER, A. (1977), 'Roman und Mysterienritual. Zum Problem eines Bezugs zum dionysischen Mysterienritual im Roman des Longos', *WJA* 3: 179–96.

GIANGRANDE, G. (1962), 'On the Origins of the Greek Romance', *Eranos*, 60: 132–51 = *Scripta minora Alexandrina*, iv (Amsterdam 1985) 339–66 = Gärtner (1974), 125–52.

——(1968), 'Théocrite, Simichidas et les Thalysies', *AC* 37: 491 ff

GILL, C. (1979), 'Plato's Atlantis Story and the Birth of Fiction', *Philosophy and Literature*, 3: 64–78.

GIRARD, R. (1961), *Mensonge romantique et vérité romanesque* (Paris).

GOETHALS, T. R. (1959), *The Aethiopica of Heliodorus* (Diss. Columbia).

GOLDHILL, S. (1995), *Foucault's Virginity: Ancient Erotic Fiction and the History of Sexuality* (Cambridge).

GOOLD, G. P. (1995) (ed.), *Chariton, Callirhoe* (Loeb Classical Library) (London).

GOUKOWSKY, P. (1981), *Essai sur les origines du mythe d'Alexandre (336–270 av. J.-C.)* (Nancy).

GOVE, P. B. (1961), *The Imaginary Voyage in Prose Fiction* (London).

GOW, A. S. F. (1952) (ed.), *Theocritus*, i–ii (Cambridge).

——and Page, D. L. (1965), *The Greek Anthology: Hellenistic Epigrams*, ii (Cambridge).

GRABAR′-PASSEK, M. E. (1969) (ed.), *Antichnyĭ roman* (Moscow).

GRAINDOR, P. (1930), *Un Milliardaire antique. Hérode Atticus et sa famille* (Cairo).

GREEN, P. (1962), 'Aspects of the Historical Novel', in *Essays by Divers Hands* (Transactions of the Royal Society of Literature NS 31) (London) 35–60.

GREEN, P. M. (1982), 'Longus, Antiphon, and the Topography of Lesbos' *JHS* 102: 210–14.

GREENBERG, J. H. (1971), 'Is Language Like a Chess Game?', in id., *Language, Culture, and Communication* (Stanford, Calif.), 330–52.

GRIFFITHS, J. G. (1978), 'Xenophon of Ephesus on Isis and Alexandria', *Hommages à M. J. Vermaseren*, i (Leiden), 409–37.

GRIMAL, P. (1958) (ed., trans.), *Romans grecs et latins* (Paris; repr. 1980).

——(1962), review of Merkelbach (1962), in *REA* 66: 483–88.

——(1967), review of Perry (1967), *Latomus*, 26: 840–5.

——(1969), *Les Jardins romains*² (Paris).

GRONEWALD, M. (1979), 'Ein Fragment aus den Aithiopica des Heliodor', *ZPE* 34: 19–21.

GRUMACH, E. (1949), *Goethe und die Antike*, i (Potsdam).

GRÜNDER, K. (1969) (ed.), *Der Streit um Nietzsches Geburt der Tragödie* (Hildesheim).

HABRICH, E. (1960) (ed.), *Iamblichi Babyloniacorum reliquiae* (Leipzig).

HÄGE, G. (1968), *Ehegüterrechtliche Verhältnisse in den griechischen Papyri Ägyptens bis Diokletian* (Cologne/Graz).

HÄGG, T. (1966), 'Die Ephesiaka des Xenophon Ephesios—Original oder Epitome?', *Class. & Med.* 37: 118-61.

——(1971*a*), *Narrative Technique in Ancient Greek Romances: Studies of Chariton, Xenophon Ephesius and Achilles Tatius* (Stockholm).

——(1971*b*), 'The Naming of the Characters in the Romance of Xenophon Ephesius', *Eranos*, 69: 25-59.

——(1972), 'Some Technical Aspects of the Characterization in Chariton's Romance', in *Studi classici in onore di Q. Cataudella*, 2 (Catania), 545-56.

——(1983), *The Novel in Antiquity* (Oxford).

——(1984), 'The *Parthenope Romance* Decapitated?', *Symb. Osl.* 59: 61-92.

——(1985), 'Metiochus at Polycrates' Court', *Eranos*, 83: 92-102.

——(1986), 'The Oriental Reception of Greek Novels: A Survey with Some Preliminary Conclusions', *Symb. Osl.* 61: 99-131.

——(1987), '*Callirhoe* and *Parthenope*: The Beginnings of the Historical Novel', *Cl. Ant.* 6: 184-204.

——(1989), 'Hermes and the Invention of the Lyre: An Unorthodox Version', *Symb. Osl.* 64: 36-73.

——(1994), 'Orality, Literacy, and the "Readership" of the Early Greek Novel', in R. Eriksen (ed.), *Contexts of the Pre-Novel Narrative: The European Tradition* (Berlin/New York), 47-81.

HAIGHT, E. H. (1943), *Essays on the Greek Romances* (New York).

——(1945), *More Essays on the Greek Romances* (New York).

——(1955) (trans.), *The Life of Alexander of Macedon* (New York).

HARTOG, F. (1980), *Le Miroir d'Hérodote. Essai sur la représentation de l'autre* (Paris).

HASLAM, M. W. (1981), 'Narrative about Tinouphis in Prosimetrum', in *Papyri Greek and Roman: Edited by Various Hands in Honour of E. G. Turner on the Occasion of his Seventieth Birthday* (1981), 35-45.

HEFTI, V. (1950), *Zur Erzählungstechnik in Heliodors Aethiopika* (Diss. Basel/Vienna).

HEINZE, R. (1899), 'Petron und der griechische Roman', *Hermes*, 34: 494-519 = Gärtner (1984), 15-40.

HEISERMAN, A. (1977), *The Novel before the Novel: Essays and Discussion about the Beginnings of Prose Fiction in the West* (Chicago).

HELM, R. (1906), *Lukian und Menipp* (Leipzig/Berlin; repr. 1967).

——(1928), review of Kerényi (1927), in *PhW* 48: 1475-81.

——(1956), *Der antike Roman*² (Göttingen; 1st edn. 1948).

HELMS, J. (1966), *Character Portrayal in the Romance of Chariton* (The Hague/Paris; Diss. University of Michigan 1963).

HENDERSON, H. B. (1974), *Versions of the Past: The Historical Imagination in American Fiction* (New York).

HENNE, H. (1936), 'La Géographie de l'Égypte dans Xénophon d'Éphèse', *Rev. Hist. Philos.* NS 4: 97-106.

HENRICHS, A. (1969), 'Lollianos, Phoinikika. Fragmente eines neuen griechischen Romans', *ZPE* 4: 205-15.

—— (1972), *Die 'Phoinikika' des Lollianos* (Bonn).

HERMANN, L. (1949), 'Recherches sur Babrius', *AC* 19: 359-61.

HERNÁNDEZ LARA, C. (1994), *Estudios sobre el Aticismo de Caritón de Afrodisias* (Amsterdam).

HEWITT, W. (1924-5), 'A Second Century Voltaire', *CJ* 20: 132-42.

HIRSCH, E. D. (1972), *Principien der Interpretation* (Munich).

HIRZEL, R. (1895), *Der Dialog*, ii (Leipzig).

HOLZBERG, N. (1984), 'Apuleius und der Verfasser des griechischen Eselsromans', *WJA* 10: 161-77.

—— (1992) (ed.), *Der Äsop-Roman* (Tübingen).

—— (1994 (1986)), *The Ancient Novel: An Introduction* (London; orig. edn. *Der antike Roman* (Munich/Zurich, 1986)).

—— (1995), 'Historie als Fiktion—Fiktion als Historie. Zum Umgang mit Geschichte im griechischen Roman', in Ch. Schubert and K. Brodersen (eds.), *Rom und der griechische Osten (Festschrift f. H. Schmitt)* (Stuttgart), 93-101.

—— (1996), 'The Genre: Novels Proper and the Fringe', in Schmeling (1996), 11-28.

—— and MERKLE, S. (1994), *Der griechische Briefroman: Gattungstypologie und Textanalyse* (Tübingen).

HOMMEL, H. (1958), 'Das hellenische Ideal vom einfachen Leben', *Studium Generale*, 11: 742-51.

HOOK, A. (1985) (ed.), *Walter Scott, Waverley* (Penguin Classics) (Harmondsworth).

HORN, L. (1934), *Due scritti di critica letteraria, la 'Vera Historia' e il 'De conscribenda historia'* (Rome).

HOUSEHOLDER, F. W. (1941), *Literary Quotation and Allusion in Lucian* (New York).

HUET, D.-P. (1671), *Traité de l'origine des romans* (Paris) = *A Treatise of Romances and their Original* (London 1672).

HUNTER, R. (1983), *A Study of Daphnis and Chloe* (Cambridge).

—— (1994), 'History and Historicity in the Romance of Chariton', *ANRW* II. 34. 2: 1055-86.

INNOCENTI, P. (1978), 'Luciano di Samosata e l'epicureismo', *Riv. crit. di stor. della filos.* 33: 30-53.

ISER, W. (1972), *Der implizite Leser* (Munich; English trans. Baltimore, 1972).

JACKSON, R. (1981), *Fantasy: The Literature of Subversion* (London).

JANNI, P. (1987) (ed.), *Il Romanzo greco. Guida storica e critica* (Bari).

JAUSS, H. R. (1970), 'Literaturgeschichte als Provokation der Literatur-wissenschaft', in id. (ed.), *Literaturgeschichte als Provokation* (Frankfurt).

——(1972), 'Theorie der Gattungen und Literatur des Mittelalters', in id. and E. Köhler (eds.), *Grundriss der romanischen Literaturen des Mittelalters*, i (Heidelberg), 107 ff.

JOHNE, R. (1996), 'Women in the Ancient Novel', in Schmeling (1996), 151–207.

JONES, A. H. M. (1940), *The Greek City from Alexander to Justinian* (Oxford).

JONES, C. P. (1978), *The Roman World of Dio Chrysostom* (Cambridge, Mass.).

——(1980), 'Apuleius' *Metamorphoses* and Lollianos' *Phoinikika*', *Phoenix*, 34: 243–54.

——(1992), 'La personnalité de Chariton', in Baslez *et al.* (1992), 161–7.

JOUAN, F. (1977), 'Les Thèmes romanesques dans l'*Euboïcos* de Dion Chrysostome', *REG* 90: 38–46.

KARL-DEUTSCHER, M. (1996), 'Heliodorstudien I: die Liebe in den *Aithiopika*', *RhM* 139: 319–33

——(1997), 'Heliodorstudien II: die Liebe in den *Aithiopika*', *RhM* 140: 341–62.

KASER, M. (1971–75), *Das römische Privatrecht*, 2 vols. (Handbuch der Altertumswissenschaften 10.3.3, 1–2) (Munich).

KAYSER, W. (1948), *Das sprachliche Kunstwerk. Eine Einführung in die Literaturwissenschaft* (Berne).

KENNEY, E. J. (1981), review of Riikonen (1978), *CR* NS 31: 282–3.

KERÉNYI, K. (1927), *Die griechisch-orientalische Romanliteratur in religions-geschichtlicher Beleuchtung* (Tübingen; rev. edn. Darmstadt, 1962).

——(1953), 'Die Papyri und das Problem des griechischen Romans', *Actes du 5ᵉ Congr. intern. de papyrologie* (Brussels, 1938), 192–209 = Kerényi, *Apollon³* (Düsseldorf), 170 ff.

——(1963), 'Ursinn und Sinnwandel des Utopischen', in *Vom Sinn der Utopie* (Eranos Jahrbuch), 9–29.

KERLIN, R. T. (1907), 'Scott's *Ivanhoe* and Sydney's *Arcadia*', *Modern Language Notes*, 22: 144–6.

KESTNER, J. (1973), 'Ekphrasis as Frame in Longus' *Daphnis and Chloe*', *Class. Weekly*, 67: 166–71.

KETTEIN, C. (1901), *Theocriti Idyliis VIII et IX cur abroganda sit fides Theocritea* (Paris).

KETTLER, G. (1882), *Nonnullae ad Herodianum . . . adnotationes* (Erlangen).

KEYDELL, R. (1966), 'Zur Datierung der Aithiopika Heliodors', in P. Wirth (ed.), *Polychronion: Festschrift für Fr. Dölger* (Heidelberg), 345–50.

KEYES, C. W. (1922), 'The Structure of Heliodorus' *Aethiopica*', *Studies in Philology*, 19: 42–51.

KIRK, E. P. (1980), *Menippean Satire: An Annotated Catalogue of Texts and Criticism* (New York/London).

KLEIN, A. (1969), *Die Krise der Unterhaltungsliteratur im 19. Jahrhundert* (Bonn).

KLINGNER, F. (1962), *Römische Geisteswelt* (Munich).

KOENEN, L. (1985), 'The Dream of Nektanebos', *BASP* 22: 171–94.

KONSTAN, D. (1994), *Sexual Symmetry: Love in the Ancient Novel and Related Genres* (Princeton).

—— and MITSIS, PH. (1990), 'Chion of Heraclea: A Philosophical Novel in Letters', *Apeiron*, 23: 257–79.

KOPPENFELS, W. VON (1981), 'Mundus alter et idem. Utopiefiktion und menippeische Satire', *Poetica*, 13: 16–66.

KORTEKAAS, G. A. A. (1984) (ed.), *Historia Apollonii Regis Tyri* (Groningen).

KÖVENDI, D. (1966), 'Heliodors *Aethiopika*. Eine literarische Würdigung', in F. Altheim and R. Stiehl (eds.), *Die Araber in der alten Welt*, iii (Berlin), 136–97.

KRENKEL, W. (1971), 'Erotica I: Der Abortus in der Antike', *WZRostock*, gesellschafts- und sprachwissenschaftliche Reihe 6: 443–52.

KREUZER, H. (1967), 'Trivialliteratur als Forschungsproblem. Zur Kritik des deutschen Trivialromans seit der Aufklärung', *Deutsche Vierteljahresschrift für Literaturwissenschaft und Geistesgeschichte*, 41: 173–91.

—— (1977), 'Gefährliche Lesesucht? Bemerkungen zu politischer Lektürekritik im ausgehenden 18. Jahrhundert', in *Leser und Lesen im 18. Jahrhundert*. Colloquium der Gesamthochschule Wuppertal (Heidelberg), 62–75.

KROLL, W. (1924), *Studien zum Verständnis der römischen Literatur* (Stuttgart).

—— (1926) (ed.), *Historia Alexandri Magni* (Berlin).

KUCH, H. (1985), 'Gattungstheoretische Überlegungen zum antiken Roman', *Philologus*, 129: 3–19.

—— (1989a), 'Die "Barbaren" und die antike Roman', *Das Altertum*, 35: 80–6.

—— (1989b), 'Die Herausbildung des antiken Romans als Literaturgattung. Theoretische Positionen, historische Voraussetzungen und literarische Prozesse', in Kuch *et al.* (1989), 11–51.

—— *et al.* (1989) (eds), *Der antike Roman. Untersuchungen zur literarischen Kommunikation und Gattungsgeschichte* (Berlin).

KUDLIEN, F. (1989), 'Kindesaussetzung im antiken Roman: Ein Thema zwischen Fiktionalität und Lebenswirklichkeit', *GCN* 2: 25–44.

KÜHN, J. A. (1958), 'Die Thalysien Theokrits (Id. VII)', *Hermes*, 86: 40–79.

KUSSL, R. (1990), 'Die *Metamorphosen* des "Lucius von Patrai": Untersuchungen zu Photius *Bibl.* 129', *RhM* 133: 379-88.

——(1991), *Papyrusfragmente griechischer Romane* (Tübingen).

KYTZLER, B. (1973), 'Utopisches Denken und Handeln in der klassischen Antike', in *Der utopische Roman* (Darmstadt), 45-68.

——(1983) (ed.), *Im Reiche des Eros. Sämtliche Liebes- und Abenteuerromane der Antike*, i-ii (Munich).

——(1996), 'Xenophon of Ephesus', in Schmeling (1996), 336-59.

LACOMBRADE, C. (1970), 'Sur l'auteur et la date des *Éthiopiques*', *REG* 83: 70-89.

LACÔTE, F. (1911), 'Sur l'origine indienne du roman grec', *Mélanges d'indianisme offerts par ses élèves à S. Lévi* (Paris), 249-304.

LAMB, W. (1961), (trans.), *Heliodorus. Ethiopian Story* (London).

LAMONT, C. (1986) (ed.), *Walter Scott, Waverley* (World's Classics) (Oxford).

LANSER, S. (1981), *The Narrative Art* (Princeton).

LAPLACE, M. M. J. (1980), 'Les Légendes troyennes dans le "roman" de Chariton *Chairéas et Callirhoé*', *REG* 93: 83-125.

——(1983*a*), 'Achilleus Tatios, *Leucippé et Clitophon*: P. Oxyrhynchos 1250', *ZPE* 53: 53-9.

——(1983*b*), 'Légende et fiction chez Achille Tatius: les personnages de Leucippé et de Iô', *Bull. Assoc. G. Budé*, 311-18.

——(1991), 'Achille Tatius, *Leucippé et Clitophon*: des fables au roman de formation', *CGN* 4: 35-56.

——(1992), 'Les *Éthiopiques* d'Héliodore, ou la genèse d'un panégyrique de l'amour', *REA* 94: 199-230.

——(1994*a*), 'Récit d'une éducation amoureuse et discours panégyrique dans les *Éphésiaques* de Xénophon d'Éphèse: le romanesque antitragique et l'art de l'amour', *REG* 107: 440-79.

——(1994*b*), 'La Parole et l'action chez Euripide, Platon et Achille Tatius: sur la "séduction" du paradoxe et du revirement romanesques, in J. M. Galy and A. Thievel (eds.), *La Rhétorique grecque* (Actes du colloque "Octave Navarre") (Nice), 233-58.

——(1997), 'Le Roman de Chariton et la tradition de l'éloquence et de la rhétorique: constitution d'un discours panégyrique', *RhM* 140: 38-71.

LASCELLES, M. (1980), *The Story-Teller Retrieves the Past* (Oxford).

LATTE, K. (1954), 'Virgil', *A&A* 4: 155-69.

LAVAGNINI, B. (1922*a*), 'Le origini del romanzo greco', *Ann. della Sc. Norm. Super. di Pisa*, 28: 1-104 (= *Studi sul romanzo greco* (Messina, 1950), 1-105).

——(1922*b*), *Eroticorum Graecorum fragmenta papyracea* (Leipzig).

LEFÈVRE, E. (1977), 'Plinius-Studien I. Römische Baugesinnung und Landschaftsauffassung in den Villenbriefen (2, 17; 5, 6)', *Gymnasium*, 84: 519 ff.

LEFKOWITZ, M. (1981), *Heroines and Hysterics* (London).

—— (1986), *Women in Greek Myth* (London).

LEGRAND, E. (1898), *Étude sur Théocrite* (Paris).

—— (1925), *Bucoliques grecs*, ii (Paris).

LEJEUNE, P. (1978), *Le Pacte autobiographique* (Paris).

LESKY, A. (1971), *Geschichte der griechischen Literatur*³ (Berne/Munich; 1st edn 1963).

LÉTOUBLON, F. (1993), *Les Lieux communs du roman. Stéréotypes grecs d'aventure et d'amour* (Leiden).

LEVEAU, PH. (1983), 'La Ville antique, "ville de consommation"? Parasitisme social et économie antique', *Études Rurales*, 89–91: 275–89.

LEVIN, D. (1977), 'The Pivotal Role of Lycaenion in Longus' Pastorals', *RSC* 25: 5–17.

LEVITAN, W. (1979), 'Plexed Artistry: Aratean Acrostichs', *Glyph*, 5: 55–68.

LEWIS, N. (1983), *Life in Egypt under Roman Rule* (Oxford).

LIGHTFOOT, C. S. (1988), 'Facts and Fiction—The Third Siege of Nisibis (AD 350)', *Historia*, 38: 105–25.

LINTVELT, J. (1981), *Essai de typologie narrative. Le 'point de vue', théorie et analyse* (Paris).

LITTLEWOOD, A. R. (1977), 'The Romantic Paradise', in Reardon (1977), 34–6.

LIVIABELLA FURIANI, P. (1988), '*Gamos e kenogamion* nel romanzo di Achille Tazio', *Euphrosyne*, NS 16: 271–80.

—— and SCARCELLA, A. (1989) (eds.), *Piccolo mondo antico: Le donne, gli amori, i costumi, il mondo reale nel romanzo antico* (Naples).

LOHSE, G. (1966), 'Die Kunstauffassung im VII Idyll Theocrits und das Programm des Kallimachos', *Hermes*, 94: 413–25.

LOICQ-BERGER, M.-P. (1980), 'Pour une lecture des romans grecs', *LEC* 48: 23–42.

LONGO, O. (1978), 'Paesaggio di Longo Sofista', *Quad. di Storia*, 4: 99–120.

LUCKE, C., and SCHÄFER, K.-H. (1985) (trans.), *Chariton, Kallirhoe* (Leipzig).

LUDVÍKOVSKÝ, J. (1925), *Recký Román Dobrodružný (Le Roman grec d'aventures: étude sur sa nature et son origine)* (Prague; Czech with French résumé).

LUKÁCS, G. (1962), *The Historical Novel*, trans. H. and S. Mitchell (London).

—— (1968), *La Théorie du roman*, trans. J. Clairevoye (Paris).

MACALISTER, S. (1991), 'The Ancient Greek Novel in its Social and Cultural Context', *Classicum*, 17: 37–43.

—— (1996), *Dreams and Suicides: The Greek Novel from Antiquity to the Byzantine Empire* (London).

MCCORMACK, T. (1969) (ed.), *Afterwords: Novelists on their Novels* (Evanston, Ill.).

McCulloh, W. E. (1970), *Longus* (Boston).

McGarry, D. D., and White, S. H. (1963), *Historical Fiction Guide* (New York).

MacMullen, R. (1967), *Enemies of the Roman Order: Treason, Unrest and Alienation in the Empire* (Cambridge, Mass.).

——(1974*a*), *Roman Social Relations 50 B.C. to A.D. 284* (New Haven).

——(1974*b*), 'Peasants during the Principate', *ANRW* II. 1: 253–61.

MacQueen, B. D. (1990), *Myth, Rhetoric and Fiction: A Reading of Longus's Daphnis and Chloe* (Lincoln, Nebr.).

Maehler, H. (1976), 'Der Metiochus-Parthenope-Roman', *ZPE* 23: 1–20.

Mandelkow, K. R. (1970), 'Probleme der Wirkungsgeschichte', *Jahrb. f. internat. Germ.* 2: 71 ff.

Manzoni, A. (1953), 'Del romanzo storico e, in genere, de' componimenti misti di storia e d'invenzione', in R. Bacchelli (ed.), *Opere* (Milan, 1953); trans. as *On the Historical Novel*, ed. S. Bermann (Lincoln, Nebr.).

Marcovaldi, G. (1969), *I romanzi greci* (Rome).

Maróth, M. (1979), 'Le Siège de Nisibe en 350 ap. J.-C. d'après les sources syriennes', *Acta Ant. Acad. Scient. Hung.* 27: 239–43.

Marrou, H. I. (1957), *Geschichte der Erziehung im klassischen Altertum* (German trans.) (Freiburg/Munich).

Mason, H. J. (1979), 'Longus and the Topography of Lesbos', *TAPA* 109: 149–63.

——(1995), 'Romance in a Limestone Landscape', *CPh* 90: 263–6.

Matte Blanco, I. (1975), *The Unconscious as Infinite Sets. An Essay in Bi-Logic* (London).

——(1982), *Illuminismo e retorica freudiana* (Turin).

Matteuzzi, M. (1975), 'Sviluppi narrativi di giuochi linguistici nella *Storia Vera* di Luciano', *Maia*, 27: 225–9.

Mazal, O. (1958), 'Die Satzstruktur in den Aithiopika des Heliodor von Emesa', *WS* 71: 116–31 = Gärtner (1984), 451–66.

——(1962–3), 'Der griechische und byzantinische Roman in der Forschung von 1945 bis 1960', *Jahrbuch der Oesterreichischen Byzantinischen Gesellschaft*, 11–12: 26–55.

——(1964), 'Der griechische und byzantinische Roman in der Forschung von 1945 bis 1960', *Jahrbuch der Oesterreichischen Byzantinischen Gesellschaft*, 13: 29–86.

Merkelbach, R. (1962), *Roman und Mysterium in der Antike* (Munich/ Berlin).

——(1977), *Die Quellen des griechischen Alexander-romans*[2] (Munich).

——(1988), *Die Hirten des Dionysos. Die Dionysos-Mysterien der römischen Kaiserzeit und der bukolische Roman des Longus* (Stuttgart).

——(1994), 'Novel and Aretalogy', in Tatum (1994), 283–95.

—— (1995), *Isis regina—Zeus Sarapis. Die griechisch-ägyptische Religion nach den Quellen dargestellt* (Stuttgart).

MERKLE, S. (1994), 'Telling the True Story of the Trojan War: The Eyewitness Account of Dictys of Crete', in Tatum (1994), 183–96.

—— (1996), 'The Truth and Nothing but the Truth: Dictys and Dares', in Schmeling (1996), 563–80.

MIGNOGNA, E. (1995), 'Roman und *Paradoxon*: die Metamorphosen der Metaphor in Achilles Tatios' *Leukippe und Kleitophon*', GCN 6: 21–37.

MILLAR, F. (1981), 'The World of the Golden Ass', *JRS* 71: 63–75.

MILLER, N. (1968), *Der empfindsame Erzähler* (Munich).

MIRALLES, C. (1968), *La Novela en la antigüedad clásica* (Barcelona).

MITTEIS, L. (1891), *Reichsrecht und Volksrecht in den östlichen Provinzen des römischen Kaiserreichs* (Leipzig).

MITTELSTADT, M. C. (1966), 'Longus, *Daphnis and Chloe* and the Pastoral Tradition', *Class. & Med.* 162–77.

—— (1967), 'Longus: *Daphnis and Chloe* and Roman Narrative Painting', *Latomus*, 26: 752–61.

—— (1970), 'Bucolic-lyric Motifs and Dramatic Narrative in Longus' *Daphnis and Chloe*', *RhM* 113: 211–27.

—— (1971), 'Love, Eros and Poetic Art in Longus', in *Fons Perennis: Saggi critici di filologia classica raccolti in onore di V. D'Agostino* (Turin), 305–32.

MODLESKI, T. (1982), *Loving with a Vengeance: Mass-produced Fantasies for Women* (New York): abridged from 'Popular Feminine Narratives: A Study of Romances, Gothics and Soap Operas', (Diss. Stanford 1980).

MODRZEJEWSKI, J. (1970), 'Zum hellenistischen Ehegüterrecht im griechischen und römischen Ägypten', ZSS (RA) 87: 50–84.

—— (1981), 'La Structure juridique du mariage grec', in E. Bresciani *et al.* (ed.), *Scritti in Onore di Orsolina Montevecchi* (Bologna), 231–68.

MOLINIÉ, G. (1982), *Du roman grec au roman baroque* (Toulouse).

—— (ed., trans.) (1989), *Chariton. Le roman de Chairéas et Callirhoé²*, rev. A. Billault (Budé) (Paris; 1st edn. 1979).

MONTAGUE, H. (1992), 'Sweet and Pleasant Passion: Female and Male Fantasy in Ancient Romance Novels', in Richlin (1992*b*), 231–49.

MONTEVECCHI, O. (1936), 'Ricerche di sociologia nei documenti dell'Egitto greco-romano', *Aegyptus*, 16: 3–83.

—— (1973), *La papirologia* (Turin).

MOODY, C. (1976), *Solzhenitsyn* (Edinburgh).

MORALES, H. (1995), 'The Taming of the View: Natural Curiosities in *Leukippe and Kleitophon*', GCN 6: 39–50.

MORGAN, J. R. (1978), 'A Commentary on the Ninth and Tenth Books of Heliodoros' Aithiopika' (Diss. Oxford).

MORGAN, J. R. (1982), 'History, Romance, and Realism in the *Aithiopika* of Heliodoros', *Cl.Ant.* 1: 221-65.

——(1983), '*Noctes Aethiopicae*: Notes on the Text of Heliodoros' *Aithiopika* 9-10', *Philologus* 127: 87-111.

——(1985), 'Lucian's *True Histories* and the *Wonders Beyond Thule* of Antonius Diogenes', *CQ* NS 35: 475-90.

——(1989*a*), 'The Story of Knemon in Heliodoros' *Aithiopika*', *JHS* 109: 99-113.

——(1989*b*), 'A Sense of the Ending: the Conclusion of Heliodoros' *Aithiopika*', *TAPA* 119: 299-320.

——(1992), 'Reader and Audiences in the *Aithiopika* of Heliodoros', *GCN* 4: 85-103.

——(1993), 'Make-believe and Make Believe: The Fictionality of the Greek Novels', in C. Gill and T. P. Wiseman (eds.), *Lies and Fiction in the Ancient World* (Exeter), 175-229.

——(1994*a*), '*Daphnis and Chloe*: Love's own Sweet Story', in Morgan and Stoneman (1994), 64-79.

——(1994*b*), 'The *Aithiopika* of Heliodoros: Narrative as Riddle', in Morgan and Stoneman (1994), 97-113.

——(1995), 'The Greek Novel: Towards a Sociology of Production and Reception', in A. Powell (ed.), *The Greek World* (London), 130-52.

——(1996*a*), 'The Ancient Novel at the End of the Century: Scholarship since the Dartmouth Conference', *CPh* 91: 63-73.

——(1996*b*), 'Erotika Mathemata: Greek Romance as Sentimental Education', in A. H. Somerstein and C. Atherton (eds.), *Education in Greek Fiction* (Bari), 163-89.

——(1996*c*), 'Heliodoros', in Schmeling (1996), 417-56.

——(1997), 'Longus, Daphnis and Chloe: A Bibliographical Survey 1950-95', *ANRW* II. 34. 3: 2208-76.

——(1998), 'On the Fringes of the Canon: Work on the Fragments of Ancient Greek Fiction 1936-94', *ANRW* II. 34. 4: 3293-3390.

——(forthcoming), *Longus. Daphnis and Chloe* (Warminster).

——and Stoneman, R. (1994) (eds.), *Greek Fiction: The Greek Novel in Context* (London).

MOST, G. W. (1989), 'The Stranger's Strategem: Self-disclosure and Self-sufficiency in Greek Culture', *JHS* 109: 114-33.

MÜLLER, C.-W. (1976), 'Chariton von Aphrodisias und die Theorie des Romans in der Antike', *A&A* 22: 115-36.

——(1981), 'Der griechische Roman', in E. Vogt (ed.), *Neues Handbuch der Literaturwissenschaft*, ii. *Griechische Literatur* (Wiesbaden), 377-412.

MÜLLER, K. (1972), *Geschichte der antiken Ethnographie und ethnologischen Theoriebildung von den Anfängen bis auf die byzantinischen Historiographen* (Wiesbaden).

MÜNSCHER, K. (1920), *Xenophon in der griechisch-römischen Literatur.* Philologus Suppl. 13/2 (1920).

NAPOLITANO, F. (1983-4), 'Leucippe nel romanzo di Achille Tazio', *Ann. Fac. Lett. Napoli,* 26: 85-101.

NEIMKE, P. (1889), *Quaestiones Heliodoreae* (Halle).

NICOLSON, M. H. (1960), *Voyages to the Moon* (New York).

NICOSIA, S. (1968), *Teocrito e l'arte figurativa* (Palermo).

NILSSON, M. P. (1955), *Die hellenistische Schule* (Munich).

NOCK, A. D. (1928), review of Kerényi (1927), *Gnomon,* 4: 485-92.

NOLTING-HAUFF, I. (1974), 'Märchen und Märchenroman', *Poetica,* 6: 129-78.

OEFTERING, M. (1901), *Heliodor und seine Bedeutung für die Literatur* (Berlin).

OERI, H. (1948), *Der Typ der komischen Alten in der griechischen Komödie, seine Nachwirkungen und seine Herkunft* (Basel).

OLLIER, F. (1962), *Lucien, Histoire Vraie* (Collection Érasme) (Paris).

ORLANDO, F. (1973), *Per una teoria freudiana della letteratura* (Turin); trans. as *Toward a Freudian Theory of Literature* (Baltimore, 1978).

—— (1980), 'Rhétorique des lumières et dénégation freudienne', *Poétique,* 11: 78-89.

O'SULLIVAN, J. N. (1980), *A Lexicon to Achilles Tatius* (Berlin/New York).

—— (1984), 'The Sesonchosis Romance', *ZPE* 56: 39-44.

—— (1995), *Xenophon of Ephesus: His Compositional Technique and the Birth of the Novel* (Berlin/New York).

PACK, R. A. (1965), *The Greek and Latin Literary Texts from Greco-Roman Egypt*² (Ann Arbor).

PADUANO, G. (1973), 'La città degli Uccelli e le ambivalenze del nuovo sistema etico-politico', *St. Class. Or.* 22: 115-44.

PAGE, D. L. (1978), *The Epigrams of Rufinus* (Cambridge).

PALM, J. (1976), *Om Filostratos och hans Apollonios-biografi* (Uppsala).

PANDIRI, TH. (1985), 'Daphnis and Chloe: The Art of Pastoral Play', *Ramus,* 14: 116-41.

PAPANIKOLAOU, A. D. (1962), *Zur Sprache Charitons* (Diss. Cologne).

—— (1973a), *Xenophon Ephesius* (Leipzig).

—— (1973b), *Chariton-Studien: Untersuchungen zur Sprache und Chronologie der griechischen Romane* (Göttingen).

PARSONS, P. (1971), 'A Greek Satyricon?', *BICS* 18: 53-68.

—— (1974), 'Narrative about Iolaus', *P. Oxy.* 42, no. 3010.

PASQUALI, G. (1966), *Orazio lirico* (Florence).

PAULSEN, TH. (1992), *Inszenierung des Schicksals. Tragödie und Komödie im Roman des Heliodor* (Trier).

PERKINS, J. (1995), *The Suffering Self: Pain and Narrative Representation in the Early Christian Era* (London).

PERRY, B. E. (1930), 'Chariton and his Romance from a Literary-Historical Point of View', *AJP* 51: 93-134 = Gärtner (1984), 237-78.

—— (1966), 'The Egyptian Legend of Nectanebus', *TAPA* 97: 327-33.

—— (1967), *The Ancient Romances: A Literary-Historical Account of their Origins*, Sather Class. Lectures 37 (Berkeley).

PERVO, R. I. (1987), *Profit with Delight: The Literary Genre of the Acts of the Apostles* (Philadelphia).

PETRI, R. (1963), *Über den Roman des Chariton* (Meisenheim am Glan).

PLEKET, H. W. (1969) (ed.), *Epigraphica II: Texts on the Social History of the Greek World* (= *Textus minores* 41) (Leiden).

PLEPELITS, K. (1976), *Chariton von Aphrodisias: Kallirhoe* (Stuttgart).

—— (1980), *Achilleus Tatios: Leukippe und Kleitophon* (Stuttgart).

—— (1996), 'Achilles Tatius', in Schmeling (1996), 387-416.

POMEROY, S. B. (1975), *Goddesses, Whores, Wives and Slaves: Women in Classical Antiquity* (New York).

—— (1977), 'Technikai kai Mousikai. The Education of Women in the Fourth Century and in the Hellenistic Period', *AJAH* 2: 51-68.

—— (1981), 'Women in Roman Egypt (A Preliminary Study Based on Papyri)', in H. P. Foley, *Reflections of Women in Antiquity* (New York/London), 303-22.

—— (1983), 'Infanticide in Hellenistic Greece', in Averil Cameron and A. Kuhrt, *Images of Women in Antiquity* (London/Canberra), 207-22.

—— (1985), *Women in Hellenistic Egypt from Alexander to Cleopatra* (New York).

POUILLOUX, J. (1983), 'Delphes dans les *Éthiopiques* d'Héliodore. La Réalité dans la fiction', *JS* 259-86 (abridged in *REG* 97 (1984), xxixf.).

PRÉAUX, C. (1929), 'Lettres privées grecques d'Égypte relatives a l'éducation, *RBPh* 8: 757-800.

—— (1959), 'Le Statut de la femme à l'époque hellénistique, principalement en Égypte', in *La femme*. Recueils de la Société Jean Bodin, 11, 127-75.

PUELMA, M. (1960), 'Die Dichterbegegnung in Theokrits Thalysien', *MH* 17: 144-641 = Effe (1986), 239-71.

PUGLIATTI, P. (1985), *Lo sguardo nel racconto. Teorie e prassi del punto di vista* (Bologna).

PULQUÉRIO FUTRE PINHEIRO, M.—*see* Futre Pinheiro, M.

RAKCIŃSKA, M. (1971), 'Chariton, représentant le plus éminent de la première phase du roman grec', *Acta Conventus XI Eirene* (Warsaw), 597-603.

RATTENBURY, R. M. (1927), 'Heliodorus, the Bishop of Tricca', *Proceedings of the Leeds Philosophical and Literary Society, Literary and Historical Section*, 1: 168-80.

—— (1933), 'Romance: The Greek Novel', in J. U. Powell (ed.), *New*

Chapters in the History of Greek Literature, 3rd ser. (Oxford), 211–57.

——(1950), review of Helm (1948), *Gnomon*, 22: 74-7.

——and LUMB, T. W. (1935–43), *Héliodore. Les Éthiopiques*, 3 vols. (Paris; 2nd edn. 1960).

REARDON, B. P. (1968a), review of Perry (1967), in *Mosaic*, 1/4: 114-18.

——(1968b), review of Perry (1967), in *AJP* 89: 476-80.

——(1969), 'The Greek Novel', *Phoenix*, 23: 291-309 = Gärtner (1984), 218–36.

——(1971), *Courants littéraires grecs des IIe et IIIe siècles après J.-C.* (Paris).

——(1974), 'The Second Sophistic and the Novel', in G. W. Bowersock (ed.), *Approaches to the Second Sophistic* (University Park, Pa) 23-9.

——(1976), 'Aspects of the Greek Novel', *G&R* 30: 118-31.

——(1977) (ed.), *Erotica antiqua: Acta of the International Conference on the Ancient Novel* (Bangor).

——(1982a), 'Theme, Structure and Narrative in Chariton', *YCS* 27: 1-27.

——(1982b), review of Molinié (1979/1989), *REG* 95: 157-73.

——(1982c), 'The Novel', in *Petronian Society Newsletter*, 12-13: 3-5 (continued: see above, Introduction, p. 34 n. 119).

——(1989) (ed.), *Collected Ancient Greek Novels* (Berkeley).

——(1991), *The Form of Greek Romance* (Princeton).

——(1994a), 'Achilles Tatius and Ego-Narrative', in Morgan and Stoneman (1994), 80-96.

——(1994b), 'Μῦθος οὐ λόγος: Longus's Lesbian Pastorals', in Tatum (1994), 135-47.

——(1996), 'Chariton', in Schmeling (1996), 309-35.

REEVE, C. (1785), *The Progress of Romance* (London).

REEVE, M. D. (1969), 'Author Variants in Longus?', *PCPhS* NS 15: 75-85.

——(1971), 'Hiatus in the Greek Novelists', *CQ* 21: 514-39.

REICH, H. (1894), *De Alciphronis Longique aetate* (Diss. Königsberg).

REITZENSTEIN, R. (1893), *Epigramm und Skolion* (Giessen).

——(1906), *Hellenistische Wundererzählungen* (Leipzig).

REYHL, K. (1969), *Antonios Diogenes: Untersuchungen zu den Roman-Fragmenten der 'Wunder jenseits von Thule' und zu den 'Wahren Geschichten' des Lukian* (Diss. Tübingen).

RICHLIN, A. (1992a), *The Garden of Priapus: Sexuality and Aggression in Roman Humor*[2] (New York).

——(1992b) (ed.), *Pornography and Representation in Greece and Rome* (Oxford).

RIIKONEN, H. (1978), *Die Antike im historischen Roman des 19. Jahrhunderts. Eine literatur- und kulturgeschichtliche Untersuchung* (Helsinki).

RIZZO, G. E. (1929), *La pittura ellenistico-romana* (Milan).

ROBERTS, C. H. (1955), *Greek Literary Hands 350 B.C.–A.D. 400* (Oxford).

ROBERTSON, D. S. (1928), review of Kerényi (1927), in *CR* 42: 230-2.

ROHDE, E. (1876), *Der griechische Roman und seine Vorläufer* (Leipzig; repr. 1900 (ed. Schöll), 1914 (ed. Schmid), 1960 (ed. Kérenyi), 1974).

——(1901*a*), 'Zum griechischen Roman', in *Kleine Schriften*, ii (Tübingen and Leipzig) 9-39 = *RhM* 48 (1893), 110-40.

——(1901*b*), review of Schwartz (1896), in *Kleine Schriften*, ii. 5-8.

——(1901*c*), 'Die asianische Rhetorik und die zweite Sophistik', in *Kleine Schriften*, ii. 75-97 = *RhM* 41 (1886), 170-90.

ROHDE, G. (1937), 'Longus und die Bukolik', *RhM* 86: 23-49 = *Studien und Interpretationen* (Berlin, 1963), 91-116 = Gärtner (1984), 361-87 = Effe (1986), 374-401.

ROJAS ÁLVAREZ, L. (1989), 'Realismo erótico en Aquiles Tacio', *Nova Tellus*, 7: 81-90.

ROMBERG, B. (1962), *Studies in the Narrative Technique of the First-Person Novel* (Lund).

ROMMEL, H. (1923), *Die naturwissenschaftlich-paradoxographischen Excurse bei Philostratus, Heliodorus und Achilles Tatius* (Stuttgart).

ROSELLINI, M., and SAÏD, S. (1978), 'Usage des femmes et autres *nomoi* chez les "sauvages" d'Hérodote. Essai de lecture structurale', *ASNP* 8: 949-1005.

ROSENMEYER, P. A. (1994), 'The Epistolary Novel', in Morgan and Stoneman (1994), 146-65.

ROSENMEYER, T. G. (1969), *The Green Cabinet* (Berkeley/Los Angeles).

ROUSSET, J. (1973), *Narcisse romancier. Essai sur la première personne dans le roman* (Paris).

RUIZ-MONTERO, C. (1979), *Análisis estructural de la novela griega* (Salamanca).

——(1980), 'Una observación para la cronologia de Caritón de Afrodisias', *Estudios Clásicos*, 24: 63-9.

——(1981), 'The Structural Pattern of the Ancient Greek Romances and the *Morphology of the Folk-Tale* of V. Propp', *Fabula*, 22: 228-38.

——(1988), *La estructura de la novela griega* (Salamanca).

——(1989), 'P. Oxy. 2466: The Sesonchosis Romance', *ZPE* 79: 51-7.

——(1991), 'Aspects of the Vocabulary of Chariton of Aphrodisias', *CQ* 41: 484-9.

——(1994*a*), 'Chariton von Aphrodisias: ein Überblick', *ANRW* II. 34. 2: 1006-54.

——(1994*b*), 'Xenophon von Ephesos: ein Überblick', *ANRW* II. 34. 2: 1088-1138.

——(1996), 'The Rise of the Greek Novel', in Schmeling (1996), 29-85.

RUMPF, A. (1953), *Malerei und Zeichnung der klassischen Antike* (Handbuch der Archäologie, 4) (Munich).

RUSSELL, D. A. (1990) (ed.), *Antonine Literature* (Oxford).

Russo, C. F. (1955), 'Pap.Ox.1250 e il romanzo di Achille Tazio', *Rend. della Classe di Scienze Mor., Stor. e Filol. dell'Accad. dei Lincei*, ser. 8ᵃ, 10: 379-403.

Saïd, S. (1987), 'La Société rurale dans le roman grec ou la campagne vue de la ville', in E. Frézouls (ed.), *Sociétés urbaines, sociétés rurales dans l'Asie Mineure et la Syrie hellénistiques et romaines. Actes du colloque organisé à Strasbourg* (Strasbourg), 149-71.

Salmon, P. (1961), 'Chariton d'Aphrodisias et la révolte égyptienne de 360 avant J.-C.', *Cd'E* 36: 365-76.

Sanchez-Wilderger, M. (1955), *Theokrit-Interpretationen* (Diss. Zurich).

Sanders, A. (1978), *The Victorian Historical Novel, 1840-1880* (London).

Sandy, G. N. (1974), 'Recent Scholarship on the Prose Fiction of Classical Antiquity', *CW* 67: 321-59.

—— (1979), 'Notes on Lollianus' *Phoenicica*', *AJP* 100: 367-76.

—— (1982a), *Heliodorus* (Boston).

—— (1982b), 'Characterization and Philosophical Décor in Heliodorus' *Aethiopica*', *TAPA* 112: 141-67.

—— (1994), 'New Pages of Greek Fiction', in Morgan and Stoneman (1994), 130-45.

—— (1996), 'The Heritage of the Ancient Greek Novel in France and Britain', in Schmeling (1996), 735-73.

Sauder, G. (1977), 'Gefahren empfindsamer Vollkommenheit für Leserinnen und die Furcht vor Romanen in einer Damenbibliothek', in *Leser und Lesen im 18. Jahrhundert. Colloquium der Gesamthochschule Wuppertal* (Heidelberg), 83-91.

Scarcella, A. M. (1968a), *La Lesbo di Longo Sofista* (Rome).

—— (1968b), *Struttura e tecnica narrativa in Longo Sofista* (Palermo).

—— (1970), 'Realtà e letteratura nel paesaggio sociale ed economico del romanzo di Longo Sofista', *Maia*, 22: 103-31 = Scarcella (1993a), ii. 241-57.

—— (1971), 'La tecnica dell'imitazione in Longo Sofista', *GIF* 23 NS 1: 34-59 = Scarcella (1993a), ii. 259-83.

—— (1972a), 'Testimonianze della crisi di un età nel romanzo di Eliodoro', *Maia*, 24: 8-41 = Scarcella (1993a), ii. 329-56.

—— (1972b), 'La donna nel romanzo di Longo Sofista', *Giorn. It. Fil.* 24: 64-84 = Scarcella (1993a), ii. 313-28.

—— (1976), 'Aspetti del diritto e del costume matrimoniale nel romanzo di Eliodoro', *MCSN* 1: 57-95.

—— (1977), 'Les Structures socio-économiques du roman de Xénophon d'Éphèse', *REG* 90: 249-62 = Scarcella (1993a), ii. 185-97.

—— (1979), 'La struttura del romanzo di Senofonte Efesio', in *La struttura della fabulazione antica* (Genoa), 89-113 = Scarcella (1993a), ii. 165-84.

—— (1981), 'Metastasi narratologica del dato storico nel romanzo erotico greco', in *Atti del convegno internazionale 'Letterature classiche e narratolo-gia'* (Materiali e Contributi per la Storia della Narrativa Greco-Latina, 3) (Perugia), 341-67 = Scarcella (1993*a*), i. 77-102.

SCARCELLA, A. M. (1992), 'Affari di cuore: Achille Tazio e l'erotologia greca dell'età (alto) imperiale', in *Studi di filologia classica in onore di G. Monaco* (Palermo), 455-70.

——(1993*a*), *Romanzo e romanzieri*, i-ii (Perugia).

——(1993*b*), 'Il romanzo greco d'amore e l'ideologia dell'amore in Grecia', in Scarcella (1993*a*), i. 47-75.

——(1994), 'Nascita, vita, caratteri e posterità del romanzo erotico greco', *GIF* 45: 279-86.

SCHEFOLD, K. (1952), *Pompejanische Malerei* (Basel).

SCHISSEL VON FLESCHENBERG, O. (1909), *Die Rahmenerzählung in den ephesis-chen Geschichten des Xenophon von Ephesus* (Innsbruck).

——(1913), *Entwicklungsgeschichte des griechischen Romanes im Altertum* (Halle).

SCHMELING, G. L. (1974), *Chariton* (New York).

——(1980), *Xenophon of Ephesus* (Boston).

——(1996) (ed.), *The Novel in the Ancient World* (Leiden).

——(1998), 'Apollonius of Tyre: Last of the Troublesome Latin Novels', *ANRW* II. 34. 4: 3270-91.

SCHMID, W. (1887-97), *Der Atticismus in seinen Hauptvertretern*, 5 vols. (Stuttgart).

——(1899-1900), 'Erwin Rohde', *Jahresb. über die Fortschritte der kl. Alt.* 103 (*Biographisches Jahrb. f. Altertumskunde*, 22): 87-114.

——(1924), *Geschichte der griechischen Literatur*, vol. 2.2⁶ (Munich).

SCHÖNBECK, G. (1962), *Der Locus amoenus von Homer bis Horaz* (Diss. Heidelberg).

SCHÖNBERGER, O. (1970) (trans.), *Longos: Hirtengeschichten von Daphnis und Chloe*⁴ (Berlin; 2nd edn. 1973, 3rd edn. 1980).

SCHREIBER, T. (1894*a*), *Die hellenistischen Reliefbilder* (Leipzig).

——(1894*b*), *Die alexandrinische Toreutik. Untersuchungen über die griechis-che Goldschmiedekunst im Ptolemäerreiche* (Leipzig).

SCHWARTZ, E. (1896), *Fünf Vorträge über den griechischen Roman. Das Romanhafte in der erzählenden Literatur der Griechen* (Berlin; repr. with an introduction by A. Rehm, Berlin, 1943).

SCHWARTZ, J. (1967), 'Quelques observations sur des romans grecs', *AC* 36: 536-52.

——(1976), 'Achille Tatius et Lucien de Samosate', *AC* 45: 618-26.

SCOBIE, A. (1969), *Aspects of the Ancient Romance and its Heritage: Essays on Apuleius, Petronius, and the Greek Romances* (Meisenheim am Glan).

——(1973), *More Essays on the Ancient Romance and its Heritage* (Meisenheim am Glan).

SEDELMEIER-STOECKL, D. (1958), *Studien zur Erzählungstechnik des Achilles Tatius* (Diss. Vienna).

—— (1959), 'Studien zu Achilleus Tatios', *WS* 72: 113-31 = Gärtner (1974), 330-48.

SEGAL, CH. (1984), 'The Trials at the End of Achilles Tatius' *Clitophon and Leucippe*: Doublets and Complementaries', *St. It. Fil. Cl.* 3rd ser. 2/77: 183-91.

SELDEN, D. L. (1994), 'Genre of Genre', in Tatum (1994), 39-64.

SERPIERI, A. (1986), *Retorica e immaginario* (Parma).

SERRAO, G. (1971), *Problemi di poesia alessandrina* (Rome).

SHAW, B. (1984): 'Bandits in the Roman Empire', *P&P* 105: 3-52.

SHAW, H. (1983), *The Forms of Historical Fiction: Sir Walter Scott and his Successors* (Ithaca, NY).

SNELL, B. (1963), 'L'Arcadia: scoperta di un paesaggio spirituale', in *La cultura greca e le origini del pensiero europeo* (Italian trans.) (Turin).

SÖDER, R. (1932), *Die apokryphen Apostelgeschichten und die romanhafte Literatur der Antike* (Stuttgart).

STANZEL, F. (1979), *Theorie des Erzählens* (Göttingen).

STANZEL, K.-H. (1991), 'Frühlingserwachen auf dem Lande', *WJA* 17: 153-75.

STARK, I. (1984), 'Zur Erzählperspektive im griechischen Liebesroman', *Philologus*, 128: 256-70.

—— (1989), 'Religiöse Elemente im antiken Roman', in Kuch *et al.* (1989), 135-49.

STEIN, F. J. (1957), *Dexippus et Herodianus rerum scriptores quatenus Thucydidem secuti sint* (Diss. Bonn).

STENGEL, A. (1911), *De Luciani veris historiis* (Diss. Rostock).

STEPHENS, S. A. (1994), 'Who Read Ancient Novels?', in Tatum (1994), 405-18.

—— and WINKLER, J. J. (1995) (eds.), *Ancient Greek Novels: The Fragments* (Princeton).

STRAMAGLIA, A. (1996), 'Fra "consumo" e "impegno": usi didattici della narrativa nel mondo antico', in O. Pecere and A. Stramaglia (eds.), *La letteratura di consumo nel mondo greco-latino* (Cassino), 97-166.

SUERBAUM, W. (1968), 'Die Ich-Erzählungen des Odysseus. Überlegungen zur epischen Technik des *Odyssee*', *Poetica*, 2: 150-77.

SUTHERLAND, K. (1985), *Walter Scott, Redgauntlet* (World's Classics) (Oxford).

SWAIN, S. (1992), 'Antonius Diogenes and Lucian', *LCM* 17: 74-6.

—— (1996), *Hellenism and Empire: Language, Classicism, and Power in the Greek World, AD 50-250* (Oxford).

—— (1999), 'Defending Hellenism: Philostratus, *In Honour of Apollonius*', in M. J. Edwards *et al.* (eds.), *Apologetic* (Oxford), 157-96.

SYME, R. (1986), *Fictional History Old and New: Hadrian* (Somerville College, Oxford).

SZEPESSY, T. (1957), 'Die Aithiopika des Heliodoros und der griechische sophistische Liebesroman', *Act. Ant. Acad. Sc. Hung.* 5: 241-59 = Gärtner (1984), 432-50.

——(1975), 'Die "Neudatierung" des Heliodoros und die Belagerung von Nisibis', in *Actes XIIe confér. intern. d'études class. Eirene* (Bucharest/ Amsterdam), 279-87.

——(1976), 'Le Siège de Nisibe et la chronologie d'Héliodore', *Act. Ant. Acad. Sc. Hung.* 24: 247-76.

——(1978), 'Zur Interpretation eines neu entdeckten griechischen Romans', *Act. Ant. Acad. Sc. Hung.* 26: 29-36.

TAIT, J. (1994), 'Egyptian Fiction in Demotic and Greek', in Morgan and Stoneman (1994), 203-22.

TATUM, J. (1994) (ed.), *The Search for the Ancient Novel* (Baltimore).

TAUBENSCHLAG, R. (1955), *The Law of Greco-Roman Egypt in the Light of the Papyri (332 B.C.-A.D. 640)²* (Warsaw).

——(1959), *Opera minora*, 2 vols. (Warsaw).

TESKE, D. (1991), *Der Roman des Longus als Werk der Kunst* (Münster).

THESAURUS LINGUAE GRAECAE (1979), *Alphabetical Keyword-in-Context Concordance to the Greek Novelists* (Irvine, Calif.).

TILLOTSON, K. (1954), *Novels of the Eighteen-Forties* (Oxford).

TODOROV, T. (1967), *Littérature et signification* (Paris).

TREGGIARI, S. (1979), 'Questions on Women Domestics in the Roman West', in *Schiavitú, manomissione e classi dipendenti nel mondo antico* (Università degli studi di Padova. Pubbl. dell'istituto di storica antica 13) (Rome).

TRENKNER, S. (1958), *The Greek Novella in the Classical Period* (Cambridge).

TREU, K. (1984), 'Roman und Geschichtsschreibung', *Klio*, 66: 456-9.

——(1989), 'Der antike Roman und sein Publikum', in Kuch *et al.* (1989), 178-97.

TREU, M. (1955), *Von Homer zur Lyrik* (Munich).

TROUSSON, R. (1975), *Voyages aux pays de nulle part. Histoire littéraire de la pensée utopique* (Brussels).

TURCAN, R. (1963), 'Le Roman "initiatique"; à propos d'un livre récent' (review of Merkelbach (1962)), *Rev. Hist. Rel.* 163: 149-99.

TURNER, J. W. (1979), 'The Kinds of Historical Fiction: An Essay in Definition and Methodology', *Genre*, 12: 333-55.

TYNJANOV, J. (1971), in J. Striedter (ed.), *Russischer Formalismus. Texte zur allgemeinen Literaturtheorie und zur Theorie der Prosa* (Munich), 393 ff., 433 ff.

UTAS, B. (1984-6), 'Did 'Adhrā Remain a Virgin?', *Or. Suec.* 33-5: 429-41.

VACCARELLO, E. (1935), 'L'eredità della poesia bucolica nel romanzo di Longo', *Mondo Classico*, 307-25.

VALLEY, G. (1926), *Über den Sprachgebrauch des Longus* (Diss. Uppsala).

VAN BREMEN, R. (1981), 'Women and Wealth', in Averil Cameron and A. Kuhrt, *Images of Women in Antiquity* (London/Canberra), 223-41.

VAN DER VALK, H. A. L. (1941), 'Remarques sur la date des Éthiopiques d'Héliodore', *Mnemosyne*, 9: 97-100.

VAN GRONINGEN, B. (1958), 'Quelques problèmes de la poesie bucolique grecque', *Mnemosyne*, 11: 293-317.

——(1965), 'General Literary Tendencies in the Second Century A.D.', *Mnemosyne*, 18: 41-56.

VAN THIEL, H. (1971), *Das Eselsroman*, i-ii (Munich).

VAN TIEGHEM, P. (1938), 'La Question des genres littéraires', *Helicon*, 1: 95-101.

VATIN, C. (1970), *Recherches sur le mariage et la condition de la femme mariée à l'époque héllénistique* (BEFAR 216) (Paris).

VEYNE, P. (1961), 'La Vie de Trimalcion', *Annales*, 16: 213-47.

——(1964), 'Le "je" dans le *Satyricon*', *REL* 42: 301-24.

VIEILLEFOND, J.-R. (1987) (ed.), *Longus: Pastorales* (Budé) (Paris).

VILBORG, E. (1955/1962), *Achilles Tatius: Leucippe and Clitophon* (Göteborg).

VISCHER, R. (1965), *Das einfache Leben. Wort- und motivgeschichtliche Untersuchungen zu einem Wertbegriff der antiken Literatur* (Göttingen).

VOIGT, E. M. (1971), *Sappho et Alcaeus* (Amsterdam).

VOSSKAMP, W. (1977), 'Gattungen als litterarisch-soziale Institutionen', in W. Hinck (ed.), *Textsortenlehre—Gattungsgeschichte* (Heidelberg), 27 ff.

WALCOT, P. (1977), 'Odysseus and the Art of Lying', *AS* 8: 1-19.

WALDEN, J. W. H. (1894), 'Stage Terms in Heliodorus's Aethiopica', *HSCPh* 5: 1-43.

WALSH, P. G. (1968), 'Lucius Maudaurensis', *Phoenix*, 22: 143-56.

WEHRLI, F. (1965), 'Einheit und Vorgeschichte der grechisch-römischen Romanliteratur', *MH* 22: 133-54 = Gärtner (1984), 161-82.

WEHRLI, M. (1942), 'Der historische Roman: Versuch einer Übersicht', *Helicon*, 3: 89-103.

WEIL, H. (1902), 'La Ninopédie', in *Études de littérature et de rhythmique grecques* (Paris), 90-106.

WEINGARTH, G. (1967), *Zu Theokrits 7. Idyll* (Diss. Freiburg i. Br.).

WEINREICH, O. (1942), 'Antiphanes and Münchhausen', *Sitzungsber. Akad. Wiss. Wien* 220.4.

——(1950), 'Der griechische Liebesroman', postscript to R. Reymer (trans.), *Heliodor, Aithiopika. Die Abenteuer der schönen Charikleia* (Zurich), 323-76 (rev. as *Der griechische Liebesroman* (Zurich, 1962)).

WEINSTOCK, F. (1934), 'De somniorum visionumque in amatoriis Graecorum fabulis vi atque usu', *Eos*, 35: 29-72.

WEITZMANN, K. (1959), *Ancient Book Illumination* (Cambridge, Mass.).

WELLEK, R., and WARREN, A. (1949), *Theory of Literature* (London; 3rd edn. 1963).

WENDEL, C. (1914), *Scholia in Theocritum vetera* (Leipzig; repr. Stuttgart 1961).

WESSELING, B. (1988), 'The Audience of the Ancient Novels', *GCN* 1: 67-79.

WEST, S. (1969), 'The Greek Version of the Legend of Tefnut', *JEA* 55: 161-83.

——(1971), 'Notes on Some Romance Papyri', *ZPE* 7: 95-6.

——(1974), 'Joseph and Asenath: A Neglected Greek Romance', *CQ* NS 24: 70-81.

WIEMKEN, H. (1972), *Der griechische Mimus* (Bremen).

WIERSMA, S. (1990), 'The Ancient Greek Novel and its Heroines: A Female Paradox', *Mnemosyne*, 43: 110-23.

WIFSTRAND, A. (1945), 'Εἰκότα V: Zu den Romanschriftstellern', *Bull. de la Soc. Royale des Lettres de Lund* 1944-45, 2 (Lund), 1-41.

WILAMOWITZ, U. (1905), *Bucolici graeci* (Oxford).

——(1906), *Textgeschichte der griechischen Bukoliker* (Berlin).

WILCKEN, U. (1893), 'Ein neuer griechischer Roman', *Hermes*, 28: 161-93.

——(1905), 'Der Traum des Königs Nektonabos', *Mélanges Nicole* (Geneva), 579-96.

WILHELM, F. (1902), 'Zu Achilles Tatius', *RhM* 57: 55-75.

WILLIAMS, F. (1971), 'A Theophany in Theocritus', *CQ* 21: 137-45 = Effe (1986), 272-85.

WILLIAMS, R. (1973), *The Country and the City* (London).

WILLIS, W. H. (1990), 'The Robinson-Cologne Papyrus of Achilles Tatius', *GRBS* 31: 73-102.

WINKLER, J. J. (1980), 'Lollianos and the Desperadoes', *JHS* 100: 155-181 (rev. in R. Hexter and D. Selden (eds.), *Innovations of Antiquity* (New York, 1992), 5-50).

——(1982), 'The Mendacity of Kalasiris and the Narrative Strategy of Heliodoros' *Aithiopika*', *YCS* 27: 93-158.

——(1985), *Auctor & Actor: A Narratological Reading of Apuleius's* The Golden Ass (Berkeley).

——(1990), 'The Education of Chloe: Hidden Injuries of Sex', in id., *The Constraints of Desire* (London), 101-126 (abbreviated as 'The Education of Chloe: Erotic Protocols and Prior Violence', in L. A. Higgins and B. R. Silver (eds.), *Rape and Representation* (New York, 1991), 15-34).

WIRTH, F. (1934), *Römische Wandmalerei vom Untergang Pompejis bis ans Ende des dritten Jahrhunderts* (Berlin).

WITT, R. (1971), 'Xenophon's Isiac Romance', in *Isis in the Graeco-Roman World* (London), 243-54.

WOJACZEK, G. (1969), *Daphnis: Untersuchungen zur griechischen Bukolik* (Meisenheim am Glan).

WOLFF, H. J. (1952), 'Die Grundlagen des griechischen Eherechts', *TRG* 20: 1-29, 157-80.

—— (1957), '*προίξ*', *RE* XXIII.1, cols. 133-70.

—— (1965), 'Recht. I. Griechisches Recht', in *Lexikon der Alten Welt* (Zurich/Stuttgart), cols. 2516-30.

—— (1973), 'Hellenistisches Privatrecht', *ZSS* (RA) 90: 63-90.

—— (1978), *Das Recht der griechischen Papyri Ägyptens in der Zeit der Ptolemäer und des Prinzipats* (Handbuch der Altertumswissenschaften 10. 5. 2) (Munich).

WOLFF, S. L. (1912), *The Greek Romances in Elizabethan Prose Fiction* (New York).

WÖRMANN, K. (1871), *Über den landschaftlischen Natursinn der Greichen und Römer* (Munich).

YOUNG, D. (1968), 'Author Variants in Longus', *PCPhS* NS 14: 65-74.

—— (1971), 'Second Thoughts on Longus' Second Thoughts', *PCPhS* NS 17: 99-107.

YOUTIE, H. C. (1971), '*Ἀγράμματος*: An Aspect of Greek Society in Egypt', *HSPh* 75: 161-76 (= *Scriptiunculae*, ii (Amsterdam, 1973), 611-27).

—— (1975), '*Βραδέως γράφων*: Between Literacy and Illiteracy', *GRBS* 12: 239-61 (= *Scriptiunculae*, ii. 629-51).

—— (1981), '*ὑπογραφεύς*: The Social Impact of Illiteracy in Graeco-Roman Egypt', *ZPE* 17: 201-21 (= *Scriptiunculae*, i. (Bonn), 179-99).

YOYOTTE, J. and CHUVIN, P. (1983), 'Le Delta du Nil au temps des Pharons', *L'Histoire*, 54: 52-62.

ZAMBRINI, A. (1982, 1985), 'Gli *Indiká* di Megastene', *ASNP* 12: 71-149 and 15: 781-853.

ZANETTO, G. (1990), 'La lingua dei romanzieri greci', *GIF* 42: 233-42.

ZEITLIN, F. I. (1990), 'The Poetics of *Erôs*: Nature, Art, and Imitation in Longus' *Daphnis and Chloe*', in D. M. Halperin, J. J. Winkler, and F. I. Zeitlin (eds.), *Before Sexuality: The Construction of Erotic Experience in the Ancient Greek World* (Princeton), 417-64 (rev. as 'Gardens of Desire in Longus's *Daphnis and Chloe*: Nature, Art, and Imitation', in Tatum (1994), 148-70).

ZIEBARTH, E. (1914), *Aus dem griechischen Schulwesen*[2] (Leipzig/Berlin).

ZIMMERMANN, F. (1936), *Griechische Romanpapyri und verwandte Texte* (Heidelberg).

—— (1949-50), 'Die *Ἐφεσιακά* des sog. Xenophon von Ephesos. Untersuchungen zur Technik und Komposition', *WJA* 4: 252-86 = Gärtner (1984), 279-94.

—— (1957), 'Kallirhoes Verkauf durch Theron: eine juristisch-philologische Betrachtung zu Chariton', *Aus der byzantinischen Arbeit der DDR*, 1: 72–81.

ZIMMERMANN, F. (1961), 'Chariton und die Geschichte', in *Sozialökonomische Verhältnisse im alten Orient und im klassischen Altertum* (Berlin).

LaVergne, TN USA
30 August 2010
195194LV00001B/81/A